Encyclopedia of Women & Islamic Cultures 2010–2020

Volume 2

Encyclopedia of Women & Islamic Cultures 2010–2020

Editors and dates of service on EWIC editorial board

General Editor

Suad Joseph (University of California, Davis) 1998–present

Associate Editors

Elora Shehabuddin (Rice University) 2009–present
Zeina Zaatari (University of Illinois Chicago) 2014–present
Sarah Gualtieri (University of Southern California) 2012–2019
Lyn Parker (The University of Western Australia) 2017–2019
Annelies Moors (University of Amsterdam) 2017–2018
Kathryn Robinson (ANU College of Asia & the Pacific) 2014–2017

Rosa De Jorio (University of North Florida) 2013–2016
Marilyn L. Booth (University of Oxford) 2012–2014
Bahar Davary (University of San Diego) 2012–2014
Amira Jarmakani (Georgia State University) 2012–2013
Hoda Elsadda (Cairo University) 2009–2012
Virginia Hooker (The Australian National University) 2009–2012
Therese Saliba (The Evergreen State College) 2009–2012

International Advisory Board

Sarah Gualtieri (University of Southern California) 2019
Lyn Parker (The University of Western Australia) 2019
Annelies Moors (University of Amsterdam) 2018
Kathryn Robinson (ANU College of Asia & the Pacific) 2017
Rosa De Jorio (University of North Florida) 2016
Marilyn L. Booth (University of Oxford) 2014
Bahar Davary (University of San Diego) 2014
Amira Jarmakani (Georgia State University) 2013

Hoda Elsadda (Cairo University) 2012
Virginia Hooker (The Australian National University) 2012
Therese Saliba (The Evergreen State College) 2012
Alice Horner (Independent Scholar) 2010
Afsaneh Najmabidi (Harvard University) 2010
Julie Peteet (University of Louisville) 2010
Seteney Shami (Social Science Research Council) 2010
Jacqueline Siapno (University of Melbourne) 2010
Jane I. Smith (Hartford Seminary) 2010

Encyclopedia of Women & Islamic Cultures
2010–2020

Volume 2
Body, Sexuality, and Health

General Editor

Suad Joseph

BRILL

LEIDEN | BOSTON

The Library of Congress Cataloging-in-Publication Data is available online at http://catalog.loc.gov
LC record available at https://lccn.loc.gov/2020027686

Typeface for the Latin, Greek, and Cyrillic scripts: "Brill". See and download: brill.com/brill-typeface.

E-ISSN 1872-5309
ISBN 978-90-04-42115-8 (hardback)

Copyright 2021 by Koninklijke Brill NV, The Netherlands.
Koninklijke Brill NV incorporates the imprints Brill, Brill Hes & De Graaf, Brill Nijhoff, Brill Rodopi,
Brill Sense, Hotei Publishing, mentis Verlag, Verlag Ferdinand Schöningh and Wilhelm Fink Verlag.
All rights reserved. No part of this publication may be reproduced, translated, stored in a retrieval system,
or transmitted in any form or by any means, electronic, mechanical, photocopying, recording or otherwise,
without prior written permission from the publisher.
Authorization to photocopy items for internal or personal use is granted by Koninklijke Brill NV provided
that the appropriate fees are paid directly to The Copyright Clearance Center, 222 Rosewood Drive,
Suite 910, Danvers, MA 01923, USA. Fees are subject to change.

This book is printed on acid-free paper and produced in a sustainable manner.

Contents

List of Contributors IX
Acknowledgments XI
The EWIC Project XV
Introduction XXVI

Breastfeeding

Breastfeeding: Malaysia 3
Siaan Ansori

Breastfeeding: Ottoman Empire 14
Tugce Kayaal

Breastfeeding: West Africa 29
Michelle Johnson

Childhood: Coming of Age Rituals

Childhood: Coming of Age Rituals: Sub-Saharan Africa 45
Michelle Johnson

Domestic Violence

Domestic Violence: Bangladesh 63
Nusrat Ameen

Violence against Women: Gulf States 76
Hasnaa Mokhtar

Domestic Violence: Indonesia 100
Lyn Parker

Domestic Violence: Malaysia 114
Maznah Mohamad

Domestic Violence: Pakistan 131
  Filomena M. Critelli

Domestic Violence: Tajikistan 145
  Muborak Sharipova

Domestic Violence: Muslim Communities: United States of America 167
  Salma Abugideiri

Female Genital Cutting

Female Genital Cutting: West Africa 185
  Elizabeth Rosner

Funerary Practices

Funerary Rites for Women Victims of "Honor Killings": Indus Valley 201
  Ghazala Anwar

Funerary Practices: Women: Palestine: Nineteenth to Early
Twentieth Century 209
  Suhad Daher-Nashif

Health Practices

Health Practices: Turkestan: 19th Century to Early 20th Century 229
  Sanavar Shadmanova

Honor

Honor: Pakistan 245
  Sabah Firoz Uddin

Mental Health

Mental Health: Pakistan   257
   Batool Fatima

Population and Health Sciences

Population and Health Sciences   277
   Hania Sholkamy

Reproduction: Health

Reproduction: Health: Bangladesh   301
   Mst Shahina Parvin

Reproduction: Health: Bangladesh and Pakistan   315
   Sanjam Ahluwalia and Hector Taylor

Reproduction: Health: India: Mid- to Late-Twentieth Century   340
   Daksha Parmar and Sanjam Ahluwalia

Reproduction: Health: Indonesia   352
   Linda Rae Bennett and Belinda Rina Marie Spagnoletti

Reproduction: Health: Indonesia   370
   Linda Rae Bennett and Emma Barnard

Sexual Harassment

Sexual Harassment: Bangladesh   397
   Hana Shams Ahmed

Sexual Harassment: Egypt   412
   Noha Roushdy

Sexualities

Sexualities and Queer Studies   435
  Samar Habib

Sexualities: Practices: Bangladesh   450
  Shuchi Karim

Sexualities: Transsexualities: Middle East, West Africa, North Africa   462
  Corinne Fortier

Space: Female Space

Space: Female Space: Arabian Peninsula   493
  *Jocelyn Sage Mitchell, Sean Foley, Jessie Moritz, and
  Vânia Carvalho Pinto*

Space: Female Space: Pakistan   510
  Sarwat Viqar

Sports

Public Spaces and Gender: Sport and Activism: United States   523
  Stanley Thangaraj

Sports: Turkey: 19th to Early 20th Centuries   538
  Ilknur Hacısoftaoğlu

Sports: Turkey   552
  Sertaç Sehlikoglu

Index of Names   567
Index of Subjects   581

Contributors

Abugideiri, Salma – Independent scholar
Ahmed, Hana Shams – York University
Ahluwalia, Sanjam – Northern Arizona University
Ameen, Nusrat – Rice University
Ansori, Siaan – Independent scholar
Anwar, Ghazala – Starr King School for the Ministry
Barnard, Emma – University of Melbourne
Bennett, Linda Rae – University of Melbourne
Critelli, Filomena M. – University at Buffalo
Daher-Nashif, Suhad – Qatar University
Fatima, Batool – International Islamic University, Islamabad
Foley, Sean – Middle Tennessee State University
Fortier, Corinne – French National Center of Scientific Research
Habib, Samar – Independent scholar
Hacısoftaoğlu, Ilknur – Istanbul Bilgi University
Johnson, Michelle – Bucknell University
Karim, Shuchi – Western University, Canada
Kayaal, Tugce – University of Michigan
Mitchell, Jocelyn Sage – Northwestern University, Qatar
Mohamad, Maznah – National University of Singapore
Mokhtar, Hasnaa – Clark University
Moritz, Jessie – Australian National University
Parker, Lyn – The University of Western Australia
Parmar, Daksha – Indian Institute of Technology Guwahati
Parvin, Mst Shahina – Jahangirnagar University
Pinto, Vânia Carvalho – University of Brasília
Rosner, Elizabeth – Independent scholar
Roushdy, Noha – Boston University
Sehlikoglu, Sertaç – University of Cambridge
Shadmanova, Sanavar – Institute of History of Academy of Sciences of
    Uzbekistan
Sharipova, Muborak – Independent scholar
Sholkamy, Hania – The American University in Cairo
Spagnoletti, Belinda Rina Marie – University of Melbourne

Taylor, Hector – Arizona State University
Thangaraj, Stanley – The City College of New York
Uddin, Sabah Firoz – Bowie State University
Viqar, Sarwat – John Abbott College

Acknowledgments

The *Encyclopedia of Women and Islamic Cultures 2010–2020* has been ten years in the making, though, in some sense it has been over two decades in the making. The EWIC Project was formally launched by Brill in 1998. EWIC 2010–2020 would not exist without Brill. All the Brill editors and staff have been immensely supportive of EWIC from the first invitation I received in 1994 to discuss the idea of an encyclopedia. EWIC 2010–2020, however, first and foremost, is indebted to Nicolette van der Hoek, our senior editor at Brill. It was her idea to produce a second print edition of EWIC, compiling all the EWIC Online articles. Nicolette has been unwavering in her understanding of our editorial work and passionate in her enthusiasm for the project. To work with an editor who believes in you and your project and who always has a positive insight to offer is the wish of any scholar in this publishing world. To Nicolette goes my deepest gratitude.

Nicolette has served as the Brill Editor for EWIC from 2013 to the present. Kathy van Vliet-Leigh served from 2010–2013; Sasha Goldstein-Sabbah from 2008–2010; and Joed Elich from 2007–2008. Maurits van den Boogert stepped in for Nicolette twice during her maternity leaves. Each brought their own perspectives, skills, and wisdom to EWIC and for each I am grateful.

Brill also offered project managers to help us orchestrate the massive routing of invitations, submissions, editing, and compiling of the supplements and volumes. For the past several years, Kristen Chevalier supported EWIC from the Boston Brill office, ushering us through Supplements 18, 19, and 20 and the publication of EWIC 2010–2020. She has been endlessly patient and persevering. I could always count on her to have the information we needed, in the form we needed it. Her contributions to EWIC 2010–2020 have been incalculable. Prior to Kristen, EWIC was also fortunate to have as project managers: Deborah Baker, Franco Alvarado, Kayli Brownstein, and Diana Steele. Though none of them stayed long on the project, they each injected energy and commitment. For them as well, I am grateful.

The EWIC Project has been most fortunate in receiving funding over the past decade. We are indebted to the Henry Luce Foundation for funding the EWIC Public Outreach Project (launched in 2012) and the Muslim Women and the Media Training Institute (launched in 2017). Toby Volkman, our program officer at Luce, has engaged with us every step of the way to think innovatively about how to make the scholarship and scholars of the EWIC Project available to diverse audiences in order to have public impact. It has been a profound experience for all of us in the EWIC Project to have this opportunity. I am most grateful to Toby and the Henry Luce Foundation for having faith in our work and supporting us.

Funding from the UC Davis Office of Graduate Studies gave further support to our work. Prasant Mohapatra and Jeffery Gibeling, past deans of Graduate Studies at UC Davis, and their dedicated officer Steven Albrecht, offered matching funds in the form of work study grants for graduate students. Without these matching funds I would not have been able to hire graduate students to support the EWIC Project. I am grateful to have had the continuous support of the Office of Graduate Studies for the EWIC Project for two decades.

At UC Davis, I am indebted to Yoke Dellenback, the most amazing grant manager I could wish to have. She keeps the accounts in the finest form that even a non-budget person like me could understand. She was unstintingly generous in meeting with me, explaining what was possible and not possible, and anticipating before me what we needed to do and plan for financially. She made it all possible, with good help from her staff, Veronica Ledesma.

The Department of Anthropology has housed the EWIC project for over a decade, after the dean's office moved the Joseph Lab back on campus. I am grateful to Anthropology chairs and staff who have given me space to continue my EWIC work as well as my many other projects. I am especially grateful to chairs Lynne Isbell and Li Zhang for the lab space, and to staff Mary Dixon and Erum Syed for management and support. Prior to the Joseph Lab's move back to campus, Dean Steve Sheffrin and Dean George Mangun had given considerable support to my off-campus lab.

The EWIC Project, since 1998, has been most fortunate to have paid and volunteer student staff from UC Davis. In the past decade, the student engagement for EWIC 2010–2020 has been inspired and inspiring. My Graduate Student Researchers (GSRs) have included: Melina Devoney, Courtney Caviness, Elizabeth Witcher, Nahrain Rasho, Aleksandra Taranov, Mash'alle Olomi, Zuzanan Turowska, Hallie Casey, Shareefa Al-Adwani, Kelsa West, Karin Root, Hazel Crawford, Rachel Diamond, Kelly Gove, and Julia Jackson. Of them, I especially thank Hazel Crawford, who worked the longest and was unbelievably dedicated, and Julia Jackson who researched funding opportunities and found the Henry Luce Foundation.

Undergraduate interns, assistants, and volunteers have included Sarah Covault, Noor Halabi, Layla Mustafa, Elise Boyle, Rawah Altuhami, Tara Saghir, Faryal Irfan, Afaaf Ebrahim, Lujain Al-Saleh, Anna Goldberg, Nida Ahmed, Jack Mizes, Karissa Oliver, To Lan Phin, Lauren Turner, Nikki Mahmoudi, Susan Flores, Niat Afeworki, Madina Stanackzai, Helen Min, Chathurika Peiris, Omar Abdel-Ghaffar, Saliem Shehadeh, Ilma Husain, Brandon Rapoza, and Lara France. They stunned me with their care and commitment and their sheer joy in working.

ACKNOWLEDGMENTS XIII

UC Davis undergraduate and graduate student IT staff have included: Randal Murphy, Yong Chong, Yash Dani, David Lin, James Zhang, Shawn Miller, George Pantazes, Justin Wong, Sailesh Patnala, Nicholas Reynolds, Sam Chou, Shobhik Ghosh, Nathan Lee, Samuel Huang, Allen Au, David Espiritu, and Nikolay Voronchikhin. Without them, we would not have had the EWIC webpage and the on-the-ground technical support our EWIC Project needed.

UC Davis IT professional staff have included Janine Carlson, Carol McMasters-Stone, Hector Sotelo, Ivy Tillich, Brandon Baker, and a host of undergraduate IT assistants who helped along the way. Their generosity with me and my many projects has seemed endless. At one point, I was told, that my "tickets" (requests for help) to the IT staff was the second highest in the whole UCD College of Letters and Sciences, just behind the Dean's. Yet they continued to have patience and offer me guidance and solutions to the on-going IT problems that a Lab with over a dozen projects and 15–25 student staff would predictably have. I cannot thank them enough and look forward each year to our annual lunches which I cook for them all, at my home.

Finally, and importantly, I am indebted to the EWIC Editors who have offered their time, intellect, wisdom, and scholarship to this project. With EWIC Print 1, we had a dedicated Board of Editors who stayed with the whole project from 1999–2007. With EWIC 2010–2020, the Editorial Board has changed over time. EWIC Associate Editors have included: Elora Shehabuddin (2009-present); Therese Saliba (2009–2012); Hoda Elsadda (2009–2012); Virginia Hooker (2009–2012); Bahar Davary (2012–2014); Marilyn Booth (2012–2014); Amira Jarmakani (2012–2013); Sarah Gualtieri (2012–2019); Rosa De Jorio (2013–2016); Zeina Zaatari (2014-present); Kathryn Robinson (2014–2017); Annelies Moors (2017–2018); Lyn Parker (2017–2019).

The EWIC Editors had regional responsibilities, as did Editors in EWIC Print 1. For the Middle East: Hoda Elsadda, Marilyn Booth, and Zeina Zaatari (who also was responsible for Europe and for Sub-Saharan Africa at different points). For the Americas: Therese Saliba, Amira Jarmakani, and Sarah Gualtieri. For Sub-Saharan Africa: Rosa De Jorio. For South and Central Asia: Elora Shehabuddin. For East and South East Asia: Virginia Hooker; Bahar Davary, Kathryn Robinson, and Lyn Parker. For Europe: Annelies Moors. Both I and Sarah Gualtieri offer a special thanks to Pauline Homsi Vinson who worked with Sarah as guest editor on EWIC Online Supplement 16. That supplement would not have come together without Pauline's dedicated commitment.

Therese Saliba wishes also to thank Hazel Crawford and Andrew Meyer for their meticulous work as EWIC research assistants. She also thanks Andrew for his help coordinating the EWIC Henry Luce Foundation training for K-12 teachers. Kathryn Robinson would like to thank Kirsty Wissing an Australian National University PhD scholar who was her EWIC research assistant. She and

Lyn Parker both thank Dr. Eva Nisa, Senior Lecturer in Anthropology at the Australian National University, for her editorial work and help with suggesting and contacting authors. Elora Shehabuddin would like to thank her editorial assistants Gemini Wahhaj and Tracy Sampiero. Tracy had been the graduate student researcher for EWIC Print I in the early years of our work at UC Davis (as well as my doctoral student). To her goes a double thanks.

Currently the Associate Editors of EWIC are: Elora Shehabuddin (Central and South Asia); Zeina Zaatari (Middle East and Africa–North Africa and Sub-Saharan Africa); Shaheen Pasha (the Americas); Nadia Fadil (Europe); Nurhaizatul Jamil (East and South East Asia). Of these Elora Shehabuddin (11 years) and Zeina Zaatari (6 years) have worked the longest. I am indebted to all my EWIC Editors for their enduring intellectual commitment to EWIC. I give special thanks to Elora and Zeina for their stalwart hard work and loving kindness. Our work is truly a collaborative feminist project. To them I add my gratitude to the 292 scholars who worked with us to author articles for EWIC 2010–2020. Their scholarship reconfirms EWIC as the highest ranked encyclopedia in its field.

I have been the General Editor of EWIC, formally since 1998, though informally from 1995 (first contact from Brill was 1994) when I was invited to become the General Editor. Over the quarter of a century of work on EWIC, I have been privileged to work with many editors and staff at Brill, many Associate Editors of EWIC, many program officers at different foundations and offices that have funded the EWIC Project (Ford Foundation, International Development Research Council, Henry Luce Foundation, University of California Davis Office of Research and Graduate Studies), many deans, many graduate and undergraduate students, and many staff at UC Davis. The EWIC Project is indebted to them all and I am grateful for the kindness, generosity, and hard work of so many who were willing to work with me and work together to create this innovative, collaborative, feminist project. I have learned so much from them all and am truly humbled by our work together. We all share in EWIC's inception, birth, growth, and maturation as a major producer of scholarly knowledge on women and Islamic cultures. As the founding and continuous General Editor and longest-serving member of this wondrous EWIC family, I take upon myself the responsibility of its shortfalls.

Finally, I would like to acknowledge and thank my beloved daughter and her family. Sara Rose and Ferguson and their magical Bear and Georgiana. Time away from them always feels like a price to be paid. I am grateful for their patience, support, and love.

Suad Joseph
June 15, 2020
Davis, California

The EWIC Project

The *Encyclopedia of Women and Islamic Cultures* (EWIC) is an interdisciplinary, transhistorical, global project bringing together scholarship on all women in Muslim-majority countries and Muslim women in Muslim-minority countries. EWIC covers research on and by women and Islamic cultures from the period just before the rise of Islam to contemporary times. EWIC's goal is to cover all disciplines, all topics, and all regions of the world for which scholarly research is available on women and Islamic cultures.

The *Encyclopedia of Women and Islamic Cultures* 2010–2020 is published in a most auspicious global moment. As I write this overview of the EWIC Project (July 2020), the world is gripped by a pandemic of the novel corona virus (covid–19) with a trajectory scientists have not been able to anticipate and whose human toll in lives lost, economies thrown into disarray, and socio/political fabrics torn asunder cannot be fully comprehended in the moment. As I write, massive protests in the United States against police brutality, especially towards African Americans, but also other peoples of color, have resonated across the globe. As I write, polarization between nativist/populist/rightist politics and liberal/radical/leftist politics has crystalized and coalesced issues around race, class, gender, religion, ethnicity, and sexuality. Across the globe, democracy and equality for all, dignity and respect for all appear to teeter on a fragile landscape with increasingly authoritarian regimes. As I write, Muslims of all colors, all too often, experience marginalization and discrimination in Muslim minority societies—from the United States to Europe to China. And Muslim women, iconically, stand in for Islam. Muslim women, homogenized, essentialized, and taken out of historical and social context, appear again and again in popular representation, and often in scholarship, as singular stick figures dis-embedded from time, cultures, and localities.

EWIC 2010–2020 highlights history, culture, time, place, locality, and specificity. There is no effort to show continuities or similarities or patterns among Muslim women across the globe and across generations. There is little in the way of continuities to show. Muslim women are as diverse as the world. There are over two billion Muslims in the world, a quarter of the world's population. Islam is the second largest world religion, just behind Christianity. Muslims are in every country of the world and have been so for centuries and centuries. Close to fifty countries are Muslim majority countries. Many Muslim minority countries have enough Muslims to create whole countries—such as India with 200,000,000, China with 30,000,000, and Russia with 20,000,000 Muslims. The population of Muslims in Europe is rapidly increasing—6,000,000 in France,

5,000,000 in Germany, 4,000,000 in the United Kingdom, and 3,000,000 in Italy. Estimates for the Muslim population of the United States range from 4–7 million—the fastest growing religion in the US, among whom African American Muslims are the largest grouping. Diversity is the material reality of Muslims and Muslim women around the world. EWIC 2010–2020 documents that diversity.

In the twenty-two years since the formal launching of the EWIC Project (1998) and the seventeen years since the publishing of Volume I of EWIC Print I (2003), an enormous body of scholarly literature has been produced about and by Muslim women, globally. The "study" of women and Islamic cultures has become a standing field of investigation. Two academic journals focus on Muslim and Middle Eastern women: *Journal of Middle East Women's Studies* (which I co-founded with Sondra Hale and miriam cooke on behalf of the Association for Middle East Women's Studies) published by Duke University Press (first volume 2005) and *Hawwa. Journal of Women of the Middle East and the Islamic World*, published by Brill (first volume 2003). EWIC Print I Volume I published a 165-page bibliography (complied by G.J. Roper, C.H. Bleaney, and V. Shepherd) of books and articles on women and Islamic cultures in European languages which had been published between 1993–2003. Seventeen years later, we might need a whole encyclopedia dedicated to a cumulative bibliography.

Why is there so much interest in Muslim women? An easy answer might be that, if Muslims are a quarter of the world's population, then Muslim women are an eighth. There are a lot of them. The Western world has been intrigued by them for hundreds of years. In many ways, Islam and the Middle East has been Europe's most immediate and proximate "other" for centuries. More immediately, in the past four decades, however, has been the increasing politicization of religion in general and of Islam in particular. With the Islamic Revolution in Iran in 1979 and the rise of armed political groupings such as Al-Qaeda, Al-Shabaab, Hamas, Hisbollah, the Taliban, ISIS, Boko Haram, and dozens of others, Western states, media, and popular culture increasingly represented Islam not just as "other" but as "enemy." Muslim men became the prime culprits of everything "bad" and "uncivilized" and "evil" about Islam. Muslim women became the "victims" of both Muslim men and of Islam, as Lila Abu-Lughod exquisitely documented in *Do Muslim Women Need Saving* (2013).

Given the power and hegemonic stature of such representations of Islam, Muslim men, and Muslim women, scholars focusing on Muslim women in the past several decades somehow have written in the shadow of that discourse. Reproducing it, challenging it, attempting to skirt around it—yet it is there. EWIC 2010–2020 works to avoid reproducing this discourse. It takes on critiques of hegemony (Western and non-Western), patriarchy, racism, sexism, Islamophobia and the like—not from a stance of political dialogue, but as questions about the production of knowledge and the production of social life. How, when, under what conditions, why, and by whom are such representations produced? How do Muslim women—and men—represent themselves? How is the production of science, literature, arts, politics, economies, and cultures by Muslim women to be understood from the stand points of history and localities—and from the standpoints of Muslim women? EWIC 2010–2020 works to historicize, situate, and contextualize what is known and what needs to be known about (and by) women and Islamic cultures across all fields of knowledge, in all regions of the world, from the period just before the rise of Islam to the present.

EWIC Print 1 (shorthand for the first six volumes of EWIC published from 2003 to 2007) created a scholarly watershed in the emergence of a field of inquiry. *Choice*, the magazine for librarians, ranked EWIC "essential" for libraries when Volume 1 was published. My Introduction to Volume 1, written with input from the distinguished EWIC Print 1 Editorial Board (Afsaneh Najmabadi, Julie Peteet, Seteney Shami, Jacqueline Siapno, Jane I. Smith), detailed at length the discussions of the Editorial Board to lay a foundation for the production of knowledge of this relatively new field of scholarship.

Conceptual work for EWIC Print 1 began in 1994 when Peri Bearman contacted me on behalf of Brill about doing an "Encyclopedia of Women in Islam." In 1995, she asked me to become General Editor. It took until 1998 to develop a basic outline for the project and write the contract. That original proposal went through many iterations (see my Introduction to EWIC Print 1 Volume 1 for a detailed history). When the EWIC Print 1 Editorial Board began meeting in 1999, we had to invent EWIC from whole cloth. It took years to think through how we wanted to frame it, how we would organize it, what kind of entries we would have, how we would solicit authors, how we would edit, and to settle on the name. We developed 410 topics with the intention of covering those topics in every region of the world. We took on the world of scholarship on women and Islamic cultures. That undertaking consumed the EWIC project from 1999–2007 during which time we published the six volumes of EWIC Print 1 (2003–2007).

EWIC 2010–2020 was built on the foundational work of EWIC Print 1. We started with the EWIC Print 1 list of entries, the entry descriptions, the author guidelines, the approach to soliciting authors (articles were by invitation only), and approximately the same regional representation on the Editorial Board, and basically the same editing process. I had begun in 2001 to build a database of scholars who had expertise on women and Islamic cultures—a searchable database that eventually housed the templates of 1,800 scholars and which I made publically available (https://sjoseph.ucdavis.edu/ewic/ewic-scholars-database).

After Volume V of EWIC Print I was completed, I worked with UC Davis student assistants to do an extensive review of what we had accomplished in EWIC Print I—how many scholars had written for EWIC; how many of them had written more than one article; how many articles on each topic; what regions of the world had been covered—and the like. The result of that analysis was published in a 153-page preface to Volume VI of EWIC Print I.

We used that analysis to think through the first years of EWIC Online. From 2007–2009, with a new Editorial Board, we focused on conceptualizing EWIC Online. Given the many areas we had not been able to cover in EWIC Print I, I invited EWIC Online Editors to solicit authors for any topic in their region to round out regional coverage with material we had not been able to solicit for EWIC Print I. We did not, at the time, know that EWIC Online would one day become nine volumes of a second EWIC print edition. As a result, EWIC Online did not try to present systematic coverage across topics or across regions. We focused on bringing forth scholarship that had not been covered in EWIC Print I, in the early years of production. EWIC Online was launched in 2009 with the uploading of all the articles from EWIC Print I. The first new online supplement published was in 2010.

The goal of EWIC Online was to produce two supplements a year, with 20–25 articles per supplement, aiming for 100,000 words per supplement. From 2010 to 2020, we produced twenty supplements, as planned, though the word length and the number of articles per supplement varied. The *Encyclopedia of Women & Islamic Cultures 2010–2020* (EWIC 2010–2020) is compiled from all the articles in the supplements of EWIC Online, plus a cumulative index.

At times, during the production of EWIC Online, I became concerned that we needed more coverage of Sub Saharan Africa. With the support of the EWIC Brill Editor, I recruited an Associate Editor specifically for that region. As more research emerged on Muslims in Europe, it became clear that we needed dedicated attention to that region. With Brill support, I recruited an Associate Editor specifically for Europe. As we shifted responsibilities, at times the Associate Editor for the Middle East also covered Europe (unless we had a dedicated editor) or Sub Saharan Africa (unless we had a dedicated editor).

EWIC Print I had 410 topics. These were developed by the Editorial Board largely between 1999 and 2003. With the launching of EWIC Online, in 2010, the new Editorial Board recognized the need to add topics that had not been conceputalized or did not exist sociologically in that earlier period—such as social media, the internet, twitter, hip-hop & rap, queer movements, security regimes, and diaspora studies. Eventually, 42 new topics were added between 2010 and 2018, giving EWIC Online Editors a total of 452 topics on which to solicit articles. EWIC Online took a sabbatical in 2020 to complete EWIC 2010–2020 and to conceptualize a new generation of EWIC Online. EWIC Online will resume its production of regular Supplements in 2021.

EWIC Print I published six volumes between 2003–2007. This innovative project brought together the research of 907 scholars who wrote 1,246 articles covering 410 topics, totaling nearly two million words.

EWIC 2010–2020 collects all the articles from ten years of EWIC Online, into a nine-volume set—eight volumes of articles and one volume for the collective index. EWIC 2010–2020 offers 289 articles, written by 292 authors, covering 126 topics. Cumulatively, this is nearly two million words.

EWIC 2010–2020 has about the same number of words as EWIC Print I, even though EWIC Print I had four and half times as many articles. The difference is this: EWIC Print I articles were mostly in the 2,000 word range. EWIC 2010–2020 articles are mostly in the 6,000-word range, allowing for far deeper analysis of each topic covered. In EWIC Print I, the editors were committed to trying to cover every single one of the 410 topics for every region of the world. While we did not achieve that, that ambition drove our guidelines for shorter articles, so we could cover more regions. We were limited by the total number of words allocated for EWIC Print I. EWIC 2010–2020, however, is built from the articles of EWIC Online where there was never a concern about limiting the number of words or the number of supplements. Brill gave us a free hand to make articles longer and to do more articles.

While the first several years of EWIC Online gave EWIC Editors free range to solicit articles on any of the 400+ topics we had accumulated, we saw an opportunity in 2012 to do something different. The tenth anniversary of the publication of EWIC Print I Volume I was in 2013. In anticipation, I proposed to Brill to produce an anniversary volume and Brill agreed. The EWIC Editors together decided that an appropriate celebration of the anniversary would be to invite the authors who had written the disciplinary articles in EWIC Print I Volume I to update their articles. We asked them to critically review what had been produced in their disciplines between 2003 and 2013 in the field of women and Islamic cultures. A number of new disciplinary articles which had not been published in EWIC Print I Volume I were additionally solicited. That exciting project produced the separate book, *Women and Islamic Cultures. Disciplinary Paradigms and Approaches: 2003–2013* (Brill 2013). It was simultaneously published as Supplement 9 of EWIC Online. As the Editors considered the best way to frame EWIC 2010–2020, we decided to spread the articles from that book throughout EWIC 2010–2020. They serve as theoretical and disciplinary introductions to the specific topics covered in Volumes 1–8.

That 2013 anniversary publication inspired the Editorial Board to consider committing some supplements to specific themes. We produced three more supplements focusing on specific themes: Supplement 10 on political violence; Supplement 12 on Sub-Saharan Africa; Supplement 15 on 19th-early 20th century history. We found that thematic supplements were both powerful and problematic. They allowed us to focus on a topic comparatively. Unfortunately, we found that it was difficult to find research on certain topics for certain regions. For example, there was little scholarship on women and Islamic cultures for 19th-early 20th centuries in North and South America in comparison to other regions of the world. For Sub-Saharan Africa, there was little scholarship on political violence specific to women and Islamic cultures.

By 2018, after supplement 18, the Editors had come to a decision that every third supplement would be dedicated to thematic solicitations, with the two in-between supplements left for open solicitation on any of the 452 EWIC topics. It was then that the Brill Editor, Nicolette van der Hoek, suggested that Brill would like to publish a second print edition of EWIC. We shifted focus from thematic supplements to prepare for EWIC 2010–2020.

EWIC 2010–2020 follows the template of EWIC Print I in organizing the volumes thematically, with articles organized alphabetically by topic within each volume. Since the supplements were not solicited with specific print volumes in mind, the coverage of topics is uneven, regionally. Yet, the articles readily fell into broad groupings which sensibly comprised eight the volumes listed below. The specific topics of each volume are listed at the end of this overview of the EWIC Project.

Volume 1 Family, Law, Religion, and Theory
Volume 2 Body, Sexuality, and Health
Volume 3 Economics, Migration, and Refugees
Volume 4 Colonialism, Education, and Governance
Volume 5 Political and Social Movements
Volume 6 Arts and Artists
Volume 7 Knowledge Production and Representation
Volume 8 Literary Studies, Media, and Communications
Volume 9 Cumulative Index

EWIC 2010–2020 comprises another watershed of research on women and Islamic cultures. The publication of two million words organized in 289 articles, written by 292 authors across all disciplines, covering 126 topics addressing women and Islamic cultures across time and locality, offers a landmark

THE EWIC PROJECT

XXI

in the production of knowledge. This landmark will become background and foundation to the next generation of EWIC, which, as I write, is being conceptualized and produced.

Suad Joseph
July 2020
Davis, California

List of Topics in the Encyclopedia of Women and Islamic Cultures
2010–2020

Volume 1 Family, Law, Religion, and Theory

1. Anthropology
2. Divorce and Custody
3. Family
4. Feminism, Islam and Gender
5. History of Science
6. Islam
7. Islamic Studies
8. Islamophobia
9. Law
   a. Articulation of Islamic and non-Islamic Systems
   b. Modern Family Law
10. Marriage Practices
11. Modesty Discourses
12. Motherhood
13. Philosophy
14. Quran
15. Religious Associations
16. Religious Practices
    a. Ablution, Purification, Prayer, Fasting and Piety
    b. Preaching and Women Preachers
    c. Zakat
16. Religious Studies
17. Secularism
18. Sociology
19. Sufi Orders and Movements

Volume 2 Body, Sexuality, and Health

1. Breast Feeding
2. Childhood
3. Domestic Violence
4. Female Genital Cutting
5. Funerary Practices
6. Health Practices
7. Honor
8. Mental Health
9. Population and Health Sciences
10. Reproduction
11. Sexual Harassment
12. Sexualities
    a. Queer Studies
    b. Practices
    c. Transexualities
13. Space
14. Sports

Volume 3 Economics, Migration, and Refugees

1. Demography
2. Development
    a. Discourses and Practices
    b. Non-Governmental Organizations
3. Diaspora Studies
4. Economics
    a. Advertising and Marketing
    b. Crafts
    c. Industrial Labor
    d. Informal Sector
    e. Islamic Banks
    f. Laboring Practices
    g. Sex Workers
    h. Small Business
    i. Social Welfare and Policies
5. Geography
6. History
7. Migration
    a. Refugee Camps

b. Refugee Regimes
c. Regional
8. Slavery
9. Social Hierarchies

Volume 4 Colonialism, Education, and Governance
1. Census Projects
2. Colonialism and Imperialism
3. Education
   a. Colonial
   b. Modern
   c. National Curricula
   d. Regional
4. Education: Religious
5. Human Rights
6. National and Transnational Security Regimes
7. Political Parties and Participation
8. Political Regimes
9. Political Science
10. Public Office
11. Sectarianism and Confessionalism

Volume 5 Political and Social Movements
1. Identity Politics
2. Muslim Women and Violent Protest
3. Political Parties and Participation
4. Political-Social Movements
   a. Academic
   b. Community Based
   c. Feminist
   d. Homosexuality and Queer Movements
   e. Revolutionary
5. Youth Culture and Movements

Volume 6 Arts and Artists
1. Arts and Architecture
2. Arts
   a. Fiction and Fiction Writers
   b. Performers and Performing Groups

> c. Poets and Poetry
> d. Theater
> e. Visual Arts and Artists
> f. Women Writers

3. Cinema
4. Film Studies
5. Music
6. Theater

Volume 7 Knowledge Production and Representation

1. Cinema
2. Production of Knowledge
   > a. International Development Agencies
   > b. Non-Governmental Organizations
   > c. States, Discourses, Policies
3. Representations
   > a. Construction of Individual Women as Iconic
   > b. Cultural Heritage
   > c. Documents
   > d. Film
   > e. Regional Articles
   > f. Theater
   > g. Proverbs, Adages, and Riddles
   > h. Visual Arts
4. Sources and Methods
5. Stereotypes

Volume 8 Literary Studies, Media, and Communications

1. Arts
2. Cultural Studies
3. Literary Studies
4. Memory, Women, and Community
5. New Modes of Communication
   > a. Online Dating
   > b. Social Networking, Text Messaging, Skype
   > c. Web Representations and Blogs
6. Oral History in the Twenty-First Century
7. Production of Knowledge

8. Representations
   a. Fiction
   b. Children's Literatures
   c. Memoirs, Autobiographies, and Biographies
   d. Romance Fiction
9. World Literatures and World Markets

Introduction

The *Encyclopedia of Women and Islamic Cultures 2010–2020* (EWIC 2010–2020), Volume 2, *Body, Sexuality, and Health* brings together thirty-three articles (212,861 words), written by thirty-seven authors on fourteen broad topics with a number of sub-topics, addressed region by region or country by country. The articles come from the twenty supplements of EWIC Online published from 2010–2020.

The EWIC Editors assembled these articles together in one volume because of the intertwining of questions of the body, sexuality, and health. Questions of health turn into questions about the body. Questions around sexuality invariably revert to issues of the body. Issues of the body often lead to questions about sexuality or health. The addition of material on sports, space, and honor aligned with these issues as well. Sports is often discussed in terms of the body and health. Space, especially female space in Islamic cultures, is often discussed in terms of the regulation of the female body. Similarly, honor, in relation to women and Islamic cultures, is commonly understood in terms of cultural practices concerning the female body. The relationships among these questions are continually theorized by scholars of population and health sciences and of sexuality.

Two disciplinary disciplinary articles are included in Volume 2: an article on Population and Health Sciences by Hania Sholkamy and an article on Sexualities and Queer Studies by Samar Habib. The disciplinary articles were solicited for the 2013 volume celebrating the tenth anniversary of the publishing of EWIC Print I Volume 1 (2003). They were simultaneously published as Supplement 9 of EWIC Online. The two disciplinary articles provide an overview and theoretical framing of many of the issues addressed in the regionally specific articles in this volume.

Topically, EWIC 2010–2020, Volume 2 presents one article on honor; three on breast feeding; one on childhood; six on domestic violence; one on female genital cutting; two on funerary practices; one on health practices; one on honor; one on mental health; five on reproductive health; two on sexual harassment; three on sexualities; two on space; three on sports; and one on violence against women. The articles cover the Middle East, Central and South Asia, East and Southeast Asia, Sub-Saharan Africa, and the Americas, offering region or country-specific empirical research contextualizing and situating the specificities of the experiences of women in these diverse cultures all over the world. They are written by scholars from all over the world, from a large range of disciplines, and from a variety of theoretical frameworks.

INTRODUCTION

XXVII

EWIC 2010–2020, Volume 2, covers a decade in which there was an enormous increase in research and profound empirical transformations in relationship to the body, sexuality, and health for women and Islamic cultures. One might suggest that decade was the decade of "the body" and its related concepts and practices. In some sense "the body" has been a central concern for scholars of women and Islamic cultures for centuries. Much of the literature on Muslim women and women in Islamic cultures has focused on women's bodies. The new literature on "the body" goes beyond the centuries old fixation with the bodies of Muslim women and re-figures issues of representation, sexualities, health, domestic violence, harassment, and the like. Research on Muslim women and sports, for example, is relatively new. Research on Muslim women and queer studies and transsexualties, similarly, is more a product of this past decade than any previous period of scholarship. While sexual harassment and domestic violence are not new topics of research, the feminist frameworks brought to these empirical issues is continually shifting to bring new contextual understandings. EWIC 2010–2020 documents a decade of these empirical changes and scholarly understandings of body, sexuality, and health in relation to women and Islamic cultures.

Suad Joseph
July 2020
Davis, California

Breastfeeding

∴

Breastfeeding: Malaysia

Siaan Ansori

Introduction

This entry examines breastfeeding practices of women in Malaysia, paying particular attention to Malay (Muslim) women. The entry begins by describing traditional pre-Islamic breastfeeding practices in Malaysia. Moving into the Islamic period, the entry highlights the importance of breastfeeding in the Qurʾān. The entry then draws on ethnographical studies to examine Malaysia's current breastfeeding practices and policies. Ethnic difference has always affected breastfeeding patterns in Malaysia, with breastfeeding rates for Malaysian-Malay women higher than those for Malaysian-Chinese or Malaysian-Indian. Nevertheless, Malaysia's modernization is shown to have created significant challenges to positive breastfeeding patterns in Malaysia, particularly for Malay women. Urbanization, modern work practices, and decreasing nuclear family size are each shown to have had a negative impact on breastfeeding patterns in Malaysia. The entry concludes by highlighting the need for revised policies to better support Malaysian breastfeeding mothers, particularly Malays.

The Social and Political Context of Islam in Malaysia

Malaysia is a multi-ethnic nation consisting of ethnic Malays and indigenous peoples (60 percent), Chinese (30 percent) and Indians (10 percent). Described as a plural society, these ethnicities live side by side with most interaction being functional only (Hefner 2001, 4). Although Malay is the national language, the ethnic groups speak different languages and practice different customs. Inter-ethnic marriage is still rare. Religion in Malaysia is also defined by these plural divisions. All Malays are Muslims as defined in Entry 160 of the Malaysian Constitution. Most Chinese are Taoist-Buddhists or Christians and the majority of Indians are Hindus or Christians. There is a very small minority of Indians and Chinese who are Muslims. Islam is the official religion of Malaysia but the Constitution allows non-Malays the freedom to practice other religions. Malaysian scholars such as Lee and Ackerman (1997, 21) have argued that Malaysian organizational analysis shows that "there is a 'real' distinction between Islam and other religions in terms of cultural and political

© KONINKLIJKE BRILL NV, LEIDEN, 2012 | DOI:10.1163/1872-5309_EWIC_EWICCOM_001430

development, structures and institutions," despite the formal endorsement of other religions. Islam shapes the political and social landscape of Malaysia, including that of non-Muslims.

Malay women have become the symbol of Malaysia's vibrant Islamic culture. Traditionally Malay women wore body-revealing *sarongs* (long skirts), tight blouses, and rarely covered their hair. In response to Islamic revivalist movements in Malaysia during the late 1970s and early 1980s, the standard female Malay costume has changed. Today the *tudung* (headscarf) and a loose, brightly colored two-piece gown (*baju kurung*) are almost universal costume. Thus, the dress code of Malay women has become the symbol of Islamic piety in Malaysia (Tong and Turner 2007).

Traditional Breastfeeding Practices in Malaysia

There is little scholarly evidence concerning breastfeeding practices in Malaysia prior to the arrival of Islam in the fifteenth and sixteenth centuries. However, study of early Islam in Southeast Asia suggests that Islam was adopted in a way that was compatible with pre-Islamic ideologies in the region (Milner 1983, 24). Given that breastfeeding is endorsed by the Qur'ān and by early Muslim scholars, we may deduce that breastfeeding was the usual form of infant feeding in early Southeast Asian societies.

The Qur'an makes explicit reference to breastfeeding and the importance of breastfeeding for fostering family relationships:

> The mothers shall give suck/ To their offspring/ For two whole years,/ If the father desires / To complete the term (2:233).
>
> Did his mother bear him/ And in years twain/ Was his weaning: (hear / The command), "Show gratitude / To Me and to thy parents"/ (31:14).
>
> In trouble did his mother / bear him, and in pain/ Did she give him birth./ The carrying of the(child)/ To his weaning is/ (A period) of thirty months (46:15).

Anthropological and medical research about the breastfeeding practices of women in the Malay archipelago was collected in an ad hoc manner in the late 1930s through to the early 1960s, with a general pattern of traditional feeding practices among Malays emerging as follows: in the supportive atmosphere of her natal home, a new mother usually established a pattern of breastfeeding on demand. Following a postpartum confinement of around 44 days, the woman returned with her child to her marital home and resumed the full range of domestic responsibilities and other productive activities. Breastfeeding continued until the child was around two years of age, although children were at times breastfed into their third or fourth year or until the mother became pregnant again. Milk supplements were rarely given, although some soft foods were introduced into the child's diet relatively early (often before six months of age). Such early foods included rice, corn flour or wheat flour porridge, mashed banana, and softened bread or biscuits. These foods were provided as a supplement to breast milk. The introduction of solid food was a gradual process and by the child's second year, the child was usually eating hard adult foods as well as rice, corn flour or wheat flour porridge, and later steamed rice, fresh or dried fish, some green leafy or root vegetables and tea or coffee. Weaning usually occurred gradually, although in some cases bitter herbs would be applied to the nipples to hasten the process (Manderson, 1984).

Modern Breastfeeding Patterns

Modern medical scientists have determined that appropriate breastfeeding and complementary feeding are among the most effective interventions to promote child health, growth and development. Among other health benefits, breastfeeding has been shown to protect infants against infectious diseases, assist with neurodevelopment, and decrease the likelihood of asthma and atopy. Breastfeeding has also been shown to have positive impacts on childhood and later life through decreased risk of chronic disease (Gartner et al. 2005).

Since 2001 the World Health Organization has recommended exclusive breastfeeding for infants up to six months of age, with continued breastfeeding along with appropriate complementary foods for children up to two years of age or beyond. Generally speaking, governments around the world have implemented maternal and child health policies to facilitate feeding for this length of time.

Despite what appears to be a fairly strong tradition of breastfeeding, in modern Malaysia the rate of exclusive breastfeeding is considered "very low." Only 14.5 percent of Malaysian mothers breastfeed their children up to six months, according to statistics from the Malaysian Ministry of Health (Bernama 2008). This compares with around 76 percent in Sri Lanka and 32 percent in Australia (WHO 2006–07, Australian Bureau of Statistics 2001). Comparable rates for Muslim countries are 32 percent in Indonesia, 25 percent in Iraq, and 28 percent for Iran (WHO 2006–07, Olang et al. 2009).

Malaysian Breastfeeding Policies

Over the past decade, the government of Malaysia has recognized the significance of breastfeeding for infant nutrition. Formulated in 1993, the National Breastfeeding Policy aimed to promote the health benefits of breastfeeding and to increase the percentage of mothers who actively breastfeed. The original policy recommended exclusive breastfeeding for the first four to six months of a child's life. The policy was revised in 2005 following new recommendations from the World Health Organization that exclusive breastfeeding should last six months and breastfeeding continue for up to two years. Some specific programs delivered under Malaysia's National Breastfeeding Policy have included the Baby Friendly Hospital Initiative, extensions of maternity and paternity leave conditions for the government sector, and a Code of Ethics for the Marketing of Infant Formula.

The impacts of Malaysia's National Breastfeeding Policy and the associated programs are questionable. The Baby Friendly Hospital Initiative is an international initiative that aims to create a health care environment where breastfeeding is the norm. The initiative includes "Ten Steps to Successful Breastfeeding" which are standards by which health services can be assessed and accredited. In March 1998, Malaysia was declared by the World Health Organization as the third country in the world where all public hospitals are "baby friendly." However, despite the high number of accredited "baby friendly" hospitals, the concrete results of the program in Malaysia have not been nearly as successful as in other countries. For example, after China implemented the Baby Friendly Hospital Initiative, rates of exclusive breastfeeding in rural areas rose from 29 percent in 1992 to 68 percent in 1994. Moreover, in urban China, exclusive breastfeeding rates rose from 10 percent in 1992 to 48 percent in 1994. In Cuba, also, the Baby Friendly Hospital Initiative had a noticeable effect on the national rate of exclusive breastfeeding. Following the implementation of the Baby Friendly Hospital Initiative, Cuban rates of exclusive breastfeeding at four months rose from 25 percent in 1990 to 72 percent in 1996 (UNICEF 1991). Malaysia has seen nothing like this level of change since the Baby Friendly Hospital Initiative was implemented.

Likewise, extended maternity and paternity leave conditions in the Malaysian government sector appear not to have met the desired goal of creating an environment conducive to breastfeeding. Extensions of maternity leave conditions in the government sector now allow for women to have between 42 and 60 days maternity leave. Although an improvement on the previous maternity leave entitlement, a 60-day maternity leave period is still well below international standards. For example, the International Labor Organization

Convention states that women should be "entitled to a period of maternity leave of not less than 14 weeks" (98 days) (ILO 2000). Moreover, paternity leave provisions in the Malaysian government sector have been extended to only 7 days. It is unlikely these "improved" maternity and paternity leave periods will have a noticeable impact on breastfeeding rates for Malaysian government officials.

Malaysia has had a Code of Ethics for Infant Formula Products since 1979. Revised in 1983, 1985 and 1999, the code aimed to "uphold the supremacy of breast milk" and "ensure proper use of Infant Formula Products where required" (Ministry of Health Malaysia 1995, 1). In 2008 the code was replaced by a Code of Ethics for the Marketing of Infant Foods and Related Products. The new code was promoted as providing a set of guidelines to control competitive promotion and advertising of commercial products which may undermine mothers' ability and intent to breastfeed.

Despite government endorsement of the successive codes, prevalence of formula feeding remains relatively high in Malaysia. A 2006 study of parental attitudes to infant feeding practices in East Malaysia found that 74 percent of mothers formula-fed their babies by one month of age; 57 percent of mothers reported giving formula to their infants immediately after birth. The predominant reason stated by parents for introducing infant formula was convenience (53 percent). The study also found that most parents (33 percent) became familiar with infant formula brands through advertisements and promotions and 21 percent of respondents learned about infant formula brands through comments made by family or friends who had used them (Chye and Chin 2006). These findings are significant as they suggest that, despite the Code of Ethics for the Marketing of Infant Foods, advertising and marketing of infant formula remains a key influence in a mother's decision concerning breastfeeding. The findings also suggest Malaysian mothers are influenced by family and friends who had already used infant formula. While rates of infant formula use remain high, it is to be expected that this places further pressure on new mothers to turn away from exclusive breastfeeding.

More generally, the key challenge for Malaysian breastfeeding policies is that breastfeeding facilities are not generally or easily available to mothers. Published research suggests that outside of the home, most Malaysian women do not have access to practical aids which would facilitate longer breastfeeding, such as a room to express breast milk, a refrigerator to store breast milk, access to a breast milk pump, a nursery, or associated working conditions such as extended maternity, paternity, or breastfeeding leave (Amin et al. 2011, 5). Even in the Malaysian public sector, which is known for being more "breastfeeding friendly" than other groups, Tan (2011 5) has found that facilities for breastfeeding are generally not acceptable or flexible. Thus Amin et al. (2001) conclude that Malaysia's breastfeeding policies will never be successful because they do not address the obstacles to breastfeeding in Malaysian society.

Factors Impacting Breastfeeding Patterns in Malaysian Society

Extensive study has been completed on the factors influencing a mother's decision to breastfeed (see for example Arora et al. 2000, Bali et al. 2009). In Malaysia alone scholars from a range of disciplines have identified a multitude of factors which influence breastfeeding patterns. This entry argues that ethnicity (religion), urbanization, modern working practices, and decreasing nuclear family size are the key factors which influence breastfeeding trends in Malaysia, particularly those of Malay (Muslim) women.

Ethnicity (Religion)

As outlined, there are three major ethnic groups in Malaysia: Malays, Chinese and Indians. All Malays in Malaysia are Muslim and the Constitution does not allow Malays to formally profess other religions. Of the three ethnic groups in Malaysia, Malays are generally identified as breastfeeding for the longest time (Amin et al. 2011). According to a study conducted in 2000 (Awang and Salleh 2000, 104), Malay-Malaysian women had a median duration of breastfeeding of approximately six months, while Indian-Malaysian women had a median duration of three months. The medium breastfeeding duration for Chinese-Malaysian women was only one month. Similarly, Tan's (2009) analysis found that Chinese-Malaysian women were more likely not to practice exclusive breastfeeding compared to Malay-Malaysian women. DaVanzo et al. (1994) have proposed that Islam promotes breastfeeding. They argue that direct Qur'ānic references to breastfeeding and its importance for motherhood and family life within other Islamic teachings lead to higher breastfeeding rates among Muslims. Thus, DaVanzo et al. conclude that the practice of Islam leads to increased uptake and longer duration of breastfeeding.

While the conclusion of DaVanzo et al. concerning the influence of Islam might perhaps explain the higher breastfeeding rates for Malay-Malaysians when compared with Chinese-Malaysians and Indian-Malaysians, it appears oversimplified when considered in the broader context of Malaysia as a modern progressive nation. Moreover, it does not explain why Malaysia has relatively lower rates of breastfeeding when compared to Western (non-Muslim) countries. Other factors must be influencing Malaysia's breastfeeding patterns.

Urbanization

It seems likely that the breastfeeding patterns of Malaysian women are being influenced by Malaysia's rapid growth and associated modern, "progressive" policies which lead to social change and added pressures on the populace. One such pressure is caused by Malaysia's rapid urbanization. Research into Malaysian breastfeeding patterns has consistently found that rural women breastfeed for longer than urban women. For example, Awang and Salleh (2000) found that the median breastfeeding duration for urban Malaysian women is three months while the median breastfeeding duration for rural Malaysian women is four months. Manderson (1984) argues that contact with urban life and the availability of the commodities of an industrialized society with greater exposure to advertisements promoting infant foods influences a women's decision to move away from exclusive breastfeeding.

Malaysia has developed rapidly since the 1970s and coinciding with this development has been significant rural to urban migration. In 1970, only 29 percent of Malaysians lived in urban areas. Today the figure is more than 71 percent (UNICEF 2009). Malaysian urbanization has had the biggest impact on Malay women who traditionally resided in rural areas. In general, Chinese and Indians were more likely to live in cities. This suggests that the breastfeeding patterns of Malay (Muslim) women will have been more strongly affected by urbanization than those of other ethnic groups.

Modern Work Practices

Statistics from Malaysia's population and housing censuses show that women's workforce participation is increasing. In 1957, women's workforce participation was only 31 percent but by 2003 it had increased to 48 percent. Since 2003 women's workforce participation has remained steady at just under 50 percent (Kennedy 2002).

Numerous studies of breastfeeding practices of Malaysian women over the last decade have shown that women who return to work are less likely to continue exclusive breastfeeding (Tan 2009, Amin et al. 2011, Manderson 1984). The second Malaysian National Health and Morbidity Survey conducted in 1996 showed the prevalence of employed women who had ever breastfed was 91 percent. However, only 25 percent of employed women practiced exclusive breastfeeding compared to 31 percent of non-working women. The mean duration of breastfeeding was 26 weeks among women working outside the home compared to 30 weeks among those who stayed at home (Fatimah et al. 2010).

As already noted, Malaysian working mothers are given less than two months maternity leave and facilities for breastfeeding at workplaces are not acceptable or flexible (Tan 2011, 5). Nevertheless, a return to work does not necessarily lead to failure to breastfeed. Additional factors such as weaning in preparation to return to work, maternal fatigue, and the difficulty in juggling the demands of work and breastfeeding also influence a mother's decision whether to breastfeed. When these additional pressures are coupled with existing poor Malaysian maternity conditions, it is more likely that a Malaysian woman may choose not to breastfeed.

Decreasing Nuclear Family Size

Decreasing family size has also affected breastfeeding patterns in Malaysia. Mothers with more children are generally more likely to breastfeed. For example, a study by Mahdiyah and Kamarulzarman (2008) found that mothers who have three or four children are more likely to breastfeed than mothers who have only one or two children. They also found that mothers with a greater number of children were more likely to breastfeed for longer. Other studies have found that mothers with only one child were less knowledgeable, less skilful and less confident in their breastfeeding skills (Chen 1978).

Confidence in breastfeeding is particularly relevant to Muslim Malaysians. To exclusively breastfeed on demand the mother must feel comfortable feeding outside of the home. It is not standard for Malaysian buildings to include breastfeeding facilities such as parents' rooms. Many Muslim mothers whom the author interviewed believed breastfeeding in public was not appropriate as it conflicted with the image of Malay women as symbols of vibrant Islam in Malaysia. There were also practical difficulties associated with breastfeeding while wearing the chest-covering *tudung* (headscarf) and knee-length blouse (*baju kurung*).

Corresponding with a decrease in the size of the nuclear family is a shift away from cooperation within the extended family. Prior to Malaysia's modernization and urbanization, it was common for families to cohabit with parents or parents-in-law. Where families did not cohabit, a new mother would often return to her natal home for the birth of her child and remain there for a period of postpartum confinement of around 44 days. Women in the extended family supported the new mother and gave guidance about breastfeeding. The extended family also assisted with providing for the physical needs of the new mother, and this was more likely to induce milk production and lead to an established pattern of breastfeeding on demand (Manderson 1984, 47).

Conclusion

Only 14.5 percent of modern Malaysian mothers exclusively breastfeed their children up to six months and this is considered very low by international standards. The percentage of breastfeeding mothers is likely to have been much higher in the premodern period and up until Malaysia's modernization. Through the Qur'ān, Islam emphasizes the importance of breastfeeding a child for up to two years. This is supported by modern recommendations from the World Health Organization.

In 1993 the Malaysian government implemented the National Breastfeeding Policy. Some specific programs delivered under the policy included the Baby Friendly Hospital Initiative, extensions of maternity and paternity leave conditions for the government sector, and a Code of Ethics for the Marketing of Infant Formula. The impacts of Malaysia's National Breastfeeding Policy and the associated programs are questionable. The National Breastfeeding Policy has not been found to have had a substantial impact on rates of exclusive breastfeeding and scholars conclude that the policy may never be successful because the sub-programs do not address the modern obstacles to breastfeeding in Malaysian society (Amin et al. 2001).

Ethnic differences continue to influence breastfeeding patterns in Malaysia, but DaVanzo's Islam-based explanation does not go far enough in explaining the current breastfeeding trends in Malaysia. The author has argued that urbanization, modern work practices, and decreasing nuclear family size are each exerting a negative impact on breastfeeding patterns in Malaysia. In short, Malaysia's modernization has created new challenges for Malaysian mothers, especially those working outside the home, who plan to breastfeed their babies for longer than a few months.

Malay (Muslim) women are the most exposed to the new challenges of modernization. More Malays have migrated from rural to urban areas, and urbanization is shown to affect breastfeeding rates. Residing in modern, urban Malaysia, Malays are also pressured to return to work earlier and are therefore exposed to the breastfeeding challenges associated with modern work practices. Urbanization and modern work practices have also affected the size of the nuclear family and relationships with extended family. In this area also, Malay women are facing challenges in coping with breastfeeding without their traditional support networks.

Islam supports breastfeeding infants and Malay women had always had higher rates of breastfeeding compared with other ethnic groups in Malaysia. However, the analyses in this entry indicate that "modernization" poses the greatest challenges to Malay (Muslim) women, especially if they have moved from their rural villages to work in cities. To return Malaysia's breastfeeding rates to premodern levels, the Malaysian government will need to give further consideration to the negative impacts of Malaysia's modernization on breastfeeding patterns. New maternal policies should be developed which better support Malaysian women, particularly Muslims, in the contemporary environment.

Bibliography

'Alī, 'Abdullah Yūsuf. *The meaning of the Holy Qur'ān*, Beltsville, Md. 1999[10].

Amin, Rahmah Mohd, Zakiah Mohd Said, Rosnah Sutan, Shamsul Azhar Shah, Azlan Darus, and Khadijah Shamsuddin. Work related determinants of breastfeeding discontinuation among employed mothers in Malaysia, in *International Breastfeeding Journal* 6:4 (2011), 1–6.

Arora, Samir, Cheryl McJunkin, Julie Weher and Phyllis Kuhn. Major factors influencing breastfeeding rates. Mother's perception of father's attitude and milk supply, in *Pediatrics* 106:5 (2000), e67.

Australian Bureau of Statistics. 4810.0.55.001 – Breastfeeding in Australia, 2001, <http://www.abs.gov.au/ausstats/abs@.nsf/mf/4810.0.55.001>, accessed 9 August 2011.

Awang, Halimah and Abdul Latif Salleh. Determinants of breastfeeding duration in Peninsular Malaysia, in *Asia Pacific Journal of Public Health* 12:2 (2000), 102–06.

Bali, Y. K., S. E. Middlestadt, C.-Y. Joanne Peng and A. D. Fly. Psychosocial factors underlying the mother's decision to continue exclusive breastfeeding for 6 months. An elicitation study, in *Journal of Human Nutrition and Dietetics* 22:2 (2009), 134–40.

Bernama. Breastfeeding rate low among Malaysian mothers, in *The Star*, 26 December 2008, <http://thestar.com.my/news/story.asp?file=/2008/12/26/nation/2008122612 5136&sec=nation>, accessed 10 March 2011.

Chen, S. T. Infant feeding practices in Malaysia, in *Medical Journal Malaysia* 33:2 (1978), 120–24.

DaVanzo, Julie, Jeff Sine, Christine Peterson and John Haaga. Reversal of the decline in breastfeeding in Peninsular Malaysia? Ethnic and educational differentials and data quality issues, in *Social Biology* 41:1–2 (1994), 61–77.

Fatimah, S., H. N. Siti Saadiah, A. Tahir, M. I. Hussain Imam and Y. Ahmad Faudzi. Breastfeeding in Malaysia. Results of the Third National Health and Morbidity Survey 2006, in *Malaysia Journal of Nutrition* 16:2 (2010), 195–206.

Gartner, L. M., J. Morton, R. A. Lawrence, A. J. Naylor, D. O'Hare, R. J. Schanler and A. I. Eidelman. Breastfeeding and the use of human milk, in *Pediatrics* 115:2 (2005), 496–506.

ILO (International Labour Organization). C183 Maternity Protection Convention, 2000, <http://www.ilo.org/ilolex/english/convdisp1.htm>, accessed 10 December 2011.

Kennedy, Jeffrey. Leadership in Malaysia. Traditional values, international outlook, in *Academy of Management Executive* 16:3 (2002), 15–26.

Lee, Raymond and Susan Ackerman. *Sacred tensions. Modernity and religious transformation in Malaysia*, Columbia, S.C. 1997.

Mahdiyah, Wan Norsiah and Ibrahim Kamarulzarman. Quartiles regression approach to identifying the determinant of breastfeeding duration, *in Journal of Applied Sciences* 8:3 (2008), 540–44.

Manderson, Lenore. These are modern times. Infant feeding practice in Peninsular Malaysia, in *Social Science and Medicine* 18:1 (1984), 47–57.

Milner, Anthony. Islam and the Muslim state, in *Islam in South-East Asia*, ed. M. B. Hooker, Leiden 1983, 23–49.

Ministry of Health Malaysia. *Code of ethics for infant formula products*, Kuala Lumpur 1995.

Olang, Beheshteh, Khalil Farivar, Abtin Heidarzadeh, Birgitta Strandvik and Agneta Yngve. Breastfeeding in Iran. Prevalence, duration and current recommendations, in *International Breastfeeding Journal* 4:8 (2009), 1–10.

Tan, Kok Leong. Knowledge, attitude and practice on breastfeeding in Klang, Malaysia, in *International Medical Journal* 8:1 (2009), 17–21.

Tan, Kok Leong. Factors associated with exclusive breastfeeding among infants under six months of age in peninsular Malaysia, in *International Breastfeeding Journal* 6:2 (2011), 1–7.

Tong, Joy Kooi-Chin and Bryan Turner. Women, piety and practice. A study of women and religious practice in Malaysia, in *Contemporary Islam* 2 (2008), 41–59.

UNICEF (United Nations Children's Fund). Malaysia – statistics 2009, <http://www.unicef.org/infobycountry/malaysia_statistics.html>, accessed 10 September 2011.

UNICEF (United Nations Children's Fund). The baby-friendly hospital initiative, 1991, <http://www.unicef.org/programme/breastfeeding/baby.htm>, accessed 10 December 2011.

WHO (World Health Organization). WHO global data bank on infant and young child feeding, 2006–07, <http://www.who.int/nutrition/databases/infantfeeding/en/index.html>, accessed 10 September 2011.

Yee, Chye Fook and Rebecca Chin. Parental perception and attitudes on infant feeding practices and baby milk formula in East Malaysia, in *International Journal of Consumer Studies* 31:4 (2006), 363–70.

Breastfeeding: Ottoman Empire

Tugce Kayaal

Introduction

As a vital source of nutrition for newborns, breastmilk had a fundamental function in the construction of womanhood in different spatial and temporal settings throughout Ottoman history. Particularly between the mid-nineteenth and early twentieth centuries, due to the pronatalist policies that placed increased importance on cultivating new and ideal Ottoman citizens, the practice of breastfeeding newborns and how it should be performed emerged as a social and political concern in religious, medical, and governmental circles. Despite diverse approaches of each of these circles towards breastfeeding, regarding its duration, frequency, and methods that nursing mothers had to deploy, the practice itself represented in Ottoman patriarchal discourse a crucial signifier of a new stage in womanhood, and it was considered the best way of building an emotional bond between the mother and child. Especially in the early twentieth century, under the government of İttihat ve Terakki Partisi [The Party of Union and Progress], breastmilk and breastfeeding were constructed as a newborn's initial connection first with its mother, and then with national and religious identities.

This article explores the politicization of breastfeeding against the backdrop of sociopolitical changes in the Ottoman Empire between the mid-nineteenth and early twentieth centuries. The alteration of the ethnoreligious composition of the empire, and the radicalization of the state's nationalist discourses (as a result of internal and international military conflicts), generated a heated debate about the nature of mothering and how it should be regulated to achieve the state's goal of creating new Ottoman men and women. Hence, particularly in the early twentieth century, breastfeeding emerged as a practice that every woman learned, beginning in her childhood, through proper training on mothering that started at home and continued in school.

This article explores two diverse yet ideologically intertwined bodies of knowledge on breastfeeding practices in the late Ottoman Empire. First, it introduces the representations of breastfeeding in Islamic theological discourses by historically contextualizing it and pointing out how it overlaps with and diversifies from teachings in Christianity and Judaism on the subject matter. Second, it explores prominent examples from the nineteenth- and

© KONINKLIJKE BRILL NV, LEIDEN, 2019 | DOI:10.1163/1872-5309_EWIC_COM_002177

twentieth-century advice literature produced by medical professionals that targeted new mothers to teach them how to nurse their newborns properly.

Religious References to Breastfeeding

Representation(s) of Breastfeeding in Christianity and Judaism
As early as in the Book of Genesis breastfeeding was considered a mother's natural and sacred duty after childbirth. The Book of Genesis condemned mothers who do not nurse their children whereas it praised those who perform this sacred duty. For instance, Lamentations cursed the "daughters of Israelites" for refusing to breastfeed their newborns: "Even the sea monsters draw out their breasts (to) nurse their young ones. (Yet) the daughters of my people (have become) cruel like ostriches in the wilderness (IV:3, Stevens, Patrick, and Pickler 2009, 32–33)." In Christianity, Mary, mother of Jesus, embodied the symbolic and practical meaning attributed to breastfeeding. In medieval and Renaissance art, Mary's breasts were generally depicted not only as full of milk but also as the source of spirituality as a connected Jesus to his mother and God, the father. (Bynum 2002, 103, Gkegkes 2012, 72).

In the teachings of Christianity, the Virgin Mary was distinguished from the ordinary Christian woman through her impregnation and the perception of her nursing the Son of God as an astral and unique experience. Different from ordinary Christian women, Mary was impregnated not by a man but the Holy Spirit. Hence, the theological interpretations of Mary's breastfeeding Jesus translated this very act as Mary's providing her body and soul for raising the Son of God. Therefore, although it was impossible for an ordinary Christian woman to attain Mary's status, the image of Mary as the virgin mother set an example for her female followers for becoming ideal mothers—desexualized beings devoted to the well-being of their children.

Breastfeeding in Islam
Representations of breastfeeding in Judaism and Christianity impacted its interpretation in Islamic theological discourses. Although Islam shared various common points with Judaism and Christianity regarding the essentiality of breastmilk for the proper physical and emotional development of newborns, certain discrepancies between Islam and these two Abrahamic religions existed concerning the nature and ingredients of breastmilk. In Islamic theological discourse, a nursing mother's sexuality and her sexual activity stand as primary concerns. Similar to the Book of Genesis and the New Testament,

several chapters in the Qur'an emphasize the significance and sacredness of breastmilk—as a source of life for being the essential nutrition for an infant's physical, mental, and emotional development. Therefore, in cases when a nursing mother involved in any form of sexual activity with her husband, it would corrupt the quality and nutritional aspect of the breastmilk. Despite the lack of direct reference in the Qur'an prohibiting nursing mothers to have sexual intercourse, there are various commentaries by Islamic scholars advising mothers to avoid having sex with their partners for the "sake of their babies." Fakhr-al-Dīn al-Rāzī (d. 606/1210), a Persian philosopher and theologian whose works remained relevant in the late Ottoman Empire as his teachings were taught at madrasas was one of these scholars who claimed that sexual intercourse harmed the breastmilk (Giladi 1999, 17, 60). Another Islamic scholar, al-Jāhiz (d. 255/868–9), from Basra, suggested that the mother of a Jāhiliyya-era poet, who had refrained from sexual intercourse with her husband for the entire period she nursed her son, should serve as an example for young Muslim mothers (Giladi 1999, 60–61).

Different from the Old and New Testaments, the Qu'ran suggests the ideal duration for a mother to nurse her baby, although it does not offer guidance on the application of proper methods for nursing or indicate an expected frequency for it. Q2:233 instructs mothers to breastfeed their infants for two years if the father approves the mother's decision to do so. According to many medieval Islamic scholars, the required duration for the completion of a newborn's physical development is two years. However, the span of a pregnancy period brought about specific nuances in how Islamic scholars interpreted the desired duration of nursing. According to Ibn 'Abbās (619–687), an early Islamic scholar and the first exegete of the Qu'ran, a mother should nurse her newborn for 21 months if her pregnancy lasts 9 months. If the pregnancy lasts 6 months, Ibn 'Abbās suggested, the she should keep nursing her baby for 24 months. In any case, the presumed 30-month development of an infant could be completed healthily only if the mother breastfed her baby (Giladi 1999, 41–45, El Tom, and Cassidy 2015, 115–19).

The Qur'an depicts breastfeeding as an instinct that emerges naturally in every woman immediately after parturition. However, certain theological interpretations of the Qur'an acknowledge that in some cases, a mother may not be able to nurse her newborn depite her urge to do so. When, for example, a mother lacks sufficient milk to breastfeed her baby, early Islamic scholars suggested that parents could legitimately hire a wet nurse, subject to certain criteria—theologians and medical professionals from all four major schools of Sunnī Islam (Mālikī, Hanbalī, Shafi'ī, and Hanafī) presumed a connection between breastmilk, blood, and sperm, and hence a kinship tie between two

BREASTFEEDING: OTTOMAN EMPIRE

people nursed by the same woman (Giladi 1999, 53–56, Fortier 2007, 16–20, Thorley 2014, 17); breastmilk as well as sperm, was only blood transformed into a different form. Like blood, both sperm and breastmilk informed the physical and moral features of a newborn. Thus, when a wet nurse suckled a newborn, her milk would affect the formation of the child's physical and moral characteristics. Due to this, many Islamic theologians and medical professionals advised families to find a wet nurse whose moral values and physical attributes resembled the infant's biological parents. According to Modanlou, Ibn Sīnā (Avicenna, d.428/1037) lists in his *al-Qānūn fī l-tibb* ("The canin of medicine") specific characteristics that parents should look for when selecting a wet nurse, including age, physical features, and moral character. A wet nurse should be a Muslim woman between the ages of 25 and 35, with breasts producing milk "moderate in quantity and consistency." Regarding the quality of the milk, "it should be white rather than dark and never greenish, yellowish, or reddish color" (Modanlou 2008, 5).

Ignoring the kinship ties that breastmilk constitutes between two individuals nursed by the same woman would harm the values of traditional family structure defined by Islam. Milk kinship between two individuals brings along the prohibition of marriage. According to the Qur'an (4:23), one could not marry someone suckled by the same woman that suckled them. Moreover, milk nieces, milk daughters, milk aunts, milk grandmothers and granddaughters were all forbidden to men in marriage. These restrictions on marriage also include the milk mother's husband and his relatives. This notion was legitimized for the husband being the source of breastmilk through his sperm (Clarke 2007, 289–90). These particular prohinitions that labeling any conjugal bond between milk relatives echoes how breastmilk's positionality is constructed as a different form of semen in Islamic judicial and theological narratives.

Islamic courts functioned as a ground for practicing the knowledge and ideologies on breastfeeding in the Qur'anic interpretations and Islamic theological studies. As the courts executed Islamic law, they were a prominent vehicle for deploying the teachings of Islam and transferring them to society through its decisions. As studies by feminist scholars in Middle East studies show, shari'a law and the courts that applied it were attractive for Muslim and non-Muslim women abandoned by their husbands with their infant children for various reasons (Peirce 2003, 167–68, Semerdjian 2008, 66–69). Because nursing a child for the first two years of its life was perceived to be vital to its well-being, the shari'a courts supported breastfeeding mothers in cases of divorce or abandonment. Especially in the provinces, remote from the imperial capital, local shari'a courts were the ultimate medium of state and served as the provincial nexus of empire-wide administrative and sociopolitical networks (Peirce 2003, 90). In central Anatolian provinces such as Konya, the shari'a court functioned as a political tool until 1917.

Even in the early twentieth century, when the Ottoman state presumably underwent a sociopolitical process replacing Islam with positivist discourses, the Islamic courts were prevalent and legitimate institutions that nursing women preferred to bring their divorce cases. In one of the cases from Konya, Beyşehir pertaining to 1913–14 that involved a young woman with a child under the age of one, one could see the reason why Islamic courts persisted to remain as the main choice for divorce issues especially for women coming from disadvantaged socioeconomic backgrounds. In her petition to the court, the woman stated that she was destitute as her husband refused to provide for her and their infant child. In the petition, she also highlighted how this unfortunate situation affected her ability to breastfeed her baby. Based on the woman's petition, the judge decided that the husband should be brought before the court, by force if need be, and in the meantime decided to assign the woman a daily payment by the state. Besides this particular example, various divorce cases involving nursing mothers demonstrate that judges often considered the delicate situation of these mothers and typically ruled for higher alimony than was offered other women.

Motherhood and Breastfeeding in Late Ottoman Advice Literature

In the late nineteenth and early twentieth centuries, medicine contributed to the promotion of breastmilk and the nursing mother's sacred imagery through a secular perspective yet by reproducing similar kind of discourses in the early Islamic theological texts. Popular medical and literary advice text were primary tools for circulating the discourses and teachings on nursing and mothering among Ottoman women in the nineteenth and early twentieth centuries. Moreover, it was not only Muslim intellectual circles who promoted the significance of breastfeeding in their publications but non-Muslim elites to focused on spreading the practice of breastfeeding among young mothers. For instance, an Armenian medical journal, Բժիշկ ("Doctor") published a series of articles on proper methods of nursing for new mothers by providing detailed schedules on the timing and frequency of breastfeeding, as well as the amount of milk that infants need according to their age (Լոգմաu, 1913). Another examples is a popular women's magazine published in the early twentieth century, Kadınlar Dünyası ("Women's World"), also published a series of articles on breastfeeding, providing information similar to that published in Բժիշկ. Despite being secular publications, such early twentieth-century journals and magazines reproduced similar discourses that we see in religious teachings on breastfeeding and at certain times did not hesitate to employ them as their reference points.

Late Nineteenth-Century Medical Advice Manuals on Breastfeeding

Despite the discursive resemblances between the early Islamic and the late nineteenth century perceptions of breastfeeding, the political transformation that the Ottoman Empire underwent attributed breastfeeding a further sociopolitical significance. Pronatalist policies took a new form in the Ottoman state's ideological landscape in the mid-nineteenth century. Beginning in the Tanzimat ("Reorganization") era (1839–76), a series of reforms, intended to execute fundamental changes in the state's administrative and judicial system, required the government and its institutional apparatuses to reformulate the notion of social and political belonging for Ottoman subjects. To achieve the aim of cultivating new Ottoman subjects, the Ottoman state deployed novel pronatalist policies, mostly inspired by Western medical discourses. This political maneuver brought about strict measures that subjected female sexuality and reproduction to medical and legal control mechanisms. As the state's main motive became promoting and preserving the female body's fertility and reproductive capabilities, evert aspect of mothering, including pregnancy and breastfeeding, became a site of ideologically motivated state intervention (Balsoy 2016, 89–93).

Nineteenth-century advice manuals on breastfeeding display the impacts of the political climate in the late Ottoman Empire. Besim Ömer (d.1940), an Ottoman obstetrician who received his higher education degree in Paris, published many booklets and newspaper articles on pregnancy and infant-feeding, as well as providing tips to young mothers on preserving maternal bodily health (Balsoy 2016, 90). In *Emzirmek* ("Breastfeeding," 1892), Ömer examined the proper methods of breastfeeding and its impacts on the infant's development. He highlighted the importance of nursing to a newborn's physical, mental, and emotional development, noting how a minor mistake in breastfeeding, usually caused by the mother's ignorance, could lead to irreversible damage. Ömer acknowledged that many young women, due to poor health, cannot breastfeed their babies even if they want to do so. Although in these cases a wet nurse was the best alternative as it was also allowed in the Islamic teachings, he also admitted that many parents cannot afford to hire a wet nurse. Different from most of his contemporaries, Ömer did not entirely rule out feeding newborns artificially, including with animal's milk. However, he stressed that parents should feed their newborns with animal's milk only if it is a necessity and that once they have used this method, the mother should pay particular attention to the preservation of the milk and the hygiene of the equipment by which she feeds her baby. Ömer also argued that the first sort of animal's milk that can substitute mother's milk is donkey's milk; cow's milk should be the last option if parents cannot supply the first.

Early Twentieth-Century on Advice Literature on Breastfeeding

In the early twentieth century, medical professionals abandoned discourses that tolerated alternative means of feeding newborns and breastfeeding once again became the only desired way to feed infants until the age of two. The sociopolitical transformation that the Ottoman state and society underwent from 1908 until the collapse of the empire, and the impact of this transformation on official pronatalist policies, played a significant role in this radical shift, especially after the declaration of the Ottoman state's participation in World War I as an ally of the Central Powers in early 1914. The government at the time deployed new measures to mobilize the empire's financial and human resources (Beşikçi 2012, 33–93, Akın 2018, 82–144, Tanielian 2018, 51–109). In order to cope with the war effort's demands for human resources, the state promoted the raising of young and physically healthy children and, with its intellectual allies, reframed mothering as every Turkish woman's national duty (Akın 2018, 144–63). Mainly during the Balkan Wars (1912–13) and World War I (1914–18), breastfeeding was considered not only the healthiest way of feeding newborns but also those newborns' primary connection to the nation. Medical journals and women's magazines published between 1913 and 1918 consistently propagated the benefits of breastfeeding and condoned recruiting wet nurses only if they shated the same ethnic background as a newborn's biological parents.

A prominent example of the impacts of the wartime ideological climate on teachings about breastfeeding is Mustafa Rahmi's (d. 1953) Çocuk Büyütmek ("Child-rearing," 1919). After graduating from the Istanbul Advanced Teachers Training School (*İstanbul Yüksek Öğretmen Okulu*), Rahmi started his teaching career as a pedagogy teacher at Skopje Training School for teachers (*Üsküp Öğretmen Okulu*). Alongside his publications on Turkish nationalism, he also produced and translated numerous works on child-rearing in the late Ottoman and early Republican era. Among these, Çocuk Büyütmek (A Turkish Translation of Rahmi's original French, with adjustments in its content) devoted a significant section to the importance of breastfeeding and how new mothers should take care of themselves while nursing their newborns. In the book's prologue, Rahmi stresses that girls should be trained, both at home and at school, as ideal mothers of the future, and adds how essential it is to keep newborns alive given the challenges faced by the wartime government. Rahmi argues that the issue of population is one of the nation's most significant and urgent concerns, and despite the challenges that the Ottoman Empire experienced with increasing the population, preventing newborn deaths was the best solution to preserving its balance. Without giving a particular reference, Rahmi gives the death rate among newborns at 50 percent, and suggests that every young girl should be properly trained in mothering. In concluding his prologue, Rahmi suggests a radical policy of developing a certificate program in mothering for young girls of every age and of allowing only those who receive an officially approved certificate to have children.

In the book's first chapter, Rahmi outlines the fundamental rules that every breastfeeding mother should follow. He defines an infant's first year as the most significant in a child's physical and mental development. He describes breastmilk as being the best substance for supporting children's current and long-term immune systems and for protecting them against fatal diseases. Breastfeeding her children should therefore be every new mother's most sacred duty. Rahmi argues that it is very rare for breastfed newborns to experience any digestion problems. However, if a mother does not know how to breastfeed her baby properly, then breastmilk can threaten her child's biological development. Rahmi suggests that mothers should pay particular attention to sufficiently breastfeeding their children according to the scientifically defined frequencies and quantities at the different stages of their development. He warns that overfeeding a newborn with breastmilk may cause severe mental and physical damage.

Rahmi provides charts to guide mothers in how often to breastfeed their newborns. A mother should start breastfeeding her baby twelve hours after childbirth—before that, the newborn and the mother need to rest. After twelve hours, mothers should nurse their babies two to four times a day on the first day after childbirth; four to six times on the second day; and six to eight times after the third day. Rahmi advises mothers to continue suckling their babies up to eight times a day for the first three months, and to gradually decrease the frequency until the age of two. According to this program, a three- or six-month-old infant should be nursed six times a day, then five times a day until the end of the sixteenth month, and then four times a day until the child reaches the age of two, which is also the age for weaning. Rahmi also offers a daily plan for splitting the breastfeeding sessions between day and night in such a way that the practice should not be detrimental to either the baby's or the mother's health. In the first week after childbirth, a mother should nurse her baby seven to eight times during the day and one to two times at night; after the end of the first week and until the fourth month, six to seven times during the day and only once or not at all at night; and after the fourth month until weaning, six times or less during the day and not at all at night.

FIGURE 1
A breastfed six-month-old baby *Çocuk Büyütmek*

The advice manuals also advised on the duration of the intervals between nursing sessions, according to a child's physical maturity. In *Çocuk Büyütmek*, Rahmi recommends regulating these intervals according to the child's weight. If the child weighs less than 2,500 grams, then the interval should be two and a half hours; for children weighing 2,500–3,000 grams, two and a half to three hours; and for those weighing more than 3,500 grams, three hours. Quantities also varied depending on age and weight. According to the instructions in *Çocuk Büyütmek*, for the first three months, the amount of milk was half a baby's total weight. For a two-month-old, this amount would be $\frac{1}{7}$ of their weight, and the amount of milk would reduce to $\frac{1}{8}$ of an infant in the third month. Alongside highlighting the significance of these calculations, Rahmi also emphasizes that, as a general rule, a mother can allow her baby as much milk as it wants, so long as it does not vomit or have unusual bowel movements.

Similar to many other advice manuals on the subject published at the time, *Çocuk Büyütmek* also deals with the importance of protecting a breastfeeding mother's physical and mental health, which was considered essential especially because it was supposed to affect the quality of breastmilk. In particular, Rahmi covers the sleep cycle, nutrition, attire, and mental health. To preserve her mental health, a breastfeeding mother should avoid any form of stress. To do so, she should not concern herself with problems of everyday life and should not stress over minor health issues that infants usually experience. To maintain healthy sleeping habits and cycle, nursing mothers should sleep for seven hours at night. To achieve this, they should not wake up to nurse their child every time it cries and should sleep in a separate room to their babies. In respect to nutrition, breastfeeding mothers should eat less than normal but frequently and should prefer nutritious and digestible foods. Any digestive problems experienced by mothers as a result of poor nutritional choices could produce the same problems in the suckling infant, so breastfeeding mothers should avoid spicy foods and should prefer chicken and meat broils, vegetable soups, fruits, and dried nuts. In terms of personal hygiene, mothers are advised to sterilize their nipples, and to wash them with a damp cloth immediately before and after nursing. As for attire—casual and formal—comfortable clothes that keep breasts warm are to be preferred.

Other advice literature published by Rahmi's contemporaries and successors echoes his methods in Çocuk Büyütmek. This consensus on proper breastfeeding methods arose partly because many medical experts of the time relied on European (mainly French and German) medical texts and advice manuals on breastfeeding and child-rearing. Another critical name, Dr. Refik Münir (d. 1940), wrote Çocuk Beslemek ("Child-feeding"). In addition to having a long and detailed section on breastfeeding, this book also addresses methods for feeding children after weaning. Among the other advice manuals on child-rearing, Münir's book had a long-lasting impact on breastfeeding teachings by having two more editions, one of which was published in 1925, immediately after the founding of the Turkish Republic. In the prologue, similar to his colleague Mustafa Rahmi, Münir highlights the importance of reducing the infant death rate as much as possible as a solution to the population crisis in the late Ottoman Empire resulting from circumstances caused by military conflict. He blames the ignorance and incompatibility of young, mostly rural, mothers and suggest public training to increase awareness about the indispensability of breastmilk to a newborn's healthy development. In addition to setting the nursing mothers in Europe as "articulated, knowledgable, and educated" examples for their Ottoman counterparts, Münir also reminds his readers that "nothing can replace the loving heart of a mother and her milk for the newborn" (Münir 1914, 9).

Unlike most of his contemporaries, including Rahmi, Münir refuses to accept any excuse for a mother's not breastfeeding her child, arguing that a mother should be prepared for any difficulties that she might encounter in raising her child, and that there is no plausible explanation or excuse, including health problems, for not breastfeeding. It was, according to Münir, very rare for a mother who genuinely wants to breastfeed her child to be unable to

FIGURE 2
"Verda is Breastfed by Her Mother" in *Çocuk Büyütmek*

do so—every female body that gives birth to a child, immediately, as a law of nature, produces the substance to feed her baby. Accordingly, even mothers who suffer from fatal diseases (such as tuberculosis and pox) are, most of the time, able to breastfeed. Mothers should be patient for the first few days after childbirth, as their breasts may not produce milk immediately. Depending on the mother's physical condition, it might take a few days for the breasts to have produced sufficient milk to feed the baby. In any case, mothers should ignore any medical or nonmedical advice to recruit a wet nurse or to feed the baby by artificial methods.

Münir includes in *Çocuk Beslemek* a short section on the consanguinity between a mother's physical features and the quality of her breastmilk. He emphasizes that a mother should pay close attention to her physical health—especially her weight, and hence nutrition—starting with the first day of her pregnancy. He suggests that a medical examination is the best way to measure the quality of breastmilk, but a mother's physical features and her health are a superficial yet efficient way to determine it. Fat women's breastmilk usually contains more fat than that of skinny mothers; and older mother's milk contains less fat, whereas a young mother's breastmilk usually contains the desired amount of fat for the child's development. Neither more fat nor less than the proper amount (4.07%) is healthy for infants; hence Münir advises women to consider their age and watch their weight before, during, and after pregnancy until weaning.

The male elite circles of the late Ottoman Empire, with a medical background, were not the only ones who aimed to regulate breastfeeding mothers' bodies and daily lives. Magazines published by elite Turkish Muslim women, such as *Kadınlar Dünyası,* reproduced contemporary medical and political discourses on breastfeeding, some of which are covered in the magazine's relevant articles (Mustafa Rahmi, Besim Ömer, and Refik Münir). An educated Muslim woman, Nuriye Ulviye Mevlan (d. 1964) founded Kadınlar Dünyası in 1913, and it became one of the earliest examples of a magazine featuring literary output exclusively by and for Ottoman women (Çakır 2007, 69–70). Stories, peoms, and advice literature produced mostly by the magazine's owner, Ulviye Mevlan, and her comrades focused on a variety of issues related to women such as fashion, childcare, and pregnancy.

Even though *Kadınlar Dünyası* promoted elite Turkish Muslim women's voices, with the aim of integrating women further into the public as well as political realm, it was not immune to elite male elite discourses about female bodies and sexuality, including patriarchal discourses. Advice literature published in the magazine, especially during World War I, projected the influence of nationalist and patriarchal discourses over how an ideal Ottoman woman, particularly a mother, should be. The magazine's fifth issue, published on 18 September 1914, included the first article in a series on breastfeeding, "Emzirmek" ("Breastfeeding"), penned by an anonymous author. The article begins by framing motherhood as every woman's most sacred duty: "The God Almighty created us, women, with an ability to feed our babies that one must consider as one of his biggest miracles." As this excerpt shows, the shift from a religious to a medical and scientific discourse on breastfeeding in the late Ottoman Empire did not necessarily mean that the elites, including women, totally abandoned early Islamic references highlighting the importance of breastmilk. The idea of the God-given sacredness of breastfeeding appears more explicitly when the author discusses mothers who, due to health problems, cannot nurse their children and mothers who prefer not to breastfeed their infant children for their "personal interests":

> Usually, it is the mother who nurses her baby [by her breastmilk]. In some instances, a mother's health problems may not allow her to suckle her baby. In this case, she can hire a wet nurse [to feed her baby]. However, we also encounter young mothers in perfect health and have abundant milk in their breasts, yet they avoid nursing their children because they do want

to continue to be a part of social gatherings and parties. We resent such woman and do not deem them worthy of the sacred title of motherhood.

EMZIRMEK 1913, 50

As the above excerpt demonstrates, although the possibly female author of *Kadınlar Dünyası* tolerates mothers who, due to health problems, cannot breastfeed their children, she condemns those who, out of personal interest, do not perform it, and she even excludes such women from the category of motherhood. Hence, similar to their male counterparts, female intellectuals framed breastfeeding as every mother's most sacred, even national, duty.

This particular article in *Kadınlar Dünyası* also discusses the benefits for a mother's body of breastfeeding. In a section titled "Irza-i Maderi" ("Breastfeeding"), the relatively thin substance coming from the breast immediately after childbirth, known as *ağız* (colostrum), was said to help to prevent the occurrence of fissures due to the large amount of milk that the breasts produce. However, in his medical manual *Kadınlık ve Analık* ("Womanhood and motherhood," 1913), Kenan Tevfik advises his audience to avoid nursing a newborn baby with colostrum immediately after birth and recommends waiting for twelve hours before suckling. He also informs readers that accumulating milk in a new mother's breasts could cause the emergence of fissures, which might harm their aesthetics. Only by breastfeeding could mothers avoid such permanent damage to the physical appearance of their breasts.

Different from the general arguments about the proper methods of breastfeeding, "Irza-i Maderi" prioritizes not only the infant's healthy development but also the mother's physical and mental health. Unlike their contemporaries, instead of imposing strict guidelines on nursing mothers determining how proper breastfeeding should be, the author allows mothers flexibility in when and how they should suckle their infants. For instance, if an infant resists being fed, the mother should wait for one or two hours to allow the infant to become hungry. Hence, the author does not insist that mothers commit to a strict schedule, unlike their contemporary male medical experts. Moreover, a mother should nurse her baby one breast at a time, so that her breasts do not suffer from any bruises caused by the suckling infant, or from fissures due to being overloaded with milk.

Conclusion

The perception that breastmilk was the best nutrition for feeding newborns was not unique to the late nineteenth and early twentieth-century Ottoman discourses—breastfeeding appears as an indispensable aspect of mothering in the sacred texts of the three monotheistic religions, Judaism, Christianity, and Islam, and the theological interpretations of breastfeeding in these texts continued to inform medical discourses in the late nineteenth century.

Beginning in the mid-nineteenth century, Ottoman advice literature on breastfeeding deployed these early Islamic interpretations and blended them with scientific discourses imported from Europe. Many prominent intellectual figures from the late Ottoman Empire, particularly during World War I, reconstructed the notion of motherhood, with a particular emphasis on breastfeeding to control the bodies and reproductivity of Turkish Muslim women with the motive of raising a desired new generation for the Ottoman nation. Even popular women's magazines of the time, produced by female intellectuals, such as *Kadınlar Dünyası* gave space to articles on breastfeeding and how to perform it correctly. Therefore, late Ottoman Empire popular and medical literature promoted breastmilk as a practice that would lead to a mother's rapid recovery after childbirth and healthy physical, mental and emotional development of her newborn.

Bibliography

Akın, Yiğit. *When the war came home. The Ottomans' Great War and the devastation of an empire*, Stanford, Calif. 2018.

Balsoy, Gülhan. *The politics of reproduction in Ottoman society, 1838–1900*, Abingdon, U.K. 2016.

Beşikçi, Mehmet. *The Ottoman mobilization of manpower in the First World War. Between voluntarism and resistance.* Leiden & Boston, 2012.

Bryder, Linda. From breast to bottle. A history of modern infant feeding, in *Endeavour* 33:2 (2009), 54–59.

Bynum, Caroline Walker. *Fragmentation and redemption. Essays on gender and the human body in medieval religion*, New York 2002.

Bynum, Caroline Walker. *Jesus as mother. Studies in the spirituality of the High Middle Ages*, Berkeley, Calif. 2007.

Carter, Pam. *Feminism, breasts, and breast-feeding*, New York 1995.

Cassidy, Tanya, and Abdullahi El Tom (eds.). *Ethnographies of Breastfeeding: Cultural Contexts and Confrontations*, London, Bloomsbury, 2015.

Chodorow, Nancy. *The reproduction of mothering. Psychoanalysis and the sociology of gender*, Berkeley, Calif. 1978.

Çakır, Serpil. "Feminism and feminist history writing in Turkey. The discovery of Ottoman feminism." *Aspasia* 1 (2007), 61–83.

Du Tamar, Comtesse. *Hayat-ı nisvanın serair-i inkişafı* [Disclosing secrets in women's lives], trans. B. Muharrir, Istanbul 1914.

Fortier, Corinne. "Blood, sperm, and embryo in Sunni Islam and in Mauritania. Milk kinship, descent, and medically assisted procreation," *Body and Society* 13:3 (2007), 15–36.

Giladi, Avner. *Infants, parents, and wet nurses. Medieval Islamic views on breastfeeding and their social implications*, Leiden 1999.

Gkegkes, Ioannis D., Vassiliki M. Darla, and Christos Lavazzo. Breastfeeding in Byzantine icon art, in *Archives of Gynecology and Obstetrics* 1:286 (2012), 71–73.

Լօզման. "Մանուկները ինչպես պէտք է սնուցնալ" [How should the infants be nursed?]. Բժիշկ 1 (1911), 18–20.

Maher, Vanessa (ed.). *The anthropology of breast-feeding. Natural law or social construct*, New York 1992.

Modanlou, H.D. Avicenna (AD 980 to 1037) and the care of the newborn infant and breatfeeding, in *Journal of Perinatology* 28:1 (2008), 1–6.

Morgan, Lisa Zaynab, and Ali Peiravi (trans.). A divine perspective on rights. A commentary on Imam Sajjad's "The Treatise of rights" by Imam 'Ali ibn al-Husayn as-Sajjad. Qum 2002.

Münir, Refik. *Çocuk Beslemek* [Child-feeding], Istanbul 1914.

Ömer, Besim. *Emzirmek* [Breastfeeding], Istanbul 1892.

Peirce, Leslie. *Morality tales. Law and gender in the Ottoman court of Aintab*, Berkeley, Calif. 2003.

Rahmi, Mustafa (trans.). *Çocuk Büyütmek* [Child-rearing], Istanbul 1915.

Semerdjian, Elyse. *"Off the straight path." Illicit sex, law, and community in Ottoman Aleppo*, Syracuse, N.Y. 2008.

Shaikh, Ulfat, and Omar Ahmad. Islam and infant feeding, in *Breastfeeding Medicine* 1:3 (2006), 164–67.

Shivram, Balkrishan. *Kinship structures and foster relations in Islamic society. Milk kinship allegiance in the Mughal world*, Shimla 2014.

Stevens, Emily E., Thelma E. Patrick, and Rita Pickler. A history of infant feeding, in *The Journal of Perinatal Education* 18:2 (2009), 32–39.

Suad, Joseph, and Deniz Kandiyoti (eds.). *Gender and citizenship in the Middle East*, Syracuse, N.Y. 2000.

Tanielian, Melanie S. *The charity of war. Famine, humanitarian aid, and World War I in the Middle East*. Stanford, California, 2018.

Tevfik, Kenan. *Kadınlık ve Analık* [Womanhood and motherhood], Istanbul 1913.

Thorley, Virginia. "Milk siblingship, religious and secular. History, applications, and implications for practice, in *Women and Birth* 27:4 (2014), 16–19.

Yalom, Marilyn. *A history of the breast*, New York 1997.

Yılmaz, Fatma Büyükkarcı and Tülay Gençtürk Demicioğlu (eds.). *Kadınlar Dünyası. Yeni Harflerle (1913–1921)* [*Women's World*. With Modern Turkish alphabet (1913–1921)], 1, 1.–50. *Sayılar* [Nos. 1–50], Istanbul 2009.

Breastfeeding: West Africa

Michelle Johnson

Introduction

In Muslim societies throughout West Africa, breast-feeding is considered to be the healthiest and most routine way to nourish one's baby. Whereas women in Western societies generally consider breast-feeding to be a choice rather than an obligation, this is not the case in West Africa: breast-feeding is often the only option available to women, and always the safest and most convenient one. Even when other options are available, such as bottle-feeding powdered milk or formula, West African women generally choose to breast-feed their babies as long as they are physically capable of doing so. Not only do mothers want to breast-feed their babies, they are expected to do so, and are often reminded of this essential maternal responsibility by members of their families and communities. Indeed, mothers consider breast-feeding one of their most important maternal duties. Muslims in West Africa also believe that babies have the right to be breast-fed, if not by their own mothers then by someone else. If a woman is not physically capable of breast-feeding, or if she dies during childbirth or at any time while she is breast-feeding an infant, the baby may be handed over to another woman, such as a relative, co-wife, or friend who has recently given birth, to be breast-fed. Not all ethnic groups embrace wet nursing, as it is termed in the West, however, and when it is practiced it is not done lightly, because it has consequences for both mothers and babies. This will be addressed in more detail later in the article.

Although Muslims in West Africa generally consider breast milk to be nutritive and essential to babies' health and proper development, they also consider breast-feeding to be about much more than just physical sustenance and nourishment. For some West African Muslims, breast-feeding is considered a form of communication between mothers and their babies. In Mande cultures throughout the region, breast milk is thought to configure relatedness and to structure or shape relationships between people who have drunk the same breast milk. Fulani and Mandinga believe that breast-feeding transmits personality characteristics from mother to baby and that it is linked to the development of personhood and religious identity through the life course.

© KONINKLIJKE BRILL NV, LEIDEN, 2016 | DOI:10.1163/1872-5309_EWIC_COM_002075

When Babies Are Breast-fed

In most Muslim societies in West Africa, babies are breast-fed for the first time shortly after birth or on the second or third day following birth. This delay can be explained by the fact that members of some societies do not give infants colostrum, the thick yellow substance that is present in a woman's breasts before her actual breast milk comes in. Although specific beliefs about colostrum differ across societies, it is rarely considered dangerous. More commonly, it is simply thought to be a worthless substance that contains little nutritive value. Mandinka in southern Senegal, for example, describe colostrum as "think and weak"; they liken it to water and equate it symbolically with amniotic fluid (Whittemore and Beverly 1996, 55). Pastoral Fulani in Cameroon feel that colostrum is "bad" because of its color; they believe that breast milk should be white like cow's milk, and associate white with purity (Yovsi and Keller 2003, 153). In contrast, Fula in Guinea-Bissau generally give their babies colostrum, feeling that it "gives babies strength and protection against diseases" (Gunnlaugsson and Einarsdóttir 1993, 285).

Mothers who don't give babies their colostrum may either express the colostrum from their breasts or simply wait to breast-feed their babies until their proper breast milk comes in. During this period, a mother might ask a lactating relative, co-wife, or friend to breast-feed her baby if the little one appears to be hungry. Not all societies, however, practice wet nursing. Mandinka in the Casamance region of Senegal, for example, contend that an infant who drinks another woman's breast milk is said to "spoil" the milk (Whittemore and Beverly 1996, 55). Mothers who reject wet nursing may instead satiate their infants with water while they are waiting for their breast milk to come in. Senegalese Mandinka mothers may sweeten water with sugar or honey before giving it to their babies. Grandmothers may also attempt to satiate their hungry grandbabies by giving them "kola milk," a bit of kola nut that they have chewed (Whittemore and Beverly 1996, 51). Not only is this nut a stimulant that is considered throughout West Africa to sharpen the mind and aid in digestion, it has profound symbolic importance and is often used in life-course rituals, including name-taking rituals, weddings, and funerals.

Although it is common, and even encouraged, in the West to breast-feed infants exclusively for the first six months, this is often not the case in West Africa, where women routinely supplement breast-feeding with other food and drink as early as the first week of life. Mothers in many societies commonly give babies water in addition to breast milk. In Côte d'Ivoire, Beng converts to Islam, for example, may still practice the indigenous custom of offering their babies one to three handfuls of cool water at a time, a practice they call *kami* (Gottlieb 2004, 86). Giving water to breast-feeding babies makes sense symbolically considering that in many African languages "breast milk" translates more accurately as "breast water," and breast milk and water are symbolically linked substances. Like breast milk, water is a highly valued substance in West Africa. It is used in many ritual practices and is considered healthy and necessary for all human beings, including babies. In some societies, offering water to babies also satisfies breast-feeding babies before their mothers' milk comes in, in between feedings, or when a mother is separated from her baby because of work or any other reason (Gottlieb 2004, 186–87). For these same reasons, Fulani mothers in Burkina Faso also commonly give their babies *basi*, a "medicinal broth" made with water and herbs (Riesman 1992, 115). Pastoral Fulani in Cameroon give their babies water immediately after birth, which they believe is both healthy and clears a newborn's throat (Yovsi and Keller 2003, 153). In addition to water, Fulani mothers throughout the region commonly offer their nursing babies cow's milk, goat's milk, or butter as early as shortly after birth (Johnson 2000, 188). Bambara and Mandinka mothers in Mali give their babies warm water daily beginning the day after birth and continuing until they are three to four months old. This is thought to "open the baby's stomach" (Dettwyler 1987, 636). Many West African mothers feed their nursing babies soft foods, including mashed cassava, yam, or plantain, as well as a thin porridge made from rice, millet, or maize as early as the first week of life.

Before breast-feeding their babies for the first time, West African Muslim mothers may wash their breasts with water and medicinal herbs. Beginning with the right breast, Mandinka mothers in the Senegambia commonly offer their right nipple to their babies while saying aloud the opening sura of the Qur'an. They also tell their babies to "suck" before breast-feeding them, especially for the first time. If they do not do this, they believe that their babies will have difficulty breast-feeding; for example, they may not appropriately latch on, or may completely reject the breast, both of which can have disastrous effects on their health and ethnic and religious identity (Johnson 2002, 78). Before nursing their babies for the first time, Fulani mothers commonly take a purgative gruel to "purify their blood" (Johnson 2000, 188). They also eat certain plants to bolster their milk supply, a widespread practice in West Africa. Which specific foods are thought to bolster breast-feeding, however, vary from one society to another. Muslim healer-diviners also make herbal or Qur'an-based medicines in the form of liquid or amulets to aid breast-feeding mothers, especially first-time mothers, mothers who struggle to breast-feed because of difficulties such as soreness, cracked nipples, and infection, and mothers whose babies struggle to latch on or refuse the breast.

Although mothers in the West tend to breast-feed their babies according to a schedule, once every two to three hours, this is not at all the case in West

Africa, where mothers breast-feed on demand. As Dettwyler (1988, 175) explains for Muslim women in Mali: "It is considered a primary right of children to be nursed whenever they want, for as long as they want, as often as they want." This attitude is typical throughout the region. Mothers throughout West Africa offer their babies the breast not only when they appear to want it or are hungry; infants who express fear or discomfort or cry for any reason at all may be offered the breast to calm them. Breast-feeding their babies at the slightest sign of distress is also a primary way by which West African mothers demonstrate care and their maternal skills, both to their babies and to relatives and community members. Other women, especially co-wives and in-laws, are quick to criticize mothers who do not immediately breast-feed their crying babies. Demanding to be breast-fed whenever they express the desire (or whenever they are distressed) is also a primary way by which babies assert themselves as agents and demand attention and care.

Muslim women throughout West Africa usually allow their babies to breast-feed for as long as they want at each feeding. At the same time, they never force their babies to breast-feed if they don't want to. A mother who is worried about her baby's long-term disinterest in breast-feeding or refusal to breast-feed, however, may fear for the little one's health, well-being, and even ethnic and religious identity, and may consult a Muslim healer-diviner for herbal or Qur'an-based remedies to discover the problem and encourage the little one to breast-feed.

Breast-feeding Beliefs and Taboos

In many Muslim societies in West Africa, breast milk is thought to be a powerful substance, and breast-feeding is thought to render both mothers and babies vulnerable in different ways. As such, breast-feeding and breast milk itself are often surrounded by taboos. Breast-feeding mothers may avoid certain foods that are thought to interfere with the production of breast milk or with the practice of breast-feeding more generally. Fulani mothers in Burkina Faso, for example, avoid foods that they consider to be too "strong," such as butter, cassava, meat, and couscous. In their view, these foods produce over-rich milk and give their babies digestive problems (Johnson 2000, 188). In many cases, however, foods are taboo due to the symbolic problems they present, which are thought to produce similar consequences: a fruit that is characteristically "dry" inside, for example, is avoided so as not to dry out a mother's breast milk. In some societies, however, foods may be thought to have little or no effect on a woman's breast milk and none are avoided.

While breast-feeding is generally a public activity in West Africa, nursing mothers may limit the exposure of their bare breasts for fear of witchcraft, because witches are thought to harm babies by poisoning breast milk. Breast milk is also treated with care: Fulani mothers, for example, contend that if even a tiny amount of breast milk drips onto a baby boy's penis, he will grow up to be impotent. Likewise, should breast milk touch a baby girl's vagina, she may have difficulty finding a partner or staying married (Johnson 2000, 188). These beliefs are found among other Muslim groups in West Africa.

Length of Breast-feeding Period and Weaning

Mothers in Muslim societies throughout West Africa believe that babies should be breast-fed for a minimum of two years. Many trace this directly to the Qur'an and feel that it is both a baby's right and a mother's responsibility to uphold this ideal so long as the mother is physically capable of doing so. Pastoral Fulani in Cameroon consider women's breasts "a precious gift of God for her children" (Yovsi and Keller 2003, 154). They contend that children who are not breast-fed for two years may lose their herds in later life and be dependent on others for a living. As a result of this belief, a Fulani husband can divorce his wife if she does not breast-feed their child for two years (Yovsi and Keller 2003, 154).

Babies are, however, commonly breast-fed until the age of three or four, or until the mother becomes pregnant again. According to LeVine et al. (1994, 25), prolonged breast-feeding is important for the health of both mothers and babies in sub-Saharan Africa: it provides infants with protein in societies where diets are often protein deficient, it provides babies with antibodies to fight disease and infection, and it allows mothers to rest after childbirth and care for their babies. Prolonged breast-feeding also plays a role in birth spacing, since postpartum amenorrhea (cessation of menstruation) is common in breast-feeding mothers across the continent. Breast-feeding thus contributes to the maintenance of longer birth intervals, which anthropologists have shown lead to healthier outcomes for both mothers and babies in societies plagued by poverty, malnutrition, and infant and maternal mortality.

Many West African Muslim mothers also uphold a 40-day taboo on sex following the birth of a child. After this period, they may resume sexual relations with their husbands. In many societies in West Africa and across the continent, Muslims also uphold various customary taboos on sexual relations until the child begins to walk. Pastoral Fulani in Cameroon believe that a man's semen will poison his lactating wife's breast milk (Yovsi and Keller 2003, 155).

Polygynous marriage also supports prolonged breast-feeding, in that a husband anxious to resume sexual relations with his wife in the postpartum period can simply visit his other wives. In many societies, lastborn children have a special status; they are typically called by special names and are often breast-fed longer than their older siblings (LeVine et al. 1994, 27).

In many West African Muslim societies, people believe that the milk that develops in a woman's breasts belongs to the developing fetus, not to the older child she is breast-feeding. Thus when a nursing mother becomes pregnant, she will wean her older child immediately. Continuing to feed a child breast milk that belongs to his or her sibling in the womb is thought to have disastrous effects on the older child. Mandinga and Fulani, for example, believe that unborn babies will become angry with their older siblings for "stealing" their breast milk, and may bewitch them by poisoning the milk. Fulani in Burkina Faso believe that a mother's failing to wean an older child when she becomes pregnant can lead to a dangerous condition called "weaning disease" (Riesman 1992, 128), which causes dysentery, rapid weight loss, and often death. As Bledsoe (2002, 103) explains, continued breast-feeding during a subsequent pregnancy is understood in The Gambia as symbolically akin to cannibalism: the older child reacts to the "polluted milk" with weight loss, nausea, and diarrhea. Members of some societies in West Africa believe that continued breast-feeding during a new pregnancy may be dangerous not only to the breast-feeding child, but also to the mother, who may become thin and tired. Others believe that when a nursing mother becomes pregnant again, her breast milk changes in either color or taste (or both), and older children may simply decide to wean themselves as a result. Muslim mothers in West Africa do their best to avoid pregnancy as they attempt to meet the Muslim ideal of breast-feeding their child for two years.

Of course, women are not always successful in avoiding pregnancy while they are breast-feeding, and some women find themselves pregnant before their babies are two years old. Bledsoe (2002, 105) reports that among Mandinka women in The Gambia, *buruu*—weaning a baby too soon because of a new pregnancy—is considered to be one of the worst things a mother can do. Women are aware that this situation usually has disastrous health consequences for their babies, such as weight loss and illness, and mothers forced to wean early due to pregnancy are often criticized by relatives and other community members. A woman in this position may attempt abortion using local herbs or Western medicines, choosing to wean her child only as a last resort if these attempts fail.

When a mother is ready to wean her toddler, she may try several different strategies, such as offering water or food instead of breast milk, or teasing the child, telling the little one that he or she is too old to nurse. If her little one resists weaning, a mother may attempt more drastic measures, such as putting hot pepper, bitter plants, or ashes on her nipples to discourage her baby from breast-feeding. Among Mandinka in southern Senegal, mothers usually wait to wean their babies until the rainy season, when they are separated from them for long periods due to intensive farm work (Whittemore and Beverly 1996, 56). A mother hoping to wean her toddler may also send the little one to grandmother's house for a week or more in the hope that he or she might simply forget about breast-feeding. When the toddler returns, the mother will tell the little one that she has no more breast milk. Grandmothers often take pity on their suffering grandchildren and may allow them to suck at their own breasts, a practice referred to as "dry nursing" (Gottlieb 2004, 203). At times, however, grandmothers can feel so much pain for their grandchildren that they actually start producing breast milk, a phenomenon documented by Riesman (1992, 121) for Fulani in Burkina Faso but one that is also common in other West African societies. Mandinka in Senegal refer to weaning as "letting go, releasing the breast" (Whittemore and Beverly 1996, 56) and they believe that the child, not the mother, ultimately decides when it is time to wean. Indeed, Senegalese Mandinka believe that a child must literally "release the breast" before his or her mother can become pregnant again, and infertility is often blamed on the failure of older children to "let go" and wean.

Configuring Relatedness and Shaping Relationships through Breast Milk

Beyond nourishing babies, breast-feeding in many Muslim societies in West Africa is believed to both create relatedness and structure relationships between different kinds of kin. For Mande peoples throughout West Africa, siblings who share the same mother are thought to share a particularly close relationship (Bird and Kendall 1980). Although anthropologists have often identified the uterus as the origin of this close relationship and often refer to these siblings as "uterine kin," the breasts and, more specifically, breast milk, is an equally important symbolic origin of this closeness among some groups. Senegambian Mandinga, for example, both imagine and describe maternal siblings not as "uterine kin" (although they recognize that they emerge from a single womb) but rather as siblings who "nursed from the same breast" or who are related "through the milk." In fact, when a woman wants to identify a relative as a maternal sibling (one with whom she shares a mother) as opposed to a paternal sibling (one with whom she shares a father) she will pull her breast out of her dress, pinch her nipple, and suck her finger. Siblings who "nursed from the same breast" are generally described as being noncompetitive and nurturing toward one another, and they do not feel shame in each other's presence. This is contrasted with paternal siblings, who are thought to be competitive toward one another and are more prone to conflict (Bird and Kendall 1980, 14–15). Mande throughout West Africa thus explain closeness or the absence of closeness in terms of the shared (or the absence of the shared) substance of breast milk.

Breast milk not only structures different kinds of relationships among biologically related kin, but can also create kinship among people who may not be at all biologically related. Furthermore, it can intensify the relatedness between distantly related kin, making them more closely related, and even preventing them from marrying one another. Khatib-Chahidi (1992, 109) explains that Islamic law specifies three types of kinship: relationship by blood, relationship by marriage, and relationship by milk. Many Muslim societies in West Africa follow this and believe that two biologically unrelated infants who drink the same breast milk actually become "milk kin." These special siblings are thought to be too closely related to marry one another and are thus prohibited from doing so. Because babies are rarely breast-fed exclusively by their biological mothers and are often breast-fed by other community members, women must keep careful track of who nursed from whom, to avoid incestuous marriages later in life. For this reason, mothers may actually proceed with caution when allowing other women to nurse their babies, because the usually helpful practice of wet nursing can turn into a harmful one by limiting a baby's potential marriage partners. This is especially important in small communities, where one's potential marriage partners may already be relatively limited. In this case, women may agree to breast-feed only those infants "who are already of 'the same blood' and therefore not marriageable" (Dettwyler 1988, 180), that is, close relatives, however closenesss may be defined in a particular society.

Beyond configuring kinship and relatedness, breast-feeding is also crucial in many West African Muslim societies for creating a special bond between mothers and babies. Fulani, for example, believe that babies who nurse for two to three years inevitably develop a closer relationship with their mothers and will be less prone to leave them later in life (Johnson 2000, 190). Muslims in Guinea-Bissau say that they feel love, which they often describe as "emotional weakness," for their children, precisely because they nursed from their breasts. This is the primary reason why Mandinga women in Guinea-Bissau say they don't climb trees to harvest palm fruit or honey: the milk that is said to be "between" a mother and her child make it too difficult for a woman to risk falling to her death and leaving her children without a mother. Fathers, who do not breast-feed, do not experience this same emotional weakness and are thus thought to be less fearful of falling.

Breast Milk and the Development of Personhood and Religious Identity

If breast milk configures relatedness and structures different kinds of relationship among kin in some Muslim societies in West Africa, in others it is believed to play a role in the development of a child's personality. Fulani throughout the region believe that personality traits and idiosyncratic behaviors—for example, talkativeness or the tendency to eat slowly or quickly—are passed from mother to child through breast milk. A "good mother" from a noble lineage who possesses a respectable (God-given) character is said to pass these qualities to her children through her breast milk. According to a Fulani proverb, "The milk that is nursed is the milk that comes back" (Riesman 1992, 163), which means that the qualities babies drink through their mothers' breast milk are the same qualities that they will manifest in later life (see also Yovsi and Keller 2003, 154).

In some Muslim societies in West Africa, breast milk is also thought to play a central role in the development of a child's religious identity. If a woman is a practicing Muslim—if she prays regularly, attends Friday prayer at the mosque, and fasts during Ramadan—then her baby is believed to literally drink these qualities through her breast milk and is thought to become an observant Muslim later in life. Throughout West Africa, women tell stories of how non-Muslim babies who were nursed by Muslim women eventually converted to Islam. At the same time, a non-observant mother may also pass this quality to her baby through her breast milk, and her baby may grow up to be non-observant or even to refuse Islam altogether.

Breast-feeding and Social Change

In West Africa, beliefs and practices pertaining to breast-feeding specifically, and infant feeding more generally, are changing as a result of urban migration and globalization. Alternatives to breast milk are increasingly available for those who can afford them and are commonly sold in stores or pharmacies in cities and towns throughout West Africa. Cerelac (a French product containing cereal made from oat, rice, or wheat mixed with infant formula), European powdered or tinned milk, and cow's milk are among the most common. Despite these alternatives, however, breast-feeding remains strong in the region due to its widespread cultural importance. In the 1980s, Nestlé aggressively marketed infant formula in some developing countries, but its efforts failed to reach Mali (Dettwyler 1987, 636): posters for infant formula were not displayed in birthing clinics in Bamako, and new mothers were not given bottles or formula samples. This was due in part to the Malian government's efforts to "promote breast-feeding and to discourage the advertising and use of infant formula" (Dettwyler 1986, 655). The continuity of many breast-feeding beliefs and practices in the midst of social change can also be attributed to economics, because many West African mothers today still lack access to or simply cannot afford alternatives to breast milk. Beyond economics, however, the majority of West Africans believe that breast milk is the best and most convenient form of nourishment for their babies and that bottle-fed babies are "weaker and more sickly" (Dettwyler 1987, 637) than are breast-fed ones.

When mothers do give their babies formula or powdered milk, they do so to supplement rather than replace breast-feeding. Dettwyler reports that Malian mothers give their babies formula or other replacements for breast milk when they feel they are not producing enough milk, when they are breast-feeding twins, or when they experience health problems associated with breast-feeding, such as sore nipples and frequent breast infections (Dettwyler 1987, 639). Since the 1980s, however, advertisements for infant formula and other alternatives to breast milk have become much more prominent. Giant roadside billboards for Cerelac, for example, are common sights in many West African cities. In some parts of the region, however, the availability of Western goods has had little effect on traditional breast-feeding patterns. In Guinea-Bissau, for example, plastic bottles, pacifiers, and infant formula are symbols of modernity and markers of social status, which relatives often present to babies as gifts. Mothers enthusiastically accept and proudly display these items even when they have no access to powdered milk or formula and have no intention of feeding their babies formula or powdered milk.

The length of the breast-feeding period in West African societies has also changed. In Mali, people from villages claim that in the past, babies were breast-fed for three to four years; nowadays, they are seldom breast-fed past two years. In Bamako, people attribute this change to the urban belief that breast-feeding a child past two years would "make the child stupid" (Dettwyler 1986, 657). In other parts of West Africa, however, people explain the two-year breast-feeding period primarily in terms of local beliefs or Islam.

Recently, international organizations and NGOs have been encouraging exclusive breast-feeding in West Africa and other parts of the developing world to address malnutrition and infant mortality. Exclusive breast-feeding has been identified as a crucial way of decreasing infant morbidity and mortality because of the nutritional and health benefits of breast milk and because breast milk is cleaner and safer than supplements, especially in areas without access to safe drinking water. According to Kakute et al. (2005, 324), "[I]nfants who are formula fed are more susceptible to infections because of lack of maternal immune factors and increased exposure to contamination and bacteria." Many people in West Africa continue to resist these efforts due to the long-standing belief that even the youngest babies cannot live on breast milk alone and mixed feeding is key for their health and wellness.

Conclusion

Among Muslims in West Africa, breast-feeding is a routine practice imbued with symbolic meaning. Although mothers are aware that breast-feeding is the easiest and most important way to feed their babies and ensure their health and well-being, breast-feeding is about much more than nutrition. As Whittemore and Beverly (1996, 47) write, "[B]reast milk is a cultural product with a cultural value." Whereas breast-feeding in the West is generally considered one of two ways of feeding young babies, in West African societies it is often the only way, and usually considered the best way. In fact, breast-feeding is considered to be one of the most important of maternal duties, and Muslims believe that it is the fundamental right of all children to be breast-fed.

Following Islamic doctrine, Muslim babies in West Africa are breast-fed ideally for a minimum of two years. This prolonged period of breast-feeding is made possible in part by a 40-day postpartum sex taboo, the practice of polygyny, and widespread customary beliefs that restrict sexual relations until breast-feeding children begin to walk and are weaned. Should a breast-feeding mother become pregnant before her child is two years old, she must wean her baby immediately because the milk that forms in her breasts is thought to belong to the fetus rather than to the older child, and continued breast-feeding is thought to be dangerous to the older child and in some societies to the mother, as well.

Breast-feeding in many West African societies is considered an important form of communication between mothers and their babies. It is also thought to structure relationships, in that two biologically unrelated people who nurse the same breast milk become related "through the milk" and thus are said to share a close emotional relationship. "Milk kin," as they are called in some West African societies, are also prohibited from marrying one another, so the practice of wet nursing is often carefully managed so as to not restrict one's children's potential marriage partners. Members of some West African Muslim societies believe that personality traits are also transmitted from mothers to babies through breast milk. In others, breast milk plays an important role in shaping personhood and religious identity through the life course.

Beliefs and practices pertaining to breast-feeding specifically and infant-feeding more generally are changing. For example, alternatives to breast milk, such as formula and powdered milk, are more readily available and more aggressively marketed today, especially in urban areas. The common length of the breast-feeding period has also decreased in some countries, from three to four years down to two years. Despite the effects of urbanization, globalization, and social change, however, many of the "traditional" beliefs and practices highlighted here are still relevant in West Africa today, even in cities and towns, as well as among West African immigrant populations living in North America and Europe (e.g., Johnson 2017).

Bibliography

Bird, Charles S., and Martha B. Kendall. The Mande hero. Text and context, in *Exploration in African systems of thought*, eds. Ivan Karp and Charles S. Bird, Washington, DC 1980.

Bledsoe, Caroline H. *Contingent lives. Fertility, time, and aging in West Africa*, Chicago, Ill. 2002.

Dettwyler, Katerine A. Infant feeding in Mali, West Africa. Variations in belief and practice, in *Social Science and Medicine* 23:7 (1986), 651–64.

Dettwyler, Katerine A. Breastfeeding and weaning in Mali. Cultural context and hard data, in *Social Science and Medicine* 24:8 (1987), 633–44.

Dettwyler, Katerine A. More than nutrition. Breastfeeding in urban Mali, in *Medical Anthropology Quarterly* 2:2 (1988), 172–83.

Gottlieb, Alma. *The afterlife is where we come from. The culture of infancy in West Africa*, Chicago, Ill. 2004.

Gunnlaugsson, Geir, and Jónína Einarsdóttir. Colostrum and ideas about bad milk. A case study from Guinea-Bissau, in *Social Science and Medicine* 36:3 (1993), 283–88.

Johnson, Michelle C. The view from the Wuro. A guide to childrearing for Fulani parents, in *A world of babies. Imagined childcare guides for seven societies*, eds. Judy S. DeLoache and Alma Gottlieb, Cambridge 2000, 171–98.

Johnson, Michelle C. Being Mandinga, being Muslim. Transnational debates on personhood and religious identity in Guinea-Bissau and Portugal, Ph.D. diss., Department of Anthropology, University of Illinois at Urbana-Champaign 2002.

Johnson, Michelle C. 2017. "Never Forget Where You're From: Raising Guinean Muslim Babies in Portugal." In A World of Babies: Imagined Childcare Guides in Eight Societies, ed. Alma Gottlieb and Judy DeLoache. Cambridge: Cambridge University Press.

Kakute, Peter Nwenfu, John Ngum, Pat Mitchell, Kathryn A. Kroll, Gideon Wangnkeh Forgwei, Lillian Keming Ngwang, and Dorothy J. Meyer. Cultural barriers to exclusive breatfeeding by mothers in a rural area of Cameroon, Africa, in *Journal of Midwifery and Women's Health* 50:4 (2005), 324–28.

Khatib-Chahidi, Jane. Milk kinship in Shi'ite Islamic Iran, in *The Anthropology of Breast-Feeding. Natural law or social construct*, ed. Vanessa Maher, Oxford 1992, 109–32.

LeVine, Robert A., Suzanne Dixon, Sarah LeVine, Amy Richman, P. Herbert Leiderman, Constance H. Keepfer, and T. Berry Brazelton. *Child care and culture. Lessons from Africa*, Chicago, Ill. 1994.

Riesman, Paul. *First find yourself a good mother. The construction of self in two African communities*, eds. David Szanton, Lila Abu-Lughod, Sharon Hutchinson, Paul Stoller, and Carol Trosset, New Brunswick, NJ 1992.

Whittemore, Robert D., and Elizabeth A. Beverly. Mandinka mothers and nurslings. Power and reproduction, in *Medical Anthropology Quarterly* 10:1 (1996), 45–62.

Yovsi, Relindis D., and Heidi Keller. Breastfeeding. An adaptive process, in *Ethos* 31:2 (2003), 147–71.

Childhood: Coming of Age Rituals

∴

Childhood: Coming of Age Rituals: Sub-Saharan Africa

Michelle Johnson

Introduction

Members of many Muslim societies throughout sub-Saharan Africa hold coming of age rituals for girls. Although the age at which these rituals take place varies considerably from one society to another, they are commonly held between the ages of 7 and 13. Because the rituals often happen around the time of first menstruation and before marriage they often have been termed puberty rituals. The Belgian folklorist Arnold van Gennep (1960 [1908], 65–66), however, demonstrated both the complex relationship between physiological puberty and "social puberty" and the fact that coming of age rituals only rarely coincide with physiological puberty. Although there are several different childhood coming of age rituals, this article focuses primarily on initiation, which is the most common and pervasive of them. It will, however, briefly address other childhood coming of age rituals, such as initiation into Qurʾānic study. The meanings of initiation rituals vary significantly across societies: they may be linked to the step from childhood to adulthood and preparation for marriage; they may construct personhood, ethnicity, or religious identity; or they may shape gender identity, ritually differentiating men from women and constructing womanhood and socially-appropriate female fertility.

While the specifics of initiation rituals also vary considerably across societies, they generally exhibit a similar structure, one originally outlined by van Gennep (1960) and later elaborated by Victor Turner (2011 [1969]). This involves: the separation of the initiates from their everyday status and routines; a transitional or "liminal" period, in which initiates are in between their old and new state; and aggregation into the community, during which their newly-attained status is publicly declared and celebrated. Among some ethnic groups, coming of age rituals are linked to formal initiation associations, which anthropologists have often termed "secret societies" (Simmel 1967), referring to the fact that some aspects of these associations (e.g. membership or activities) are often kept hidden. In other societies, however, initiation rituals take place without formal associations. The majority of these rituals for Muslim girls in sub-Saharan African societies involve some form of female circumcision, which is often also referred to as female genital cutting, excision,

---

© KONINKLIJKE BRILL NV, LEIDEN, 2016 | DOI:10.1163/1872-5309_EWIC_COM_002082

or clitoridectomy. In the vast majority of societies, initiation rituals pre-date Islam, and Islam has simply absorbed the rites, albeit often transforming both their structure and associated meanings. The complicated dynamic between initiation rituals, female circumcision, and Islam will be discussed in more detail later in this article.

Coming of age rituals, like all rituals, are dynamic and constantly subject to change. This change has recently intensified, however, as a result of urbanization, religious change and conversion, globalization, and efforts to eradicate female circumcision practices. In some societies, for example, female circumcision has become divorced from the initiation rituals that traditionally accompanied it. Girls may be circumcised when they are very young, as early as infancy, either at home or at a clinic by a traditional circumcizor or midwife. Then, around puberty, they may undergo an initiation ritual. Unlike boys, who in many parts of sub-Saharan Africa today are circumcised in hospitals by medical practitioners, hospital circumcisions for girls are illegal in many countries and thus rarely an option. In other societies, especially in parts of East Africa, girls may be circumcised without any elaborate ritual at all. In this latter case, female circumcision *is* the initiation ritual, and marks the transition from being an uncircumcised to a circumcised girl in light of the specific meanings that accompany this change of state.

Structure and Timing of Coming of Age Rituals

Arnold Van Gennep (1960, 3) described rites of passage as rituals "whose essential purpose is to enable the individual to pass from one defined position to another which is equally well defined." Coming of age rituals, including initiation, typically fall within this category of rites. These rituals all have a tripartite structure, which Van Gennep deemed universal. In the first phase, called separation, initiates are removed from their daily routines and previous states. Commonly, they are taken from the place of human dwelling (i.e., their village or town) to the sacred forest. The forest is deemed sacred because of its connection to the spirit world and as it is said literally to house the power necessary for transforming the initiates from one state to the next. Depending on the society, initiates may spend several weeks to several months in the sacred forest, where they live with their fellow initiates in a structure often built especially for the rituals. In some Muslim societies in sub-Saharan Africa, however, especially many in East Africa who circumcise but do not initiate girls, there is no sacred forest and girls are simply circumcised in the house, courtyard, or clinic.

In the second phase of the rituals, called transition or limen, the initiates occupy an ambiguous space between states; although stripped of their old state they have not yet attained their new one. In short, they are "betwixt and between" (Turner 1967, 93) and their ambiguous status is often accompanied by elaborate symbolism, which is marked on their bodies. For example, their heads may be shaved, they may be dressed in specific clothing, and they may be likened to infants, corpses, or sexless/genderless beings. In Sande initiations in Sierra Leone, for example, Mende girls are covered with *hojo* (white clay associated with beauty and representative of Sande society) "to indicate that they are under the Sande's control and protection and are subject to the full authority of Sande law and punishment" (Boone 1986, 21). Because of their ambiguous position between states, initiates may be considered dangerous, vulnerable, or polluting, and strict taboos govern communication or contact with them. As Mary Douglas (1966, 96) has argued, "Danger lies in transitional states, simply because transition is neither one state or the next, it is undefinable." It is during this phase of initiation that girls often learn secret knowledge that is taboo for the uninitiated, such as knowledge pertaining to menstruation and childbirth, as well as other traditional skills, including dancing, singing, cooking, and sexual techniques. During this second phase, initiates may also undergo physical trials, such as sleep deprivation, beatings by elders, scarification, or female circumcision. According to Turner, the initiates' previous differentiated statuses dissolve during this phase and a strong, egalitarian bond develops among them, a phenomenon that he terms "communitas" (Turner 2011, 96).

During the final phase of the rituals, called aggregation, the initiates—no longer ambiguous—are welcomed back into society as changed individuals. Dancing and feasting may accompany the reunion of the initiates with their families and community members. During this final phase, which is often referred to in local languages as "coming out," the initiates may don new clothing or hairstyles that mark their transformation. Muslim Jola women, for example, wear colorful outfits, wigs, jewelry, make-up, and high-heeled shoes, as well as carry colorful handbags and umbrellas (de Jong 2007, 48). From this point onward, the initiates' behavior may also change, as a way of further highlighting their altered status. For example, girls may no longer be allowed to socialize casually with boys, they may be required to wear a headscarf or always have their hair plaited, they may no longer expose their bare breasts, or they may be expected to sit in prescribed ways (e.g. with their legs together and stretched out in front of them). After they are initiated or circumcised, girls may experience pressure to behave as proper Muslims. For example, they may be expected to pray five times daily, to attend Friday prayer at the mosque rather than simply to pray at home, and to fast during the month of Ramadan. Some recently-initiated or circumcised girls may also be expected to begin formal Qurʾānic education, if they have not already. In some societies, initiation into a Qurʾānic school might be considered an important coming of age ritual for the attainment of adulthood and the construction of Muslim identity. As such, it will be considered later in this article.

Initiation rituals in Muslim societies in sub-Saharan Africa generally take place in the dry season, following the harvest. This is true in both rural and urban areas. At this time of year, food is plentiful and people—liberated from their intense agricultural work routines—have more leisure time and energy to engage in ritual. But this time of year is significant for symbolic reasons as well, as Ahmadu (2000, 288) explains: "[I]t represents a new season of fruitfulness, fertility, abundance, and the possibilities of new life—just as initiation seeks to give birth to new, fertile, culturally transformed young women and men." In some societies, girls' initiation rituals may take place according to a strict cycle; for example, once in a certain number of years or a certain number of years following the boys' rituals. In other societies, however, they may be held more frequently, perhaps yearly or at a time when the elders determine there is a need for them; that is, when there are enough girls in the village or town who are of age but have not yet been initiated.

It is important to note, however, that not all Muslim groups hold initiation rituals for girls. Susan Rasmussen (1997, 45) explains that Tuareg peoples in Niger hold no special ritual for a girl's menarche and Tuareg girls are not initiated or circumcised. This was not always the case, however. In the past, when a girl began to menstruate, she was force-fed a special gruel made of pounded millet, dates, goat cheese, and water, as a way of imparting blessings (al-baraka) on her. This ritual was also thought to bolster her maturation and fertility, preparing her for marriage. Although this ritual of force-feeding is no longer practiced in Tuareg society today, fatness is still a desired cultural quality for women, one that is equated with womanhood, health, and fertility. In societies where initiation is not practiced, other coming of age rituals (e.g., initiation into Qurʾānic study, marriage, or first childbirth) mark the transition from childhood to adulthood.

Secrecy and Secret Societies

Coming of age rituals, especially those occurring in societies with formal initiation associations, often involve secrecy. In many Muslim societies in West Africa, formal associations that initiate boys and girls have often been termed "secret societies" (see Simmel 1950, Bellman 1984). The role that secrecy plays in coming of age rituals varies according to the society. Summarizing Simmel's (1950) foundational work on this subject, Beryl Bellman (1984, 47) outlines the two major types of secret societies; those "whose presence is known but whose membership is confidential" and "those in which the membership is known but the activities are secret." In sub-Saharan Africa, secret societies are thought to commonly own, manage, and impart secret knowledge to initiated members. This knowledge is often considered sacred (that is, it is distinct and set apart from everyday knowledge) and has ontological power, meaning it is believed to actually play a role in transforming the initiates from one state to another. For Muslim Jola in Senegal, separation between the sexes is crucial to society and secrecy serves to maintain this distinction. Everything associated with the girls' initiation, for example, is kept secret from the men and the reverse is also true. In performing secrecy, Muslim Jola mark the ritual separation between men and women (de Jong 2007, 27).

Bellman (1984) argued that secrecy does not necessarily refer to a body of concealed knowledge itself but rather prescribes when and how concealed knowledge may be revealed. For example, all initiates in a given society may know the content of a secret associated with initiation—that there is a human being behind the masked figure—but they are forbidden to reveal this "secret" to the uninitiated, who will learn it for themselves when they are initiated. In some Muslim societies in West Africa, such as the Mende of Sierra Leone, secrecy pertains not just to ritual contexts but is a culturally important and pervasive concept in everyday life. As Boone (1986, xv) writes: "Mende believe that information about Mende life should not be transmitted to those not subject to its laws." This pertains not just to Sande and Poro initiations but rather to all things Mende.

Female Circumcision

Many initiation rituals for Muslim girls throughout sub-Saharan Africa incorporate some form of female circumcision. Anthropologist Ellen Gruenbaum (2001, 2–3) identifies and describes the three main types, which vary in severity. The least severe form is generally referred to as *sunna*, which involves pricking, cutting, or removing the clitoral hood or a portion of the clitoris. Local people often describe this as a "reduction" of the clitoris. *Sunna* means "tradition" in Arabic and the term is used to refer to those things that the prophet Muḥammad did or advocated during his lifetime. The second type is excision or clitoridectomy and is more severe. It includes the removal of the clitoral prepuce, the clitoris, and sometimes most or part of the labia minora. Pharaonic circumcision or infibulation is the name for the third type, which is the most severe. It is practiced in northeast Africa, in Somalia, Djibouti, Sudan, Egypt, and some parts of Ethiopia and Eritrea. It involves the removal of all of the external female genitalia, the clitoral prepuce, the clitoris, the labia minora, and the labia majora. The two sides of the wound are then sewn together and a small opening is left for the passage of urine and menstrual blood. Women who undergo this type of circumcision have to be deinfibulated and reinfibulated each time they give birth. Although infibulation is actually the rarest form of female circumcision practiced on the continent, it is often the form that people most often imagine when they think of the practice and it also receives the most media attention.

Initiation, Female Circumcision, and Islam

The relationship between initiation rituals, female circumcision, and Islam is a complicated subject that many anthropologists have explored (e.g., Dellenborg 2004, Gruenbaum 2001, Johnson 2000). Both coming of age rituals and the practice of female circumcision pre-date Islam and the Qur'ān makes no mention of the latter. There is one sentence addressing female circumcision in the *hadīth*, statements purported to have been made by the prophet Muḥammad. It warns: "Do not go deep. That [the clitoris] is enjoyable to the woman and is preferable to the husband" (cited in Gruenbaum 2001, 64). As there are several versions of this statement, however, its meaning has been interpreted in different ways. For example, both pro- and anti-female circumcision activists have used the passage to support their opposing stances on the practice. The situation is even more complicated in that not all Muslims practice female circumcision and many non-Muslims do.

Although scholars and activists alike often attempt to disentangle the practice of female circumcision from Islam, Muslims in local contexts often link it explicitly with their religion. Muslim Jola in Senegal, for example, consider both excision and initiation, which take place separately and are rather recent practices, as "Islamic obligations" (de Jong 2007, 49). For Mandinga peoples in Guinea-Bissau as described by Johnson (2009, 209), female circumcision is a "cleansing rite that enables women to pray in the proper Muslim fashion, making them 'true Muslims.'" Specifically, Guinean Mandinga believe that uncircumcised women's genitals produce an odor that makes them unfit for prayer. In similar fashion, Senegalese Muslim Jola believe than an uncircumcised woman's prayers do not "take" or are worth less in the eyes of God than the prayers of circumcised women. In their eyes, "a circumcised woman is considered a better Muslim" (Dellenborg 2004, 82). In Mali, *seliji*, or "prayer water," is a common euphemism for both male and female circumcision, and refers to the water that Muslims use for ablutions before prayer (Gosselin 2000, 54). In cutting their bodies in the name of Islam as men do (through the practice of male circumcision), Muslim women in these societies are increasingly demanding full participation in their religion.

Despite the explicit link made in some societies between female circumcision and Muslim identity, not all Muslim women in sub-Saharan Africa practice it and many disapprove of it. Tuareg peoples in Niger (see Rasmussen 1997) and Wolof peoples in Senegal are two examples of Muslim ethnic groups that practice circumcision for men but not for women. Lively debates about the practice of female circumcision, including but certainly not limited to its relationship to Islam, are currently taking place across sub-Saharan Africa, as well as in African immigrant populations in North America and Europe. These debates will be addressed later in this article.

Sexuality

There are many local meanings attached to initiation rituals and the practice of female circumcision. In many societies, female circumcision is linked either explicitly or implicitly to sexuality. Boddy (1982, 686) explains that, in rural northern Sudan, Pharaonic circumcision or infibulation ensures that a girl is a virgin when she marries for the first time, even though this is not the officially-stated purpose of the practice. It is thus a way of controlling female sexuality, as it decreases the likelihood that women will have extramarital affairs. The need to decrease or control female sexuality is especially important in Muslim societies where, in contrast to the West, people "maintain that women have a greater sexual urge than do men" (Gottlieb 2002, 177). Taming female sexuality is also one of the meanings behind the less severe practice of (partial) clitoridectomy among Muslim groups in Guinea-Bissau. Mandinga women, for example, maintain that female circumcision "calms" women, making them better, more faithful wives and more dedicated and attentive mothers (see Johnson 2007, 216–18). The effects of female circumcision on women, however, remain complicated. Non-Muslims in Guinea-Bissau, for example, believe that female circumcision intensifies a woman's sex drive and they link the practice with promiscuity and higher rates of prostitution, a view that contradicts Muslim women's own views of the effects of the practice.

Adulthood, Marriageability, and Fertility

In many societies in sub-Saharan Africa, initiation rituals are linked—either explicitly or implicitly—to the attainment of adulthood. Although physical maturation in the West is considered a "natural" process, the presence of initiation rituals highlights the cultural dimension of this transition. As van Gennep (1960, 65) wrote in his classic book on rites of passage, "physiological puberty and 'social puberty' are essentially different and only rarely converge." Considering this, coming of age rituals do not necessarily coincide with physical maturation. In some societies, physical maturation is not considered complete until it is marked culturally, through initiation. That is, a girl may be recognized as a physically mature woman, but she is not considered able to become pregnant until she has been initiated or circumcised.

Among Mende peoples in Sierra Leone, initiation is believed to transform girls into women and make them eligible for marriage (MacCormack 1979, 27). During their initiation, girls learn how to be proper wives and mothers and how to get along with their co-wives and husbands' relatives. This is especially important in societies with virilocal marriage, where, at marriage, women leave the comfort of their natal kin group to reside with their husband's relatives, who are strangers to them. In these societies, initiation rituals—especially those that are managed by members of formal associations—provide women with a network of support that can help them as they struggle to live in their husbands' villages, away from their own kin. Through Bundu initiation, as described by Ahmadu (2000, 288–89), Kono girls in Sierra Leone are ritually "'reborn'... as new persons with full social membership in the adult world."

For many Muslim women in sub-Saharan Africa, initiation—and for some groups, female circumcision—renders a girl eligible for marriage. In Sudan, for example, members of many ethnic groups require that women are virgins at the time they are married. Infibulation is taken as proof of virginity, since the practice is said to inhibit premarital sex (see Gruenbaum 2001, 78). It is important to note that in Sudan, circumcision for girls takes place without an elaborate ceremony or accompanying initiation ritual. Instead, Sudanese girls receive an anesthetic injection, undergo infibulation, and afterwards drink tea and are adorned with "ritual ornaments" that are said to protect them from harm as their wounds heal (Boddy 1982, 684). Although Sudanese girls are not considered full women until they marry, circumcision is considered necessary for marriage and is linked to the construction of culturally appropriate womanhood, sexuality, and fertility.

Personhood, Ethnicity, and Class

For members of some ethnic groups, initiation rituals are linked to the cultivation of personhood, the process of becoming a social person and full member of one's ethnic group. Among Mandinga peoples in Guinea-Bissau, for example, initiation for both boys and girls is a process whereby people come to "know the eye." These people are aware of "their position in society and the correct way of acting in a variety of social situations relative to their gender and age" (Johnson 2000, 222). Knowing the eye also means being socially graceful and aware of the needs and desires of others, even before they articulate them. In short, it is about possessing the understanding and empathy necessary to belong to a community. An uninitiated person is considered foolish, socially unaware, and someone who may behave in ways that are contradictory to their gender or age. For Mandinga, as well as for members of other ethnic groups that initiate youth, personhood often has an ethnic aspect to it: becoming a fully-fledged person involves acting within the boundaries of accepted behavior established by the elders of a particular ethnic group.

In some societies, female circumcision marks ethnic or class distinctions between groups. In her book *The female circumcision controversy* Gruenbaum (2001, ch. 4) presents a case study from Sudan demonstrating this, involving two ethnic groups, the Kenana and the Zabarma. The Kenana people were historically nomadic but today practice a mixed economy of pastoralism and farming. They imagine themselves as "true Arabs" who are descended from the prophet Muḥammad. They practice Pharaonic circumcision and infibulation, which they claim increases men's sexual pleasure and prepares women for marriage. The Zabarma people, in contrast, trace their origins to West Africa and are ethnically related to Songhay peoples in Niger and Mali. They migrated to East Africa in the nineteenth century to make the *hajj*, the pilgrimage to Mecca, and ended up settling in Sudan. They practice a mild form of *sunna*, removing only the clitoral prepuce or a small portion of the clitoris, a practice they associate with Islam.

The Kenana people call the Zabarma people *Fallata*, a derogatory term for peoples of West African descent, whom they consider to be socially and morally inferior. They also consider the Zabarma people to be uncircumcised because they practice such a mild form of female circumcision. Ten years after her original research, Gruenbaum returned to her field-site. She observed that inter-ethnic visitation had increased considerably and the lower-status Zabarma peoples had adopted many practices of the higher-status Kenana; for example, the Zabarma women's Arabic had improved. The two ethnic groups' respective female circumcision practices, however, remained unchanged, and continued to serve as an ethnic marker that distinguished them from each other. As Gruenbaum (2001, 128) asserts, "the Kenana remained convinced that their ethnic superiority was manifest in their practice of infibulation."

Gender Identity

For members of some societies in sub-Saharan Africa, initiation rituals—especially those that include circumcision for both sexes—are linked to the creation of unambiguously gendered subjects (see Gosselin 2000, for an example from Mali, Meinardus 1967, cited in Gruenbaum 2001, for Egypt, Boddy 1989, for Sudan, van der Kwaak 1992, for Somalia). The foreskin of the penis is often associated with female genitalia and is thus cut away in the practice of male circumcision, rendering boys fully male. Likewise, the clitoris is, for members of many ethnic groups, thought to resemble a penis, and cutting it away as part of the practice of female circumcision is said to render girls unambiguously female. Gosselin (2000, 54) writes that among Mande peoples of Mali, the clitoris is thought to contain excessive concentrations of energy, which is said to be dangerous for men during intercourse, as well as to babies during childbirth. The practice of female circumcision thus removes gender ambiguity, creating fully differentiated male and female genitalia, and thus full male and female persons.

Coming of Age in Qur'ānic Schools

In some Muslim societies in West Africa, initiation into Qur'ānic schools is ritualized and constitutes an important coming of age ritual for both girls and boys. Indeed, the start of Qur'ānic study can, to some extent, resemble initiation rituals, as it constructs Muslim identity and is linked (though only implicitly) to the attainment of adulthood, especially in the sense of religious roles and practices. Muslim children in Mali, as described by Mommersteeg (2012, 36–39), begin Qur'ānic study when they are seven years old. Before teaching children, a *marabout* asks God to "open" their heads. He then writes a text, usually the opening verse of the Qur'ān, on the children's wooden Qur'ānic slates and on their hands. The students then lick the verses from their hands, literally ingesting God's word. In Guinea-Bissau, as described by Johnson (2006), the *bulusafewo*, or "writing-on-the-hand ritual," initiates Mandinga children into Qur'ānic study, something that has become even more elaborate in the Mandinga immigrant community in Lisbon. In this ritual, a holy man dips a fountain-pen in ink, writes Qur'ānic verses on the children's right palms, sprinkles salt over the ink, and instructs the children to lick the mixture from their palms three times. Next the holy man points to the letters of the Arabic alphabet, reciting each letter and instructing the children to repeat it. Relatives and friends join the children in their recitation while placing offerings of money and kola nuts on their heads. *Munkoo*—pounded rice-flour sweetened with honey—is then distributed to guests and everyone takes part in a feast. This ritual is crucial to the construction of children's religious identity: it initiates them into Qur'ānic study, begins their life-long relationship with angels, and pardons their sins, opening their heads and purifying their hearts in order to prepare them to study Islam's most sacred text. Like circumcision for some Muslim groups, initiation into Qur'ānic study inscribes Muslim identity onto children's bodies, paving the way for a more responsible, adult-like practice of Islam.

In some societies, coming of age rituals are only loosely connected with the attainment of adulthood. Girls do not officially become full adult women until they have given birth to their first child in the final stage of marriage; that is, when they are residing in their husbands' compounds. Coming of age rituals such as initiation and the start of Qur'ānic study are, however, both considered important steps in the journey to adulthood (Johnson 2000, 222–23, Johnson 2006).

Continuity, Conflict, and Change

Coming of age rituals throughout sub-Saharan Africa, like all rituals, are dynamic and have long been undergoing change. This change has intensified, however, following increased urbanization, religious conversion and change, and globalization. Among Jola peoples in Senegal, as explained by de Jong (2007), girls' initiation has always taken place in the sacred forests, where women traditionally gave birth, a taboo subject for Jola men. In the past, Jola sacred forests contained spirit shrines that were actively venerated. Although Jola converts to Islam today claim they praise Allah instead of venerating spirits, the shrines continue to have a cultural and religious importance and "palm wine libations have been replaced by sacrifices of kola nuts and prayers to Allah" (de Jong 2007, 35). In the Jola case, aspects of initiation rituals—such as where they are performed and libations—remain constant, even though the meanings attached to these activities have changed following conversion to Islam.

Coming of age rituals—such as initiation and female circumcision—and Islam often exist in tension with one another, and their relationship is the subject of lively contemporary debates. Although the contours of these debates are similar across societies, the actual effects on ritual practices vary considerably depending on the society concerned. Among Mandinga peoples in Guinea-Bissau, for example, women associate the practice of female circumcision with Islam. Men, however, especially those who are knowledgeable about the Qur'ān and who have made the pilgrimage to Mecca, argue that that it is an "animist" practice that is contradictory to Islam. They maintain that women's ignorance of Islam has led them to inaccurately construct a customary practice as a Muslim one and worry that women are ruining their reputations as "good Muslims" (see Johnson 2000, 2007). Ferme (1993) describes changes to Sande girls' initiation rituals when "Alhaji Airplane" made the pilgrimage to Mecca and returned. He banned, for example, the *sowei* mask from the rituals, claiming that he "did not see it in Mecca" (Ferme 1993, 37). Among Dyula peoples in Mali, excision ceremonies were abolished as early as the 1970s because Dyula, who were very concerned about their status as good Muslims, deemed the rituals "pagan" and "religiously improper" (Launay 1992, 114). In Sudan, as described by Gruenbaum (2001, Ch. 7), some men deem the practice of infibulation unnecessary, since the Qur'ān does not require it. They also consider it to be harmful, linking the practice to problems with women's health, sexual intercourse, and childbirth. As a result, some people are encouraging change. For example, during her research, Gruenbaum met an urban midwife who had created an alternative form of female circumcision that was less severe than infibulation, and even clitoridectomy. In this alternative form, a small portion of the clitoral prepuce is removed, leaving most of the erectile tissue intact (Gruenbaum 2001, 184). Many Sudanese women, however, are resistant to this innovation and prefer the "traditional" form of Pharaonic circumcision because of its link to marriageability.

In response to global campaigns against "female genital mutilation," as well as specific efforts to eradicate female circumcision across the continent, various forms of "symbolic circumcision" (Shell-Duncan and Hernlund 2000, 5) have emerged in some parts of sub-Saharan Africa. Hernlund (2000), for example, discusses a case of "ritual without cutting" in The Gambia, where female activists have advocated for "the revitalization of girl's adolescent initiation minus the element of genital cutting" (2000, 235). In other parts of Africa and among immigrant African populations in the contemporary African diaspora,

Muslim women themselves are critiquing the practice of female circumcision. In a five-day conference dedicated to gender issues in Mali, for example, de Jorio (2009, 104) reports that Muslim women criticized patriarchal interpretations of Islam, as well as practices they consider to be "animist," and not Islamic, such as excision.

Conclusion

Throughout sub-Saharan Africa childhood coming of age rituals—especially initiation and female circumcision—vary considerably in content and meaning. They do, however, tend to share a similar structure. Some take place in the presence of formal initiation societies (often termed "secret societies"), such as the Sande of West Africa, or they can take place in the absence of these societies. Although in some sub-Saharan African societies initiation rituals are either explicitly or implicitly linked to the transformation of children into adults, the timing of the rituals does not always coincide with physical adolescence. In some societies, female circumcision is an important component of initiation rituals, while in others this is not practiced.

Initiation rituals have a variety of meanings that vary according to the society in which they are practiced. They may be linked to the attainment of adulthood and preparation for marriage. In a similar vein, they may be linked to womanhood and the construction of socially-appropriate fertility. In other societies, these rituals have to do more with the construction of personhood, ethnicity, or gender identity. For example, in many societies girls are not thought to be full female persons until they have been initiated and circumcised, acts which are said to remove gender ambiguity. Other childhood rituals, such as the start of Qur'ānic study, resemble initiation rituals in that they are linked to the attainment of social adulthood and Muslim identity.

Childhood coming of age rituals in sub-Saharan Africa, like all rituals, have been undergoing change as a result of religious conversion, urbanization, and globalization. For example, in some societies the rituals have been shortened to accommodate children's school schedules. In other societies, female circumcision has been divorced from the initiation rituals that traditionally accompanied it. In this case, girls may be circumcised as infants or young children and may (or may not) experience a curtailed form of initiation when they are older. In other societies, female circumcision has undergone change or has been abolished altogether because the practice has been deemed contradictory to Islam.

Bibliography

Ahmadu, Fumbai. Rites and wrongs. An insider/outsider reflects on power and excision, in *Female "circumcision" in Africa. Culture, controversy, and change,* ed. Bettina Shell-Duncan and Ylva Hernlund, Boulder, Col. 2000, 283–312.

Belman, Beryl L. *The language of secrecy. Symbols and metaphors in Poro ritual*, New Brunswick, NJ 1984.

Boddy, Janice. Womb as oasis. The symbolic context of Pharaonic circumcision in rural Northern Sudan, in *American Ethnologist* 9:4 (1982), 682–98.

Boddy, Janice. *Wombs and alien spirits. Women, men, and the Zar cult in Northern Sudan*, Madison, Wis. 1989.

Boone, Sylvia Ardyn. *Radiance from the waters. Ideals of feminine beauty in Mende art*, New Haven, Conn. 1986.

De Jong, Ferdinand. *Masquerades of modernity. Power and secrecy in Casamance, Senegal*, Edinburgh 2007.

De Jorio, Rosa. Between dialogue and contestation. Gender, Islam, and the challenges of a Muslim public sphere, in *Journal of the Royal Anthropological Institute* 15 (2009), 95–111.

Dellenborg, Liselott. A reflection on the cultural meanings of female circumcision. Experiences from fieldwork in Casamance, Southern Senegal, in *Re-thinking sexualities in Africa*, ed. Signe Arnfred, Uppsala 2004, 79–97.

Douglas, Mary. *Purity and danger. An analysis of the concepts of pollution and taboo*, London 1966.

Ferme, Mariane. What "Alhaji Airplane" Saw in Mecca, and What Happened When He Came Home. Ritual Transformation in a Mende Community (Sierre Leone), in *Syncretism and anti-syncretism. The politics of religious synthesis*, ed. Charles Steward and Rosiland Shaw, London 1994, 27–44.

Gosselin, Claudie. Feminism, anthropology and the politics of excision in Mali. Global and local debates in a postcolonial world, in *Anthropologica* 42 (2000), 43–60.

Gottlieb, Alma. Interpreting gender and sexuality. Approaches from cultural anthropology, in *Exotic no more. Anthropology on the front lines*, ed. Jeremy MacClancy, Chicago, Ill. 2002, 167–89.

Gruenbaum, Ellen. *The female circumcision controversy. An anthropological perspective*, Philadelphia 2001.

Hernlund, Ylva. Cutting without ritual and ritual without cutting. Female "circumcision" and the re-ritualization of initiation in the Gambia, in *Female "circumcision" in Africa. Culture, controversy, and change*, ed. Bettina Shell-Duncan and Ylva Hernlund, Boulder, Col. 2000, 235–52.

Johnson, Michelle C. Becoming a Muslim, becoming a person. Female "circumcision," religious identity, and personhood in Guinea-Bissau," in *Female "circumcision" in Africa. Culture, controversy, and change,* ed. Bettina Shell-Duncan and Ylva Hernlund, Boulder, Col. 2000, 215–33.

Johnson, Michelle C. "The proof is on my palm." Debating ethnicity, Islam, and ritual in a new African diaspora, in *Journal of Religion in Africa* 36:1 (2006), 50–77.

Johnson, Michelle C. Making Mandinga or making Muslims? Debating female circumcision, ethnicity, and Islam in Guinea-Bissau and Portugal, in *Transcultural bodies. Female genital cutting in global context*, ed. Ylva Hernlund and Bettina Shell-Duncan, New Brunswick, NJ 2007, 202–23.

Launay, Robert. *Beyond the stream. Islam and society in a West African town*, Long Grove, Ill. 2004.

MacCormack, Carol P. Sande. The public face of a secret society, in *The new religions of Africa*, ed. Bennetta Jules-Rosette, Norwood, NJ 1979, 27–37.

Meinardus, Otto. Mythological, historical, and sociological aspects of the practice of female circumcision among the Egyptians, in *Acta Ethnographica Academiae Scientiarum Hungaricae* 16 (1967), 387–97.

Mommersteeg, Geert. *In the city of Marabouts. Islamic culture in West Africa*, Long Grove, Ill. 2012.

Rasmussen, Susan J. *The poetics and politics of Tuareg aging. Life course and personal destiny in Niger*, DeKalb, Ill. 1997.

Shell-Duncan, Bettina, and Ylva Hernlund. Female "circumcision" in Africa. Dimensions of the practice and debates, in *Female "circumcision" in Africa. Culture, controversy, and change*, eds. Bettina Shell-Duncan and Ylva Hernlund, Boulder, Col. 2000, 1–40.

Simmel, Georg. The secret and the secret society, in *The sociology of Georg Simmel*, ed. Kurt H. Wolff, New York 1950, repr. 1967.

Turner, Victor. *The rites of passage. Structure and anti-structure*, New Brunswick, NJ 1969, repr. 2011.

Turner, Victor. *The forest of symbols. Aspects of Ndembu ritual*, Ithaca, NY 1967.

Van der Kwaak, Anke. Female circumcision and gender identity. A questionable alliance?, in *Social Science and Medicine* 35:6 (1992), 777–87.

Van Gennep, Arnold. *The rites of passage*, Chicago 1908, repr. 1960.

Domestic Violence

∴

Domestic Violence: Bangladesh

Nusrat Ameen

Introduction

In the 40 years since the country's independence in 1971, the government of Bangladesh has taken a variety of legal steps to curb violence against women, in response both to international conventions and intense activism by women's rights groups within Bangladesh. The most recent is the Domestic Violence Act of 2010. Unfortunately, these laws have not proven sufficiently effective. The record of actual implementation has been poor and the incidence of domestic or family violence remains high for a number of reasons. This entry focuses on the problems in the legal attempts to address the problem.

Violence against Women

A sample survey of 3,130 women conducted in Bangladesh as part of a multi-country project for the World Health Organization by ICDDR, B (International Centre for Diarrheal Disease Research, Bangladesh, an international health research institution) and Naripokkho (a women's activist group), and funded by the government of Bangladesh, found that the majority of women (60 percent) reported having experienced either physical or sexual abuse or both at some time in their life (Naved 2003). Two specific forms of violence against women in Bangladesh that have received both national and international media attention are fatwa-related violence and acid attacks.

Islamic jurisprudence dictates that only those muftis (religious scholars) who have expertise in Islamic law are authorized to declare a fatwa (judicial opinion) on matters of marriage and divorce, for perceived moral transgressions, and other religious issues. Yet, village religious leaders sometimes make declarations in individual cases and call the declaration a fatwa. Such declarations can result in extrajudicial punishments against women. In 2001, the Bangladesh High Court declared all fatwas illegal, but fatwas have become a means of moral policing that operates by subjecting women to violence in order to constrain their behavior and choices (ASK 2006).

Acid attacks also remain a serious problem. Assailants throw acid in the faces of women and men, leaving victims disfigured and often blind. From January to December 2007, according to the human rights organization Odhikar, 161 persons were attacked with acid. Of these, 96 of the victims were women,

© KONINKLIJKE BRILL NV, LEIDEN, 2012 | DOI:10.1163/1872-5309_EWIC_EWICCOM_001431

42 were men, and 23 were children. According to Amnesty International USA's Annual Report 2008, in Kushtia district in the month of June alone, police and hospital records revealed that at least 19 women committed suicide and 65 more attempted suicide because of violence by their husbands or family members.

Table 1 shows the acts of violence in the years from 2005 to 2009.

TABLE 1   Acts of violence 2005–09

Type of violence	2005	2006	2007	2008	2009
Acid violence	130	142	95	80	63
Domestic violence	689	635	577	608	281
Violence for Dowry	356	334	294	296	285*
Rape	585	515	436	486	446**
Fatwa	46	39	35	20	35

SOURCE: *PROTHOM ALO* (MOST POPULAR DAILY BANGLA NEWSPAPER), 7 MARCH 2010.
* 194 women were murdered in dowry violence.
** 62 women were killed after rape; 158 were gang raped; 244 rape cases were filed.

Table 2 shows the statistics of violence against women in 2011, compiled by the Bangladesh National Women Lawyers' Association.

TABLE 2   Violence against Women and Children in Bangladesh (January–December, 2011)

SL	Type	Number	Deaths
1.	Sexual harassment	556	79
2.	Public violence	1,451	728
3.	Fatwa/punishment without trial	52	0
4.	Rape	603	86
5.	Acid throwing	78	0
6.	Trafficking	554	0
7.	Domestic violence	646	493
8.	Dowry	367	257
9.	Violence against domestic workers	114	81
10.	Political violence	11	4
	Total	4,432	1,728

SOURCE: STATISTICS FROM 14 NATIONAL DAILY NEWSPAPERS COMPILED BY BNWLA, JANUARY 2012

The Constitution and International Conventions

The constitution of Bangladesh guarantees equal rights for men and women in public life but this guarantee does not extend to the private sphere, which is governed by personal laws based on male-biased interpretations of religion (not only Islam but also Christianity and Hinduism). These discriminatory laws govern matters such as marriage, divorce, inheritance, and guardianship. At the same time, the constitution does recognize the unequal situation of women and has made special provisions that treat them as a specially disadvantaged category.

Moreover, Bangladesh is a signatory to international conventions such as CEDAW. This obligates those countries that have ratified or acceded to it to take "all appropriate measures" to ensure the full development and advancement of women in all spheres: political, educational, occupational, medical, economic, social, legal, and domestic (marriage and family relations). It also calls for the modification of social and cultural patterns of conduct in order to eliminate prejudice, customs, and all other practices based on the idea of inferiority or superiority of either sex. Bangladesh signed the Convention in 1984 with reservations on four Articles: 2, 13(a), 16(1)(c) and (f). The government of Bangladesh later withdrew its reservations to Article 13(a) and 16(1)(f), but did not reconsider its stand on Article 2, pursuing a policy on the elimination of discrimination against women, and Article16 (1)(c), which provides for the same rights and responsibilities during marriage and at its dissolution. This was clearly in deference to the government's understanding of religious sentiments in the population regarding the distribution of rights between the sexes. While some reforms and modifications have been made to protect the rights of women, the CEDAW provisions can be invoked before a court of law only if they have been transformed into national laws or administrative regulations.

Religion and Domestic Violence

In Bangladesh religion plays a vital role in the context of social life; both rural and urban Muslims claim to be influenced by religious beliefs (Banu 1992). Popular, male-biased interpretations of religious texts add to the misery of women in cases of domestic violence. In one study, 76.3 percent of the men interviewed men claimed there was a religious basis for the common local saying, "heaven lies under the husband's feet." Another oft-cited local saying is that "the parts beaten by the husband go to heaven" (Ameen 2005).

There are numerous verses in the Qur'ān as well as several *hadith*s that call for a stop to cruelty against women. Qur'ānic scholars such as Amina

Wadud and Asma Barlas, and women's rights activists throughout the world, have spilled much ink and devoted much time and energy to focus attention on the egalitarian message of the Qur'ān and of the Prophet's own practice and sayings. Throughout the Muslim world, the Qur'ānic verse 4:34 has been most heavily quoted by those who wish to argue that men are the guardians and rulers of women and that a husband has the right to beat an errant wife. Barlas has questioned this interpretation, arguing that this verse describes "men as women's protectors and maintainers, not guardians or rulers" (Barlas 2002, 184–85). Wadud has questioned the apparent "provision allowing husbands to *daraba* a disobedient wife" later in the same verse, arguing that the Qur'ān "never orders a woman to obey her husband. It never states that obedience to their husbands in a characteristic of the 'better women'." She also points out that *darraba* means "to strike repeatedly or intensely" but it is possible to translate *daraba* as "to set an example" (Wadud 1999, 76; see also Barlas 2002, 187–89).

Domestic Violence in Bangladesh

Feminist perspectives on men's abuse of women have shown that it can be understood only in the wider social context. It is an extension of normal, condoned behavior in a context of social inequality. Men wield power over women and all men (and some women) benefit from this through "differential access to important material and symbolic resources, while women are devalued as secondary and inferior" (Bograd 1988). Men remain the dominant group. Virtually all men can use violence to subdue women and keep them subordinate if they choose or allow themselves to do so. Globally, this is played out in public and in private in ways that lead to the deaths and suffering of many millions of women, and yet that are condoned and regarded as normal (Davies 1994).

In the Bangladeshi context, ethnographic and survey research shows that most women, both Hindu and Muslim, think of themselves as physically and morally bound to their husbands and their in-laws. Women are taught two virtues, patience and sacrifice, seen as the ideal traits of Bengali womanhood across religious lines. When a young woman moves into the home of her parents-in-law, she has very little status. She is subject to the "law" of her husband and his father because they are males. Several studies have found that for most women across class lines, independence remains something to fear rather than strive for, that women accept a subordinate role, and rarely challenge the authority of their fathers, brothers, husbands, and, later, even their sons (Hartmann and Boyce 1983, Ameen 2005). In the case of domestic violence, various social practices, religious beliefs as well as state policies, operate to treat some incidents or events as "personal," "shameful," and not to be spoken of in public. It is not a coincidence that most of these incidents concern women. Thus a wife may think that if her husband beats her, it is her personal problem. After all, religious codes seem to give men a certain right over their spouse. The common Bengali sayings mentioned earlier indicate the wide social acceptability of such violence.

Such views are further reinforced by state policies that assume men are the primary breadwinners and consider women's income to be essentially supplementary in a male-headed household. A survey conducted in 1976 among a cross-section of 270 men in the capital city Dhaka found that they considered household work and domestic employment (sewing, private tuition, toy-making) to be the most suitable areas of work for women. Next in order of preference was teaching, followed by medicine. These male respondents believed that, in these occupations, women would be able to cater for female clients only and they would "avoid conversing with men and therefore preserve [their] chastity" (Chowdhury and Ahmed 1980: 75). The attitude remained unchanged almost 20 years later: according to women interviewed in Ameen's 1997 study, their husbands held a similar view, thereby limiting their scope of work. Indeed, even women respondents who were doctors reported being constantly harassed by their husbands because their work involved interaction with men (Ameen 1997).

More often than not, women are taught that, for the sake of family honor, they should not leave their husbands even in the face of abuse. They are then compelled to quietly accept and find satisfaction in the circumstances of their marriage. Conformity to the conventional social norms and the prevailing order is ensured within the family level through the use of force, which in turn faces no sanction from society. Even highly educated women are bound by these expectations. As a doctor noted, "For the sake of society, women have to marry and remain married. The marriage sign is like a label which gives women a status in Bangladeshi society. Therefore, even when the marriage is abusive, women have to endure it" (Ameen 1997).

In Bangladeshi society then, sociocultural and religious traditions can collude to produce the ideal woman as submissive, dependent, and all-compromising. Their roles as wife and mother are the only goals in her life. In other words, she is there to cater to the needs of all others first. A woman's "inferior" status, as defined by the patriarchal society and supported and propagated by a section of that society in the name of religion, only increases her vulnerability and makes her a potential target for violence. The prevalence and acceptability of dowry both reflects and reinforces women's subordinate status and is also directly related to acts of violence against women (Ameen 2005).

Legal Solutions for Situations of Domestic Violence

Legal solutions that ignore social norms cannot alone guarantee the rights of women. Analyses of recent court cases show that social concerns such as family honor and the importance of marriage prevent the proper prosecution of the acts of violence. The case of Mossammat Julekha Begum vs. Md. Shamsul Alam (Family Suit no. 133/2003, 5th Additional Judge Court, Dhaka) is a good illustration of this.

After the marriage of the contesting parties in 1990, the father of Mossammat Julekha Begum, bore all expenses to send Md. Shamsul Alam to a foreign country for work. The defendant returned home permanently in the year 2000. After his return, he started to put pressure on the plaintiff by abusing her and her parents for Tk. 100,000. He threatened that if they failed to provide this amount, he would take a second wife who could bring a dowry of that sum. Julekha went to her parents because of the abuse. Julekha's parents sent her back to Alam because they were worried about the social stigma that would result from their separation or divorce. The abuse increased, however, and Alam took a second wife in May 2000. The plaintiff then filed a complaint through an NGO, which served a notice on her behalf. The defendant first pressured the plaintiff to withdraw the complaint. As a last resort, the plaintiff filed a petition before the family court for the dower that had not been paid to her by her hsband and maintenance for her three minor children and herself. The issues of the suit were decreed *ex parte* against the defendant without cost.

In case after case, the violent abuse becomes a secondary issue with the victims focusing on recovering maintenance or dower. Julekha, like many respondents in Ameen's (2005) study, was doubly trapped: on the one hand by the abusive relationship and on the other by society. Julekha's vulnerability was further reinforced by her parents, who wanted her to remain in the abusive relationship. She sought neither divorce nor redress for the violence, but simply payment of maintenance and dower.

In the end, the legal solutions available at any given time have been constrained by a number of practical factors: the weak economic position of women affected; the reluctance of the police to become involved in marital disputes; the difficulty of enforcing and sometimes obtaining injunctions; the problems of providing protection against husbands seeking "revenge"; a lack of alternative accommodation; and the presence of assisting agencies (lawyer, doctors, social services department) who tend to emphasise reconciliation and compromise over separation and divorce. The emphasis on mediation, arbitration and *shalish* (informal adjudication of petty disputes) by legal aid workers, professionals, as well as by clients, reflects the formal legal system's inability to remedy a wrong to the satisfaction of those seeking legal assistance. Indeed, 85 percent of lawyers opted for compromise or mediation over taking the husband to court for abuse. However, mediation is not always the best solution either (Ameen 2005).

Are women in Bangladesh then to be left unprotected by criminal law and other legal remedies in their own homes? If privacy is to be maintained and respected, what are the implications of this for the people concerned, not just the couple but also their children (if any) and larger family? Who is being protected when privacy is respected? At what point and at whose request is it appropriate for public agencies to intervene in the private world of marriage? The weakness of the law in Bangladesh lies in the fact that neither substantive nor procedural law is gender-neutral. The laws governing women's private lives are discriminatory. They discriminate against women vis-à-vis the men of the same community; for example, women have either delegated right of divorce or the court has to be satisfied on their behalf in order for the husbands to release them from the marriage contract. The laws also differ across religious communities; for example, a Hindu woman does not have the same rights to divorce as does a Muslim woman in Bangladesh.

Therefore sometimes, it would appear that even the fullest application or implementation of these laws cannot deliver justice to women. The procedures to be followed in the court process are complicated and often systematically and inherently discriminatory to women. Because of the prevalent male bias among the police, in most cases they do not even record complaints, and because evidence is then hard to produce or establish, there is a very slim chance of obtaining proper judgment. And when there is judgment, there is almost no guarantee of its execution. The husband very often escapes punishment.

A major obstacle for women who wish to take legal action against their abusive husbands is that cases of domestic violence tend to be inadequately dealt with within the police force and the judiciary. Owing to the ambiguity in law, domestic violence cases are often filed under inappropriate legal provisions (for example as dowry offences). This happens because the police are ignorant of the issue as a public crime and may not know under which law it should be filed. Thus, they misuse the law, and this leads to a miscarriage of justice. This suggests that a law reform is needed to increase the focus on domestic violence.

In Bangladesh the law is primarily concerned with "public" violence against women, for example, murder, rape, or trafficking, but quite silent in the case of domestic violence (except grave dowry offences), which is perhaps the most evident and prevalent form of oppression against women.

Thus, at every level, the implementation of the law is fettered by the attitude of actors in the legal system. There is a general reluctance to intervene in the family unit, a reluctance that again reflects the ideologies of the sanctity and the privacy of the family. It is therefore important to consider non-legal strategies also. Human rights agencies have a significant role to play here. Through their legal aid activity, movement, and advocacy, they can portray a positive image in society regarding the equal rights of men and women. As women have hardly any opportunity to use the formal legal system, these agencies can process their grievances through their legal aid programs. The mere existence of agencies that offer assistance to abused wives seems to have had a positive effect on women's situation. Field experience shows that while women generally try to cope on their own, in extreme situations, they do come to these agencies for mediation. The agencies successfully help them recover dower or maintenance money from the husbands. Formal legal remedies remain out of these women's reach because of their illiteracy, economic dependency, as well as the attitude of law enforcement officials regarding intervening in marital situations. Laws governing violence against women are themselves also problematic because they recognize violence committed by strangers anywhere and dowry-related violence within the home. There is no easy way to prosecute regular acts of domestic violence by members of a woman's own family.

Special Laws

The last two decades of the twentieth century might well be called a golden era for women in Bangladesh in terms of the creation of legal instruments to combat violence against women. Between 1980 and 2001, which saw periods of both military and democratic rule, eight special laws for women were enacted: Women and Children Repression Prevention (Amendment) Act, 2003; Acid Crime Prevention Act, 2002; Acid Control Act, 2002; Women and Children Repression Prevention Act, 2000; Repression Against Women and Children (Special Provision) Act, 1995; Family Court Ordinance 1985; Cruelty to Women (Deterrent Punishment) Ordinance, 1983; and Dowry Prohibition Act 1980.

The passage of these laws conveys a positive sense of accomplishment. Statistics, however, reveal a more complicated story. Despite the increasing number of reported cases of rape and unnatural death, the number of convictions under these laws has been minimal. Moreover, none of these laws deal directly with domestic violence, but rather with offences such as murder, rape, trafficking, kidnapping and dowry. In theory, in most jurisdictions, a woman who is a victim of family violence has a number of legal remedies at her disposal, under both criminal and civil law.

Criminal and Civil Law

In practice, criminal law has proven to be of little assistance to victims of family violence (Flavia 1999). Since the state is the prosecuting body in criminal offences, strict procedures of investigation have to be followed. Therefore, even if husbands could be convicted under the Penal Code, for murder, abetment to suicide, causing hurt and wrongful confinement, and so on, these provisions fail to take account of the sensitive situation of victims who encounter violence within the home. Moreover, it is almost impossible to prove family violence, be it by husband or in-laws "beyond reasonable doubt" as required by the criminal jurisdiction.

Interviews with lawyers reveal that the evidence is hard to obtain because witnesses are unwilling to testify in private matters (Ameen 2005). In many cases, the issue is mental trauma as a result of habitual beatings, rather than specific incidents resulting in grievous injuries, but the law is only equipped to consider the latter. Different criteria need to be developed in order to tackle domestic violence.

A 1998 survey carried out by Ain-O-Shalish Kendra (Law and Mediation Center, a legal aid organization) revealed that of 1,691 women subjected to violence in 75 unions (the smallest administrative unit of local government), 72 percent were severely beaten by their husbands. In Bangladesh, a woman faces domestic violence not only from her husband, but also from her in-laws, with whom the couple often resides. Up to 50 percent of all murders in Bangladesh have been attributed to marital violence (UN Report 1997). Yet only 10.5 percent had filed a case against the perpetrator (ASK 1998).

As in other contexts, women in Bangladesh are generally reluctant to file a report against their husbands (Ameen 2005, Khan 2001, 123). In one study of 313 women, all of whom had suffered physical injury, 256 refrained from reporting abuse to the police and 57 did contact the police. Of the 57, only 7 women got a positive response from the police, and 8 women were urged simply to leave their husband (Ameen 2005). Even women suffering from wrongful confinement, or who have been forced to have abortions, often do not bring any case in a criminal court for such offences (Ameen 1997).

Jan Pahl (1985) has noted that law enforcement officials treat violence within the home, by a marital partner, quite differently from violence by a stranger on the street. The former is seen as occurring within the private sphere and hence, less worthy of their attention. Research shows that assaults on the street are entered into the police records but assaults on women within their homes are either directed to agencies for mediation or rejected but hardly recorded.

There is no specific criminal law on domestic violence in Bangladesh. This gives rise to ambiguity and ignorance regarding the role of the police vis-à-vis such cases. Traditionally, the police have been blamed for the gap between the victim's abstract legal rights and her remedies in practice. Similarly, courts have been criticised for their reluctance to view violence between spouses as a crime comparable to public crime, for example, murder, rape or assault. Courts are also unwilling to accept the premise that traditional criminal law is inappropriate in the context of intimate relationships. These perceptions have led, it is believed, to easy bail and lenient sentences (Ameen 1997, 2005). Moreover, criminal law does not protect a woman by giving her the right to the "matrimonial home," nor does it offer her shelter during the proceedings. She is thus compelled to reconcile with her husband. It is also evident that for any legislation to be effectively implemented, especially to combat violence against women, it is necessary for the entire criminal justice system to be modified and interrelated with the welfare, health and community sector. Clearly there are significant difficulties in dealing with domestic abuse through standard criminal law and it is understandable why abused wives have hesitated to seek redress through criminal law.

There are also no specific civil law provisions for dealing with domestic violence. The only option within civil law in the event of abuse is to seek a divorce under the Dissolution of Muslim Marriage Law of 1939 and, in connection with that, make claims for dower, maintenance, and child custody. Field research reveals that wives abused by their husbands, finding no alternative, are compelled to seek divorce, and that lawyers themselves have tended to prefer using civil rather than criminal laws in cases of domestic violence (Ameen 2005).

There are several special laws to deal with violence against women in Bangladesh. There is, however, no law that deals specifically with domestic violence. Women's rights groups in Bangladesh have been so preoccupied with finding a way to respond to horrific offences against women such as acid throwing, rape, and murder, that they have not been able to give adequate attention to the issue of domestic violence. As a result, there has not been any serious initiative so far, either from women's groups or from the government, to produce even a draft bill or proposal to enact a law to deal with domestic violence. "Violence in the family is perhaps as old as the institution itself, yet this grave social problem has received inadequate attention from Bangladeshi researchers, so far ... family violence has remained and still remains the most under-reported crime in the country" (Jahan 1994).

It is evident from the general and special laws protecting women against violence that there is a gap in these laws that prevents them from dealing effectively with the particular issue of domestic violence. For any legislation that seeks to combat violence against women to be effectively implemented, it is necessary for the entire criminal justice system to be modified and coordinated with the welfare, health, and community sectors.

Nasrin Sultana's case is a good example of the misuse of law due to ignorance. Nasrin came to a legal aid organization in September 2003 seeking relief against her abusive husband. The agency mediated the matter by reminding her husband of his duty to maintain her. The parties came to a decision in March 2004 and Nasrin moved back home. But the abuse continued. Nasrin informed the police, who advised her to prosecute her husband for having demanded dowry from her and her family, and she ended up filing a case under the dowry law. However, in this case, dowry was not the main issue; the real issues were the husband's own frustration at being unemployed and his suspicions regarding her interactions with men in her office, and his decision to act on these through violence directed at Nasrin. This case demonstrates clearly how both the police and victims have creatively resorted to various laws in the absence of specific laws for dealing with domestic abuse.

The Domestic Violence (Resistance and Protection) Act 2010

Finally, in 2010, the Domestic Violence (Resistance and Protection) Act was passed into law. According to the law, a victim may complain to the court after facing domestic violence; the court then directs the state to ensure her security through different mechanisms. The accused (especially when it is the husband) is brought under a process of counseling and correction to bring an end to the practice of violence, according to Salma Ali, Executive Director of BNWLA. The law has been designed to be preventive rather than punitive, "to motivate people against domestic violence," to empower "a woman or witness to complain to the court and realise her right to have shelter and necessary maintenance cost from a husband" (Urmee 2010). This law thus seeks to address many of the problems inherent in the older laws against violence against women discussed earlier.

The new law has given domestic violence long-awaited recognition. It is of course too soon to assess the effectiveness of the new legislation. For the law to work and actually help abused women, law enforcement officers will have to take domestic violence complaints seriously and help the victims to escape the violent situation. The judiciary, for its part, will have to safeguard the rights provided under the legislation. This will require that officials in law enforcement and the judicial system are properly re-educated such that they recognize the seriousness of domestic violence and consider legal remedies as opposed to mediation and reconciliation in all instances (Ameen 2005).

Bibliography

Ain-O-Shalish Kendra (ASK). *Gender justice and discrimination*, Dhaka 1998.

Ameen, Nusrat. Keeping a wife at the end of a stick. Law and wife abuse in Bangladesh, Ph.D. thesis, University of East London 1997.

Ameen, Nusrat. *Wife abuse in Bangladesh. An unrecognised offence*, Dhaka 2005.

Ameen, Nusrat. Convention on the Elimination of Discrimination Against Women. Bangladesh situation, paper presented on behalf of NGOs for Bangladesh government, September 2006.

Bangladesh Gazette, 12 October 2010.

Banu, U. A. B. Razia Akhter. *Islam in Bangladesh*, Leiden and New York 1991.

Bograd, M. Feminist perspectives on wife abuse. An introduction, in *Feminist perspectives on wife abuse*, ed. K Yllö and M. Bograd, Newbury Park, Calif. 1988, 11–26.

Chowdhury, R. H. and Nilufer R. Ahmed. Women and law, in *Female status in Bangladesh*, ed. R. H. Chowdhury and Nilufer R. Ahmed, Dhaka 1980.

Davies, Miranda. Understanding the problem, in *Women and violence. Realities and responses worldwide*, ed. Miranda Davies, London 1994, 1–9.

Flavia, Agnes. Violence against women. Review of recent enactment, in *In the name of justice. Women and law in society*, ed. Swapna Mukhopadhyay, New Delhi 1999, 55–80.

Freedman, Lucy N. et al. Domestic violence. The criminal justice response, in *Victims of crime. Problems, policies, and programs*, ed. Arthur J. Lurigio, Wesley G. Skogan, and Robert C. Davis, London 1990, 87–103.

Hartmann, Betsy and James K. Boyce. *A quiet violence. View from a Bangladesh village*, Dhaka 1983.

Jahan, Roushan. *Hidden danger. Women and family violence in Bangladesh*, Dhaka 1994.

Khan, Saira Rahman. *The socio-legal status of Bengali women in Bangladesh. Implications for development*, Dhaka 2001.

Naved, Ruchira Tabassum. *A situational analysis of violence against women in South Asia* (for UNFPA Country Support Team for South and West Asia), Kathmandu 2003.

UNFPA. The right to choose. Reproductive rights and reproductive health, in *Human Rights Report of the Ain-O-Salish Kendra*, Dhaka 1997.

Pahl, Jan. *Private violence and public policy. The needs of battered women and the response of the public services*, London 1985.

Urmee, Farhana. A new law against domestic violence, in *Star Magazine*, 29 October 2010.

Violence against Women: Gulf States

Hasnaa Mokhtar

Introduction

The rich history of the Gulf states (Bahrain, Kuwait, Oman, Qatar, Saudi Arabia, and the United Arab Emirates) remains engulfed in stereotypical modern-day imagination. The prevailing view is that the Arabia of the past was an empty desert and that today it is a reservoir of oil run by authoritarian regimes. Despite being under the British colonial influence for over a hundred and fifty years, from 1820 until 1971, little is known about the region's history of indirect rule or colonization by proxy,[1] which disrupted social and gender relations and produced a neopatriarchy (Sharabi 1992). Widespread racism, clichés, and stereotypes embedded in Western discourse about the region continue to shape discussions on women's issues in the Gulf. In general, contemporary English-language research on the six Gulf states is devoid of nuanced gender analyses (al-Rasheed 2013, Sonbol 2014a).

This article provides an overview of the structural and interpersonal forms of violence that women experience in the region, including legal frameworks on violence against women, state and political violence, and societal perceptions and understandings of the problem. Researchers have noted that violence against women in these countries is underreported, under-researched, and poorly documented, despite its prevalence (Nazar and Kouzekanani 2007, al-Ghanim 2009, Afifi et al. 2011, al-Fazari 2011, Aldulijan et al. 2017, Alzahrani, Abaalkhail, and Ramadan 2016, AlFazari 2016, Aldosari 2017, Halawi et al. 2017, Volgare 2017). Available studies are mostly quantitative and focus on measuring attitudes to violence against women (al-Fazari et al. 2016). The marked improvement in women's economic lives following the discovery of oil contrasts with a notable deterioration in gender relations: "Violence is a living reality faced by women in Gulf society" (Sonbol 2014a, 23).

Understanding the complex and multifaceted nature of violence requires raising questions about the historical, political, economic, and social processes linked to its prevalence. Direct and visible forms of violence—such as intimate partner violence and domestic violence—cannot be studied and tackled in isolation from indirect and invisible structural violence—such as sexism,

---

1   Colonization by proxy is an analytical framework that describes how British colonizers established their administrative systems through pre-existing indigenous male power structures and in alliance with Muslim elites giving them more authority and considerable power (Vaughan, 2015).

racism, classism, colonialism, and militarism: "Personal violence is built into the system" (Galtung 1969, 184). In recent years, several national campaigns have emerged for the first time in the Gulf states that have raised awareness of violence against women. A number of states have also introduced legal reforms criminalizing this violence. Yet data remain scarce, and "resources to assist and support women are limited" (al-Fazari 2011, 1). This article provides a few examples of different forms of violence and how they are connected to structures of violence at the global and local levels. Readers should exercise caution in taking these details at face value and should avoid treating Gulf women as a homogeneous group. Attention must be given to situated knowledge on how social classes, racial and ethnic groups, religious and tribal affiliations, nationalities, rural and urban communities, geography, and politics shape women's individual experiences (Allaghi and Almana 1984, al-Mughni 2001): "Women's lives show us just how varied and complicated the sources of any one woman's suffering might be" (Abu-Lughod 2013, 24).

The Male Guardianship Laws

Post-oil modernization, the rise of capitalism, and the establishment of the modern-day Gulf states have provided women with access to professional and economic opportunities. However, the codification of laws, which continues to evolve in various ways in each country, affecting Sunni and Shiʻi women differently, coupled with new divisions of labor, has led to a general deterioration in women's situation, resulting in the policing of women's public attire, mobility, and autonomy. These processes have created and institutionalized the male guardianship system that grants men (fathers, husbands, brothers, or sons) legal authority over a woman's body, life, and decisions to varying degrees in each country. The guardianship system is based on the concepts of male authority (*qiwāma*) and male guardianship (*wilāya*). *Wilāya*, discussed in the Qur'an, is often interpreted as meaning the responsibility of men to provide for the family, which implies that they are thus superior to women, in charge of their affairs, and have authority to discipline them. This interpretation has been challenged and refuted by many Islamic feminists (al-Hibri 2003, Musawah 2016, Mogahed, AlKiek, and Brown 2017). The culturally and legally accepted understanding of male guardianship is the result of a patriarchal reading of Islamic sources by Muslims who adopted Western-style codes and interpreted Islam "through Victorian lenses" (Sonbol 2014a, 314). The law, with its different applications, "not only protects the state envisioned gender roles ... but also entrusts the state to act as the guardian of the family" (Aldosari 2016b, 6). However, this relationship between familial and state-level patriarchy is upheld but not well defined (Weiner 2016). Women are regarded as second-class citizens and the property of their male guardians, to be controlled, disciplined, and oppressed in the name of nationalism and Islam. This system of male authority represents the ideal model for indirect structural violence, which leads to visible forms of domestic violence against women and girls: "The male guardianship system creates an environment ripe for abuse" (Beckerle 2016, 32).

According to Human Rights Watch's report for 2018 (HRW 2019), the male guardianship system impedes women's right to marriage, travel, and custody to varying degrees in each Gulf state. Under the Kuwaiti personal status law, which applies to most Sunni Kuwaitis, a woman requires her male guardian's consent to marry, and a Kuwaiti man can prohibit his wife from working if he decides it negatively affects his family's affairs. In Oman, a mother can lose custody of her children if she remarries, while her ex-husband continues to have guardianship of the children (HLO 2017, HRW 2019). The Qatari personal status law allows a male guardian to divorce his daughter from her husband if he decides they are incompatible, even if she wants to remain married to him (al-Bahāwīd 2018). Qatari women also need to obtain their guardian's consent for employment and cannot travel without his permission unless they are over 25 years of age (al-Malki 2018). In Bahrain, a woman does not need her male guardian's permission to obtain a passport or civil identity card, but she needs him to accompany her if she is 45 or younger when traveling to perform hajj or *umra* (almost a full hajj ritual performed during other times of the year). In some cases, women need their guardian's permission to work outside the house (BCHR 2017). In the UAE, a woman needs her male guardian to conclude the marriage contract and is required to obey her husband (HRW 2019). Saudi Arabia's male guardianship laws are by far the most severe. Regardless of age, all women are required to get their male guardian's permission to travel, marry, be released from prison or a governmental institution, and obtain personal identification documents: "Many officials in public or private institutions, including health facilities, require the permission even when not required by law" (Aldosari 2017, 6). These are some examples of how Gulf women are subject to coerced choices under the male guardianship framework, placing them in the position of a legal minor.

Laws Pertaining to Intimate Partner Violence/Domestic Violence

One of the most dangerous repercussions of the vast authority granted to male guardians over women is violence against women and girls. Male guardianship plays a central role in institutionalizing, justifying, and sustaining a patriarchal model of the family. This results in many cases of husbands or fathers disciplining women physically, psychologically, or sexually if they do not comply. The arrest of Maryam al-Otaibi in Saudi Arabia on 19 April 2017, after her father filed a formal charge against her when she decided to leave her family's house and live independently, is one example. After receiving the complaint, the state acted on the father's behalf and arrested her, which led to her being fired from her job (Doaiji 2017). This patriarchal state-guardian model is reinforced through male religious authorities (judges and jurists) in much of the Gulf, who employ the concepts of guardianship derived from the most controversial verse in the Qur'an (4:34), which has been termed by scholars "the hitting verse." The patriarchal interpretations of the verse imply that men, as guardians, have the right to physically punish their women and correct their behavior if women disobey whatever rules are set for them. In 2010, the UAE's most senior judge, Chief Justice Falah al-Hajeri, made headlines worldwide when he gave a man, who slapped his wife and broke her tooth and left bruises on his daughter's body, a fine of approximately $112 (Newling 2010).

Article 53 of the penal code in the UAE allows the imposition of "chastisement by a husband to his wife and the chastisement of minor children" as long as he does not harm his wife or children. The country has no laws that criminalize any type of violence inflicted on women, including marital rape and female circumcision, even though the Ministry of Health has issued regulations prohibiting the practice of the latter in hospitals and clinics (CEDAW 2010, HRW 2019). A 2013 study measured the severity of hospitalized interpersonal violence-related injuries in Al-Ain Hospital Trauma Registry in Abu Dhabi. The estimated annual injury hospitalization of interpersonal violence was 6.7 per 100,000 population, and women were significantly more involved in domestic violence and injury at home by a family member (Osman et al. 2014. In 2018, Dubai's Foundation for Women and Children reported 1,027 cases of domestic violence against women and children (Ryan 2019).

In Saudi Arabia, the government issued the first law generally criminalizing domestic violence, "The Law on the Protection from Abuse," in 2013. Researchers have noted that several articles in the law reduce its effectiveness and that institutional resistance to implementing the law, as well as a lack of awareness, remain a challenge (Alhadban 2015, Aldosari 2017). A study examining the impact of gender norms and the male guardianship system on women's health in Saudi Arabia found that women's medical care was compromised, and that women sometimes lost their lives because institutions denied them medical care due to gender segregation norms or the guardianship system. A female student died after a heart attack because university administrators blocked male paramedics access to an all-women campus. Another university student was forced to deliver her baby in the campus dressing room after the attending female physician refused to transfer her without her male guardian's consent (Aldosari 2017, 6). In 2014, 1,088 cases of domestic violence against women were reported to social services, "but only 64 of those cases were referred to shelters, while 300 were returned to their families after a mediation process" (Aldosari 2017). A study on 511 women in al-Dammām and al-Aḥsā', Saudi Arabia, found a high prevalence of social anxiety and female abuse, which included verbal and physical violence (Aldulijan et al. 2017). In 2015, the Ministry of Labor and Social Development revealed that there were 8,016 reported cases of physical and psychological abuse, most of which involved violence between spouses. The ministry recorded 961 cases of domestic violence in one year in one major city, with most cases involving women and children being denied their basic rights to education, health care, or personal identification documents (Musawah 2018).

Although Article 29 of the Kuwaiti constitution prohibits gender discrimination, women are subject to discriminatory laws and procedures in the country's personal status law. Kuwait has no law that protects women from violence. Procedures to report cases of domestic violence are similar to those followed in other standard cases, which do not afford confidentiality or protection for the person reporting the case (HLO 2017). There is no law that criminalizes domestic violence in Kuwait, including marital rape. In cases of kidnapping, a person convicted of kidnapping a woman can be sentenced to between 3 and 15 years of imprisonment and may receive the death penalty as per Articles 178[80] and 180[81] of the penal code. However, the same law "excludes in Article 182, the kidnapper who legitimately marries the woman he has abducted with the consent of her guardian and a request from the guardian for not punishing the kidnapper" (HLO 2017). In a recent survey of 767 people in Kuwait, 53 percent of female respondents stated that they had been subjected to some form of violence. The husband or fiancé was considered the most frequent perpetrator of violence, with physical and psychological violence being the most prevalent forms (al-Salem 2018). Additionally, Article 153 of the penal code reduces the penalty for any man who finds his wife, mother, sister, or daughter in an act of adultery and kills her and/or the man committing the act with her.

The first national survey in Qatar, of 2,787 female students (Qatari and non-Qatari, aged 15–64) at Qatar University in 2009, revealed that 596 students had been subjected to violence. Beating was the most widespread form of violence, with 381 women having been physically battered. Of those who had been victims of violence, 14 percent had been subjected to sexual harassment; over half of this group had been raped (al-Ghanim 2009). Women's rights advocates in Qatar have noted that sexual harassment in the workplace needs to be urgently addressed since it is a social taboo and is often swept under the rug: "Far too many incidents go unreported, resulting in women choosing to leave their jobs because of their justifiable fear of getting blamed for harassment" (al-Malki 2018, 23).

The legal system in Qatar has no provisions for dealing with violence against women. In 2013, the first law school clinic focusing on domestic violence was established in the country, and the students drafted legislation designed to criminalize domestic violence in Qatar. Yet the country remains without any laws to protect women from violence (Treuthart and Rosenbaum 2013, Kassem, al-Malek, and Ali 2014), despite reports suggesting that the number of domestic violence incidents in Qatar is "perceived to have risen in recent years" (Saeed 2015, Badawi 2016).

Bahrain had no law that criminalized violence against women until 2015, when the government issued Law No. 17/2015, "Protection Against Domestic Violence Law," to protect women from violence (al-Fardan 2016). The law covers physical, sexual, psychological, and economic violence within the domestic sphere. Additionally, labor laws in Bahrain criminalize sexual harassment against women in the workplace. Articles 350 and 351 of the penal code both stipulate imprisonment or a fine for the perpetrator (al Gharaibeh 2011). However, the law does not specifically criminalize marital rape (Musawah 2018, HRW 2019). Moreover, Article 353 of the Bahraini penal code allows the rapist to escape punishment if he marries his victim. This law, like others with similar tendencies, was based on colonial British and/or French laws. In 2016, when the *Almajlis Al'aelaa Lilmar'a* (Supreme Council of Women) recommended to the *Majlis an-nuwab* (Council of Representatives) that Article 353 be abolished, a majority of Bahraini MPs voted to repeal it, but their efforts were blocked by a governmental reservation under which the government claimed that the article had "been established to preserve the honor of the family" (Aljballi 2017). In 2004, in a survey of 620 Bahraini wives, almost 30 percent of the women surveyed had been subjected to violence by their husbands (al-Romaihi 2012). Officially recorded statistics for domestic violence showed that in 2015, 1,655 cases of violence were against women and that incidents of violence were on the rise. In the first half of 2016 the number of reported cases of violence reached 859, more than half the cases reported the previous year, "and 73 percent of them were against women" (al-Fardan 2016). A more recent survey of 293 men and 294 women of various ages revealed that 78 percent of the women surveyed were victims of more than one type of domestic violence (*Arabian Business* 2016).

Human Rights Watch reported in 2019 that Oman's 2018 penal code has no provisions prohibiting violence against women. Instead, the law explicitly allows parents to scold underage children (HRW 2019). In 2011, a study on family violence in Oman conducted by Sultan Qaboos University surprisingly blamed both wives and husbands for the incidents of violence:

> The problem is to do with a commanding wife having her husband under her thumb, ignoring her role in the family, disrespecting her husband and his relatives, and children, and neglecting herself. On the other hand, a violent husband shows signs of wife abuse, disrespect, lack of communication, volatile temperament, sense of irresponsibility, and excessive force against wife and children.
>
> *Oman Daily Observer* 2011

The Ministry of Social Development in Oman in 2017 surveyed 200 men and women about the prevalence of and solutions to violence in Omani society. Of 250 cases filed in different courts, only 6 percent were related to violence against women, and physical violence was the most prevalent (al-Watan 2018). However, a study conducted in 2014 on female genital mutilation indicated that 20–30 percent of Omani women get circumcised (al Hinani 2014). Additionally, the Penal Code of 1974 in Oman does not criminalize marital rape. In fact, Article 38(2) states that disciplining a woman "within the limits of public custom" is permissible. Article 252 allows a man who finds his female relative in an adulterous relationship to kill or injure her or her partner without punishment (Musawah 2018).

In-country legislative differences to criminalize violence against women in the Gulf region indicate how gender norms and decision-making continue to be dominated by patriarchal perceptions. Despite some progress, implementation where laws have been passed is a challenge, and reporting violence against women is still stigmatized due to societal norms.

State, Administrative, and Political Violence against Gulf Women

Violence enacted by the state or its subsidiary bodies against women in the Gulf states takes multiple forms, including depriving children born to Gulf women married to non-Gulf men of the right to citizenship, imprisoning women for their activism and promotion of women's rights, and suppressing any form of protest against oppression, especially by Shi'i minorities. With the exception of Emirati women, no Gulf woman can pass on her citizenship to her children if she marries a non-Gulf citizen, unlike Gulf men married to non-Gulf women, who can easily pass on their citizenship to their children (Kinninmont 2013,

Seikaly, Roodsaz, and van Egten 2014, Weiner 2016, Al Fassi 2018, Al Gurg 2018). This type of administrative violence "is defined as the use of all possible administrative means to de-legitimise the claims to citizenship by anybody feeling some sense of entitlement" (Beaugrand 2011). The UAE Nationality Law stipulates that the children of an Emirati woman who marries a foreign man at least six years after they are born, can obtain citizenship "in accordance with the regulations determined in the Executive Regulations" (UAE Government 2019). However, there is no mention of what the executive regulations are that determine if the children can actually obtain Emirati nationality.

Daughters of Gulf women who cannot obtain citizenship based on their mother's nationality are often subjected to more violence than their male siblings. For example, in Saudi Arabia the law grants only the son of a Saudi woman the right to apply for Saudi citizenship, when he turns 18 (BBC News 2016). In Kuwait, *bidūn* women (women who are "without" citizenship or nationality or who are stateless—have no legal identification papers) are subject to structural and state violence. They are left without access to educational, medical, and legal resources or any social benefits due to their status. There is hardly any reliable data on the numbers of stateless people in the region. There are estimates that Kuwait hosts 93,000 stateless persons, Saudi Arabia 70,000, and Qatar 1,200, but there are no estimates on the number of stateless persons in Bahrain, Oman, or the UAE (Fisher 2015). Additionally, a Gulf woman who marries a non-Gulf man can risk losing custody of her Gulf children. In the UAE, an Emirati woman lost custody of her four Emirati children after marrying a foreign man. Her Emirati ex-husband argued that his three girls and one boy should not be allowed to live with their mother, who had married a man "from a different culture and traditions"; the court ruled in his favor (*The New Arab* 2018).

In what the government called a crackdown on terrorists and dissidents with affiliations to terrorist organizations, Saudi authorities, a few weeks before lifting the ban on women driving on 24 June 2018, arrested prominent women's rights activists and academics and accused them of treason. Despite not being told what the charges against them were, the women were moved to the Riyadh criminal court to await trial. In March 2019, human rights organizations and international media outlets reported that some of the imprisoned Saudi women activists had been subjected to mistreatment, electric shocks, flogging, and sexual assault (Kalin 2019). As of May 2019, authorities had temporarily released seven of the eleven women activists standing trial for charges related to their women's rights activism (Qiblawi 2019). Saudi scholar and feminist Hatoon Al Fassi is one of the recently released detainees. In a 2018 article, she had explained that the Saudi culture of misogyny based on a patriarchal reading of Islam, mixed with a harsh capitalist economy, has exploited women for centuries. She explained that recent developments—like allowing Saudi women to drive—were empowering, but she thought they were insufficiently sincere to address structural and political violence against Saudi women and so free them from their second-class citizenship status (Al Fassi 2018).

The Shi'i–Sunni ethno-sectarian struggle is another powerful tool that states use to inflict violence against Gulf women: "The sectarian narrative justifies the employment of overwhelming force and violence in order to overcome such powerful sectarian forces" (Dixon 2017, 12). In 2007, *Arab News* reported the case of seven men who had gang-raped a 21-year-old girl 14 times, in what later became known as the Qatif rape case. Qatif, Saudi Arabia, where the teenage girl lived, is majority Shi'i, and its residents are often subjected to political arrests, imprisonment, and oppression by the state. A Sunni judge at the time ordered that the rape victim receive 100 lashes, doubled to 200 for appealing the lenient sentences given to the rapists, and six months in jail—because on the night of the rape the victim had met with a man who was not a relative. The girl's fiancé and her lawyer pressured the judicial authorities to drop the charges against her, but both were accused of being disruptive to the court, and her lawyer's license was revoked for a time. The case received international attention from human rights agencies and political figures and raised further controversy because the girl was Shi'i (*BBC* 2007). In December 2015, a Saudi Shi'i woman activist, Israa al-Ghomgham, was arrested for protesting against the systematic oppression of the country's Shi'i minority. In October 2018, international media reported that she faced the death penalty for her human rights work; she would be the first female human rights defender to be executed in Saudi Arabia, if the sentencing is carried out (Selsky 2018). *Gulf Business* reported in February 2019 that Saudi Arabia is not seeking to execute al-Ghomgham, according to an official's confirmation, but she faces "trial before Saudi Arabia's specialised criminal court which deals with counter terrorism cases" (*Gulf Business* 2019).

In a crackdown on peaceful political protests and continued oppression of Bahrain's Shi'i majority, the Bahraini government arrested Maryam al-Khawaja in 2014. The government threatened her with up to seven years' jail time for trying to visit her father in prison. Her father, imprisoned human rights defender and co-founder of the Bahrain Center for Human Rights (BCHR) Abdulhadi al-Khawaja, was on hunger strike at the time of his daughter's visit. As the acting president of BCHR, Maryam al-Khawaja played a key role in the democratic protests in Bahrain in 2011. She was sentenced in absentia to one year in prison by Bahraini authorities in 2014 on charges related to an alleged assault on a police officer in Bahrain's airport. Following a rapid decline in her father's health, al-Khawaja travelled to Bahrain in hopes of visiting him, but she was detained on arrival. She was subsequently held in prison for 19 days and was released whilst the investigation was ongoing (BCHR 2017).

Zainab al-Khawaja, Maryam's sister, has also been subjected to violence at the hands of the Bahraini government. Since 2011, she has been detained many times, and 13 cases have been brought against her in Bahraini courts. She was arrested on 14 March 2016 following a house raid. She was sentenced to jail for 3 years and one month and to pay a fine. She was charged over tearing a photo of the king. Because she had a young boy at the time, he was kept with her in prison. Her sentence was suspended, and she was released in May 2016, on humanitarian grounds, but she was forced into exile and now resides in Denmark, to where her sister also relocated a few years later for fear of prosecution and pending sentencing (BCHR 2017).

Authorities start targeting women activists as they become more visible. Violence is weaponized against female human rights defenders, who are threatened during interrogation with rape, sexual assault, and detention. Bahraini Shi'i citizen Ayat al-Ghermeizi was arrested and severely tortured for reading publicly a poem criticizing the government for its anti-Shi'a oppression. According to the BCHR, more than 300 women have been arrested since 2011. In 2016, 3,445 women were detained in Bahrain; nine women were arrested in the first two months of 2017 alone (BCHR 2017). Additionally, Nazeeha Saeed, a well-known Bahraini female journalist, was tortured while being questioned in Bahrain in 2011. BCHR states that "Saeed was beaten with plastic tubing, had her head put down a toilet that was then flushed to simulate drowning, and had a caustic liquid, believed to be urine poured on her body" (2017, 20). After her release, Saeed reported the torture to the authorities, and although she could identify her attackers, only one was put on trial, and none were held accountable for the incident (BCHR 2017).

The so-called Arab Spring of 2011 created domestic implications for the Gulf states. Some rulers raised wages to sustain the status quo and maintain order, while others used violence against peaceful political protests to curb any opposition (Ulrichsen 2013). Women led many of these protests, calling into question restrictions placed on women (Seikaly, Roodsaz, and Egten 2014). However, hardly any data or studies explore the gendered impact of state and political violence or the impact the Gulf wars had on women. One study that examined the health of young Kuwaiti adults in 2006 revealed that thinking about the 1990 Iraqi invasion and occupation of Kuwait became increasingly traumatic for teenagers following the 2003 war in Iraq. Young adults reported "dramatic changes in their self-perceived health during that time" (Casey 2015, 84–85). Navigating postwar memories of violence created tensions and double lives for the younger generation, which obscured and hid the destructive forms of violence in Kuwait and in the region: "In Kuwait, acknowledging psychological distress has ... been highly stigmatized with consequences for family reputation, marriage, and extended family relations" (Casey 2015, 92).

Societal Attitudes and Perceptions of Violence

Rigid gender roles, gendered laws and policies, the male guardianship system, gender segregation, religious norms, educational backgrounds, and the socioeconomic status of women play a huge role in determining society's acceptance or rejection of violent behavior toward women: "Gender standards are constantly built and reproduced at various levels, including households, communities, and state institutions, or within health care and legal systems. Violence and coercion are frequently used to enforce gender standards, putting girls and women's well-being at risk" (Aldosari 2017, 7). A study conducted in 2015 in Riyadh, Saudi Arabia, concluded that men who abuse their wives have low levels of education. According to the female victim's perspective, violent men were described as having a strong personality and low flexibility in dealing with and trusting others (al-Harby 2015). A health care survey of Saudi women revealed that they mostly held gender attitudes that did not support equality. Of those surveyed, 81 percent believed that family problems should not be disclosed to outsiders, 59 percent believed a husband is the head of the family, and 55 percent thought people outside the family should not interfere if a husband mistreats his wife. The use of violence was tolerated by 30 percent of Saudi men, who admitted to using violence against women in their families, mostly for answering back or perceived immoral behavior (Aldosari 2017). In 2017, a survey of 758 Saudi women from 13 Saudi governorates revealed that drugs and alchohol were the most common risk factor for being abused. Alternately, unemployment and low income of husbands seemed to be the most important variables that caused violence (Halawi et al. 2017). One out of ten women were estimated to be victims of violence in al-Ṭā'if, Saudi Arabia; the husbands either had been exposed to violence in childhood or had struggled with drug addiction. About 56 percent of the abused women resorted to talking to family or friends; only 3 percent complained to the authorities (Alzahrani, Abaalkhail, and Ramadan 2016).

In Kuwait, a study of the attitudes of primary health care physicians to violence against women surveyed 899 physicians, interviewing 565 of them. The results revealed that male physicians tended to have a higher tolerance of violence against women, giving reasons such as that violence is a private issue, or that the woman was abused for good reasons. Female physicians, though, tended to be less tolerant of violent attitudes (Alkoot et al. 2010). A recent survey of 1,050 Kuwaitis revealed that half of the respondents agreed that physical violence is justified as punishment for female adultery; a third of both men and women said they would support a law permitting violence against a female adulterer (Gengler, Alkazemi, Alsharekh 2018).

In Qatar, a study revealed that some women tolerate violence for fear of losing their children or being divorced (al-Ghanim 2009). In Bahrain, barriers cited to women reporting violence or speaking up include a lack of protection measures, considering violence to be a normal part of family life, maintaining the reputation of the woman or family, and fear of losing custody of children (al-Fardan 2016). Another study in Bahrain also noted a link between increased violence due to alcohol and drug abuse in men. As for the role of education, although the likelihood of violence was greater among the less educated, the husband's educational background did not prevent the practice of all forms of violence against the wife (Mahrous and al Ansari 2016). Many Bahraini men believed that using force against women is justified (*Arabian Business* 2018). In Oman, women in urban areas experience more violence than those in rural areas, as a result of increased work pressure in the city, marital responsibilities, and greater social expectations (al-Fazari 2016).

National Campaigns and Colonial Legal Legacies

All Gulf states have ratified the Convention on the Elimination of All Forms of Discrimination Against Women (CEDAW), but with reservations due to the convention's "incompatibility with Islamic Shari'a" (Seikaly, Roodsaz, and van Egten 2014, 64). With this commitment to CEDAW, global pressure is high on Gulf state governments and NGOs to end all forms of gender violence to meet the UN's fifth sustainable development goal, which promotes gender equality. The Oxford Gulf and Arabian Peninsula Studies Forum's Spring 2018 issue of *Gulf Affairs* analyzes the persistent gender imbalances in the Gulf societies, with commentaries from Gulf women advocates in Saudi Arabia, Kuwait, Oman, Qatar, and the UAE, including an interview with the regional director of UN Women Arab States, Mohammad Naciri, in which he states that the Gulf countries are far behind on data and legislation around violence against women. He highlights that violence against women remains a major obstacle to gender equality (*Gulf Affairs* 2018a). In the same publication, Moodhi al-Suqair, treasure and board member of the Kuwaiti Women's Cultural and Social Society, stresses the need to pass legislation that criminalizes violence against women in Kuwait and other Gulf countries (*Gulf Affairs* 2018b).

Following calls from activists and civil society advocates to create a legal framework that better protects women from violence, a few national campaigns have emerged, breaking the silence around violence against women and leading to public discussions of this taboo topic. In 2015, *Zahrat al-Khaleej* ("The flower of the Gulf"), a women's magazine, relaunched its nationwide campaign "#DontCoverItUp," first launched in 2014, to discuss gender violence publicly in the region (Lakhpatwala 2015). In 2018, the Naseem Initiative of the Bahrain Youth Forum Society, a local NGO for human rights founded in 2015, launched the campaign "We Respect Her" aimed at raising awareness of violence against women. It was launched following the approval of Bahrain's Family Violence Law of 2015, which focuses on preventing violence in households and protecting victims of domestic violence. In 2016, the "I Am My Own Guardian" campaign emerged via social media demanding an end to the male guardianship system. The campaign was launched by Saudi women to coincide with the release of the Human Rights Watch "Boxed In" report (Beckerle 2016), which shared stories of Saudi women's lived experiences of the guardianship system. Activists noted that in response to this campaign, the Saudi government issued a royal decree on 17 April 2017 instructing all public institutions to not require a male guardian's approval for women to access government services (Doaiji 2017).

In Kuwait, a group of Kuwaiti women established the campaign "Abolish Article 153" to lobby the Kuwaiti parliament (*majlis*) to abolish the said article (of the penal code). It sentences a man who kills his female relative or her partner after finding them in an adulterous relationship, to no more than three years in jail and/or a fine of around 225 Kuwaiti dinars (Omar 2015). The campaign's founder, Alanoud al-Sharekh, describes this law as "colonial baggage" derived from the Napoleonic Code's crime of passion (al-Shammaa 2017). The legal system in Kuwait is based on Islamic law, French civil law, Egyptian law, and British common law. In the French civil code of 1810, "A man who, in a fit of passion, murdered his spouse in the midst of a sexual activity was guilty of no crime" (Holmberg 2007. Therefore, Article 153 is not "derived from the provisions of the Islamic Shariah" (HLO 2017).

The law has been attacked by activists because it allows "honor killings." The media frequently use this category to report on crimes in Muslim-majority countries such as Kuwait. For example, the BBC reported that a Kuwaiti man, Adnan Enezi, cut the throat of his 14-year-old daughter over suspected adultery, citing thousands of honor crimes in the Middle East (BBC News 2005). In 2014, it reported that Kuwaiti citizen Faleh Ghazi Albasman, 59, stabbed his 13-year-old daughter before stabbing himself, claiming, "it's about honor" (BBC News 2014). Postcolonial and decolonial feminists have argued against the use of the "honor crimes" label to describe such crimes, because it reinforces the divide between the civilized West and uncivilized other: "The obsession with honor crimes erases completely the modern state institutions and techniques of governance that are integral to both the incidents of violence and the category by which they are understood" (Abu-Lughod 2013). Additionally, post 9/11 the category has been deployed to stigmatize entire cultures with terrorist associations—hence the mentioning of "honor crimes" in the travel ban that the Trump administration signed in 2017 on the premise of protecting the United States from foreign terrorists. Researchers should exercise caution and avoid using problematic labels such as "honor crimes" to describe violence against women in Gulf states because it stigmatizes not specific acts of violence but entire cultures and communities. The use of such labels perpetuate racist and colonial logic that the sole reason for the prevalence of such violence is backward cultures: "an approach that obscures the multiple factors that give rise to and sustain the violence" (Razack 2004).

Violence against Female Domestic Migrant Workers

The wealth that has resulted from the "international petroleum regime" (Téreault 2003, 215) in the Gulf states has enabled upper- and middle-class families to recruit foreign domestic workers or housemaids to serve, clean, babysit, and perform home chores. Most of these workers are women who live in the same household with the family they work for: "Alien labor in the form of low-paid household workers constitutes perhaps the greatest contribution to the standard of living of Kuwaiti women and the chief support for those employed outside the home" (Téreault 2003, 215). Female domestic workers in the Gulf region are considered the most vulnerable and least protected population from abuse, violence, and injustice, inflicted on them by their employers. Physical, psychological, verbal, and financial violence against female migrant workers in the Gulf is another example of how gender-based violence is built into legal and social systems in the region. Local embassies and human rights organizations have reported accounts of stabbings, murders, rape, deportation, confinement, physical abuse, extortion, suicides, suicides under suspicious circumstances, workplace injuries, debilitating illness, and more: "Although there are certainly religious, gender, and class aspects to this violence, the most reliable pattern underpinning these events pits citizens against foreign laborers" (Gardner 2010, 2).

Laborers are employed in the Gulf states under the *kafāla* legal system (visa sponsorship), which ties migrant workers' residency permits to national or local "sponsoring" employers, whose written consent is required for workers to change employer or leave the country under normal circumstances. The workers come mostly from South and Southeast Asian countries such as India, Bangladesh, Sri Lanka, Indonesia, Nepal, and the Philippines in hope of earning a better income and improving the lives of their families back home: "Most of these workers come from impoverished, poorly-educated backgrounds and work as ... domestic workers ... care givers" (Mostofi 2012, 1). Driven by poverty and harsh conditions in their home countries, some of these workers pay recruitment agencies in their respective countries fees or bribes to land contracts in the Gulf. Once they arrive to their destination, migrant workers are subjected to slavery-like labor and legal systems, under which the employer has complete control over the worker's life, official documents, wages, mobility, health, safety, and so forth. In Bahrain, domestic workers reported having experienced sexual abuse and harassment, "such as unwanted advances, groping, fondling, and rape ... by their recruitment agents, employers, or employers' sons" (Mostofi 2012, 3). In a 2017 study that measured violence toward health workers in Bahrain Defense Force Royal Medical Services' emergency department, responses from 100 staff members (doctors, nurses, and support personnel) revealed that 78 percent of staff had experienced verbal abuse; 11 percent reported physical abuse, and 3 percent, sexual abuse (Rafeea et al. 2017).

In 2014, Amnesty International reported that due to the violence some female workers were subjected to in Qatar, they had tried to escape their employer's household. After conducting investigations with housemaids and drivers who had escaped from their sponsors, they stated that "maltreatment, domestic violence, over-work (in Ramadan) and no day-off in the week" to be some of the major violations that prompted them to escape (Amnesty International 2014, 7). Due to multiple incidents of abuse, torture, and murder of domestic workers in the Gulf states, some governments banned their nationals from working or traveling to some Gulf countries. In 2012, the BBC reported that Nepal had banned its female citizens under the age of 30 from working in Middle Eastern countries, including the Gulf states, due to reported cases of physical and sexual abuse. Gulf News reported in 2016 that Indonesia had informed 19 countries in the Middle East, including all the Gulf states, of a ban on recruiting Indonesian citizens as domestic workers due to abuses and inadequate labor laws. The more than 154,000 migrant domestic workers in

Oman often report falling victim to employer exploitation, through the confiscation of passports, delayed or unpaid salaries, or denial of adequate food and living conditions, and sometimes physical violence (HRW 2019). In Saudi Arabia, female domestic workers face a range of abuses, including forced confinement, nonpayment of wages, food deprivation, and psychological, physical, and sexual abuse (HRW 2019).

But international pressure seems to be pushing for minor changes, and local campaigns are trying to shed some light on the problem. In 2015, Kuwait issued a new standard contract for migrant workers, and a 2016 administrative decision allowed some migrant workers to transfer their sponsorship to a new employer after three years of work, without their employer's consent (HLO 2017). In Qatar, after partial reforms in 2018, the government announced plans to abolish exit visas for all its foreign workers by the end of 2019 (Harwood 2019).

Reliable data that capture the scope of violence against female domestic workers in the Gulf states are scarce (Gardner 2010). In 2008, the Saudi advertising agency Full Stop ran a regionwide campaign called Rahma (Mercy), highlighting the mistreatment of and abuses committed against migrant workers in the Gulf. Saudi-owned satellite channels broadcast the campaign's public service announcements, and local print media published the posters. One Rahma poster depicted a housemaid crouching to eat food from a dog's bowl placed next to her employer's shoe; another servant peeked out from a doghouse with metal chains around her neck. "Don't strip me of my humanity" was the message written in Arabic on these posters. al-Arabiya.net (2008) reported that there was a backlash in response to Rahma, and Saudi columnists and government officials slammed the campaign as overdone and biased. Employers of domestic workers claimed they were also victims of workers' abuse, theft, and running away schemes. In Kuwait, One Roof is the country's national campaign to raise awareness of domestic workers' rights. It has provided a legal guide in 15 languages to increase domestic workers' knowledge of their legal rights and responsibilities so that they are familiar with the rules that regulate their work and are able to demand their rights in case they are violated (One Roof 2018).

Conclusion

Incidents of violence against women are underreported and data remain scarce, except for a handful of quantitative studies conducted by graduate students and physicians with access to hospital records. As al-Ghanim suggests, "The topic of violence against women has been treated as marginal, the sample studies have been very small, and some of the studies have been mere surveys of the problem" (2009, 80). A few of the Gulf states have introduced legislation to criminalize violence against women, but implementation remains a challenge, and people's rigid gender perceptions and the persistence of the male guardianship system impede change. Female domestic workers endure the worst violence due to the intersection of their class, religion, ethnicity, and legal residency. There is an urgent need for research that examines violence against women in the Gulf states in relation to larger structures of power and that produces more nuanced analyses of the problems. As Lila Abu-Lughod has emphasized, cultural humility and respectful feminist curiosity are vital qualities in research, especially when addressing women's problems in Muslim-majority countries: "We have to keep asking hard questions about who or what is to blame for the problems that particular women face. What responses might be most effective for addressing problems that we do find, and who is best situated to understand or respond to these problems?" (Abu-Lughod 2013, 16).

Bibliography

al-Arabiya.net. Saudi mercy campaign higlights Islamic values, in *alarabiya.net*, 23 December 2008, <https://www.alarabiya.net/articles/2008/12/23/62654.html#/>. 17 September 2019.

Abu-Lughod, Lila. *Do Muslim women need saving?* Cambridge, Mass. 2013.

Afifi, Emam M., Nouriah S. Al-Muhaideb, Nina F. Hadish, Faten I. Ismail, and Fatema M. Al-Qeamy. 2011. "Domestic Violence and Its Impact on Married Women's Health in Eastern Saudi Arabia." *Saudi Medical Journal* 32 (6): 612–20.

Aldosari, Hala. Royal women in the Gulf. Agents of change or defenders of the status quo?, in Agsiw.org, 24 June 2016a, <https://agsiw.org/royal-women-in-the-gulf -agents-of-change-or-defenders-of-the-status-quo/>. 17 September 2019.

Aldosari, Hala. The personal is political. Gender identity in the personal status laws of the Gulf Arab states. Issue Paper No. 8/2016, The Arab Gulf States Institute in Washington, 29 August 2016b, <https://agsiw.org/the-personal-is-political-gender -identity-in-the-personal-status-laws-of-the-gulf-arab-states/>. 17 September 2019.

Aldosari, Hala. The effect of gender norms on women's health in Saudi Arabia. Policy Paper No. 1/2017, The Arab Gulf States Institute in Washington, 2 May 2017, <https:// agsiw.org/wp-content/uploads/2017/05/Aldosari_Womens-Health_Online-1.pdf>. 17 September 2019.

Aldulijan, Fajar Abdulrazzak, Abdullatif Sami Al Rashed, Asmaa Ibrahim Al Khamis, Marwah Mohammed Al-Jumaiah, Zainab Ali Al Ammar, Zainab Yousef Al Shaqaq, and Seema Irshad. 2017. "The Impact of Female Abuse on Social Anxiety Among

Females of Al Ahsa, Saudi Arabia: A Pilot Study." *EC Psychology and Psychiatry* 5 (4): 110–16.

Al Fassi, Hatoon. Despite worthy reforms, Saudi women are still second-class citizens, in *Gulf Affairs*, Spring 2018, 24–25, <https://www.oxgaps.org/files/gulf_affairs_spring_2018_full_issue.pdf>. 17 September 2019.

AlFazari, Manal Khasib Hamdan. 2016. "Wife Abuse in the Oman Society: An Interdisciplinary Psycho-Social Study." *Journal of Arts and Social Sciences: Sultan Qaboos University*, 105–13.

Al-Fazari, Manal, B. Sullivan, D. Walsh, and P. Newcombe. 2011. "Qualitative Research Helps Explore Attitudes towards Domestic Violence in Oman." *Conference: 6th International Qualitative Research Convention, Malaysia.*

Al Gurg, Muna. The UAE is making strides in closing the gender gap, in *Gulf Affairs*, Spring 2018, 28–29, <https://www.oxgaps.org/files/gulf_affairs_spring_2018_full_issue.pdf>. 17 September 2019.

Alhadban, Sahar. Domestic violence in Saudi Arabia. Ph.D. diss., Indiana University, 2015, <https://www.repository.law.indiana.edu/etd/27/>. 17 September 2019.

Al Hinani, Habiba. 2014. "Female Genital Mutilation in the Sultanate of Oman." http://www.stopfgmmideast.org/wp-content/uploads/2014/01/habiba-al-hinai-female-genital-mutilation-in-the-sultanate-of-oman1.pdf.

Aljballi, Samia. 2017. "The Rapists in the Gulf States: Friends of the Law." *Gulf House: Studies and Publishing* (blog). May 17, 2017. https://gulfhouse.org/posts/1865/.

Alkoot, Ibtisam M., M. I. Kamel and M. Shazly. Attitude of primary health care physicians in Kuwait towards domestic violence against women, in *Alexandria Faculty of Medicine* 46:4 (2010), 335–41.

Allaghi, Farida, and Aisha Almana. Survey of research on women in the Arab Gulf region, in *Social science research and women in the Arab world*, Paris 1984, 14–40.

Alzahrani, Turki A., Bahaa A. Abaalkhail, and Iman K. Ramadan. Prevalence of intimate partner violence and its associated risk factors among Saudi female patients attending the primary healthcare centers in western Saudi Arabia, in *Saudi Medical Journal* 37:1 (2016), 96–99.

Amnesty International. "My sleep is my break." Exploitation of migrant domestic workers in Qatar. Report index number MDE 22/004/2014, 23 April 2014, <https://www.amnesty.org/download/Documents/8000/mde220042014en.pdf>. 17 September 2019.

Arabian Business. Majority of men in Bahrain say 'use of force against women justified'—survey, in *Arabian Business Industries*, 23 October 2016, <https://www.arabianbusiness.com/majority-of-men-in-bahrain-say-use-of-force-against-women-justified-survey--649906.html/>. 17 September 2019.

Arabian Business. Majority of men in Bahrain say "use of force against women justified." Survey, in *Arabian Business*, 23 October 2016, <https://www.arabianbusiness

.com/majority-of-men-in-bahrain-say-use-of-force-against-women-justified-survey--649906.html>. 17 September 2019.

Badawi, Nada. Qatar-based NGO joins global fight against domestic violence, in *Doha News*, 28 November 2016, <https://dohanews.co/qatar-based-ngo-joins-global-fight-against-domestic-violence/>. 17 September 2019.

al-Bahawid, Shaykha. Laysat al-Saʿudiyya faqaṭ. Mādha taʿarruf ʿan al-walāya ʿalā l-maraʾ fī l-Khalīj? (Not just Saudi Arabia: What do you know about guardianship of women in the Gulf?), in Manshoor.com, 25 January 2018, <https://manshoor.com/people/male-guardianship-over-women/>. 17 September 2019.

Bahrain Center for Human Rights (BCHR). The legal status of women in Bahrain, 2017, <http://bahrainrights.org/sites/default/files/NEW%20BCHR%20Legal%20Status%20of%20Women%20in%20Bahrain.pdf>. 17 September 2019.

Beckerle, Kristine. Boxed in. Women and Saudi Arabia's male guardianship system, 16 July 2016b, <https://www.hrw.org/report/2016/07/16/boxed/women-and-saudi-arabias-male-guardianship-system>. 17 September 2019.

BBC News. Kuwaiti "slit daughter's throat," 26 January 2005, <http://news.bbc.co.uk/1/hi/world/middle_east/4209463.stm>. 17 September 2019.

BBC News. 2014. "Faleh Ghazi Albasman Detained Indefinitely for Killing Daughter." 2014. https://www.bbc.com/news/uk-england-dorset-29559155.

BBC News. Nepal women banned from Middle East over exploitation. 09 August 2012, <https://www.bbc.com/news/world-asia-19196245>. 17 September 2019.

BBC News. Saudi king 'pardons rape victim'. 17 December 2007. <http://news.bbc.co.uk/2/hi/middle_east/7147632.stm>. 28 October 2019.

Beaugrand, Claire. Statelessness and administrative violence. *Bidūns'* survival strategies in Kuwait, in *The Muslim World* 101/2 (2011), 228–50.

Casey, Conerly. Remembering and ill health in postinvasion Kuwait. Topographies, collaborations, mediations, in *Genocide and mass violence. Memory, symptom, and recovery*, ed. Devon E. Hinton and Alexander L. Hinton, New York 2015, 83–104.

CEDAW. 2010. "Women's Rights in the United Arab Emirates (UAE)."

Dixon, Paul. Beyond sectarianism in the Middle East? Comparative perspectives on group conflict, in *Beyond Sunni and Shia. The roots of sectarianism in a changing Middle East*, ed. Frederic Wehrey, New York 2017, 11–36.

Doaiji, Nora. Saudi women's online activism. One year of the "I am my own guardian" campaign. Issue Paper No. 11/2017, The Arab Gulf States Institute in Washington, 19 October 2017, <https://agsiw.org/saudi-womens-online-activism-one-year-guardian-campaign/>. 17 September 2019.

Doumato, Eleanor Abedlla. Women in civic and political life. Reform under authoritarian regimes, in *Political change in the Arab Gulf states. Stuck in transition*, ed. Mary Ann Téreault, Gwenn Okruhlik, and Andrzej Kapiszewski, London 2011, 193–223.

al-Fardan, Enas. Study of the reality of domestic violence against women in the Kingdom of Bahrain, in *Tafawuq center for women and gender*, 2016, 1–28.

al-Fassi, Hatoon Ajwad. Women in eastern Arabia. Myth and representation, in *Gulf women*, ed. Amira El-Azhary Sonbol, Doha 2014, 25–47.

al-Fazari, Manal. Qualitative research helps explore attitudes towards domestic violence in Oman. Conference presentation at the 6th International Qualitative Research Convention, Malaysia, 13–15 November 2011.

Fisher, Betsy L. Statelessness in the GCC. Gender discrimination beyond nationality law. Statelessness Working Paper Series No. 2015/01, Institute on Statelessness and Inclusion, December 2015, <https://files.institutesi.org/WP2015_01.pdf>. 17 September 2019.

Fromherz, Allen. Tribalism, tribal feuds and the social status of women, in *Gulf women*, ed. Amira El-Azhary Sonbol, Doha 2014, 48–68.

Gardner, Andrew M. 2010. *City of Strangers: Gulf Migration and the Indian Community in Bahrain*. USA: Cornell University Press.

Galtung, Johan. Violence, peace, and peace research, in *Journal of Peace Research* 6:3 (1969), 167–91.

Gengler, Justin. A survey of knowledge of and attitudes toward Article 153 among Kuwaiti citizens, in the LSE Middle East Centre blog, 15 December 2017, <https://blogs.lse.ac.uk/mec/2017/12/15/a-survey-of-knowledge-of-and-attitudes-toward-article-153-among-kuwaiti-citizens/>. 17 September 2019.

Gengler, Justin, Mariam Alkazemi, and Alanoud al-Sharekh. Who supports honor-based violence in the Middle East? Findings from a national survey of Kuwait, in *Journal of Interpersonal Violence* (2018), 1–27.

al-Ghanim, Kaltham Ali. Violence against women in Qatari society, in *Journal of Middle East Women's Studies* 5:1 (2009), 80–93.

Al Gharaibeh, Fakir (2011). Women's Empowerment in Bahrain. Journal of International Women's Studies, 12(3), 96–113. Available at: http://vc.bridgew.edu/jiws/vol12/iss3/7

Government.ae. Acquiring UAE Nationality. <https://www.government.ae/en/information-and-services/passports-and-traveling/uae-nationality>. 24 October 2019.

Gulf Affairs. Interview with Mohammad Naciri, regional director, UN Women Arab States, in *Gulf Affairs*, Spring 2018a, 32–35, <https://www.oxgaps.org/files/gulf_affairs_spring_2018_full_issue.pdf>. 17 September 2019.

Gulf Affairs. Interview with Moodhi Mohamed al-Suqair, treasurer and board member, Women's Cultural and Social Society, Kuwait, in *Gulf Affairs*, Spring 2018b, 39–41, <https://www.oxgaps.org/files/gulf_affairs_spring_2018_full_issue.pdf>. 17 September 2019.

Gulf Business. Saudi says not seeking death penalty against female activist Israa Al-Ghomgham, in *Gulf Business*, 3 February 2019, <https://gulfbusiness.com/saudi -says-not-seeking-death-penalty-female-activist-israa-al-ghomgham/>. 17 September 2019.

Halawi, Azhar Ahmed, et al. Prevalence and risk factors for abuse among Saudi females, KSA, in *The Egyptian Journal of Hospital Medicine* 68:1 (2017), 1082–87.

al-Harby, Sarah Fawaz. 'unf alrajul dida almar'a fi almujtama' al-Saudi (Man's violence against women in the Saudi society), Doctoral Thesis, King Saud University 2015, 1–191.

Harwood, Anthony. Qatar to abolish exit visas for all foreign workers, in *Global Construction Review*, 30 April 2019, <http://www.globalconstructionreview.com/ news/qatar-abolish-exit-visas-all-foreign-workers/>. 17 September 2019.

Hibri, Azizah Y. al-. 2003. "An Islamic Perspective on Domestic Violence." *Fordham International Law Journal* 27 (1): 195–224.

Holmberg, Tom (transc.). France. Penal code of 1810, in *Napoleon Series*, April 2007, <https://www.napoleon-series.org/research/government/france/penalcode/c_penal code3b.html>. 17 September 2019.

Human Line Organization (HLO). The Human Line Organization's parallel report to the State of Kuwait's report submitted to the Committee Concerned with the Convention on the Elimination of All Forms of Discrimination against Women, August 2017, <https://tbinternet.ohchr.org/Treaties/CEDAW/Shared%20 Documents/KWT/INT_CEDAW_NGO_KWT_28643_E.pdf>. 17 September 2019.

Human Rights Watch (HRW). World Report | 2019 Events of 2018. <https://www.hrw .org/sites/default/files/world_report_download/hrw_world_report_2019.pdf>.

Kalin, Stephen. Saudi women activists detail torture allegations in court, in *Reuters*, 27 March 2019, <https://uk.reuters.com/article/uk-saudi-arrests/saudi-women -activists-detail-torture-allegations-in-court-idUKKCN1R80M4>. 17 September 2019.

Kassem, Lina M., Tamadher S. al-Malek, and Fatema M. Ali. Domestic violence legislation and reform efforts in Qatar. Conflict and intl. politics, in Heinrich Böll Stiftung (Beirut), 3 March 2014, <https://lb.boell.org/en/2014/03/03/domestic-violence-legis lation-and-reform-efforts-qatar-conflict-intl-politics>. 17 September 2019.

Kinninmont, Jane. Citizenship in the Gulf, in *The Gulf states and the Arab uprisings*, ed. Ana Echagüe, Madrid 2013, 47–57, <https://www.chathamhouse.org/sites/default/ files/public/Research/Middle%20East/0713ch_kinninmont.pdf>. 17 September 2019.

Lakhpatwala, Zaira. Zahrat Al Khaleej campaigns against domestic violence, in *Communicate Online*, 29 November 2015, <https://www.communicateonline.me/more/cam paigns/zahrat-al-khaleej-campaigns-against-domestic-violence/>. 17 September 2019.

al-Malki, Amal. *Gender equality constraints in the Qatari workplace*, Oxford 2018.

Mahrous, Fadeela, and Hala Mohammed Al Ansari. 2016. "National Strategy for Women's Protection from Domestic Violence." Supreme Council for Women: Kingdom of Bahrain.

Mogahed, Dalia, Tesneem AlKiek, and Jonathan Brown. 2017. "Islam and Violence Against Women: A Critical Look at Domestic Violence and Honor Killings in the Muslim Community." 12th Annual Conference on Crimes Against Women: Yaqeen Institute for Islamic Research.

al-Mughni, Haya. *Women in Kuwait. The politics of gender*, London 2001.

Musawah. Thematic report on Muslim family law and Muslim women's rights in Saudi Arabia. Prepared for the 69th CEDAW Session, Geneva, Switzerland, February 2018, <https://www.musawah.org/wp-content/uploads/2019/02/Saudi-Arabia-Thematic-Report-2018-CEDAW69.pdf>. 17 September 2019.

Musawah. 2016. "Women's Stories, Women's Lives: Male Authority in Muslim Contexts." Malaysia: Musawah for equality in the Muslim family. http://www.musawah.org/ . http://www.musawah.org/women%E2%80%99s-stories-women%E2%80%99s-lives-male-authority-muslim-contexts.

Mostofi, Mani. For a better life. Migrant worker abuse in Bahrain and the government reform agenda, 30 September 2012, <https://www.hrw.org/report/2012/09/30/better-life/migrant-worker-abuse-bahrain-and-government-reform-agenda>. 17 September 2019.

Nazar, Fatima, and Kamiar Kouzekanani. Attitudes towards violence against women in Kuwait, in *Middle East Journal: Middle East Institute* 61:4 (2007), 641–54.

The New Arab. Emirati woman loses custody of four children after marrying foreigner, in *The New Arab*, 20 November 2018, <https://www.alaraby.co.uk/english/news/2018/11/20/emirati-woman-loses-custody-of-children-after-marrying-foreigner>. 17 September 2019.

Newling, Dan. Men allowed to beat their wives and young children (as long as they don't leave any marks), rules UAE court, in *Mail Online*, 18 October 2010, <https://www.dailymail.co.uk/news/article-1321504/UAEs-highest-court-rules-men-beat-wives-long-leave-marks.html>. 17 September 2019.

Omar, Faten. Honor killing law under attack, in *Kuwait Times*, 21 May 2015.

Qiblawi, Tamara. Saudi Arabia temporairly releses three women activists, in *CNN*, 28 March 2019, <https://www.cnn.com/2019/03/28/middleeast/saudi-women-activists-released-intl/index.html />. 17 September 2019.

One Roof. Domestic worker's legal guide, 2018. <http://secureservercdn.net/160.153.137.59/mk4.ee6.myftpupload.com/wp-content/uploads/2019/07/Domestic_Worker_Legal_Guide_2019.pdf>

Osmana, Ossama T., Alaa K. Abbasb, Hani O. Eidb, Mohamed O. Salemc, and Fikri M. Abu-Zidanb. Interpersonal violence in the United Arab Emirates, in *International Journal of Injury Control and Safety Promotion* 21:3 (2014), 260–65.

Rafeea, Faisal, A. Al Ansari, E. M. Abbas, K. Elmusharaf and M. S. Abu Zeid. Violence toward health workers in Bahrain Defense Force Royal Medical Services' emergency department, in *Open Access Emerg Med* 9 (2017), 113–121.

al-Rasheed, Madawi. *A most masculine state. Gender, politics, and religion in Saudi Arabia*, Cambridge 2013.

Razack, Sherene H. Imperilled Muslim women, dangerous Muslim men and civilized Europeans. Legal and social responses to forced marriages, in *Feminist Legal Studies* 12 (2004), 129–74.

Begum, Rothna. "I was sold." Abuse and exploitation of migrant domestic workers in Oman, study for Human Rights Watch (HRW). 13 July 2016, <https://www.hrw.org/report/2016/07/13/i-was-sold/abuse-and-exploitation-migrant-domestic-workers-oman>. 17 September 2019.

Al-Romaihi, Mohammed. 2012. "Domestic violence and its security implications." Bahrain: Academy of Royal Police: Ministry of Interior.

Ryan, Patrick. Dubai shelter sees more than 1,000 victims of domestic violence and human trafficking, in *The National*, 19 March 2019, <https://www.thenational.ae/uae/dubai-shelter-sees-more-than-1-000-victims-of-domestic-violence-and-human-trafficking-1.838750>.

Saeed, Marium. When it comes to love and marriage, more Qataris taking their time, in Doha News, 31 May 2015, <https://dohanews.co/when-it-comes-to-love-and-marriage-more-qataris-taking-their-time/>. 17 September 2019.

al-Salem, Fatima. Attitudinal survey on violence against women in Kuwait. Report prepared for Abolish 153, 20 July 2018, <http://abolish153.org/community/RAMA/uploads/2018/11/Abolish-153-Attitudinal-Survey-on-VAW_English.pdf>. 17 September 2019.

al-Sayegh, Fatma. Women of the Gulf during the first half of the twentieth century. A comparative study of American missionary archives and local memory, in *Gulf women*, ed. Amira El-Azhary Sonbol, Doha 2014, 241–76.

Seikaly, May, Rahil Roodsaz, and Corine van Egten. The situation of women in the Gulf states. Study for the Femm Committee, October 2014, <http://www.europarl.europa.eu/RegData/etudes/STUD/2014/509985/IPOL_STU(2014)509985_EN.pdf>. 17 September 2019.

Selsky, Sam. A Saudi Shia woman faces death for her activism, in Freedom at Issue blog, 25 October 2018, <https://freedomhouse.org/blog/saudi-shia-woman-faces-death-her-activism>. 17 September 2019.

al-Shammaa, Khalid. Abolish 153 campaign seeks to rid Kuwait of archaic law, in *Gulf News*, 20 October 2017, <https://gulfnews.com/world/gulf/kuwait/abolish-153-campaign-seeks-to-rid-kuwait-of-archaic-law-1.2106442>. 17 September 2019.

Sharabi, Hisham. *Neopatriarchy. A theory of distorted change in Arab society*, Oxford 1992.

Sonbol, Amira El-Azhary. Introduction. Researching the Gulf, in *Gulf women*, ed. Amira El-Azhary Sonbol, Doha 2014a, 1–24.

Sonbol, Amira El-Azhary. The family in the Gulf history, in *Gulf women*, ed. Amira El-Azhary Sonbol, Doha 2014b, 310–42.

Toumi, Habib. Six Gulf countries informed of Indonesia domestic workers ban, in *Gulf News*. 27 January 2016, <https://gulfnews.com/world/asia/six-gulf-countries-informed-of-indonesia-domestic-workers-ban-1.1661460>. 17 September 2019.

Téreault, Mary Ann. Kuwait. Sex, violence, and the politics of economic restructuring, in *Women and globalization in the Arab Middle East. Gender, economy, and society*, ed. Eleanor Abdella Doumato and Marsha Pripstein Posusney, Boulder, Colo. 2003, 237–255.

Téreault, Mary Ann. Bottom-up democratization in Kuwait, in *Political change in the Arab Gulf states. Stuck in transition*, ed. Mary Ann Téreault, Gwenn Okruhlik, and Andrzej Kapiszewski, London 2011, 73–98.

Téreault, Mary Ann, Andrzej Kapiszewski, and Gwenn Okruhlik. Twenty-first-century politics in the Arab Gulf states, in *Political change in the Arab Gulf States. Stuck in transition*, ed. Mary Ann Téreault, Gwenn Okruhlik, and Andrzej Kapiszewski, London 2011, 1–18.

Treuthart, Mary Pat, and Stephen A. Rosenbaum. Engendering a clinic. Lessons learned from a domestic violence clinical course in Qatar, in *International Review of Law* 1 (2013).

Ulrichsen, Kristian Coates. Domestic implications of the Arab uprisings in the Gulf, in *The Gulf states and the Arab uprisings*, ed. Ana Echagüe, Madrid 2013, 35–46.

Volgare, Vittoria. A long and winding road. Fighting gender-based violence in Kuwait, in *Your Middle East*, 11 April 2017, <https://yourmiddleeast.com/2017/04/11/a-long-and-winding-road-fighting-gender-based-violence-in-kuwait/>. 17 September 2019.

al-Watan. A study that examines the reality of violence against women in society and examines solutions to reduce it, in al-Watan.com, 21 January 2018, <http://alwatan.com/details/239468>. 17 September 2019.

Weiner, Scott. 2016. "Rethinking Patriarchy and Kinship in the Arab Gulf States." Women and Gender in Middle East Politics. George Washington University: The Project on Middle East Political Science: Institute for Middle East Studies.

Domestic Violence: Indonesia

Lyn Parker

Introduction: Terminology and Recent History

The nation-state of Indonesia is the largest Muslim-majority country and the fourth largest in the world in terms of population: 238 million in 2010. Muslims make up about 87 percent of the population of Indonesia (BPS 2011). In this entry, the statistics do not distinguish Muslims from those of other religions.

Domestic violence is probably the most common form of gender-based violence in Indonesia (Bennett et al. 2011, 160). It has only very recently been named in Indonesia, and is still a novel and controversial topic in public discourse. Some people believe that what happens within the family is a private matter and that, as heads of households, men have the right to physically abuse or punish their wives.

In Indonesia, the most common terms are *Kekerasan Terhadap Perempuan* (Violence against Women) and the acronym KDRT (*Kekerasan Dalam Rumah Tangga*, Violence in the Household *Kekerasan Dalam Rumah Tangga* was the official term used in ground-breaking legislation in 2004 when Law no. 23/2004 was given the title *Penghapusan Kekerasan Dalam Rumah Tangga* (The abolition of violence in the household). "KDRT" is commonly used in headlines in the national newspapers, but it is known and understood mainly by educated people; in local newspapers, the full phrase is used, with the acronym in brackets, as though the newspapers are educating the reading public about the concept.

However, the concept was not new to many activists in the women's movement. In 1993, in Yogyakarta, Muslim academics and activists had set up Rifka Annisa (Women's friend), an anti-violence group, which provided a women's shelter and counseling service that were to become famous across Indonesia. In 1995, the Mitra Perempuan (Women's friend) Crisis Centre was established in South Jakarta, and had branches in Bogor and Tangerang. As well as providing private counseling, it also ran a telephone helpline. In 1995, LBH-APIK (Legal aid institute—association of Indonesian women for justice) was set up to work for women's human rights in law. It has been very active and effective, in advocacy, for instance, on behalf of victims of gender-based violence.

Ironically, it took violence against women in the public sphere to push Indonesia toward legislation that made domestic violence a crime. The New Order of President Suharto (1966–1998) came to an unexpected and sudden

© KONINKLIJKE BRILL NV, LEIDEN, 2013 | DOI:10.1163/1872-5309_EWIC_EWICCOM_001452

end in May 1998, following an economic crisis and the resignation of Suharto. The mass, and apparently systematic, rape of Chinese women that occurred in May 1998 was the single most important event leading to the "outing" of rape, and eventually domestic violence, as forms of gender-based violence in Indonesia (see Blackburn 1999). The event attracted worldwide concern and international pressure on the Indonesian government. Inside Indonesia, activists in the human rights and women's movements began extraordinary efforts to campaign against race rape, rape as a form of state violence against women in disputed areas such as East Timor, West Papua and Aceh, and violence against women in general (Blackwood 1999, 440). It became clear that the New Order had not only failed to protect women against violence by not adequately recognizing rape and domestic violence, but it had also perpetrated violence against women, for instance, in military violence (Blackwood 1999, 441–43, Blackwood 2004, Chapter 8 "Violence").

As women's groups made violence a focus of their agenda, activists, academics and NGO representatives formed People Opposed to Violence Against Women, which successfully petitioned President Habibie. In October 1998 he set up Komnas Perempuan, the National Commission on Women, to investigate violence against women and the mass rapes of May 1998 (Komnas Perempuan website, Robinson 2009, 154). Komnas Perempuan has been an outstanding advocate for women against violence and continues the work of research, advocacy and reporting today.

Following the resignation of Suharto in 1998, Indonesia moved rapidly toward democratization: severe censorship of the press was lifted, women's groups flourished and a wide range of topics, formerly proscribed, were given free rein. Domestic violence was among them. From almost complete silence about gender-based violence, violence against women—state and public violence toward women as well as domestic violence—became a frequent topic in the press. Major new coalitions of women's organizations were set up; there was a revitalization of formerly non-political women's organizations; and well-established organizations began to take action on domestic violence (Robinson 2009, 155).

This is the context in which activists successfully lobbied for a law against domestic violence. Passed in 2004 as Law No. 23/2004 on the Abolition of Violence in the Household, it defines domestic violence as: "any act against anyone, particularly women, bringing about physical, sexual or psychological misery or suffering, and/or negligence in the household, including threats to commit acts, the use of force, or constraint of freedom in a manner against the law within the scope of the household" (ROI 2004, author's translation).

This is a broad and comprehensive definition, but it remains to be seen if some of the more ambitious aspects of the definition, such as psychological suffering, will stand up in court. With the passing of Law No. 23/2004 the National Commission on Women (Komnas Perempuan) declared, "In 2004, Indonesian women proved that the personal is political" (Komnas Perempuan 2005).

The Incidence and Prevalence of Domestic Violence in Indonesia

There is no one institution charged with responsibility for the collection of data on domestic violence in Indonesia. It is common for NGOs and institutions such as Komnas Perempuan to classify domestic violence together with other forms of violence against women, such as rape or sexual harassment, in the one category, as gender-based violence or violence toward/against women (VAW). Cases of domestic violence, however, commonly constitute about 95 percent of all such cases. Data are collected by various agencies—police, hospitals and other health centers, crisis centers and shelters, and other institutions such as courts and counseling services. Komnas Perempuan issues annual statistics based on their data collection (in 2011, they collected data from 395 institutions in 30 provinces, see Komnas Perempuan 2012, 1).

There are statistics on VAW going back to 2001. While all reports claim that the incidence of violence is increasing, the figures seem to have peaked in 2009, with 143,586 cases of violence toward women reported, and to have declined to 119,107 cases in 2011 (Komnas Perempuan 2012, 6). However, all authorities agree that these cases represent only the "tip of the iceberg," and that the figures do not reflect the true situation. There are also indicative data from several Indonesian provinces. For East Java, for example, Andajani-Sutjahjo (2003) reported that 29 percent of women interviewed had experienced violence from their husbands; Hakimi et al. (2001) reported that 27 percent of women had experienced partner violence. Andajani-Sutjahjo (2003) also found that 32 percent of women had reported having unwanted sex within marriage in the past 12 months (MOH et al. 2008, 46). In the provinces of East and West Nusa Tenggara, two of the poorest provinces in Indonesia, a survey of 1,004 married women in four districts reported an average of 50 percent of women who had been physically or emotionally abused by their partners (MOH et al. 2008, 46).

Domestic Violence, Marriage and Masculinity

To understand domestic violence in Indonesia it is necessary to understand the construction of marriage. (For Indonesia the level of domestic violence outside of marital domestic violence—for example, violence toward children, housemaids or the elderly—is not yet known.) Marriage is almost universal in Indonesia. For both men and women, marriage marks the attainment of social adulthood. The age at marriage is rising, but society expects most Indonesians to marry and to have children.

The legal and Islamic construction of marriage in Indonesia not only creates conditions that enable men to think that being violent toward their wives is natural and normal, but also makes it very difficult for abused wives to escape the violence. The 1974 Marriage Law states that husbands are the heads of families, and that wives are housewives (ROI 1974, Article 31 (3)). Although the implementation of law is commonly weak in Indonesia, this statement, that husbands are the heads of families, is universally known and widely accepted there. The Marriage Law remains current, despite criticism over decades for its domestication and subordination of women (for example, Suryakusuma 1996, Blackburn 2004) and recent attempts to revise it (see LBH-APIK 2010, Robinson 2009, 162). The law provides a legal basis for men to enjoy authority over their wives, and many men take advantage of this to assume that they can do whatever they like with their wives.

More broadly, the Indonesian authorities during the New Order period promulgated an ideal of the happy and harmonious family, and the nation-state was perceived as the family writ large. For instance, Law 10/1992 concerned "Population Development and the Development of Happy and Prosperous Families," and shows that harmonious relationships within the family (i.e., in line with the wishes of the father/husband) were considered to establish ideal conditions for national development; internal family conflicts were considered an obstacle to development and unpatriotic (Sciortino and Smyth 2002, 102).

The ideological foundation of the Indonesian nation-state is the "family foundation" (*azas kekeluargaan*) (Parker 2003, Chapter 1). The family foundation ideology presumed an automatic harmony of affective ties between family members and assigned to each family member a "natural" place and role to play. Aside from assigning husbands as heads of households, the Marriage Law of 1974 lays out the rights and responsibilities of husbands and wives. The economic role of the husband is clearly articulated: "husbands are responsible for protecting their wives and for providing all the necessities of life for the household, in keeping with their capability" (ROI 1974, Article 34, 1). Article 34, 2 clearly lays out the wife's territory: "Wives are obliged to organize the household as well as possible" (ROI 1974). The ideological framework of *kekeluargaan* (family-ness) provided a vision of an integrated nation and state: the nation-state was to be a happy family.

The main reason for marriage in Indonesia is procreation. In Islam, marriage is an act that follows the actions of the Prophet Muhammad; if one does not marry, one is not a follower of the Prophet (Idrus 2004). Marriage is a "benevolent and purified act that establishes the rights and duties for both husband and wife, and protects any children born from the marriage" (Idrus 2004). Muslim Indonesians often say that marriage is an act of worship (*ibadah*).

The construction of maculinity is also relevant. Recent research on men who are violent to their wives shows that they "believe that Islam gives them the right and authority to lead and educate their wives" (Hidayat 2012). As one Muslim man in Central Java said, "Being the men of families, we are the blessed, beloved and chosen ones" (Hidayat 2012). They believe that to be "a real man, one must be the leader of one's family," and that this leadership role is "a duty for which men themselves will be held directly accountable by God."

Further, many people believe that male violence to wives is countenanced by the Qur'ān. They are following an interpretation of verse 34 of *Surat al-Nisā'* (Chapter of women) in the Qur'ān: "Men are in charge of women, because Allah has made some of them excel over the others, and because they spend some of their wealth. Hence righteous women are obedient, guarding the unseen which Allah has guarded. And those of them that you fear might rebel, admonish them and abandon them in their beds and beat them. Should they obey you, do not seek a way of harming them; for Allah is Sublime and Great!" (Dunn and Kellison 2010, 15). Although this verse has many possible translations and interpretations (see, for example Bauer 2006, Dunn and Kellison 2010, Mahmaoud 2006), many *ulama* and violent men assume that "beating" a wife who challenges their authority is allowed, and even correct, in Islam. Research among men in the Indonesian cities of Pekanbaru and Makassar shows that they "regard domestic violence as quite normal. In the words of a market trader in Pekanbaru, 'Domestic violence happens inside the family. It's only natural'" (Nilan 2012). Coupled with this picture of the place of the man in the family is the idea of the ideal "righteous" (*sholehah*) wife, a woman who is obedient, submissive to her husband and sexually attractive.

Thus, the national Marriage Law is in harmony with the widely accepted teachings of Islam—though it is important to remember that many progressive Muslims do not share the the interpretations mentioned here and have an understanding of marriage as an equal, companionate relationship of mutual respect (see Hasyim 2006, Munir 2005). In addition, Indonesia's many ethnic groups have local versions of *adat* (custom), which variously reinforce, cross-cut or accommodate these authoritative versions of family life. For instance, in Bali, the patrilineal kinship system and virilocal residence pattern mean that women marry out of their natal families and go to live with their husbands' families, a system which can leave wives quite vulnerable to domestic violence. In West Sumatra, the matrilineal kinship system and uxorilocal residence tend to protect women from domestic violence. However, increasingly, all over Indonesia, through urbanization for education and employment, a neolocal residence pattern is followed, with newly-weds setting up house on their own. The effect of this trend on rates of domestic violence is not known.

Although Indonesia does not have the honor killings that are reported for many patriarchal Islamic cultures, in some Indonesian ethnic cultures, "honor" (*siri'*) is an important feature of marriage. For instance, in Bugis/Makassarese society (Sulawesi), which is quite hierarchical, marriage can enhance or lower one's social status. The woman is "the symbol of family *siri'* (honor) ... A woman determines or stabilizes the degree of nobility of her family" (Idrus 2004). Like honor elsewhere, the concept of *siri'* connotes both honor and shame, and has multiple meanings: shyness, fear, humility, disgrace, envy, self-respect and morality.

Women's Experience of Domestic Violence in Indonesia

Domestic violence in Indonesia occurs within the understandings of marriage described above. The view that violence is a private matter which does not necessarily require intervention from outsiders is held by many Indonesians, including some women who have experienced domestic violence. In this view, conflict and disagreement within marital relationships are natural, and husbands and wives are expected to resolve their problems within the family. In Makassar, for instance, it is commonly believed that speaking out about domestic violence to others, even to authorities or women's organizations, causes a woman to feel *siri'* (shame) which undermines family honor. It is not uncommon for the victims of domestic violence, rather than the husbandly perpetrators, to experience social stigma. Many women are unwilling to make reports against abusive husbands because of the social stigma associated with domestic violence (for example, *Jakarta Post* 16 April 2006 and 17 December 2004). This is because they could be seen as troublesome women, who have failed to maintain harmony and good relations within the family.

It is thus common for people to believe that domestic violence is normal, and that it is a private matter. Usually men think that their violence is their way of disciplining their wives, and that it is justified. When women are perceived to be disobeying their husbands—for instance, if they have gone outside the home without first asking their husband's permission, or if they have not prepared dinner for their husband when he wants it—men can feel that their authority is being challenged and that they need to show their wife who is in charge. These are the sorts of everyday acts that can trigger men's domestic violence. Often, of course, men hit their wives in order to win an argument; the consumption of alcohol can also be a factor.

Typically, each battered wife's story is complicated, with many different strands woven together. The following excerpt from an interview in Makassar shows a woman's typically densely-woven narrative that combines many strands: challenges to male authority, conflict over gender roles, alcohol abuse, conflict over control of money, and finally, the pain of having to compete with another woman:

> My husband beats me if I interrupt or talk while he is speaking, or if the children fall down, or after drinking alcohol or if I am looking for him at a drinking site ... I cannot make decisions about family expenditure and when the money is insufficient he keeps asking "How has the money been spent?" My husband often hits me if I purchase something which he dislikes. Also, my husband is having an affair with another woman. (S1, 4 March 2004, Aisyah and Parker forthcoming)

In addition, women often accept that marriage entails presumed consent for sexual intercourse, whenever a husband demands it. This was also reported by Idrus and Bennett (2003, 51):

> He believes that as a husband, he has the right to be sexually served by his wife whenever he pleases. If I refused him, he would throw me onto the bed, take off my clothes, and force me to have sex. He also forced me to make sounds to stimulate his passion. He treated me not like a wife, but like a whore. If I resisted him, he would become angrier and hit me without any thought or respect.

The language of "serving" is frequently used. While women generally accept that they should serve their husbands with food and drink, opinion is divided over sexual services. Many women believe that Islam teaches that men have a right to have sex with their wives at any time outside of menstruation. Bennett et al. (2011, 157) note that, "We believe that the extremely high prevalence of unwanted sex in marriage is related to a lack of awareness by both men and women that Muslim women are entitled to exercise sexual consent and to refuse sex in marriage" (see Hasyim 2006, 99–102). They provide testimony from a newly-wed, 20-year-old woman, pregnant with her first child:

> When he gets drunk with his friends on a Saturday night he always expects sex. He wakes me up very late and he smells bad and is clumsy

and aggressive. The first time it happened I was very shocked, because he never drank alcohol when we were engaged and he had never been rough with me before. I tried to resist him physically and to leave the room, but it made him very angry and he shouted and called me very bad names and I was embarrassed because his parents were in the next room. I was sure they could hear everything.

Now I just try to avoid him, I sleep in the kitchen or hide in the bathroom when I hear him come home. But if I am asleep in our bed he will always wake me up if he wants it. When he is drunk he is very aggressive and it [intercourse] hurts inside, now I understand if I resist him he is rougher, even until I have bled.

The worst time was when he forced himself in from behind [anal sex], it really hurt and I cried. I think there must be something wrong with my husband but I am too scared to confront him and too embarrassed to make a scene in front of his parents.

Until now I have told no one about his behavior but I feel so angry and depressed and I think it is ruining our marriage (recorded by field interviewer, March 2007.)

BENNETT et al. 2011, 157

Domestic violence has also been commonly associated with polygyny and divorce in Indonesia. The 1974 Marriage Law and associated regulations made early marriage, divorce and polygyny more difficult. Nurmila's recent study of polygyny in Indonesia (primary data were from 39 cases of polygynous marriages) revealed that polygyny was consistently associated with "significant degrees of emotional and physical violence" for women (Nurmila 2009, 14).

While Indonesia's Law on Domestic Violence 2004 does recognize acts that cause "sexual or psychological misery or suffering" as domestic violence, this is not to say that Indonesia recognizes polygyny as necessarily entailing domestic violence (ROI 2004). However, there does seem to be a strong link between polygyny and female suffering, and between polygyny and divorce. For instance, Suhandjati's (2002) research examined the cases of 50 women who self-registered as having experienced domestic violence, and 12 of these were women who filed for divorce because of violence toward them that involved polygyny or *selingkuh* (unofficial wives, mistresses or long-running affairs).

It is very clear that many women who are the victims of violent abuse by their husbands have to put up with sexual infidelity—through their husbands having affairs or through polygyny, which is sometimes kept secret. The cultural logic that causes men who are having affairs to be violent to their wives seems to be related to the fact that their wives can take the moral high ground. The men have no defense: such behavior is not condoned by religious or social norms, and indeed is a major sin (*zina*) in Islam. A common "explanation" is that men's sexual drive (*nafsu*) is stronger than women's, and cannot be denied. This is extended to become a justification for polygyny. Islam, it is claimed, provides a "solution" to this problem of the male sex drive: take more than one wife, lest the husband commit *zina*.

In taking a mistress or having affairs, a man is clearly contravening social and religious norms. A female interviewee in Makassar said: "I never complain or tell anyone when my husband physically abuses me, but when he engages in a sexual scandal, I let others know about that" (S1, 4 March 2004, cited in Aisyah and Parker forthcoming). Thus, while sexual infidelity can be made public, domestic violence is often a silent crime.

Women of all educational backgrounds and socioeconomic statuses can and do experience domestic violence. The study by Rowe et al. (2006) of academic women in Medan who experienced domestic violence makes it clear that professional standing and higher education do not protect women from violent husbands. Even "financially independent women experienced financial abuse, including dishonesty, unfairness and in some instances their husbands' outright refusal to support the family" (Rowe et al. 2006, 44). Idrus and Bennett (2003) found that if wives enjoyed a higher educational and financial status than their husband, husbands were jealous and felt threatened, leading to domestic violence. Idrus's study of eight cases of marital rape in Makassar revealed a wide range of education and socioeconomic status (1999, 11). Nevertheless there are some class-related patterns. For instance, Suhandjati found that women with higher education (for example, senior high school or above) were more likely to express their feelings and to file for divorce than those with only primary school or junior high school education (2002, 96–97).

Government and NGO Action

Following the enactment of the Law for the Abolition of Violence in the Household in September 2004, the Indonesian government released its Zero Tolerance Policy, which aimed at nationwide, multiple-sector coverage. It provided one-off training for civil servants in various government ministries, support for the establishment of integrated crisis centers, and the development of guidelines for police and medical staff to show them how to respond sensitively to incidents of rape and domestic violence (MOH et al. 2008). The government has made some real progress, particularly in the provision of special reporting desks in police offices and dedicated services such as shelters and crisis centers in hospitals. In 2012, the Ministry of Women's Empowerment and the Protection of Children reported the existence of the following services:

DOMESTIC VIOLENCE: INDONESIA

1. P2TP2A (Integrated Service Centers for Women and Children) in 20 provinces and 117 districts/towns
2. UUPA (Service Units for Women and Children) in 305 police locations
3. PKT (Integrated Crisis Centers) for female victims of violence in 22 public hospitals
4. PPT (Integrated Service Centers) in 42 "police hospitals"
5. 29 Safe Houses/Trauma Centers
6. 42 Crisis Centers/Women's Trauma Centers (Kementerian Pemberdayaan Perempuan dan Perlindungan Anak 2012)

However, Komnas Perempuan worries that the situation is "stagnating" (Komnas Perempuan 2012). The rate of official reporting of incidents of domestic violence remains low; rates of prosecution of crimes of VAW in the courts are even lower; the availability of safe accommodation for women living with violence is severely limited; and the number of integrated rape crisis centers in operation is "completely inadequate" for the size of Indonesia's population (Bennett and Andajani-Sutjahjo 2007, Bennett et al. 2011, 147). Despite strenuous efforts on the part of some government agencies, NGOs and activists, the legal process for women who report violent partners can often be called "revictimization" (Komnas Perempuan 2012, 29).

In different places, there are different facilities. In Makassar, the PPT is the result of various initiatives developed by the Ministries for Women's Empowerment, Health Services, Social Welfare and the National Police (POLRI). It is a special unit with workers employed at a local hospital. It aims to provide integrated services for women and children as survivors of violence. These services comprise medical examinations undertaken by medical staff, psychological counseling, legal assistance and police investigations. It is coordinated by the police medical services and is run by trained female staff and professionals. The PPT has specific roles and responsibilities such as providing medical or psychological treatment to women and children who have experienced violence; keeping medical records for police investigation purposes; investigating the incident if it relates to criminal charges; and offering psychological and legal support for the victim, including access to a shelter if necessary. To achieve these aims, the PPT works closely with and has established networks with other agencies such as police psychologists, RPK (Ruang Pelayanan Khusus—Special Service Shelter) for legal and advocacy purposes, social security for shelters, the health bureau for medical referrals, and the Ministry for Women's Empowerment and its affiliated offices at the regional level and with NGOs. Thus, the PPT aims to offer a comprehensive and efficient hospital-based service for women and children experiencing violence, coordinated by police medical staff.

The respected agency Komnas Perempuan (2008) has examined Indonesia's legal code for compliance and consistency with the 2004 Law and identified several issues. One is the inadequacy of the definition of rape and the legal framework for dealing with rape; another is the absence of legislation regarding sexual harassment; and there is a range of issues surrounding poor implementation of Law 23, lack of understanding about the concept of domestic violence, and problems of jurisdiction. One major problem is that the religious (Islamic) courts deal with 30–40 per cent of domestic violence cases, because domestic violence is made public through cases of divorce among Muslim couples, and the religious courts seem to be unaware of the 2004 Law and fail to direct their clients to the relevant authorities (Komnas Perempuan 2008).

Recently some NGOs have begun working with violent men, in order to bring about behavioral changes. Since 2007, the women's NGO Rifka Annisa has established a counseling service especially for abusive men. Male activists are increasingly being used as a resource. Violent men rarely see their behavior as a problem, and tend to "deny, minimize and excuse their violence, frequently blaming the victims" (Hidayat 2012). A national network, the Alliance of New Men (LLB), has been established, aiming to change the discourse about masculinity toward non-violence.

Escaping Domestic Violence

Leaving a husband is a very big step to take in Indonesia. There are enormous practical difficulties for women who have violent partners. There may be nowhere to escape to: women in rural areas cannot access the few refuges and crisis centers, and the number of such shelters is inadequate even for urban populations. If their natal family is not supportive (and this is often the case, for reasons of family honor as well as women's shame), there is usually a lack of physical refuge and emotional support, as well as economic support. Sometimes women have to leave their children behind, and this tie tends to drag them back to violent husbands. Financial support is often an issue, especially when the woman is not earning an income; many women have no experience of supporting themselves.

Most "women have ... no concepts of rights against such violence" (Blackburn 2004, 195). Women who suffer abuse often want to conceal it in order to present an image of family harmony. The family and the community often lack respect and sympathy for the victims and blame the victim for having provoked the violence. Women who experience domestic violence often feel there is no way to end the violence. If a woman escapes briefly and then is forced to return to her husband, she may well experience further violence.

DOMESTIC VIOLENCE: INDONESIA

Thus, feelings of hopelessness, vulnerability and isolation are reinforced. The characterization of divorced women as "bad" and "shameful" means that it is difficult for abused wives to leave their violent husbands, thus contributing to the perpetuation of domestic violence.

However, even if they understand that they have the right to leave, and to be safe, the option of divorce or separation is not an attractive one. The divorced or separated woman is strongly stigmatized in Indonesian society. As Wieringa notes, "Non-married women such as widows or divorced women ... are seen as deviant or abjected and face various kinds of harassment" (2009, 21–22). Divorce is restricted by the state, not only through the Marriage Law but also through discourses of shame (O'Shaughnessy 2009, chapter 3). The secular courts are embedded in a gender order which defines female-initiated divorce as shameful and sees divorce as an attack on men's superior social status. Women who want to escape marriage are constructed as transgressive: if they initiate divorce, they are exhibiting impropriety. Women bear the brunt of public humiliation and shame for failed marriages as well as for their husband's affairs. Where marriage is a matter of family honor, as in Bugis (Makassarese) society, a failed marriage is a public disgrace, especially for the woman.

Finally, as Blackburn notes (2004 195), women have no faith in the legal system and cannot see that anything is to be gained by "going public." They perceive the police as corrupt and untrustworthy and this view is often quite justified: the police have a reputation for failing to treat women with respect and sensitivity, and often compound women's problems through revictimization. There are few successful stories or model cases. It is hardly surprising that most women just accept the abuse.

Bibliography

Aisyah, Siti and Lyn Parker. Problematic conjugations. Women's agency, marriage and domestic violence in Indonesia, in *Asian Studies Review* (forthcoming).

Bauer, Karen. "Traditional" exegeses of Q 4:34, in *Comparative Islamic Studies* 2:2 (2006), 129–42.

Bennett, Linda, Sari Andajani-Suthahjo and Nurul I. Idrus. Domestic violence in Nusa Tenggara Barat, Indonesia. Married women's definitions and experiences of violence in the home, in *Asia Pacific Journal of Anthropology* 12:2 (2011), 146–63.

Blackburn, Susan. Gender violence and the Indonesian political transition, in *Asian Studies Review* 23:4 (1999), 433–48.

Blackburn, Susan. *Women and the state in modern Indonesia*, Cambridge 2004.

BPS (Badan Pusat Statistik). 2011 sensus penduduk 2010 [Population census 2010], http://sp2010.bps.go.id/, accessed 11 April 2013.

Dunn, Shannon and Rosemary B. Kellison. At the intersection of scripture and law. Qur'an 4:34 and violence against women, in *Journal of Feminist Studies in Religion* 26:2 (2010), 11–36.

Hakimi, M., Nur Hayati, E., Marlinawati, V. U., Winkvist, A., & Ellsberg, M. C. (2001). Membisu demi Harmoni: Kekerasan terhadap Istri dan Kesehatan Perempuan di Jawa Tengah, Indonesia [Silent for the Sake of Harmony: Violence towards Wives and Female Health in Central Java, Indonesia]. Yogyakarta: LpkGm-FK-UGM (Indonesia), Rifka Annisa Women's Crisis Centre (Indonesia), Umea University (Sweden), Women's Health Exchange (USA).

Hasyim, S. *Understanding women in Islam. An Indonesian perspective*, Jakarta 2006.

Hidayat, Rachman. We are the blessed ones, in *Inside Indonesia* 107 (January–March 2012), <http://www.insideindonesia.org/current-edition/we-are-the-blessed-ones>, accessed 15 October 2012.

Idrus, Nurul Ilmi. *Marital rape (Kekerasan seksual dalam perkawinan)*, Ford Foundation with Pusat Penelitian Kependudukan, Universitas Gadjah Mada, Seri Laporan No. 88, Yogyakarta 1999.

Idrus, Nurul Ilmi. Behind the notion of *siala*. Marriage, *adat* and Islam among the Bugis in South Sulawesi, in *Intersections: Gender, History and Culture in the Asian Context* 10 (2004), available at <http://intersections.anu.edu.au/issue10/idrus.html>, accessed 2 May 2011.

Idrus, Nurul Ilmi and L. R. Bennett. Presumed consent. Marital violence in Bugis society, in *Violence against women in Asian societies*, ed. L. Manderson and L. R. Bennett, London 2003, 41–60.

Kementerian Pemberdayaan Perempuan dan Perlindungan Anak [Ministry for women's empowerment and the protection of children]. Pemerintah pantang berpangkutangan untuk mewujudkan pengarusutamaan gender [Government abstaining from applause on realizing gender mainstreaming], Press Release, 14 June 2012, <http://menegpp.go.id/V2/index.php/component/content/article/52-info/391 -press-release-mewujudkan-pengarusutamaan-gender-di-palangkaraya>, accessed 25 October 2012.

Komnas Perempuan. Annual Note, 2005, <http://www.komnasperempuan.or.id/en/ 2011/09/annual-note-2005/>, accessed 15 Ocober 2012.

Komnas Perempuan. Stagnansi sistem hukum. Menggantung asa perempuan korban. Catatan tahunan tentang kekerasan terhadap perempuan 2011 [Stagnation of the legal system. Suspending hope for women as victims. Annual note on violence toward women 2011], Jakarta (photocopy).

LBH-APIK (Lembaga bantuan hukum—Asosiasi perempuan Indonesia untuk keadilan [Institute for legal aid—association of Indonesian women for justice]. Usulan amandemen UU perkawinan No. 1 tahun 1974 [Suggestion for Amendment to Marriage Law No. 1/1974], <http://www.lbh-apik.or.id/amandemen_UUP-usulan .htm>, accessed 15 October 2012.

Mahmaoud, Mohamed. To beat or not to beat. On the exegetical dilemmas over Qur'an, 4:34, in *Journal of the American Oriental Society* 126:4 (October–December 2006), 537–51.

MOH Ministry of Health, Provincial Government of West Nusa Tenggara, Provincial Government of East Nusa Tenggara and GTZ. Measuring the fulfillment of human rights in maternal and neonatal health using WHO tools in 2 cities and 2 districts in West and East Nusa Tenggara, Indonesia. Report on provincial and district laws, regulations, policies and standards of care, GTZ, Jakarta 2008, <http://www.unfpa .org/sowmy/resources/docs/library/R415_MOHINDONESIA_2008_Human_Rights_ and_MNH_in_Indonesia-Survey.pdf>, 25 October 2012.

Munir, Lily Zakiyah. Domestic violence in Indonesia, in *Muslim World Journal of Human Rights* 2:1 (2005), 1–37.

Nilan, Pam. The winds of change in *Inside Indonesia* 107 (January–March 2012), <http://www.insideindonesia.org/current-edition/the-winds-of-change>, accessed 8 October 2012.

Nurmila, Nina. *Women, Islam and everyday life. Renegotiating polygamy in Indonesia,* London and New York 2009.

Parker, Lyn. *From subjects to citizens. Balinese villagers in the Indonesian nation-state,* Copenhagen 2003.

Rifka Annisa [Women's friend]. Website, <http://www.rifka-annisa.or.id/>, accessed 15 October 2012.

Robinson, Kathryn. *Gender, Islam and democracy in Indonesia,* London and New York 2009.

ROI (Republic of Indonesia). Marriage Law No.1/1974, <http://id.wikisource.org/wiki/ Undang-Undang_Republik_Indonesia_Nomor_1_Tahun_1974>, accessed 1 August 2011.

ROI (Republic of Indonesia). Law on the Abolition of Domestic Violence No. 23/2004, <http://www.djpp.depkumham.go.id/inc/buka.php?czoyNDoiZDoyMDAwKzQmZ judTIzLTIwMDQuaHRtIjs=>, 1 August 2011.

Rowe, William S., F. Sutan Nurasiah and Iryna M. Dulkha. A study of domestic violence against academic working wives in Medan, in *International Social Work* 49:1 (2006), 41–50.

Sciortino, Rosalia and Ines Smyth. The myth of harmony. Domestic violence in Java, in *Violence and vengeance. Discontent and conflict in New Order Indonesia,* ed. Frans Hüsken and Huub de Jonge, Nijmegan Studies in Development and Cultural Change, Saarbrücken 2002, 95–115.

Suhandjati, Sri. *Kekerasan dalam rumah tangga terhadap perempuan (studi kasus gugatan cerai di pengadilan agama Semarang)* [Violence toward women in the household (a case study of divorce suits in the Semarang religious court)], Proyek PTA/ IAIN Walisongo, Semarang 2002.

Suryakusuma, Julia. The state and sexuality in New Order Indonesia, in *Fantasizing the feminine in Indonesia,* ed. Laurie J. Sears, Durham, N.C. and London 1996, 92–119.

Domestic Violence: Malaysia

Maznah Mohamad

Introduction

This article explores the roots of the Malaysian Domestic Violence Act 1994 (DVA). It traces the many ways in which the courts conceived of and defined marital violence. Legal judgments in the Sharia and civil systems reveal that Muslim and non-Muslim women were treated differently when they sought justice against their abusers in court. This inconsistent and inappropriate implementation of justice formed the basis for much gender angst and unity. By the mid-1990s, domestic violence began, slowly, to be recognized and named as a grave offense; the right to guard the body against harm was recognized. This period saw an intense contestation involving the government, media, police, and civil society interests. In this spirited discursive terrain, and largely through the organizational weight of autonomous women's groups, the DVA was shaped, contested, and claimed, in a pattern similar to that observed in the East and the West (Htun and Weldon 2012, Spehar 2012). It was an unmistakable moment for gender consolidation. Although epic in nature, the outcome of the struggles led by feminist organizations resulted in a law that reflected numerous compromises and accommodations. Although it was an historic law, the relevance of its provisions and the effectiveness of its implementation are continually being assessed and critiqued. There continue to be difficulties in resolving family matters, ranging from the seemingly simple procedure of obtaining a protection order to intimidating court procedures unsuitable for family deliberations, as well as the dilemmas around intervention and the autonomy of victims to decide if and how violence visited upon them should be criminalized.

The article discusses how the impact of a domestic violence law can be assessed in two ways. On the one hand, it has been a potent force in raising rights consciousness and in providing legal clout to the erstwhile unnamed subjectivities of intimate agony. On the other hand, it is also a manifestation of the limited capacity of law and the state in effecting social transformation within the lives of families. However, like most statutes introduced in the modern nation-state, the Malaysian DVA took on a life of its own: its most meaningful impact in Malaysia has been to sustain a secular women's movement in competition with forces tending toward ethnic and religious separatism and exclusiveness.

© KONINKLIJKE BRILL NV, LEIDEN, 2018 | DOI:10.1163/1872-5309_EWIC_COM_002160

Domestic Violence in Its "Pre-Criminalization" Period

Before the DVA was passed, domestic violence was not classified as a criminal offense and was interpreted differently by various courts in Malaysia. The civil, or secular, court had access to the penal code, under which battery and assault were considered criminal offenses, causing hurt and liable to be punished under the law. Nevertheless, wife-battery was not a chargeable offense under this law. Women could only use battery as grounds to apply for restraining orders against their husbands, and only in the case of a pending divorce application could the penal code be applied to restrain abusers. Judges were also able to cite judgments from British courts as precedents, as long as the applicable English common law came into existence before 1956. Such legal moves favored women's application for protection, as in the cases of *Jayakumari a/p Arul Pragasam v. Suriya Narayanan a/l v. Ramanathan* (1996) and *Chan Ah Moi v. Phang Wai Ann* (1995).

In the *Jayakumari* case, for example, the applicant, Jayakumari, got a court order to evict her violent husband from their matrimonial home. This was in 1996, before the DVA came into effect. Jayakumari first left her matrimonial home after being assaulted by her husband. However, in March 1996, she filed a petition for judicial separation and sought an order to restrain her husband from further assaulting her and to force him to vacate the matrimonial home. Although the DVA was not yet in force, the judge applied a precedent used in an English court. He cited a 1953 case, in which the English judge noted that it is the right of the wife to stay in the matrimonial home while keeping the husband away from it, as "otherwise the wife will be bullied out of her remedy or deterred by pressure from seeking the help of the court."

In the *Chan Ah Moi* case, Chan applied for a non-molestation order pending the release of her convicted husband from jail. He had earlier been convicted of causing her serious injuries and had been imprisoned for two years. The order was to exclude him (after his release from prison) from any part of the matrimonial home and its vicinity. English cases were cited to grant Chan the exclusion order to prohibit her husband from entering her home. The judge held that "there is no provision in the Act for an exclusion order. However, where there is a lacuna in Malaysian law, English common law principles can be invoked as provided under Section 3 of the Civil Law Act 1956."

That was how judgments were handed down to women who sought justice from their intimate but violent partners. Domestic violence was wholly attached to a matrimonial condition, and it was only if women decided to end the marriage that spousal abuse could be used as a justification. The above cases dealt with women plaintiffs who were ready and able to do so. If they chose to stay in a violent marriage, no amount of complaints over wife-battery could lead to conviction, since the law did not recognize it as an offense.

However, there were some highly inconsistent court rulings in cases of violence against Muslim women. In all cases, a complaint of violence could only be made to the Sharia court upon application for divorce under either *taklik* or *faskh*. *Taklik* divorce is automatically and judicially granted to a woman (without spousal consent) if the court is satisfied that a husband has breached stipulations inserted in the marital contract, wife-beating being one of them. If wife-beating is not so stipulated, a wife can apply for a *faskh* divorce. One of the conditions for a *faskh* divorce is cruelty and wife-beating.

Nevertheless, in earlier legislation, in order to be valid as grounds for divorce, wife-abuse had to be interpreted as a form of cruelty traversing the bounds of "Islamic law and adat." In *Hasnah v. Saad* (1983), Hasnah complained of being beaten on the face, right ear, chest, and back. A doctor's report was also submitted as evidence as grounds for divorce by *taklik*, as her marriage certificate had listed a condition, or vow from the husband, to qualify for her automatic divorce:

I cannot assault, beat or torture or hurt my wife Hasnah bt. Hashim by any means that exceeds the bounds of Islamic law and adat. Whenever I commit any of these, and that she files a complaint with the qadi and upon verification of her allegations, the qadi shall witness the divorce of one *talaq* on my wife Hasnah bt. Hashim.

Hasnah's divorce application was granted based on the qadi's (the judge of an Islamic court) assessment that the assault had "exceeded the bounds of Islamic law and *adat*" (*melebehi hukum syarak dan adat*). Clearly, this stipulation seemed to indicate that some form of "violence" may even be interpreted as acceptable and within the bounds of Islam.

If the judge was not convinced that the violence was "habitual," the application would be rejected, as in the case of an application for *faskh* divorce in *Hairun v. Omar* (1993). The evidence of assault was supported by reports from two doctors. The qadi accepted the veracity of Hairun's allegations, but did not grant the divorce as he was not satisfied that the offense committed could be classified as being "habitually hurting" (*lazim menyakiti*). In the legislation, a *faskh* divorce shall be affected under the following conditions: "when a husband abuses his wife, among others through i) habitually hurting or causing her life to suffer due to his abusive behavior" (Section 52(1)(h)(i) of the Selangor, Islamic Family Law Enactment, 1984).

Since the beating was inflicted twice (as admitted by the husband), the qadi interpreted that this did not indicate habitual assault.

Islamic stipulations, such as the rejection of female witnesses and the acceptance of sworn oaths as claims to truth in courts, were also applied to deny women their right to be free from their violent husbands. In the case of *Adibah v. Abdul Rani* (1986), Adibah was denied *faskh* despite providing a witness to the assault and submitting a medical report as evidence of her injury. The qadi ruled that the testimony of Adibah's witness, her female domestic helper, was not considered credible. According to the qadi, under Islamic law (*hukum Syarak*), only the testimonies of two male witnesses, or of one male witness together with two female witnesses, can be accepted in court. To add insult to injury (literally), the qadi then asked if Abdul Rani would swear upon the Quran (*sumpah Syarie*) to deny his wrongdoing. He did, and read out the following oath: "I hereby named swear that I did not assault or beat or torture or hurt my wife ... as alleged by her in this case." Based on this declaration, Adibah's application to leave her abusive husband was rejected.

It was only in the mid-1980s, when Islamic family law statutes (such as the Administration of Islamic Family Law Enactment 1985 of Selangor) were passed in almost all states, that Muslim women were able to securely use domestic violence as grounds for divorce. Under Islamic family law statutes, the definition of wife abuse was expanded to include nonphysical hurt, and the notion of "habitual assault" was no longer applied to verify or deny women's claims of spousal violence against them.

In *Hairun v. Omar* (1993), Hairun's divorce application was rejected (before she appealed) by the qadi court on the grounds that she was not "habitually assaulted" by her husband. She appealed against this decision to the Selangor Sharia Appeals Committee (Jawatankuasa Ulang Bicara Syar'iah), and her appeal to obtain divorce under *faskh* was granted. The committee ruled that the term "habitually assaults," as contained in the legislation, had been wrongly interpreted by the qadi, and that the beatings suffered by Hairun fulfilled the *faskh* clause. This judgment expanded the definition of cruelty to wives to include nonphysical hurt, such as "refusal to speak with one's wife, ignoring her or turning away one's face away from hers in bed, preferring to be hospitable to other women other than the wife, any form of beating which brings hurt and it does not mean that the beating has to be done repeatedly or habitually."

By 1995, the judicial system appeared more accepting of wife abuse as grounds for divorce. At the Sharia High Court of Terengganu, a woman's application for divorce in *Hasnah v. Zaaba* (1995) was granted without reference to the habitual nature of the abuse or if the beating was within Islamic limits. The judge even acknowledged that the husband "had not only beaten and disparaged his wife, but also forced violent sexual intercourse on her." The judgment seemed to draw on the precedent set in the *Hairun* case. The definition of cruelty to wives as extending beyond physical assault was restated in this case.

Protection against Violence Only Applied to Non-Muslims

To protect themselves against violence by their spouses while a divorce was pending, women could apply for a restraining order through the civil courts. For the most part, only non-Muslim women could make use of this right, as in the *Jayakumari* and *Chan* cases. Muslim women, on the other hand, were unable to do so, as in *Faridah bte Dato Talib v. Mohamed Habibullah bin Mahmood* (1990). Faridah had sought divorce by *faskh* at the Sharia court on the grounds of assault and battery by her husband, Mohamed Habibullah. However, she had to apply to the civil court for an injunction to restrain her husband from further abusing her. The High Court judge considered assault and battery as a civil and criminal wrong and ruled that although it involved a Muslim marriage, such an offense did not fall within the jurisdiction of the Sharia enactment and court. As the acts of battery and assault had caused hurt, they were considered criminal offenses under the penal code.

However, on 28 April 1989, Faridah's husband challenged the High Court order by appealing to the Supreme Court. The question posed in *Mohamed Habibullah bin Mahmood v. Faridah bte Dato Talib* (1992) was whether the High Court had the jurisdiction to hear the case—it involved a Muslim marriage, so should have been heard in a Sharia court, it was argued. The judges referred to an amendment to the Constitution, Article 121 (1A), which came into effect on 10 June 1988. Under this new provision, in cases involving Muslim personal law, the jurisdiction of the civil court was separated from that of the Sharia court. In trying to decide if the case fell within the jurisdiction of the civil or Sharia courts, the judges referred to the Islamic Family Law (Federal Territory) Act 1984, which gave the Sharia court power to "order any person to refrain from forcing his or her society on his or her spouse or former spouse and from other acts of molestation." Faridah's allegation of assault and battery was thus interpreted to fall within the jurisdiction of the Sharia court, and the interim injunction granted to Faridah by the High Court was overturned. According to the judges, the complaint was related to the husband's conduct during the course of a Muslim marriage; it was thus considered neither a civil nor a criminal matter, as suggested by the High Court judge. To the Supreme Court judges, the alleged assault and battery merely constituted a matrimonial offense or misconduct to be dealt with by the Sharia court. Faridah was also not entitled to sue her husband for damages, since the Married Women Ordinance 1957

DOMESTIC VIOLENCE: MALAYSIA

considered a husband and wife one entity, so taking up a suit would be like suing oneself. The Married Women Ordinance 1957 was subsequently amended, allowing a husband and wife to "sue each other in tort or damages in respect of injuries to his or her person, as the case may be in the like manner as any other two separate individuals" (Section 4A in the Married Women Act 1957).

Faridah's husband had the law on his side based on the following legal concepts of being married and Muslim: (1) Muslim couples come under the jurisdiction of the Sharia, as there are clauses under Islamic statutes to protect women from assault by husbands; (2) civil courts cannot adjudicate on matters under the Sharia court because of the amendment to Article 121 (a) of the Constitution; and (3) spouses cannot sue each other under tort (for claims arising from injury to person or reputation) under Section 9(2) of the Married Women Ordinance 1957.

As a whole though, both the Sharia and civil legal systems treated violence against married women as mere matrimonial misconduct rather than as an offense punishable by law. The Married Women Ordinance 1957 considered a man and a woman in marriage to be one person and, therefore, not entitled to damage claims against one another when an injury is inflicted upon their persons (or body). This law allowed the couple to sue one another if there was damage to their property, but not to their bodies or reputation.

Yet another law that worked against Muslim women at that time was the separation of civil and Sharia jurisdictions on matrimonial matters. This proved to be a great obstacle in Faridah's attempts to obtain justice, compelling her to renounce her status as a Muslim during the course of her legal action. It was stated in the court statement that Faridah believed that "Islam could not provide enough protection for battered wife [sic]," and thus took steps to revoke her faith by means of a statutory declaration before a commissioner of oath. It was ascertained later that she retracted this renunciation. (A document was provided to the court in the form of a letter from the qadi of Petaling Jaya, Selangor, notifying that on 16 May 1989, Faridah had retracted her renunciation of Islam and renewed her faith in the religion, at his office.) Nevertheless, it suggested that at that time, the Sharia court was less reliable in guaranteeing women safety from their abusive spouses.

The Beginnings of the Campaign against Domestic Violence

Rising awareness about the battery of women in their own homes, the unequal treatment that abused women experienced under different jurisdictions, and the accumulated experiences of women's shelters in dealing with domestic abuse cases were some of the many reasons for public support for a domestic violence law in Malaysia. One of the first few conceptual issues that arose was whether this law, covering family matters, should be drafted as a criminal or a civil law, and whether it should cover Muslims as well. In Malaysia, it was the legal aspect of family that was being debated rather than its cultural significance. This was because Malaysia did not have an explicit "family code" or any written constitutional provision extolling family as the moral fibre of the nation (as in the Indian, Philippine, and Indonesian cases); instead, the family's supposed sanctity was guarded by civil or Islamic law. In the 1970s, a Royal Commission was set up to study and propose reforms to marriage and divorce laws affecting non-Muslims. This resulted in the Law Reform (Marriage and Divorce) Act 1976, which, among other stipulations, abolished polygamy and set eighteen as the minimum age of marriage for non-Muslims. Although the commission's brief did not cover Muslims, Islamic marriages were also scrutinized around the same concerns. This resulted in the first Islamic Family Law Acts, with three state enactments passed in Kelantan, Malacca, and Negri Sembilan in 1983, and one covering the Federal Territory in 1984 (Siraj 1994, 563–65). Hence, the delineation of jurisdictional turfs between the "Islamic family" and the "Other family" was established. Much of the campaign to push for the DVA was thus taken up by advocacy, debates, and resistance around the question of who had jurisdictional authority over the family, regardless of their religion. There followed a long, combative, and arduous process of organizing and negotiating as to what should constitute the appropriate law against domestic violence in Malaysia.

The Passage of the Domestic Violence Act in 1994

By 1994, the Domestic Violence Bill was finally tabled in the national parliament, dubbed the "Cinderella Act" because of its "turbulent midnight passage" through the House of Representatives (Padman 1995a). On the very last day of the parliamentary session, amidst opposition from other legislators, Minister Napsiah Omar was determined to push the bill through before the stroke of midnight since failure to do so would mean presenting it at another sitting, to be held two months later. Such a wait, although not long, could spell uncertainty for the future of the bill.

Although the DVA was finally approved by parliament, the struggle to have it gazetted and implemented continued for several more years. It was only in 1996 that the "Cinderella Act" of 1994 could be enforced. English dailies such as the *New Straits Times* steadfastly supported women's interests in getting the DVA enforced. Women journalists at these publications carefully strategized the publication of public debates to suit the agenda of the law's final adoption. In 1995, the paper started running a fortnightly column under its Woman's Desk section called "Women Behind Closed Doors." The column carried news and features on domestic violence as a means of exerting pressure to have the act enforced (Padman 1995b).

By mid-1996, the DVA was still not in force. Islamic religious authorities, who were represented at meetings to draft the act, were purported to be changing their minds. A new minister for women's affairs, who took over from the previous minister (who had been involved in the passage of the law), hesitant about implementing the DVA, was quoted as saying that the Islamic faction was "not in favour of the Act applying to Muslim women," as all matters pertaining to Muslims "should come under the jurisdiction of the syariah court, the power of which they fear could be undermined if the Act applies to all" (Muharyani 1996). This news was met with furious reactions from women's groups. The JAG-VAW (Joint Action Group against Violence Against Women) swiftly shot off a memorandum to the minister reiterating that domestic violence is a criminal offense, hence it is the civil and not the Sharia court that should preside over the cases (New Straits Times 1996a).

Religion seemed to have come between the bill and its passage. There was a lot of resistance, not just from the Muslim/Sharia faction (or the Sharia Islamists), which considered anything pertaining to Muslim marriage within their jurisdiction, but also from those reluctant to accept domestic violence as a criminal offense.

Uncertainty remained over whether the original DVA was meant to be civil or criminal—some sections believed that family offenses did not deserve criminal treatment. More immediately, the committee had to find a way to avoid the conflict of jurisdiction between Muslims and non-Muslims. Ostensibly the way out, to include all Muslims and non-Muslims under a common law, was to have the DVA drafted as a criminal law (Afida Mastura 2000, 79, Ng, Maznah, and Tan 2006, 52–57). However, the bill also needed to accommodate the views of Islamic scholars who had expressed dissatisfaction with marital rape being included in the definition of domestic violence, claiming that this was unacceptable under Islamic law (Mohd Shahrizad 1994). Whether the DVA were to be civil or criminal, it seemed unlikely that it would please all factions all the time.

The debates persisted for a month after the minister's agreement. Rahmah Hashim, head of the Women's Affairs Bureau of the Muslim Youth Movement of Malaysia (or ABIM – *Angkatan Belia Islam Malaysia*), wrote to the press insisting on the primacy of the Islamic position on this issue, condoning some form of violence, and "stealthily" using the disciplining of children as an example:

Islam has its own perspective on the roles of parents and children ... a parent is allowed to a limited extent to physically discipline a child who is 10 years old and above who refuses to carry out the obligation of the five daily prayers.... The extent to which this duty can be carried out by the parent and his defences will be relevant only in a Syariah Court.... Islam does not take an apologetic stance in the face of the move in some Western countries to totally abolish physical disciplining by parents towards their children even to educate them (Rahmah 1996).

Zainah Anwar, one of the founders of Sisters in Islam, retorted by asking if the "murder and rape of family members" was also considered to "fall within the jurisdiction of the Islamic Family Law of each State" and that the "DVA and Muslim women should not be turned into victims, yet again, in the battle over turf" (Zainah 1996).

By mid-1996, the government's waffling and Muslim scholars' diatribes over jurisdiction finally came to an end. However, amidst the seemingly positive atmosphere surrounding the acceptance of the DVA, a new controversy erupted in 1997. The police, perhaps playing its role as the de facto vanguard of the patriarchal state, seemed to resist the law's implementation. Oddly enough, Minister Zaleha Ismail, who had been hesitant about the DVA's enforcement, found herself at the receiving end of police and male "power." It started with women politicians from the ruling party, the National Front (the Barisan Nasional), expressing concerns about the police not taking women's complaints of abuse seriously (New Straits Times 1997a). The stance of the women leaders displeased the inspector general of police, Rahim Nor, who set up a police team to interview the said women, all of whom were high-ranking officials within their political parties—Ng Yen Yen, secretary-general of Wanita MCA (Malaysian Chinese Association); Sarasa Pasamanickam, head of Wanita MIC (Malaysian Indian Congress); and Zaleha Ismail, the minister (New Straits Times 1997b). The chief of police insisted that his men had acted professionally in dealing with these cases, claiming that the women politicians had not provided evidence to prove their allegations (Raja 1997). The minister responded by identifying three police stations—in Klang, Petaling Jaya, and Gombak— as being responsible for the actions that spawned the allegations (Singh and Nelson 1997). A supporting news report by Shareem Amry verified these allegations, noting that "those who have been witnesses in the frontlines of spousal abuse argue that Zaleha has a strong case" (Amry 1997).

Ultimately, the exchange of accusations took a disconcerting turn. Amry was called in for questioning. A police report had reportedly been lodged against her for "malicious publication of false news," making her liable to be charged under Section 8(A) of the Printing Presses and Publications Act.

After she was interviewed on 3 July 1997, others who were cited in her article, were also called in for questioning by the police. In reaction to this show of police high-handedness, 21 organizations issued a statement expressing their concern over police treatment of this matter (New Straits Times 1997b). The "women versus police" conflict had become so heated that Lim Kit Siang, the opposition leader, brought the issue up for debate in parliament. The motion was turned down by the speaker, but this only sparked even greater public interest in the issue (New Straits Times 1997c).

The dispute was finally settled when then acting prime minister, Anwar Ibrahim, intervened, noting that the police should have conducted their investigations into reports of domestic violence "in a manner acceptable to all" (Ashraf and Ainon 1997). Police officers were subsequently asked to attend courses on public relations, so that they could be "more courteous" and "hopefully, help improve the public image of the police" (Deutsche Presse-Agentur 1997). All these measures appeared to have worked, according to a subsequent report about the police becoming more cooperative in accepting reports lodged by women (Muharyani 1997).

With the termination of the conflict between the police and the women activists, the system seemed to be on the women's side. However, the DVA was still not a satisfactory piece of legislation. It was a version that accommodated the interests of many parties. It was not the law envisaged by its initiators, who had wanted to introduce a bill that explicitly recognized domestic violence as an offense.

This unease was justified. For example, soon after the DVA was enforced in June 1996, a case came up before the High Court in Kuala Lumpur. In September of that year, the court quashed an interim order sought by a Muslim woman to restrain her husband from assaulting her. The judge found no mention of any pending investigation in the notes of the proceedings in the magistrate's court, where she was granted the protection order (New Straits Times 1996d). In another case, the judge confirmed that any investigation into domestic violence must involve criminal proceedings. In *Ngieng Shiat Yen v. Ten Jit Hing* (2001), Ngieng failed to obtain a protection order against her husband, Ten, despite her harrowing experience.

A protection order and the arrest of a perpetrator are guaranteed only when grave and obvious physical hurt has been inflicted. Yet, a bigger conundrum facing advocates of the law is that many survivors of domestic violence do not persist in convicting their offenders (Hare 2010, Noraida 2011a). In Malaysia, from June to December 1997, only 27 out of 1,611 cases were prosecuted; 113 reports were withdrawn (New Straits Times 1997d). Those who lodge reports with the police differ from those who actively use the services of women's organizations and shelters. Those seeking help from the latter do so with the serious intention of taking practical action. Women's shelters report that of the 64 battered women they dealt with in one year, 24 (or less than half), decided to return to the abusive situation (Chin 2007). That the number of cases handled by women's centers was lower than the reports lodged with the police has been said to indicate that many more women prefer to use the police channel to serve as a warning to husbands rather than take action against their abusers (Siti Hawa 2010).

The availability of protection orders under the DVA is perhaps the most significant, and also the most elusive, of the benefits arising from the Act. Women's groups and service counsellors complain about how difficult it is to get a protection order for women, often due to the ignorance of police personnel about protection orders or their perception of the offense itself. Investigations are hence abandoned once the abused person retracts the report, something that would not happen with other crimes. Ivy Josiah, the executive director of WAO (Women's Aid Organisation), has expressed her indignation that domestic violence is not equated to other crimes: "If I make a police report that 'A has stolen my car,' and later A comes forward and says how sorry he is, well, the police will still have to prosecute, right? But it's not the case when it comes to wives retracting their reports!" (Chin 2007).

The DVA's inadequacy as a tool for dealing with the prosecution process is aggravated by the method of justice itself. The mode of enquiry, examination, interrogation, cross-examination, and inquisition in the courtrooms would be enough to separate the extremely determined plaintiff from the fainthearted and under-resourced victim. In Malaysia, the adversarial system is used in courts, through a method of examination and cross-examination for the extraction of evidence. Much significance is given to individual autonomy and dignity in the presentation of arguments and evidence. Judges are also expected to remain impartial. Such a system actually works against victims of domestic violence, who expose themselves to greater danger and stigmatization if forced to testify against their partners and family members. This is in contrast to the inquisitorial system, where systems and procedures are said to be less rigidly applied and more conducive to resolving family-related cases (Tan 2009, 406–7).

Reviewing the DVA, Post 2000s

Issues such as those discussed above resulted in a call to review the DVA as early as 1999. The drive was initiated by the WCC (Women's Crisis Cetre) of

DOMESTIC VIOLENCE: MALAYSIA

Penang, which submitted a 20-point memorandum to the government. Loh Cheng Kooi, the executive director of the WCC, highlighted that some of the recommendations advocated for a broader definition of domestic violence, to encompass mental, psychological, and emotional harm (New Straits Times 1999).

The call seemed to have been heeded by then-prime minister Abdullah Badawi (2003–2009), who accepted the recommendation for review, remarking that he was proud that Malaysia was the first Asian and Islamic country to introduce domestic violence legislation. The seriousness of the problem was backed up by police statistics that showed an increase in reported domestic violence cases, from 1,409 cases in 1995 to 5,799 cases in 1997 (Senyyah 2000). Azalina Aziz, who had just been made head of Puteri UMNO (United Malays National Organisation), the newest UMNO wing for young women, touted the DVA as a government achievement. In her first keynote address as Puteri UMNO chief, at the movement's maiden assembly, she cited the DVA as an example of government-formulated laws that were not discriminatory to women and rebuked the opposition PAS (Islamic Party of Malaysia) for their inability to do the same (New Straits Times 2003). The DVA was indeed useful as a political platform for upcoming politicians to gain legitimacy in an important constituency, women. Abdullah Badawi had just taken over as prime minister after Mahathir Mohamad suddenly stepped down in 2002 and was seeking a mandate on his leadership through the 2004 general election. So too was Azalina, as she prepared for her first contest in a general election.

In 2005, in response to the high-level endorsement of the DVA reform, the Parliamentary Select Committee on the Penal Code and Criminal Procedure Code proposed that the DVA get its separate section in the penal code to enable the criminalizing of not just physical assault, but also sexual, emotional, mental, and financial abuse. The committee considered amending both the DVA and the penal code to take into account various forms of domestic violence (New Straits Times 2005).

Another six years passed before the amendments to the 1994 DVA were effected. In June 2011, a bill cited as the Domestic Violence (Amendment) Act 2011 was tabled for debate in parliament by the deputy minister for women, family, and community, Heng Seai Kie. The amendments were not in accordance with the proposal of the Parliamentary Select Committee in 1995, but included some of the following new provisions (Ganesh and Mazlinda 2011):

- Recognizing psychological abuse, including emotional injury, as a form of abuse.
- Recognizing the illegal use of intoxicating substances to cause victims, including children, to suffer delusions as a form of domestic violence.

- Extending protection orders to include a safe place and shelter in the list that the perpetrator is prohibited or restricted from entering.
- Prohibiting or restricting the perpetrator from communicating with the protected person, not just using "written or telephone communication" but other means of communication technology.

The amendments to the DVA were passed, without much objection, debate, or fanfare, in October 2011. In spite of having come a long way, the DVA reforms have yet to succeed in criminalizing domestic violence. The amended law still prioritizes protecting victims over punishing offenders. The definition of domestic violence, although stretched to include nonphysical forms of abuse, has been useful only to protect victims subjected to various degrees of cruelty. In the end, punishment still depends on how an offender's acts are read by the penal code. More important, the procedures for getting protection remains as circuitous and discouraging as before.

Continuing Issues around the DVA

Although the definition of domestic violence has been expanded to cover acts such as emotional and psychological hurt, a distinction is still made between a "seizable" and "non-seizable" offense. A "seizable" offense is one where the victim's hurt is physical, with injuries such as cuts, wounds, lacerations, or broken bones being evidenced. Malaysia's DVA has to be read together with the penal code for the act of battery itself to be charged as a criminal offense (Amirthalingam 2005, 685–90). The penal code only empowers the police to investigate "seizable" offenses, which means that violent spouses inflicting other forms of assault may still not warrant an arrest under the law. Perpetrators can only be arrested automatically when there is a "seizable" offense, although women can be battered regularly without any visible evidence of grave physical injury. Given that the post-reporting period can be even more traumatic for the victim, since a protection order is not immediately granted, there is a high dependence on shelter facilities to provide pre-protection or protection before the protection orders (Noraida 2011b, 156–161).

Another controversial exclusion of a form of gendered violence from the definition of domestic violence is marital rape. The DVA does not recognize forced sexual intercourse between married persons as an act of violence. Hence, Section 2 (c) of the Act implies that a victim does not have the right to be protected against the imposition of certain conduct (namely, sexual intercourse) even if inflicted by force or threat upon the victim. This is because domestic violence is still treated as falling within the ambit of matrimonial law (Noraida 2011b, 56).

As the DVA needs to be read with the penal code, the law is quasi-criminal, combining civil and criminal procedures (Ng, Maznah, and Tan 2006, 53). It is also referred to as "a strange hybrid of criminal law with provisions pertaining to civil law remedies," such as the nonlegal remedy of counselling (Afida Mastura 2000, 79). The ambiguity of the law, being both civil and criminal, is not the actual obstruction to the solution. Even if gendered violence is defined within the ambit of the penal code, it will not be sufficiently addressed by it, given the complex nature of "hurt" and "harm" inflicted by intimate partners on each other.

The Persistent Problem of Criminalizing Domestic Violence

Thus, dilemmas continue as to how to treat domestic violence as a crime. If domestic violence is to be considered a crime (like burglary or murder), then the victim does not have the right to decide whether or not the alleged offender should be prosecuted. This stance takes away the autonomy of wives and mothers, whose lives could worsen if their only source of support, their perpetrators, are incarcerated. If victims lack autonomy in determining whether the system should intervene in their lives, the results (such as mandatory imprisonment for their partners) could be rather painful for the entire family. Hence, while punishment of offenders is the preferred option among feminist advocates of the law, given its deterrence value, this could mean taking away victim "autonomy." Concerns such as this probably explain why very few cases actually go from reporting to seeking actual intervention to prosecution. Much to the dissatisfaction of the DVA's advocates, domestic violence has remained a "quasi-crime" because of "victim ambivalence or hesitancy" in acting against their abusers. If domestic violence is to be fully criminalized, then the victim cannot assume autonomy in the matter (Bailey 2010, 1271).

Home and marriage are often still women's only source of sustenance, social networks, and status. A criminal justice system that includes mandatory punishment for domestic violence will only work well if we can assume that victim autonomy does not create further misery for the victim. To arrive at that conclusion the body as sovereign needs to be freed from the fetters of family, community, and state. However, it is not in a position to do so, as the subjectivities of self and its material sustenance are still entrenched within the very sites that it seeks freedom from—family and the state.

Conclusion

The campaign for the DVA in Malaysia allowed for much rethinking around the question of one's own subjectivity (and empowerment) in relation to gender, family, ethnicity, religion, and nation. However, the implications of the DVA also drove home the realization that domestic violence has yet to be deeply understood as a form of gendered violence and explicitly criminalized under the Malaysian legal system. Yet, criminalizing this offense does not alone resolve the multifaceted nature of the problem, rooted as it is in the ambiguity of family. Home is the site of many "domesticities," the violent one being one of these, and filled with complex emotions where, for some, only a thin line separates passion from aggression (Das 2008). This ambiguity is the root of the ineffectiveness of the law, although the effectiveness of women's agenda in public life has been enhanced by the possibility of further reforms around this issue.

Bibliography

Afida Mastura, Binti Muhammad Arif. A study on remedies for domestic violence in Malaysia. Ph.D. diss., School of Law and Politics, University of Hull, 2000.

Amirthalingam, Kumaralingam. Women's rights, international norms, and domestic violence. Asian perspectives, *Human Rights Quarterly* 27:2 (2005), 683–708.

Amry, Shareem. Making sure women are protected under Domestic Violence Act, in *New Straits Times*, 2 July 1997, 2.

Ashraf, Abdullah, and Ainon Mohamad. Exercise care in abuse cases, Anwar tells police, in *New Straits Times*, 18 July 1997, 2.

Bailey, Kimberly D. Lost in translation. Domestic violence, "the personal is political," and the criminal justice system, *Journal of Criminal Law and Criminology* 100:4 (2010), 1255–300.

Chin Mui Yoon. Home is where the hurt is, in *The Star*, 25 November 2007, <www.thestar.com.my/lifestyle/story.asp?file=/2007/11/25/lifefocus/19548266&sec=lifefocus>. 15 October 2012.

Das, Veena. Violence, gender, and subjectivity, *Annual Review of Anthropology* 37 (2008), 283–99.

Deutsche Presse-Agentur. Malaysian cops to undergo ethics course to polish image, in *Deutsche Presse-Agentur*, 27 August 1997, <http://www.lexisnexis.com.libproxy1.nus.edu.sg/ap/academic/>. 15 October 2012.

Ganesh, V. Shankar, and Mazlinda Mahmood. Protection from emotional abuse, in *New Straits Times*, 30 June 2011, p. 10.

Hare, Sara C. Intimate partner violence. Victims' opinions about going to trial, *Journal of Family Violence* 25:8 (2010), 765–76. <https://doi.org/10.1007/s10896-010-9334-4>.

Htun, Mala, and S. Lauren Weldon. The civic origins of progressive policy change. Combating violence against women in global perspective, 1975–2005, *American Political Science Review* 106:3 (2012), 548–69.

Mohd. Shahrizad, Mohd. Diah. The legal and social issues of wife battering and marital rape in Malaysia. A comparative view with Islamic law. M.A. thesis, Kulliyah of Laws, International Islamic University, Malaysia, May 1994.

Muharyani, Othman. Still waiting for the Act, *New Straits Times,* 1 February 1996, 8.

Muharyani, Othman. Controversy has positive effects, in *New Straits Times,* 24 November 1997, 7.

New Straits Times. DVA should apply to all races, in *New Straits Times,* 9 March 1996a, 4.

New Straits Times. Order restraining man from harassing wife quashed, in *New Straits Times,* 14 September 1996b, 6.

New Straits Times. Police. We are serious in dealing with abuse reports, in *New Straits Times,* 26 June 1997a, 6.

New Straits Times. 21 organizations express concern over police response, in *New Straits Times,* 11 July 1997b, 3.

New Straits Times. Kit Siang's debate bid fails, in *New Straits Times,* 15 July 1997c, 9.

New Straits Times. Police on why domestic cases left hanging, in *New Straits Times,* 14 June 1997d, 4.

New Straits Times. Plan for drive to review Domestic Violence Act, in *New Straits Times,* 22 February 1999, 15.

New Straits Times. Get feedback from women says Azalina, in *New Straits Times,* 19 June 2003, 7.

New Straits Times. Penal code section on domestic violence, in *New Straits Times,* 3 August 2005, 22.

Ng, Cecilia, Maznah Mohamad, and Tan Beng Hui. *Feminism and the women's movement in Malaysia. An unsung (r)evolution,* London 2006.

Noraida, Endut. The nature and impact of domestic violence. A study of survivors of wife abuse in Malaysia, in *Our lived realities. Reading gender in Malaysia,* ed. Cecilia Ng, Rashidah Shuib, and Noraida Endut, Penang 2011a, 43–64.

Noraida, Endut. Women, law and justice. The case of domestic violence in Malaysia, in *Our lived realities. Reading gender in Malaysia,* ed. Cecilia Ng, Rashidah Shuib, and Noraida Endut, Penang 2011b, 150–63.

Padman, Padmaja. Legal protection for the battered, in *New Straits Times,* 16 February 1995a, 39.

Padman, Padmaja. Interim protection order help for abuse victims, in *New Straits Times,* 2 March 1995b, 13.

Raja, Gerlad. IGP: Zaleha could not prove allegations, in *New Straits Times,* 29 June 1997, 1.

Rahmah, Hashim. Consider complexities before implementation Act, say group, in *New Straits Times,* 11 May 1996, 15.

Senyyah, Patrick. Domestic violence laws for review, in *New Straits Times,* 5 April 2000, 2.

Singh, Satwant and Charlotte Nelson. Zaleha identifies three stations that refused to accept reports, in *New Straits Times,* 30 June 1997, 1.

Siraj, Mehrun. Women and the law. Significant developments in Malaysia, *Law and Society Review* 28:3 (1994), 561–72.

Siti Hawa, Ali. Preserving family values. Experience of WCC in challenging violence against women. Paper presented at workshop, "Domestic Violence in Asia: The Ambiguity of Family as Private-Public Domain," Asia Research Institute, National University of Singapore, Singapore, 7–9 October 2010.

Spehar, Andrea. Women's movements as agents of change. The politics of policymaking and the reform of domestic violence laws in Croatia and Slovenia, 1991–2004, *Journal of Women, Politics and Policy* 33:3 (2012), 205–38.

Tan Seng Teck. Battered women, provocation and the criminal justice system. An inherent mismatch, *The Law Review* (2009), 403–13.

Zainah, Anwar. Polemics on jurisdiction obscuring issue of justice, in *New Straits Times,* 20 May 1996.

Legal Cases Accessed through LexisNexis Academic Database

Chan Ah Moi v. Phang Wai Ann (1995) 3 MLJ 130

Faridah bte Dato Talib v. Mohamed Habibullah bin Mahmood (1990) 1 MLJ 174

Jayakumari a/p Arul Pragasam v. Suriya Narayanan a/l V Ramanathan (1996) 4 MLJ 421

Jennifer Patricia A/P Thomas v. Calvin Martin A/L Victor David (2005) 6 MLJ 728

Mohamed Habibullah bin Mahmood v. Faridah bte Dato Talib (1992) 2 MLJ 793

Ngieng Shiat Yen v. Ten Jit Hing (2001) 1 MLJ 289

Legal Cases Reported in *Jurnal Hukum* (JH), a Journal for Reporting Sharia Cases in Malaysia

Adibah v. Abdul Rani (1986): Adibah Yasmi lwn Abdul Rani (1986) 3 *JH* 44

Hairun v. Omar (1993): Hairun bt Mohd Shariff lwn Omar bin Mohd Noor (1993) 8 *JH* 289

Hasnah v. Saad (1983): Hasnah Bt Hashim lwn Saad B. Arof (1983) 3 *JH* 84

Hasnah v. Zaaba (1995): Hasnah Bt. Omar lwn Zaaba bin Mohamad Amin (1996) 10 *JH* 59

Domestic Violence: Pakistan

Filomena M. Critelli

Pakistan is a strongly patriarchal society where male power manifests itself in a high incidence of domestic violence. Violence takes a variety of forms, some of which are common across cultures, as well as other forms of violence that are rooted in traditional customary practices such as so-called honor killings, stove deaths, acid attacks, and nose cutting. Women may also be treated as property or as objects of exchange between families in order to enhance social status or settle disputes. In spite of recent legal and policy reforms and advocacy efforts of civil society organizations, there still has been limited progress in delimiting domestic violence. Dramatic improvement is required in the legal framework and efficacy of applications of the law. Laws criminalizing domestic violence and the repeal of discriminatory laws that contradict the intent of CEDAW and the Pakistani Constitution as well as broad-based education programs to modify societal attitudes that condone domestic violence and promote awareness of rights are essential.

Prevalence and Scope

It is difficult to assess the prevalence of domestic violence in Pakistan because the government does not routinely collect data about gender violence. Moreover, collecting accurate data is difficult because incidences of violence are highly underreported, and women are not easily accessed for research interviews. Gender violence is also largely condoned in society and viewed by police and law enforcement institutions as a private matter. Even overt incidents of violence such as acid throwing, stove burnings, or murders are regularly recorded as "accidents" or not recorded at all by the authorities. Thus, much of what is currently known about gender violence in Pakistan is based upon anecdotal and broad-based reports of human rights and women's non-governmental organizations (NGOs) or from small-scale micro-studies.

Pakistan is a diverse country with great disparities in social development, therefore the nature and degree of domestic violence vary widely and are dependent on the intersections of social class, region and location. Thus, while a large proportion of Pakistani women across social classes suffer from varying degrees of violence, those vulnerable to the most severe acts of violence tend to be poor women and those in rural and tribal settings, where local customs

© KONINKLIJKE BRILL NV, LEIDEN, 2013 | DOI:10.1163/1872-5309_EWIC_EWICCOM_001453

often prevail over national law, patriarchal structures are much stronger and access to education and other resources is limited (Human Rights Watch 1999, Mumtaz and Shaheed 1987). Patriarchal social norms are embodied in strict codes of behavior, rigid gender separation, patrilineal and patrilocal family and kinship patterns, where inheritance of descent flows through the male line and married couples reside with or near the husband's parents. Family honor is linked to female virtue which is used to maintain control over women's sexuality (Moghadam 2003). In the rural and tribal settings patriarchal customs establish male authority and power over women's lives to such an extreme that women may be sold and bought in marriages, exchanged to settle disputes or murdered in the name of honor with impunity (Mumtaz and Shaheed 1988, Amnesty International 2002). In contrast, upper-class educated women have a wider range of resources and options available to them and greater knowledge of their rights, although strong societal disapproval and lack of support exists for women who attempt to live independently without family or male relatives in the home.

Gender violence in Pakistan takes a variety of forms, some of which are common across cultures such as marital violence, which includes verbal abuse, hitting, kicking, slapping, rape and murder, and economic and emotional abuse. Other forms of violence are rooted in traditional practices that continue under the guise of social conformism and religious beliefs such as so-called "honor killings" (called *karo-kari* in the Sindh province, literally meaning "black male" [*karo*] and "black female" [*kari*], which are metaphoric terms for perceived immoral behavior), forced marriage, child marriage, exchange marriage (*watta-satta* or "give-take," which involves the simultaneous marriage of a brother-sister pair from two households and is a contributing factor to child marriages), death by burning (stove deaths, which are presented as accidents), acid attacks, and nose cutting (a form of humiliation and degradation). In rural and tribal settings, local customs may also treat young girls and women as property or as objects of exchange between families (known as *vani* or *swara*) in order to enhance social status, gain resources, or settle disputes (Amnesty International 2002, Jilani and Ahmed 2004). Polygamy is legal in Pakistan, and psychological abuse can be inflicted by the threat of divorce or taking of another wife. Since it is common for women to move into the home of her husband's family after marriage, an additional cultural variation in the Pakistani context is that abuse may also be perpetrated by extended family members, including by the women of the family, such as mothers-in-law. In addition to the physical dangers, there is evidence of pervasive mental health consequences of domestic violence that contribute to high rates of depression and attempted suicide (Fikree and Bhatti 1999). Heightened suicide rates of women in Pakistan are interpreted as "more a result of being denied the right to express themselves as human beings and a denial of bodily rights" than due to poverty or hopelessness (Human Rights Commission of Pakistan [HRCP] 2011).

A 2010 report released by the Aurat Foundation, a major NGO working for women's rights, revealed over 8,000 reported incidents of violence against women in 2010, which represents a 13 percent increase over the last several years. The highest number of reported cases took place in Punjab with 5,492 incidents, followed by 1,652 cases in Sindh, 650 in Khyber Pakhtunkhwa, 127 in Islamabad, and 79 in Balochistan. More recently, HRCP (2011) also documented 2,900 cases of sexual assault and rape of women and over 4,400 cases of domestic violence against women in 2011, which included incidents of extreme violence such as 47 cases of women who were set on fire, 10 cases of women who reportedly had their heads shaved as part of public humiliation, and 9 cases of women who had their noses or other parts of the body amputated as punishment.

Since the late 1990s honor killings have been an important focus of the movement against gender violence in Pakistan. The issue was projected into the national and international arenas when Samia Sawar, a 29-year-old woman from an influential family in Peshawar who sought a divorce, was shot dead in the office of her attorney. In spite of subsequent legislation enacted to punish these crimes, HRCP (2011) reported that nearly 1,000 Pakistani women and girls were victims of honor killings in 2011, an increase of 100 cases from the previous year. A majority of the victims are married women and are killed by their husbands or brothers because they are considered to have damaged the family name, having been accused of having "illicit relations" or marrying without permission. Many cases are covered up by relatives and sympathetic police officers or reported as suicides.

Violence against women in Pakistan was once again projected into the international media in 2002 when Mukhtār Mai, a woman from the village of Meerawala in Punjab, was gang raped as a form of honor revenge on the orders of a *panchayat* (tribal council) of a local clan. Defying expectations that she would commit suicide in shame, Mai instead came forward to prosecute her attackers. The case was an embarrassment for then President Pervez Musharraf and raised questions about the government's commitment to the protection of women from violence, especially after a series of court decisions that resulted in the acquittal of all but one of her attackers. Sexual violence is not infrequent, and 445 incidents of gang rape of women were documented in 2010 (HRCP 2011). Women are also raped and abused while in police custody, which further deters them from reporting incidents of violence (Amnesty International 2002, Jilani and Ahmed 2004).

Acid attacks against women have also garnered increased international attention as a result of the film "Saving Face," which won a 2012 Academy Award and was co-directed by Pakistani filmmaker Shireen Obaid-Chinoy. It is reported that 200 acid attacks occur annually in Pakistan, most of them in southern Punjab and northern Sindh areas. Acid-related incidents are generally committed by jealous suitors, close family members, or enraged husbands (Acid Survivors Foundation 2012).

It must be noted that these figures do not account for all the thousands of cases that are not reported due to taboos associated with various forms of domestic violence, especially rape. Women's activists and government officials call for more gender aggregated census data including data on violence against women and dedicated police stations where women feel secure reporting crimes against them and are assured that action will be taken.

Historical, Legal and Political Context

Pakistan achieved nationhood in 1947 with a powerful military bureaucracy and a weak political framework and has since been under the rule of military regimes longer than the rule of civilian governments, from 1957–68, 1977–88 and 1999–2008 (Mumtaz and Shaheed 1987, Weiss 2003). From the time of independence in 1947, however, women had the right to vote, and Muslim women had the right to inherit property. Shortly after Pakistan's founding, women's groups pushed for legal reforms toward protecting women's rights within the family, which resulted in the Muslim Family Law Ordinance (MFLO) of 1961. The MFLO fell short of the goal to eliminate polygamy but did place constraints on it. The MFLO made marital practices more transparent; it instituted specific protections for women entering into marriage by establishing a minimum marriage age of 18 years for men and 16 years for women (Mumtaz and Shaheed 1987). The MFLO established penal sanctions for contracting child marriages; required registration of marriage contracts; and placed regulations on *talaq*, unilateral verbal divorce by repudiation that is initiated by a husband (Mumtaz and Shaheed 1987, Weiss 2003). The MFLO also required the consent of both the man and the woman for a marriage to occur in order to deter traditional practices that allow families to marry off their underage daughters (Mumtaz and Shaheed 1987). The MFLO is regarded by activists as one of the few pieces of legislation that safeguards women's rights within the family, but it continues to be challenged by conservative religious groups claiming that sections of it are un-Islamic (Women Living Under Muslim Laws 2006).

The civilian government of Zulfikar Ali Bhutto that lasted from 1971 to 1977 facilitated the next significant expansion of women's rights in Pakistan (Shaheed and Warraich 1998). During this period, the 1973 Constitution of Pakistan was promulgated, which granted women equal status and participation and guaranteed a number of women's rights, including freedom from violence. It specifically states: "All citizens are equal before [the] law and are entitled to equal protection of law...There shall be no discrimination on the basis of sex alone" (Constitution of Pakistan 1973).

Bhutto's presidency was followed by the military dictatorship of General Muhammad Zia ul-Haq, who seized power in 1977 and initiated an Islamization process that heralded a major step backward in the movement for women's rights. Zia enacted a set of criminal laws in 1979, known as the Hudood Ordinances, which govern the punishment for crimes involving theft, rape and adultery, among others, based on strict interpretations of Islamic law. The Hudood Ordinances criminalized all forms of extramarital sex (*zina*) and failed to legally distinguish between extramarital sex and rape (*zina bil-jabr*). The laws also provided standards for how sexual crimes were heard in court by disallowing a woman's testimony as legal evidence to a sexual crime and instead requiring the testimony of four adult Muslim men (Jahangir 2000). Women who could not meet this standard could be prosecuted for extramarital sex, and thousands of women, especially poor and uneducated women, have been imprisoned as result. Families have also used the Hudood Ordinances to punish women for refusing arranged marriage or seeking a divorce, and the laws have been linked to a rise in gender violence (Jahangir 2000, Amnesty International 2002, Jilani and Ahmed 2004). In 1984, Zia introduced further discrimination against women through the Law of Evidence (*Qanoon-e Shahadat*), which required the testimony of two women to counter the testimony of one man in court.

The Qisas and Diyat Ordinance, which was proposed in 1984 under Zia's Islamization program and implemented in 1990 by his protégé Nawaz Sharif, further undermined women's rights to safety and security by privatizing violent crimes of murder and bodily harm. The law replaced sections of the Pakistan Penal Code that cover offenses relating to physical injury, manslaughter, and murder, making these crimes against the person rather than against the state. Under the Qisas and Diyat law, the victim or his heir has the right to determine whether to exact retribution (*qisas*) or financial compensation (*diyat*) or to pardon the accused (Jilani and Ahmed 2004, UN Secretary General 2012). Thus, crimes of honor, where a woman is murdered by her father, brother, or other family member, may result in impunity. Families are usually complicit in these crimes, and the perpetrators may actually stand to profit if they do not seek formal justice (Human Rights Watch 1999, Jilani and Ahmed 2004).

Women's Activism against Domestic Violence

The oppressive conditions of Zia's military regime provoked a strong surge in the women's movement in Pakistan and marked the beginning of women's activism on gender violence. During this period, women activists played a critical role in shaping Pakistan's human rights movement, as the connections between violence against women and human rights became clear early on. The key focus of activism was state-sponsored violence against women, which was seen as responsible for increasing gender violence at large. The first cases of a guilty verdict under the newly passed Hudood Ordinances were Fehmida and Allah Bux, who in 1981 were sentenced to 100 lashes and stoning to death, respectively. Shortly thereafter, a blind teenage rape victim was charged with illegal intercourse (*zina*) when she became pregnant as a result of rape and was unable to provide the necessary identification of the accused to support her case because of her disability. The sentence of flogging (used interchangeably with lashing or whipping), three years imprisonment and a fine provoked outrage among women's groups regarding the manner in which the state and society implemented legal mechanisms to punish and control women who asserted their rights. These initial cases served as a catalyst for a wide spectrum of women's rights groups to form a lobby-pressure group known as the Women's Action Forum (WAF), which held numerous protests despite a ban on all forms of political protest. As a result of national and international pressure from women's rights organizations the young rape victim's sentence was later overturned.

Within this political context, there emerged the notions of women's rights as human rights and gender violence as "crimes against women," many years prior to the United Nation's 1993 Vienna Declaration recognizing that women's rights are human rights. Although violence was attributed to patriarchal structures in Pakistani society, the movement against domestic violence emerged in response to the new forms of legalized violence against women and was unlike movements in many other countries, especially in the West, where groups first directed their efforts against interpersonal violence. The conceptualization of violence expanded with increased awareness of the interconnectivity of different forms of violence against women that encompassed both individual and family level acts of physical and psychological violence as well as systemic and structural violence (Shaheed and Hussain 2007). During the 1990s, the focus

DOMESTIC VIOLENCE: PAKISTAN

of activism centered on domestic violence, especially honor killings and rape. As a result of The Fourth World Conference for Women in 1995, Pakistani feminists connected to the burgeoning international debates on violence against women and global human rights standards, and Pakistan adopted the Beijing Platform for Action (BPA).

Policy and Legislative Initiatives

Much of the policy framework that shapes the actions and interventions of the government of Pakistan to combat violence against women was developed as a follow-up to Pakistan's participation in the 1995 World Conference on Women, where women's human rights and empowerment emerged as central themes. The Pakistani government enacted a National Plan of Action (NPA) in 1998 to set priorities for action for the implementation of the various commitments of the Beijing Declaration and the BPA. The NPA lead to the formation of the National Commission on the Status of Women (NCSW) in 2000 to serve as a monitoring body of the government on women's issues. The commission's mandate is to examine policy, programs and other measures taken by the government for women's development and gender equality, to assess their implementation, and make recommendations to the relevant authorities, as well as to monitor mechanisms and institutional procedures for redress of violations of women's rights. In 2005, as another outcome of the NPA, a Gender Reform Action Plan (GRAP) was instituted as a project of the Government of Pakistan housed in the Ministry of Women's Development (MoWD). Five GRAPs have been established, one the national level and one for each of the four provinces. At the national level, one of GRAP's main purposes is to target key federal government ministries and set up gender equity positions or sections in each ministry at a senior level. GRAP also promotes institutional reforms and departmental restructuring to create gender-sensitive operations, political reforms to facilitate effective participation of women in the political sphere and reforms in public sector recruitment process and working conditions to encourage women's employment in the public sector throughout the country (Khan 2009). These policy bodies have improved the research capacity and advisory roles to the government on women's issues, but a lack of authority and adequate funding limits the impact of their efforts to promote women's empowerment and freedom from gender-based violence (Khan 2009, Shirkat Gah 2007).

Pakistan has adopted many of the international commitments to protect basic human rights and gender equality, which provide a platform for advocacy in courts and set standards against which to measure national laws. Gender violence against women is specifically addressed through international treaties such as the Convention on the Rights of the Child (CRC), which was ratified by Pakistan in 1990, and the Convention for the Elimination of All Forms of Discrimination against Women (CEDAW), signed by Pakistan in 1996. While CEDAW does not directly address the question of violence against women, it obliges the state to eliminate all forms of discrimination against women. CEDAW Article 5, in particular, instructs states to work toward modifying social and cultural patterns of individual conduct with the goal of eliminating prejudices and practices that discriminate against women.

In recent years, Pakistan has enacted some positive legal and policy reforms to delimit gender violence and promote women's rights. Pakistan's Penal Code began to recognize honor killings as premeditated murder in 2004. For years, a key demand of women activists was the repeal of the Hudood Ordinances in order to conform to CEDAW. In 2006, the Women's Protection Act (WPA) amended the Hudood Ordinances and reformed the most controversial parts. Rape was placed under Pakistan's Penal Code, which is based on civil rather than religious law, and the requirement for victims to produce four male witnesses or be prosecuted for adultery was eliminated. Adultery and extramarital consensual sex continue to be criminal offenses, and spurious charges of these acts continue to be used by husbands and families to punish women when they assert their rights. The Hudood laws were revised rather than repealed as a capitulation to objections from religious parties, and although women's rights advocates considered this a positive step forward, they continue to demand total repeal of the Hudood laws and other discriminatory legislation (Jilani and Ahmed 2004, Shirkat Gah 2007).

Other progressive legislation includes the Prevention of Anti-Women Practices Bill, passed in the National Assembly in 2006, which calls for abolition of customary practices such as giving women away in settling disputes, forced marriages, and marriages with the Holy Qur'ān. Moreover, the Acid Control and Acid Crime Prevention Act of 2010, which introduced potential liability of up to 14 years imprisonment and a 1 million rupees fine for individuals charged with the crime of acid throwing, was widely perceived as a robust legislative measure created by female politicians to empower women victims of acid violence. However, despite the passage of this law, acid attack incidents continue to occur. NGO activists call for the government to provide greater control and registration of acid sales across the country and to make those who sell the acid to attackers accountable as a party to the crime (Acid Survivors Foundation 2012).

Finally, a Gender Crime Cell (GCC) was established in 2006 under the umbrella of the National Police Bureau (NPB) to improve data collection on cases of violence against women, to render policy advice to government on particular cases or proposed legislation on violence against women, to investigate cases on the request of the Ministry of Interior, and to oversee other related activities such as police trainings (Khan 2009).

In spite of laws and international treaties, legal scholars and human rights organizations agree that girls and women in Pakistan continue to confront profound disadvantages and lack of rights protections (Ali 2000, Amnesty International 2002, Jilani and Ahmed 2004). There is a large gap between the rights established by statutes and the women they purport to protect. Weak governance and lack of rule of law renders much of the population beyond the scope of the formal legal system so that customary practices may carry greater significance than the rights granted in the formal law (Women Living Under Muslim Laws 2006, Shirkat Gah 2007). Written laws, particularly those protecting and guaranteeing women's rights, are often unknown, ignored or broken rather than honored and enforced. Women are constrained from taking action against violence and/or from accessing rights by a lack of knowledge of formal, especially constitutional rights (Ali 2000, Amnesty International 2002). Norms and accepted social practices based on custom may be presented as "law" to women or believed to have religious sanction. Parallel legal systems such as tribal courts continue to operate in remote areas because the formal state law and its machinery have not penetrated into all parts of society (Women Living Under Muslim Laws 2006). Statutory law is accepted and increasingly used by citizens in urban areas, but in rural or remote areas laws such as the MFLO are rarely used and enforced (Ali 2000). Despite the seriousness and prevalence of gender-based violence, the government has failed to make concerted efforts to initiate public awareness programs or gender sensitization programs of government functionaries (Asian Development Bank 2009). Civil society organizations have initiated legal education and awareness programs but have limited capacity to accomplish this enormous task.

Debates over the roles and rights of women and which interpretation of Islam should play in society have also intensified (Weiss 2003). Increasing violence and insecurity fueled by the growth of fundamentalism affect women's education and participation in other activities outside the home and contribute to the increased vulnerability of groups that support women's empowerment and human rights (Shirkat Gah 2007, Amnesty International 2010). Militant campaigns launched by armed groups have denounced women's shelters, contraceptives, and girls' education as un-Islamic; girls' schools and NGOs have been attacked or forced to limit their activities (Shirkat Gah 2007).

Over the last decade there have been attempts to pass a law criminalizing domestic violence in Pakistan. Pakistan lags behind other nations in the region such as Sri Lanka, India, Nepal and Bangladesh, which have passed laws specifically prohibiting domestic violence. Women's rights advocates criticize the culture of tolerance toward domestic violence whereby it is treated as a private family matter and legal institutions as well as individuals are routinely complicit in either perpetrating or perpetuating gender violence (Amnesty International 2002, Jilani and Ahmed 2004, Shirkhat Gah 2007). The police continue to treat domestic violence as a matter of marital dispute and encourage women to reconcile with their husbands, and the civil courts continue to mitigate the sentences of those who kill in the name of honor (Jilani and Ahmed 2004).

In 2009, the Domestic Violence (Prevention and Protection) Bill (DVB) was passed in the National Assembly but lapsed after Pakistan's senate failed to pass it within 90 days as is constitutionally required. Since the bill failed to be adopted in this time frame, rules stipulate that it can only be passed in a joint sitting of parliament. The government attempted to reintroduce the long-pending bill in February 2012. It passed in the senate but was again deferred due to strong resistance by opposition parties such as the Pakistan Muslim League Nawaz (PML-N) and Jamiat Ulema-e-Islam-Fazl (JUI-F) who refuse to pass the bill through the parliament without further amendment. These parties object to the law on the grounds that it is harmful to the family, will cause a rise in divorce rates and undermines Islamic values. The debate on the DVB continues in Pakistan's parliament (Shah 2012).The proposed law defines domestic violence as: "All intentional acts of gender-based or other physical and psychological abuse committed by an accused against women, children or other vulnerable persons, with whom the accused person is or has been in a domestic relationship." The law also classifies domestic violence as acts of physical, sexual or mental assault, force (psychological or physical), criminal intimidation, harassment, hurt, confinement, and deprivation of economic or financial resources. Violators will be punished with jail terms and fines paid out to victims. Monetary compensation and other relief will be provided to victims, and protection orders will be mandatory (National Assembly of Pakistan 2009).

Access to Legal and Support Services

Despite improved legislation, many factors such as cultural norms, tradition, high illiteracy rates, lack of knowledge, lack of initiative on the part of the government to enforce laws and educate the public, and the absence of other support mechanisms prevent women from claiming their rights. Pakistan's legal system is very confusing to its citizens and operates with parallel judicial systems. The formal legal system operates under Civil law, which is based on a combination of English common law and Islamic law and is administered in a secular, procedural framework (Ali 2000). In rural and tribal areas, customary laws continue to be implemented in tribal courts, although these laws are not accepted within the formal legal system in the event that a case is presented there (Women Living Under Muslim Laws 2006). A majority of women throughout the country do not understand how to take action to protect their legal rights and lack of legal aid systems or the availability of affordable legal representation further limits access to justice (Asian Development Bank 2009, United Nations Development Program 2007). The government must make a greater effort to fully honor the state's commitments under international treaties such as CEDAW and to enforce other existing laws to ensure that women's rights are sufficiently protected.

Women in Pakistan must navigate a multitude of structural, familial and individual level barriers to obtain social assistance with regard to gender violence. The availability of support in the form of shelters or follow-up services such as counseling for women seeking to leave situations of domestic violence is highly inadequate. For example, there is only one government supported shelter in the entire province of Balochistan, which has a population of 7,914,000 inhabitants and is marked by high rates of poverty, illiteracy, infant and maternal mortality and great gender disparities in development (Haider 2010). In any case, state-run shelters (*darulamans*) are of poor quality, lack trained staff, and function like jails where women are kept under custodial restraint and offered no support services to assist them in rebuilding their lives. A small number of shelter programs operated by NGOs provide an array of legal and/or supportive services, but few organizations have the resources to develop such programs (Bari 1998, Khan 2009). There is a growing recognition for increased government initiatives to expand services for victims of domestic violence. During 2007–2008 the Ministry of Women's Development added 25 new women's crisis centers throughout the country (now named Shaheed Benazir Bhutto Centres for Women), which provide temporary shelter, medical aid and counseling, legal assistance, relief, and support on an emergency basis to victims of domestic violence, with plans to create more. However, some of the centers in Sindh are facing severe financial crisis and have stopped functioning.

Moreover, only a small minority of women are willing to risk the social rejection and stigma that results from leaving abuse and seeking assistance. The high incidence of rape and abuse of women in police custody is also a deterrent, despite designated police stations for women in a few major cities. Thus, even though increasing numbers of women are becoming aware of their rights and coming forward to seek services (Critelli and Willett 2010, Gillani 2003), there are many women who continue to believe that they have no recourse but to accept domestic violence. A recent study on Pakistan found that 42 percent of women accepted violence as part of their fate; 33 percent felt too helpless to stand up to it; 19 percent protested against it; and only 4 percent took action against it (Amnesty International 2005). Furthermore, there is limited evidence of the positive impact of recent legal and policy changes such as the Women's Protection Bill and laws to prevent honor crimes and acid attacks. Women's advocates, although supportive of legislation as an important tool for women's protection, are concerned that it serves as mere window dressing without adequate implementation and enforcement.

Conclusions

Substantial changes that will ensure the protection and safety of women from domestic violence have yet to be implemented in Pakistan. Accurate data on domestic violence must be collected by the government and shared with the public. Dramatic improvement is required not only in the legal framework in Pakistan but also in the efficacy of applications of the law. Of utmost priority is passage of the Domestic Violence Bill and the repeal of discriminatory laws, such as the Law of Evidence 1984, the Hudood Ordinances of 1979, and the Qisas and Diyat law, which contradict the intent of CEDAW and the Pakistani Constitution. Stronger measures to enforce penalties for harmful practices against women must be implemented.

Ensuring women's rights and eradicating violence from their family lives also requires reforms in social attitudes that sustain or contribute to the problem of impunity. Currently, the government of Pakistan provides no public information programs or mechanisms to disseminate information about laws and regulations that would enable citizens to understand their rights and obligations (Asian Development Bank 2009). There is a persistence of social attitudes, traditional practices, and religious precepts that discriminate against women as well as a failure of the state to enforce laws and promote societal attitudes and police and judicial practices conducive to the recognition of women's fundamental rights (Ali 2000, Jahangir 2000, Jilani and Ahmed 2004).

Today, there are numerous vibrant and committed feminist, women's and human rights activists and NGOs engaged in influencing policy and legal reform and raising societal awareness against gender-based violence in Pakistan, including the Aurat Foundation, AGHS Legal Aid Cell, Shirkat Gah Women's Resource Center, which also houses a branch of the highly effective transnational feminist network Women Living Under Muslim Laws (WLUML), the All Pakistan Women's Association (APWLA), War Against Rape (WAR) and Simorgh Women's Research and Publication Center. While there has been some limited progress, civil society organizations cannot accomplish all that is required. The government must take assertive action and commit itself to securing the rights of women, or domestic violence will continue to hinder the capacity development of women and that of the nation.

Bibliography

Acid Survivors Foundation. Acid attacks statistics, 1999–2012, <http://www.acid survivors.org/statistics.html>, accessed 5 May 2012.

Ali, Shaheen. Using law for women in Pakistan, in *Gender, law and social justice*, ed. Ann Stewart, London 2000, 139–59.

Amnesty International. Pakistan. Insufficient protection of women, 16 April 2002, <http://www.amnesty.org/en/library/info/ASA33/006/2002>, accessed 26 July 2006.

Amnesty International. Amnesty International Report 2005 – Pakistan, <http://www .unhcr.org/refworld/docid/429b27f120.html>, accessed 26 July 2006.

Asian Development Bank. Pakistan. Access to Justice Program, ADB Completion Report, 2009, <http://www.adb.org/Documents/PCRs/PAK/32023-01-pak-pcr.pdf>, accessed 12 January 2011.

Bari, Farzana. *Voices of resistance. The status of shelters for women in Pakistan*, Islamabad 1998.

Critelli, Filomena M. and Jennifer Willett. Creating a safe haven in Pakistan, in *International Social Work* 53:3 (2010), 407–22.

Fikree, Fariyal and Lubna Bhatti. Domestic violence and health of Pakistani women, in *International Journal of Gynaecology and Obstetrics* 65:2 (1999), 195–201.

Gillani, Waqar. Domestic abuse and violence force women to leave home, in *Daily Times*, 30 November 2003, <http://www.dailytimes.com.pk/default.asp?page=story _30-11-2003_p7_10>, accessed 15 July 2009.

Government of Pakistan. The Constitution of Pakistan, 1973, <http://www.pakistani .org/pakistan/constitution/>, accessed 15 July 2009.

Haider, M. Sindh – Balochistan lowest and most neglected in Pakistan, in *Indus Asia Online Journal*, 2 June 2010, <https://iaoj.wordpress.com/tag/human-development -index/>, accessed 2 October 2012.

Human Rights Commission of Pakistan (HRCP). *State of human rights in 2011*, <http:// www.hrcp-web.org/pdf/AR2011/Complete.pdf>, accessed 10 May 2012.

Human Rights Watch. *Crime or custom? Violence against women in Pakistan*, 1999, <http://www.hrw.org/sites/default/files/reports/pakistan1999.pdf>, 5 November 2009.

Jahangir, Asma. Human rights in Pakistan. A system in the making, in *Realizing human rights*, ed. Samantha Power and Graham Allison, New York 2000, 167–94.

Jilani, Hina and Eman Ahmed. Violence against women. The legal system and institutional responses in Pakistan, in *Violence, law and women's rights in South Asia*, ed. Savitri Goonesekere, Thousand Oaks, Calif., 148–206.

Khan, Rabia. Situational analysis and mapping of women's human rights in Pakistan. CIDA Pakistan Program, 2009, <http://www.researchcollective.org/Documents/Final%20Report_on_Women.pdf>, accessed 5 May 2012.

Moghadam, Valentine. Patriarchy and the politics of gender in modernizing societies, in *International Sociology* 7:1 (2003), 35–53.

Mumtaz, Khawar and Farida Shaheed. *Women of Pakistan. Two steps forward, one step back?* London 1987.

National Assembly of Pakistan. Domestic Violence Protection (Prevention and Protection) Bill 2009, <www.na.gov.pk/uploads/documents/1300322603_188.pdf>, accessed 18 May 2012.

Shah, Bina. Time to pass the Domestic Violence Bill, in *Express Tribune*, 12 April 2012, <http://tribune.com.pk/story/363696/time-to-pass-the-domestic-violence-bill/>.

Shaheed, Farida and Sohail Warraich. The context of women's activism, in *Shaping womens lives. Laws, practices and strategies in Pakistan*, ed. Farida Shaheed, Sohail Warraich, Cassandra Balchin, and Aisha Gazdar, Lahore 1998.

Shaheed, Farida and Neelam Hussain. *Interrogating the norms. Women challenging violence in an adversarial state*, Colombo 2007.

Shaikh, Masood. Is domestic violence endemic in Pakistan? Perspectives from Pakistani wives, in *Pakistan Journal of Medical Sciences* 19:1 (2003), 23–28.

Shirkat Gah. *Talibanization and poor governance. Undermining CEDAW in Pakistan*, Second Shadow Report, Lahore 2007.

UN Secretary-General's Database on Violence against Women. Qisas and Diyat Ordinance 1990, <http://sgdatabase.unwomen.org/searchDetail.action?measureId =18083&baseHREF=country&baseHREFId=997>, accessed 19 July 2012.

Weiss, Anita. Interpreting Islam and women's rights. Implementing CEDAW in Pakistan, in *International Sociology* 18:3 (2003), 581–601.

Women Living Under Muslim Laws. *Knowing our rights. Women, family, laws and customs in the Muslim world*, 2006[3], <http://www.wluml.org/english/about.shtml>, accessed 26 July 2011.

Domestic Violence: Tajikistan

Muborak Sharipova

Introduction

For over a millennium, the Tajik people have played an important geopolitical role as mediators of the cultural and trade centers of the Silk Route, the crossroads between the "West" and the "East," a role that has had dramatic consequences for the people of this landlocked land. Throughout their history, the Tajiks have been invaded by many different forces, which, in turn, has led to internal rebellions, state-led aggression, and the general spread of violence. Tajikistan in its current territorial form was established in 1929, and today, the Republic of Tajikistan exists as a sovereign and secular state since gaining independence after the fall of the Soviet Union in 1991. Soviet rule (1918–1991) had established Soviet-style educational, social, and health care infrastructure in Tajikistan, replacing Islamic law (sharia) with a Western civil legal code in a country in which 95 percent of people are at least nominally Muslim (Rose 2002, 106). The fall of the Soviet system was marked by a deep political and economic crisis and followed by a civil war (1992–1997). Today Tajikistan remains among the world's poorest countries. Despite grand declarations in the Tajik Constitution, according to which citizens are granted all the freedoms and rights called for by UN conventions, including equal rights for men and women, Tajikistan continues to have a poor human rights record, dramatic gender inequality, and widespread incidence of violence especially against women and children.

Studies on Domestic Violence in Tajikistan

Domestic violence (DV) is a fairly new topic of research in Tajikistan. There were no statistical data or information about DV during the Soviet period because the topic was considered taboo, and it was prohibited to study it or to bring the issue to public discourse. DV was neither officially acknowledged as a social problem nor was it defined in the legal system (Sharipova 1998a, 2000a). However, recent studies, witness testimonies, and oral histories show that Tajik society and families were saturated with violence during the Soviet period (Sharipova 2000c, 2001). Experts agree that during the Soviet era DV was a widespread and an accepted mechanism employed by the Communist Party's metropolitan and local power-holders to preserve women and children's sense of inferiority for controlling their behavior (Sharipova 2007, Tlostanova 2009).

© KONINKLIJKE BRILL NV, LEIDEN, 2012 | DOI:10.1163/1872-5309_EWIC_EWICCOM_001447

The current attention to DV began under the influence of international organizations that were engaged in humanitarian assistance during the civil war of the 1990s. Between 1999 and 2000, the research center Open Asia conducted two comprehensive studies on DV, "Violence against Women" (VAW; supported by the World Health Organization or WHO, United Nations Development Program or UNNDP, and the Swiss Agency for Development and Cooperation or SDC) and "Violence Against Children in Tajikistan" (VACH; supported by UNICEF). These studies for the first time provided detailed quantitative and qualitative data and knowledge about the magnitude, factors, and consequences of the different forms of DV in Tajikistan (Sharipova 2000a, 2000b, 2001, 2002).

Defining Domestic Violence

For the purposes of this entry, domestic violence may be defined as any intentional action by a family or household member aimed at gaining or maintaining control over another family or household member. It may also include any lack of action such as the abandonment or neglect of a young, sick or elderly family member, or the withholding of care, food, or medication that may lead to significant negative consequences for the physical or mental health and development of the victim(s).

In the majority of DV cases, perpetrators use one or more of the following forms of abuse and neglect: physical, sexual, economic, and psychological/emotional (dominance, humiliation, isolation, threats, denial, and blame, among others). It is important to mention that (in)actions of DV can take place between any persons in a relationship of mutual obligation and support: husbands, wives, brothers, sisters, (grand)parents, children, in-laws, other relatives, people who live together, or members of a small community (friends, neighbors, acquaintances, or informal authorities close to the family). Moreover, such actions may not only be directed toward the victim(s) of DV, but also toward people, animals, or things significant to him/her.

In Tajikistan, DV is deeply embedded in political and socioeconomic inequalities and usually targets those household members who have low status in the family or community along economic, gender, age, familial, or ethnic lines (that is, they are unemployed, are women, children, the elderly, sick, disabled, or in-laws, or belong to ethnic or social minority groups).

Family Characteristics in Tajikistan

Family life in Tajik society is organized by the *avlod*, an extended patriarchal community of relatives (Bushkov 1991). An *avlod* is a traditional extended kinship network that differs from a nuclear family not only in size, but also in its vertical hierarchies of generation and gender and horizontal networks encompassing neighborhoods and relatives. Under Soviet rule, in 1989, the average household size in Tajikistan was 6.1 members, while the average for the USSR as a whole was 3.5 (Social Development of USSR 1990).

The *avlod* is the most powerful traditional institution in Tajikistan, providing physical, social, and economic support as well as emotional security in the form of a total sense of belonging. An *avlod* typically comprises several generations mainly related by blood or intimate relation to each other (for example, parents with their married children's families), often but not necessarily living in the same household or in the same neighborhood. An *avlod* can include a neighbor, an orphan child, or an individual who is not related to an *avlod*, but who nonetheless is entitled to the *avlod's* care and protection.

The social institution of the *avlod* is relevant to a discussion about DV in Tajikistan because it leads to a broader definition of DV. Because the *avlod* encompasses a wider range of relations than does the typical Western nuclear family model, the understanding of what counts as DV or who is a party to DV is quite different. Thus, an incident of DV in an *avlod* may involve actors (perpetrator, witness, and victims) who may not be intimately related, for example, in-laws or an adopted child. In addition, the post-Soviet revival of pseudo-Islamic marriages and polygyny in Tajikistan complicates matters further by extending the family, and thus the possibility for DV, in even more directions, as the *avlod* takes in the first, second, third, and fourth wives, along with their children and in-laws.

Domestic Violence in Tajikistan: a Historical Perspective

Spread of Violence under Soviet Rule (1918–1991)

The high rates of DV in Tajikistan may be understood as part of the massive spread of structural violence that began with the Russian colonization of Tajikistan (1868–1917) and followed into the conquest of the Red Army and the period of Soviet rule (1918–1991). During the 1920s, Stalin's national policy of reorganizing or fragmenting regional and national communities and political entities gave rise to anti-Soviet Islamic and nationalistic opposition. This policy created ongoing conflict between different regional ethnic groups and separated Tajik people from their main historical and cultural centers, especially Samarkand and Bukhara, which became part of Uzbekistan (Masov 1996, Bleuer 2012). Although the majority of Tajik intellectuals remained in these cities, eventually most of them either left or fell victim to the wars and related violence (Masov 1996, Shirin 1997). The civil war between Islamic-nationalist forces and the supporters of the Soviets raged into the early 1930s and was quickly followed by the cultural revolution during which communist ideology was absorbed into Tajik education, literature, arts, and language. The cultural revolution also included the destruction of mosques and old schools, the forced liberalization (unveiling) of women (*hujum*, literally attack, referring to the Soviet attack on "old and harmful" religious norms, including a dress-code, that kept women inferior), the burning of millions of books, and the severing of the Tajik people from their heritage, language, and cultural roots. Political repression culminated in forced collectivization and resettlement and persecution for religious beliefs or political opposition (Masov 1996, Rosefielde 1996, Shirin 1997). The Second World War, the Cold War, and the war in Afghanistan expanded Soviet militarism, saturating Tajik people's lives with the state's militarized discourse (Sharipova and Fabian 2010).

During Soviet rule, a general atmosphere of discipline and fear marked everyday life, with ever-present suspicion, neighbor spying on neighbor, and daily lineups for scarce basic goods. These conditions contributed to a rise in mental illnesses, changes in social norms, and, in many ways, to the direct and indirect spread of DV in Tajikistan (Sharipova 2008). In interviews conducted between 1998 and 1999, the majority of both old and young Tajiks revealed that they viewed DV as a normal part of their daily lives (WHO 1999, Sharipova, 2000b, 2001).

The Independence Years (1991–Present)

In the 1960s, the USSR launched a variety of programs aimed at creating a new type of Soviet individual among its constituent states. However, these efforts to change individuals and their ways of life proved to be inadequate and misdirected. For the Tajiks, these efforts resulted in an identity crisis whose unresolved nature contributed to the outbreak of civil war when Soviet tutelage ended in the 1990s. According to a variety of reports, the war inflicted significant damage on the country's population. At least 40 percent of the Tajik population was affected directly by the conflict: more than 100,000 civilians were killed, 55,000 children were orphaned, and 20,000 women were widowed (Falkingham 2000). There are no official data on how many women and children were raped, wounded, or killed during military actions. There are also no reliable statistics on how many women and children were among the more than 700,000 refugees that resulted from the war. Many displaced and refugee Tajik women and their children were exposed to violence and discriminatory treatment based on their gender and ethnicity within the refugee camps and other locations to which they fled (WHO 2000, Richters 2001).

DOMESTIC VIOLENCE: TAJIKISTAN

The civil war also led to the destruction of all kinds of infrastructure. The southern part of Tajikistan suffered the most damage during the war, where hundreds of school buildings, hospitals, bridges, and homes were partially or completely ruined. The economic cost of the war is generally estimated at US$7 billion (UNDP 1998). Moreover, the violent conflict inflicted a significant negative impact on gender disparities and the marriage market. Compared to the data for the year 1989, "during the first few years of war, the mortality rate due to injuries among young adults, ages 15–19, increased by 225 percent ... The mortality among boys in the age group 5–14 increased substantially during the same period and was higher than that of females of the same age" (Shemyakina 2009). Even today, more than fifteen years after the end of the war, war-related mortality and morbidity patterns continue to have a negative impact on the "marriage market" and on women's reproductive rights and behaviors, which continue to reflect post-war trends of forced and child marriages as well as polygamous and informal marriages and prostitution (Kasimova 2006, Shemyakina 2009).

Tajikistan's socioeconomic situation has not significantly improved since the end of the war in 1997. And although the Tajik government has signed international conventions such as the Convention on the Elimination of Discrimination Against Women (CEDAW) and the Convention on the Rights of the Child (CRC) and has publicly declared its commitment to women and children's welfare and rights, it has failed to provide social security, efficient education, and social and health care, and has failed to generally maintain gender equality. In fact, for all these measures, Tajikistan has registered a significant regress (–8.9 percent) in the Gender Equality Index (2008; State Statistics Committee 2009).

With the support of international financial institutions, reforms started after the collapse of the Soviets and rebuilding followed the civil war that included the liberalization of the economy and an unbridled and sudden wave of privatization. These reforms produced massive negative social and gender-specific consequences, including high levels of unemployment and deep and feminized poverty. Many men and women lost or quit their former jobs and engaged in informal markets consisting of small-business activities, such as buying and selling goods in the local bazaars or making "shuttle-business" trips to the former Soviet successor states and other neighboring countries. Children also quit school in order to help out at home (Sharipova 2000). Recent data show that the gender gap in education is growing: the coverage ratio of basic education (grades 1–9, ages 7–15) is 99.8 percent for boys and 93 percent for girls. The gap is especially stark for secondary education (grades 10–11, ages 16–17) for which the ratio is 56.5 percent for boys and 37.1 percent for girls (States Statistics 2007).

In 2009, 53 percent of the population, most of them women and children, lived below the poverty line (CIA 2012). In 2007, less than two-thirds of the population had access to safe drinking water. The rapidly increasing prices of basic goods and services – food, clothes, health care and medicine, childcare and education, transport, electricity, water, and communication – further deteriorated quality of life and especially affected women and children. Food insecurity reached dramatic proportions both during and after the civil war, producing high rates of malnutrition and child and maternal mortality. During the war more than 200,000 professionals left the country, and this number has increased significantly since, resulting in ill-equipped and poorly managed hospitals and schools. According to a report by UNIFEM (United Nations Development Fund for Women), lack of infrastructure, necessary equipment, supplies, drugs as well as lack of skilled health care workers are limiting access to health care, especially for women and children (UNIFEM 2012). Although there has been some improvement since the war, still, lack of health care contributes to a very high infant mortality rate (52.2 deaths/1,000 live births in 2010; UN Inter-Agency Report 2011) and a high maternal mortality rate (65 deaths per 100,000 births; World Bank World Development Indicators 2010); and it is estimated that one in three children in Tajikistan is malnourished (UNICEF 2008).

Lack of employment opportunities in the post-war period has pushed half of all working age Tajik men and an increasing number of Tajik women to seek employment out of the country, primarily in Russia (IFES 2006, U.S. Department of State 2012). An estimated 30 percent of the Tajik labor force migrates out of the country for work, and there are reports that more than 25 percent of these labor migrants are women. Experts agree that given existing economic and political conditions, women's migration from Tajikistan will increase in the coming years.

As men left, were displaced, or died in the war, women took the principal role as head of household and breadwinner, working mainly in low-skill occupations and in agriculture with poor wages and hard manual labor (World Bank 2005). Surveys show that though the majority of agriculture laborers are women, only one of ten heads of agricultural farms is a woman (UNICEF 2007). This is because of existing traditional norms and gender disparity in access to land and property, which limit women's ownership of land and property. That is also why, despite the fact that Tajik law recognizes all women's rights to land and property, widowed or divorced women often lose the right to their husband's property and can be thrown out of the deceased or ex-husband's home.

The "best case" scenario for a widowed or divorced woman is that she has a son because then she is responsible for the property until her son comes of age. She is expected to take care of the household until her son marries, after which the wife or wives are expected to obey and take care of the mother-in-law (Sharipova 2008).

In 2000, 5 percent of all households in Tajikistan consisted of single mothers with children, and this number has increased dramatically since, due to the extensive out-migration of men. Reports show that female-headed households tend to be more food insecure, and in Tajikistan, a woman heads almost half of all severely food-insecure households (TLSS 2007).

Another post-civil war trend was the development of prostitution and human trafficking circles (International Organization for Migration 2001, Sulaimatova 2004). Drug dealers increasingly used women and girls as "mules" for smuggling, and this led to state-mandated discriminatory practices, such as routine strip-searches and gynecological exams, against women crossing national borders (Sharipov 2002, Vandenberg 2007).

Despite the moves toward democratization, Tajik people and especially women still have very limited access to the legislative machineries that could protect them from discrimination, violation of their rights, and widespread crime and corruption. Very few, if any, Tajik women would be in a position to safely rely on the judicial system to defend their reproductive rights, rights to work and education, and freedom of expression (Sharipova and Fabian 2010).

As trust in governmental institutions remains low (Dadabaev 2006), Tajik society is falling back on the support of traditional institutions, such as the *avlod*, which were limited to some extent during Soviet times. Given the dearth of health and welfare services, many women have turned to Islam and its institutions for psychological and material help. While traditional and Islamic institutions undoubtedly provide a sense of belonging and security, they have also brought an increase of patriarchy into Tajik society. The Tajik government, for its part, has been alternating between ignoring (and thus supporting) and controlling/oppressing Islamic institutions. Official legislation has started to lose ground to *adat* (a customary practice based on a mixture of Islamic and common law), and the issues the government has recently tackled show an increasing symbolic and actual power of Islam in politics and everyday life. Similarly to many countries struggling to establish a balance between secularism and religious freedom, the Tajik government has taken steps to limit religious appearance and activity, for example, by banning (Islamic) headscarves in schools in 2005. However, the state has also shown itself willing to play in the field of religion, especially under the current fragile economic and political conditions. For instance, with the support of other Islamic countries, the Tajik government is building a mosque in Dushanbe that is planned to be the biggest mosque in Central Asia. The government is also calling upon developed Muslim countries "to help their brothers ... in the Islamic world to develop their energy, communications, transport and agrarian sectors" (Asia Plus, 5 April 2011). This political strategy could further fan the forces of religious radicalization and cause the breakdown of the state, leading to disastrous consequences, especially for already vulnerable populations.

Findings on DV in Tajikistan

The WHO Study
In 1999 the UN's World Health Organization (WHO), together with a local non-governmental organization (NGO), Open Asia, initiated a survey on "Violence against Women in Tajikistan" (WHO 1999) to produce a record of the violence women faced during and after the end of the civil war. The study was also supported by the Swiss Agency for Development and Cooperation, the gender program of the UNDP, and the Italian government. This study successfully brought together different local and international experts and actors to survey the nature and scope of violence against women. WHO experts on violence against women supervised the survey. The questionnaire covered socio-demographics, opinions on and experience of violence, and health status. Eventually, 900 women and girls (aged 14–65 years) were interviewed. In addition to the 900 interviews, the qualitative data consisted of the interviewers' daily journal entries and additional focused interviews with victims of violence and their responses to open questions. Quantitative and qualitative data, its analysis and other results of the study were presented in several reports and recommendations in a national conference on "Violence against women" The author was the national head of the study program, the author of study program, data analysis and most of the reports presented during the conference on "Violence against Women" held in Dushanbe in 2000. held in Dushanbe in 2000. Among the important practical results of the study were the establishment of many local NGOs working on issues of domestic violence, the 1999 Presidential Decree on "Improving Women's Role in Tajik Society" that established the "National Plan of Actions to Decrease Violence against Women" and later the broader "National Plan of Action on Improving Women's Status in Tajikistan" (2000), as well as many other follow-up programs and actions.

Psychological Violence
The 1999 WHO study examined the emotional environment in families right after the end of the civil war. Analysis of some of the yet unpublished data that

has been used in this entry shows that of the 900 women who participated in the survey, 45 percent reported having previously experienced psychological violence during girlhood or adolescence, 31 percent reported currently experiencing a tense atmosphere at home, and 14 percent reported open conflicts, in which members of their families were aggressive or used physical violence against them. Participants reported that when there were quarrels in their families, the quarrels often (32 percent) or seldom (54 percent) ended in physical violence. Only 13 percent of respondents reported no use of physical violence when there were quarrels in their families. Interestingly, when asked about the level of physical violence present in their parental families, the women reported similar levels: 25 percent reported that physical violence occurred often; 60 percent reported seldom; and 13 percent reported never. Moreover, the data received from women regarding their children being witnesses to physical violence during quarrelling also revealed a similar breakdown: 31 percent reported often; 61 percent reported seldom; and 8 percent reported never. The data suggests that the cycle of violence repeats itself intergenerationally.

The data also shows that many women were exposed to threats, offensive language, and insults. Women reported that their husbands threatened them and their children in the following ways: 30 percent of women reported that their husbands threatened to leave their families, 33 percent reported that their husbands threatened to beat them, and 17 percent reported that their husbands threatened to kill them. Moreover, 17 percent of the women reported that the husbands used the children against their wives, and 15 percent reported that their husbands and his relatives specifically threatened them that if the women left their families, the women would never see their children again. The women also provided accounts of restrictions on their freedom: 43 percent reported that their husband and his relatives limited the women's freedom in dress, 29 percent reported that they were prohibited from meeting with relatives and friends, and 32 percent reported being subject to accusations based on unjustified jealousy. Finally, 18 percent of participants reported that they were constantly offended, criticized, dishonored, and insulted by their own or their husband's relatives (Sharipova unpublished).

Materials of the focus group discussions (FGD) in the VACH study documented that many children were afraid of their parents, relatives, brother, sister, or grandfather. The children were afraid that with "wrong" behavior, they could provoke an irritation or even a rage in their loved ones that may incur unwanted penalties (Sharipova 2001).

Physical Violence

Even though there are no official age- or gender-specific statistics about losses during the civil war, the VAW and VACH studies show that the prevalence of

DV, especially against women and children, was exceptionally high during and right after the war (Sharipova 2002). In 1999, two years after the end of the war, 45 percent of women reported that their husband used physical violence against family members. One in three women reported experiencing physical abuse at the hands of family and non-family members during girlhood and adolescence (WHO 1999). In studies carried out in 1999–2000, immediately after the end of the civil war, experts have noted the increase of incidence of suicide among children. The studies have also noted that it is common for parents in Tajikistan to know from personal or others' experience about cases of severe physical abuse of children. One in five parents admitted that her/his children were beaten by her/his partner; one in ten indicated that children were beaten by relatives; and one in five parents admitted that they themselves often use physical violence as a form of punishment. This data is supported by the general belief among many Tajik parents that physical punishment is a normal act and a necessary method in raising a child: 22 percent of parents agreed that "it is normal if a child is beaten by a parent, it is necessary for the proper upbringing, sometimes, without it, [parenting] does not work." At least three out of the ten children participants of FGD reported being subjected to physical violence (Sharipova 2002).

More recent studies have confirmed this data on physical violence. For example, in standardized interviews with 800 Tajik men and women based on a national sample and FGD with eighty women, 62 percent of women and 60 percent of men stated that physical violence that causes victims pain, injury, or feelings of intimidation is widespread or very widespread in Tajikistan (Shoismatulloev 2005). Another study found that three out of four married Tajik women (ages 15–49) accepted physical violence from their partner, stating that their partner had the right to beat or hit them; such acceptance was even higher among younger women (85 percent among women ages 15–29; Tajikistan SCS 2005).

Sexual Violence, Reproductive Rights, and Polygyny

Testimonies of women show that common forms of DV during and since the end of Soviet period include forced marriages, elimination of reproductive choices through violence, marital rape, and forced pregnancies or abortion. Moreover, old traditions and customs, such as lower age at marriage and, especially, polygyny, although prohibited by both Soviet-era and post-Soviet Tajik laws, are becoming widespread again in Tajikistan (Sharipova 2000c, Kasimova 2006). In the 1999 WHO survey, 10 percent of respondents reported entering into a *nikah*, the traditional Islamic marriage contract, which leaves open the possibility of polygyny (WHO 1999). According to Shemyakina (2009), the spread of polygyny is directly connected to the loss of lives during the civil war, which left behind a large number of widows and a dearth of marriageable men. Traditional expectations about marriage, economic need, and concerns about personal security compelled many women to wed already-married men.

Since polygyny is not legal in Tajikistan, the second, third, and fourth marriages are not registered with the state. Consequently, in the case of divorce from the second, third, or fourth wife, the husband's family can avoid the division of property. These divorced or widowed women are often driven out of their homes for trivial reasons and often cannot even take their own things with them. Once they are out of the family compound, the woman and her children lose all rights to the house and other property. Children born in unregistered marriages are not registered with the state, have no official documentation or certification of birth, and therefore cannot receive proper prenatal or postnatal medical care. If they die, their deaths go unregistered. The long-term consequences for unregistered children can be dire. Children without official papers have trouble attending school, and they can encounter many difficulties in plans to officially marry or find a job. Women in polygynous marriages are more likely to face abuse, including sexual abuse. Interviewees reported, "A woman has to put up with a man's mockery or abuse so as not to be abandoned by him. A man would say to a woman: if your behavior is bad, keep in mind that there are many widows nowadays and it is very easy to replace one wife for another" (WHO 1999, interview diaries).

A 1999 study also found that more than 22 percent of women were entered into forced marriages and another 5 percent got married out of fear of public opinion and to avoid being labeled a spinster. One in six women reported that they got married because they wanted physical protection and some sort of economic support in the highly insecure political and economic environment in the war and post-war periods. During the civil war, the militia often forced young women to marry. Other women were forced into sex and consequently bore children; in order to avoid scandal, these women reported such incidents as forced marriages, even if the act of marriage did not actually take place (WHO 2000).

Studies also provide evidence that exposure to armed conflict was a significant factor in increasing the incidence of forced and child marriages in Tajikistan and in girls dropping out of schools when families became afraid of such a future for their daughters (Sharipova 2002, Shemyakina 2009). At the beginning of the civil war, the age of consent for girls was lowered to 17, although many girls were and continue to be married in religious ceremonies even before their 16th birthday. Increasing numbers of married Tajik "women" under the age of 17 have one or more children (Sharipova 2002). Studies have noted that the marriageable age for girls in Tajik society is declining and the child marriages have become widespread in Tajik society, increasing steadily since 1995 (Sharipova and Fabian 2010). During the civil war, in order to avoid rape and the humiliation of the family, parents favored marrying off their daughters at an early age. At the time, arranged marriages involved girls as young as 10 years old, some of whom became second or third wives to much older men simply in order to avoid the shame associated with the loss of *nomus* (honor). In this context, a woman who is not chaste is regarded as having dishonored her family, and especially her male relatives. In Tajikistan, as in many other societies, families and communities condemn girls who have lost their virginity before marriage and married women who engage in extramarital relationships. Traditional Tajik culture views sexual intercourse as a dirty act after which one must wash one's body. In the case of women and girls who have been forced to have sex against their will, there is little sympathy for them; rather they are seen as having brought great shame to themselves as well as their family and community. Only 14 percent of the parents surveyed reported that they would be willing to support their daughter if she were to lose her virginity before marriage, 5 percent said they would kill her, and most of them believed that sex outside of marriage is contrary to religion and tradition (UNICEF 2000, Sharipova 2002).

Tajik legislation makes rape punishable by up to 20 years in prison, and there are also laws against prostitution; brothels; procuring, making, or selling pornography; infecting another person with a sexually transmitted disease; and the trafficking of women for sexual exploitation. Despite these laws, sex workers operate openly at night in designated urban areas, and the trafficking of women remains a serious problem. Official statistics about sexual crimes are absent, and there are no special police units for handling such crimes. Studies show that sexual abuse is widespread and growing, and the threat of rape is often used to intimidate women. One in four women reported having been raped by her husband. Analysis of the figures by marriage type revealed that 62 percent of women in a polygamous marriage had been sexually abused by their husbands, compared to 42 percent of women in a monogamous marriage (WHO 2000). In interviews, many married women reported that they were afraid to even raise the issue of contraception for fear of being beaten. Among those who had experienced an unwanted pregnancy, 7 percent were forced to continue the pregnancy by their husbands or other relatives; 5 percent wished to terminate the pregnancy but did not for "fear of God and public opinion"; and 7 percent did not know of any alternatives to continuing the pregnancy (WHO 2000).

Incidents of sexual violence against children are also rarely registered by law enforcement agencies, as such cases are usually committed within the family

Causes of DV

"Women and children are fragile creatures, they have to be cared for" and "raising a hand against a woman or a child is shameful!" are a couple of the many Tajik traditional norms that call for caring and respectful behavior toward women, children, the elderly, orphans, and the disabled. What factors, then, can explain the high levels of DV that have existed and continue to exist in Tajik society?

As mentioned earlier, the totalitarian Soviet regime was characterized by particular forms of violence involving militarism, enforcement of internal cohesion and integration through consistent and aggressive assertion of Soviet patriotism and communist ideology, and elimination of other forms of ideology including national identity and cultures. The post-Soviet state followed with authoritarianism based on excessive use of power against non-submissive individuals and groups and human rights violations, among other violent tactics. Against both forms of state-led violence emerged a previously suppressed nationalism and traditional fundamentalism. These, however, led to the tightening of control over women and children and were manifested in cruel forms of domestic violence. As in other parts of the world (Göle 1997), within these ideological struggles, Soviet-style patriotism and post-Soviet authoritarianism, on the one hand, and nationalism and traditional fundamentalism on the other hand, women and their sexuality were abstracted both as symbols of modernity and progress as well as symbols of national culture, tradition, and the motherland. Concern for the motherland was expressed by enforcing special care over women and especially over their sexuality and bodies. In this process, women's bodies often became arenas of violent struggle, wherein each side tried to show to whom these bodies belong (Saigol 2008).

During the independence years, the modern legislative machinery and the education, health, and social care systems deteriorated along with the main achievement and matter of pride of Soviet rule, the presence of women in the public sphere. Women's presence in leadership positions, politics, mass media, and the legal and engineering professions decreased significantly. The general fall in women's status was the result of at least two sets of factors, political-economic and socio-cultural, that influenced processes immediately after the fall of the Soviets.

The first set of factors, political-economic ones, involved the rapid, unequal, and corrupt process of distribution of previously nationalized assets mostly among the post-communist elites, warlords, nationalists, and Islamic leaders. Due to lack of information, political skills, and basic resources, women across classes had little chance to take part in the redistribution of previously public goods, which led to their poor economic status.

The second set of factors involved the difficult post-Soviet cultural process of redefining national identities in the newly independent country, which contributed to a revival of traditional institutions, customs, and norms that did not consider women's role to be crucial in the society. This complex process led to resettling traditional gender roles and gender-specific socialization with values that empowered men with rights over women and girls, putting women in an inferior and subordinate position not only in the *avlod*, but also in the post-Soviet public domain.

Political-economic Factors of DV

Studies have shown that the civil war combined with political and economic instability, insecurity, and growth in crime, unemployment, poverty, and hunger had a major role in spreading DV in Tajik society. Government policies both during and after the Soviet period also had a major impact by legitimizing and normalizing the use of violence (Sharipova 2000c, 2008).

DV has been encouraged by the destruction of social infrastructure, which has resulted in a lack of adequate governmental care facilities for families and the absence of psychological institutions to provide individuals and families with ways of managing stress and trauma. Among other socioeconomic factors, experts also point to poor sanitation and the spread of disease; the presence of feelings of apathy and mental and moral exhaustion among people; and increased rates of alcoholism, drug abuse, and and other conditions relating to poor health and well-being. The deterioration of general conditions for the development of children, the appearance of a lost generation, and the large numbers of orphans and street children, in turn, contributed further to greater violence and crime against children and by children.

These factors are all interconnected and have prompted growing feelings of frustration, depression, mental illness, hopelessness, anger and out-of-control behavior among adults and children that lead in turn to conflicts in the family and to incidents of DV.

Legal and Policy Factors

Though the Tajik Constitution and other official laws regarding divorce, child custody, maintenance and inheritance, rape and abuse provide some norms to ensure gender equality and domestic safety for family members, the existing mechanisms of these written laws are not working. This is due primarily to the low level of legal literacy and gender education not only among the general population, but also among the police and judicuary (Sharipova 2010). The Soviet totalitarian regime did not encourage legal literacy, and the current state has not done so either. During Soviet rule in Tajikistan, as in other Soviet countries, issues of public and domestic violence were considered taboo. Thus, neither received much attention and the resultant silence pushed public, structural, and institutional violence into the domestic sphere.

Studies have reported problems of underreporting and underestimations of DV in Tajikistan, especially as a result of taboos and the influence of norms that encourage women to keep silent about what are considered negative family experiences. Data showed that women perceive beating by husbands, constraints on their dress, and other forms of violence as "normal and common practice in the family," and that is why they "do not meddle in other people's lives, even if you know that somebody is being abused" because "even the doorstep laughs at the quarrel between husband and wife." Moreover, women reported that it is a "sin for a woman to divorce," and public attitudes to a divorced woman are "worse than the attitude to a widow or even a prostitute." Thus women avoid public condemnation by not divorcing (Sharipova 2008).

Lack of state supported policies to combat DV and growing influence of Islamic ideology in the society has also empowered the concept of men's control and ownership over women and often has legitimized DV. This is why, given the enormous power and respect enjoyed by the heads of the *avlod*, as described below, it is very hard to formally prosecute or sanction members of the *avlod* for acts of DV. The punishment, whether physical or mental, of "bad" members of the family that "defile the honor" of the *avlod* is only justified when it is in response to transgressions of the code of the *avlod*. The violence is thus legitimated.

Sociocultural Factors

One major response to the end of Soviet rule was the strengthening of local patriarchal and religious values and traditions. With the civil war, these traditions gained further ground in a dramatically unstable and materially and physically insecure environment and contributed to changes in the status of men and women. One such change was the rise of an attitude of hostility toward girls' education. This attitude was particularly problematic for preventing the spread of DV, as girls' education is known to serve as a bulwark against DV especially in rural areas.

Studies conducted in Tajikistan provided evidence and showed that traditional institutions, such as the *avlod*, and religious or traditional customs, for example polygyny or forced marriage, were bolstered by political and economic factors (Shemyakina 2009, Tyomkina 2005, Sharipova Fabian 2009). Experts noticed that amidst the insecure political and economic circumstances during and after the civil war, Tajik society survived to a great extent as a result of the informal structures of the *avlod*, which continued to carry out their essential traditional functions (Bushkov 1991, Tyomkina 2005, Sharipova and Fabian 2009). As a central feature of Tajik society, the *avlod* lays the foundation for the roles and rights of its members, and especially for the contradictory attitudes toward women and children's social status. On the one hand, the *avlod* relieves women of the heavy responsibility to provide for their own and their children's financial future and protects them from some of the most dire and direct interventions of the state (such as the "liberalization campaign" or obligatory employment and public activity, for example in elections, during the Soviet rule). In the *avlod* the burden of social and economic security is placed squarely on the men in the family.

On the other hand, women and children's so-called protected status within the *avlod* results in their isolation, economic dependence, and subjugation. The *avlod* represents a strict patriarchal ideology that oppresses women and children as individuals and deprives them of initiative, education, and development. Heads of *avlod*, for example, control women's income-generating activities, restrict marriages between different religions and ethnicities, decide at what age and whom their children should marry, and enforce traditional norms that decree that women and girls should be obedient, calm, patient, and forgiving. Traditional norms authorize sex-segregating public facilities, such as mosques and most entertainment places, prohibit most women and girls from establishing social contacts outside of their extended family, deny women's right to public (socio-political) activity and their access to economic and social capital. Men of the *avlod* (father, brother, husband, and his relatives) maintain control over women's every step and restrict women's outdoor movements and public activity (Sharipova and Fabian 2009).

Respect for the elderly, interpreted as the subordination of the younger to the older generation, and women's submission to the family men are central features of the *avlod*. The underlying assumption is that women, like children and young people, are physically and emotionally less developed than men, which is why they not only need protection, but also need their behavior to be governed by men. There is evidence, however, that while norms of absolute respect to elders are changing somewhat, the norm of a woman's complete subservience to her husband's authority remains very strong in society (Tyomkina 2005).

The need to organize marriage with the consent of the parents is one of the most significant manifestations of patriarchy (Therborn 2004). It is widely understood in Tajik society that the elders of an *avlod* have a "sacred duty" to protect the *avlod*'s noble name and wealth for posterity. Therefore the proper upbringing of members of the *avlod*, such that none of them would abuse or tarnish this name, is a very important responsibility. And since with every new marriage, the *avlod* expands its kinship net, sharing each other's name and wealth, there is need for strict control over such marriages and to guard connecting with an *avlod* that has a bad reputation or poor wealth. That is why light or moderate forms of DV are sanctioned in traditional culture as tools of nurturing and raising children or controlling behavior of members of the family/*avlod*. However, other forms of physical violence, especially sexual violence towards children and other members of the family/*avlod* who are not in a marital relation, are strictly prohibited (Sharipova 2002).

Traditionally, while a girl child is looked down upon as a liability, she is also seen as family property and a potential source of income. A bridegroom must pay a *kalym* (bride-price) as a "gift" to his future wife's family. The girl's parents and relatives determine the sum of the *kalym* as the price of her dignity, virginity, physical potential to serve the husband's family and bear children, and her "professionalism" in managing housework, among other things. In some cases, in addition to the *kalym* the bridegroom has to make payments for "good parenting," for example, for "the cost of mother's milk" given to a daughter or the price for "mother's care" (Sharipova and Fabian, 2010) Many parents regard a daughter as a very profitable item when they try to "sell" her for more money, depriving her of a childhood and, just as importantly, a free choice.

Strictly gendered social expectations explain why parents bring up their daughters in a dramatically different way than their sons. Strict moral, religious, and socio-cultural codes govern all aspects of conduct, especially of women. The worst crime is to engage in behavior that would be a disgrace to one's community. This is reflected in the peculiar hierarchy of values and norms reflected in the common saying that it is less shameful to be a thief than to be a man whose sister spoke to a man outside the family.

The members of an *avlod*, especially women, can expect to suffer ostracism if they are caught engaging in premarital or extramarital sex. In fact, fear of public opinion and *avlod* sanction result in some of the most serious and cruel forms of DV. Sexually explicit behaviors elicit the most violent responses, such as parents killing their daughters and relatives torturing women for "dishonoring" their family or *avlod*. Family conflicts often arise based on mere suspicions about "unchaste" sexual behavior, and these conflicts can end in tragedy.

Of course, an *avlod* can also provide women and children with significant moral and financial support and security. This sense of externally validated security provided by *avlod* is the main reason why women do not easily consider leaving their family, even when they face various forms of DV, or why both girls and their parents consider marriage as a main avenue for establishing their future (Sharipova and Fabian 2010).

Changes in the Traditional Gender Order

It is important to mention that some trends in contemporary Tajik society do point to turbulent changes in the traditional gender order. For example, some young men have rejected the traditional role of family provider, especially in the current political and economic situation in Tajikistan, where high levels of unemployment and a severe lack of economic opportunities have led to increasing labor migration out of the country. One trend resulting from this emigration is SMS-divorces: young male labor migrants send the word *talaq* (divorce) to their wife back home via text messages on mobile phones (Najibullah 2009). Another recent trend is migrants not calling or remitting income to their children, wives, and parents for several months in a row (Tursunzade 2010). These trends have forced women to take on roles as heads of households and providers for their family and facilitated women's involvement in social and economic activities. An increasing number of Tajik women are also marrying foreigners, a relatively new phenomenon that has raised concerns for both religious and nationalistic groups who have called to protect Tajik culture and restrict such marriages (Kasimova 2009, Olamafrouz and Khushbakht 2011).

The emigration of large segments of the population is a significant threat to traditional Tajik culture, in that it undermines the traditional institutions, separates members of families and members of the *avlod*, and loosens strict control over *avlod* members. Many families have responded by tightening traditional norms and rules and punishment for those remaining inside the culture. Migration has thus had a significant effect on society, especially in terms of encouraging different forms of DV, including the neglect of children and the elderly, and forms of psychological and economic violence.

Conclusion

For over two centuries, the Tajik people lived under Russian colonial rule, followed by Soviet totalitarian rule, both periods characterized by high levels of structural and societal violence. The enforced nature of Sovietization, militarization, repression, and political violence exerted a lasting effect on Tajikistan. It isolated the Tajik people from their spiritual and cultural sources; created an environment of aggression, intimidation, and fear; and further scarred the emerging national consciousness, leaving many raw personal and social traumas that diffused into the private spheres and came to be manifested in acts of DV. The current situation in Tajikistan can be characterized as one of great political and economical instability. Lack of state support, poverty, its feminization, lack of social and economic security, high levels of unemployment, limited access to education, and high levels of migration all contribute to the increasing of DV.

Precisely because of the interlocking social and economic support prevalent in traditional social structures and Islamic institutions, the impact of and respect for these institutions has increased during and since the civil war. Islam's influence is indisputably increasing in Central Asia, but religion is only one influence among many, starting with the family and extending to kin networks, regional loyalties, and to allegiance to the newly independent states, as well as to political affiliations. As a result, gender roles, in particular, have become further bifurcated, resulting in increased restrictions on women's political and economic opportunities, lack of women's access to social and economic capital, lack of quality education for children, a gender gap in education, and the enhanced seclusion of the majority of women and girls. There is evidence that these larger trends continue to contribute to a high prevalence of physical, sexual, psychological and economic forms of DV in Tajikistan.

Bibliography

Bleuer, Christian. State-building, migration and economic development on the frontiers of northern Afghanistan and southern Tajikistan, in *Journal of Eurasian Studies* 3 (2012), 69–79.

Bushkov, Valentin. Tadjik avlod [Thousands of years later], in *Vostok* 5 (1991), 72–81.

Dadabaev, Timur. Public confidence, trust, and participation in post-Soviet Central Asia, in *Central Asia-Caucasus Institute Analyst*, 31 May 2006, <http://www.caci analyst.org/?q=node/3977/print>, accessed April 2012.

Falkingham, Jane. *Women and gender relations in Tajikistan*, Country briefing paper, Asian Development Bank, Dushanbe 2001.

Göle, Nilüfer. The quest for the Islamic self within the context of modernity, in *Rethinking modernity and national identity in Turkey*, ed. Sibel Bozdogan and Resat Kasaba, Seattle 1997, 81–94.

International Foundation for Electoral Systems (IFES). Political engagement and enfranchisement of labor migrants from Tajikistan, <http://www.ifes.org/publications detail.html?id441>, accessed April 2012.

International Organization for Migration (IOM). Deceived migrants from Tajikistan. A study of trafficking in women and children, Geneva 2001, <http://www.iom.tj/pubs/trafficking_2001.pdf>, accessed June 2012.

Kasymova, Sofia. Tajikskoye obshchestvo. Traditsiya i praktika mnogozhenstva [Tajik society. Tradition and practice of polygamy], in *Vestnik Evraziya* 4 (2006), 97–115.

Masov, Rahim. The history of a national catastrophe, ed. and trans. Iraj Bashiri, Minneapolis 1996, <http://tajikistanfocus.wordpress.com/2011/10/18/the-history-of-a-national-catastrophe-by-rahim-masov/>, accessed April 2012.

Najibullah, Farangis. "SMS divorces" cut Tajik migrants' matrimonial ties to home, in RFE/RL, 6 December 2009, <http://www.rferl.org/content/SMS_Divorces_Cut_Tajik/1896511.html>, accessed April 2012.

Olamafruz, Faromarz and Yasmin Khushbakht. Tajikistan tightens marriage rules, Central Asia Human Rights Reporting Project, RCA Issue 643, 3 March 2011, <http://iwpr.net/report-news/tajikistan-tightens-marriage-rules>.

Richters, Annemiek, Gender, violence, health, and healing in situations of ethnonational conflicts. The cases of the former Yugoslavia and Tajikistan. Hommes armés, Femmes aguerries, http://66.102.1.104/scholar?hl=en&lr=&q=cache:qWHy8gfVciUJ:www.unige.ch/iued/new/information/publications/pdf/yp_hommes_armes_femmes/12-conflits-richters.pdf, accessed 19 April 2012.

Rose, Richard. How Muslims view democracy. Evidence from Central Asia, in *Journal of Democracy* 13:4 (2002), 102–11.

Rosefielde, Steven. Stalinism in post-Communist perspective. New evidence on killings, forced labor and economic growth in the 1930s, in *Europe-Asia Studies* 48:6 (1996), 959–87.

Saigol, Rubina. Militarization, nation and gender. Women's bodies as arenas of violent conflict, in *Deconstructing sexuality in the Middle East. Challenges and discourses*, ed. Pinar Ilkkaracan, Burlington, Vt. 2008.

Sharipov, Orzu. Alive containers, 2002, in Open Society Archives, http://www.osa archivum.org/filmlibrary/browse/country?val=69, accessed April 2012.

Sharipova, Muborak. Opening remarks. Speech at the First National Conference on "Violence Against Women" in Dushanbe, Tajikistan 1998a.

Sharipova, Muborak. War widow in Tajikistan, Census, 1998b.

Sharipova, Muborak. Violence against women. Pilot survey in Tajikistan. World Health Organization (WHO), unpublished quantitative and quantitative material, 1999.

Sharipova, Muborak. *Violence against women in Tajikistan*. National report. Dep. УДК343.54/57: 316.52 (575.3), Dushanbe 2000a.

Sharipova, Muborak. *Prevalence and risk factors of violence against children in Tajikistan. Results of the national survey*, Dushanbe 2000b.

DOMESTIC VIOLENCE: TAJIKISTAN

Sharipova, Muborak. Report on violence against women in Tajikistan. Analysis of quantitative and qualitative data, WHO Regional Office for Europe, Copenhagen 2000c.

Sharipova, Muborak. *Status of children in Tajikistan*, national report for UN GMC, Dep. УДК 321. (575.3): 351.766.2), Dushanbe 2001.

Sharipova, Muborak. Theoretical and practical problems of violence against children based on national surveys implemented in Tajikistan, Ph.D. thesis, Russian Academy of Science, Institute of Sociology, Moscow 2002.

Sharipova, Muborak. Problems of gender violence in Tajikistan, in *Violence and social change* (in Russian), ISBN-5-94101-082-6, Moscow 2003.

Sharipova, Muborak. Women in Tajikistan. Between the hammer of Sovietization and the anvil of traditional culture, presentation at Copenhagen University 2007.

Sharipova, Muborak. One more war against women in Tajikistan, in *Gender politics in Central Asia. Historical perspectives and current living conditions of women*, ed. Christa Herausgegeben von Hämmerle, Nikola Langreiter, Margareth Lanzinger and Edith Saurer, Cologne 2008, 67–95.

Sharipova, Muborak. Some factors of gender inequalities and violence against women in Central Asia, presentation at EU EIDHR, Brussels 2010.

Sharipova, Muborak and Katalin Fabian. Changes in gender regime. The case of Tajikistan in comparative perspective, presentation at CESS, Toronto 2009.

Sharipova, Muborak. From Soviet liberation to post-Soviet political and economic segregation. Women and violence in Tajikistan, in *Domestic violence in postcommunist states*, ed. Katalin Fábián, Bloomington, Ind. 2010, 133–70.

Shemyakina, Olga. The marriage market and Tajik armed conflict, HiCN Working Paper 66, October 2009, <http://www.hicn.org/wordpress/wp-content/uploads/2012/06/wp66.pdf>.

Shirin, Akiner. Between tradition and modernity, in *The dilemma facing contemporary Central Asian women/post-Soviet women. From the Baltic to Central Asia*, ed. Mary Buckley, Cambridge 1997, 261–304.

Shoismatulloev, Shonazar. *Violence against women. Past and present*, Dushanbe 2005.

Social Development of USSR (finances and statistics) [Социальное развитие СССР (Статистический сборник)], Moscow 1990.

Tajikistan. *CIA world factbook* via the libraries of the University of Missouri-St. Louis, <http:///www.cia.gov/cia/publications/factbook/geos/ti.html#Econ>, accessed 19 April 2012.

Tajikistan State Committee on Statistics. *Findings from Tajikistan monitoring the situation of children and women Multiple Indicator Cluster Survey. Preliminary report*, Dushanbe 2006.

Tajikistan State Committee on Statistics. *Women and men in the Republic of Tajikistan*, Dushanbe 2009.

Therborn, Goran. *Between sex and power. Family in the world 1900–2000*, London 2004.

Tlostanova, Madina. *Decolonial gender epistemologies*, Moscow 2009.

Tursunzade, Mehrangez. *Plight of "abandoned wives" in Tajikistan*, Central Asia Human Rights Reporting Project, RCA Issue 637, 15 December 2010.

Tyomkina, Anna. Gender order. Post-Soviet transformation in north Tajikistan, in Gender. Tradition and contemporaneity. Collected articles on gender, ed. Safia Kasimova, Dushanbe 2005, 27.

United Nations Inter-agency Group for Child Mortality Estimation. Levels and trends in child mortality. Report 2011, <http://www.childinfo.org/files/Child_Mortality_Report_2011.pdf>, accessed April 2012.

UNICEF, Tajikistan. Country statistics, 2006, 2008, http://www.unicef.org/infoby country/Tajikistan_statistics.html, accessed April 2012.

UNICEF, Tajikistan. *Tajikistan. Living standards measurement survey, 2007*, Dushanbe 2009.

UNIFEM. Country gender profile – Republic of Tajikistan, <http://www.untj.org/docs/country_context/gender/Policies/Gender_profile.pdf>.

United Nations Development Programme (UNDP). Human development report, Tajikistan, 1995, 1999, http://www.undp.org/rbec/nhdr/tajikistan/chapter7.htm, accessed April 2012.

Vandenberg, M. Women, violence, and Tajikistan, Eurasia Policy Forum, 2001, http://www.eurasianet.org/policy_forum/vand022001.shtml, accessed April 2012.

Vandenberg, M. *World Bank world development indicators*, <http://search.worldbank.org/data?qterm=Tajikistan&language=EN>, accessed April 2012.

World Health Organization. *Violence against women. Report on the 1999 WHO Pilot Survey in Tajikistan*, WHO Regional Office for Europe, Copenhagen 2000, <http://socialtransitions.kdid.org/library/violence-against-women-report-1999-who-pilot-survey-tajikistan>.

Domestic Violence: Muslim Communities: United States of America

Salma Abugideiri

Domestic Violence: United States

Domestic violence is a social issue that affects people of all faith groups, ethnicities and races. There are victims from every socioeconomic bracket, educational level and professional background. While there is no single agreed upon definition of domestic violence, particularly in the way it is measured in research studies, a core component is a pattern of behaviors by one person in an intimate relationship designed to coerce or control another person in the relationship. The broadest definitions of domestic violence include spousal abuse, child abuse and sibling abuse. Domestic violence includes verbal, emotional, financial, physical and sexual abuse and can range from threats that cause the victim to live in a state of fear and anxiety, to beatings, rape and even murder.

While great strides have been made in the United States to provide services for victims and treatment for batterers, there are many segments of American society that are underserved, with few benefiting from the existing resources. Muslims are one of these populations. Although Muslims affected by domestic violence have a great deal in common with other Americans in terms of the types of abuses experienced and the types of services that are needed to deal with the abuse, Muslims also have some unique issues and needs related to their religio-cultural background.

The study of domestic violence in Muslim communities in the United States is relatively recent. While the mainstream movement against domestic violence began in the 1960s, documented research related to Muslims began in the 1990s. Among the general population in the United States, approximately 30 percent of women in intimate partner relationships are victims of domestic violence (Collins et al. 1999). To date, there is relatively little research about the prevalence of domestic violence among Muslims in the United States, the manifestations of domestic violence in this group, how Muslims in the United States are dealing with domestic violence, and best practices for intervention. Yet in the past 10–15 years, there has been growing attention given to this issue as is evident in both scholarly and community-based literature, as well as in the development of domestic violence services for Muslims (Alkhateeb and Abugideiri 2007).

© KONINKLIJKE BRILL NV, LEIDEN, 2010 | DOI:10.1163/1872-5309_EWIC_EWICCOM_0690

Recently, Muslim communities across the United States were spurred into action by the case of a Muslim television producer who killed his wife after she sought a divorce following years of documented abuse. The nationally publicized tragedy of Aasiya Hassan forced many Muslim communities to recognize that domestic violence is a real threat to them and to the lives of abuse victims, and that Muslim communities need to become more active in understanding and responding to domestic violence (Abugideiri 2009, Ghayyur 2009, Grewal 2009).

Demographics

A recent major study of Muslim Americans describes this population as "youthful, racially diverse, generally well-educated, and financially about as well off as the rest of the US public" (Pew Research Center 2007, 15). Determining the exact number of Muslims in the United States has been problematic, with great variability in survey outcomes, depending on who is conducting the survey, and with no one survey being completely reliable (Leonard 2003). The most commonly cited figures indicate that there are anywhere from 5 to 8 million Muslims in the United States (*World Almanac* 2009; Bagby, Perl and Froehle 2001; Esposito 2010; Smith 1999). The bulk of these Muslims consist of first, second or third generation immigrants (Smith 1999),[1] mostly South Asian Americans and Arab Americans. Among Muslims born in the United States, a large majority are African Americans. This population also includes converts (African American, Caucasian, Latino and Caribbean), who comprise about one-fourth of the United States Muslim population (Bagby, Perl, and Froehle 2001). Significantly, more than three-fourths of Muslims in the United States are American citizens (Pew Research Center 2007). Muslims are therefore an extremely diverse group, representing a wide range of cultures, which are reflected in a variety of attitudes, opinions and behaviors. According to a recent Gallup poll, Muslim Americans are the most racially diverse religious group in the United States (Muslim West Facts Project 2009).

---

1 The Pew Research Center's study (2007) reported there are 2.35 million Muslims in the United States, a figure standing in stark contrast to the more commonly cited figures of 5–8 million (World Almanac 2009; Bagby, Perl, and Froehle 2001; Smith 1999). The discrepancy may be a result of any number of problems, including defining who is counted as Muslim (Smith 1999), lack of scientific surveys (Pew Research Center 2007), and differences in sampling procedures.

Cultural and Religious Identity

Both religion and culture are very important in the understanding of domestic violence among Muslims because both of these factors contribute significantly to people's perceptions, interpretations and responses to the phenomenon of domestic violence (Alkhateeb and Abugideiri 2007). It is often hard to separate religion from culture as they inform each other and are deeply intertwined. The diverse cultural backgrounds of Muslims in the United States lead to many variations in the ways Islam is interpreted and sometimes practiced, especially in rituals related to marriage, divorce and the birth of a child. Immigrants from Muslim-majority societies may presume some of their familiar practices are Islamic, when in fact those practices may have predated Islam. Converts to Islam, including whites, blacks and Latinos, are frequently educated by immigrant Muslims about Islamic beliefs and practices, and they may adopt some of the interpretations and practices of Islam that are a result of cultural influences.

Religion is reported to be important to between 72 and 80 percent of Muslims in the United States, with 47 percent identifying themselves first as Muslim, second as American (Pew Research Center 2007, Muslim West Facts Project 2009). In comparison, 65–82 percent of Americans in general report religion to be important in their lives (Newport 2009; Pew Forum on Religion and Public Life, 2009). For this reason, it is critical to understand the religious impact on the occurrence of domestic violence, as well as the ways in which religion can be used as a deterrent and preventive resource.

As far as religious affiliation is concerned, about half of the Muslims in the United States are Sunni, 22 percent report no particular affiliation, and 16 percent are Shi'i. While 50 percent of Muslims believe the Qur'ān is to be read literally, 60 percent believe that there is more than one way to interpret Islamic teachings. Almost 70 percent of Muslims believe that Islam treats men and women equally, while 23 percent believe Islam treats men better than women (Pew Research Center 2007).

Muslims in the United States cover the entire continuum of religiosity, from extremely conservative to extremely liberal. Some Muslims are more secular than others. Nadir and Dziegielewski have suggested a typology that categorizes Muslims according to degree of practice, while Alkhateeb has suggested a matrix that categorizes Muslims according to the degree of literalism by which they interpret the Qur'ān (Alkhateeb and Abugideiri 2007).

Prevalence

It is difficult to ascertain the prevalence of domestic violence among Muslims for many reasons. Research specifically considering Muslim Americans and domestic violence is emerging, although it is more common to find studies focusing on particular ethnic groups that tend to be heavily Muslim, such as South Asian or Arab American, without always providing a breakdown of how many participants were Muslim. Readers should note that while the majority of Arabs in the Arab world are Muslim, the 2002 Zogby International Survey found the majority of Arab Americans to be Christian (Arab American Institute n.d.). However, research studies mentioned in this article have focused on communities in the United States, such as Dearborn, Michigan, that have large numbers of immigrant Arab Muslims. Studies of South Asian Americans and Arab Americans have focused more on the ethnicity and cultural factors than the religious identity of the target population. While this research certainly has helped tremendously in beginning to understand some of the cultural variables that affect domestic violence, it has not focused on the importance that religious identity has for many Muslim Americans. Those studies that have focused on issues that may be specific to Muslim Americans have emphasized the significance and impact of their understanding of religious teachings and practices within their cultural contexts (Abugideiri 2007).

The first documented survey of domestic violence among Muslim Americans was conducted by Sharifa Alkhateeb in 1993 (1999), looking at a range of abuse from hitting to incest. In this study, 10 percent of respondents reported experiencing some type of abuse, not including verbal or emotional abuse. In a 2009 survey of 241 Muslims, approximately one third of respondents reported feeling afraid of a current or previous spouse. In terms of physical abuse, 14 percent reported experiencing abuse in a current marriage, and almost 18 percent had experienced it in a prior marriage. In addition, 4.3 percent of the women reported miscarriages due to abuse (Ghayyur 2009). In a study of 190 Muslims (mostly Arab and South Asian) who had sought counseling mainly for family and relationship problems or for depression, 50 percent of the clients had experienced physical abuse; 63 percent had experienced emotional abuse; and 14 percent had experienced sexual abuse. Three percent of these clients reported the death of a family member due to domestic violence (Abugideiri 2007). Among Americans in general, one in four women (or 25 percent) report experiencing abuse by an intimate partner (Family Violence Prevention Fund n.d.), and more than half of women accessing mental health services have experienced either current or past abuse by an intimate partner (Warshaw and Barnes 2003).

Contributing Factors

Although there is no single cause for domestic violence, and no single theory that explains it, it generally occurs as a result of inequality and the desire on the part of the abuser for power and control. There are cultures in which oppression of women is more tolerated than others, with highly patriarchal cultures more susceptible to the abuse of women. In addition to the systemic risk factors, research on Muslim Americans seems to suggest the possibility of certain risk factors that may also contribute to domestic violence.

While the research is still quite limited, some of the risk factors that seem to be associated with Muslim Americans' experience of domestic violence include a family history of abuse, as well as poverty, isolation, and tenuous legal status (Abdallah 2007; Kulwicki and Miller 1999; Maker, Shah and Agha 2005). Other factors that need to be researched and that may exacerbate the potential for or existence of domestic violence are related to the historical and geopolitical contexts of many Muslim American sub-groups. Muslims who have come to the United States to escape war, political persecution, torture in refugee camps, or other types of violence may be suffering from traumatic disorders that could lead to emotional instability, making them either more likely to tolerate abuse or more likely to be abusive. In this author's clinical experience working with refugees, women who had experienced torture or witnessed extreme forms of violence due to war dismissed the beatings or threats they sustained from their husbands as minor irritants compared to what they had already endured. In terms of their perceptions of and responses to abuse, African American Muslims may be affected by their history of slavery and oppression, as well as contemporary societal racism they have experienced in the United States (Alkhateeb and Abugideiri 2007). These are just a few examples that highlight aspects of the Muslim American experience that need further study in order to determine scientifically the contribution these factors make to the occurrence of domestic violence. Researchers also emphasize the importance of considering the impact of the intersections of race, class and gender, which also influence the ways people perceive and respond to domestic violence (Sokoloff and Dupont 2005).

Cultural and Religious Attitudes and Beliefs

Cultural belief systems typically include contradictory values that can be either supportive of abusive practices or liberating from abusive practices (Ammar 2000; Kasturirangan, Krishnan and Riger 2004). For example, many majority-Muslim societies place a high value on the integrity of the family unit and the role of women in maintaining the well-being of the family. The honor of the family is tied to women's reputations, and men are generally tasked with controlling women's behavior as a way to protect their reputations by limiting their access to anything that might mar their reputations. Shame is often used as a regulating factor in South Asian and Arab cultures to maintain behaviors within acceptable social norms.

At the same time, these societies also subscribe to religious beliefs of individual accountability and the fact that God hates injustice and oppression and sides with the oppressed. The health and well-being of children are highly valued. In addition, Islam sets conditions for marriage that are preventive of abuse, such as terms that can be set in the marriage contract guaranteeing a woman's right to education, a certain standard of living, and so on. Islam highlights the accountability of each human being directly to God, as well as the importance of critical thinking and freedom of choice. These are examples of beliefs that can be used to empower women and create systemic change (Alkhateeb and Abugideiri 2007; Faith Trust Institute 2007).

Immigrants bring their cultural legacies with them when they come to the United States, and although the process of acculturation certainly can dilute cultural norms, beliefs and attitudes over time, the deeply engrained values related to shame and honor in Arab and South Asian cultures can be seen even in second and third generation Muslim Americans. Women coming from highly patriarchal cultures where they have limited rights may not even recognize behaviors that constitute abuse simply because they may be prevalent or condoned in their native culture (Ahmad et al. 2004). To further complicate matters, some Muslims confuse their cultural norms with Islamic teachings, misusing certain Islamic teachings to enable and maintain abusive relationships.

For example, the high value placed on marriage from both a cultural and Islamic perspective can lead many parents to focus on encouraging their daughters to be patient and endure an unhappy marriage, even if the marriage is abusive. These parents rely on Islamic teachings that value marriage and women's patience in order to avoid the shame of a failed marriage, to the exclusion of Islamic values of mutual satisfaction in marriage, justice, and accountability. Parents may not realize that their pressure, in and of itself, is a form of abuse of their daughters who are also experiencing abuse from their husbands (Ayyub 2000).

Among Muslims in the United States, there is a wide range of interpretation of Islamic teachings. Certain Ḥadīth and Qur'ānic verses have sometimes been used to justify wife-beating, the submission of women to their husbands in general, and the husband's right and responsibility to discipline his wife. These teachings are sometimes used out of context; at other times, the problem arises from translations of Qur'ānic text that are informed by the translator's geocultural and historical context. The most frequently misused and misunderstood Qur'ānic verse in this case is 4:34. Problematic issues can be seen in the commonly used translation of 'Abdullah Yūsuf 'Alī (1989), which ostensibly instructs men to "spank" their wives if they are disobedient to them:

> Husbands are the protectors and maintainers of their wives because Allah has given the one more strength than the other, and because they support them from their means. Therefore the righteous women are devoutly obedient, and guard in the husband's absence what Allah would have them guard. As to those women on whose part you fear disloyalty and ill-conduct, admonish them first, next refuse to share their beds, and last spank them lightly. But if they return to obedience, seek not against them means of annoyance, for Allah is Most High, Great (above you all).
>
> ALĪ 1989, 195

An alternative translation, which reflects greater internal consistency with the rest of the Qur'ān, as well as greater congruence with the model of the Prophet Muḥammad's life, is written by Laleh Bakhtiar:

> Men are supporters of wives because God has given some of them an advantage over others and because they spend of their wealth. So the ones (f) who are in accord with morality *are* the ones (f) who are morally obligated, the ones (f) who guard the unseen of what God has kept safe. But those (f) whose resistance you fear, then admonish them (f) and abandon them (f) in their sleeping place then go away from them (f); and if they (f) obey you, surely look not for any way against them (f); truly God is Lofty, Great.
>
> BAKHTIAR 2007, 94; f denotes feminine gender pronoun

This translation in no way suggests any kind of violence; rather it suggests constructive steps for dealing with the serious disruption in marriages that can occur when one partner (in this verse, it is the wife) violates the moral obligations outlined by God.

This verse has been interpreted in at least four ways, ranging from permitting wife-beating under certain conditions and with certain restrictions to having nothing to do with beating at all (Ammar 2007). The degree to which Muslims' interpretations of Islamic teachings are influenced by patriarchal values is an important factor in the degree to which domestic violence will be tolerated in any given family or community.

In one sample of a group of Arab Americans, 98 percent of which was Muslim, with limited education and lower socioeconomic status, more than half of the respondents approved of a man slapping his wife if she hit him first during an argument. More women than men believed that a man should slap his wife if she had been unfaithful. In the case of a wife's affair, 20 percent of the women believed a man could kill her (Kulwicki and Miller 1999). Another study of a similar population (85 percent Muslim) found that 25 percent of women believed husbands were justified in beating their wives in the case of infidelity, disobedience, or insulting the husband (Abu Ras 2007). While this research is helpful in beginning to develop a picture of attitudes regarding domestic violence among American Muslims, it should be noted that the samples in these two studies are not reflective of the broader American Muslim population in terms of education and socioeconomic status, nor are they reflective of the general Arab American population.

Mental health counselors who served Arab American women (a majority of whom were Muslim) reported that abused women cited religious beliefs to support the values of placing the needs of the family above their own, maintaining an intact family for the sake of the children, and men's right to discipline their wives. At the same time, women who condemned domestic violence used religious beliefs to support their position (Halabu 2006).

African American Muslims and converts to Islam may be influenced by all the values mentioned here if they are framed as Islamic and if their primary source of learning about Islam is from those immigrant Muslims who espouse attitudes and values that can lead to the oppression of women in the home. On the other hand, African American Muslims are a distinctive group and have their own heritage, cultural values and beliefs that shape their perceptions and attitudes toward violence. Their experiences with racism have contributed to sometimes antagonistic or ambivalent attitudes toward immigrant Muslims and other groups. African American Muslims are a diverse group in terms of their journey to Islam. While approximately 10–15 percent of the Africans brought as slaves to the United States were Muslim, they were unable to retain Islam more than a few generations. The history of African Americans as Muslims has had multiple influences, including the Ahmadiyya movement and the Nation of Islam. Currently, the majority African Americans are Sunni (Leonard 2003; Turner 2004).

Despite the existence of misogynist attitudes and practices in the Muslim world, nearly 70 percent of Muslims interpret Islam to be egalitarian in its treatment of men and women (Pew Research Center 2007). Muslim survivors, advocates, community leaders and imams who are working to end domestic violence rely heavily on Islamic teachings to change cultural attitudes or religious interpretations that foster abuse (Alkhateeb and Abugideiri 2007; Faith Trust Institute 2007).

It is important to recognize that there are significant differences in the ways subgroups of the ethnicities mentioned vary in their interpretation and practice of Islam. There are also significant generational differences between immigrants and their children, who may adopt some, all or none of their parents' values and beliefs.

Culture-specific Manifestations of Abuse

Domestic violence can be manifested in many different ways. The key factor in determining whether behavior falls under the category of domestic violence is that the behavior is designed to control or wield power over another person in the family, and generally contributes to a climate of fear or intimidation. Abusers can accomplish this goal in many ways, including physical, sexual, psychological, financial and verbal abuse. While these categories of abuse exist in every culture, the meaning that is ascribed to particular behaviors is dependent on the cultural context in which it occurs (Sokoloff and Dupont 2005). There are some behaviors and practices that occur in Arab and South Asian cultures that may appear abusive to Westerners but may not be abusive at all. For example, while some Saudi women may long for the opportunity to drive, others may be grateful to have chauffeurs and feel no need whatsoever to drive themselves.

At the same time, some abusive practices may have more impact on Muslim American women than other American women. For example, accusing a woman of having a boyfriend in a culture that normalizes boyfriend/girlfriend relationships will not feel as threatening as it will to a Muslim woman whose reputation will be ruined if such an accusation is made about her. In order to capitalize on the significance that reputation holds in many Muslim communities, abusers may threaten to tell others that she is guilty of immoral or loose behavior, or threaten to broadcast secrets he has learned about her family, as a way to control her behavior. Despite the fact that Islam allows divorce, many Muslims from immigrant cultures feel a great deal of shame about divorce. Muslim men who are abusive might utilize the threat of divorce, or actual repeated divorces, to manipulate their wives into doing what they want.

Furthermore, the structure and hierarchy in many immigrant families sometimes leads to abuse by family members other than the husband (Dasgupta

2000; Halabu 2006). This abuse can come from the victim's family (brother, father, uncle) who may believe that she should be obedient to her husband and remain in the family at any cost. In addition to pressuring her, family members may actually physically abuse her. In other cases, the abuse may come from the husband's family members, either to reinforce his position or as unrelated abuse because of her lower status in the family.

On the other hand, family members can often be extremely supportive of the victim and may intervene, provide refuge, or even confront the abuser or help the wife end the marriage when they learn of the abuse. In some cases, the husband's family may be the wife's strongest allies. Extended families can be the source of multiple types of support, and can be a great resource for many women who might otherwise feel isolated and forced to remain with the abuser for financial and other reasons.

Religious Abuse

Religious or spiritual abuse occurs in all faith groups and refers to the use of religious values or teachings in a manner that is manipulative and controlling. Although in some ways this type of abuse overlaps with the culture-specific manifestations of abuse, and technically falls under the category of psychological abuse, it warrants attention and understanding because advocates and professionals from secular backgrounds may not easily understand the significance and the impact this type of abuse has on women of faith. In fact, because of the relative unfamiliarity of mainstream service providers with Islamic teachings, it is not uncommon for these providers to believe batterers who claim a religious right to abuse their wives. This can lead to biased treatment, collusion with the abuser, and re-victimization of the abused woman if she and/or her religious beliefs are blamed for the abuse.

Religious abuse includes a wide range of behaviors that include taking Ḥadīth or Qur'ān out of context to manipulate the wife or to give authority to the husband, calling the wife a bad Muslim, and telling the wife she will go to hell if she does not obey her husband in all matters. It also includes preventing her from practicing her religion or forcing her to practice in ways that are not comfortable to her. For example, in considering the issue of *hijab*, it becomes abusive if the husband either forces his wife to wear it when she does not want to, or prevents her from wearing it if she chooses to.

Muslim women themselves may not be knowledgeable about their religious teachings and may believe that their husbands have the right to beat them. Many Muslim women do not know they have the right to initiate a divorce (*khul'*), or that domestic violence is grounds for *ṭalāq* (divorce initiated by the husband or ordered by a judge in which the wife retains financial rights). They may also not be aware of the ways Islamic values can be used as resources. For example, while patience (*ṣabr*) has typically been used to encourage women to endure a bad marriage somewhat passively, the Qur'ān uses it in association with action. With this understanding, Muslim women can utilize the same value of *ṣabr* to motivate them to seek help and explore their options.

Regarding the actual marriage process, there are some Muslim Americans who prefer to have only an Islamic marriage contract, or *nikāḥ*, without registering the marriage in court. This preference may exist for many reasons, but one of these is related to polygyny. In the United States, the practice of polygyny creates a potential area for abuse because of its prohibition under US law. While some women, and particularly African American women, may view polygyny as a solution to the shortage of eligible or compatible men that is experienced by Muslim American sub-cultures, the fact that the marriage is illegal in the United States automatically creates a system with built-in abuses. The second wife cannot have any marital rights enforced in court, including the provision of *mahr* (gift given by the groom to the bride), and she must often keep her marriage a secret, which in and of itself violates the conditions of an Islamic marriage. Abusive men may use the threat to take a second wife as an effective control tactic for those women who do not want to practice polygyny.

Culturally Appropriate Services

Some of the first organizations to provide culturally sensitive services to Muslim Americans were established in the late 1980s and were primarily ethnic-specific, serving South Asian Americans or Arab Americans, for example. In the 1990s, Muslim-focused organizations that incorporate the Islamic paradigm were also gradually being established around the country (Alkhateeb and Abugideiri 2007; Dasgupta 2000). Because of the limited number of these organizations, and their often limited resources, many Muslim American survivors of abuse continue to need to rely on mainstream American services.

Domestic violence advocates have found that Muslim Americans are more likely to trust and utilize the services of individual advocates and domestic violence organizations that are aware of their religious and cultural values. Some strategies that have been effective in serving Muslim victims of domestic violence include working in a non-judgmental fashion, recognizing that culture and religion contain many positive values that can be enlisted to empower women and to lend credibility to the services being provided, and building collaborative relationships with Muslim communities, to increase trust and opportunities for education and effective intervention.

Responses to Domestic Violence

Muslim Americans' responses to domestic violence are quite varied. At the individual level, most women who are abused remain in the relationship (M. Alkhateeb 2009; Halabu 2006). They cope by avoiding dealing with the problem, relying on their faith or distracting themselves by focusing on children or work. Despite the fact that many women believe that the most effective response to domestic violence is to have the husband arrested, few women choose this option, especially after the attacks of 11 September 2001 (Abu Ras 2007). Muslim women may not reach out for help for many reasons, some of which include valuing the family's privacy, perceiving the services to be culturally insensitive, fearing that their immigration status will be compromised or that they will be reported if they are undocumented, or that the children will be removed from the home. Other obstacles include racism, language barriers, lack of familiarity with available services, and perceptions that Americans are hostile to Muslims (Abu Ras 2007; Grewal 2009; Halabu 2006).

Those women who do take some action involve others, seek professional services, or try to change their own behavior in the hopes that the violence will be reduced (Halabu 2006). African American Muslims tend to use more counseling services than immigrant Muslims, and because they are more familiar with American culture, may have more resources than their immigrant counterparts that will allow them to be more independent. At the same time, because many are converts, they may be alienated from non-Muslim family members and feel more isolated than their immigrant counterparts (Abdallah 2007).

In a recent survey of Muslim Americans, most respondents reported that mosques are not doing enough to address the issue of domestic violence (Ghayyur 2009). Responses from community and family members range from getting absolutely no support, to getting the support they needed at some point during the abusive relationship or upon leaving (M. Alkhateeb 2009; Halabu 2006). Unhelpful responses from religious leaders include an insistence that women remain in abusive relationships, discouragement from seeking counseling, blaming the victim for the abuse, and conducting assessments or counseling with the abuser present. Because there is no unified policy for imams regarding how to deal with domestic violence, and no oversight body to regulate how imams and community leaders respond to cases of abuse, responses are varied and inconsistent, often leading to frustration on the part of victims and their advocates (Abdallah 2007; Abugideiri 2007).

At the same time, Muslim women have reported to this author that their imams played critical roles in their ability to leave an abusive relationship, in making them feel supported and validated even when family members have not been supportive, and in pressuring the abusive husband to seek treatment. As imams and community leaders are being confronted with the reality of domestic violence in their communities, they are responding by learning more appropriate methods of intervening and are beginning to collaborate with others who have more expertise in the matter (Faith Trust Institute 2007). Following the murder of Aasiya Hassan in February 2009, many Muslim organizations responded immediately by sending out press statements denouncing the murder and the preceding abuse, while organizations such as the Muslim Alliance of North America have developed healthy marriage initiatives to prevent domestic violence (Grewal 2009), which are being practiced by a growing number of mosques around the country. National organizations such as the Peaceful Families Project and the Islamic Social Services Association have developed resources and training workshops to address the needs of Muslim American communities regarding domestic violence.

The Muslim American community, though widely diverse, is becoming more aware of the phenomenon of domestic violence and its impact. With this growing awareness and understanding has come a response that is beginning to address the needs of those affected by domestic violence. Continuing research must be conducted to determine accurate prevalence rates, to further identify and mitigate risk factors, and to develop best practices for prevention and effective intervention.

Bibliography

Abdallah, Keilani. A peaceful ideal, violent realities. A study on Muslim female domestic violence survivors, in *Change from within. Diverse perspectives on domestic violence in Muslim communities*, ed. M. B. Alkhateeb and S. E. Abugideiri, Great Falls, Va. 2007, 69–89.

Abugideiri, Salma E. Domestic violence among Muslims seeking mental health counseling, in *Change from within. Diverse perspectives on domestic violence in Muslim communities*, ed. M. B. Alkhateeb and S. E. Abugideiri, Great Falls, Va. 2007, 91–115.

Abugideiri, Salma E. Domestic violence in the Muslim community, in *FAVTEA Bulletin*, 2009, <http://favtea.com/news-archives/FallWinter09.pdf> (accessed 19 September 2009).

Abu Ras, Wahiba. Cultural beliefs and service utilization by battered Arab immigrant women, in *Violence Against Women* 13 (2007), 1002–28.

Ahmad, Farah, Sarah Riaz, Paula Barata, and Donna E. Stewart. Patriarchal beliefs and perceptions of abuse among South Asian immigrant women, in *Violence Against Women* 10: 3 (2004), 262–82.

'Alī, 'Abdallah Yūsuf. *The meaning of the holy Qur'ān*, 10th ed., Beltsville, Md. 1999.

Alkhateeb, Maha B. DV organizations serving Muslim women. Preliminary results of a 2009 quantitative survey, Peaceful Families Project, 2009, <http://www.peacefulfamilies.org/DVOrgsSurvey.pdf> (29 accessed September 2009).

Alkhateeb, Maha B. and Salma E. Abugideiri. Introduction, in *Change from within. Diverse perspectives on domestic violence in Muslim communities*, ed. M. B. Alkhateeb and S. E. Abugideiri, Great Falls, Va. 2007, 13–30.

Alkhateeb, Sharifa. Ending domestic violence in Muslim families, in *Journal of Religion and Abuse* 1: 44 (1999), 49–59.

Ammar, Nawal H. Simplistic stereotyping and complex reality of Arab-American immigrant identity. Consequences and future strategies in policing wife battery, in *Islam and Christian Muslim Relations* 11 (2000), 51–71.

Ammar, Nawal H. Wife battery in Islam. A comprehensive understanding of interpretations, in *Violence Against Women* 13:5 (2007), 516–526.

Arab American Institute. Arab Americans, <http://www.aaiusa.org/arab-americans/22/demographics> (accessed 13 December 2009).

Ayyub, Rukhsana. Domestic violence in the South Asian Muslim immigrant population in the United States, in *Journal of Social Distress and the Homeless* 9:3 (2000), 237–48.

Bagby, Ihsan, Paul M. Perl, and Bryan T. Froehle. *The mosque in America. A national portrait. A report from the mosque study project*, Washington, D.C., 26 April 2001, <http://www.cair.com/Portals/0/pdf/The_Mosque_in_America_A_National_Portrait.pdf> (accessed 15 September 2009).

Bakhtiar, Laleh (trans.). *The sublime Quran*, Chicago 2007.

Collins, Karen S., Cathy Schoen, Susan Joseph, Lisa Duchon, Elisabeth Simantov, and Michele Yellowitz. *Health concerns across a woman's lifespan. The Commonwealth Fund 1998 survey of women's health*, New York, May 1999, <http://www.cmwf.org/publications/publications_show.htm?doc_id=221554> (accessed 13 December 2009).

Dasgupta, Shamita. Charting the course. An overview of domestic violence in the South Asian community in the United States, in *Journal of Social Distress and the Homeless* 9:3 (2000), 173–85.

Esposito, John L. *The future of Islam*, Oxford and New York 2010.

FaithTrust Institute and Peaceful Families Project, *Garments for one another. Ending domestic violence in Muslim families*, (DVD and study guide), Seattle, Wash. 2007.

Family Violence Prevention Fund. Get the facts. The facts on domestic, dating, and sexual violence, <http://endabuse.org/content/action_center/detail/754> (accessed 13 December 2009).

Ghayyur, Taha. Domestic violence survey analysis February–March 2009, in *SoundVision*, 2009, <www.soundvision.com/cgi-bin/print.asp?url=/info/domestic violence/2009survey.asp> (accessesd 31 July 2009).

Grewal, Zareena. *Death by culture? How not to talk about Islam and domestic violence*, July 2009, <http://ispu.org/files/PDFs/ISPU%20-%20Domestic%20Violence.pdf> (accessed 19 September 2009).

Halabu, Hilda. Domestic violence in the Arab American community, Ph.D. diss., University of Michigan 2006.

Leonard, Karen I. *Muslims in the United States. The state of research*, New York 2003.

Kasturirangan, Arati, Sandhya Krishnan, and Stephanie Riger. The impact of culture and minority status on women's experience of domestic violence, in *Trauma, Violence, & Abuse* 5 (2004), 318–32.

Kulwicki, Anahid D. and June Miller, Domestic violence in the Arab American population. Transforming environmental conditions through community education, in *Issues in Mental Health Nursing* 20 (1999), 199–215.

Maker, Azmairi H., Priti V. Shah, and Zia Agha. Child physical abuse. Prevalence, characteristics, predictors, and beliefs about parent–child violence in South Asian, Middle Eastern, East Asian, and Latina women in the United States, in *Journal of Interpersonal Violence* 20 (2005), 1406–28.

Muslim West Facts Project, *Muslim Americans. A national portrait*, 2009, <http://www .muslimwestfacts.com/mwf/116074/Muslim-Americans-National-Portrait.aspx> (accessed 25 September 2009).

Newport, Frank. State of the states. Importance of religion, in *Gallup*, 28 January 2009, <http://www.gallup.com/poll/114022/state-states-importance-religion.aspx> (accessed 13 December 2009).

Pew Forum on Religion and Public Life/US Religious Landscape Survey, *Religious beliefs and practices/Social and political views*, Chapter 1, June 2008, <http://religions.pew forum.org/pdf/report2religious-landscape-study-chapter-1.pdf> (accessed 13 December 2009).

Pew Research Center. *Muslim Americans. Middle class and mostly mainstream*, Washington, D.C., 22 May 2007, <http://pewresearch.org/pubs/483/muslim -americans> (accessed 19 September 2009).

Smith, Jane I. *Islam in America*, New York 1999, 2nd ed. 2010.

Sokoloff, Natalie J. and Ida Dupont. Domestic violence at the intersections of race, class, and gender, in *Violence Against Women* 11 (2005), 38–64.

Turner, Richard B. Mainstream Islam in the African American experience, Muslim American Society, 2004, <http://www.masnet.org/news.asp?id=1572> (accessed 1 November 2009).

Warshaw, Carole and Holly Barnes. Domestic violence, mental health and trauma. Research highlights, Domestic Violence and Mental Health Policy Initiative, April 2003, <http://www.dvmhpi.org/Research%20Highlights.pdf> (accessed 13 December 2009).

The world almanac and book of facts, New York 2009.

Female Genital Cutting

∴

Female Genital Cutting: West Africa

Elizabeth Rosner

Introduction

Female genital cutting (FGC), female genital mutilation (FGM), and female "circumcision," or *l'excision* in francophone countries, is a highly contested practice that continues to be performed throughout parts of West Africa. It is a complex issue, deeply rooted in local conceptions of gender and the body. The recent transnational movement for abandoning FGC seeks to end a practice viewed as violent and harmful while highlighting broader political and social implications. This entry explores the continued practice of FGC throughout West Africa with a focus on its significance in Senegal and The Gambia. It examines religion, ethnicity, political marginality, and the appropriation of human rights discourse as some of the contributing factors leading to FGC's continued importance in shaping individual identities, whether people ultimately retain or reject the practice. International policies directly impact communities throughout West Africa, as national governments and non-governmental organizations (NGOS) establish place-specific human rights policies. While NGOS and governmental agencies continue to advocate for its abandonment, FGC remains an important rite of passage and performance of womanhood for many.

Overview

The World Health Organization (WHO) has estimated that over 100 million women and girls worldwide have undergone FGC. While widely debated, it is still practiced throughout parts of West Africa and is documented in Benin, Burkina Faso, Côte d'Ivoire, The Gambia, Ghana, Guinea, Guinea-Bissau, Mali, Mauritania, Niger, Nigeria, Sierra Leone, Senegal, and Togo. The prevalence of FGC ranges widely in West Africa, from affecting over 80 percent of women and girls in Mali and Guinea to fewer than 10 percent of women in Ghana and Togo. Its pervasiveness varies not only between nations but is also subject to disparities within each country. It is best understood in the context of site-specific religious and ethnic identities rather than national identity alone, which is not the only determining factor. Other variables, including economic status, rural or urban context, as well as education opportunities, have been linked to rates of FGC but cannot be separated from other contributing factors.

© KONINKLIJKE BRILL NV, LEIDEN, 2015 | DOI:10.1163/1872-5309_EWIC_COM_002021

FGC is practiced for reasons stemming from religious and cultural obligations, rites of passage, and reasons of purity, hygiene, and preserving virginity.

A biomedical approach to female genital cutting categorizes all genital modifications into four classifications. Type I defines a procedure altering or completely removing the clitoris, known as clitoridectomy. Type II, or excision, involves a modification or complete removal of the clitoris and the labia minora. The removal of the labia majora may also be a part of this procedure. Type III, or infibulation, is considered the most invasive of the procedures, involving the restricting of the vaginal opening through a seal formed by altering the labia minora or majora. The fourth category catalogs all other female genital operations used for non-medical purposes, including the pricking or incising of the external genitals. All four types of FGC have been documented throughout West Africa, but the occurrence and specific procedure are dependent upon the location and practitioners involved.

The side effects of the practice identified by the World Health Organization include infection, shock, pain, hemorrhaging, infection, with long-term side effects involving cysts, infertility, and complications during childbirth. Reports of decreased sexual pleasure have been documented; however, because of social taboos and the subjective nature of the subject, it is difficult to confirm to what extent. Studies have also shown a correlation between FGC and HIV rates as a result of unsterile environments and tools. Complications of the procedure have, in particular cases, led to death. While the side effects are serious and potentially life-threatening, some scholars critique the validity of statistical studies of the effects of FGC on the grounds of insufficient sample sizes and the failure to consider other contributing environmental and health factors affecting mortality rates.

While 15 African countries have outlawed the practice, including Benin, Burkina Faso, Côte d'Ivoire, Ghana, Guinea, Niger, Nigeria, Senegal, and Togo, FGC still occurs. Laws often have little impact at the local level given that many practicing communities are in rural areas, far from the reaches of government officials. National legislature may serve as an ideological stance, aligning nations with international policies rather than rather than creating feasible laws. Where legislation exists, limited judicial options for prosecuting those who practice FGC may inhibit enforcement. Without state monitoring, local civic and spiritual leaders are charged with policing and addressing these issues. The difficulty remains in changing the perceptions of local leaders so that they stand in solidarity with national policies. Female genital cutting is so deeply grounded into community life that practitioners knowingly break the law in order to enact what they view as an indispensable component of being a woman. While Senegal and The Gambia share common national borders, the prevalence, reasons, and programs for ending the practice diverge greatly.

FGC and Human Rights Agendas

Although there is evidence showing that international organizations have known about female genital cutting from as early as the 1950s, it is an issue recently problematized as a violation of human rights. By the late 1990s, the United Nations shifted its attention to women's social and economic development. A woman's economic opportunities coincide with her ability to make other decisions about her well-being, leading to self-empowerment and more informed decision-making. The 1995 Fourth World Conference on Women hosted by the United Nations in Beijing was a groundbreaking international event that discussed and established the groundwork for a transnational feminist movement. The declaration from the conference states that the creation of economic opportunities for women contributes to worldwide gender equality. Economic prosperity and self-reliance will enable women to make decisions regarding their own sexual and reproductive health. The preservation of one's bodily autonomy is not just an issue of women's rights but of universal human rights. NGOs, aid organizations, and international governing bodies have prioritized women's rights as human rights by establishing policies which protect women and girls from acts of sexual violence including FGC and child marriage.

Policies, laws, and programs framed to eradicate FGC as human rights violation do not alone deter individuals from ending the practice. Studies have shown that while individuals may be aware of the existence of the ban on FGC, few understand the details of the law or the consequences of legal persecution. While it has caused some to continue in secrecy, other families will travel across borders where it is not illegal to have the procedure done. This is an issue of growing concern in the diaspora of Western Europe, as families will send their children to be circumcised in countries where the practice is still legal. The laws are being challenged in some instances because it is perceived as another form of Western neo-colonialism rather than a reflection of place-specific processes and structures.

The establishment of laws and policies, however, does not accurately reflect the internal struggles women and their families face when deciding whether or not to excise their daughters. The debate occurs in both private and public domains as individuals and families make decisions affecting their daughters. Anti-FGC laws support the messages of abandonment campaigns and justify the total abandonment of the practice for families who were struggling with the decision. Acknowledging the challenges individuals face in making these decisions, and providing room for these opinions to waiver, undermines the commonly perceived dichotomy presented in scholarship and media.

Multiple agencies and NGOs including the United Nations Population Fund Africa (UNFPA), the United Nations Children's Fund (UNICEF), the World Health Organization, Tostan, the Orchid Project, and World Vision, among others, have executed interventions throughout West Africa. Anti-FGC campaigns have historically failed to convince communities to abandon a necessary rite of passage. Accusations of reinstating Western, colonial views of the female body onto African women have been a major criticism of these organizations. Programs apply different approaches including payment to excisers to stop working, retraining performers of FGC so that they have alternative economic means, community meetings, education classes, and lobbying for national legislation. The lack of success of many programs is often due to their approach and their failure to convince communities to abandon what they view as a necessary rite of passage for young girls to become gendered women in the community. With the influx of foreign NGOs, many communities feel that the individuals conducting these programs have little connection to those at the center of these debates and do not grasp the significance of the ritual within the cultural context. NGOs who have been successful tend to focus on changing cultural norms through the use of public anti-FGC declaration ceremonies and the redirection of social pressures to have girl children undergo FGC.

In order to facilitate change, NGOs are increasingly using the visual and performing arts as tools for addressing the taboo subject. The radio, for instance, serves as a practical means of disseminating information to larger audiences quickly. Other forms of visual and performing arts are used to demonstrate the compatibility of human rights agendas with local contexts. Many organizations turn to folkloric music and dance during classes and at public declaration ceremonies whereby communities denounce the practice of genital cutting. Public performances may encourage local ownership over the decision to end FGC within a community and can be seen as facilitating a transfer of power to participants in NGO programs. Other organizations such as Tostan, World Vision, the Orchid Project, and the UNFPA partner with popular musicians such as Senegalese hip-hop artist Sister Fa as a way of connecting to the interests of young people. Within popular music performances, musicians address the goals of human rights interventions by framing them in a culturally appropriate and more broadly appealing manner. The aim of many organizations is to promote human rights agendas through education programs in the hope that communities will change their cultural practices, and are doing so, through the adoption and appropriation of local art forms.

FEMALE GENITAL CUTTING: WEST AFRICA   189

FGC and Religion

Female genital cutting is a rite of passage a young girl must complete to be considered a fully developed woman within the community. The act of altering a girl's genitals is a physical change that marks her as an adult, ready for marriage and childbirth. Many anti-FGC campaigns fail to recognize the symbolic importance of FGC, leading to the ineffectiveness of programs that assume individuals can abruptly change their worldview. Anti-FGC programs do not just end a cultural practice, but a central symbol representing foundational aspects of the female experience. NGOs with the most success acknowledge the cultural significance of FGC while rearticulating social norms without the necessity for it to occur. As the lives of African women change based on economic and social development, so will gender beliefs and practices.

Communities throughout West Africa are more frequently citing religious obligation as the rationale for FGC. Traditionally, girls would not be circumcised individually but instead in groups where they would be isolated for days or weeks. FGC would be but part of a larger ritual that involves preparing a girl for the responsibilities of womanhood. The more individualized practice of FGC reflects the cultivation of new forms of subjectivity that result from globalization and the spread of world religions. Some religious communities view FGC as a religious obligation intended for preparing girls for life as pious, productive members of society. Female genital cutting is not a static tradition; it instead fluctuates within cultural and historical contexts.

Although some Christian communities have been known to practice it, Western media have increasingly connected FGC to Islamic obligation. The Qur'an does not mention FGC; however, the association with Islam is challenged. A passage in the Hadith forms the basis of the dispute and translates to "Reduce, but do not destroy." The Prophet Muhammad purportedly made this statement to a midwife who conducted pharaonic infibulation in Medina; there are multiple interpretations and variations in circulation. Its presence in the Hadith is used to argue for FGC as Sunna, or religious tradition based on Muhammad's actions. Another position views the passage as allowing FGC, but only less invasive forms compared to Type III or pharaonic infibulation. Those who do not consider FGC to be a religious obligation either interpret the passage as an overt disapproval of the rite or inconclusive evidence regarding Muhammad's beliefs and therefore not Sunna.

FGC is not a specifically Islamic practice as there is evidence of its practice prior to the Islamization of sub-Saharan Africa. There is no definitive connection between FGC and Islam in religious texts, and yet it has become a real part of Islamic practices for many communities such as the Jola in Senegal and Mandinka in The Gambia. It is a vital part of becoming a devout Muslim regardless of its appearance in religious texts. While men play a significant role in perpetuating a culture that views FGC as the social norm, it is important to recognize that FGC is often a woman-centered and perpetuated tradition. Women are the excisers and the cultural bearers of the tradition who adopt it for multiple reasons. A discussion of FGC in relation to Islam requires a nuanced approach because it can reinforce a homogeneous and inaccurate image of Islam. Instead of being an active participant, the Muslim woman becomes a homogenized symbol of patriarchal oppression when viewed through this lens. Rather than condemn a singular vision of Islam which promotes FGC, it must be understood within a specific geographic and historic space. Wolof are predominantly Muslim and yet in general reject FGC, whereas other ethnic groups such as the Mandinka have interwoven pre-Islamic traditions such as FGC into modern Islamic practices to address their changing identities and shifting gender roles.

The Gambia

In The Gambia, a recent study reveals that approximately 76.3 percent of women aged 15–49 of both Christian and Islamic backgrounds undergo FGC. The Mandinka ethnic groups, however, comprises the ethnic majority with 40 percent of the total population. FGC is common practice amongst approximately 98 percent of the ethnic majority. Other practicing ethnic groups in The Gambia include Fula and Wolof, as well as ethnic minorities such as the Sarahule, Serer, Aku, Tilibonka, and Karonika. Approximately 10.6 percent of the population is made up of the Jola and Karonika communities combined. The procedure identified as Type II or excision is most commonly practiced in The Gambia.

According to a survey of Gambians practicing FGC, 90 percent of the given population identifies as Muslim and correlates their Muslim faith to the practice. In contrast to other African countries, there is a higher rate of younger Gambian women, under the age of 49, who have experienced FGC as a result of the abandonment of the practice in many other communities throughout West Africa. The ritual can be traced back to pre-colonial times and has become closely associated with Muslim devotion although it is performed by some Christian communities as well. A Muslim woman is expected to undergo FGC if she is going to be accepted as a religious woman in her community.

Unlike many neighboring countries, there is no national ban on FGC in The Gambia. In 1999, Gambian President Yaya Jammeh argued that FGC is a definitive part of Gambian culture and undergoing it is a decision Gambian women make for themselves. Jammeh's statement was in reaction to Senegal's federal ban on the cultural rite as well as to the influx of foreign NGOs in the area. While the official positioning of the government in power focuses on FGC as a significant cultural practice and encourages people to make autonomous decisions, the vice president has more decidedly supported the eradication of this practice. The retention of FGC, despite international pressure, functions as a political tool and symbol referring to the rejection or adoption of Western assumptions and values with an emphasis on Gambian nationalism. Genital cutting is imbued with not only personal or local meaning, but national importance.

There is no national support in the form of legislation for abandoning FGC. However, in recent years, the office of the vice president as well as government organizations such as the National Women's Bureau have partnered with NGOs to establish campaigns throughout the country. Tostan began their Community Empowerment Program in The Gambia in 2007 and continue to work with 32 communities of varying ethnic diversity in the hope that they create generational change and ensure that younger generations will no longer continue with the tradition through human rights education programs. Most recently, they have established a community meeting of both southern Senegalese and northern Gambian communities to jointly discuss human rights issues, including the abandonment of FGC.

Mandinka

The Mandinka comprise the ethnic majority in The Gambia and the great majority of Mandinka women practice FGC, stating religious obligations as a fundamental reason. While formerly it was a part of a rite of passage, scholars have noted that more girls are being excised without the accompaniment of a ritual and instead are being cut at earlier ages. A common trope in practicing communities is to cut girls at earlier ages individually without the ritual itself partly due to the emphasis placed on individual expression of religious devotion as well as the fear of legal repercussions from governing bodies.

While some find their Mandinka and Muslim identities analogous, Manding identity in its modern context was founded in the nineteenth and twentieth centuries during various conflicts and the conversion of Mande states to Islam. In regard to Mandinka women, FGC is viewed as a vehicle for physically expressing religious devotion, and as a necessity for women to be able to pray effectively. It allows women to participate in religious prayer while menstruation and childbearing often exclude them from the same religious obligations as men. The rite can be partly read as a form of female assertion of power through the physical inscription on their bodies as it alters their participation in religious and other social contexts. To not be excised is to be considered unclean and improper. Community beliefs establish cultural norms in which all girls are expected to undergo FGC if they are to become pious Muslim women. Because of the cultural debate concerning FGC, NGOs now focus on developing new rites that do not involve genital cutting while still promoting cultural identity. The Association for Promoting Girls' and Women's Advancement in The Gambia (APGWA), for example, restores the importance of the ritual by creating youth camps where girls are initiated without being circumcised. In The Gambia, the debate concerning FGC is most often a discussion of maintaining cultural identity, as it is elsewhere. The symbols of rites of passage are changed to fit a new context and resist pressures to abandon a former symbol of womanhood.

GAMCOTRAP

The Gambia Committee on Traditional Practices (GAMCOTRAP) was established in 1984 to investigate and create awareness regarding traditional practices impacting on women's sexual and reproductive health, including the practice of FGC and the spread of HIV/AIDS. The non-profit is one of the leading organizations focusing on FGC abandonment in The Gambia, working with traditional excisers and communities. GAMCOTRAP works with religious advisers to talk about FGC in a culturally sensitive manner, focusing on educating women and men about the dangers of the practice while addressing its role and incompatibility within Islam. The organization represents a grassroots campaign to engage both women and men in the discussion, providing a space to break the cultural taboo of silence surrounding the issue.

The first public declaration of FGC abandonment took place in 2007 in an event held by the NGO called Drop the Knife. Seven districts participated in the declaration ceremony including excisers, community members, and local cultural groups. The ceremony was the result of a three-day training session with excisers who were targeted by GAMCOTRAP. Many excisers rely for their livelihoods on the money they earn from performing FGC and so the organization established the Alternative Employment Opportunities Project (AEO), which provided excisers with alternative training and skills for economic growth that does not involve excising. The Drop the Knife celebration occurred again in 2009, with 60 excisers and 351 communities declaring their abandonment of FGC.

Senegal

Despite large-scale investment from the national government and external sources, female genital cutting continues to be practiced in Senegal and is similarly linked to Islamic practices and rites of passage with 94 percent of the population identifying as Muslim. According to a 2014 national study, 25.7 percent of Senegalese women reported having personally experienced it. Among these women, mostly Muslim Soninke, Manding, and Pulaar populations widely practice FGC. In 2014, 29 percent of Muslim women indicated undergoing FGC as compared to 11 percent of Christian women and 16 percent of animist women. Wolof are the ethnic majority in Senegal and although largely Muslim, rarely practice female genital cutting, representing the tension and contradiction of associating FGC as a universal tenet of Islam. Jola communities in the Casamance, who comprise approximately 5 percent of the Senegalese population, count nearly 60 percent of women as having undergone excision. Populations performing FGC in Senegal most commonly practice Types II and III dependent upon ethnicity and geographic location. FGC has a significantly higher rate of occurrence in the southern and eastern states of Matam, Tambacounda, Kedougou, Kolda, Sedihou, and Ziguinchor regions than in the northern and western regions of the country including Thies, Fatick, Koalack, Diorbel, Louga, and Saint Louis. The areas with the lowest reporting of FGC include the capital city of Dakar and the central state of Kaffrine.

In 1997, the women of Malicounda, Senegal publicly declared their abandonment of female genital cutting. The women of the rural village were working with the Senegalese-based human rights organization Tostan at the time. The NGO previously taught non-formal education classes in literacy and finance until the women asked for a module on women's health. The unit included a discussion of FGC and the bio-medical risks it carries. As a result of this course and the conversation it started, both men and women in the community pledged to abandon FGC, encouraging neighboring villages to follow suit. The declaration ceremony was the first public denunciation of its kind in Senegal and was important because the community of Malicounda made the decision themselves, without government or NGO intervention.

The FGC controversy is an international conversation, including political, economic, and social pressures, and the Senegalese government has coordinated a response. Senegal nationally banned FGC soon after Hillary Clinton's speech in 1998 declaring FGC an act of injustice towards women and young girls, coinciding with the release of the US foreign aid for the coming year. In 2010, the *Plan d'action national pour l'accélération de l'abandon de l'excision 2010–2015* was created by the Senegalese national government for ending FGC within Senegal by the year 2015. The national plan was influenced by Tostan's model and sought to mobilize targeted communities and states where FGC is practiced by utilizing NGOs, communities, and local governments in educating individuals about human rights agendas.

Jola

The Jola are an ethnic minority in the Lower Casamance region of Senegal who did not adopt FGC until the conversion to Islam as recently as the 1940s. They practice female genital cutting in an effort to prove themselves good Muslims. Jola sought out aspects of Islam from dominant neighboring Manding communities following the proselytization by marabouts in the late nineteenth and early twentieth centuries. Through the process of adopting Manding cultural practices and religion, new constructions of gender and gendered performance were developed. The women's circumcision ritual is an essential part of contemporary Jola communities, and this reflects its function within the gendered spaces of everyday life. FGC becomes an expression of one's womanhood and ultimately one's place within the social hierarchy. Anti-FGC programs argue for the abandonment of the cultural practice and the abandonment of aspects of Jola constructions of womanhood.

Jola participate in *sunay*, or clitoridectomy, in bio-medical terms, borrowing the practice from Mandinka women as part of a larger initiation practice for women. The adoption of FGC is recent in some Jola communities as a form of Muslim obligation. The naming of the practice as *sunay* makes a clear connection to Islamic Sunna. Women believe that FGC is an expression of female Muslim devotion, maintaining that they must undergo the procedure in order to have their prayers heard. The adoption of Islam and Manding cultural traits has altered both male and female rite of passage ceremonies and served to place Jola communities in alignment with those historically with the most political power. Men and women do not lose their ethnic identity as a result of cultural adaption but instead inform their customary practices with new traditions, reflective of new social structures and hierarchies.

The southern region of Senegal, known as the Casamance, is geographically and culturally distant from the northern political center of Senegalese life. The Casamance maintained relative control during the colonial era because of its distance from the French colonizers in the north. After independence, the Casamance remained autonomous, separate from the northern part of the country. Casamançais people felt that the government had failed to address or consider their needs for economic development. This distance has created tensions within Senegal, as communities feel marginalized by ruling ethnic

FEMALE GENITAL CUTTING: WEST AFRICA

groups in the north. With over 90 percent of the Senegalese population identifying as Muslim, Jola were, until recently, marginalized in both religious and geographical spheres.

Ziguinchor, the capital of the Casamance state, is targeted as one of the twelve intervention sites for national abandonment of FGC. A national ban does not affect Wolof communities in the northern part of the country, instead disproportionately affecting Jola and Mandinka living in the Casamance. While Jola adopt Islam, their profession of faith through FGC is in opposition to a national law, which furthers cultural and political tensions between the northern and southern regions. The federal ban in Senegal reinforces transnational policies on human rights and women's health but also reiterates a political message, which targets communities with little impact on governmental discourse. As a marginalized community, Jola adopted Islam in order to become closer in proximity to power in the manner of neighboring ethnic groups. The act of abandoning the process again concerns power relations because it aligns Jola with the dominant values of the country and national legislation.

Tostan

Tostan has successfully convinced communities to abandon FGC through a grassroots approach. The organization claims that their aim is not to end female genital cutting but to empower communities to make their own informed decisions. The organization, founded by former Peace Corps worker Molly Melching, prides itself on being Senegalese-based and focusing on local interests. Tostan provides education modules on women's health comprising a unit concerning the bio-medical risks of FGC. Community leaders including imams are brought in to speak about the harmful effects of FGC as well as child marriage. The engagement of religious and civic leaders serves as an important component in empowering communities to sustain significant change.

Currently, 175 communities in Senegal are involved in Tostan's Community Empowerment Program. At the end of the three-year program, members of the community can officially announce their abandonment of the practice. This may result in a community-wide declaration of abandonment of female genital cutting after completing the process of health care education with Tostan activists. The NGO also offers classes in parenting, sustainable agriculture, finance, and literacy, believing that a holistic human rights education is the path to locally-driven, long-term change.

Tostan's philosophy requires the entire community to abandon female genital cutting, not just the pledges of a few individuals. Public declaration ceremonies involve the whole community and take place in front of representatives from neighboring villages. At the end of Tostan's program, a committee of community members is placed in charge of monitoring the town, ensuring the enforcement of the declaration. At these public declaration ceremonies, folkloric music and dance as well as declarations from local leaders are important components of the public event. The NGO enables communities to regulate themselves by establishing local committees charged with ensuring the abandonment of FGC, putting into place new structures of power and accountability. Studies have found that Tostan's Community Empowerment Program has not completely eradicated FGC but has had a profound impact in communities, citing a decrease from 54 percent to 40 percent in FGC rates from women who participated in the program.

Conclusions

Female genital cutting is a controversial practice, in which locally and historically specific contexts are needed for understanding the complexity of the issue. It encompasses a variety of genital modification procedures and serves multiple purposes for practicing communities. For many families, the justifications for FGC are varied but often concern the preparation of a girl child for a successful life in a community where social norms dictate it. Reasons for continuing the rite include, among others, religious obligation, assertion of gendered experience, rite of passage, and political considerations. FGC continues to be practiced throughout parts of West Africa although the transnational intervention coupled with the inflence of NGOs and other local initiatives are changing the climate and culture surrounding the practice. Local initiatives encourage the cessation of FCG while developing new practices such as the youth camps in The Gambia which allow women to retain their cultural identity and reclaim bodily autonomy.

FGC remains contentious because human rights agendas juxtapose human rights against core beliefs about the female body and performance of womanhood. Anti-FGC programs do not end just a discrete cultural practice, but also a core symbol representing the fundamental aspects of women's experience. NGOs finding most success acknowledge the cultural significance of FGC and attempt to replace the ritual with alternative but locally grounded gendering practices, which demonstrate that human rights agendas are applicable in local contexts, rather than being another form of Western encroachment in the area. Continuing financial support and pressure to end the practice in the diaspora complicates the issue by taking a practice out of its site-specific context and discussing it on a transnational level in terms of human rights violations.

FEMALE GENITAL CUTTING: WEST AFRICA

While FGC is discussed elsewhere, it continues to be debated within West African countries. Factors of religion, ethnicity, location, and political marginality all affect the reasons for continuing to engage in the practice of female genital cutting, as well as the motivations for convincing communities to comply with international human rights policies by ending it. As governments, human rights NGOs and other aid organizations continue to work with, rather than against, practicing communities, the form and significance of the rites of passage will also change, as they have previously.

Bibliography

Diop, Nafissatou J. and Ian Askew. Strategies for encouraging the abandonment of female genital cutting. Experiences from Senegal, Burkina Faso, and Mali, in *Female circumcision. Multicultural perspectives*, ed. Rogaia Mustafa Abusharaf, Philadelphia 2006, 125–41.

Diop, Ndeye Khady. Plan d'action national pour l'accélération de l'abandon de l'excision 2010–2015, Ministère de la Famille, de la Sécurité alimentaire, de l'Entrepreneuriat féminin, de la Microfinance et de la Petite enfance. République du Sénégal 2005, <http://tostan.org/sites/default/files/imce/PLAN%20D'ACTION%20 EXCISION%20version%20imprimée.pdf>, accessed 6 March 2014.

Easton, Peter, Karen Monkman and Rebecca Miles. Social policy from the bottom up. Abandoning FGC in Sub-Saharan Africa, in *Development in Practice* 13 (November 2003), 445–58.

Gambia Committee on Traditional Practices Affecting the Health of Women and Children. Organization profile, <http://www.gamcotrap.gm/>, accessed 7 June 2014.

Gillespie, Diane and Molly Melching. The transformative power of democracy and human rights education. The case of Tostan, in *Adult Education Quarterly* 60 (2010), 477–98.

Gruenbaum, Ellen. *The female circumcision controversy. An anthropological perspective*, Philadelphia 2001.

Hernlund, Ylva. Cutting without ritual and ritual without cutting. Female "circumcision" and the re-ritualization of initiation in the Gambia, in *Female "circumcision" in Africa. Culture, controversy and change*, ed. Ylva Hernlund and Bettina Shell-Duncan, London 2000, 235–52.

Hernlund, Ylva and Bettina Shell-Duncan. Contingency, context, and change. Negotiating female genital cutting in Senegal, in *Africa Today* 53:4 (Summer 2007), 43–57.

Jain, Devaki. *Women, development, and the UN. A sixty-year quest for equality and justice*. Bloomington, Ind. 2005.

Johnson, Michelle. Making Mandinga or making Muslims? Debating female circumcision, ethnicity, and Islam in Guinea-Bissau and Portugal, in *Transcultural bodies. Female genital cutting in global contexts*, ed. Ylva Hernlund and Bettina Shell-Duncan, New Brunswick 2007, 202–23.

Koroma, J. M. *Female genital mutilation in The Gambia. A desk review*, Banjul, The Gambia 2002, <http://www.unicef.org/wcaro/wcaro_gambia_FGM_Desk_Review.pdf>, accessed 7 June 2014.

Monjok, Emmanuel et al. Female genital mutilation. Potential for HIV in Sub-Saharan Africa and prospect for epidemiologic investigation and intervention, in *African Journal of Reproductive Health* 11:1 (April 2007), 33–42.

Orchid Project. Country file. The Gambia, <http://orchidproject.org/category/resources/country-pages/page/8/>, accessed 10 February 2014.

Shell-Duncan, Bettina et al. Legislating change? Responses to criminalizing female genital cutting in Senegal, in *Law and Society Review* 47 (2013), 803–35.

Shweder, Richard A. What about "female genital mutilation"? And why understanding culture matters in the first place, in *Daedalus* 129:4 (Fall 2000), *The end of tolerance. Engaging cultural differences*, 209–32.

Tostan. Senegal, <http://www.tostan.org/country/senegal>, accessed 26 February 2014.

UNICEF. Female genital mutilation/cutting. A statistical overview and exploration of the dynamics of change, <http://data.unicef.org/corecode/uploads/document6/uploaded_pdfs/corecode/FGMC_Lo_res_Final_26.pdf>, accessed July 2013.

United Nations. Beijing Declaration and Platform for Action, in United Nations Entity for Gender Equality and the Empowerment of Women, 1995, <http://www.un.org/womenwatch/daw/beijing/pdf/BDPfA%20E.pdf>, accessed 14 October 2014.

United Nations. Resolution on Ending Female Genital Mutilation, 2008, <http://www.un.org/womenwatch/daw/csw/csw52/AC_resolutions/Final%20L2%20ending%20female%20genital%20mutilation%20-%20advance%20unedited.pdf>, accessed 14 October 2014.

World Health Organization. Female Genital Mutilation Fact Sheet, <http://www.who.int/mediacentre/factsheets/fs241/en/>, accessed 10 February 2014.

Funerary Practices

∵

Funerary Rites for Women Victims of "Honor Killings": Indus Valley

Ghazala Anwar

Introduction

It is the right of a child and a father to know of and honor their biological bond. Mechanisms for ascertaining biological paternity need not be violent or restrictive toward the mother. In patriarchal societies, however, this right becomes an oppressive metasymbol that forms the cornerstone of an integrated system of subjugation, domination, and oppression of women, an extreme form of which is the ritualized killing of women suspected of infidelity in order to protect male honor. Pakistan may have the highest per capita incidence of honor killings in the world (Knudsen 2004, 2), despite the fact that this practice is believed by a majority of Muslims to violate the teachings of the Qur'ān and the Sunna. It also violates contemporary international standards of justice.

Qur'ān and *Ḥadīth* on "Honor Killings"

> The testimony of men who accuse their wives but do not have any witnesses except themselves is to testify by Allah four times that he is being truthful, and a fifth time that the curse of Allah will be upon him, if he should be a liar. She will avoid punishment if she testifies by Allah four times that he is a liar, and a fifth time, that the wrath of Allah shall be upon her if he should be telling the truth.
>
> Qur'ān 24:6

Contemporary Pakistani religious scholars agree that in Islam, a person who witnesses a relative engaged in illicit sexual behavior does not have the right to kill him or her (National Commission on the Status of Women 2005, 38). The Qur'ān verses related to adultery (after it has been established through due judicial process) prescribe a punishment of one hundred lashes or forgiveness for those who repent (Anwar 2006). Thus medieval *sharī'a* law's penalty of stoning to death for adultery would appear to be against both the letter and the spirit of the Qur'ān. Moreover, the procedural requirement by *sharī'a* law

© KONINKLIJKE BRILL NV, LEIDEN, 2010 | DOI:10.1163/1872-5309_EWIC_EWICCOM_0654

of four eyewitnesses makes a conviction of adultery impossible in the case of private sexual contact between consenting adults.

> The sunna with us is that those who curse each other [after an accusation of infidelity] may never return to be remarried. If the man calls himself a liar [takes back his accusation], he is flogged with the ḥadd-punishment, and the child [whose paternity he had questioned] is given to him, and his wife can never return to him [otherwise the child is given to the mother].
>
> IBN MĀLIK 1982, 263–64

There is no concept of male or family honor in the Qur'ān and the *ḥadīth*, neither is reproduction a concern. Suspicion of infidelity is grounds for dissolution of marriage but not for the murder of the suspected wife. Moreover, early Muslim jurists agreed that when a woman accused of adultery or a child born of adultery dies they are to be given a normal burial. "Ibn Mālik [said], 'I have not seen any person of knowledge disapproving of praying over either a child born of adultery or its mother'" (Ibn Mālik 1982, 113).

The Sindhi Custom of *karo kari*

The psychosocial complex of *karo kari*, enforced by death, restricts a woman's autonomy over her own body, sexuality, and life and demands her complete subordination to the male members of her family. Marital infidelity or engagement in extramarital sex is the main reason for the accusation of *karo* (blackened or shamed man) or *kari* (blackened or shamed woman), but there are many other recognized grounds for leveling this charge against a person. A woman's right to marry against the will of the family, to refuse a forced marriage, to divorce, and to live after being raped, while categorically recognized under Islamic law and international human rights conventions, are all denied by tribal customary laws governing female sexuality. Any woman asserting her right in these matters may be seen as compromising the family honor, declared *kari*, and murdered by the family. Since no evidence is required to bring an accusation of *karo kari* against another, it serves as a convenient cover for murders motivated by reasons that would not be justifiable even under tribal custom. The following are some of the hidden motives documented in the case of *karo kari* murders: a male enemy was declared *karo* with a woman from the accuser's family, and both were killed; a woman who refused to work for the local landlord without pay was called *kari* and beaten to death; a woman who incurred severe physical disability through domestic violence was declared *kari* by the husband and killed; a man killed his divorced first wife as *kari* in order to prevent her from marrying a second time; a female family member was killed as *kari* to prevent her from marrying and taking her share of family property with her; a woman was killed as *kari* in order to extract money from the accused man, the *karo*; and a woman was killed as *kari* by her relatives because they wanted to obtain a woman in compensation from the accused *karo's* family (National Commission on the Status of Women 2005, 39–43). The life of a woman in rural Sindh may be of less worth to the man who rules over her than that of a domestic animal. Women in certain districts of rural Sindh live under the constant fear of the fatal consequences of an arbitrary accusation of adultery or fornication. Many are murdered with impunity in the name of male honor. Everyone this author interviewed in Sukkur city and region knew women victims of *karo kari* who had been murdered and their bodies disposed off unceremoniously in a river or a ditch. The woman was never mentioned again. One poor woman was accused of being *kari*, completely unexpectedly by her husband, while she prepared the morning tea for her family. She then had to leave immediately and seek refuge in the house of the tribal elder (*sardar*). Her older sister had been accused of being *kari* and had been murdered. She did not know where her sister was buried. In her case, however, a settlement was reached, and she was later married off to a widower significantly older than herself.

The ritualized violence of *karo kari* involves five key parties: the accuser/aggressor; the *kari* (accused woman/victim) and the *karo* (accused man/victim); the families of the aforementioned three parties and the community; the *jirga* (all-male tribal council); and the police and justice system. Any man may accuse his wife or sister of being an adultress or fornicatress, *kari*, without having to provide any evidence. The customary principle is that if a man accuses his wife of having committed adultery even with the wooden leg of a *charpoy* (traditional rope bed), she is deemed an adultress. His is the last word. Nothing she can say or do will prove her innocence, and the accusation may be made at any time with no prior notice. The husband or brother who levels the charge and even murders the *kari*, expects to gain money or young virgins or both from the family of the *karo*, and he may be elevated to the status of a local hero.

A woman accused of being *kari* faces the possibility of death, the loss of her children and family, bonded labor, sexual slavery, and sale to an older man. If she has no education, no personal income, and no way to travel far away, then even if she escapes death, she will not escape the other consequences. Interviewees commented that the irony is that the women who actually engage in adultery, those who are better-off in socioeconomic terms, are usually not the ones who are accused of being *kari*. This suggests that the death penalty is not so much a deterrent against adultery but rather a means of violating and abusing the most vulnerable women. The *karo*, for his part, faces death, harassment, mental torture, destruction and loss of property, and the "payment" of female members of his family to the accuser. However, because men are more mobile and have more access to resources than women, they are more likely to escape and to ransom their lives by giving their property and/or their virgin sisters to the accuser.

The family of the *kari* often hesitates to give shelter to their daughter or sister because this would make their homes a target of violence by the accuser and other villagers who may rise to support him. That is why a poor accused woman can only find refuge in the mansion of a *sardar*. However if her family is educated, urbanized, and stands by her, and if the community sees it as a clearly unfounded accusation, the accused woman might be able to live out her life with her family of origin though it is quite possible that she may never see her children again. The family of the *karo* often consents to the transfer of its property and the "marriage" of one of its young girls to the accuser if that is the only way to save his life. One such family, which was forced to give away a young girl to save a wrongly accused son, went on to educate their remaining daughters and sons who then formed an organization dedicated to the eradication of the custom of *karo kari*.

The *jirga* reflects the mentality, perspectives, wisdom, and compassion, or lack thereof, of the men who sit in judgment. The *jirga* is paid for its services by the disputants and solves problems at a local level. It is an alternative to a costly, ineffective, and equally discriminatory court and justice system. Since *jirga*s are embedded in the local tribal system they can be more effective than the police and courts. In the absence of governance and rule of law they are a much needed stopgap measure. However, they uphold a system of tribal retributive justice that perpetuates the cycle of violence and is considered grossly iniquitous by both Qur'ān and international standards. The tribal *sardar*s, who are also feudal landlords, confine the accused women in their mansions if they survive the accusation. Whereas this may be seen as providing shelter for the accused woman, in practice it may amount to bonded labor and even sexual slavery till she is sold off to an older man who lacks the means to secure a virgin. There are many women in illegal confinement in rural Sindh. Recently some *jirga*s have discontinued the practice of giving away minor girls from the family of the accused *karo* to the accuser/murderer as part of the settlement. But in general the transfer of girls to the family of the accuser persists.

The police and justice system, the last actor in this ritual of violence and violation, is either far removed and inactive or tends to collaborate with the accuser/murderer (Burney 1999; Khan 2006, 225–52). According to those interviewed by this author, at times the murderer bribed the police beforehand to keep them out of what he considered his personal business. Current laws and customs protect the murderer and there is hardly ever a conviction (Knudsen 2004). Through defense under "sudden provocation" and through the *razinama* (settlement between the families) the murderer is never brought to justice (Shah and Malick 2002). He is either never arrested or is released after a few days or months and may even become a local hero. The attitude of the men who judge the case in their capacity as police, judges, or elders is "Why kill a man for the sake of a mere woman?"

Funerary Rites for *kari*s

Funerary rites honor the life of the deceased and console the families by responding with reverence and beauty to the seemingly insurmountable grief that accompanies an ultimate loss. No specific funerary rites are mentioned in the Qur'ān except for the instruction to the Prophet not to pray over the bodies of hypocrites and wrongdoers who strove to undermine his mission while pretending to be his followers:

> And never [O Muḥammad] pray [funeral prayer] for any of them [hypocrites] who dies, nor stand at his grave. Certainly they disbelieved in Allah and His Messenger, and died while they were *fāsiqūn* (wrongdoers).
> Qur'ān 9:84

The majority of Muslims agree that a person enters the fold of Islam by declaring "There is no god but God and Muhammad is the Prophet of God," and that it is impossible to ascertain the state of faith of a Muslim, for only God knows and is able to judge what is in a person's heart. Thus the Qur'ānic instruction to the Prophet not to pray over the bodies of hypocrites cannot be generalized to include all Muslims. Moreover, as seen in the earlier quotation, Ibn Mālik's juristic opinion specifically allows for funerary prayers for children born of adultery and their mothers.

The Prophet performed funerary rites (*ṣalāt al-janāza*) not only for Muslims but also for members of other faith communities. He prayed in absentia, in Medina, for the soul of Najashi, the Christian king who protected the first Meccan Muslim refugees, on the day of his demise in his native Abyssinia (Ibn Mālik 1982, 112). The burial of the Prophet was not the first concern for the Medinan elders, distracted by the conflict over who was to succeed him. There was no congregational funerary prayer for him, perhaps because no agreement could be reached as to who would lead the prayer. His followers prayed individually over his body (Ibn Mālik 1982, 114). Similarly, prayers can be offered for the souls of *kari*s even when their time of death or their place of burial remains unknown.

Muslim funerary rites are simple and impersonal in keeping with the egalitarianism and simplicity characteristic of Islam. The five funerary rites for the deceased are: *taghsīl* (washing); *takfīn* (shrouding); *ṣalāt al-janāza* (ritual funeral prayer); *tadfīn* (burial); and benedictions (Qur'ānic recitations and prayers for the departed soul). The same five rites are followed regardless of whether the deceased is a man or a woman. In Pakistan, fragrant native red roses and rose petals, natural perfumes, and incense accompany the last rites. The *taghsīl* of the deceased is undertaken by close family members of the same sex who then shroud the body in an unsewn white cotton cloth. There is no priestly or ordained class in Islam, but religious leadership is a male preserve, and men with religious knowledge lead the community in religious rites, including funerary rites. Like the leading of ritual prayers in general, leading of the *ṣalāt al-janāza* is exclusively the domain of men. Women cannot lead *ṣalāt al-janāza*, nor is there provision of space for them to participate in it. Women are also forbidden to accompany the body to the burial ground no matter how closely they might be related to the deceased. They may visit the grave afterwards but this is also discouraged. If a woman tries to remain close to the dead body of a male relative or to follow it to the graveyard, she is physically held back. Thus for women there is an added cultural dimension to the natural grief of bereavement. This exclusion of women from ritual leadership and from congregational prayers is symptomatic of the discrimination against women in family and in life in Pakistan.

The customary exclusion of women from funerary rites in Pakistan is justified by the belief that women give birth and are more invested in life, and it would be unfair to expose them to death and to burden them with end of life rites as they are particularly fragile at such moments of grief. This justification would have been more credible had it been the case that women were seen more fit to lead the life-affirming rites accompanying birth, puberty, and marriage. In the end, a woman is denied the right to choose having her last rites conducted and led by family or community members who cared for her and contributed at least equally to her well-being. Moreover, this tradition supports the situation where a woman's last rites may be conducted by those who may have treated her as less than equal or mistreated her during her lifetime and, in certain cases, even refuse outright to grant her a proper burial. There are no safe spaces to raise, discuss, and reflect on this issue of deep existential significance before the crisis of death hits and, at that time, the bereaved fall back on the received tradition because it is an inappropriate time to question funerary arrangements.

Qur'ānic recitations accompany the entire funerary process. Thus family members recite Sūra Yā Sīn (Qur'ān 36), considered the heart of the Qur'ān, at the bedside of the deceased and throughout the process of *takfīn* and *tadfīn*. After the burial, private and communal recitations of Yā Sīn and even the entire Qur'ān are held in the home or in the mosque, according to the wishes and means of the family, to send blessings to the soul of the deceased. This may be repeated on the third and the fortieth day after the death and continued thereafter on the anniversary of the death. When the communal recitations are held at home, both women and men participate, although they are segregated. But when they are held in the mosque, only men participate as mosques in Pakistan are a male preserve. Food is served and distributed among the poor at the end of such ceremonies.

For *kari*s killed by their husbands after being accused of adultery, there is no washing of the body, shrouding, or funerary prayers. There are no recitations and prayers to ease the journey of their souls after death. Their unwashed, often mutilated bodies are thrown into rivers or ditches or buried in forbidden *kari* graveyards: women who are killed because they are perceived to have brought dishonor to their male relatives are either not provided with a grave or it remains unmarked and prohibited to visitors. This absence of funerary rites for *kari*s leaves a gaping and unhealed wound of tragedy and fear, which haunts the bereaved and permanently terrorizes all women in the community. *Kari* women remain dishonored even after death. *Karo*s, by contrast, are buried in the communal graveyard (National Commission on the Status of Women 2005, 39).

Activism

Many Sindhi men are of course actively involved in the struggle to eradicate the custom of *karo kari*. Some have even risked their own lives. The driver, guide, and companions who rode with this author along sandy tracks to a very remote area to visit a *kari* graveyard were all men. Among them was a journalist who had published a news item regarding a separate "graveyard" for *kari*s that even the women's female next of kin were not allowed to visit. The guide was so afraid that he remained in the car when the group left the car to walk through cotton fields (irrigated by a canal system that has recently reclaimed parts of the Sindh desert) to an unexpected clearing with a burial site much older than the cotton fields. The journalist pointed to a sand dune in the far corner of the graveyard where, according to him, the bodies of the *kari*s were unceremoniously dumped. Except for the fear of all the local men in the group, there was no evidence that the unmarked sand dune was a *kari* graveyard.

Bibliography

[No primary sources (except in *ḥadīth* literature) on funerary rites for Muslim women were found. This is especially the case concerning funerary rites for victims of *karo kari*.]

Amnesty International, Pakistan. *Violence against women in the name of honor*, New York 1999.

Anwar, Ghazala. Religious pluralism and Shariah in Indonesia, in *Understanding Indonesia*, ed. S. Epstein, Wellington, N.Z. 2006, 77–92.

Burney, Samya. *Crime or custom? Violence against women in Pakistan*, New York 1999.

Ibn Anas, Mālik. *Al-Muwaṭṭa'*, ed. I. Mears, trans. A. Abdurrahman and Y. Johnson, Norwich 1982.

Khan, Tahira S. *Beyond honour. A historical, materialist explanation of honour related violence*, Oxford 2006.

Knudsen, A. J. *License to kill. Honour killings in Pakistan*, Bergen 2004.

Malik, N., I. Saleem, and I. Hamdani (eds.), There is no "honour" in killing, National seminar report, Shirkat Gah, 25 November 2001, Lahore 2003, <www.boell-pakistan .org/downloads/Karo_Kari_Tor_Tora.pdf>.

National Commission on the Status of Women, *The concept of justice in Islam. Re. Qisas and Diyat Law*, Islamabad 2005.

Niaz-Anwar, Unaiza. *Violence against women. Women's rights are human rights*, Karachi 1995.

Patel, Sujay and Amin M. Gadit, Karo-kari. A form of honour killing in Pakistan, in *Transcultural Psychiatry* 45:4 (2008), 683–94.

Shah, H. Q. and N. Malick, *Don't let them get away with murder. Booklet on criminal procedures. Basic questions answered*, Lahore 2002.

Funerary Practices: Women: Palestine: Nineteenth to Early Twentieth Century

Suhad Daher-Nashif

Introduction

This article examines women's rites of passage following natural and suspicious or unnatural deaths and the differences between men and women's rites of passage in Palestine in the late nineteenth and early twentieth centuries. The article reveals how social and religious factors affected postmortem examination and investigation practices, and intersected with medicolegal rules. The article reveals how in many cases a woman's unnatural death was declared as a natural death to avoid postmortem practices. This desire to avoid postmortem examinations resulted from social attitudes and religious ideologies about female bodies, and toward corpses in general.

Drawing on archival data published in books, academic articles, and online historical documents, the article examines these factors, with a special focus on women. It begins with a general description of Muslim women's rites of passage following natural death. It examines the sources of the Islamic rules and customs surrounding women's death, explaining how these practices were used in most Arab-Muslim societies, including Palestine. The article clarifies the meaning of postmortem practices and identifies which practices are considered medicolegal. Then it describes generally the developments in postmortem practices during the Ottoman Empire. Since postmortem practices following unnatural deaths alter the familiar death customs and socioreligious processes, social reactions are documented and explained. The article then describes which and how postmortem practices were performed in Palestine during the nineteenth and early twentieth centuries, explaining the differences in practices for men versus women. These differences are further discussed in the final section, which describes and examines postmortem examination and investigation practices during the British Mandate in Palestine (1922–48).

Muslim Women's Rites of Passage in Natural Death Cases

In Muslim societies, death rituals are governed by several rules mainly derived from the Qur'an and from the Prophet Mohammad's behavior and hadith; what

© KONINKLIJKE BRILL NV, LEIDEN, 2017 | DOI:10.1163/1872-5309_EWIC_COM_002100

is referred to as *al-Sunnah al-Nabawiyya* [the Prophetic Sunna] (Al-Suh'eri Ben-H'atira 2008). For female corpses, these practices include:

- turning the corpse toward Mecca, straightening the arms and legs, and closing the mouth and eyes;
- covering the corpse with a sheet until the beginning of the purification process;
- ritually bathing and purifying the corpse before burial;
- the woman's corpse can be washed by her husband (covering the woman's genitals); or, if the husband cannot do so, or if the woman does not have a husband (such as if she is a widow or has divorced or has never married), another woman washing her;
- covering the private body parts (the trunk area, including the genitals and breasts) during washing and purification;
- respected elderly woman, who's also experienced in Muslim burial customs, draping the corpse with a simple white cloth made up of three pieces, called a *kafan*; and
- burying the corpse as soon as possible (see Gatrad 1994, Sheikh 1998).

These practices should usually be conducted on the Muslim woman's corpse following an expected or natural death. In men's cases, the wife can wash his body; if this is not possible, then another man must conduct the purification and washing process. Most of these customs were derived from the way the Prophet Muhammad dealt with his daughter's and his sons' bodies after their deaths (Al-Suh'eri Ben-H'atira 2008). The Prophet Muhammad gave instructions to Um Atiyyah, the woman who washed and purified his dead daughter, Um Kulthoum, and he washed his sons after their deaths (Al-Suh'eri Ben-H'atira 2008). As a result, these practices were conducted on the corpse in Muslim societies throughout Islamic history, with minor differences, including in the Ottoman Empire's various Muslim societies.

Although the Ottoman Empire was a multinational, multilingual state comprising many religions, with diverse customs around death rituals and funerary practices, in most respects Ottoman death rituals were consistent with fundamental Sunni Islamic principles. In women's cases, the corpse was washed before being placed in a *kafan*. The shrouded body was then carried in a coffin to a mosque, where a funeral prayer was held in the presence of the entire community's men. The body was then carried to the grave to be laid to rest, in direct contact with the earth, facing Mecca, toward the *qibla* (Agoston and Masters 2009). Male relatives and friends carried the woman's corpse from her home to her grave because Muslim women were never allowed to attend burials (Gatrad 1994).

The Ottomans shared the faith of other Muslims in terms of the meaning of death and their idea of an afterlife. Islamic eschatology was simple: death was not an end, but rather the beginning of another form of life. The dead wait in the grave until resurrection on Judgment Day, when souls would be subjected to the final test and sent either to paradise or to hell. One important principle was that of total submission to death, seen as the irrevocable will of God (Agoston and Masters 2009).

Anthropologists consider death customs to be a rite of passage through which a person passes from one state of existence to another. Belgian anthropologist Arnold Van Gennep notably coined the notion of "rite of passage." In 1908, he published *Les rites de passage*, in which he described and analyzed social aspects of humans' transition from one life status to another. The notion of "rites of passage" emerged as a way to interpret ritual events marking social changes experienced by members of a society as they progress through life (Davis 1994). Death and giving birth are each considered a rite of passage that women must pass through, during which social and religious norms are inscribed onto their bodies (Van Gennep 1960).

In cases of suspicious or unnatural death—when murder or suicide is suspected—medical and legal practices interfere in this process, whereby socioreligious norms interact with scientific and formal laws. While Van Gennep and other social scientists, such as Mary Douglas (2002) and Julia Kristeva (1982), have addressed prevailing meanings, practices of death rituals, and transitions, little attention has been paid to cases wherein rites differ from the norm to become restructured, as in cases of suspicious death, when formal systems such as forensic medicine systems intervene in constructing these rites.

Postmortem Practices in the Ottoman Empire: General Review

Modern forensic medicine lies at the intersection between medicine and law, constituting an arena whereby medical knowledge and experience serve the legal system (Vij 2008). These practices include externally examining and dissecting the corpse and medically evaluating lived bodies for legal issues (Rao 2006). Historically, forensic medicine has been used in different parts of the Arab and Islamic world, mostly on male corpses, and less so on female corpses. Modern forensic medicine practices generally appeared in the mid-nineteenth century in parallel with the rise of the modern nation-state, which accompanied interactions between the Islamic world and Europe (Kharoshah et al. 2011).

Ottoman scientists began to adopt European practices beginning in the seventeenth century, gaining momentum in the mid-nineteenth century at a time of many innovations in Europe (Kemal 2015). Postmortem examinations were rarely undertaken in the sixteenth-century Ottoman Empire, but this is unsurprising given they were not part of the empire's official laws and legal rules. Toward the mid-nineteenth century, the Ottoman Empire's health system began to be affected by the West due to interaction with European militaries, science, and commerce (Fahmy 1998). Some Western ideas replaced Islamic shari'a in commercial legal processes, in civil, and in criminal law (Davidovitch and Greenberg 2007; al-Madani et al. 2012). The definitive Islamic law or doctrine for Muslims, shari'a, derives from four sources: the Qur'an (Islam's Holy Book), hadith (the Prophet Mohammad's statements and practices), *ijmā'* (deduction of laws through juristic consensus), and *qiyās* (reasoning by analogy).

During the fourth decade of the nineteenth century, physicians from the Habsburg Empire (the Austrian Empire) played a decisive role in reforming medical structures in the Ottoman Empire. The Austrian health care structure constituted a model for those Austrian physicians who came to work in the Ottoman Empire, establishing the Austrian Hospital in Istanbul (Chahrour 2007). In 1838 more than a thousand books on medicine were bought in Europe and shipped to the school of medicine in Istanbul (then called Constantinople), and medical equipment was bought from London with funding from the sultan (Chahrour 2007).

In 1839 Austrian doctor Carl Ambrose Bernard was the first to lecture on forensic medicine in the Ottoman Empire at the newly established first school of medicine in Istanbul. In 1843 with Sultan 'Abd al-Majīd's permission, Dr. Bernard performed the first autopsy in the history of the empire, at the Austrian hospital in Istanbul (Çelik 2015)). The autopsy conducted to a construction worker who died after being stuck by a pole, and medical students were present during the autopsy (Çagdir et al. 2004). In 1857, 'Abd al-Majīd founded a committee addressing forensic medicine, which evolved into the Forensic Medicine Authority (Inanici et al. 1998).

The first dissections were performed on male corpses, not female corpses, even if the woman died from the same cause as the man. One example of this distinction occurred surrounding deaths from tuberculosis. When a sultan (like Sultan Mehmet VI, d. 1922) died, he was dissected, but a woman from the sultan's harem who died for the same reason was not dissected (Baris and Hillerdal 2009). This indicates that attitudes toward women and women's bodies continued after their death and that they did not possess the same rights to have the truth of their death stories uncovered.

While these developments and dynamics describe the field of forensic medicine in the empire's capital, the question remains as to what was happening in its provinces. In Egypt, for example, Mohammad ʿAlī Pāshā established the School of Medicine in Abi Zaʿbal in 1827, recruiting foreign doctors such as the French physician Anthoine Barthelemy Clot, who later gained the Ottoman title of Bey for his lengthy and loyal service to ʿAlī (Aksakal 2003). Dr. Clot initiated forensic education in the School of Medicine as part of its internal medicine program. In 1862, Khedive Ismail sent Dr. Ibrahim Pasha Hassan to France and Austria to specialize in forensic medicine. He returned to teach the subject as an independent science in the School of Medicine at Eini Palace (Kharoshah et al. 2011, 10–13). In that period, social and religious opposition to autopsy, and to postmortem in general, offered fertile ground for larger disputes between men and women regarding the proper position of women in society (Fahmy 1998).

Social and Religious Opposition to Autopsies and Postmortem Practices

Anthropological research on medicolegal systems in various contexts examines the interaction between the formal medicolegal institutes and the local population (Prior 1989). It was common for Ottoman religious authorities and social systems to reject modern medicolegal practices, particularly for female corpses. A discussion of family dynamics when a request was made for a mother's body to undergo autopsy after she was buried can be found in Khaled Fahmy's analysis of historical women's status and role in the medical field (1998, 54–56).

Local communities refused to adopt Western and new or different medical practices, even if they had been sanctioned by the government. For example, autopsies were an integral part of Dr. Clot's medical pedagogy and anatomical studies, and they sparked considerable controversy. Dr. Clot felt compelled to teach anatomy lessons in secret because of fierce opposition to the practice of dissection (Aksakal 2003). One medical student was so outraged that he attacked Dr. Clot with a knife as he performed an autopsy in a class in 1829. The opposition to autopsies derived from the importance of keeping the body whole because of the Muslim belief in resurrection on Judgment Day (Kuhnke 1990).

To deal with the social rejection of autopsy and postmortem practices, fatwas were issued by religious scholars. In 1910 the Egyptian religious scholar Moḥammad Rashīd Riḍa published a fatwa on "postmortem examinations and the postponement of burial," which seems to have been the first treatment of the topic in nineteenth-century Arab-Muslim countries (Rispler-Chaim 1993, Fahmy 1999). In his fatwa, Riḍa allowed some extension of the time between death and burial because in "natural" deaths, shariʿa encourages burial as soon after death as possible "in order to bring the dead person closer to what God prepared for him/her" (Rispler-Chaim 1993, 165). Muslim scholars often use fatwas to express contemporary responses to "new" questions, questions for which there is no direct answer in the Qurʾan or in the hadith or in any of the pre-twentieth century Islamic legal literature.

The next section examines developments of medicolegal practices in Palestine and concludes discussion of women's rites of passage following murder.

Postmortem Practices in Palestine: "Rites Of Passage" following Unnatural Death

Scholarly literature on forensic medicine within Palestinian society is scarce. Most of the Israeli, Palestinian, and Jordanian scholarship on the topic that does exist begins with the British Mandate (1922–48), incorrectly implying that forensic medicine began in Palestine during that time (De-Paz 2002). Postmortem examination practices in the Levant, including in Palestine, were indeed in use throughout the Ottoman Empire, beginning in the seventeenth century. Some historical resources mention cases of autopsy and postmortem examinations in the Levant, including in Palestine, even during the sixteenth century. In *Ottoman medicine. Healing and medical institutions, 1500–1700* (2009), Miri Shefer-Mossenson notes that even during the sixteenth century, the historian Mustafa ʿAlī identifies autopsy as a means for demonstrating local physicians' inferiority in comparison to their European colleagues (60).

Although autopsies were very rarely conducted at that time, especially on female corpses, other methods for assessing or "examining" corpses were practiced. These external examinations were conducted in order to determine what had happened to individuals in death, to locate their wounds, and to identify the instruments used to kill them (Erer, Düzbakar, and Erdemir 2006). Reports were written on these examinations' findings, specifying the locations of wounds and the means that had caused them (Wecht 2005).

Dror Zeʾevi (1995) examined how postmortem practices on male and female corpses differed. Drawing on travelers' memoirs on Jerusalem, court records, and local sources, Zeʾevi describes women's lives in Ottoman Jerusalem. He found that Jerusalem and Nablus shariʿa courts' *sijillāt* (records) revealed women's rites of passage in cases of suspicious death. Zeʾevi also found court records to be silent on many issues where social norms did not coincide with the written law as upheld by the court. We therefore have only a vague picture of issues such as puberty, virginity, and relations between wives and concubines, because families tended to confine such women's issues to the private domain. For example, Ze'evi found no record of daughters, wives, or sisters having been murdered after "shaming" their families by "sexual promiscuity." But he did find numerous reports of women who had slid into wells, fallen off roofs, or had been buried by stone avalanches, certainly many more than such cases involving men. As Ze'evi explained: "A clue to the silence [around murders of women] might be found in the relative abundance of reports of accidents involving women and girls in the city and surrounding villages" (1995, 161).

In cases of unnatural deaths a team of investigators was sent to the scene. The evidence supplied by (usually male) relatives was deemed sufficient, even when the circumstances surrounding the death were unusual. Male relatives mostly described women's unnatural deaths as *"bi qaḍā' allah wa qadarihi"* [by God's will], hoping to discourage inquest and bury the women as soon as possible. Such dynamics between the formal and the informal systems enabled family members to use socioreligious arguments to conceal women's murder and manipulate the legal process.

Furthermore, determining whether a death resulted from accident, suicide, or murder was not possible because autopsies were very rarely undertaken, even less so in women's cases. The medicolegal apparatuses mainly included externally examining a covered female corpse, examining the death scene, and investigating family members and others present at the scene, mainly men. Following this process, and with the judge's permission, female corpses were purified as prescribed by Islam and buried according to Islamic death customs. We can conclude that women's rites of passage in suspicious death cases continued to be affected by social norms and attitudes toward women, their bodies, their behavior, and the family's reputation.

These practices continued to be performed within the same sociolegal structure from the seventeenth century until the mid-nineteenth century, when the Ottoman Empire adopted modern Western medical practices. At that time, under Ottoman sovereignty, the local Palestinian population of farmers (*fellāḥīn*), city people (*ḥaḍar*), and settled and nomadic Bedouin tribes (*badu*) relied primarily on folk medicine, which employed medicinal herbs, bonesetting, burns, bloodletting, leaches, amulets, and cupping therapy. Practitioners included religious healers and midwives (Davidovitch and Greenberg 2007).

Palestine was part of the Levant (*bilād al-shām*), whose administrative-military center was in Syria. Between 1860 and 1865, the Ottoman government appointed several foreign doctors (including Italians, Greeks, Hungarians, and Poles) to the province to work as military surgeons, health officials, and municipal doctors, as part of legal and administrative district reorganizations

(Sa'di, Sarton, and Van Dyck 1937, Shaw 2000). Through that period, Medical unions were created in the Palestinian cities of Jaffa and Jerusalem, with doctors holding social and educational roles, in addition to medical responsibilities (al-Barghouthi 1932).

Although remote from the seat of the empire, because of its spiritual importance Jerusalem continued to attract many doctors, who contributed greatly to the development of its modern medicine (Amar 2002). Due to Jerusalem's centrality and religious status, Ottoman interest in the city also began to increase. Jerusalem's importance for the Ottoman regime stemmed from its appeal to Europeans and Americans, who came to establish welfare and religious institutions and foreign consulates, which also turned Jerusalem into an arena of power struggles among different forces (Abu-Manneh 1990, 8). Jerusalem's increasing importance enhanced all of Palestine's importance because, among other reasons, the Ottomans feared losing the city's administration and sovereignty to foreigners (Abu-Manneh 1990, 274). Palestine's centrality led several governors, charged with carrying out reforms and upholding the law, to work emphatically to maintain order and safety (Abu-Manneh 1990, 277). Ottomans used forensic medicine to support their legal system, especially where they held interests of order and control. This intent may explain their use of postmortem practices in Palestine in the late nineteenth century.

In Beersheba, for example, the authorities appointed a local mayor, as well as a pharmacist, who lived in the city and arranged and planned medical examinations required by courts of law in cases of homicide and injuries following confrontations occurring among feuding bedouin tribes (Abu-Rabia 2001, 52–53). Limiting these practices to victims of tribes' clashes indicates that cases of killed women and unnatural deaths of women were not issues to be investigated. Perhaps women's unnatural deaths did not cause the kind of social disorder that could threaten the empire's control over society. Some scholars even mention that in some Arab countries under Ottoman rule, a woman's killer would "sprinkle his victim's blood on his clothes and parade through the streets displaying the bloody murder weapon to increase his honor," attracting community respect rather than condemnation for taking a life (Kressel et al. 1981). If a murdered woman's family and relatives celebrated her murder and honored her murderer, it is unlikely they would want answers or societal upheaval. The archival research seems to be rather silent on funerary and burial ceremonies conducted for women killed by male relatives.

According to court records, the municipal doctor's main forensic role was to give medical or legal advice following the *nā'ib*'s (attorney) request (Yazbak 1998, 80). Sometimes, when murder was suspected, a doctor was sent to the scene. One document reports: "The doctor concluded upon examination that the cause of death was stabbing with a sharp instrument" (Yazbak 1998, 80). In another report, the municipal doctor declared: "The dead baby found in one of the town's streets is 42cm. long, has blond hair and blue eyes. He has six fingers on each hand and is 37-days-old. Cause of death was diarrhea. This is what the examination of the body revealed" (Yazbak 1998, 80). These descriptions of two male cases exemplify the kinds of external examinations of corpses, which were rarely performed on women because of social attitudes about revealing their bodies to strangers. Yazbak (1998) claims that according to the records of the German consulate in Jerusalem, autopsies were not performed, but only external examinations.

Based on the various documentation mentioned here, in the Palestinian context, until the final third of the nineteenth century, forensic medical practices were very traditional, were performed by the municipal doctor, and involved external examination of the corpse with medical assessment for legal needs. Actual autopsies were likely performed only after the rebuilding of Jerusalem by the Ottomans in the early twentieth century. This assumption follows scholars such as Orit Navot (2003), who notes that by that time, doctors in public medicine could make independent decisions regarding all health issues except for in three fields, one of which was the performance of autopsies for legal needs (52–53), implying that autopsies were indeed at that time performed under certain circumstances.

To conclude, medicolegal practice rarely intervened in the case of murdered women, likely because the Ottomans used forensic medicine practices to maintain social order, and conducting a postmortem on a female corpse might have been expected to induce social rejection and disorder. Therefore, women's death practices in such cases are expected to have been similar to cases where women died naturally.

The next section will describe how postmortem practices were instituted and conducted during the British Mandate, including in which cases and under what conditions medicolegal apparatuses were used. It will particularly examine how these tools were used in cases where women were murdered.

Postmortem Practices in Palestine in the Early Twentieth Century: the British Mandate (1922–48)

In the early years of the British Mandate, the legal system in Palestine rested on a variety of laws whose principles at times conflicted. Ottoman law, which formed the constitutional basis of Palestinian law, leaned toward Islam and Islamic customs, whereas laws enacted by the British Mandate originated from

English common law. Mogannam explains how the law in force in Palestine was comparatively complex. It was an amalgam of various laws and contradictory principles. Shari'a had the sanction of Muslim religion and custom, while the laws introduced by the Mandate were derived for the most part from colonial and English legislation (Mogannam 1932). Rejecting the colonial powers by the local Palestinian community resulted in rejecting and resisting practices such as autopsy (Karplus 1969).

The penal code, however, contained some traces of Islamic principles. It provided, for example, for the payment of *diya*, or blood money, to a victim's relatives in cases where death was caused either willfully or by negligence (Bentwich 1938). When blood money was paid, the legal process stopped. As a result, we can conclude that in these cases, the rites of passage—funerary and burial customs—were performed the same as in natural deaths.

The British Mandate divided medical administration in Palestine into four regions: Jerusalem, Nablus, Haifa, and Jaffa, and eighteen subregions (Abu-Rabia 2001; 2005). A senior health official, usually British, headed each area. He managed and supervised health activity and was assisted by a junior official, usually a Palestinian, whose job was to carry out assignments dictated by the senior official (Abu-Rabia 2001, 421). Mortality rates decreased following the establishment of this public health system. In 1917, Palestine's population was characterized by high rates of fertility and mortality. These high mortality rates were due to recurring epidemics of smallpox, malaria, typhus, and cholera. Between 1926 and 1947, the total fertility rate of Muslims remained the highest in Palestine. In addition, Palestine's total mortality rate dropped during the mandate from 25.1 in 1923 to an average of 16.8 between 1940 and 1942 (El-Eini 2004).

Experienced local pathologists were engaged by British officials to perform autopsies, albeit there were conflicts of interest between various groups of the population and the British Mandate forces (Karplus 1969). Another expression of rejecting the British existence was the silence of the Muslim 'ulama' when a woman was murdered (Faqir 2001). Faqir notes how "the protection of *'ird'* or women's honour was perceived as the last resort against Western influence and modernization during the British Mandate in Palestine and Jordan" (2001, 76). Faqir claims that the silence of the 'ulama' on women's murders was perceived as an act of defiance against British colonialism. It prioritized resisting colonialism over applying Islamic law, which rejected murdering women. Village heads were responsible for reporting deaths to British officials (El-Eini 2004). Therefore, it is expected that they did not report a woman's murder because they rejected postmortem dissection of woman's dead body by their colonizers.

During that period, when forensic autopsies took place, they were performed by British government doctors, who acted on behalf of the Crown's delegates in Palestine and usually had some training and experience in postmortem diagnosis (Hiss 1998). These doctors were appointed by regional authorities and functioned as coroners (Hiss, Kahana, and Arensburg 1997). The law governing examination of the cause of death and the coroner's work writ large was based on the ancient English institution of the coroner (De-Paz 2002). This institution within English law began in the Anglo-Saxon period (450–1066), which founded the English nation (Al-Hadidi and Hamdi 2003). In Palestine, coroners' training was mainly legal, and judges also did not come from the field of medicine. Therefore, investigations were unscientific and limited, especially in cases where medical experience and knowledge were necessary (Skeels 1936).

In *Forensic medicine and its function in applying criminal law in Palestine*, Moa'men al-Hadidi and Nazeeh Hamdi (2003, 52–53) cite the Coroner's Ordinance, published on September 1, 1926. It includes the following articles:

Article 1: The ordinance will be named the coroners' ordinance in cases of suspicious death.

Article 2: The high commissioner has the authority to appoint, from time to time, one man or more as a coroner for cases of suspicious death in every district.

Article 3.1: If the coroner investigating cases of suspicious death knows of the presence of a dead body in his district, and there is suspicion that the person was murdered or died an unnatural death, or a sudden death the cause of which is unknown, or died while in prison or hospital or a place the circumstances of which require an investigation of the causes of death, then the coroner must investigate the causes of death as quickly as possible.

Article 3.2: The coroner has the authority to postpone the burial of the deceased in his district until the end of the investigation of the causes of death. If he cannot abandon the investigation, the deceased will not be buried until the coroner issues a burial order.

Article 4.1: If the cause of death is unknown and there is suspicion that the death is the result of use of violence or unnatural means, the coroner has the authority to demand the autopsy from one of his district's doctors, and the authority to order one of the specialists to conduct an examination of the stomach's content. The doctor will perform an autopsy of the organ he sees as vital for the inquiry of the suspicion during the medical examination he is conducting.

Article 4.2: The doctor asked by the coroner to perform an autopsy must go to where the deceased is, examine the body and confirm the cause of death unless he finds another doctor to do this, and in this case he must file a detailed report to the coroner, in which he describes the appearance of the body and the conclusions and results he reached regarding the cause of death. This report is initial evidence of the event. According to mandatory law, if a person addresses the coroner and swears under oath that the cause of death, in part or in full, is the negligence of a doctor or another person who attended to the deceased wrongly, that doctor or attendant will not be entitled to examine the body or assist in examining it.

Article 5.1: If the doctor testifies in his report that the death is natural, and there are no marks on the body indicating that the death occurred or was caused by the use of unnatural means or force, or negligence, the coroner is entitled to request a statement under oath of said doctor as an appendix to the report. After this the coroner is entitled to issue an order permitting burial while relinquishing investigation processes.

Article 5.2: The doctor is entitled to collect monetary compensation if the coroner has decided to abandon the investigation based on the report submitted to him.

Through the British Mandate in Palestine, the police system was weak, which made maintaining law and order nearly impossible (Kolinsky 1993). The weakness of the system, the weakness of autopsy professionals, the power of village heads to report deaths, and socioreligious opposition to forensic medicine practices on female corpses meant female corpses passing through natural death rites of passage with no intervention by the medicolegal institution. It could be concluded that many women's death narratives were erased and that justice did not take place in the many cases of murdered women. The Palestinian women's memories of the British Mandate period reflect different views on the nature of the British rule and the impact of that rule on their lives (Fleischman 2003, 58). Although Palestinians viewed the period as one of liberalization, in that it increased women's mobility, independence, and life options, Palestinian women faced obstacles in local community traditions, and obstacles, too, from the colonial powers (Fleischman 2003). These had a major role in structuring the Palestinian Women's Movement. The 1920–29 period is noteworthy for the emergence of the women's movement in the context of growing opposition to Zionism and the British Mandate (Peteet 1991, 61). This activism addressed women's social rights and was faced with opposition. The political context, from the British Mandate to the beginning of Zionist encroachment, excluded women's social justice from the public scene, unless women were involved in national issues. Therefore, the women's movement did not prioritize women's murders at the time.

Conclusion

Women's rites of passage in funerary and burial customs during the late Ottoman Empire and early British Mandate in the Palestinian region were structured through Islamic rules. These rules derived mainly from the Qur'an, and the *sunna*. In cases of suspicious death, where murder or suicide were suspected, in addition to socioreligious practices, the structure of these rites is constructed by medical and legal practices. In Palestine, medicolegal practices such as death scene investigation and external body examination began to be practiced beginning in the seventeenth century. This orientation gained momentum in the mid-nineteenth century as many innovations were also made in Europe and autopsying the corpse was added to them. These practices were conducted mainly on men. Differences in performing these practices between men and women indicate that social norms and attitudes toward men and women play a role in the use of medicolegal practices in cases of suspicious death. Based on the fact that most examples of dissection noted in different sources were conducted on men, and that few sources discuss these gendered differences (Ze'evi 1995), women's unnatural deaths received far less interest than men's. Thus intersectionality existed between social attitudes toward women's bodies and their postmortem treatment, indicating cooperation between the medical and the social systems and between the formal and informal systems in efforts to prevent social disorder and to protect families from dishonor.

Throughout the Ottoman Empire, shari'a constructed the rites of passage in natural death cases, for men and for women. In unnatural death cases, postmortem investigation took place on both male and female corpses, but far less so on female corpses. Female corpses rarely passed through postmortem examination, and death reports drew instead on testimony attained at the scene of death from male family members of the deceased. As a result, many cases of killed women were reported as accidents, such as from a fall. Since female corpses were neither examined directly nor dissected, it is suggested that many murders of women were recorded as accidental deaths. As a result, many women's murder narratives were silenced.

Later, when the forensic medicine practices and autopsy were part of the Ottoman Empire's new reforms performed in Palestine, bodies that were dissected were mainly those of men killed in tribal clashes. During that period, doctors performed medicolegal practices. Still later, under the British Mandate, legal professionals conducted postmortem investigations, and many questions arise as to the degree of truth of their written reports. During that same period women were also rarely dissected, and funerary and burial customs continued according to Islamic rules familiar to the local community.

Additional historical and archival work is needed in order to build a clearer narrative of women's rites of passage in unnatural death cases and to understand how power relations structured women's existence between death and burial. Palestinian women's death stories have been excluded from the narrated history of Palestine, their deaths only narrated when they resulted from confrontation with the enemy or the colonial powers, narrated only when they killed for the nation, and excluded or even erased when they paid with their lives for their social and individual rights.

Bibliography

Abu-Manneh, Butrus. Jerusalem in the Tanzimat period. The new Ottoman administration and the notables, in *Die Welt des Islams* 30:1 (1990), 1–44.

Abu-Rabia, Aref. *A Bedouin century. Education and development among the Negev tribes in the twentieth century*, Oxford 2001.

Abu-Rabia, Aref. Bedouin health services in Mandate Palestine, in *Middle Eastern Studies* 41:3 (2005), 421–29.

Agoston, G'abor, and Bruce Masters. *Encyclopedia of the Ottoman Empire*, New York 2009.

Aksakal, Layla J. The sick man and his medicine. Public health reform in the Ottoman Empire and Egypt, Third-year paper, Harvard Law School, 26 April 2003, <http://nrs .harvard.edu/urn-3:HUL.InstRepos:10015270>.

Amar, Zohar. *The history of medicine in Jerusalem*, Oxford 2002.

al-Barghouthi, O. B. Local self-government. Past and present, in *Annals of the American Academy of Political and Social Sciences* 164 (1932), 36–37.

Baris, Izzetin, and Gunner Hillerdal. Tuberculosis in the Ottoman harem in the nineteenth century, in *Journal of Medical Biography* 17 (2009), 170–73.

Bentwich, Norman. The new criminal code for Palestine, in *Journal of Comparative Legislation and International Law* 20:1 (1938), 71–79.

Chahrour, Marcel. "A civilizing mission"? Austrian medicine and the reform of medicine structures in the Ottoman Empire, 1838–1850, in *Studies in History and Philosophy of Biological and Biomedical Sciences* 38 (2007), 687–705.

Çagdir, Sadi, Celbis Osman, Aydin Engin and Soysal Zeki. Evolution of forensic autopsy and current legal procedures in Turkey, in *The American Journal of forensic Medicine and Pathology* 25 no. 1 (2004), 49–51.

Çelik, Nermin. The start of of conducting dissection in Ottoman Empire, in *International Journal of Basic and clinical Medicine* 3 no.1 (2015), 53–59.

Davidovitch, Nadav, and Zalman Greenberg. Public health, culture, and colonial medicine. Smallpox and variolation in Palestine during the British Mandate, in *Public Health Reports* 122 (2007), 398–406.

Davis, Douglas. Introduction. Raising the issue, in *Rites of passage*, eds. Jean Holm and John Bowker, London 1994, 1–9.

De-Paz, Moshe. Netihot Refueyot Meshpatiyot bi-Yesrael [Medicolegal autopsies in Israel], in *Refuah Omeshpat* 26 (2002), 57–61.

Douglas, Mary. *Purity and danger: An analysis of concepts of Pollution and Taboo.* Routledge, London, 2002 [1966].

El-Eini, Roza. *Mandated landscape. British imperial rule in Palestine, 1929–1948,* New York 2004.

Erer, Sezer, Ömer Düzbakar, and Ayşegül Erdemir. A forensic autopsy case belonging to the nineteenth century in Turkey, in *Journal of the International Society for the History of Islamic Medicine* 5 (2006), 40–45.

Fahmy, Khaled. The anatomy of justice. Forensic medicine and criminal law in nineteenth-century Egypt, in *Islamic Law Society* 6:2 (1999), 224–71.

Fahmy, Khaled. Women, medicine and power in nineteenth-century Egypt, in *Remaking women. Feminism and modernity in the Middle East*, ed. Lila Abu-Lughod, Princeton 1998, 35–72.

Faqir, Fadia. Intrafamily femicide in defence of honour, in *Third World Quarterly* 22:1 (2001), 65–82.

Fleischman, Ellen. *The nation and its "new women." The Palestinian women's movement, 1920–1948,* Berkeley, Calif. 2003.

Gatrad, Abdul Rashid. Muslim customs surrounding death, bereavement, postmortem examination, and organ transplants, in *British Medical Journal* 309:6953 (1994), 521–25.

al-Hadidi, Moo'men and Nazeeh Hamdi.*Forensic medicine and its function in applying criminal law in Palestine*, Bir Zeit 2003.

Hiss, Jehuda. Forensic medicine in Israel, in *Medicine and Law* 19 (1998), 71–73.

Hiss, Jehuda, Tzipi Kahana, and Baruch Arensburg. Forensic medicine in Israel, in *American Journal of Forensic Medicine and Pathology* 2 (1997), 154.

Inanici, M. A., N. Birgen, M. Ercüment Aksoy, N. Alkan, G. Batuk, and O. Palut. Medico-legal death investigations and autopsies in Istanbul, Turkey, in *Journal of Clinical Forensic Medicine* 5:3 (1998), 119–23.

Karplus, H. Present-day forensic services in Israel. Their development and legal background, in *Proceedings of the Fifth International Medico-Legal Seminar*, eds. C. H. Wecht and H. Karplus, Pittsburgh 1969, 17–22.

Kemal, Namik. The start of conducting dissection in the Ottoman Empire, in *International Journal of Basic Clinical Medicine* 3:1 (2015), 53–59.

Kharoshah, Magdy, Mamdouh Zaki, Galeb Sherien, Moulana Ashraf, and Elsebaay Elsebaay. Origin and development of forensic medicine in Egypt, in *Journal of Forensic and Legal Medicine* 18:1 (2011), 10–13.

Kolinsky, Martin. *Law, Order and Riots in Mandatory Palestine, 1928–35*, London 1993.

Kressel, Gideon M., Alessandro Bausani, Joseph Ginat, Roger Joseph, A. M. Khazanov, Simha F. Landau, Emanuel Marx, and Moshe Shokeid. Sororicide/Filiacide. Homicide for family honour, in *Current Anthropology* 22:2 (1981), 141–58.

Kristeva, Julia. *Powers of horror. An essay on abjection*, trans. Leon S. Roudiez, New York 1982.

Kuhnke, LaVerne. *Lives at risk. Public health in nineteenth-century Egypt*, Berkeley, Calif. 1990.

al-Madani, Osama, Magdy Kharoshah, Mamdouh Zaki, Sherien Galeb, Salah Moghannam, and Ashraf Moulana. Origin and development of forensic medicine in the kingdom of Saudi Arabia, in *The American Journal of Forensic Medicine and Pathology* 33:2 (2012), 147–51.

Mogannam, Mogannam. Palestine legislation under the British, in *Annals of the American Academy of Political and Social Science* 164 (1932), 47–54.

Navot, Orit. A historical overview of the developing medical ethics culture in the new Jewish settlements in Israel during the years 1840–1914, in *Eubios: Journal of Asian & International Bioethics* 13 (2003), 52–53.

Peteet, Julie. *Gender in crisis. Women and the Palestinian Resistance Movement*, New York 1991.

Prior, Lindsay. *The social organization of death. Medical discourse and social practices in Belfast*, New York 1989.

Rispler-Chaim, Vardit. The ethics of postmortem examination in contemporary Islam, in *Journal of Medical Ethics* 19 (1993), 164–68.

Sa'di, Lufti M., George Sarton, and W. T. Van Dyck. Al-Hakim Cornelius Van Dyck (1818–1895), in *ISIS: A Journal of the History of Science Society* 27:1 (1937), 20–45.

Shaw, Stanford J. The origins of representative government in the Ottoman Empire. An introduction to the provincial councils, 1839–1876, in *Studies in Ottoman and Turkish history. A life with Ottomans*, ed. Stanford J. Shaw, Istanbul 2000, 25–28.

Shefer-Mossenson, Miri. *Ottoman medicine. Healing and medical institutions, 1500–1700*, New York 2009.

Sheikh, Aziz. Death and dying. A Muslim perspective, in *Journal of the Royal Society of Medicine* 91 (1998), 138–40.

Skeels, Bernard. Correspondence: Medical Coroners, in *The British Medical Journal* 2 (1936), 845–846.

al-Suh'eri Ben-H'atira, Sofiya. *Al-jasad wa al-mujtama'* [*The body and society*], Lebanon 2008.

Van Gennep, Arnold. *The rites of passage*, trans. Monika B. Vizedom and Gabrielle L. Caffee, Chicago 1960.

Vij, Krishan. *Identification textbook of forensic medicine and toxicology principles and practices*, New Delhi 2008.

Wecht, Cyril. The history of legal medicine, in *Journal of the American Academy of Psychiatry and the Law* 33:2 (2005), 245–51.

Yazbak, Mahmoud. *Haifa in the late Ottoman period, 1864–1914. A Muslim town in transition*, Leiden 1998.

Ze'evi, Dror. Women in seventeenth-century Jerusalem. Western and indigenous perspectives, in *International Journal of Middle East Studies* 27:2 (1995), 157–73, <doi: https://doi.org/10.1017/S0020743800061869>.

Health Practices

∵

Health Practices: Turkestan: 19th Century to Early 20th Century

Sanavar Shadmanova

Introduction

The local population in Turkestan relied on different forms of medicines in the nineteenth and early twentieth centuries, among them folk medicine, mystical pre-Islamic medicine, and Islamic medicine. Starting in the late nineteenth century, when ambulatories and hospitals were established in the region, European medicine began to play a more important role in Turkestan.

Folk, Mystical Pre-Islamic, and Islamic Medicine

Information about folk medicine, or traditional medicine (*khalq tabobati*), is based on data about how people identify disease, how they protect themselves from illness, and the methods they use to treat it. Folk medicine relied on pharmaceuticals taken from plants, animals, and minerals. Patients were treated by massage, mineral water, therapeutic mud, and surgical procedures. Modern medicine also draws on some aspects of folk medicine. Practitioners of folk medicine included *tabib* (a doctor who treated by using herbal medicine), *dzharakhchi* (surgeons), *rishtachi* (surgeons who specialized in the removal of the guinea worm), *sinikchi* (trauma surgeons), *doya* (midwives), and *zulukchi* (hirudo-therapists, those who treated using leeches). Mystical medicine originated before the advent of Islam in the region and was based on petitions, visits to places of worship, and the wearing of tiger claws, wild boar fangs, various stones, and many other items as talismans, which were believed to rescue the person wearing them from various diseases. Islamic medicine used prayers from the Qur'an to treat its patients. Amulets and talismans with incantation were written in long, narrow strips of paper rolled into a tube, worn, sewn in silk cloth, or in special cases, and called a *duo-tumar* (the amulet with incantation). It was believed that this condition protected from evil and affected physical health. The prayer requests served to protect against future illnesses and to treat existing conditions (Gabdrafikova 2013, 126).

© KONINKLIJKE BRILL NV, LEIDEN, 2017 | DOI:10.1163/1872-5309_EWIC_COM_002114

European Medicine in Turkestan

Starting in the late nineteenth century, the population of Turkestan began to use European medicine alongside local medicine. In December 1882, women doctors N. N. Goondius, A. V. Poslavskaya, and E. N. Mandelstam addressed the governor of Turkestan by written report about offering their services in medicine. As a result, they became the first European female doctors in Turkestan in that time when the first ambulatory opened. On December 4, 1883, the first ambulatory for women and children in the region opened in Tashkent. Later, this type of ambulatory began to open in other cities in Samarkand (1885, paid for from the city's budget); in Khodjent (September 1886); and later in Andijan (1888); in Namangan (1888); in Kokand (1888); in Marghilon (1891).

In the early twentieth century, one of the urgent issues in Turkestan medicine was establishing a gynecological ambulatory. On December 1916, a 24-bed gynecological department was opened in the Tashkent city hospital. The surgery block was brought from the surgical department of the Imperial Institute in Saint Petersburg; obstetric-gynecologic instruments were provided by Antonina Alekseevna Shorokhova who finished Women Medicine Institute in St. Petersburg in 1909 and came to Tashkent in 1916. Shorokhova was professor-gynecologist in Central Asia. She notes that the department initially served only Russian women. Later, it started to address the birthing and gynecological needs of local women, too (O'zRI-TTHMDA fond 192, r. 1/295, 1–2).

The first head of Tashkent's ambulatory was a female doctor. She was selected by Ivan Petrovich Suvarov, the regional military-medical inspector and confirmed by Michael Grigorovich Cherniyayev, Turkestan's governor-general. The staff of this ambulatory consisted of two doctors, one nurse, one translator, and one servant. Doctors and nurses who worked in the medical field in Turkestan were provided some privileges, such as two horses for transportation, a residence, or a financial allowance of a half-year salary. The newspaper *Turkestanskiye vedomosti* published the regulation of the Tashkent ambulatory on 25 October 1883. It stated that the staff of the ambulatory should consist only of women and that all types of medical assistance—pharmaceuticals, uncompounded operations, and closing a blood vessel with a ligature—should be free for women and children.

Moreover, European hospitals in the region were badly understaffed. Thus, 25 doctors and 60 *feldsher* (medical assistants) worked in three provinces of Turkestan in 1890, compared to a total of 642 medical practitioners serving three other provinces of the Russian Empire, of which 243 were doctors and 399 worked as medical assistants. In other words, one doctor served 135,000 people in Sirdarya province, 100,000 people in Fergana province, and 97,100 people in Samarkand provinces. In contrast to this, there was one doctor for 18,000 people in Tula, 21,000 people in Kharkov, and 35,000 people in Vyatskaya provinces of the Russian Empire (Vasilyev 1895).

Childbirth Numbers, Prenatal Care, and Infant Care

Fertility
According to estimates by Russian doctors, between 1883 and 1894, Muslim women in Tashkent had on average 5.13 childbirths. Medical specialists from that era calculated that the reproductive age of Muslim women was approximately 30 years, and 17.1 children were born to every 100 women in a year in Tashkent. Compared with other provinces in the Russian Empire, this number was high—according to Yu E. Janson's comparative statistics, fertility ranged from 5.7 to 12.2 per 100 women in other parts of the Russian Empire. In general, an important reason for the high fertility in Turkestan was that local people believed that a baby was a gift from God, making abortion a sin. Also, almost all women got married and had children.

In general, available statistics suggest that the number of infertile women in Tashkent was very low. Particularly, one calculation from the Tashkent women's ambulatory shows that between 1883 and 1894 around 7 percent of patients were infertile or, put differently, one in fourteen marriages suffered from infertility. This compares with the 15 percent of infertile patients in England in the late nineteenth century (Poslavskaya 1894, 92).

Prenatal Care
During the nineteenth and early twentieth centuries, most women in Turkestan gave birth in their homes. Women in large cities often employed midwives (*doya*); women in the countryside relied on female relatives during delivery. Only in the event of a difficult delivery did the immediate family seek the assistance of Russian doctors. In difficult cases, medical assistance was given by male as well as female doctors. For example, the Benevolent Society's doctor, Dorofey Stepanovich Paliyenko, wrote in 1893 that male doctors such as D.S. Gimmer, Muhammad Khanafiy Alyukovich Batyrshin, and Johansson often assisted birthing mothers. Dorofey Stepanovich Paliyenko who worked in Tashkent from 1886 to 1894 also frequently assisted birthing mothers (Paliyenko 1893, 88).

A labor ward was established in Tashkent in 1880 under the patronage of the Benevolent Society. In its first 30 years (1880–1910), the ward assisted 3,210 births, averaging 140 births each year. In 1905, construction began for a new building for the labor ward. The cost of the building was estimated at 38,000 rubles and made possible by the emir of the Bukharan Emirate, Seyid Abdulahadhan (1859–1910), who donated his embassy house on Romanovsky street and capital proceeds from its sale (O'zRMDA fond I1, 12/1741, 5).

At the same time, in order to train midwives from among the local women, there was an attempt to establish a school for midwives and the matter was actively discussed in the periodical press in 1890s. In 1893, Dorofey Stepanovich Paliyenko presented a list of 17 females from the local population, aged between 18 and 45, who expressed a desire to learn the obstetric business. Among them were one *doya* and a female teacher (Paliyenko 1893, 76). Because of a lack of funds, however, this idea was not realized until the 1990s.

Although Dorofey Stepanovich Paliyenko mentioned the facts of reference of Muslim women to the male doctors, especially to male doctors-Europeans, but it was rather an exception than the rule. This fact was noted by Vladimir Petrovich and Maria Vladimirovna Nalivkin, Russian ethnographers and researchers of Central Asian history: "Midwives especially those who involved in this process were available mostly in big cities" (Nalivkin and Nalivkin 1886, 170). The *doya* stayed in the pregnant woman's house long before delivery, especially, when he expectant mother had few immediate female family members at home to rely on. Post-birth, the mother was prohibited from going up 8–9 days and she was considered as a patient during *chilla* (meaning "40 days" in Persian). During *chilla*, she was prohibited from leaving the house or working. The reasoning behind this custom was that it helped with the involution of the uterus and with the new mother's general recuperation after childbirth.

The colonial administration of Turkestan considered obstetrics to be extremely difficult, and on 1 June 1890 Tashkent's city council (duma) established two midwife positions in the Muslim quarter of the city. Each midwife would receive 880 rubles per year, comprising a salary of 600 rubles, 100 rubles to rent an apartment, and 180 rubles to hire interpreters. Because no Muslim midwives existed, two Orthodox midwives, Blumfeldt and Raykova, were hired. These two women submitted in 1891 suggest that they attended 42 births that year (with one attending 18 births and the other 24). Each of the midwives received no more than two visits a month from expectant mothers (O'zRMDA fond I718, 1/17, 329ob–330ob).

That the official midwives attended so few births may be partly attributed to the local Muslim women's secluded lifestyle and their complete estrangement from European women. The Muslim population also likely did not understand the benefits of professionally practiced obstetrics and educated midwives. As important, however, was that European midwives did not speak in the local language, Uzbek —although Blumfeldt and Raykova received money from the city council to hire interpreters, there were few interpreters for them to hire because it was difficult to find women who knew both Russian and Uzbek. This made it difficult for them to render medical assistance to the local population. And because patients did not understand Russian, most medical instructions were not followed. Until the appointment of the two Russian-speaking, local women had long relied on the services of Fotima Kurmysheva, a Tatar Muslim and the former interpreter of the city obstetrician (O'zRMDA fond I36, 1/3149, 2).

City officials tried to respond with assistance. For example, records show that the city council decided to provide a translator for three months to meet the request of Dr. Luiza Ash, who worked in Tashkent in the 1880s (O'zRMDA fond I718, 1/17, 89–890b). To alleviate the situation of Muslim women in childbirth, the city's administrative board, which managed organizations, established the position of urban midwife in 1897 in the Muslim part of the city. The position was given to a Muslim midwife, Fotima Bulatova, who had graduated in 1895 from the Nadezhdinskye Medical and Obstetrical courses in Saint Petersburg and then returned to Tashkent (O'zRMDA fond I718, 1/17, 3290b–3330b).

On 24 September 1897, Tashkent's city council approved rules regarding midwives in the old part of the city. According to these rules, midwives had to be Muslim, had no right to work in other places or in other facilities, or have a free practice anywhere except in the old part of Tashkent city. The midwife had to rent, at her own expense, a private apartment in that part of the city, and specifically in the area around the central market (O'zRMDA fond I718, 1/17, 354–355).

Despite these efforts by the council, it appears that the language barrier persisted as late as 1914, when the newspaper *Sadoi Farghona* discussed the language issue in an article published on 3 September 1914. Among these was simply that patients did not visit doctors at all. Another problem, according to the author of article, was the lack of health workers from the local population ("Need for *tabib*" 1914). Furthermore, most locals remained unwilling to take pregnant female relatives to the hospital for medical services, even in the severest of cases. For example, in December 1916 Antonina Alekseevna Shorokhova was forced to perform a caesarean section in a private home in the old part of the city on a woman who was clearly in a critical condition but whose close relatives had flatly refused to take her to the hospital. Fortunately, the operation went well (O'zRI-TTHMDA fond 192, 1/296, 17–18).

Infant Care

Islamic tradition recommends breastfeeding children until the age of two. This is both beneficial for the children's health and can delay further pregnancy, allowing mothers a respite between pregnancies. It was not uncommon to see children of three or four years, who had already started running, still being given access to their mother's breast. The move from maternal milk to adult food came without any training or transition period. As soon as a child started to walk by himself, he gradually became accustomed to chewing solids and drinking from a drinking bowl. On the whole, in the opinion of Russian doctors, the general condition of local children aged under two years who were fed breast milk was "good." Children between two and five who suffered from gastrointestinal problems such as diarrhea usually looked emaciated and more death among children took place at exactly this age. Russian doctors who worked at the ambulatory for women and children in Tashkent estimated that only 42 percent of children survived this age (Poslavskaya 1894, 29–30).

Illness Statistics

For most illnesses, individuals underwent treatment in their own homes using herbs and minerals given by *tabib*s. For this reason, there are no records of their medical conditions. Starting in the late nineteenth century, sick people began to go to the hospital for treatment. But even then the records are incomplete. As a result, it is very difficult to know with any accuracy how many people suffered from a particular illness at any given time in the nineteenth and early twentieth centuries in Turkestan.

Children and Women

Some diseases were fairly rare among children in Turkestan. For example, over a period of ten years, from 1883–1894, the ambulatory in Tashkent saw only 56 pediatric patients seeking medical assistance for rickets. This figure represents only 0.3 percent of the population; the disease afflicted up to thirty percent of the population in western parts of the Russian Empire (Poslavskaya 1894, 45). The reason for the far lower incidence of this disease among the children of Turkestan may lie in the climate, as well as in the prolonged breastfeeding of children (see above), extended play outdoors, plentiful sunshine, and a tradition of families growing many of their fruits and vegetables (Poslavskaya 1894, 45).

As children approached adolescence, some diseases occurred more frequently among girls than among boys. Under the age of five, girls and boys did not differ in terms of afflictions; between five and ten, more girls than boys suffered from thyroid gland disease. Among children aged ten to fifteen, the number of girls suffering from thyroid disease was four times that of boys

("Санитарные очерки города Коканда" 1899; Shishov 1904, 463). In fact, women up to the age of 25 often sought medical advice in Kokand ambulatory about precisely this disease ("Санитарные очерки города Коканда" 1899). Records from 1883–94 show that 214 children in Tashkent had goiter; of these, only nine were boys. Another common medical problem was skin disease. Records show than almost thirty percent of pediatric patients suffered from various skin diseases (Poslavskaya 1894, 33–34, 62).

Women and girls visited the ambulatory more frequently than men and boys did. Of the 18,558 pediatric patients who visited the Tashkent ambulatory for women and children between 1883 and 1894, the majority (about 63 percent) were girls. While there is no difference in the visits of children under five years of age, this begins to change after age ten, with fewer boys seeking medical help. It was quite rare to receive visits from boys beyond the age of twelve. Of the 1,749 women who visited the Tashkent ambulatory in 1885, 149 were young girls (Poslavskaya 1894, 33–34).

In the higher age bracket age, too, some diseases were more common among women than among men. Statistics show that the incidence of childbirth among women in Turkestan was fairly high, and this figure had important consequences for women's health. According to the data collected by the Kokand female ambulatory between 1887 and 1897, morbidity among women decreased between the ages of 30 and 40, when a woman's body was fully developed and had reached its high fertility.

One ambulatory doctor, Aleksandr Lvovich Schwarz, noted that among the 389 goiter patients he treated were 24 men, 281 women, and 84 children (Shishov 1904, 475). Goiter disease typically coincided with the onset of puberty and the age of childbearing. Evidence from Samarkand and Kokand also suggests that thyroid disease was quite common among young women and afflicted women far more than men (Likoshin 1892, 419–20).

Starting in the early twentieth century, men also started seeking medical treatment at these ambulatories. The second ambulatory for women and children to be opened, in the Beshagach district of Tashkent in 1900, soon found that 10 percent of its patients were men.

Who Goes to the Doctor?

A. V. Poslavskaya, who was head of Tashkent's ambulatory for women and children from 1885 to 1894, recorded that in 1885, a total of 1,749 women sought medical advice over 3,812 visits (Poslavskaya 1886). In 1886, the Samarkand ambulatory saw 3,213 patients, of which 2,142 were women and 1,071 were children ("Отчет о деятельности лечебницы для туземных женщин и детей в г. Самарканде за 1886 г" 1887).

In 1885, 95.5 percent of patients at the Tashkent ambulatory were Uzbek. The rest comprised Kazakh, Tatar, and Jewish women (Poslavskaya 1886, 16). At the Samarkand ambulatory, the vast majority of the 1,756 patients at the Samarkand ambulatory were Uzbek, but a greater proportion were Jewish and Kazakh; several were Persian and Arab women ("Отчет о деятельности лечебницы для туземных женщин и детей в г. Самарканде за 1886 г" 1887). It is clear, then, that the ambulatories were visited by women of different nationalities, and their composition reflected well the composition of Turkestan's population.

Diseases among Women in Tashkent

The Tashkent Muslim increasingly visited the ambulatory, but very few of them sought medical advice for acute infectious diseases. According to the data collected by Tashkent physician Aleksandr Lvovich Schwarz, 531,435 patients visited ambulatories in the old part of the city between 1897 and 1908. Of them, only 221 sought treatment for acute infectious diseases (specifically, smallpox, diphtheria, measles, and scarlet fever). These numbers remained low even though this period saw major outbreaks in Tashkent of diphtheria (1890), scarlet fever (1898), and smallpox (1901) ("Успехи русской медицины среди туземцев" 1909). It seems that the local population turned to mystical remedies, too, in such times. For example, treatment for whooping cough included burying five blue dolls in the ground, hanging feathers on the patient, hanging blue rags on saints' graves, and feeding patients eggs painted in blue (Shishov 1904, 467).

Various kinds of skin diseases were the most common ailment among Tashkent women in the nineteenth to early twentieth centuries. In 1885, nearly a third of women who sought medical advice from the Tashkent ambulatory had a skin disease (Poslavskaya 1886, 16). Most common were scabies, eczema, different types of tetter, leprosy, and white spot disease. The doctors at the ambulatory attributed these conditions to the difficult lifestyle and low socioeconomic status of the population—in effect, the patients' abject poverty. Medical treatment was further complicated by Muslim women's initial distrust of Russian doctors. In its first years, the Tashkent ambulatory witnessed a large number of patients with skin disease on their heads, but the doctors could not treat them because the patients refused to allow the doctors to cut their hair. But after a certain time, after seeing the results of the treatment, the patients came already prepared for treatment (mothers started to bring their daughters to the clinic with their hair already cropped).

The second most prevalent set of diseases were of the gastrointestinal tract. For example, between 1883 and 1894 the Tashkent ambulatory was visited by 3,143 patients with such types of disease (12.7 percent of all patients)

(Poslavskaya 1894, 103). It was connected to undernourishment and low quality drinking water, as well as with the consumption of rich foods. Within the category of gastrointestinal diseases, a large proportion of patients had contracted oral catarrhal diseases in the mouth cavity. This was usually the result of eating very spicy foods and of dipping tobacco, which directly irritated mucous membranes. The smoking of kalian, which was local smoking apparatus, also contributed to the diseases of the mouth cavity. Dipping tobacco was popular mainly among older women. The third most common disease was syphilis, which constituted some 8 percent of the total number of patients seen at the Tashkent clinic (Poslavskaya 1886, 16). The Russian doctors attributed the prevalence of syphilis to a lack of education in health and hygiene among the local women. The doctors were particularly concerned that their patients did not know how contagious the disease was or that it could be transmitted through nonsexual contact. Thus they continued to eat out of the same dish as the infected person and share towels, as well as breastfeed other people's children ("Извлечение из отчета Маргиланской амбулаторной лечебницы для туземных женщин и детей за 1891" 1893). *Tabib*s often treated syphilis using mercury, which was both ineffective and dangerous.

Frequent childbirth and prolonged breastfeeding (up to the age of three or four) also resulted in a high incidence of anemia. In addition, the women of Tashkent also often suffered from various kinds of gynecological, infectious, oncological, and thyroid diseases. Most patients who visited gynecological doctors did so because of infertility.

Types of Treatment

In the nineteenth and early twentieth centuries, patients went primarily to *tabib*s. In the late nineteenth century, many also began to go to European doctors. *Tabib*s and European doctors provided outpatient care at the ambulatories and also visited patients in their homes. In a medical emergency, many families preferred to have a doctor come to their home rather than send their wives and daughters to a doctor, so home visits were quite common. For example, in Samarkand in 1898, doctors made 16 house calls; a year later, they made 40 (Pakhomova 1902, 84). The early twentieth century also saw the establishment of private hospitals in the region for inpatient care.

Treatment in Local Medicine

According to Islamic traditions, women were not forbidden from seeking medical help from a *tabib*. *Tabib*s performed treatment that was not associated with the discovery of the body parts, which, according to the shari'a, should be closed. *Tabib*s were allowed to treat the closed part of the body only as a last resort—when they showed the symptoms of any disease and these same symptoms clearly pointed to the fact that the disease could cause death (Kamol 2004, 89).

Sources tell us about local treatment practices in Turkestan in the nineteenth and early twentieth centuries. Local medical practitioners used coral, pounded into a powder and mixed with amber or gray, as a medical treatment for goiter. The patients usually took about 10 grams of the powder twice a day. Corals were purchased from pilgrims returning from Mecca. In addition to corals, treatment for goiter also relied on a type of seaweed. Both *tabibs* and ambulatory doctors performed surgery to address thyroid nodules. For example, in 1886, a woman was referred to the Samarkand ambulatory with a thyroid tumor. She reported that she had twice visited a *tabib*. On both visits, the *tabib* had severed the tumor and drained it of all fluid, stopping the pain and shrinking the tumor. When European methods employed at the ambulatory proved unhelpful, the ambulatory's doctors severed the tumor, as the *tabib* had done. *Tabibs* also treated goiter by cauterizing it with a hot iron ("Отчет о деятельности лечебницы для туземных женщин и детей в г. Самарканде за 1886 г" 1887).

To seek treatment for infertility, women first visited the holy places scattered over Turkestan, giving generously of alms and providing funds to the sites' caretakers, and slaughtering sacrificial animals whose meat was usually then distributed. In addition to prayers, women performed different rituals at each place. For example, in the area of Hazrat Ayub (the Fergana Valley), the childless women had to embrace a nearby stone. Near Marghilan was a mountain down which childless women would slide in hopes of becoming fertile (Likoshin 1892, 419–20).

Turkestani Muslim Women in European Medicine
Part of the population of Tashkent regarded the intrusion of European medicine into the lives of Turkestan women with some disfavor; most of the rural population regarded it with extreme hostility. Only in exceptional circumstances did rural women use the services of Russian doctors, and even then it was very difficult to organize everything. According to information provided by physician T. A. Kolosov of the Turbat ambulatory of Tashkent, women who had serious problems with their teeth did not want to uncover their face. In such cases, it became necessary to tear the *chimmat* (hair net) that covered the face at the level of lips ("О народном врачевании" 1903, 112). It was precisely such attitudes toward male doctors on the part of Turkestani women that accelerated the opening of medical institutions staffed with female doctors.

The ambulatory opened on 4 December 1883, and the staff wondered if Muslim women would come and what their attitude would be to the new medicine and ambulatory. As it turned out, three women came for medical advice on the first day, and ten the second day. In the first month, 200 women visited. Initially, only nonelite women came. Rich and aristocratic women did not want to wait their turn, and for this reason they did not visit until later (Poslavskaya 1894, 4–5).

Inpatient Care

Women in Tashkent could seek medical care not only in the ambulatories but also in the city hospitals. According to Dr. Paliyenko, 30 to 40 women a day sought medical care at the hospitals for a variety of ailments, including surgical procedures. Of the 223 patients seen in the third city hospital in the old part of Tashkent city in 1906, 85 were women and children of local nationalities ("Успехи русской медицины среди туземцев" 1909). Paliyenko performed several surgeries, and women spent several weeks at the hospital in the post-operative period. The hospital had no female staff.

By 1904, the Tashkent ambulatory had four beds for mothers and seriously ill women, though under special circumstances 22 patients could be accommodated. From 1909, Tashkent's city council granted permission to have 15 beds at the hospital. Later, stationary hospitals treated up to 120 patients per year. In 1908, an exceptional year, the number of hospitalized patients reached 455, who spent a total of 5,632 days. By that time, not only were Muslim women being treated by Russian-speaking doctors, but they were also being treated alongside Russian women. Thus, of the 455 patients treated in 1908, 281 women were Russian-speaking women (O'zRMDA fond I1, 12/1741, 33).

Treatment at the Private Hospitals

Starting in the early twentieth century, private hospitals began to cater to female patients in the region, alongside local *tabibs* and state ambulatories and hospitals. In 1908, Dr. A. N. Predtechenskaya opened the first private hospital for women in Tashkent, with just five beds. If needed, capacity could be expanded to twelve beds. As many as 220 women a year stayed at the hospital. About half of these were birthing mothers who paid from 25 to 40 rubles for their stay (Dobrosmislov 1912, 341). The doctor M. I. Gorenstein and midwife Kovaleva also opened a private gynecological hospital with four beds and a maternity ward with six beds (fond I17, 1/29494, 6).

Research in Medicine

In addition to their clinical practice, the female Russian doctors studied the physiology of local women. Their research revealed that women in Turkestan attained sexual maturity between the ages of 15 and 16, and that early marriage negatively impacted the physical development of girls and led to different functional disorders of the body (Poslavskaya 1886, 1894). Articles often appeared in the periodical press of Turkestan of that period warning about the danger of early marriages for young women's health. Moreover, early marriages did not correspond to Russian legislation ("Ранние браки у туземцев" 1899, "Эрта никоҳларга қарши мусулмонлар ҳаракати" 1914). Members of the local intelligentsia were among those who wrote about the dangers of early marriage. For example, in 1915, one of the prominent figures of the Jadid movement, Abdurauf Fitrat, published *The family and family management order*, which discussed these dangers in considerable detail (Fitrat 2000, 43–44).

Conclusion

In the nineteenth and early twentieth centuries, Muslim women in Turkestan used services of various medicine such as folk medicine, mystical pre-Islamic medicine, Islamic medicine and "European" medicine. Particularly, Muslim women in countryside in the region used more folk medicine, when local women in big cities began to use "European" medicine together with folk medicine. "European" medicine started its work in the territory of Turkestan by establishing ambulatories. If we say more clearly, first ambulatory in Turkestan was organized for women, not for men. Furthermore, staffs of these ambulatories consisted of women doctors in order to consider local attitude. Moreover, in few cases, we may see from available sources that local women were treated by men doctor. Furthermore, surgical intervention practiced for Muslim women, particularly, pregnant woman was sometimes delivered by caesarean section. Despite to coming new medicine, local Muslim women still were using services of folk medicine. In some cases, doctors were called to patient's home for treating. In the same time, *doya* usually did medical assistance to pregnant woman in her house.

Bibliography

Dobrosmislov, A. I. *Ташкент в прошлом и настоящем. Исторический очерк* [*Tashkent at past and present. Historical essay*], Tashkent 1912.

Fitrat, Abdirauf. *Оила ёки оила бошⷠариш тартиблари* [*Family or rule in managing a family*], Tashkent 2000.

Gabdrafikova, Lilia. *Повседневная жизнь городских татар в условиях буржуазныхпреобразований второй половины XIX—начале XX вв* [*Everyday life of urban*

Tatars in the condition of bourgeois transformations at the second half of 19th century and early 20th century], Kazan 2013.

Kamol, Muhammad. *Аёлларга доир фатволар* [*Fatwas concern women*], Tashkent 2004.

Likoshin, Nil Sergeevich. Население и смертность в туземной части г.Ташкента [People and mortality in native part of Tashkent], in *Сборник материалов для статистики Сырдарьинской области* [*Collected materials for statistics of Sirdarya province*], ii, Tashkent 1892, 419–20.

Nalivkin, Vladimir Petrovich, and Maria Vladimirovna Nalivkin. *Очерк быта женщины оседлоготуземного населения Ферганы* [*Essay on the daily life of women in the sedentary local population of Fergana*], Kazan 1886.

О народном врачевании сартов и киргиз Туркестана. Медицинская помощь инородцам Туркестана и их отношение к русским врачам [*About folk medicine of sarts and Kirgiz in Turkestan. Medical help for Turkestani people and their attitudes toward Russian doctors*], Saint Petersburg 1903.

Pakhomova, E. Из записной книжки женщины-врача [From the notebook of a female doctor], in *Справочная книжка Самаркандской области* [*Reference book of Samarkand province*], vii, eds. M. Virskiy, Samarkand 1902, 84–90.

Paliyenko, D. О подготовлении повитух из туземок [About preparing midwives from local people], in *Turkestanskiye vedomosti* (*Turkestan bulletin*), *29 September 1893, 76*.

Paliyenko, D. Моим оппонентам [My opponents], in *Turkestanskiye vedomosti* (*Turkestan bulletin*), *10 November 1893, 88*.

Poslavskaya, A. V., and E. N. Mandelstam. *Обзор десятилетней* (*1883–1894*) *деятельностиамбулаторной лечебницы для женщин и детей в Ташкенте* [Review of ten-year activity (1883–94) of an outpatient ambulatory for women and children in Tashkent], Tashkent 1894.

Poslavskaya, A. V. Отчет о деятельности лечебницы для туземных женщин и детей за 1885 год [Report about activities of the hospital for local women and children for 1885], in *Turkestanskiye vedomosti* (*Turkestan bulletin*), *29 April 1886, 16*.

Shishov, Aleksandr Polikarpovich. *Сарты. Этнографическое и антропологическое исследование.* (*Sarts. Ethnographic and anthropological research*), in *Сборник материалов для статистикиСырдарьинской области* [*Collected materials for statistics of Sirdarya province*], xi, Tashkent 1904, 467–75.

Положение об амбулаторной лечебнице для туземного женского населения в г. Старом Ташкенте [Regulation on outpatient ambulatory for local women in old part of Tashkent], in *Turkestanskiye vedomosti* (*Turkestan bulletin*), *25 October 1883, 42*.

Положение об амбулаторной лечебнице для туземных женщин и детей в г. Самарканде [Regulation on outpatient ambulatory for local women and children in Samarkand], in *Turkestanskiye vedomosti* (*Turkestan bulletin*), *17 September 1885, 37.*

Несколько слов о медицинской помощи туземцам [Some words about medical help for local people], in *Turkestanskiye vedomosti* (*Turkestan bulletin*), *31 December 1886, 51.*

Отчет о деятельности лечебницы для туземных женщин и детей в г. Самарканде за 1886 г [Report about activities of the hospital for local women and children in Samarkand for 1886], in *Turkestanskiye vedomosti* (*Turkestan bulletin*), *17 November 1887, 46. 24 November 1887, 47.*

Извлечение из отчета Маргиланской амбулаторной лечебницы для туземных женщин и детей за 1891 [Retrieval from the report of Marghilan outpatient ambulatory for local women and children for 1891], in *Turkestanskiye vedomosti* (*Turkestan bulletin*), *20 October 1893, 82.*

Ранние браки у туземцев [Early marriage among local people], in *Turkestanskiye vedomosti* (*Turkestan bulletin*), *28 January 1899, 8.*

Санитарные очерки города Коканда [Sanitary essay of Kokand city], in *Turkestanskiye vedomosti* (*Turkestan bulletin*), *11 March 1899, 19.*

Vasilev, N. Наша общая беда и как помочь ей [Our common misfortune and how to help it], in *Okraina* (*Outskirt*), *13 August 1895, 61. 17 August 1895, 62.*

Успехи русской медицины среди туземцев [Success of Russian medicine among local people], in *Turkestanskiy kuryer* (*Turkestan courier*), *6 August 1909, 172. 7 August 1909, 173.*

Табибга муҳтожлик [Need for tabib], in *Sadoi Farghona* (Echo of Fergana), *3 September 1914, 55.*

Эрта никоҳларга қарши мусулмонлар ҳаракати [Muslim attempts against early marriage], in *Turkiston viloyatining gazetasi* (*Newspaper of Turkestan province,*) *March 9 1914, 20.*

Archival Documents

Central State Archive of the Republic of Uzbekistan (Oz'RMDA)

Fond I1, register 12, folder 1741.

Fond I17, register 1, folder 29494.

Fond I36, register 1, folder 3149.

Fond I718, register 1, folder 17.

Central State Archive for Scientific-Technical and Medical Documentation of the Republic of Uzbekistan (Oz'RI-TTHMDA)

Fond 192, register 1, folder 295.

Fond 192, register 1, folder 296.

Honor

∵

Honor: Pakistan

Sabah Firoz Uddin

Mothers of the Nation

A historical survey of state discourse shows that, since the 1940s, Pakistani women have been constituted as symbols of national identity and of cultural and religious authenticity (Ali, 1975; Hassan, 1990; Mandelbaum, 1988; Mumtaz and Shaheed, 1987). Against a colonial backdrop, the religio-cultural practices of Islam and South Asian tradition with respect to women emerged as central to the Western narrative of the inferiority of Islam and ultimately to the conflict between the cultures of the colonizers and the colonized. Fundamentally, colonialist discourse was organized around the project of civilizing the colonized and reforming what the discourse described as barbaric and oppressive customs, sanctioned by religious tradition. The colonizers believed that Islam was innately oppressive and that measures such as segregation and the veil not only epitomized that oppression but also were fundamental in characterizing the backwardness of Islamic societies.

In response to the colonial narrative of women and Islam, an oppositional narrative in Pakistan, engineered in resistance, emerged. Refusing to negotiate "the woman question" with the colonial state, and further rejecting the state imperative to push their particularized religio-cultural edicts aside in favor of those of the West, the colonized chose to reaffirm the value of their indigenous customs. Reforming tradition/religion/culture, as historically demanded by Britain, could not mean the wholesale appropriation of Western values. Instead, Pakistan needed to distinguish between the West and the East to maintain a visibly unique native cultural and religious collective identity. The woman, her traditional role as wife and mother, and her body became symbolic representations of the nascent Muslim community. To preserve the religio-cultural identity, the ideal Pakistani woman was tasked with protecting and nurturing the spiritual essence of the national culture by ensuring that she maintained a marked difference between social spaces. Home became an important site to politicize a woman's national consciousness, without maligning her role as wife and mother. The home/world, spiritual/material, feminine/masculine dichotomies in Pakistan were firmly established through a cultural agenda that regulated the strict control of the woman's dress and education and her roles inside and outside the home.

© KONINKLIJKE BRILL NV, LEIDEN, 2019 | DOI:10.1163/1872-5309_EWIC_COM_002200

Pakistani state discourse underscoring the distinction between public and private for women became more acute in the 1970s, under the rule of General Muhammad Zia-ul-Haq. On 1 January 1978, General Zia-ul-Haq, using the emotive appeal of religion, launched an Islamization campaign directed at women. Its stated intent was "to bring all laws into conformity with Islamic tenets and values" (Weiss 1985, 7). The legislation advocated for women's roles as mothers, the complete segregation and exclusion of women from the public, and, in turn, their exclusion from any decision-making processes. This campaign for "Islamic morality" introduced a series of reforms that in effect formalized women's secondary status in society, including a law of evidence, laws of *qiṣāṣ* (retaliation) and *diya* (financial compensation paid to victims or their heirs), and, more importantly, the Hudood Ordinance.

The Hudood Ordinance is "a collective term for four ordinances concerning enforcement of prohibition of drinking, and punishments for adultery, slander and theft" (Pal 1990, 459). For example, with a particular focus on sexual mores, Pakistani women were most impacted by the second ordinance—the offense of *zina* (unlawful sexual intercourse). The legal definition of *zina* liable to punishment is "a sane adult man and a sane adult woman are said to commit *zina* if they willfully have sexual intercourse without being validly married" (Weiss 1985, 8) and includes the offenses of adultery, fornication, rape, and prostitution. For the crime of *zina*, the maximum punishment, *hadd* (the measure of punishment as fixed by the Quran), is death by stoning or 100 lashes. It requires for evidence either the voluntary confession of the perpetrator or the testimony of four morally upstanding Muslim men, who must have witnessed the act of penetration.

The process of Islamization under Zia-ul-Haq extended primarily to measures centered on chastity and honor that emphasized the strict control of women. Zia-ul-Haq focused particularly on restoring the sacredness of the "*chadder aur chardiwari* (women veiled and within the four walls of the house)" (S.S. Ali 2000, 110). By restricting women's mobility to the private sphere, women's access to economic, social, and political power was adversely affected.

Honor

In Pakistan, the family's, and nation's, honor is closely linked to women's *izzat* (honor), which is located in her body and measured by her sexual purity. There is a cultural belief that the protection and control of women and female sexuality maintains familial honor, social order, and cultural continuity in the community. In this exercise, its members (men and women) are self-appointed guardians of the moral purity of "their" women. Men calculate their *izzat* by the behavior of the women in their family rather than by their own behavior. A woman's *izzat* is linked with her sexuality and intact virginity. As a man possesses a woman, by extension, he possesses honor. Nawal El Saadawi identifies the hymen as the most essential part of a girl's body, more valuable "than one of her eyes, an arm or a lower limb" (El Saadawi 1980, 26). A girl's honor, and her family's, depend on the preservation of her virginity. If virginity is lost, "this brings almost everlasting shame which can be only be 'wiped out in blood,' as the common Arab saying goes" (El Saadawi 1980, 27). It is commonly believed that God has provided women with hymens as a means to prove their virginity and that, as long as female members of his family keep their hymens intact, a man's honor is safe. His honor is related to the behavior of the women in his family rather than to his own behavior. Accordingly, the Islamic social system is configured to protect her honor through social control devices such as segregation and the veil.

The system of purdah (state of screening or seclusion) remains rooted in current Pakistani society. Inherited from the Arabic *harem*, purdah is a regulatory mechanism to forestall the interaction between unrelated men and women. Space is delineated according to gender: the public space is strictly male, while the private space is the domestic realm of women. These physical boundaries often function to curtail the movement of women, and in doing so, the boundaries ensure few women trespass into the public male world (Mernissi 1991, Mills 2003). Purdah is a cultural instrument that not only moderates spatial arrangements but also intervenes in social relations, permitting who can to speak to whom.

Household Design

The household is described as essentially a private unit within which honor and the dependence of women have been maintained through the institution of purdah. From a root word meaning "veil" or "curtain," and starting at puberty according to the dictates of Pakistani culture, "decent" women must observe the rules of purdah, inside and outside the home. The physical manifestations of purdah include the concealment of a woman's body from head to toe in public, a spatial enclosure, and "the beliefs and values about the behavior of women, including the restrictions in their movements outside the home and the requirements for their respectful and deferential demeanor within the home" (Mandelbaum 1988, 2). The practice of purdah communicates a strong message to women: its goal is to protect them from male strangers outside their own household, and it is "usually couched in terms of showing respect and order inside the home" (Mandelbaum 1988, 72).

A Pakistani woman is denied an identity of her own and derives her status from her family. They are "known as the sister, daughter, mother or wife of a man and depend entirely on him for their economic needs" (Mumtaz and Shaheed 1987, 30). According to Parveen Shaukat Ali, the purdah system symbolizes the three impulses of human nature: status, dominance, and dependence. She points to a secluded woman's behavior as a major determinant of a man's status in society:

> She is considered to be the IZZAT (pride) of the family and the extent to which a woman abides by the rules of segregation would determine the intensity of this pride, and this intensity in turn will determine the status which a man would command in society. A nonconformist woman would endanger the family pride, which might entail social humiliation for its male members.
>
> P.S. ALI 1975, 168

Additionally, within a purdah society, hierarchy pervades gender as the dominance of men is accepted as natural, and the dependence of women within a familial context is seen as a source of personal pride. Women are socialized to accept marriage as the only purpose in life and, as such, "a woman is only a visitor in her father's family to be kept in trust until claimed" (Mumtaz and Shaheed 1987, 23). Accordingly, a girl in her parents' house is often labeled as *paraya dhan* (not one's own property), denoting her as someone else's property. Therefore in efforts to guard the reputation of women, seclusion is regarded as necessary, as the actions of women need to be supervised, family honor needs to be protected, and outside dangers need to be minimized. A woman outside in "public" life, incompletely covered, and without the protection of her male relatives contravenes the rules of society and thus faces the risk of verbal or physical harassment. In effect, purdah acts as "a type of social insurance" (Warwick 1991, 464)—a way to safeguard against potential human weakness.

Izzat is highly valued and "always refers to how a person carries out the group's values, and how he/she realizes them in actual behavior" (Mandelbaum 1988, 20). In Pakistan, *izzat* echoes sentiments of prestige, rank, and respect, avoiding *sharm* (shame). A man's *izzat* is measured by the conduct of his women and, as such, where a woman's honor has been lost, in instances of illicit sexual behavior, there are significant implications for both her marital and natal family's public position. Hence, a woman's observance of purdah is integral to her family's *izzat*.

While the public space remains male-dominated, the design of the household also draws upon the purdah system, thereby creating gender divisions within the home. Multigenerational homes, where large families divide space and resources, reflect Muslim modesty, and gender relations within the home are defined in relation to space. Although no singular space is reserved for one person, and women mostly exercise control of household management, access to space is determined by who is occupying the house at a particular time. Social prescriptions about gendered behavior operate within private space as well, and thus, to prevent accidental contact between unrelated men and women, entry to certain parts of the home continues to be policed. Social events within the home are mostly gender segregated, where men will eat and socialize in one room, and women and children in another. Some homes have gender-specific entrances, whereby men enter through the front and women can enter, leave, and welcome guests through the back entrance (Zakaria 2015). This ensures that an uncovered woman is shielded from unrelated men, including her brothers-in-law.

Dress

Ever since the inception of Pakistan, dress has played a central role in the nation's ideological construction and (re)presentation of the ideal "Pakistani Muslim woman." The essential components of Pakistani dress for both men and women are the tunic (*kameez*) and trousers (*shalwar*). The size, fabric, and color have varied according to the sartorial style of the time. However, it is the *duppatta* (thin gossamer veil) in particular that has remained constant as the Pakistani trope of modesty and *izzat*. The *duppatta* can be draped over the shoulder (covering the breasts) or loosely placed over the hair. It took on enhanced significance during the Zia-ul-Haq years. As part of his Islamization vision, he discouraged Western clothing and launched a campaign to "look Pakistani." The *duppatta* was depicted as a symbol of Islamic modesty. State-run propaganda campaigned

> against obscenity and vulgarity and extolled the virtues of the good self-sacrificing woman, domestic and domesticated, and blamed "other" public visible women (particularly working women) for the disentegration of the family, of moral rectitude and values as well as for corruption and other social ills.
>
> SHAHEED 2010, 859

Government school students, teachers, and female state employees were expected to uphold public morality by being properly covered and dressed in public spaces. Teachers could refuse to teach girls who were immodestly uncovered. On TV, women newscasters and hosts on state-run television were expected to cover their heads. Those who defied the orders were fired. In 1982, the government issued the following directive:

> The Federal Government has decided that in all institutions under its control, girls from Class IX upward will henceforth wear a proper dupatta as headcover, rather than the thin strip of cloth which is generally in use at present. It has further been decided that all female staff in schools and colleges will be modestly dressed and will wear a chador over their dress.
>
> MUMTAZ and SHAHEED 1987, 79

Even former prime minister Benazir Bhutto was compelled to embrace the *duppatta* as a way to look "Islamic" to bolster voter appeal. Since the end of the 1980s, the hijab, transplanted from Iran or the West, has been a conservative alternative for women who want fully to cover their hair instead of the loose draping of a cloth.

Education and Work

The very definition of what constitutes public space changes with class and geographical location. For example:

> On farms where their labor is essential for survival, women work openly in the fields, yet in the villages the bazaar area remains out of bounds; women enter only if heavily veiled. In cities, the restrictions vary according to the class of the woman and the size of the place itself. In general, the higher the class of the woman, the fewer restrictions she faces. Larger, more cosmopolitan cities such as Islamabad and Lahore have a freer atmosphere than smaller ones in the more conservative regions of Baluchistan and the Northwest Frontier Province.
>
> WARWICK 1991, 462

The degree to which a girl or woman is threatened by other influences determines her access to space, a space marked by an invisible inside/outside border. Paradigmatic to this border is the ideological assumption that women, as agents of the cultural nation, are repositories of honor, such that their virginity and sexuality need to be protected. Breaches of honor are unambiguous: any contact with an unrelated male can violate moral codes. Accordingly, many Pakistanis choose to strike a delicate balance between fear of disturbing the line between public and private, and the wholesale prohibition of women's access to the public sphere. This is perhaps most evident in girls' access to education. Post partition, there was an awakening to literacy. Whereas early thoughts of education centered on preparing girls to be good wives (cooking and sewing), there was a shift in thinking, whereby girls' education was viewed as social currency. As such, when school fees were not a financial burden on the family, and when a girl's help was not needed at home, girls were permitted to attend all-girls schools and colleges. In her memoir, Rafia Zakaria describes the schools as "fortress[es] of high walls and gates designed to enclose girls yearning to learn and keep men outside" (2015, 132). However, education remains a precursor to marriage—it serves only to bolster a girl's value as a potential wife and mother. Norms of mobility continue to determine girls' access to education. For example, for many, girls' schooling is a viable option only when an all-girls school is located close to the home.

Living under the constraints of purdah, women are mostly excluded from public economic activities and instead are responsible for reproductive activity. However, Pakistani women living in poverty have found ways to participate in the informal economy. In particular, many women engage in cottage industries such as sewing and embroidery (Weiss 1992). Others engage in small-scale manufacturing in the home. Weiss points to work such as glueing straps to shoes, fashioning for floral *sehra*s (wreaths) for weddings, stringing flowers, and preparing desserts and samosas (Weiss 1992). In this way, women can earn an income within the private sphere of their home and maintain respectability.

A consequence of the purdah system, where contact between men and women is limited, is that it necessitates a separate space for female medical staff and teachers. As a result, there are limited, culturally sanctioned labor opportunities for women outside the home, providing "contact services," including teaching and medicine, to women who otherwise would not have access to such services because of segregation restrictions. The social need for separate women's professions also enables girls to enter these jobs, as they themselves are removed from men when working (Papanek 1971).

Social Rituals

A female's selfhood in Pakistan is derived from her roles as a wife, mother, daughter, and sister, and, to a lesser extent, from her relationship with distant kin. To nurture this sense of social identity, women are responsible for maintaining social bonds and commemorating and participating in social events such as births, marriages, and deaths. Amineh Ahmed characterizes it is a "sub-society ... an alternative, quasi-autonomous female network of circulation" (2005, 931). Here, women work to ensure cultural and religious practices continue to flourish. Closely associated with the purdah system, for example, is the tradition of arranged marriages, which are typically brokered between families. As girls are shielded from unrelated men, a bride will have very little contact with the groom until after her wedding day. The wedding, then, is an event to commemorate the transfer of symbolic guardianship from a girl's father to her husband. As such, social life is mediated through these events (many female only), where women spend weeks preparing and attending wedding celebrations and rituals. In funerals, as well, women remain inside. Women are not permitted to attend burial prayers at the mosque. The task for women, instead, is to recite Quranic verses for the dead for three days, in the home. A widow, in particular, enters a period of seclusion (*iddah*) for three months and ten days (three menstrual periods), during which she remains sequestered from all unrelated men. Should a woman die, a woman of authority will bathe and shroud the body, preparing it for men to take to the mosque and from there to the burial site (Zakaria 2015).

Modern-Day Pakistan

There has been little restructuring of family and community since the early years of Pakistan. While there are notable exceptions, the majority of Pakistani women are reluctant to stand in opposition to the cultural norms that determine existing gendered hierarchies. As such, feminized gendered roles in the private sphere continue to prevail, and education instead works mostly to support family cohesion. This is particularly evident, for example, in the modern phenomenon of "doctor brides," where a rising number of Pakistani women attend medical school to increase their value not in the job market but in the marriage market. A recent government report from the Pakistan and Medical Council states that although 80% of medical students are women, only 23% of registered doctors are female (2017). Ayesha Masood attributes this trend to the perception that by culturally connecting medical education and chastity, the profession is considered "honorable primarily because its educational climate conforms to the gender norms of Pakistani society" (2019, 113). Where arranged marriages are still desirable, a potential spouse's medical degree—a time-consuming, gender-segregated education—can suggest not only her self-discipline and practical comportment but also that she has kept her attention narrowly focused on her studies, and not on the opposite sex. Moreover, practicing medicine is seen to conform to norms of modesty, where, for example, a female doctor can construct a separate sphere of work by opening a clinic for female patients within the home (Masood 2019). By continuing to place limits on female mobility, cautiously encouraging education, and further entrenching Pakistani women within the home, this larger cultural discourse, which seeks to preserve family honor, continues to underpin the construction of the female subject in Pakistan.

Bibliography

Ahmed, Amineh. Death and celebration among Muslim women. A case study from Pakistan, in *Modern Asian Studies* 39:4 (2005), 929–80.

Ali, Parveen Shaukat. *Status of women in the Muslim world*, Lahore 1975.

Ali, Shaheen Sardar. *Gender and human rights in Islam and international law. Equal before Allah, unequal before man?* The Hague 2000.

El Saadawi, Nawal. *The hidden face of Eve. Women in the Arab world*, London 1980.

Hassan, Riffat. *An Islamic Perspective. Women, Religion and Sexuality*. Edited by J. Becher. Geneva: Kitab Bhavan World Council of Churches Publications, 1990.

Mandelbaum, David G. *Women's seclusion and men's honor*, Tuscon, Ariz. 1988.

Masood, Ayesha. Influence of marriage on women's participation in medicine. The case of doctor brides of Pakistan, in *Sex Roles* 80 (2019), 105–22.

Mernissi, Fatima. *The Veil and the Male Elite: A Feminist Interpretation of Women's Rights in Islam*. Cambridge: Perseus Books, 1991.

Mills, Sarah. *Gender in Colonial Space. Feminist Postcolonial Theory: A Reader*. Edited by Reina Lewis, and Sara Mills. New York: Routledge, 2003: 692–720.

Mumtaz, Khawar, and Farida Shaheed (eds.). *Women of Pakistan. Two steps forward, one step back?* London 1987.

Pakistan Medical and Dental Council. 2017, <http://www.pmdc.org.pk/Statistics/tabid/103/Default.aspx>. May 10, 2019.

Pal, Izzud-Din. Women and Islam in Pakistan, in *Middle Eastern Studies* 26:4 (1990), 449–64.

Papanek, Hanna. Purdah in Pakistan. Seclusion and modern occupations for women, in *Journal of Marriage and Family* 33:3 (1971), 517–30.

Shaheed, Farida. Contested identities. Gendered politics, gendered religion in Pakistan, in *Third World Quarterly* 31:6 (2010), 851–67.

Warwick, Ellen D. The veil is hard to lift. Women's place in Pakistan, in *Commonweal* 118:14 (1991), 462–64.

Weiss, Anita M. Women in Pakistan. Implications of the current program of Islamization. Working Paper No. 73, Office of Women in International Development, Michigan State University, January 1985.

Weiss, Anita. *Walls within walls. Life histories of working women in the Old City of Lahore*,
Boulder, Colo. 1992.

Zakaria, Rafia. *The upstairs wife. An intimate history of Pakistan*, Boston, Mass. 2015.

Mental Health

∴

Mental Health: Pakistan

Batool Fatima

Introduction

With a population of over 200 million, Pakistan is the sixth most populous country in the world. It has an annual population growth rate of 3 percent. It is situated in South Asia and borders India, China, Afghanistan, and Iran. Pakistan is a federation of four provinces, Punjab, Sindh, Khyber Pakhtunkhwa, and Baluchistan, as well as a capital territory and a group of federally administered tribal areas in the northwest, including the frontier regions. Although Pakistan is a rapidly developing economy, the country's adult literacy rate is only 58 percent. Male literacy is 70 percent, and female literacy is 48 percent. According to 2018 statistics, life expectancy at birth is 67.4 years for females and 65.7 years for males.

Health should be understood not simply as an absence of illness, but also as encompassing a healthy mind, the ability to utilize one's own potential, and psychosocial well-being. The World Health Organization (WHO) recognizes mental, social, and physical well-being as important elements of health. Although the impact of mental health issues on general health and well-being has received particular attention in recent years, there is still no general agreement on any single cause of mental disorders, and a worldwide biopsychosocial model is used to explain the causes behind mental illness. In Pakistan, most mental health professionals also use and practice Western concepts of psychiatry and psychology to understand, diagnose, and treat mental illness. A few professionals, however, have started to use the concepts of Islamic psychology, and have integrated prayer therapy into their clinical practice to cater to clients' needs and to make clients comfortable with practice of religious healing. These approaches need to be studied from the perspective of the patients to assess their effectiveness.

It is generally estimated that 10 to 16 percent (circa 21 million) of the population of Pakistan have mild to moderate mental health disorders, while 1 percent suffer from severe psychiatric illnesses. However, studies conducted in both rural and urban areas of Pakistan present a far grimmer situation. Ilyas Mirza and Rachel Jenkins conducted a systematic review that reported a prevalence of 34 percent (range 29–66 percent for women and 10–33 percent for men) of common mental illnesses, which is far higher than other developing countries (Mirza and Jenkins 2004). In their study in three major cities of Pakistan,

© KONINKLIJKE BRILL NV, LEIDEN, 2019 | DOI:10.1163/1872-5309_EWIC_COM_002193

Amin Gadit and Gerry Mugford found 46 percent prevalence of depression in the adult population (Gadit and Mugford 2007). Mental illnesses in Pakistan have grown at an alarming rate, particularly among women in the recent past. Besides genetics and biological influences, this rise is attributable to a lack of awareness about mental illness, stigma, discrimination, untreated mental illness in the family, adverse childhood experiences, other chronic illnesses, poor nutrition, poverty, violence, natural disasters, displacements, urbanization, political instability, gender discrimination, early marriages, multiple pregnancies, high number of children, and marital difficulties. The situation is exacerbated by a lack of mental health services.

According to one estimate, 10–44 percent of people in developing countries suffer from depression and anxiety disorders. Of the approximately one million suicides committed every year, 86 percent occur in low-income and middle-income countries. The World Health Organization reported 13,377 suicides in Pakistan in 2012, of which 7,085 were by women and 6,021 by men). Even this figure very likely reflects underreporting, given underdeveloped reporting systems and the Islamic prohibition against suicide and the cultural stigma attached to it. In addition to the cultural and religious taboos that contribute to underreporting are the complications of the Pakistani legal system, which requires each case to be reported to the police, and stipulates a fine and imprisonment for attempting suicide. Studies show that, of those who die by suicide, 80–100 percent have a psychiatric disorder, with depression the most common primary diagnosis. Under-recognized and untreated mental disorders (especially depression) are undoubtedly the main reason behind suicidal tendencies.

The Global Burden of Diseases, Injuries, and Risk Factors Study 2015 (Charara et al. 2017) reported that women in Pakistan lose over twice as many disability-adjusted life years (DALY) to common mental disorders as compared to their male counterparts. In Pakistan, more women than men are brought to the hospital following parasuicide and attempted suicide (Khan, Islam, and Kundi 1996). This suggests that mental illness in women is more likely to go unnoticed, undiagnosed, and hence untreated, leading them to attempt suicide (Shahid et al. 2009). Left untreated, mental disorders can deteriorate, and can lead to comorbid disorders, disabilities, occupational difficulties, and loss of productivity.

Gender and Mental Health

Pakistan has one of the worst gender disparities in the world (WEF 2018). Traditional cultural and family norms specify very clear and limited gender roles, whereby women must be good daughters, sisters, wives, and mothers over everything else. They are at a much greater gender disadvantage due to sociocultural factors, which often result in less access than men to education, lack of decision-making power, domestic violence, and low social status. Often, women are confined to their homes in the name of protection, which further restricts their social support, political engagement, and access to health and other facilities.

This complex web of sociocultural factors—economic dependence, limited control over their own lives, lack of outside employment and a heavy workload at home, limited mobility, and a cultural preference for sons—puts them under constant stress and at risk of developing mental illness (Patel 2005, Levinson and Ifrah 2009). For example, the strong preference for sons in Pakistani culture means that the birth of a girl child is a cause for stress and postpartum depression in women, especially if there are already more than two girls in the family (Rahman, Iqbal, and Harrington 2003). Many women have reported being afraid of divorce or of their husband taking on another wife if they are infertile or do not produce a male child (Fatima et al. 2015, Fatima 2016). Gender discrimination and stressful life events increase the incidence of depression, mental illness, and suicide attempts among women (Patel et al. 2006, Maselko and Patel 2008, Devries et al. 2011).

At the same time that many who need professional help for mental health problems go undiagnosed and untreated, there is evidence of family members describing a woman as crazy or mentally ill if she flouts family traditions and cultural norms or demands her rights—in order to avoid social stigma and save their "honor." It has also been observed that patients were admitted to confined facilities after family members declared them mentally ill in order to seize control of their property. This happens more with women, because family members do not want them to marry outside the family and take their share of the property to their husbands' families.

Maternal Mental Health

Stressful life events combined with low social support lead to high levels of anxiety, depression, and other mental illnesses among Pakistani women (Mirza and Jenkins 2004), but these women are also the least likely to get the treatment they need. The risk for depression and other mental illness in women increases at various points throughout their reproductive life. This is due in part to physical and hormonal changes, such as during the premenstrual, prenatal, postnatal (postpartum), premenopausal, and postmenopausal stages. Continuously changing and demanding social roles and stressors related to puberty, marriage, childbirth, increasing responsibility, and gender roles also increase the risk of mental illness.

The interaction between women's reproductive process and mental health is often ignored (WHO 2009). Psychological distress related to reproductive issues (e.g., premarital or unwanted pregnancies, miscarriages, abortions, lack of control over contraceptive use, surgery, or removal of reproductive organs, sexually transmitted infections, fistula, and infertility) makes women even more vulnerable to mental illness, particularly depression (WHO 2009). Women in all societies are at higher risk than men of childhood sexual abuse and rape. Unsurprisingly, the rate of depression in women survivors of sexual abuse is much higher than that in other groups of women (Bifulco et al. 1998).

Given some five million deliveries in Pakistan each year, a large number of women are at risk for stress, maternal depression, and other illnesses that need intervention for positive reproductive mental health. Over 25 percent of women are reported to suffer from depression in the antenatal period and 28 percent in the postnatal period, as compared to approximately 10–15 percent of all mothers in Western societies. Women who are prenatally depressed give birth to lower birth-weight babies than do other mothers, which puts children at risk of behavioral and other health problems throughout their lives. A clinic-based study conducted in Pakistan found that maternal mental distress (such as antenatal or postnatal depression) was connected to undernutrition and poor health in infants (Rahman et al. 2004). This finding points to an important avenue of intervention in the high malnutrition rate (almost 50 percent) among children under five years of age in Pakistan—if maternal depression were eliminated from the population, 30 percent of infant stunting could be reduced in children less than a year old (Rahman et al. 2004). Infants with depressed mothers in Pakistan have also been reported to have higher rates of diarrhea and lower rates of immunization. Addressing the issue of depression, anxiety, and other debilitating mental illnesses in mothers would be tremendously beneficial for mothers' as well as children's health.

Sociocultural Factors

The sociocultural factors that have been identified as posing a greater risk for mental disorders in Pakistan are being female and middle-aged; holding certain cultural beliefs; having a low level of education, financial difficulties, and interpersonal problems (for women, particularly with husbands or in laws).

Poverty and Socioeconomic Disparity

Data from around the world indicate that low income and low socioeconomic status are associated with high rates of mental illness. In Pakistan, where 35 percent of the population lives below the poverty level (<2$ per day/ per person), it is no surprise that mental disorders are so high. A new measure of multidimensional poverty recently reported 4 out of every 10 Pakistanis live below the poverty line. This new measure looks at the intensity as well as the incidence of poverty. Economic and housing problems are the most important social challenges, faced by 49 percent and 67 percent of depressed patients; these figures are much higher than in other developing countries. A lack of access to basic needs keeps people engaged in a constant struggle to acquire the necessities they need to survive. A lack of water and sanitation facilities, a lack of power supply for extended stretches in scorching heat, a lack of gas at cooking time even in large urban areas—all of these disrupt the day-to-day routine, sleep, and general functioning. The result is stress and irritability. Husain et al. (2007) found a significant association between overcrowding in the home (due to poverty and a lack of basic necessities) and depression. It can also work in the other direction, with mental illness leading to poverty. Those who suffer from mental illness are more at risk of losing or not finding jobs, becoming homeless, and losing their relationships.

A recent study from Pakistan reports that debt, food insecurity, and lower assets significantly increase the risk of maternal depression in women as compared to those belonging to a higher socioeconomic status (Maselko et al. 2018). Earlier studies from Pakistan reported that women who are poor and have depressive symptoms during pregnancy are more likely to remain depressed even after a year of the child's birth (Rahman and Creed 2007).

Low Level of Education

Common mental illnesses have also been found to be linked with low levels of education in Pakistan. Low levels of education are connected to low economic and social status in society, which puts people under stress at each stage of life, as well as leaving them with poor problem-solving and communication skills, leading to increased risk of stress due to an inability to handle problems. Given the gender gap in literacy in Pakistan, women in Pakistan are at a higher risk than their male counterparts.

In addition to those who suffer from more common mental disorders, around one million Pakistanis suffer from serious psychiatric disorders, but a low level of education, especially mental health literacy, means that it takes longer to recognize mental illness and look for treatment options. This delay increases the complexity of the illness and increases the stress and burden for carers and family members (Batool et al. 2015, Fatima 2016). Again, women, more than men, often do not understand their own illness and lack information about where to go for treatment or whom to consult. Often, people fail to understand their own feelings, and express their problems in somatic symptoms like headaches and chest pains and persist in getting medications for headache, different kinds of pains, insomnia, upset stomach, and so forth. Some lucky ones might have access to a general practitioner, but even these health professionals often lack proper training in the diagnosis and treatment of mental illness. Thus, they fail to treat patients correctly or to refer them to mental health care providers. Many general practitioners simply treat their patients' physical symptoms or prescribe sleeping or anti-anxiety pills to relieve them from stress, without educating them about their illness or the medicine they give them.

Extended and Nuclear Family Systems

In Pakistan living together in an extended family has been the norm. Although this has started to change, it is still highly prevalent and valued. As within most families, the burden of care likely falls on the mother. Studies have reported that mothers living in extended families in Pakistan had more mental health problems than did their nuclear family counterparts. The caring burden associated with combining the demanding roles of mother, wife, and daughter-in-law becomes too exhausting for women. Disagreement over child-rearing between mothers and grandmothers is also strongly related to maternal distress and anxiety, as women feel powerless and develop feelings of helplessness in the presence of domineering and interfering grandmothers with whom they disagree over childcare. Care of elderly and sick family members is considered the female's responsibility only, and often the elderly in the home are in need of special care. This additional carer responsibility can lead mothers to emotional burnout and physical exhaustion.

The type of family system plays a critical role in the mental health of Pakistani women according to their age and position in the family. Living in a nuclear family system is a strong independent predictor of depression among the elderly in Pakistan (Taqui et al. 2007). The prevalence of depression in the elderly Pakistani population is moderately high and a cause for concern. The transition in family systems toward nucleation may have a major deleterious effect on the physical and mental health of the elderly in Pakistani society. While living in extended families appears to have positive effects on grandparents and children, it seems to place mothers at risk. The challenge, therefore, is to address the threats to the welfare of mothers without jeopardizing the benefits to members of the other generations.

Being Single, Divorced, or Separated

Women living without a male partner—whether because they have never married or are divorced or separated—are stigmatized in Pakistan and are thus particularly vulnerable to mental illness, including depression. Although Islam clearly permits separation and divorce, it is strongly discouraged religiously, culturally, and socially (Mirza and Jenkins 2004).

In Pakistan, women are identified and respected as part of a family, mostly in relation to their husband. For a woman to lose her husband is to lose the status she enjoyed through him. Women tend to be stigmatized for being divorced or separated—they are seen as having been unable to manage a relationship—though they do get some sympathy if widowed. The sympathy is usually for the loss of support (intimate, social, and financial), which also increases stressors and difficulties in their lives and hence increases their susceptibility to mental disorders.

Interpersonal Conflicts and Domestic Violence

Social relations, more so than social conditions, are the main determinant of mental illness for people, and particularly for women, in Pakistan (Kazi et al. 2006). Women who lack support from their husbands, in-laws, and families are more likely to suffer from mental illness (Nisar, Billoo, and Gadit 2004, Husain et al. 2007). Although marriage is considered a protective factor from mental illness, married women are found to suffer from mental illness or experience stressors that put them at risk of mental illness in greater numbers than single women or married men.

Domestic violence is a serious social and public health problem in Pakistan, which is considered to be the third worst country in the world for women. Studies report that at least one-third of women have suffered from domestic violence, which includes physical, verbal, and psychological abuse. The husband as well as in-laws or other relatives are often involved in the abuse. Domestic abuse leads not only to severe psychological issues, such as anxiety, fear, post-traumatic stress disorder, and major depression, but very often also to severe physical injuries, requiring emergency treatment, or even to death.

Most women who experience domestic violence at the hands of their in-laws and husbands cannot obtain any support, let alone help leaving an abusive situation, because many in the community consider such acts of violence to be acceptable. Many women themselves have internalized patriarchy and consider domestic violence to be acceptable and in keeping with local cultural norms. The police and law enforcement agencies, for their part, are usually reluctant to intervene, considering these incidents to be personal or family disputes. Women tend to remain in abusive relationships because, given the stigma attached to divorce or separation, their own (parental) families are unlikely to support such measures (Niaz 2004). Interpersonal conflicts and domestic issues are considered to be the most common reason for self-harm and suicide in Pakistan.

High Number of Children

A large number of children is also associated with a high level of distress. A study undertaken in a small village near Islamabad found that inhabitants with mental illness had significantly more children than people without mental illness. A study conducted in a fishing community of Karachi also found that adult married women who were illiterate, had more than four children, and had financial difficulties were at significantly higher risk of depression (Nisar, Billoo, and Gadit 2004). This is likely because more children usually mean a greater economic, social, and health burden on the family. Not only are more resources required to raise more children but so is more time and effort on the part of parents in order to take care of them. Multiple deliveries also take a toll on the mother's physical and mental health, and, given her childcare responsibilities, she has little time left to take care of herself.

Stigma

There are negative attitudes toward people with mental illness across classes, educational levels, and communities in Pakistan, such that family members try to hide people with severe mental illness, often keeping them chained or locked inside the house.

The fear of being stigmatized, labeled "mad," and socially isolated leads people with mental illness and their families to avoid seeking treatment for fear of being seen at a psychiatric facility. They are afraid to share the diagnosis or problems with others because they are afraid they might lose their job and, in the case of women especially, that they will be unable to get married or their marriage might end. Women have reported forgoing treatment because of cultural factors—thinking that they can handle their problems on their own; that it is their fate or God's will; fear of stigma; and even a lack of confidence in mental health treatments (Anderson et al. 2006, Sartorius 2007, Grote et al. 2007). Stigma also makes it difficult for general practitioners to refer patients for psychiatric treatment. Indeed, psychiatrists and psychologists themselves face the stigma for being mental health care providers.

This stigma is common not only among ordinary people but also health professionals, including public health professionals. It arises from a lack of professional knowledge and understanding at health professional's level about the relationship between mental health and all other health conditions, such as the activation of genetically predisposed illnesses in the face of stressful life events.

Religious Interpretations

Religious belief is an integral part of most Pakistanis' lives. How people interpret religious teachings impacts many aspects of their lives, including health. Mental illness, particularly depression, is interpreted as an indication of being ungrateful to God, and of having moved away from religion, so many people often blame the patient herself for not trusting God enough and not being thankful. Women are regularly told simply to be thankful, avoid stress, and offer more prayers, in order to feel better.

A lack of awareness about mental illness leads many women to believe they have no option other than to seek help through prayer. For some women, seeking help from religion and trusting God helps them feel that they have some support, and that is enough for them to start feeling better. However, relying on faith alone prevents many women from considering other causes and solutions to their problems, and this serves to prolong their suffering in the long run.

Many women believe their illness comes from God, that it is their destiny, so interpret events in their lives as fate and accept them as God's will. This means that many also believe that they have no control over their illness and health and, indeed, that to quietly accept their illness is itself a sign of their religiosity.

The Alternate Practitioners/Shamans

A large number of people, women more so than men, also consider supernatural phenomena to be behind their physical and mental illnesses. They seek help from traditional, Sufi, and other kinds of faith healers. Illiterate and educated women alike frequent such healers for their mental illnesses because of a lack of awareness, because of the stigma associated with going to a mental health worker, and for cultural and religious reasons. They describe mental illness as possession by an evil spirit, *jinn*, or other supernatural influence. The usual treatment comprises wearing or burning amulets, reciting special chants and prayers, or drinking water over which the healer has uttered prayers. A shaman is usually called a *baba* or *pir*. The religious healers or Sufis tend to be well-respected in their communities and offer relief through reciting Quranic verses and religious services.

Given the severe shortage of mental health care providers in Pakistan, as well as the low level of education, the prevalent stigma around mental illness, and the poor socioeconomic conditions of the majority of the population, it is easy to understand why people depend so heavily on religious and traditional treatments for mental illnesses. Visiting traditional healers is culturally acceptable, less expensive, and more convenient. However, adverse outcomes have been reported, including maltreatment, adverse reactions from the drugs that they use, delay in getting appropriate mental health treatment, physical and sexual abuse by these healers, and even death during their healing ceremonies.

Use and Abuse of Psychiatric Medication

The dearth of appropriate mental health services has led to the misuse of psychiatric medication, which is easily available over the counter in Pakistan. One study conducted in an outpatient clinic reported that 40 percent of the sample was using psychoactive drug, mainly for sleep and relaxation, without any doctor's advice (Ali, Khuwaja, and Zafar 2009). The community health center of an urban tertiary care center found that 20 percent of the patients received psychiatric treatment. Fifty percent of them, however, had no idea about their diagnosis, and most patients were not given information about potential alternative treatments, referral options, the treatment process of the disease, and for how long they were supposed to take their medication (Ganatra et al. 2009).

The use of benzodiazepines in particular is on the rise. A study undertaken in Karachi found that 14 percent of the sample (which had significantly more women) reported using benzodiazepines (Iqbal et al. 2011). Of these, only 3 percent had seen a psychiatrist, and 40 percent used them on the prescription of general practitioners. Only 22 percent of the sample used them on genuine complaints; others used them mainly to relieve symptoms of distress. Very often, general practitioners prescribe these medications without proper counseling regarding the duration of use and the side effects of long-term use. As a result, many patients take these medications for much longer than they are supposed to and end up suffering from addiction or substance abuse disorder (Naqvi, Hussan, and Dossa 2009).

State of Mental Health Systems and Services in Pakistan

The resources available for mental health care in Pakistan are in desperate need of expansion and improvement. Pakistan, with its population of 210 million, has fewer than 500 registered psychiatrists, an estimated 125 psychiatric nurses, and 480 clinical psychologists to support the feeble mental health care infrastructure across Pakistan (Gadit 2007). The brain drain has been instrumental in diminishing the existing services as many psychiatrists have emigrated overseas (Khan 2004). Moreover, these mental health care providers are heavily concentrated in the major cities, while 70 percent of the Pakistani population lives in the rural areas, where mental health facilities are almost nonexistent. There is a dearth of qualified and trained mental health professionals, and even more so of specialist services, such as child, forensic, and geriatric mental health.

Despite the urgent need to provide mental health care to people in Pakistan, and women in particular, the measures taken at present are insufficient and inefficient. Pakistan's health budget has been consistently less than 1 percent of GDP, and there is no separate mental health budget (Government of Pakistan 2019). This is almost the lowest percentage in the world for health expenditure as a percentage of GDP, much lower than Iran, India, and other neighboring countries. Although the government sector provides free consultation, at most of the places patients need to buy medication, beside bearing the cost of travel. As a result of the inadequacy of public health care, nearly 70 percent of health care is provided by the private sector—usually at a high cost. A study on the financial burden of mental illness in Pakistan reported that, often, the direct and indirect cost of mental illness exceeds the resources available (Malik and Khan 2016). This situation reflects the inefficiency and weakness of poor mental health services in Pakistan.

Mental health has been mentioned as a main priority area in Pakistan's national health policy. The National Mental Health Ordinance 2001 provided a framework for protecting the human rights of people with mental illness and their families, but its implementation remained a challenge. In April 2010, the National Assembly passed the 18th Amendment to give autonomy to the provinces, and hence the Federal Mental Health Authority was promptly dissolved. Two of the provinces, Sindh and Punjab, have since passed their own mental health legislation but have not been able to begin implementation. There remains an urgent need to remove barriers to affordable and high-quality mental health care for all Pakistanis.

Barriers to Accessing Mental Health Services

Evidence-based and effective treatments exist for most forms of mental illness, yet almost 90 percent of patients in the developing world go untreated (Wells 1996, Rubenstein et al. 1999, Bower 2005, Patel et al. 2007, 2009). In a single-site study in Karachi, Haider Naqvi and Murad Khan (2006) reported an average 3.8 years of delay in seeing a mental health care provider after the onset of symptoms. Karachi, it should be noted, is the largest city in Pakistan and arguably has better mental health services than the rest of the country (Naqvi and Khan 2006). The lack of medical insurance coverage and the high cost of out-of-pocket mental health services also pose significant barriers to seeking treatment. Women face additional instrumental barriers, such as the limited availability of transport, the inconvenient location of clinics childcare needs, and a lack of family support. As noted earlier, many women's lack of awareness and misconceptions about mental illness; the prevalence of self-medication among the population generally; and women's lack of agency and general economic dependence, all also make it difficult for women to seek out and access mental health services. Primary health care providers' lack of training in the treatment of mental illness, and the lack of a referral system, also make it difficult for women to gain access to mental health services.

In the end, despite the high incidence of mental health problems among Pakistani women, mental health and suicide prevention is not a priority—neither for the government, which appears indifferent to this problem, nor for medical professionals, who appear to have a "mental block" toward mental illness, perhaps because of the nature of their professional training. Psychiatry is not yet fully integrated in the teaching of medical and allied professionals' curriculum, hence primary and general health care providers, as well as other specialists, are unable to detect, diagnose, and treat mental illnesses.

Conclusion

Mental illness puts an enormous burden on individuals, families, and society in Pakistan. For a variety of reasons, women tend to suffer more but are also less likely to see treatment. Mental health problems among women lead to a loss in productivity due to the affected women's—and, often, family members'—inability to carry out daily responsibilities; conflicts and disruption within families; slower growth and poorer health among infants and children of affected mothers; increased burden on care givers; and premature death. Pakistan continues to work to overcome the challenges of communicable diseases, so the country's health programs are very much focused on those. It is imperative, however, that the government (and medical schools) quickly recognize the high prevalence of and the high cost to the country of mental health illnesses, and set about working to destigmatize both the illnesses and the treatments for them.

Bibliography

Ali, Niloufer Sultan, Ali Khan Khuwaja, and Abdul Moeed Zafar. Characteristics of patients using psychoactive drugs in Karachi, Pakistan, in *Pharmacy World & Science: PWS* 31:3 (2009), 369–72. <https://doi.org/10.1007/s11096-009-9279-y>.

Anderson, Carol M., Cynthia S. Robins, Catherine G. Greeno, Helen Cahalane, Valire Carr Copeland, and R. Marc Andrews. Why lower income mothers do not engage with the formal mental health care system. Perceived barriers to care, in *Qualitative Health Research* 16:7 (2006), 926–43. <https://doi.org/10.1177/1049732306289224>.

Batool, F., U. Boehmer, F. Feeley, and S. Foster. Nobody told me about it! A qualitative study of barriers and facilitators in access to mental health services in women with depression in Karachi, Pakistan, *Journal of Psychosomatic Research* 78:6 (2015), 591. <https://doi.org/10.1016/j.jpsychores.2015.03.022>.

Bifulco, A, G.W. Brown, P. Moran, C. Ball, and C. Campbell. Predicting depression in women. The role of past and present vulnerability, in *Psychological Medicine* 28:1 (1998), 39–50.

Bower, P. Managing common mental health disorders in primary care. Conceptual models and evidence base, in *BMJ* 330:7495 (2005), 839–42. <https://doi.org/10.1136/bmj.330.7495.839>.

Devries, Karen, Charlotte Watts, Mieko Yoshihama, Ligia Kiss, Lilia Blima Schraiber, Negussie Deyessa, Lori Heise, et al. Violence against women is strongly associated with suicide attempts. Evidence from the WHO multi-country study on women's health and domestic violence against women, in *Social Science & Medicine* 73:1 (2011), 79–86. <https://doi.org/10.1016/j.socscimed.2011.05.006>.

Charara R, Forouzanfar M, Naghavi M, Moradi-Lakeh M, Afshin A, Vos T, et al. The burden of mental disorders in the eastern mediterranean region, 1990–2013. Maulik PK, editor. *PLoS One* [Internet]. 2017 Jan 17 [cited 2019 Sep 18]; 12(1):e0169575. Available from: https://dx.plos.org/10.1371/journal.pone.0169575.

Fatima, Batool. Facilitators and barriers in access to mental health services for women with depression in Karachi, Pakistan. Ph.D. diss., Boston University School of Public Health, 2016. <https://open.bu.edu/handle/2144/19588>.

Fatima, B., B. Ulrike, S. Foster, and F.G. Feeley. Key informants' perspective on barriers and facilitators in access to mental health services for women with depression in urban area of a low-income country, in *European Psychiatry* 30 (2015), 1290. <https://doi.org/10.1016/S0924-9338(15)31009-9>.

Gadit, Amin A. Mental health model. Comparison between a developed and a developing country, in *Journal of Medicine* 1:1 (2007). <http://www.scientificjournals.org/journals2007/articles/1047.htm>.

Gadit, Amin A. Muhammad, and Gerry Mugford. Prevalence of depression among households in three capital cities of Pakistan. Need to revise the mental health policy, in *PLoS ONE* 2:2 (2007), e209. <https://doi.org/10.1371/journal.pone.0000209>.

Ganatra, Hammad Ashraf, Hadi Bhurgri, Roomasa Channa, Fauzia Ahmad Bawany, Syed Nabeel Zafar, Rafia Ishfaq Chaudhry, Syeda Hina Batool, Abdul Basit, Mehmood Asghar, Sarah Saleem, and Haider Naqvi. Educating and informing patients receiving psychopharmacological medications. Are family physicians in Pakistan up to the task?, in *PLoS ONE* 4:2 (2009), e4620. <https://doi.org/10.1371/journal.pone.0004620>.

Government of Pakistan. *PAKISTAN ECONOMIC SURVEY 2018–19.* Islamabad; 2019. http://finance.gov.pk/survey/chapters_19/11-Health and Nutrition.pdf. Accessed September 17, 2019.

Grote, Nancy K., Allan Zuckoff, Holly Swartz, Sarah E. Bledsoe, and Sharon Geibel. Engaging women who are depressed and economically disadvantaged in mental health treatment, in *Social Work* 52:4 (2007), 295–308. <https://doi.org/10.1093/sw/52.4.295>.

Husain, N., I.B. Chaudhry, M.A. Afridi, B. Tomenson, and F. Creed. Life stress and depression in a tribal area of Pakistan, in *The British Journal of Psychiatry* 190:1 (2007), 36–41. <https://doi.org/<p>10.1192/bjp.bp.106.022913>.

Iqbal, S.P., S. Ahmer, S. Farooq, Y. Parpio, A. Tharani, R.A.M. Khan, M. Zaman, et al. Benzodiazepine use among adults residing in the urban settlements of Karachi, Pakistan. A cross sectional study, in *Substance Abuse Treatment, Prevention, and Policy* 6:1 (2011), 1–7.

Kazi, Ambreen, Zafar Fatmi, Juanita Hatcher, Muhammad Masood Kadir, Unaiza Niaz, and Gail A. Wasserman. Social environment and depression among pregnant women in urban areas of Pakistan. Importance of social relations, in *Social Science & Medicine* 63:6 (2006), 1466–76. <https://doi.org/10.1016/j.socscimed.2006.05.019>.

Khan, Murad M. The NHS International Fellowship scheme in psychiatry. Robbing the poor to pay the rich?, in *Psychiatric Bulletin* 28:12 (2004), 435–37. <https://doi.org/10.1192/pb.28.12.435>.

Khan, M.M., S. Islam, and A.K. Kundi. Parasuicide in Pakistan. Experience at a university hospital, in *Acta Psychiatrica Scandinavica* 93:4 (1996), 264–67. <https://doi.org/10.1111/j.1600-0447.1996.tb10646.x>.

Levinson, Daphna, and Anneke Ifrah. The robustness of the gender effect on help seeking for mental health needs in three subcultures in Israel, in *Social Psychiatry and Psychiatric Epidemiology* 45:3 (2009), 337–44. <https://doi.org/10.1007/s00127-009-0079-4>.

Malik, Muhammad Ashar, and Murad Moosa Khan. 2016. "Economic Burden of Mental Illnesses in Pakistan." *The Journal of Mental Health Policy and Economics* 19 (3): 155–66. http://www.ncbi.nlm.nih.gov/pubmed/27572143.

Maselko, Joanna, Lisa Bates, Sonia Bhalotra, John A. Gallis, Karen O'Donnell, Siham Sikander, and Elizabeth L. Turner. Socioeconomic status indicators and common mental disorders. Evidence from a study of prenatal depression in Pakistan, in *SSM—Population Health* 4 (2018), 1–9. <https://doi.org/10.1016/j.ssmph.2017.10.004>.

Maselko, Joanna, and Vikram Patel. Why women attempt suicide. The role of mental illness and social disadvantage in a community cohort study in India, in *Journal of Epidemiology and Community Health* 62:9 (2008), 817–22.

Mirza, Ilyas, and Rachel Jenkins. Risk factors, prevalence, and treatment of anxiety and depressive disorders in Pakistan. Systematic review, in *BMJ* 328:7443 (2004), 794–800. <https://doi.org/10.1136/bmj.328.7443.794>.

Naqvi, H., S. Hussan, and F. Dossa. Benzodiazepine. Slow sand of addiction, in *The Journal of the Pakistan Medical Association* 59:6 (2009), 415–17.

Naqvi, Haider A., and Murad M. Khan. Pathway to psychiatric care in Karachi, in *Journal of the College of Physicians and Surgeons—Pakistan* 16:6 (2006), 438–39. <https://doi.org/6.2006/JCPSP.438439>.

Niaz, Unaiza. Women's mental health in Pakistan, in *World Psychiatry* 3:1 (2004), 60.

Nisar, N., N. Billoo, and A.A. Gadit. Prevalence of depression and the associated risk factors among adult women in a fishing community, in *The Journal of the Pakistan Medical Association* 54:10 (2004), 519–25.

Patel, Vikram. Poverty, gender and mental health promotion in a global society, in *Promotion & Education* 12:2 (2005), 26–29. <https://doi.org/10.1177/10253823050120020104x>.

Patel, Vikram, Ricardo Araya, Sudipto Chatterjee, Dan Chisholm, Alex Cohen, Mary De Silva, Clemens Hosman, Hugh McGuire, Graciela Rojas, and Mark van Ommeren. Treatment and prevention of mental disorders in low-income and middle-income countries, in *The Lancet* 370:9591 (2007), 991–1005. <https://doi .org/10.1016/S0140-6736(07)61240-9>.

Patel, Vikram, Betty R. Kirkwood, Sulochana Pednekar, Bernadette Pereira, Preetam Barros, Janice Fernandes, Jane Datta, Reshma Pai, Helen Weiss, and David Mabey. Gender disadvantage and reproductive health risk factors for common mental disorders in women. A community survey in India, in *Archives of General Psychiatry* 63:4 (2006), 404–13. <https://doi.org/10.1001/archpsyc.63.4.40 4>.

Patel, Vikram, Gregory Simon, Neerja Chowdhary, Sylvia Kaaya, and Ricardo Araya. Packages of care for depression in low- and middle-income countries, in *PLoS Med* 6:10 (2009), e1000159. <https://doi.org/10.1371/journal.pmed.1000159>.

Rahman, A., and F. Creed. Outcome of prenatal depression and risk factors associated with persistence in the first postnatal year. Prospective study from Rawalpindi, Pakistan, in *Journal of Affective Disorders* 100:1–3 (2007), 115–21.

Rahman, A., Z. Iqbal, and R. Harrington. Life events, social support and depression in childbirth. Perspectives from a rural community in the developing world, in *Psychological Medicine* 33:7 (2003), 1161–67. <https://doi.org/10.1017/S003329170 3008286>.

Rahman, A., H. Lovel, J. Bunn, Z. Iqbal, and R. Harrington. Mothers' mental health and infant growth. A case-control study from Rawalpindi, Pakistan, in *Child: Care, Health and Development* 30:1 (2004), 21–27. <https://doi.org/10.1111/j.1365-2214.2004 .00382.x>.

Rahman, A, Zafar Iqbal, James Bunn, Hermione Lovel, and Richard Harrington. 2004. "Impact of Maternal Depression on Infant Nutritional Status and Illness: A Cohort Study." *Archives of General Psychiatry* 61(9):946–52.

Rubenstein, L.V., M. Jackson-Triche, J. Unutzer, J. Miranda, K. Minnium, M.L. Pearson, and K.B. Wells. Evidence-based care for depression in managed primary care practices, in *Health Affairs* 18:5 (1999), 89–105.

Sartorius, Norman. Stigma and mental health, in *The Lancet* 370:9590 (2007), 810–11. <https://doi.org/10.1016/S0140-6736(07)61245-8>.

Shahid, Muhammad, Murad M. Khan, Muhammad Saleem Khan, Yasir Jamal, Aaref Badshah, and Rifat Rehmani. Deliberate self-harm in the emergency department. Experience from Karachi, Pakistan, in *Crisis* 30:2 (2009), 85–89. <https://doi.org/ 10.1027/0227-5910.30.2.85>.

Taqui, Ather M., Ahmed Itrat, Waris Qidwai, and Zeeshan Qadri. Depression in the elderly. Does family system play a role? A cross-sectional study, in *BMC Psychiatry* 7 (2007), 57. (https://doi.org/10.1186/1471-244X-7-57).

Wells, Kenneth B. *Caring for depression*, Cambridge, Mass. 1996.

WEF (World Economic Forum). *Global Gender Gap Report 2018*, <http://reports .weforum.org/global-gender-gap-report-2018>.

WHO (World Health Organization). *Mental Health Aspects of Women's Reproductive Health: A Global Review of the Literature*. Geneva, 2009.

Population and Health Sciences

Population and Health Sciences

Hania Sholkamy

Introduction

Population and health sciences have shifted focus from reproduction, fertility, and the medicalization and systemization of populations to a political economy paradigm. The last decade has witnessed a radicalization of social sciences in general and the disciplines of population have followed suit. The overtly medicalized tenor that marked population and health till 1994 has given way since then to a concern with gender, youth, poverty and governance. These last ten years have culminated in a number of revolutions in the Arab Muslim world and have also witnessed a series of crises in the world at large. The problems of population growth have become closely associated with the crisis of impoverishment and inequality. The relations of reproduction are now addressed as gender inequalities. The issues that relate to services, access to information and rights to health are subsumed by radical political overhauls and loud calls for social justice. In brief, the arena of population and health studies now studies politics, ideologies, gender and social rights, as well as poverty and deprivation. In the Muslim world there has also been a significant shift in the preponderance of religion as a frame of reference and of the resurgence of its jurisprudence as a source for policy directions. The old contradictions between renditions of religion and those of modernities are once again on the surface but are perhaps on their way to a complex and nuanced resolution.

The Muslim world and the worlds of Muslims seem to have become more radicalized, more dangerous, more urgent, and fractured by unrelenting competitions around identity, resources, rights and bodily integrity. Half a billion Muslim women inhabit some 45 Muslim-majority countries, and another 30 or more countries have significant Muslim minorities, including, increasingly, countries in the developed West (Offenhaur 2005). The tensions that define the demographic and daily life of hundreds of millions of women are precipitated by a changing real world and by the shift in the world of research and ideas. On the one hand, scholarship has come to encompass the economic and social determinants of population health and well-being or of deprivation and inequality. On the other hand, the growing importance of religion and religious identity have brought added attention to the individual, to sexuality and to agency.

© KONINKLIJKE BRILL NV, LEIDEN, 2014 | DOI:10.1163/1872-5309_EWIC_COM_00017

These two almost contradictory trends are delineated by political contestations and economic deprivations and inequalities. The work of Livia Wick (2008) exemplifies these changes well. Wick worked on birthing practices, looking at the medicalization of birth in Palestine and at the impact of politics of protest and liberation on Palestinian health services. In telling the stories of Palestinian women's birthing experiences as determined by the checkpoints that fragment the landscape of their homeland, Wick has illustrated the unnecessary suffering and risks taken by Palestinian women giving birth while at the mercy of checkpoint schedules or the checkpoints themselves. The increased risk to the health of both mother and newborn are mitigated by the brave and innovative efforts of local midwives. Besides registering the birth stories themselves, Wick historicizes the intersection between the professional politics of medicine and national politics during the second Palestinian uprising, which erupted in 2000, and brings to bear the significance of the Palestinian political movements of steadfastness (ṣumūd) and of the popular health movement on the practices of health professionals (Wick 2008). Her work and that of others has yielded a popular campaign called "VisualizingPalestine" that has produced posters to express the horrendous neonatal mortality associated with restricted mobility precipitated by checkpoints. (Between 2000 and 2005, 67 Palestinian mothers were forced to give birth at Israeli military checkpoints; 36 babies died.)

Population and health studies have been defined by two sets of relationships of production. The first are from the world of donor aid and oversees funding. Much of population research has been motivated by an anti-natalist agenda that identifies population growth as a development burden. The scholarship produced in this context tends to be problem and policy oriented and to be dominated by statistics and prescriptions. The second emanate from critical knowledge production networks and movements. This body of work references overtly political projects such as those of feminism, national liberation, bodily rights and integrity, and anti-globalization movements. These divergent worlds of scholarship often intersect and usually inform one another. This entry will trace some of the important trends in population and health studies that have emerged in the past decade in both the world of policy that is relevant and critical scholarship. The approach adopted focuses on examples of initiatives, literatures and ideas that have shaped the field and does not attempt a comprehensive summation or rendition of this large area of scholarship and action. The entry highlights areas of intersection between health and population and considers the influence of gender ideologies on both.

The scope of this entry falls short of EWIC's mandate because the focus here is primarily on the Arab world; therefore many aspects of health and

POPULATION AND HEALTH SCIENCES

population studies in Africa, Asia and Europe are overlooked. There are three reasons for this oversight. The first concerns the articulation of health and population with policy. There are such differences between the situation and experiences of women in these contexts and their explication that a broad sweep analysis is impossible. Muslim women in non-Arab Asia and Africa experience life through diverse cultural lenses that determine their status, rights, health, work and reproductive norms and practices. Second, the character of the state and of state institutions varies enormously between these countries and locations. The rights availed to women by legal and moral regimes are significantly different for Muslim women in India than they are for Nigerians in the north. Muslim women in Europe have access to services that enable them to make reproductive decisions that are remarkably different from services available to Muslims in Ghana. Third, the revolutions and transformations taking place in Arab countries have to some extent overwhelmed this entry; the dramatic and unfinished revolutions and the ongoing wars and displacements have warranted reflection on the relationships between social, gender and political transformations and their implications for our understanding of health and population.

Reproductive and Public Health

In a summary of the state of reproductive health and population research after the 1994 International Conference on Population and Development, Huda Zurayk (1999) noted a number of future directions. These included an engagement with health services to ensure quality of care and investigations into the economic and political contexts in which health and population policy is drafted. These recommendations also highlighted the intersections between reproductive and public health in general.

Population and reproductive health have always featured as a core component of public health programs and research. The past decade confirmed the importance of macro-level conditions to health and well-being. The collection edited by Michael Marmot and Richard G. Wilkinson (2009) presented hard evidence of the importance of social and political factors to individual health. The Whitehall study that tracked thousands of British public sector employees over time proved that people's social and economic circumstances strongly affect their health throughout life. Junior office workers were found to suffer double the disease burden of senior office workers, despite the advantage of youth (Brunner 1997). This landmark study filtered into policy discourses in the past decade whereby the social determinants of health became a key approach to addressing health burdens. Health is affected by conditions and structures that limit or enhance well-being, security and opportunity (Marmot and Wilkinson 2009).

These macro-level determinants affect the distribution of health and well-being and the risks and vulnerabilities that cause morbidity and mortality. Thus, poverty, inequality, environmental pollutions, deprivations, racism, and biases all impact health and the distribution of disease. They also impact the care that people receive at the hands of health systems (Farmer 1999). While public health programs alone cannot ameliorate the social forces that are associated with poor health outcomes, developing a better understanding of the social determinants of health is critical to reducing burdens of disease. Working with this approach, WHO launched a major effort to document the social determinants of health and to encourage governments to reorganize their health systems so as to address these causal factors. The important influence of Iran in shaping this agenda should be noted as it is one of the countries that has long adopted a social approach to health care (WHO 2008).

More than any other field of health, reproductive health is immersed, not only in material and social conditions, but also in personal and social relations. Beliefs, family relations, material conditions, as well as political choices all condition reproductive health and how it is experienced or pursued. For example, maternal mortality is a construct of a number of social determinants— the practice of letting women eat last and least; early marriage and early pregnancy; lack of decision-making power within the household; low demand for prenatal care and for attention—that can lead to increased exposure to maternal death. Community factors also impinge on health, so access to water, sanitation, employment, public services and resources are important determinants of health outcomes.

The connections with poverty and war are clear when looking at women's health outcomes in Arab and Muslim countries. Of maternal deaths in the Arab region, 77 percent occur in Somalia, Sudan, and Yemen; these are three countries that have been recently ravaged by war and poverty, and where contraception use is low (Roudi-Fahimi et al. 2012). The impact of violence on the quality of life of peoples in occupied and war-torn countries has been amply documented, particularly in Iraq, Palestine and in Lebanon (Giacaman et al. 2012, Rawaf and Rawaf 2012, Nuwayhed et al. 2012). Gender disparities as determinants of poor health outcomes have also been discussed (DeJong 2006), since gender is recognized as a primary category in health research and analysis.

There are many other ongoing conflicts in the Arab region, including the bloody and protracted war in Syria and the recently ended conflict in Sudan

POPULATION AND HEALTH SCIENCES

that split the country into two. The impact of violence and insecurity has shaped the field of population studies in these societies not only in terms of their impact on mortality and morbidity, but also in the effect of the dramatic cost of war on stability and livelihoods. These and other conflicts in the region have produced vast numbers of forced migrants and refugees making the Arab region one of the largest refugee producing areas in the world. There are reportedly one million Syrian refugees now scattered on the borders in Lebanon and in Turkey. Iraqi refugees have been pouring into Jordan, Syria and Egypt over the past decade (Fargues 2013, 2012).

Structural adjustment and the impoverishment of health systems is another political/economic determinant of health. The impact of globalization and liberalization on population in general has been a feature of recent scholarship. The policies that have been associated with rising social and economic inequalities are blamed on the structural adjustment programs dictated by international economic agents such as the International Monetary Fund and the World Bank, who have promoted what some label as market fundamentalism. These programs are dictates of the so called Washington Consensus, which is a recipe for policy changes that enable countries to rationalize public spending, liberalize their markets so as to enable the private sector, attract foreign investment and thereby realize high levels of economic growth which could/should decrease poverty, provide employment and enhance well-being.

However, these SAPs (structural adjustment programs) have had a devastating impact on livelihoods and on public health and other public services to the poor, leading to a "new intensity of immiseration" (Pfeiffer and Chapman 2010). The World Bank has promoted user fees for services, for example, as a way to improve quality, reduce waste, and create the correct incentive structure for service providers that would ensure a better quality of care; but this has resulted instead in the privatization of basic services (Turshen 1999). These policies have been shown to fail the poor and the vulnerable and to create inequalities and social disruptions (Castro and Singer 2004).

The impact of macro-level policy direction on the production of health inequalities has been noted for countries such as Egypt (Shukrallah 2012) and Senegal (Foley 2001; see also Desclaux 2004). These policies have also led to the commodification of social relations, while unemployment and falling incomes have affected the reproductive behavior and choices of women in, for instance, Mongolia (Janes and Oyuntsegtseg 2004), and Egypt (Hatem 1992, Pfeiffer and Chapman 2010). This is a growing field of interest as it affects vulnerable people everywhere, and women in particular as reproductive health services that serve women and primary health care services that benefit children are being undermined or priced out of their reach. The recent and ongoing financial crises will further limit the ability of states to finance and develop health and reproductive care services.

The edited collection *Public Health in the Arab World* has made a significant contribution to health studies in Arab countries (Jabbour et al. 2012). The chapters cover the gamut of public health scholarship from the characteristics of different population groups to the gaps in scholarship and the specificities of contextual actors in Arab countries. The chapter on gaps in knowledge is a particularly important one as it points the way toward future scholarship that investigates the linkages between social and health actions and measurements to promote a health equity lens to examine policy and research interventions (Rashad and Khidr 2012).

Despite the proliferation of disease burdens amongst women as a result of reproductive health burdens, deprivations, the high cost of immobility, and the lack of access to resources, there is little in terms of new scholarship that further investigates the excess disease burdens of women and the relevance of nation and society to this relationship. Recent work on gender and violence has, however, paid specific attention to the ideological and moral connections of Islam and the justifications for violence in wars of occupation (Abu Lughod 2002), as well as to suicide bombing and acts of struggle (Das 2008, Asad 2007).

The Changing Profiles, Positions, and Problems of Women

The situation of women in Arab and Muslim countries and societies has been central to population research, particularly over the last decade. There are three strands of research that focus on women. The first concerns the changing demography of families and societies, which is forcing a re-imagination of gender roles and responsibilities. The second concerns debates over Islamic laws and whether their interpretations are compatible with demands for more personal freedoms and socioeconomic rights for women. The third concerns narratives of sexuality, of the body and of health rights and bodily integrity. This third area of work also involves the development of rights groups and movements.

There are convergences between the situation of women in Muslim-majority and Muslim-minority countries. Gender as a religious and moral construct has crossed borders and adapted to a variety of socioeconomic, linguistic, and political contexts. This section will, however, focus on Arab-majority and Muslim-majority countries since many of the debates concerning women are contingent on national legal and political frameworks; therefore the patriarchal character of the state and of the political and economic institutions of society shape the debate on the situation of women.

The new demographic reality of the Arab family has been a focus of interest for scholars. The dynamic changes in family formations, size, and function have created new contexts in which gender roles are enacted. Several studies have shown evidence of lower fertility levels, higher educational attainment, longer years spent single, and lower rates of nuptiality amongst Muslim and Arab women.

Studies based on numerous data sources include the book-length 2004 UNIFEM report, *Progress of Arab Women*, the *Arab Human Development Report 2005: Empowerment of Arab Women*, Philippe Fargues's 2005 article on women in Arab countries and challenges to the patriarchal system (Fargues 2005), and a 2012 edited volume on *Population Dynamics in Muslim Countries: Assembling the Jigsaw* (Groth and Alfonso 2012). Together, they draw a picture of change and tensions. Although there are a few people who insist that "demographics are destiny" or base analysis solely on the basis of demographic determinism, still there some hard facts that demonstrate the inevitability of a reformulation of gender roles.

The most striking finding that emerges from such studies pertains to reproduction, namely fertility, female reproductive health (and related contraceptive prevalence), and the age and type of family formation. Current research reveals that a "demographic transition" is underway in many Muslim areas. The theory, which has governed population policies since the 1970s, holds that societies in general eventually abandon the strategy of high fertility when mortality drops because of health improvements and the pressures of urbanization and modernization. For demographic researchers, the evidence of Muslim countries bears out this theory, in that most have seen a sharp fertility decline as well as improvements in child survival and overall life expectancy (Offenhaur 2005, 45, Eberstadt and Shah 2012, 11–14).

Philippe Fargues pointed to a falling fertility rate that may, on average, be high by global standards, but is much lower than it was in the recent past. He cites the example of Iran, which saw a drop from a pre-transitional 6.4 children per woman in 1986 to a below-replacement level of 2.06 in 1998. All Muslim-majority countries have witnessed such sharp drops, leading researchers to focus on the implications of transition to social and family life. A particular effort has been made to link this transition not only to falling fertility but also to delayed marriage as a driver of lower fertility.

The New Arab Demography project alluded to earlier has yielded a number of studies on nuptiality transition. The first aspect of nuptiality that has undergone significant changes is the proportion of women who never marry. In the 1960s and 1970s, between 15 percent and 26 percent of women aged 15–49 were never married. These proportions increased considerably in the 1990s, ranging from 24 percent to 61 percent, except for Oman, which has a proportion of

18 percent. The figure has reached at least 40 percent in half of Arab countries. Thus, for many Arab countries, two out of every five women in the age group 15–49 have never married (Rashad and Osman 2003, 8). More than a third of the Arab countries have experienced an increase in the median age at marriage for the cohort 25–29 from 4.7 to 7.7 years during a span of 20 years. Estimates of the time spent in not-married state during 35 years between ages 15 and 50 show that in nearly half of the Arab countries, a female spends around a third of her prime 35 years of life in the unmarried state (Rashad, Osman and Roudi-Fahimi 2005, 10–11).

The timing of marriage has important implications for social life in general and family life in particular. Women who marry young are fertile for longer than those who marry later. They may not be able to begin or sustain careers or work opportunities. They are more likely to be destined for a lifetime of dependency. The ideological valorization of women's work at home as daughters, mothers and wives is the mainstay of patriarchal ideologies and policies (whether of individuals or of the state). It is this "work" that enables women to claim rights, dignity, recognition, and influence. But homemaking and care-giving roles are least prized by the cultures that theoretically venerate stay at home women. This is evident in legal codes that do not compensate women for these gender roles and which provide social security covers only through markets and families rather than as a natural right of citizenship, even for stay at home mothers and wives (UNIFEM 2004). Decades of cultural scrutiny have shown that women have not claimed the benefits of the patriarchal bargain.

The shift in age of marriage and in the patterns and timing of family formation are therefore a key element in political and social transitions in Muslim countries. An Egypt labor market panel study notes that women exit labor markets almost automatically upon marriage (and rather than in relation to motherhood as has been noted in other parts of the world (Assad and Hamidi 2009). Not only is this the practice, but it is also the expectation. Another survey of laborers also found that the vast majority of young women workers expect to leave work once married (World Bank 2009). Despite the entry of millions into the labor market as a strategy to provide basic needs and enable young women to save up for marriage, paid work outside the home is not pursued or promoted for women. Women's rights as workers have also been neglected (ITUC 2012). A large cohort of women has joined labor markets although, unfortunately and often, as in the case of Egypt and Turkey, in informal or home-based employment (Assaad and Hamidi 2009, Buğra and Özkan 2012, Sholkamy 2012a).

In sum, significant change in the familial roles of women is in progress because of delayed marriage, even in areas that have tended to be the most resistant to such change (Rashad and Osman 2003, 55, Hasso 2011). Feminists have problematized the meaning and implications of paid work and questioned its viability as an unconditional route to women's liberation. The issue now surely should be how to make work empowering and not whether the right to work is a right worth having or not (Kabeer et al. 2013, Sholkamy 2012a).

Education is another area that exemplifies important changes in the status of women. The *Arab Human Development Report 2005* cites education as the only arena in which discrimination against women is overturned as there are increasingly higher levels of enrollment in, and attainment of, education amongst women than there are amongst men (AHDR 2005; see also UNFPA 2010); for example, in Iran, 54 percent of recent entrants to universities were women, and in Kuwait, in 2003, female registrations in higher education exceeded men's by 30 percent (Hosseini-Chavoshi and Abbasi-Shavazi 2012). These changes have been the focus of scholars working at the intersection of population and gender research.

There are also significant changes taking place at the level of prevalence of contraception and the concomitant changes in reproductive behavior. Four in ten married women of reproductive age in Arab countries use modern contraception (Roudi-Fahimi et al. 2012). As well as addressing the general trend of declining fertility that contributes to "demographic transition," researchers have taken up the related issues of desired levels of fertility and of family planning by means of contraception and abortion. In an effort to understand the demographic transition, research on these well-documented issues deploys both quantitative and qualitative approaches. Straightforward quantitative research reveals widespread growth in the rates of the adoption of modern contraceptive methods, but with respect to Islamic countries, rates of contraception are highly variable and often counterintuitive. For example, religiously conservative Iran shows a respectable contraceptive prevalence rate of 55 percent, while conservative Yemen shows only 10 percent. The main factors determining contraceptive prevalence are the availability of services and their quality; poverty and culture also play a very important role (Roudi-Fahimi et al. 2012).

Exceptional cases of high fertility that have received scholarly attention include diaspora populations, most notably the Palestinians. Other counter-examples of persisting or renewed high fertility include Islamist sub-populations in Egypt. Such cases, however, in the view of many demographers, are indeed exceptions, in which a high birth rate is best explained as a strategy whose meaning is highly situation-specific. Amongst Palestinian families, according to Rita Giacaman and her colleagues, high fertility is an act of political engagement and an assertion of national identity (Giacaman et al. 2012), while in Islamist Egyptian sub-groups, it is a marker of political dissent and dissonance (Offenhaur 2005, 114). These researchers are not convinced of the explanatory primacy of Islam, Islamic traditions, or even Islamic family laws, because Islam itself has proven to be adaptable on issues of family planning under wider socioeconomic and other pressures.

The problem of "unmet need," or the situation whereby women do not want to get pregnant but are not using contraception, remains one of much importance (Bradley et al. 2011, Roudi-Fahimi et al. 2012). Failures in reproductive health services, in the quality of care received by women, and in the ability of the state and civil society as well as service providers to communicate the ideals of smaller families to the population at large are cited as the reasons for continued contraceptive failures (Roudi-Fahimi et al. 2012). Abortion as a right and as an indicator of unmet need has also been a recent focus of research and of action (Dabash and Roudi-Fahimi 2008).

Whatever their causal dynamics, changes such as the postponement of marriage, the growing proportion of never-marrieds, declining childbearing, increasing contraceptive usage, and mass schooling for females spell erosion of the traditional kinship-based and patriarchal extended family. Fargues suggests that such changes undercut key pillars of the kinship-based family structure (Fargues 2013; see also Offenhaur 2005).

These shifting demographic sands have created a demand for a moral and political investigation of women's rights in Islam and of the religious constructions of gender. Recent scholarship from the Arab Families Working group, for example, is providing ample evidence of changes in the family which is the building block of the Muslim *umma*. The tensions between moral desires and modernities' mandates have been a feature of all literatures on Islamic social transformations and on stagnations in Muslim societies (Rogan 2009, Soroush 2000).

Although an established tradition since the 1970s, Islamic feminism has gained a larger following from observers and a deeper scrutiny by scholars in the past decade. In 2011, the revolutions of Tunis, Egypt and Libya changed existing political orders and, with them, overthrew the structures of state-led feminisms that had obfuscated the relationships between religion and gender (Sholkamy 2012b). The replacement of secular, albeit conservative, elites with new cadres of religiously inclined and informed voices and agents is one expression of a decade-long tussle between the religious and the secular in which women were a prime territory for the display of an often adversarial relationship. The prevalence of formal and physical displays of modesty and piety has long been a feature of qualitative work on Muslim communities and countries (for example, Mahmood 2005). But beyond these "veils" lie varied

POPULATION AND HEALTH SCIENCES

constructions of gender rights. Recently, observers and activists have questioned the validity of assumptions concerning the moral determinisms of idioms of piety (Sholkamy 2010).

Changing Age Structures of the Population and Their Consequences

The third and perhaps most dynamic and urgent field of recent scholarship concerns the implications of changing age structures of populations. The youthfulness of populations or so-called demographic gift has been a focus of surveys and analysis. The political protests, revolutions and tensions seen all over the world, and which have resulted in regime change in several Arab countries, were led by youth and mounted in the name of social justice and the right to work. Those who stress that demographic factors are at the heart of the Arab spring focus mostly on the so-called youth bulge theory (Urdal 2006, Cincotta 2012, Puschmann and Mattjis 2012). According to this theory, the risk of revolutions and armed conflicts increases if there is an excess of young people, especially young men, in the age group 15–24. The demographic gift in this case was a poisoned chalice for autocrats. The situation for several Arab countries shows a younger, better-educated population with fewer opportunities for mobility and employment.

For example, the ratio of those entering the labor force to those leaving it is 3:1 in Egypt, 5:1 in Jordan, 8:1 Saudi Arabia. Millions of young Arabs between the ages of 15 to 29 years have acquired an education, but have not found jobs or a means to support themselves, start families, or gain voice and citizenship rights. The Survey of Young People in Egypt (Population Council 2011) predicted the problems of economies and society out of synchronization with demographic upheavals. The characteristics of youth have also been analyzed in other studies. Recent scholarship in the field of health has noted the lack of health services and access to care and the heavy burdens placed on youth by unhealthy lifestyles (see Jabbour et al. 2012).

The politics of revolt have been addressed by some recent scholarship, but mostly in the context of political science research and transition theory. Youth anger and frustration have been noted by Diane Singerman in Egypt and explained by the lingering state of liminality caused by the pressures of culture and economy whereby the attainment of adulthood and full respect via marriage (the cultural gate) or employment (the economic avenue) are both denied to young men and women (Singerman 2007, 29). As Miriam Marks observes, "Even as these youth voice their disapproval of authoritarian regimes and corrupt governments, marriage is not an issue far from their minds. Rather, it is perhaps the most important institution in the life of a young person, and its relevance to political activity and even extremism should not go understated" (Marks 2011, 23). Population sciences have confronted the consequences of an un-addressed youth bulge for the future of social security and protection. While Arab societies are now young they are only growing older. By 2025 the percentage of those aged over 60 in Egypt will be over 12 percent; in Bahrain, Qatar, and the United Arab Emirates it will be 25 percent; and in other Arab states it is projected to be around 10 percent of the population.

The family has also been studied in connection with the acceleration in aging and the various needs for social protection and security. Because families are such vital social institutions, valuable cultural assets and an integral part of the Arab self perception, this changing institution has been the subject of extensive study, not only in terms of demographic changes and theory, but also as an economic institution that provides welfare and protection for both the young and unemployed, for women who remain single or whose marriage is delayed and for the elderly (Yount and Sibai 2009, Olmsted 2005, Rashad, Osman and Roudi-Fahimi 2005). Few people in the Arab region, for example, will be able to rely on retirement payment (Kárpáti 2011, Puschmann and Mattjis 2012). This situation can increase poverty burdens as well as pose a challenge for health systems. Also of concern is that what may be seen as a lessening of both personal and geographic ties between generations means that a revival of extended families is less likely to occur.

Analysts in the field of population are of the opinion that demographic factors played a decisive role in the outbreak of the Arab Spring (Cincotta 2012). Others have pointed to the inadequacy of any models based on the youth bulge theory to explain the timing of revolutions, while retaining the notion that demographics provide the most relevant explanations of political transformation and disruptions. The inability of youth to find work and a marriage partner are key to understanding the politics of Arab countries in particular and Muslim countries in the global South in general (Puschmann and Mattjis 2012).

Reports, Networks, Benchmarks and Goals

This entry coincides with the flagging of policy initiatives in the fields of population and reproductive health. A new international conference of population will be convened in 2014. In 2015 the end of the Millennium Development Goal initiative will be celebrated and the achievements of the initiatives in terms of poverty, health, population and gender equity assessed.

POPULATION AND HEALTH SCIENCES

The Millennium Declaration commits itself to gender equality as part of its broader vision of human rights and social justice. The goals set by this agenda include several that relate to population issues. However, since population has been linked to the development agenda, it is fair to argue that all the goals are relevant to population. The commitment to gender equality that is key to the achievements of all these goals is expressed in terms of two rationales: one *intrinsic*, seeing gender equality as a fundamental human right, the other *instrumental*, recognizing the powerful contribution that women make to the eradication of poverty in all its dimensions—and indeed to development itself (Sholkamy 2010, Kabeer et al. 2012).

The goal of gender equality and women's empowerment, even in the narrow sense that it is defined in MDG 3, will not be achieved without progress on equalizing access and control in relation to paid work, education at all levels, health, water, sanitation, housing, and political participation. Equally, progress on the other MDGs, particularly those related to hunger, health, education and poverty reduction, are likely to be accelerated as a result of progress on gender equality. All development interventions need to be formulated with a view to transforming these structures, whether through radical interventions such as land reform or incremental interventions such as building separate toilets for girls and boys in schools (Kabeer et al. 2012).

A number of reports have been issued, which cover different regions in which Muslim women live and report on the situation of women and of population. The ICPD (International Conference in Population and Development)/15 reports have gauged the progress on the population agenda. The BPFA (Beijing Platform for Action) reports focus on the advancements in the situation of women. In the Arab world, two important reports that focus on women have been produced. The first, by UNIFEM (now UN Women), called *The Progress of Arab Women*, was published in 2004. The second is the *Arab Human Development Report: The Empowerment of Arab Women*, published in 2005. All of these documents combine statistics and narrative to describe the situation, characteristics and options/choices facing women in particular and populations in general. The surveys on youth have also been an important reference for scholars and have proven to be precursors of a critical field of investigation in which Muslim countries seem to be following their own trajectory of population transition as the impact of delayed marriage on youth is seen as the key to understanding all elements of transition including the demographic, the social and the political (Puschmann and Mattjis 2012).

The next two years will witness a new cycle of pledges, global initiatives, and covenants. The legacy of the ICPD has been honored in terms of the mainstreaming of reproductive health and gender equality as essential approaches to population policy and services. The focus on quality of and access to care has proven to be more problematic as health services continue to be of uneven quality or unaffordable to millions of women. The ascendance of political Islam in many Arab countries and the preponderance of ultra-orthodox renditions of Islam amongst groups such as Salafists have also posed a challenge to the values that have hitherto held sway in population policy circles. One newspaper article in February 2012 noted that 6 percent of the newly elected parliamentarians had more than ten children (*al-Masry al-Youm* 2012).

In the Arabic-speaking world, there are now more venues for the discussion of issues relating to population and to public health. *Reproductive Health Matters* continues to be published in Arabic. Recently, the *Lancet* has begun to appear also in Arabic. Breaking the hegemony of European languages on scholarship may well yield a more dynamic and broader-based engagement with population sciences and also garner a different audience to these disciplines.

In addition, there are digital platforms for discussing and sharing information and experiences on the issues of development and population. These blogs and sites may not yet be fully recognized as sources of scholarship, but it is a matter of time before this becomes the case. *Jadaliyya* (<http://www.jadaliyya.com>), which mixes academic, activist, and journalistic content, has become one of the few places where issues of sexuality in the Arab world are freely expressed. *Muftah* (<http://www.muftah.org>) is another site that hosts "free and open debate from Morocco to Pakistan" and invites contributions on issues that matter to people. While these are not explicitly population-related fora, they are becoming instrumental in facilitating the voices of actors and activists engaged in the work of development and social change. A third noteworthy source of opinion and scholarship is *Contestations* (<http://www.contestations.net/>), an electronic newsletter devoted to presenting the opposing opinions of scholars on contentious questions related to women's empowerments and gender rights.

A number of activist networks are approaching the gender aspects of population. Musawah (<http://www.musawah.org/>) works in African, Asian, European and Middle Eastern contexts and is focusing on the gender pact and constructions of gender within marriage as defined by a progressive Islamic frame of reference. These scholars have made significant contributions towards equality in the Muslim family through work on guardianship, maintenance, the nature of the marriage contract, and the constructions of gender as designed and sanctioned by scripture and Qur'ānic texts (Mir-Hosseini 2009).

Pathways of Women's Empowerment (<http://www.pathwaysofempowerment.org/>) is a consortium of researchers working on identifying the development and policy interventions that empower women. Researchers from this network have addressed women's empowerment in Islamic contexts in Egypt (Sharmani 2010), Pakistan (Khan 2010), and Bangladesh (Azim and Sultan 2010, Nazneen and Tasneem 2010).

There is evidence from this work that gender equality is strengthened through key resources that enable women's agency and bargaining power. These include women's share of employment, particularly formal employment; post-primary education and life-learning opportunities; access to a broad range of financial resources, including microfinance; access to land and housing on a secure joint or individual basis; access to organizational resources across a range of spheres of life (natural resources management, women's organizations, microfinance groups, trade unions, co-operatives); sexual and reproductive health and rights, including access to safe abortion, contraception and treatment for HIV and sexually transmitted infections; access to safe water and sanitation; and access to opportunities for voice and representation, and to participation in governance (Kabeer 2012, UN Women 2004).

Another important network is that of the Arab Families Working Group, which has nurtured new generations of scholars working on the dynamics of Arab families in a variety of contexts. The Reproductive Health Working Group has also continued its association and scholarship and investigated new areas in this field, including the constructions of masculinity in Turkey, prostitution and the leisure industry, as well as playing an instrumental role in the contributions to public health in the Arab world.

The field of population has also been defined by the activism of civil society, in particular health, human, and women's rights groups. The social power of movements has been an important signifier of the politics of this decade (Bayat 2007, Batliwala 2012). Women's movements have been key to peace-building, as in the case of the Sudanese Women Empowerment for Peace (SuWEP), and in promoting reproductive health and women's political rights, as in the case of Iran (Hoodfar 2012). International networks for reproductive rights, such as Women's Global Network for Reproductive Rights (WGNRR) and Realizing Sexual and Reproductive Justice (RESURJ), undertake research, produce evidence, and lobby for sexual and human rights.

Such networks and organizations have also emerged at the national and local levels. In Egypt, for example, due to the proliferation of sexual harassment as both a planned and opportunistic mode of violence against women, a number of organizations not only combat harassment and document its incidence, but also operate as research centers, producing activist scholarship on women's rights and conditions, such as the New Women Research Centre, Women and Memory Forum, and Nazra for Feminist Studies.

Conclusion

Linking demographic change with its social implications is not new. However, doing so in a framework that is dynamic and illustrates how population transitions can be burdens or opportunities is a more interesting alternative that places populations in political economy contexts. Thus one can see how the link between population changes and socio/political ones is neither causal nor simple. Rather, it is a dynamic change that has multiple connections that can be causal, complementary, or competitive.

The first decade of the second millennium was marked by a number of revolutions in the Arab Muslim world. Egypt, Tunis, Libya and Yemen toppled their autocratic rulers. There is ongoing or recently ended conflict in Palestine, Syria, Lebanon, Sudan, Iraq and Afghanistan. And many other Muslim-majority countries have witnessed rebellions, protests or civil unrest, as is the case in Bahrain, Iran, Pakistan and Bangladesh. The Muslim world is unsettled and the populations within these societies are almost all somehow touched by turmoil and change.

Analysts have linked the demographics of these societies with their political trajectories and transitions. A young cohort has come of age in many if not all Arab Muslim countries where youth and children now form the majority of the population. These anticipated changes in the demographics of countries that enjoyed/endured high fertility rates have been noted in the vast literature on population and reproductive health of Arab and Muslim countries. The problems of population growth have become closely associated with the crisis of impoverishment and inequality. The relations of reproduction are now addressed as gender inequalities. The issues that relate to services, access to information, and rights to health are subsumed by radical political overhauls and loud calls for social justice. In brief, the arena of population and health studies now studies politics, ideologies, gender, and social rights as well as poverty and deprivation.

The Muslim world and the worlds of Muslims seem to have become more radicalized, more dangerous, more urgent, and fractured by unrelenting competitions around identity, resources, rights, and bodily integrity. The field of population and health sciences has embraced the social, economic and political contexts in which issues of reproduction, movement, and health are transacted. The past decade bears testimony to the eclectic and critical outputs of scholars and practitioners in this field. It is, however, unfortunate that other social sciences and fields of development have not reciprocated by considering the demographic and human health dimensions of their own subjects of study.

POPULATION AND HEALTH SCIENCES

Bibliography

Abu-Lughod, Lila. Do Muslim women really need saving? Anthropological reflections on cultural relativism and its others, in *American Anthropologist* 104:3 (2002), 783–90.

Abu-Odeh, Lama. Crimes of honor and the construction of gender in Arab societies, in *Comparative Law Review* 2:1 (2011).

Asad, Talal. *On suicide bombing. What is to be done?* New York 2007.

Assaad, Ragui and Fatma Hamidi. Women in the Egyptian labor market. An analysis of developments, 1988–2006, in *The Egyptian labor market revisited*, ed. Ragui Assaad, Cairo 2009, 219–58.

Azim, Firdous and Maheen Sultan (eds.). *Mapping women's empowerment. Experiences from Bangladesh, India and Pakistan*, Dhaka 2010.

Batliwala, Srilatha. *Changing their world. Concepts and practices of women's movements*, 2nd edn., 2012, <http://www.awid.org/eng/Library/Changing-their-World-Concepts-and-practices-of-women-s-movements-2nd-Edition>, accessed 23 May 2013.

Bayat, Assef. *Making Islam democratic. Social movements and the post-Islamist turn*, Stanford, Calif. 2007.

Bradley, Sarah E. K., Trevor Croft and Shea Rutstein. The impact of contraceptive failure on unintended birth and induced abortions. Estimates and strategies for reduction, September 2011, <http://www.measuredhs.com/publications/publication-as22-analytical-studies.cfm>, accessed 23 May 2013.

Brunner, Eric J. Stress and the biology of inequality, in *British Medical Journal* 314:7092 (1997), 1472–76.

Buğra, Ayşe and Yalçin Özkan (eds.). *Trajectories of female employment in the Mediterranean*, New York 2012.

Castro, Arachu and Merrill Singer. *Unhealthy health policies. A critical anthropological perspective*, Lanham, Md. 2004.

Cincotta, Richard. Life begins after 25. Demography and the societal timing of the Arab spring, Foreign Policy Research Institute E-Notes, January 2012, <http://www.fpri.org/enotes/2012/201201.cincotta.demography_arabspring.html>, accessed 23 May 2013.

Courbage, Youssef. Does demographic revolution lead to democratic revolution? The case of the Middle East and North Africa region, paper presented at the workshop "Population Change and Europe: Thinking beyond the Demographic Divide", University of Antwerp, 9–11 May 2012.

Dabash, Rasha and Farzaneh Roudi-Fahimi. Abortion in the Middle East and North Africa, September 2008, <http://www.prb.org/Publications/PolicyBriefs/abortion-mena.aspx>, accessed 23 May 2013.

Das, Veena. Violence, gender and subjectivity, in *Annual Review of Anthropology* 37 (2008), 283–99.

DeJong, Jocelyn. Capabilities, reproductive health and well-being. An application of Sen's and Nussbaum's capabilities framework, in *Journal of Development Studies* 42:7 (2006), 1158–79.

DeJong, Jocelyn and Golda El-Khoury. Reproductive health of Arab young people, in *British Medical Journal* 333:7573 (2006), 849–51.

Desclaux, Alice. Equity in access to AIDS treatment in Africa. Pitfalls among achievements, in *Unhealthy health policy. A critical anthropological examination*, ed. Arachu Castro and Merrill Singer, Lanham, Md. 2004, 115–32.

Eberstadt, Nicholas and Apoorva Shah. Fertility decline in the Muslim world, c. 1975–c. 2005. A veritable sea-change, still curiously unnoticed, in *Population dynamics in Muslim countries. Assembling the jigsaw*, ed. Hans Groth and Alfonso Souza-Posa, New York 2012, 11–30.

Fargues Phillipe. Women in Arab countries. Challenging the patriarchal system?, in *Reproductive Health Matters* 13:25 (2005), 161–65.

Fargues Phillipe. International migration and the nation state in Arab countries, in *Middle East Law and Governance* 5 (2013), 1–31.

Farmer, Paul. *Infections and inequalities. The modern plagues*, Berkeley, Calif. 1999.

Foley, Ellen. No money, no care. Women and health sector reform in Senegal, in *Urban Anthropology and Studies of Cultural Systems and World Economic Development* 30:1 (2001), 1–50.

Giacaman, Rita, Rana Khatib, Luay Shabaneh, Asad Ramlawi, Belgacem Sabri, Guido Sabatinelli, Marwan Khawaja and Tony Laurance. Health status and health services in the Occupied Palestinian Territory, in *Public health in the Arab world*, ed. Samer Jabbour, Rita Giacaman, Marwan Khawaja and Iman Nuwayhid, New York 2012, 312–30.

Groth, Hans and Alfonso Souza-Posa (eds.). *Population dynamics in Muslim countries. Assembling the jigsaw*, New York 2012.

Hasso, Frances. *Consuming desires. Family crisis and the state in the Middle East*, Palo Alto, Calif. 2011.

Hatem, Mervat. Economic and political liberation in Egypt and the demise of state feminism, in *International Journal of Middle East Studies* 24:2 (1992), 231–51.

Hoodfar, Homa. Against all odds. The building of a women's movement in the Islamic Republic of Iran, in *Changing their world. Concepts and practices of women's movements*, ed. Srilatha Batliwala, 2nd edn. 2012, <http://www.awid.org/eng/Library/Changing-their-World-Concepts-and-practices-of-women-s-movements-2nd-Edition>, accessed 23 May 2013.

Hosseini-Chavoshi, Meimanat and Mohammad Jalal Abbasi-Shavazi. Demographic transition in Iran. Changes and challenges, in *Population dynamics in Muslim* countries. *Assembling the jigsaw*, ed. Hans Groth and Alfonso Souza-Posa, New York 2012, 97–116.

International Trade Unions Council, Trade union rights violations around the world in 2011, <http://survey.ituc-csi.org/>, accessed 23 May 2013.

Jabbour, Samer, Rita Giacaman, Marwan Khawaja and Iman Nuwayhid (eds.). *Public health in the Arab world*, New York 2012.

Janes, Craig and Oyuntsetseg Chuluundrj. Free markets and dead mothers. The social ecology of maternal mortality in post-socialist Mongolia, in *Medical Anthropology Quarterly* 18:2 (2004), 102–29.

Kabeer, Naila, Andrea Cornwall, Jerker Edstrom, Rosalind Eyben, Marzia Fontana, Lyla Mehta and Hilary Standing. Gender equality and the MDGs. Pathways to a transformative agenda, unpublished manuscript, Institute of Development Studies, University of Sussex 2012.

Kabeer, Naila, Ratna Sudarshan, and Kirsty Milward (eds.). *Organizing women workers in the informal economy. Beyond the weapons of the weak*, London 2013.

Kárpáti, Jozsef. The pension systems of Arab countries in the light of socio-economic risks, in *Public Finance Quarterly* 56:2 (2011), 179–92.

Khan, Ayesha. Lady healthworkers and social change in Pakistan, in *Economic and Political Weekly* 46:30 (2011), 28–31.

Mahmood, Saba. *The politics of piety. The Islamic revival and the feminist subject*, Princeton, N.J. 2005.

Marks, Miriam. Determinants of delayed male marriage in Egypt, in *Avicenna: The Stanford Journal on Muslim Affairs* 2:1 (2011), 22–29.

Marmot, Michael and Richard Wilkinson (eds.). *The social determinants of health*, 2nd edn., Oxford 2009.

al-Masry al-Youm, daily newspaper, Cairo, 23 February 2012.

Mir-Hosseini, Ziba. Muslim women's quest for equality. Between Islamic law and feminism, in *Critical Inquiry* 32:4 (2006): 629–45.

Mir-Hosseini, Ziba. Towards gender equality. Muslim family laws and the shariʻa, in *Wanted. Equality and justice in the Muslim family*, ed. Zainah Anwar, Selangor, Malaysia 2009, <http://www.musawah.org/wanted-equality-and-justice-muslim -family-english>, accessed 10 April 2013.

al-Nasr, Tofol Jassim. Gulf Cooperation Council (GCC) Women and *misyar* marriage. Evolution and progress in the Arabian Gulf, in *Journal of International Women's Studies* 12:3 (2011), 43–57.

Nazneen, Sohela and Sakiba Tasneem. Legitimacy enhances capacity, in *Capacity: Local Government for Gender Equality* 40 (2010), 10–11.

Nazneen, Sohela, Maheen Sultan and Naomi Hossain. National discourses on women's empowerment in Bangladesh. Enabling or constraining women's choices?, in *Development* 53:2 (2010), 239–46.

Nuwayhid, Iman, Huda Zurayk, Rouham Yamout and Chadi S. Cortas. Summer 2006 war on Lebanon. A lesson in community resilience, in *Public health in the Arab world*, ed. Samer Jabbour, Rita Giacaman, Marwan Khawaja and Iman Nuwayhid, New York 2012, 345–53.

Offenhaur, Priscilla. *Women in Islamic societies. A selected review of social scientific literature*, Washington, D.C. 2005.

Olmsted, Jennifer C. Is paid work the only answer? Neoliberalism, Arab women's well-being and the social contract, in *Journal of Middle Eastern Studies* 1:2 (2005), 112–41.

Pate, Muhammad Ali and Joel Schoppig. Africa's growing giant. Population dynamics in Nigeria, in *Population dynamics in Muslim countries. Assembling the jigsaw*, ed. Hans Groth and Alfonso Souza-Posa, New York 2012, 211–25.

Pfeiffer, James and Rachel Chapman. Anthropological perspectives on structural adjustment and public health, in *Annual Review of Anthropology* 39 (2010), 149–65.

Population Council (West Asia and North Africa Office). Survey of young people in Egypt, 2011, <http://www.popcouncil.org/pdfs/2010PGY_SYPEFinalReport_FrontMatter.pdf>, accessed 23 May 2013.

Puschmann, Paul and Koen Matthijs. The Janus face of the demographic transition in the Arab world. The decisive role of nuptiality. Working paper WOG/HD/2012 -4D/2012/1192/9, <https://lirias.kuleuven.be/bitstream/123456789/361994/1/The+Janus +Face+of+the+Demographic+Transition+in+the+Arab+World.pdf>, accessed 23 May 2013.

Rashad, Hoda and Zeinab Khadr. Knowledge gaps. The agenda for research and action, in *Public health in the Arab world*, ed. Samer Jabbour, Rita Giacaman, Marwan Khawaja and Iman Nuwayhid, New York 2012, 106–15.

Rashad, Hoda and Magued Osman. Nuptiality in Arab countries. Changes and implications, in *The new Arab family*, ed. Nicholas Hopkins, Cairo 2003, 20–50.

Rashad, Hoda, Magued Osman and Farzaneh Roudi-Fahimi. Marriage in the Arab world, Population Reference Bureau, 2005, <http://www.prb.org/Publications/PolicyBriefs/MarriageintheArabWorld.aspx>, accessed 23 May 2013.

Rawaf, Salman and David Rawaf. Public health crisis. Iraq, in *Public health in the Arab world*, ed. Samer Jabbour, Rita Giacaman, Marwan Khawaja and Iman Nuwayhid, New York 2012, 331–44.

Rogan, Eugene, *The Arabs. A history*, London 2009.

Roudi-Fahimi, Farzaneh. Child marriage in the Middle East and North Africa, Population Reference Bureau, 2010, <http://www.prb.org/Articles/2010/menachild marriage.aspx>, accessed 23 May 2013.

Roudi-Fahimi, Farzaneh, Ahmed Abdul Momen, Lori Ashford and Maha el-Adawy. Women's need for family planning in Arab countries, 2012, <http://www.unfpa.org/worldwide/family-planning-arab-countries-2.pdf>, accessed 23 May 2013.

al-Sharmani, Mulki. Egyptian family courts. A pathway of women's empowerment?, in *Hawwa* 7:2 (2009), 89–119.

Sholkamy, Hania. Gender and population, in *International Conference on Population and Development in Cairo, 15 years later*, ed. Hassan Zaky, Egyptian Cabinet Information and Decision Support, Evidence-Based Population Policy and UNFPA, Cairo 2009, 22–36.

Sholkamy, Hania. Creating conservatism or emancipating subjects? On the narrative of Islamic observance in Egypt, in *IDS Bulletin* 42:1 (2010), 47–55.

Sholkamy, Hania. How private lives determine work option. Reflections on poor women's lives in Egypt, in *Trajectories of female employment in the Mediterranean*, ed. Ayse Bugra and Yalçin Özkan, New York 2012a, 114–36.

Sholkamy, Hania. Women are also part of this revolution, in *Arab spring in Egypt. Revolution and beyond*, ed. Bahgat Korany and Rabab el-Mahdi, Cairo 2012b, 153–74.

Sholkamy, Hania (ed.). Islam and feminism, in *Contestations. Dialogues on women's empowerment* 1 (2010), <http://www.contestations.net/issues/issue-1/>, accessed 23 May 2013.

Shukrallah, Alaa and Mohamed Hassan Khalil. Egypt in crisis. Politics, health care reform, and social mobilization for health rights, in *Public health in the Arab world*, ed. Samer Jabbour, Rita Giacaman, Marwan Khawaja and Iman Nuwayhid, New York 2012, 477–88.

Singerman, Diane. The economic imperatives of marriage. Emerging practices and identities among youth in the Middle East, Middle East Youth Initiative working paper no. 6, 2007, <http://papers.ssrn.com/sol3/papers.cfm?abstract_id=1087433>.

Soroush, Abdelkarim. *Reason, freedom and democracy in Islam. Essential writings of Abdelkarim Soroush*, trans. Mahmoud Sadri and Ahmad Sadri, Oxford 2000.

Turshen, Meredeth. *Privatizing health care in Africa*, New Brunswick, N.J. 1998.

UNDP. Arab human development report 2005. Empowerment of Arab women, 2005, <http://hdr.undp.org/en/reports/regionalreports/arabstates/name,3403,en.html>, accessed 23 May 2013.

UN Women. Progress of Arab women, 2004, <http://www.unifem.org/materials/item_detail4863.html>, accessed 23 May 2013.

Urdal, Henrik. A clash of generations? Youth bulges and political violence, in *International Studies Quarterly* 50:3 (2006), 607–30.

Wick, Livia. Building the infrastructure, modeling the nation. The case of birth in Palestine, in *Culture, Medicine, and Psychiatry* 32:3 (2008), 328–57.

World Bank. Egypt investment climate assessment 2009. Accelerating private enterprise-led growth, 2009, <http://www.aucegypt.edu/research/src/Documents/Egypt_ICA_Policy_Brief.pdf>, accessed 23 May 2013.

World Health Organization/Iran Ministry of Health. The social determinants of health in Iran, May 2008, <http://behdasht.gov.ir/uploads/291_1041_SDH%20 SITUATION%20ANALYSIS.pdf>, accessed 22 May 2013.

Yount, Kathryn M. and Abla M. Sibai. A demography of aging in Arab countries, in *International Handbook of Population Aging*, ed. Peter Uhlenberg, New York 2009, 277–315.

Zurayk, Huda. Reproductive health in population policy: a review and look ahead, in *Reproductive health: program and policy changes post-Cairo*, ed. Axel I. Mundigo. Liege, 1999.

Zurayk, Huda, Rita Giacaman and Ahmed Mandil. Graduate education in public health. Toward a multidisciplinary model, in *Public health in the Arab world*, ed. Samer Jabbour, Rita Giacaman, Marwan Khawaja and Iman Nuwayhid, New York 2012, 429–44.

Reproduction: Health

∴

Reproduction: Health: Bangladesh

Mst Shahina Parvin

Introduction

In the 1960s and 1970s, second-wave white feminist activism in the Global North focused on contraceptive access as a way to establish women's rights over their bodies and sexualities (Heise 1993). While this has remained an important strategy for many European and American feminists, for most Bangladeshi women, in particular impoverished women, access to contraceptives has not led to greater freedom and rights (Parvin 2016). Instead, during the late twentieth century, large numbers of women were targeted by population control programs run by the Bangladeshi government and donor agencies. Women's access to contraceptives does not always mean that they have control over their bodies. Similarly, while assisted reproductive technologies (ARTs) help many couples to conceive, these technologies also establish control over women's bodies by reinscribing childbearing and motherhood as the ultimate goal and achievement in Bangladeshi women's lives (Sultana 2014, Parvin 2016). Additional issues with the technologies include their low success rates, their harmful side effects, and the high cost of treatment. This article discusses how, in the Bangladeshi context, reproductive technologies might actually contribute to women's suffering and to their loss of control over their bodies rather than ensuring their reproductive rights.

In its exploration of how reproductive technologies contribute to Bangladeshi women's stress and suffering, this article begins with a brief history of the population control program in what is today Bangladesh. This is followed by a discussion of some of the ways in which population control workers and medical professionals have violated Bangladeshi women's reproductive rights. The third section explores the ways that fertility clinics and the media in Bangladesh represent women's identity in society today. The final section discusses the commercial aspects of the media's and selected fertility clinics' endorsement of ARTs.

© KONINKLIJKE BRILL NV, LEIDEN, 2019 | DOI:10.1163/1872-5309_EWIC_COM_002184

Population Control Programs and Bangladeshi Women's Rights to Contraceptives

Bangladesh emerged as an independent country in 1971, following some two hundred years of colonization by the British and then 24 years of documented economic exploitation and cultural suppression by West Pakistan. The new nation very quickly became dependent on foreign aid, particularly from the Global North, and aid agencies began to intervene by means of a variety of development projects. The population control program, funded primarily by the United States, enjoyed a prominent place in these efforts (White 1992, Parvin 2006).

In East Pakistan in the 1960s (as Bangladesh was then called), women generally received access to birth control methods from the government's population control program, which was presented as a family planning program. This family planning program was linked with the international population reduction program. During the 1950s, awareness had been raised internationally about the problems of the rapid global population increase (Lane 1994). The Malthusian notion of the tragic consequence of increased uncontrolled population contributed to tension in the West, particularly in the United States. In 1962, the United Nations' resolution "Population Growth and Economic Development" showed that fertility rates in the countries of the Global South were noticeably higher than in the Global North (p. 1307). In mainstream Western discourse, large populations were seen as a major reason for the poverty in the world's poorer countries and, by this logic, better controlled fertility would lead to "development." This fear about overpopulation prompted President Lyndon Johnson to call for the funding of a global population control program. The United States began to provide funding for such a population control program through USAID in 1965. In 1967, the United Nations' Fund for Population Activities (UNFPA) also began to coordinate funding and contraceptive distribution to the countries of the Global South, East Pakistan among them.

In 1960, the UN began to provide aid for population control programs in East Pakistan (Parvin 2006). Starting in the mid-1960s, family planning health assistants were appointed to motivate rural women to plan their families using contraceptives (Parvin 2006). These health assistants also used the global discourse that overpopulation was the reason for the poverty of impoverished Bangladeshi people. From the beginning, ideas and assumptions about class and gender informed population control programs, and impoverished women have always been the primary target of population control programs. The government of independent Bangladesh continued to receive funds and technological assistance from different donor agencies to provide contraceptives to its population free of cost (F. Akhter 1992). Since 1974, the UNFPA has played a key role both in ensuring the availability of contraceptives in Bangladesh and also in making decisions about which contraceptives the government should provide to its population (F. Akhter 1992).

In order to legitimize its interventions in this arena, the Bangladeshi government also resorted to discourses of reproductive well-being (Parvin 2006). Health professionals told women that giving birth frequently was harmful for their health, while contraceptive use could help them to plan childbirth, enhance their reproductive health, and establish autonomy over their own bodies. The United Nations' Decade of Women (1975–85) helped the population control establishment to use women's freedom and sexual rights discourses in its population reduction program in Bangladesh (Parvin 2016). The third United Nations' decennial conference, the International Conference on Population and Development (ICPD), held in Cairo in September 1994, developed a new definition of population policy, which particularly focused on women's reproductive freedoms, health, and sexual rights (McIntosh and Finkle 1995). The UN conferences had a significant impact on women's development programs in Bangladesh; following the Decade of Women, foreign donors began to allocate aid for women's empowerment issues (White 1992). This resulted in both governmental and nongovernmental organizations focusing their work on the issue of women's rights in order to access financial aid, such that, in 1980, most "funds allocated for women's empowerment was invested into women's use of contraceptives in the name of women's empowerment" (Parvin 2016, 4).

Early efforts in Bangladesh to foster women's empowerment by encouraging them to use contraceptives came up against many obstacles (Parvin 2006). There was concern that contraceptive use would simply be a license for women to engage in promiscuous behavior. Some Islamic groups opposed contraceptives on the ground that any practice that prevented pregnancy was tantamount to infanticide (Roudi-Fahimi and Ashford 2006). They declared that Islam preaches a high level of procreation because it helps to increase the size of the Islamic community and thereby expands and strengthens the power of Islam. Other groups rejected contraceptives because they were manufactured in the West, so their use might establish the dominance of Western beliefs and practices over Islamic ones and contribute to the abolition of the so-called Islamic way of life. Other Islamic groups, however, advocated for family planning by arguing that there is no Quranic statement regarding the use of contraceptives. Additionally, some Islamic groups insisted that Islamic belief is not static and accommodates changes for the betterment of society (Roudi-Fahimi and Ashford 2006). In Bangladesh, as in other societies, imams

Contraceptives and Violation of Bangladeshi Women's Reproductive Rights

The Bangladeshi government primarily targeted impoverished rural families in its birth control efforts. Health workers generally motivated poor rural women to use long-term and provider-dependent contraceptives, such as intrauterine devices (IUDs), sterilization, and Norplant, usually without adequate warnings about possible side effects (F. Akhter 1992, Parvin 2009).

Both men and women were encouraged to undergo sterilization—usually, in exchange for a small sum of money—but men resisted and refused more often, out of concern that such a procedure would lead to diminished sexual pleasure. In the end, women accepted the procedure in far greater numbers than did men, perhaps because of societal ideas that women, as the bearers of children, were ultimately responsible for the family's fertility (Parvin 2006).

Healthcare workers also emphasized the greater ease of methods such as Norplant, arguing that, once the Norplant had been inserted, women were spared having to worry regularly about taking a pill—offered at low or no cost since the 1970s—or having to rely on their partners' use of condoms (Parvin 2009). Critics were quick to point out that these methods were problematic precisely because the women required outside, trained assistance to remove them, and because they could not remove them on their own if they decided to stop (F. Akhter 1995, Parvin 2009). In rural areas, illiterate, impoverished women relied on healthcare workers to choose for them the "right" kinds of contraceptives, but more often than not, the healthcare workers' decisions were based on the government's interests rather than on women's reproductive health. Health professionals have generally claimed that, because impoverished, illiterate women lack the ability to make a better plan for themselves, they are morally obligated to make better life plans for these women, and that the latter should follow medical professionals' advice for their own betterment (Parvin 2006). This attitude rationalizes and legitimizes the medical professionals' control over women's bodies. It also helps health professionals to promote contraceptives that the government or donors want to provide to women in Bangladesh.

Perhaps most notorious among the contraceptives encouraged by the government of Bangladesh and family planning workers on the ground was Norplant-1, which, as Farida Akhter points out, had already been rejected by middle-class white women in the Global North (F. Akhter 1995). The economically vulnerable Bangladesh government, for its part, was of course working with donor priorities and concerns in mind. UNFPA funds to the Bangladesh government, for instance, have often been accompanied by a contract to distribute certain contraceptives (F. Akhter 1995). UNFPA funds have also come with directives on how much to reduce the population in the ensuing period. Unsurprisingly, such external pressures manifest themselves on the ground in the form of medical professionals' reluctance to remove the implants even when women have adverse reactions (F. Akhter 1995, Parvin 2009).

That impoverished rural women exercise limited control over their own bodies becomes obvious upon closer scrutiny of a Norplant-1 clinical trial, was implemented in 1985, involving 600 women run by the Bangladesh Institute of Research for Promotion of Essential and Reproductive Health and Technologies (F. Akhter 1995). Although the institute reported that most Bangladeshi women in the trial were satisfied with Norplant-1, there is evidence that many women experienced negative side effects, among them nausea, headaches, spotting, anxiety, vomiting, dizziness, change of appetite, weight gain, infection, pain and itchiness at the implant site after using Norplant—and crucially, they did not receive proper services (F. Akhter 1995). Feminists worldwide protested against this trial, but the US Food and Drug Administration approved Norplant for the broader market in the 1990s, and UNFPA and the Bangladesh government continued to provide Norplant in Bangladesh until 2004. While the positive findings of UNFPA-supported research on Norplant trial was used to support the marketization of Norplant, UBINIG's research on Norplant users' experiences in Tangail in Bangladesh revealed that some women had not even been informed that they were implanted with Norplant as part of a clinical trial (Parvin 2009).

By 1996, approximately 6,000 American Norplant users had registered complaints of severe medical consequences, leading the United States to finally stop distribution of Norplant in 2002 (Mosher and Crnkovich 2012). The Bangladeshi government stopped providing Norplant in 2007, only to launch distribution of the hormonal contraception Norplant II, also called Jadelle, in 2008 (Parvin 2009). Research suggests that because Jadelle has the same hormonal formulation as Norplant-1, users can expect similar adverse effects. Indeed, when the USFDA approved Jadelle, it relied on the trials of Norplant (Mahboob-e- Alam, Hossain, and Searing 2012, Pfizer 2014).

As the above discussion suggests, the Bangladeshi government and health professionals have been eager to promote contraceptive technology in order to reduce fertility levels in the country, even at the cost of women's health and reproductive rights. An interesting, and indeed contradictory, development in recent years has been the aggressive promotion of assisted reproductive technologies (ARTs) by the media and health professionals among childless women of all socioeconomic backgrounds.

The Portrayal of Women's Subject Positions as Mothers in the ARTs Promotional Materials

Drawing on Stuart Hall's (1977) work on the fundamental role that the media plays in reflecting and shaping people's views in society, and on Michel Foucault's (1972) insights about how human beings are produced through discourses, and how discourses are about the production of knowledge and concepts through language, it is possible to see the power of texts and images in the media to produce a specific discourse about a particular issue (Helstein 2007). Foucault notes that not everybody is authorized to make statements; people who possess power generally construct knowledge, which has a disciplinary role in society, and, starting in the eighteenth century, medical professionals began to hold power in producing knowledge about "normal," "perfect," and "abnormal" bodies. These notions of "normal" and "abnormal" have disciplinary power because they shape people's views about "normal" and "abnormal" and prompt people to adopt "normal" behaviors and achieve "perfect" bodies by following medical professionals. However, medical professionals become able to obfuscate their disciplinary power over human bodies through the notion of their well-being. Examining health professionals' representations about ARTs in the Bangladeshi context is pertinent in order to learn how they desire to produce knowledge about "normal" and "perfect" bodies in their representations of ARTs.

Much of the material currently in circulation in Bangladesh is produced primarily by fertility centers. While these publications begin by discussing childless couples' desire to have children, they often conclude by suggesting that women desire children more than men do (Purabi 2015). For instance, Dr. Purabi states:

> In married life children are like an anchor between the father and mother. A woman possesses a dormant desire to be a mother. In most cases, this desire exceeds everything including her career development or physical beauty. In case of a man the outer expression can be less but he also wants to live through his children.
>
> PURABI 2015

Images in these publications tend to stress the woman's primary relationship with babies, while the man is depicted in a protective role vis-à-vis his wife and child, arguably reiterating the traditional "ideal" notions of gender performativity in Bangladeshi society, with women responsible for providing care to children and men for providing protection. The notion that women have "natural" qualities of caring and rearing contributes to women's burden by pushing them to act like some ideal care provider and also by stigmatizing those who are unable to bear children or to provide the level of care for children and family expected (Abel and Nelson 1990). Images can also reinforce the social perception that infertility is a woman's issue.

Sarah Franklin's (1990) research on representations of ARTs in the United Kingdom finds similarly gendered portrayals. While the media has discursively been producing knowledge regarding infertility to encourage childless couples to use ARTs, the discursive claims are selective, and they shore up the normative gendered order, whereby women are naturally meant to desire children, and children are naturally positioned as the progeny of heterosexual, married couples. For Franklin, medical and psychiatric publications act to pathologize decisions to remain childless, portraying infertility as "failed femininity," and the source of great sorrow or frustration (Franklin 1990, Hadfield, Rudoe, and Sanderson-Mann 2007). Janice Raymond (1987) also argues that, in the name of women's choice and benevolence, reproductive technologies confirm women's reproductive subject position. Further, ARTs as beneficial for women is confusing because once women begin fertility treatments, their bodies undergo a series of invasive and painful tests. ARTs thus ensure and extend medical intervention in women's bodies, which began "with the nineteenth-century establishment of the specialties of gynecology" (Raymond 1987, 12). Similarly, Robyn Rowland (1987) notes that it is hard for women to refuse reproductive technologies in the context of a complete medicalization of reproduction, and a male-dominated medical profession. She argues that medical science often possesses and extends the patriarchal ideology of the necessity of motherhood in women's lives, as new reproductive technology focuses mostly on women's reproductive capabilities. In Bangladesh, too, the fertility centers focus on women's reproductive capabilities.

Perhaps more surprising is that there is no sense of contradiction between such a pronatalist approach—understood as "an ideology that incorporates beliefs, attitudes, and actions that implicitly or explicitly support parenthood and encourage fertility" (Rich et al. 2011, 228)—and active support of population control programs. Reproduction is regarded as the primary goal of married life, and it is seen as one of the necessities required to continue a marital relationship (Nahar 2012, 23, Sultana 2014, 1–4). Marriage is almost synonymous with parenthood and, perhaps even more so, womanhood is associated with motherhood (Nahar 2012). Childlessness, then, contributes to women's suffering. As Shameem Akhter (2012) observes, "Infertile women often receive disrespectful treatment by husbands, and the husbands and families may encourage them to divorce or take a second wife. In more extreme cases, acts of violence are committed against them." In Bangladesh, childless women often encounter violence because, as a nation, Bangladesh is interested in women's subject position as mothers and encourages women to be "good" mothers. "Good mothering" is connected with producing "good," productive citizens of the future.

In Bangladesh, most households, and women, are represented in public by the men in the family, whether husbands, fathers, brothers, or sons. After marriage, producing children is seen as the principal responsibility of women, often certifying their rights in their husbands' households (Nahar 2012). Before 1980, the Bangladeshi economy was predominantly agricultural, and producing children was important as children were valued for the labor (F. Akhter 2010). In the neoliberal economy that has emerged since 1980, producing economically productive children has become an imperative for the socioeconomic development of the nation (Parvin 2016). Women in Bangladesh have now become responsible for and encouraged to produce "good" citizens using the power of their "perfect" mothering. The public valuing of motherhood can be seen as linked with the broader political and economic systems of Bangladesh. There is an annual celebration of the "best mothers" in Bangladesh. Women with multiple well-established children are nationally recognized as a *ratnagarbha ma,* a mother who bore talented jewels, on International Mother's Day (*Prothom Alo,* 10 May 2015). Such practices reflect the ways in which Bangladeshi women's honor depends mainly on their successful participation in motherhood, suggesting that they may be prompted to police their own behavior not only to become mothers but also to do their utmost to achieve "perfect motherhood." In this context, it is easy for IVF (in vitro fertilization) proponents to deploy conceptualizations of women's identity as mothers to encourage them to use ARTS.

Commercialization of ARTS

In Bangladesh, the general perception is that women are responsible for infertility. They are thus encouraged by friends and family to use the treatments and are targeted by companies offering these services. As Shameem Akhter (2012) notes,

> When a couple cannot have children, the woman is usually blamed in Bangladesh. In our society, only woman is being generally considered responsible for child bearing and bears the brunt of being infertile irrespective of with whom the cause of infertility lies. When women do not conceive, they get insulted from family and also are under immense pressure to seek medical help without considering the need of investigation of their male counterpart.

While some infertility centers have recently started to pay greater attention to men—by incorporating men's voices about their joys of having their babies by using ARTs from the center (http://harvestinfertility.com/success-stories/)—it is clear that commercial motivations are behind this change. While women are still regarded as responsible for the couple's infertility, there is a recognition that men are the decisionmakers in most families (Nahar 2012). The websites of fertility centers in Bangladesh compare the quality of care they provide to centers located in such places as India and Singapore, popular medical destinations for the local socioeconomic elites, but there is no discussion of the specific costs or detrimental effects of these treatments, the worst of which are typically experienced by women. ARTs, mainly IVF, can contribute to ovarian cancer due to superovulation, infection, bleeding, and damaged fallopian tubes (Shildrick 1997, McWhorter 2010). In their publicity materials, fertility centers focus on their ability to reduce harm using technology to monitor and manage risks, thereby encouraging couples to keep faith in the ability of the medical professionals' technological interventions. One center even constructs superovulation as beneficial for childless couples, affirming:

> Since most IVF/ICSI programs superovulate patients to grow many eggs, there are often many embryos.... It is now also possible to freeze these embryos and store them in liquid nitrogen ... so that [they] can have another embryo transfer cycle done without having to go through superovulation and egg collection all over again. (http://harvestinfertility.com/service/)

The text addresses frozen embryo technology as a one-time intervention that offers new hope for childless couples. It also endeavors to normalize the regularly occurring failure of the first attempt of IVF and encourage couples to try several cycles. Moreover, by preserving the embryo, specialists are becoming the authority in controlling conception (Basen 1993), all the while portraying fertility treatments as harmless and risk free (Franklin 1990, Sultana 2014).

Feminists around the world have long criticized the controlling aspects of ARTS (Franklin 1990, Corea 1993, F. Akhter 2010, Sultana 2014, Parvin 2016). They have drawn attention to the physical and emotional harms associated with these technologies, associated with their experimental nature and high risk and failure rate (Corea 1993, F. Akhter 2010). For instance, the superovulations common as a result of IVF treatments have contributed to many women's deaths, yet, as Gena Corea points out, this ethical issue is not taken into consideration in the IVF industry (Corea 1993). Instead, the manipulation of eggs and embryos is promoted as "care and cure" (24). The limiting of this kind of information is problematic regarding "informed choice," and it is a form of violence over women's bodies in the name of assisting women to become mothers. Corea calls for a disruption of this technological intervention in women's bodies for the sake of women's well-being (21).

ART centers in Bangladesh reassure clients that their procedures are in accordance with Islamic principles. Many in Bangladesh are reluctant to use ARTS because they fear that doctors might use the wrong sperm to fertilize the egg, which they believe would violate Islamic rules (Amin 2014). Also, there is a clear preference for female gynecologists among the women clients themselves as well as their male relatives. For example, the Harvest Infertility Care Ltd. Clinic highlights the availability of their female doctors during treatments and that "patients will be fully covered before ultrasonography is carried out by specialists" (Harvest Infertility Care Ltd. Clinic, 2019). By emphasizing its adherence to its understanding of Islamic principles regarding women's modesty and sexuality, the center reassures clients and potential clients it does not pose a threat to the "sanctity of women and their position within Muslim society" (Parvin 2016, 114). In Bangladesh, as in Egypt, as Marcia Inhorn (2003) has shown, sperm and egg donations are not acceptable, as they involve a third person in addition to a heterosexual couple, and involving a third party is seen by many interpretations of Islam as constituting adultery. In Egypt, similarly, IVF is only acceptable within a heterosexual married couple, and donor insemination is illegal (Inhorn 2003). Mirza Sultana (2014) observes that doctors in Bangladesh are hesitant even to speak about these options, as "the government of Bangladesh will never permit the option of donor's egg and/ or sperm" (305). Thus, it is important to maintain the appearance that health professionals are not "doing anything" that contradicts religion (305). Some doctors are known to provide the services privately, reflecting that they themselves have no objection to the practice, but are hindered from doing so openly out of "fear of criticism and [of] being labelled as practicing something that is haram" (Parvin 2016). Despite the increased regulation of women's bodies by medical professionals in Bangladesh, few social science researchers or feminists in Bangladesh are as critical of fertility treatments as they have been of population control programs. Instead, they often concur with the notion that motherhood is necessary for Bangladeshi women's lives and propose a better public health policy for democratizing ARTs (Nahar 2012, 24), which eventually emphasizes women's subject positions as mothers.

Conclusion

This article demonstrates how aspects of reproductive technologies, in particular contraceptives and fertility treatments, exercise control over Bangladeshi women's bodies. Impoverished women's bodies have long been the site of population control programs. Such women are encouraged to use long-term and provider-dependent contraceptives to establish long-term control over their fertility, advice that often ignores their general health and contributes to their suffering. Indeed, health professionals, more concerned with the interests of population control programs regulated by the Bangladeshi government and donor agencies, have tended to ignore the detrimental effect on women's health and well-being. Instead, the power has been legitimized through the discourse of women's freedom and empowerment over their fertility.

While impoverished Bangladeshi women's fertility is the subject of Bangladeshi government and donors' population control programs, infertility has become a matter of commercial business for ART clinics, which, given the cost of the treatment, target women of a higher socioeconomic stratum. These clinics rely on polished publications and websites to provide assurances that their procedures are safe and in accordance with Islamic principles, but here too, it is women who are presumed to be the reason for a couple's infertility and the object of increasing regulation.

Bibliography

Abel, Emily K., and Margaret K. Nelson (eds.). *Circles of care. Work and identity in women's lives*, Albany, NY 1990.

Akhter, Farida. *Depopulating Bangladesh. Essays on the politics of fertility*, Dhaka 1992.

Akhter, Farida. *Resisting Norplant*, Dhaka 1995.

Akhter, Farida. "Doctor's babies" in Bangladesh, Ubinig.org, 20 March 2010, <http://ubinig.org/index.php/home/showAerticle/14/english/Farida-Akhter>. 23 April 2018.

Akhter, Shameem. Only women bear the brunt of infertility, in *The Daily Star*, 1 December 2012, <https://www.thedailystar.net/news-detail-259414>. 3 July 2019.

Amin, Mortayez. Male infertility. [Video file]. 2014, <https://www.youtube.com/watch?v=YZtaRnh4gB0>. 24 August 2019.

Ashraf, Shamim. First frozen embryo baby born in Bangladesh, in *The Daily Star*, 20 September 2008, <http://www.thedailystar.net/news-detail-55656>. 3 July 2019.

Based, M.A. Dealing with infertility, in *The Daily Star*, 11 January 2015, <http://www.thedailystar.net/dealing-with-infertility-59295>. 3 July 2019.

Basen, Gwynne. Following Frankenstein. Women, technology and the future of procreation, in *Misconceptions. The social construction of choice and the new reproductive and genetic technologies*, ed. Gwynne Basen, Margrit Eichler, and Abby Lippman, Toronto 1993, 27–38.

Corea, Gena. Introduction, in *Misconceptions. The social construction of choice and the new reproductive and genetic technologies*, ed. Gwynne Basen, Margrit Eichler, and Abby Lippman, Toronto 1993, 13–26.

Foucault, Michel. *The archaeology of knowledge and the discourse on language*, New York 1972.

Franklin, Sarah. Deconstructing "desperateness." The social construction of infertility in popular representations of new reproductive technologies, in *The new reproductive technologies*, ed. Maureen McNeil, Ian Varcoe, and Steven Yearley, London 1990, 200–29.

Frye Helzner, Judith. Men's involvement in family planning, in *Reproductive Health Matters* 4:7 (1996), 146–54.

Harvest Infertility Care Ltd. Clinic. First Consultation <http://harvestinfertility.com/services/proin-consequat-placerat-tortor-at-interdum/> 24 August 2019.

Hadfield, L., N. Rudoe, and J. Sanderson-Mann. Motherhood, choice and the British media. A time to reflect, in *Gender and Education* 19:2 (2007), 255–63.

Hall, Stuart. Encoding/decoding, in *Encoding and decoding in television discourse*, cccs Stenciled Paper no. 7. 1977.

Heise, Lori L. Reproductive freedom and violence against women. Where are the intersections? in *Journal of Law, Medicine & Ethics* 21:2 (1993), 206–16.

Helstein, Michelle T. Seeing your sporting body. Identity, subjectivity, and misrecognition, in *Sociology of Sport Journal* 24:1 (2007), 78–103.

Inhorn, M.C. *Local babies, global science. Gender, religion, and in vitro fertilization in Egypt*, New York 2003.

Lane, Sandra D. From population control to reproductive health: an emerging policy agenda in Social science & medicine 39:9 (1994), 1303–1314.

McIntosh, C. Alison, and Jason L. Finkle. The Cairo conference on population and development. A new paradigm?, in *Population and Development Review* 21:2 (1995), 223–60.

McWhorter, Ladelle. Darwin's invisible hand. Feminism, reprogenetics, and Foucault's analysis of neoliberalism, in *Southern Journal of Philosophy* 48 (2010), 43–63.

Mahboob-e-Alam, Dr. Sharif Hossain, and Hannah Searing. Acceptability of sino-implant (II) in Bangladesh: Final report on a prospective study. USAID: The RESPOND Project Study Series, Report No. 8., December 2012, <https://cdn2.sph .harvard.edu/wp-content/uploads/sites/32/2014/05/Acceptability-Final_Engender Health_Rep_2012.pdf>. 3 July 2019.

Mosher, Steven W., and Elizabeth Crnkovich. Norplant is back—under a different name, Population Research Institute, 22 October 2012, <https://www.pop.org/ content/norplant-back-under-different-name>. 3 July 2019.

Nahar, Papreen. The link between infertility and poverty. Evidence from Bangladesh, in *Human Fertility* 15:1 (2012), 18–26.

Parvin, Mst. Shahina. Use of gender and class relation in population control programme, in *Nribigyan Potrika* [*Journal of Anthropology*] 11 (2006), 95–116.

Parvin, Mst. Shahina. Use of gender and class relation in population control programme, in *Nribigyan Potrika* [*Journal of Anthropology*] 14 (2009), 43–63.

Parvin, Mst Shahina. Assisted reproductive technologies. The discourses of motherhood and childlessness in Bangladesh. MA thesis, Department of Sociology, University of Lethbridge, 2016.

Pfizer. Novel agreement expands access to Pfizer's contraceptive, Sayana Press, for women most in need in the world's poorest countries (press release), 13 November 2014, <https://www.pfizer.com/news/press-release/press-release-detail/novel_agree ment_expands_access_to_pfizer_s_contraceptive_sayana_press_for_women_most_ in_need_in_the_world_s_poorest_countries>. 15 September 2016.

Purabi, Nowsheen Sharmin. Know the reasons of infertility, in *The Daily Star*, 7 June 2015, <https://www.thedailystar.net/health/health-tips/know-the-reasons -infertility-93094>. 3 July 2019.

Raymond, Janice. Preface, in *Man-made women. How new reproductive technologies affect women*, ed. Gena Corea et al., Bloomington, Ind. 1987, 74–87.

Rich, Stephanie, Ann Taket, Melissa Graham, and Julia Shelley. "Unnatural," "unwomanly," "uncreditable," and "undervalued." The significance of being a childless woman in Australian society, in *Gender Issues* 28:4 (2011), 226–47.

Roudi-Fahimi, Farzaneh, and Lori Ashford. Investing in reproductive health to achieve development goals. The Middle East and North Africa. Policy brief prepared for PRB, 1 January 2006, <https://www.prb.org/investinginreproductivehealthto achievedevelopmentgoalsthemiddleeastandnorthafrica>. 23 April 2019.

Rowland, Robyn. Motherhood, patriarchal power, alienation and the issue of "choice" in sex selection, in *Man-made women. How new reproductive technologies affect women*, ed. Gena Corea et al., Bloomington, Ind. 1987, 74–87.

Shildrick, Margrit. *Leaky bodies and boundaries. Feminism, postmodernism and (bio) ethics*, London 1997.

Square Fertility Centre. One stop comprehensive service provider, <https://www.squarehospital.com/page/1/square-fertility-centre>. 3 July 2019.

Staff Correspondent. "Ratnagarbha Ma" conferred on 25 mothers, in *Prothom Alo*, 10 May 2015, <https://en.prothomalo.com/bangladesh/news/65995/Ratnagarbha-Ma-conferred-on-25-mothers>. 3 July 2019.

Sultana, Mirza T. Without a child my world does not end. IVF and childlessness in Bangladesh. Ph.D. diss., University of Lancaster, 2014.

White, Sarah. C. *Arguing with the crocodile. Gender and class in Bangladesh*, Dhaka 1992.

Reproduction: Health: Bangladesh and Pakistan

Sanjam Ahluwalia and Hector Taylor

Introduction

Pakistan emerged as a new nation, on the heels of British colonial retreat from the subcontinent, in August 1947, as East and West Pakistan, two distant wings flanking India. Until December 1971, it existed as a single nation, using Islam as a principle of nationhood, glossing over the geographical, linguistic, and cultural differences between its two halves. But the fratricidal Indo-Pakistani War of 1971 witnessed its breakup into two nations, Pakistan and Bangladesh. The war challenged Muhammad Ali Jinnah's (25 December 1876–11 September 1948) "two-nation theory," deployed by the British colonial state to justify the partition of the territories that it had controlled prior to 1947.

As a short-lived project, Pakistan and its breakup, scholars have argued, challenges the idea of singling out Islam as a legitimate basis for Pakistani nationalism (Oldenburg 1985, Nazneen 2018). In hindsight, many writers and political commentators have offered a teleological and determinist historical framing to understand the partition of Pakistan. For instance, in his novel *Shame*, Salman Rushdie paints unified Pakistan as an ill-conceived project, "that fantastic place of a bird, two Wings without a body, sundered by the landmass of its greatest foe, joined by nothing but God." (Rushdie 1983, 178) Others pejoratively referred to this national project as a "freak of history," one that was "an unstable state" from its inception (Raghavan 2013, 6). Without suggesting that the fragmentation of Pakistan was a foregone conclusion given its geospatial composition and cultural differences, this article centers reproductive health and natality as specific historical analytics. This focus highlights the distinct trajectories within unified Pakistan and, later, across the two nations, tied to their intersecting histories of sexuality, bodies, communities, class, religion, nation, and global geopolitics. By mapping the different histories of politics and advocacy on reproductive health, the article captures important distinctions in the trajectories of reproductive governance and reproductive outcomes across Pakistan and Bangladesh, determined as these were by complex dynamics across the abovementioned intersecting variables of power.

In reviewing the histories of reproductive health across the two nations, it is useful to recall Hannah Arendt's insightful observation that "natality and not mortality, may be the central category of political, as distinguished from metaphysical, thought" (Arendt 1958, 9; Tyler 2009). Acknowledging that concerns over birth determine national and global politics permits us to recognize that the dynamics of sexual and reproductive bio-economies have underwritten national histories in Pakistan and Bangladesh. Feminist scholars have extensively documented the limits placed on women's procreative liberties, given how access to contraceptive technologies are differentially managed across lines of class, caste, community, ethnicity, race, ability, and nation (Hartmann 1995, Roberts 1997, Ahluwalia 2008, Takeshita 2012). Fears over a looming danger of "overpopulation" have differently shaped the dominant terrain of reproductive politics in Pakistan and Bangladesh—as they have in other parts of the Global South—and the rights-bearing feminine reproductive subject has been disadvantaged in many ways within these two locations (Hartmann 1995). It is important to highlight that there are two parallel and competing traditions of research and scholarship on reproductive health in Pakistan and Bangladesh: numerical and algorithmic obsession with computing demographic shifts co-exists with revisionist feminist scholarship invested in highlighting inequities in access to reproductive and sexual health across various axes of power. This article engages with both.

Research has pointed to the pluralities of reproductive histories and politics across Pakistan and Bangladesh. Warren Robinson, for instance, has argued that "Pakistan has a long, interesting, expensive and generally unsuccessful history" of family planning (Robinson 1987). In contrast, the narrative on Bangladesh has shifted from identifying it as a "basket case" to celebrating what some refer to as "Bangladesh's health revolution," marking its emergence as a new Asian Tiger (Abed 2013–14, Hossain 2017). Markers of this "health revolution" within contemporary Bangladesh, highlighted by state and international observers such as Amartya Sen, include a lowering of the birth rate, declining maternal and infant mortality rates, and increased rates of contraceptive acceptance and usage. Bangladesh has surpassed most South Asian nations in achieving the Millennium Development Goals (MDGs), including those related to improving maternal health. Sen has lauded Bangladesh for its record on gender equality and for its stronger record in every aspect of the Human Development Index (HDI) compared to both Pakistan and India, attributing this transformation to investment in the health and education of Bangladeshi women (Sen 2013). In contrast, the newly elected prime minister of Pakistan, Imran Khan, in his inaugural speech in July 2018, commented on the abysmal state of Pakistani women's health, especially its high maternal mortality rate. According to a recent UNICEF report, the maternal death rate recently recorded for Pakistan is 178 deaths/100,000 live births. (UNICEF, 2017)

Reproductive health has become an important marker of a nation's standing in the world. Feminist scholars have drawn attention to competing and overlapping state and global investments in the contemporary governance of reproduction. Various state and global entities deploy multiple modalities to govern, regulate, seize, restrain, and control the reproduction of populations around the world. Within global biopolitical governance, most nation-states singularly burden and identify the woman as the reproductive subject. Consequently, most contemporary contraceptive technologies align with national and global demographic initiatives, to mark the woman as the principal contraceptive subject. Moreover, the global "population establishment" has been most successful in its continual discursive mapping of demography, reproductive practices, and contraceptive acceptance as significant markers of national growth and development into the new millennium (Hartmann 1997, Ahluwalia 2008, Murphy 2012).

The commentary below on the trajectories of reproductive health in Pakistan and Bangladesh over the last five decades captures both the similarities and the differences between these two South Asian countries. Even while Islam is a shared variable, the politics and practice of Islam have varied not only across but also within Pakistan and Bangladesh for the period under review. Beside Islam, many other intersecting axes have worked to determine the different modalities of governing reproduction within these two nations (and continue to do so). A simplistic paradigm of Islamic exceptionalism is therefore inadequate for understanding the heterogeneous reproductive experiences and histories of women and men in Pakistan and Bangladesh. According to World Bank data, Pakistan has the highest fertility rate in Asia, coupled with a low contraceptive prevalence rate (CPR), whereas Bangladesh has witnessed an impressive sevenfold increase in its CPR, from 7.7% in 1976 to close to 62.4% in 2014. In comparison, Pakistan, from a CPR of 5.5% in 1969, reached a CPR of only 35.4% in 2013. Scholars argue that political leaders have justified their lackadaisical approach to these issues with false claims to political backlash and the absence of political will to support the use of contraceptives and advocacy of family limitation (Adil 2015).

Given the plurality of historical outcomes around fertility management, contraceptive technologies, and access to these, existing scholarship has highlighted some important features that have shaped the different reproductive histories in Pakistan and Bangladesh. A focus on the histories of the two nations, especially the birth of Bangladesh at the end of Pakistani neocolonial control in 1971, captures the different state policies toward women as reproductive citizens. Trained "lady health workers" emerge as important actors within these two locations. Female health workers in both countries have long provided the first line of treatment and been the primary source of information about contraception, as well as about maternal and infant well-being, in rural areas as well as poorer urban neighborhoods. An interrogation of sociocultural ideas that uphold son preference and daughter aversion highlights differences within and between these two nations. Scholars such as Riddell have probed the role of Islam and religious leaders in shaping family planning politics and reproductive behaviors across these two nations. (Riddell 2009). Scholarship has also interrogated the merits of the autonomy model, which recognizes the woman as the primary contraceptive subject, especially as this overlooks the prevalence of the couple-method in Pakistan. (Husain, Husain, and Izhar 2019) In the early years in Pakistan, from 1960 to 1970, male vasectomy, along with IUDs, was the preferred contraceptive method, adopted and advanced through the state Family Planning Board and foreign (mainly American) organizations (F. Akhter 1992b). The singular focus on women within family planning programs more recently in Pakistan is identified as a primary reason behind the country's failure to achieve the targeted CPR and the overall lowering of the fertility ratio from 3.6 to 2.2. Some scholars have argued that the near exclusive focus on women is the reason for the slow progress that Pakistan has made in family planning, even though a somewhat similar focus has achieved different results in Bangladesh (Schuler, Hashemi, and Jenkins 1995, Abed 2013–14).

Pakistan, 1947–71

Begum Saeeda (Saida) Waheed, a member of the All Pakistan Women's Association (APWA), is recognized as one of the early female advocates of family planning and birth control in independent Pakistan. She founded the Family Planning Association of Pakistan (FPAP) in Lahore as early as 1952, with support from the International Planned Parenthood Federation (IPPF). The FPAP operated as a small nongovernmental organization (NGO), with branches in Lahore, Karachi (West Pakistan), and Dhaka (East Pakistan). Elite educated middle-class Pakistani women were thus early pioneers in advocating and promoting family planning. The Pakistani state, for its part, at best paid lip service to the cause of providing women with better reproductive health, especially in terms of enabling women to exercise control over their reproduction through access to contraceptive technologies. Based on information from the FPAP's webpage, Katrina Riddell highlights the modest beginnings of advocacy work that the organization undertook, using donkey carts and bicycles to spread the message of family planning (Riddell 2009, 157) According to Riddell, the organization initially encountered much resistance in its advocacy work—the dominant sentiment among the populace was that human intervention to deliberately manage reproduction was haram (forbidden within Islam). Despite such opposition to family planning initiatives, the Pakistani state allocated five lakh rupees in state funds in its first Five-Year Development Plan (FYDP). Family planning was identified as important to the nation and, to this effect, the National Planning Board in 1956 stated: "The country must appreciate that population growth is a rock on which all hopes of improved conditions of living may flounder. It admits of no approach except that the rates of growth must be low" (Riddell 2009, 159).

Despite this allocation of public sector funds to family planning initiatives during the early years of independence in Pakistan, it was civil society members, chief among whom were the FPAP, private citizens, and other NGOs, that undertook most of the groundwork to promote family planning interventions. The first FYDP suffered a setback with the political coup of 1958, which installed Ayub Khan as president (1958–69), in the first of the many coups that would punctuate Pakistani politics for several decades.

A "military modernizer," Ayub Khan was committed to promoting family planning as necessary to national growth and development. He is on record as identifying "overpopulation" as a national "menace" that should be combatted through education (A Khan 1996). Although he was personally committed to promoting family planning initiatives to reduce population growth, international funding agencies such as the US Agency for International Development (USAID) exerted much political pressure on him and his government to actively and monetarily advance pro-family planning state policies. During the second and third FYDPs, covering the period from 1960 to 1970, political discourse consolidated around the idea that national development, modernization, and well-being were closely tied to a lower fertility rate. Pakistani state machinery collaborated with the international population establishment to advance population control through fertility regulation. The IPPF, the Population Council, the Ford Foundation, and USAID worked with the Pakistani government to lower the fertility rate, starting from the early years of independence. There was a push for what Farida Akhter refers to as a mass scale operation to advance the acceptance and use of contraceptive technologies to lower the birth rate. From the 1960s, financial incentives were adopted as a means to expand the acceptance of IUDs and vasectomies; acceptors and recruiters were both paid. It is unclear if the introduction of such incentives led to the subsequent increase in the use of IUDs (from 96,000 cases in 1963–66 to 227,000 cases in 1969–70). Vasectomies also increased (from 5,000 cases in 1965–66 to 314,000 cases in 1969–70) (F. Akhter 1992a).

The state directive to expand the use of contraceptives was carried through with slight variations from Ayub Khan through to Zulfiqar Ali Bhutto leadership in the 1970s. From a focus on a supply-based initiative for contraceptives to incentive-based directives, the state and the international population establishment worked within the framework of biopolitics to determine the size of the nation's population. Leaning upon neo-Malthusian ideas from the 1950s to 1970, they identified a high population growth rate as a major hindrance to enriching the nation and expanding its GNP. Reproductive health, equality, and rights did not shape national and/or international population establishment understanding of demographics during this period.

The Pakistani state and leadership engaged differently with Islamic orthodoxy. In 1956, Pakistan promulgated its constitution, which declared the new country an Islamic republic. Ayub Khan adhered to a modernist interpretation of Islam but conceded that contraceptives should be used only to limit procreation within matrimonial sex. Nonetheless, anti-presidential sentiment during the last few months of his presidency specifically targeted his family planning policies. Both the left wing, represented by Bhutto's Pakistan People's Party (PPP), and the right wing, led by Jamaat-i-Islami, accused his administration of encouraging promiscuity, chanting "Family planning for those who want free sex!" (Finkle 1972, 122).

Ayub Khan's successor as president Yahya Khan's short rule (1969–71) oversaw the separation of West and East Pakistan. In 1969, Pakistan undertook the Sialkot experiment, which focused on contraceptive inundation and the supply side, but rather than IUDs, the emphasis was now on condoms and the pill. In the absence of a well-planned national family planning framework, the overly centralized supply system failed to increase the national CPR. The war of 1971 disrupted national policies and the implementation of family planning, but, more importantly, was marked by genocidal violence unleashed on Bengali women's bodies in the form of mass rape and the resultant pregnancies (discussed below).

Pakistan Since 1971

Given that state efforts in the pre-1971 era only haltingly and haphazardly lent support to fertility management, Pakistan saw little-to-no change in its national birth rate. There was also no significant decline in the high infant and maternal mortality rates. Variations between urban and rural areas in contraceptive adoption and practices were registered, with contraceptive use differing along class lines and according to educational qualifications. Even though Zulfiqar Ali Bhutto, the first prime minister after 1971, supported family planning, he did not actively advocate for or direct state resources to the expansion of contraceptive usage. The civilian leadership under Bhutto sought to push a socialist state, being careful not to alienate Islamic sentiment and domestic political factions. Bhutto's successor, General Zia-ul-Haq (1978–88), pursued a state policy of greater Islamization of Pakistani society and culture, with significant implications for women's reproductive access and health.

Zia-ul-Haq, after toppling the civilian government through a bloodless coup in 1977, worked with the Islamic faction to institute a greater Islamization of law and the state within Pakistan. The Hudood Ordinances, passed in 1979, were part of the state's intent to Islamicize its structures and its ideological underpinning. Feminist scholarship has pointed out how the Zina Ordinance (from Ar. *zina*, illicit sexual relations), which falls under the umbrella of the Hudood Ordinances, sought to police Pakistani women's sexuality and limit their mobility. In practice, these laws impacted working-class and low-income women much more severely than other women, and many of them were imprisoned under its provisions (S. Khan 2005). It would be fair to argue that they shaped the dominant discourse around sexuality and gender starting in the late 1970s, criminalizing nonmarital sex and further restricting unmarried women's access to contraception.

Under Zia-ul-Haq's *zina* laws, the popular idiom "Chadar aur chardiwari" (Women in veil and behind four walls) gained greater cultural credence, demarcating the distinction between the public and the private, and restricting women's access to public spaces. Despite these restrictions on women's mobility during Zia-ul-Haq's presidency, according to Riddell and other scholars, the population program did not disappear completely. Some have argued that even as Zia-ul-Haq ostensibly sought to distance himself from Bhutto and the PPP's support for family planning, he appointed Dr. Attiya Inayatulla as his advisor on population in 1980. He gave Inayatulla, who had served as head of the FPAP, full independence in her new position, though no doubt on the understanding that she would be discreet in her activities and not draw the attention of family planning critics. Riddell has remarked upon the "discrepancy and disparity" in Zia-ul-Haq's public position and his "silent," tacit support for family planning and population policy (A. Khan 1996, Riddell 2009). It was also during Zia-ul-Haq's presidency, in 1987, that Dr. Nafis Sadik became the executive director of the UN Fund for Population Activity (UNFPA). The appointments of these two high-profile Pakistani women to head family planning initiatives within Pakistan and at the UN, while also accepting large funds from members of the international population lobby, such as USAID, belie Zia-ul-Haq's stated antipathy toward family planning and his support for the Council of Islamic Ideology (CII) and its religiously determined pronatalist politics.

The leaders who followed Zia-ul-Haq sought to internalize the dominant international discourse on population and its connections to development, sustainability, and security (Riddell 2009). Under prime minister Benazir Bhutto (1988–90, 1993–96), the government once again took up what was presented as a "great battle ... to save Pakistan from the population bomb which is ticking away" (Riddell 2009). In 1994, Bhutto attended the International Conference on Population Development (ICPD) in Cairo and received unanimous applause with the following statement:

> I dream of a Pakistan, of an Asia, of a world, where every pregnancy is planned and every child conceived is nurtured, loved, educated and supported. I dream of a Pakistan, of Asia, of a world, where we can commit our social resources to the development of human life and not its destruction.
>
> KHAN and SHAH 2016

Under her regime, Pakistan relaunched its ambitious scheme of women health workers to promote women's overall reproductive health outcomes. Generally, however, issues related to national population and fertility patterns have received fragmented national attention in the three decades since Zia-ul-Haq's military rule. Those concerned that "the population bomb is ticking" have been countered repeatedly by ulema opposed to national initiatives promoting family planning. At the London Family Planning Summit in 2012, Pakistan committed to increasing its CPR to 55% by 2020, but the state has yet to implement any concrete policy or action in this direction, and no province has issued a population policy. Pakistan today has lower contraceptive usage than most other Muslim countries.

Bangladesh Since 1971

Reproductive concerns shaped the very genesis of Bangladesh. At the birth of the new nation, Bangladeshi women reported an unprecedented scale of reproductive crimes committed against them by the neocolonial Pakistani army and their Bengali collaborators (*razakars* during the nine-month war of independence. According to historical records, an estimated 200,000 to 400,000 Bangladeshi women experienced wartime rape. (Mookherjee 2015) The new state was thus confronted with the urgent need to acknowledge the enormous scale of the reproductive crimes committed against its female-bodied citizens. Under the leadership of the first Bangladeshi president, Sheikh Mujibur

Rahman (1971–72), the state publically designated the survivors of rape as *birangona* (war heroines). At its very moment of inception, the Bangladeshi state could not escape acknowledging the modalities of sexual violence that marked the lives of many of its female-bodied citizens. Both the perpetrators and the state identified the womb as a national incubator. Pakistani soldiers had acted on their leader's command and raped Bengali women, in doing so, realizing the slogan "Pehle inko Mussalman karo" (First, make them Muslim). The Bangladeshi leaders, in turn, wanted to ensure that there were no legal or legitimate claims of "Pakistani bastards" on the nation's women and other resources. The popular sentiment among West Pakistani leaders during the war had been that the emasculated Bengalis needed to be remade in the image of the masculine Pathans and Punjabis, whereas the new Bangladeshi state was determined to cleanse its citizenry of questionable parentage, in turn reclaiming their masculinity. In this historical moment, Bangladeshi women's reproductive bodies became the sites for enacting the competing masculinist nationalist aspirations of the two sides (Mookherjee 2007, Saikia 2011, D'Costa 2013).

Even as the newly independent Bangladeshi state eulogized the raped women and established *punorbashon* (rehabilitation) centers for them, it was not prepared to entirely trust the women to determine their own reproductive futures. Hetero-patriarchal politics understands women's reproductive expressions as fundamental in determining the future of the nation. Given the backdrop of this nationalist patriarchal politics, in the first year of its independence, the Bangladeshi state addressed the reproductive disruptions of its citizens by temporarily suspending the prohibition against abortions. The state oversaw, with the support of many international organizations and actors, an unprecedented, "industrial scale" undertaking of abortions between December 1971 and October 1972. A team of doctors from the IPPF, along with their Bangladeshi, Australian, and Indian colleagues, terminated unwanted pregnancies after the war. In her oral history account of the 1971 war, Yasmin Saikia also mentions the plight of women who defied the government injunction and carried their pregnancies to term. (Saikia, 2011) The state intervened in these instances, too, preventing the women from keeping their babies. Mother Teresa and the Sisters of Charity stepped in to "rescue the war babies" and facilitated their adoption by families in the Netherlands, other European nations, and Canada. Moreover, in seeking to rehabilitate the raped women, the state provided some of them with professional training as health workers. The state and other health agencies employed these trained women to advocate for and promote family planning advice and devices (D'Costa 2005, Mookherjee 2007, Saikia 2011).

In this one historical moment, as well as in its longer trajectory of reproductive politics, Bangladesh not only provincializes Western experiences but also simultaneously illuminates the incredible variations among Muslim women's sexual and reproductive experiences and histories. In 1971, a genocidal intent, underlined by a putative agenda to Islamicize the bloodline of Bengalis, captured the deep fault lines within the Islamic Republic of Pakistan. Centering this history of reproductive disruption and state intervention discredits homogeneous, simplistic, and ahistorical narratives about Islam and sexualities. Bangladesh embraced technology and science to "cleanse" pregnancies caused by rape during its war of independence. Islam notwithstanding, since the dawn of the nation, the Bangladeshi state, along with international aid agencies and many NGOs, has aggressively intervened and managed reproduction through the adoption of science and contraceptive technologies.

In its very first Five-Year Plan (1973–78), the Bangladeshi government incorporated population control into its model for growth, development, and modernization. In 1975, however, Bangladesh entered a period of army rule that ended only in 1990. The army rule coincided with a heavy state emphasis on managing the nation's reproductive future through population control. General Hussain Muhammad Ershad (1982–90) repeatedly identified "population" as the nation's greatest source of suffering and its "worst enemy." Population control, he argued, was "a question of the survival of Bangladesh" (Weaver 1984, Helmore 1987). He prioritized population control, according to Betsy Hartmann, considering it "more important than boosting agricultural production, increasing literacy, improving health care, or feeding hungry children" (Hartmann 1995, 213).

International donor agencies and large NGOs worked with staunch support from the highest level to determine Bangladesh's biopolitical engagement and, in the process, undermine the reproductive autonomy of its impoverished citizens. Many international donors pressured the government to make population control a central directive of the state. Hartmann argues that these donor agencies pushed the army not only to promote family planning in rural areas but also to enhance incentives for sterilization in order to transform reproductive behaviors among Bangladeshis (Hartmann 1995). As early as 1979, the government framed a National Population Policy, whereby they integrated advocacy and promotion of family planning into its overall national health services. Demographers such as John Cleland argue that Bangladesh benefitted from innovative government policies in reducing its fertility rate, especially the community-based approach adopted since the 1970s. This is when Bangladesh witnessed what Farida Akhter refers to as the "notorious inundation program," spearheaded by USAID. Feminist activists write about this period, when the

REPRODUCTION: HEALTH: BANGLADESH AND PAKISTAN

population plan adopted a "simple" strategy—to "flood the country with pills and every woman should get them whether she needs them or not, as long as they are taking the pills they cannot get pregnant" (F. Akhter 1992). A pluralistic health system made it possible to underwrite the contraceptive and larger reproductive initiatives in Bangladesh from the early years of its independence. Instead of a "purity of approach," public and private sectors,, along with numerous NGOs, such as the International Center for Diarrhoeal Disease Research (ICDDR-B), Johns Hopkins University, and USAID, worked together to create the much touted "success" of Matlab *thana* (administrative unit) among demographers and other constituents within the population control lobby. Matlab *thana* is a rural area of study with a cluster of 149 villages with a population of 180,000 (Ahmed et al. 2013). Feminist scholars and activists have brought to light the human costs associated with the success in Matlab, referring to it as "the world's longest-running experimental field site for fertility research" (Murphy 2012, 164–65). Revisionist scholarship by Hartmann has focused on women's bodily experiences in redesigning national fertility rates, primarily achieved through the adoption of various contraceptive technologies and the intervention of a pluralistic health system.

In the 1970s, IUDs were identified as the ideal contraceptive technology in Bangladesh. The UN World Population conference held in Mexico City in 1974 was a significant publicity campaign that favored the introduction of IUDs. The population control lobby embraced the IUD as a one-time and long-term contraceptive, since it followed the simple idea of "fit-them-and-forget-them" (Takeshita 2012). Bangladesh continued its enthusiastic embrace of the technology even despite increasing disenchantment with it elsewhere in the world by the early 1980s and despite a host of problems with it even in Bangladesh. The IUDs exacerbated reproductive tract infections among many low-income Bangladeshi women, who then struggled to find someone to remove the item. Following a WHO investigation, feminist scholar and activist Betsy Hartmann has argued that this technology was inappropriate and unsuitable for Bangladeshi women, given that in "most health centers where IUDs are being inserted asepsis is poor, appropriate instruments are lacking, lighting is not adequate and above all FWVs' (family planning workers) knowledge and insertion technique of IUDs are inadequate" (Hartmann 1995, 218).

The injectable contraceptive Depo-Provera, made by the pharmaceutical company Upjohn, failed to get approval from the US Federal Drug Administration (FDA) for use in that country in the 1970s. In Bangladesh, however, the NGO Gonashyastha Kendra (People's Health Center) started distributing it among its clients. By 1979, about 10-15 thousand Bangladeshi women were using Depo (F. Akhter 1992, Hartmann 1995).

The Population Council in New York helped fund the development of Norplant, which it introduced as a clinical trial among 600 women in Dhaka in 1985. This contraceptive was provided free to women and promoted for its long-term efficacy, as it provided protection from pregnancy for five years. Many women chose Norplant precisely because of its "worry-free long-term" appeal. But the rural women who adopted Norplant as a form of birth control faced a lack of information on what to expect or any follow-up clinical support. The family planning workers who recruited adopters were not trained to provide follow-up information to women on what to expect and how to take care of themselves (Rashid 2001). In the BBC documentary *Human Laboratory*, Bangladeshi women share their experiences with Norplant, and Farida Akhter narrates the callous response of a medical doctor to a Bangladeshi woman's plea to have the Norplant removed: "'I'm dying, please help me get it out' ... 'OK, when you die you inform us, we'll get it out of your dead body'" (*Human Laboratory* 1995).

Incentives underwrote sterilization in Bangladesh. Although it was not officially a state-sanctioned initiative, local officials eager to reach their target number of sterilizations often tied the sterilization procedure to food relief for poor women. Hartmann strongly criticizes what she refers to as the "sterilization at starvation point" approach in Bangladesh. The emphasis of this program was on population control, with a focus on recruiting female clients in deeply compromised economic situations. Although it was based on the principle of "voluntarism," some within the global population lobby, such as Walter Holzhausen, the UNFPA's Bangladesh representative, advocated a shift away from this voluntarism in a confidential letter to Dr. Nafis Sadik in New York: "Certain Governments in Asia using massive incentive schemes, including disincentives and other measures of pressure, still deserve international support" (Hartmann and Standing 1985).

As a result of its aggressive promotion of population control since the 1970s, Bangladesh has achieved a significant decline in its population growth. It boasts an impressive CPR of 62%, higher than many other countries on the subcontinent. A singular focus on these figures, however, obscures the biopolitics of top-down, state-directed population control that is technologically and financially underwritten by foreign pharmaceutical companies and donor agencies. Bangladesh's historical trajectory has limited the abilities of subaltern women and their families to make autonomous reproductive decisions. Despite these challenges, birth control has been celebrated as a "solution" to many social, economic, cultural, and political ills. According to James Grant, of UNICEF, "Family planning could bring more benefits to more people at less cost than any other single 'technology' now available to the human race" (UNICEF Annual Report 1992).

Female Health Workers' Programs in Pakistan and Bangladesh

Both Pakistan and Bangladesh have long relied on lady health workers (LHWs) to provide much-needed knowledge about women's maternal and reproductive health. LHWs also deliver contraceptives, such as condoms and pills, door-to-door in rural communities and to working-class women in urban areas. Instead of singularly relying on state actors, the introduction of LHWs fostered a robust community partnership while also investing in women at the local level and empowering them to become "managers of health and development" (Abed 2013-14).

Under Ayub Khan, Pakistan sought to recruit a new cadre of paramedical women family planning visitors to serve as IUD inserters, but his government was overthrown before the scheme could be adopted across the country (A. Khan 1996). Finally, under Benazir Bhutto's leadership in 1994, Pakistan set up what proved to be one of the greatest assets to the advancement of women's maternal and reproductive health at the grassroots level through its Lady Health Workers Program (LHWP). The LHWP provided important pathways for quality reproductive health care and basic curative services for many rural women in Pakistan. In their report on the LHWP, Nina Zhu et al. commend the program for providing a "springboard for female empowerment." As one of the largest community health worker programs—the Ministry of Health deployed 110,000 LHWs—they see the LHWP as providing a replicable model for the global community (Zhu et al. 2014). According to a 2018 report, the number of LHWs has grown to 125,000 (Adil 2015).

The ideal LHW is a local resident, is married, is at least 18 years old, and has a minimum of 8 years of education. According to external reviewers of the LHWP, "Women who are served by LHW are 11% more likely to use modern contraceptives, have 13% higher rates of tetanus vaccination, 15% more likely to attend a medical facility within 24 hours of birth and immunize children under 3 years" (Zhu et a. 2014). These reviewers point out that, in addition to improving maternal and infant health among the most impoverished communities within Pakistan, the program has also empowered women by providing professional training and opportunities for female health workers to earn a living in a patriarchal society (Zhu et al. 2014).

Other commentators dispute the LHWP's role in expanding family planning in Pakistan. According to Adnan Adil, despite the extensive network, LHWs were not adequately tapped to extend the reach of family planning, for this area is placed at the bottom of their training. If properly trained, he argues, they could contribute significantly to strengthening the family planning program in Pakistan. Given that LHWs have access to women clients, they could help raise awareness and remove reservations and misunderstandings about available contraceptives and their side effects (Adil 2015). Although Nina Zhu and her colleagues insist that LHWs have increased contraceptive usage among women in rural Pakistan, in some places even doubling the usage within a decade (1990–2000), others point out that LHWs do not reach out to lower caste women such as those belonging to the Kammi caste in northern Punjab (Mumtaz et al. 2014, Zhu et al. 2014).

Even Zhu and her colleagues highlight some of the challenges faced by the LHWP, such as the inability to hire local women, low wages, and lack of job security for existing LHWs. LHWs are often threatened and verbally abused, and "vilified for carrying out tasks deemed un-Islamic by local leaders." The recent shooting of two LHWs while on duty in Quetta had only made recruitment harder (Adil 2015). Many LHWs also face resistance from their families, who disapprove of their working and entering homes and interacting with strangers, which, at times, include men. Given that many of LHWs are familiar with their local milieu, they are careful not to breach cultural boundaries and provide contraceptive information to women only after they have had their first child; nor do they openly seek to dissuade parents from marrying off their daughters before the age of 18. Despite carefully navigating their cultural milieu and providing the first line of medical assistance, LHWs routinely face "accusations, slurs, and disapprovals from the communities they serve" (Adil 2015). Although many laud the convenience of the door-door campaign, some critics have pointed out by their very nature, these visits are short and not informative enough. This health delivery modality ultimately reinforces women's isolation and powerlessness "through its accommodation of the existing gender dynamics and norms of mobility" (Mumtaz et al. 2003). Following the US-led military operation in Abbottabad to capture Osama bin Laden in 2012, LHWs encountered heightened local suspicion and harassment. Many locals accused the women of being American agents in their advocacy for vaccinations and birth control. Some LHWs regard the patriarchal culture of their communities as a major hindrance to their work, even as Zhu and others see this program as empowering some poor and rural Pakistani women.

Bangladesh, too, has a history of using community health workers (CHWs). Its Shasthya Shebika program is similarly rooted in a gendered perspective. BRAC (formerly the Bangladesh Rural Advancement Committee, now sometimes known as Building Resources Across Communities), the largest NGO in the world, has almost 100,000 CHWs in Bangladesh, who work to bridge the gap between public health and local community needs (Perry et al. 2017). According to Mushtaque Chowdhury, through a gendered redesign of Shasthya Shebika, Bangladesh yielded tremendous health benefits—maternal mortality has by 75% since the 1980s, infant mortality has halved since 1990, and life expectancy has increased to 68.3 years, surpassing neighboring India and Pakistan. Female health workers continue to provide door-to-door family planning services as a mostly female front line of health workers. Other researchers, such as Cleland and Rozario, have also credited the work done by female health workers who visit women at home, for many of their clients observe purdah (seclusion). According to Rozario, these health workers were able to reach out to Bangladeshi women who would otherwise have had little access to health care (Rozario 1992).

Starting in the mid-1970s, Bangladesh adopted a community-based approach, recruiting married, literate village women trained in basic medicine and family planning to go door-to-door dispensing contraceptive pills and condoms and referring women for clinical contraception. "They acted as a bridge between the modern medical world and the village world," writes Cleland. "Because they were literate, they were part of the elite, and as villagers, they had credibility among a suspicious and very religious population" (Cleland 1823,2006). These female CHWs have worked tirelessly to "maintain one of the longest-running and most detailed health and population data sets" in the Matlab *thana*, a rural region close to Dhaka (Weiss 2014). Originally established to address the spread of cholera and run trials for the cholera vaccine in 1960, Matlab was repurposed after the 1971 war for longitudinal research on health and population. NGOs and Bangladeshis, who have helped expand the network and flow of health and contraceptive information, refer to Matlab as the "population laboratory." As a human laboratory, Matlab became a site for both experimentation and massive documentation for global consumption and research (Murphy 2017). One of the many reasons for the success of CHWs in Matlab is that these women work with their allocated communities, building trust through many hours of patient, empathetic, and necessary support related to the health care of women, children, and families. Mohammad Yunus, who ran the Matlab center for 40 years, describes Bangladesh as "a success story for family planning and reducing infant mortality." Among the global population lobby and public health researchers, Matlab is "something of a mecca," given its success with increasing contraceptive adoption and lowering fertility and maternal and infant mortality rates (Weiss 2014).

Although the Matlab experiment, with its trajectory of a declining birth rate and increasing contraceptive usage, is touted as a model for "poor nations" to replicate, it is sobering to note the increasing reliance on NGOs and foreign funding within Bangladesh that has helped achieve these outcomes. Feminist anthropologist Lamia Karim documents the often-untold sad stories related to the NGO-led initiatives, especially in the arena of microcredit, showing that although they often empower women, such initiatives can lead to economically vulnerable families losing their homes (Karim 2011). Nancy Fraser presents a broader critique of how the embrace of NGOs has led to the state retrenching and abandoning macrostructural efforts to address poverty and the displacement of vulnerable citizens (Fraser 2013). This critique speaks to the Bangladeshi experience of regulating reproduction through techno-medical socialization around contraceptive usage. State and nonstate actors have worked in partnership to achieve this much-celebrated Bangladeshi model of development, and many among the international development lobby think it is ready to be implemented in countries such as Malawi (Hossain 2017).

Selective Procreation: Son Preference and Daughter Neglect/Aversion

Socioeconomic factors influence the preference for sons, and this preference generally cuts across religious affiliations in South Asia. Researchers report a candid preference for sons over daughters in Pakistan and Bangladesh, and this affects contraceptive adoption. This cultural preference for sons, however, has not significantly shaped the sex ratio at birth in either Pakistan or Bangladesh. Although there is a skewed sex-ratio for 1- to 5-year-old children for a number of reasons, mortality among girls below the age of 5 has been declining in Bangladesh since the 1990s (Kabeer, Huq, and Mahmud 2014).

Economist Naila Kabeer and her colleagues have found important distinctions between Bangladesh and neighboring India around connections between declining fertility and gendered preferences for children in the composition of desired families. In Bangladesh, in contrast to India, the declining fertility rate has not led to an "intensification of discrimination against girls." Women's education, Kabeer and her colleagues find, has played an important role in mediating the cultural preference for sons in Bangladesh: lower educational levels among women aligned with stronger son preference. When tracking this preference along religious affiliation, Hindus, they argue, have a stronger preference for sons than do Muslims. In their research they point out that since the 1990s, there appears to have been a "widespread weakening" of son preference in Bangladesh. This shift in son preference has led to a 3–5% point drop in "missing women" in Bangladesh and Pakistan, compared to a much more modest 1-2% point drop in India (Kabeer, Huq, and Mahmud 2014).

Within Pakistan, son preference varies across communities, with a higher incidence among Baloch and Pathan communities than in Urdu- and Punjabi-speaking communities. Unlike in India, there is no legislation in

Pakistan that outlaws divulging information about the sex of the fetus. Expectant parents demand this information of their medical providers, who are willing to disclose it. Research has not found female feticide occurring in Pakistan at any comparable scale compared with India. Some families do rely on ultrasound technology to determine the sex of the fetus and selectively abort female fetuses. India's Pre-Conception and Pre-Natal Diagnostic Techniques Act of 1994, India's law prohibiting the disclosure of fetal sex, was further strengthened by an amendment in 2003 (Sathar et al. 2015).

Abortion laws in Pakistan date back to the British penal code of 1860, revised minimally in 1997. Very few providers in Pakistan appear to be familiar with the law. In practice, access to abortion seems relatively easy. The law permits abortions to protect the health of the mother and until such time that the fetus has not developed its limbs. Within much Islamic jurisprudence, this has been recognized as occurring in the fourth month of pregnancy. Researchers have argued that sex-selection abortions do not occur that often in an Islamic context since the sex of the fetus cannot be determined using ultrasound technology until 18-20 weeks (Sathar et al. 2015). Although sex-selection abortion is one of the modalities through which sex ratios are manipulated at birth across the border in India, it is not something that occurs with much frequency either in Pakistan or in Bangladesh. Existing research on Pakistan and Bangladesh has found that even with son preference being part of the cultural landscape, it has not led to widespread abuse of amniocentesis and ultrasound scanning technology for prenatal sex-selection abortions (Kabeer, Huq, and Mahmud 2014).

The harrowing accounts of rape among the Rohingya refugees have revived the history of gendered violence during the genocidal war of 1971 discussed earlier (Adams 2018). Although a proposed abortion bill failed in Bangladesh's parliament in 1976 in spite of the 1971 experience, a provision for "menstruation regulation" (MR) to remove the contents of the uterus before a positive pregnancy test remains an accepted and legal option. MR is framed as a backup to contraceptive failure, and Bangladesh is exceptional within South Asia for integrating it and family planning services into its overall health-care infrastructure, available through its multi-sectoral health-care provision comprising the public, NGO, and private sectors. Even as some scholars have questioned the access and efficacy of MR in promoting Bangladeshi women's reproductive health, it does provide an entry point for women's access to maternal health care (Dixon-Mueller 1988, Chowdhury and Moni 2004, Murphy 2012, Guttmacher Institute 2017). Moreover, MR enables organizations such as International Project Assistance Services (IPAS) to train health workers in Bangladesh to provide what they refer to as "abortion in humanitarian settings," especially for the displaced Rohingya women refugees from neighboring Myanmar (https://www.ipas.org/our-work/humanitarian-settings).

Although both Pakistan and Bangladesh fall within what some scholars have referred to as the "classic belt of patriarchy," there are very different histories of abortion across these two nations (Kandiyoti 278, 1988). Nationalist patriarchal considerations determined a very distinct history and politics of abortion in Bangladesh during its inception in 1971. The legal provisions of MR within Bangladesh have proven useful in making abortion available to the the raped and displaced Rohingya women. In both nations, legal restrictions on abortion date back to the colonial code of the 1860s, but Bangladesh has had MR in place since 1979. In Pakistan, despite a long history of legal restrictions on abortion, women continue to avail themselves of this with some ease, especially given physicians' lack of familiarity with national legal provisions that limit the terms and conditions for terminating an unwanted pregnancy. The high incidence of abortion in Pakistan, some scholars have argued, is evidence of the weak role of religious opposition in fertility behavior (Kamran et al. 2013). Although there are somewhat different trends in sex ratio and cultural preference for sons between Bangladesh and Pakistan, both countries have witnessed a greater drop in the phenomenon of "missing women" since the 1990s (Kabeer, Huq, and Mahmud 2014).

Conclusion

Narrating the histories of Pakistan and Bangladesh through the lens of natality and reproductive politics, the commentary above captures distinct trajectories across these two nations. Today, the world celebrates Bangladesh as one of development's biggest success stories, as captured in the comments of scholars such as Nobel laureate Amartya Sen cited earlier. Research highlights the changes across measurable reproductive health indices such as contraceptive usage and fertility to map this successful trajectory within Bangladesh, especially in comparison to neighboring South Asian nations. Recent revisionist feminist scholarship, however, has alerted us to the history of "experimental exuberance," where Bangladesh operated as the world's "aid lab," contributing significantly to underwriting this success (Murphy 2012, Hossain 2017). Since its inception following the genocidal war of independence, Bangladesh has allowed foreign organizations, aid, and NGOs to help alleviate its citizens' challenges in the face of infrastructural limitations. Bangladesh, in this instance, has successfully experimented with adopting a multi-sectoral approach in making health care available to its citizens (Kumar and Bano 2017).

This history is not one of linear progression, however, despite the remarkable upward swing in many human development indices. Although Bangladeshis adopted experimental and new Western contraceptive technologies such as IUDs, Depo-Provera, and Norplant, they did not do so necessarily as empowered sovereign citizens exercising autonomous control over their reproductive bodies (Hartmann 1995, Murphy 2012, Hossain 2017).

Pakistanis, on the other hand, lament what they refer to as "our family planning failure," something that the recently elected prime minister Imran Khan alluded to in his inaugural speech. One measure of this "failure" is the vastly contrasting CPR between Bangladesh and Pakistan. Bangladesh's CPR (63%) is nearly double that of Pakistan's (36%). This wide difference, some have argued, might have to do with Pakistan's failure to recruit Islamic leaders to help promote family planning in the country. This is in contrast to the ways that religious leaders in countries such as Bangladesh and Iran have facilitated the state's advocacy and promotion of family planning. Some Pakistani scholars have analyzed the singular reliance on women's autonomy as shortsighted. The focus on women, they argue, has overlooked recognizing men as reproductive subjects and the need for their greater participation in fertility regulation.

In the transition toward modernization, there are high stakes involved in mapping demographic shifts as tied to politics of natality. Leaning on algorithmic calculations of reproduction, international bodies such as the United Nations rank nations across the globe as being either successful or not. Within this narrative, Bangladesh represents a success story, whereas Pakistan lags behind in meeting an "objective," universalized measure of desirable reproductive patterns. Feminist scholars have drawn attention to the dangers underlying biopolitics tied to state and nonstate actors' regulation, management, and discipline of human reproduction. As is amply evident in the discussion above, there emerged vastly differing political trajectories of reproduction and natality within Pakistan and Bangladesh from the 1970s onward. This article highlights the terrain upon which these differing histories of reproductive politics have unfolded in the two nations, despite their shared past.

Bibliography

Abed, Fazle Hasan. Bangladesh's health revolution, in *The Lancet* 382:9910 (2013–14), 2048–49.

Adams, Patrick. How Bangladesh made abortions safer, in *New York Times*, 28 December 2018, <www.nytimes.com/2018/12/28/opinion/rohingya-bangladesh-abortion.html>. 1 August 2019.

Adnan, Adil. Our family planning failure, 15 November 2015, <www.thenews.com.pk/print/73301-our-family-planning-failure>. 21 February 2019.

Ahluwalia, Sanjam. *Reproductive restraints. Birth control in colonial India 1877–1947*, Chicago, Ill. 2008.

Ahmad, Wajihuddin. Field structure in family planning, in *Studies in Family Planning* 2:1 (1971), 6–13.

Ahmed, Syed Masuda, Timothy Evans, Hilary Standing, Simeen Mahmud. Harnessing pluralism for better health in Bangladesh, in *The Lancet* 382:9906 (2013), 1746–55.

Akhter, Farida. The eugenic and racist premise of reproductive rights and population control, in *Issues in Reproductive and Genetic Engineering* 5:1 (1992a), 1–8.

Akhter, Farida. *Depopulating Bangladesh. Essays on the politics of fertility*, Dhaka 1992b.

Akhter, Farida. "Doctor's Babies" in Bangladesh, 25 March 2010, <ubinig.org/index.php/home/showAerticle/14/english/Farida-Akhter/>. 21 February 2019.

Akhter, Halima, and Md. Ershadul Haque. The role of son preference on modern contraceptive use in Bangladesh, in *Journal of Humanities and Social Science* 19:7 (2014), 89–96.

Alam, Sultana, and Nilufar Matin. Limiting the women's issue in Bangladesh. The western and Bangladesh legacy, in *South Asia Bulletin* 4:2 (1984), 1–10.

Ali, Moazzam, Mohammad Bhatti, and Chusi Kuroiwa. Challenges in access to and utilization of reproductive healthcare in Pakistan, in *Ayub Med* 20:4 (2008), 3–7.

Al Jazeera News. Iman Khan's inauguration speech in full, 26 July 2018, <www.aljazeera.com/news/2018/07/imran-khan-speech-full-180726124850706.html>. 21 February 2019.

Arendt, Hannah. *The human condition*, Chicago, Ill. 1958.

Avan, Iqbal Bilal, and Saima Akhund. Role of family type in the idealization of a larger number of children by husbands in Pakistan, in *Journal of Biosocial Science* 38:2 (2006), 203–20.

BBC Television. Human Laboratory Documentary Transcript, 5 November 1995, <http://www.oldthinkernews.com/2010/12/09/human-laboratory-documentary-transcript/>. 19 February 2019.

Bishwajit, Ghose, Shangfeng Tang, Sanni Yaya, Seydou Ide, Hang Fu, Manli Wang, Zhifei He, Feng Da, and Zhanchun Feng. Factors associated with male involvement in reproductive care in Bangladesh, in *BMC Public Health* 17:3 (2017), 1–8.

Biswas, Kamal, Erin Pearson, S.M. Shahidulla, Sharmin Sultana, Rezwana Chowdhury, and Kathryn L. Andersen. Integrating postabortion care, menstrual regulation and family planning services in Bangladesh. A pre-post evaluation, in *BMC Reproductive Health* 14:37 (2008), 1–10.

Caldwell, John, and Pat Caldwell, What does the Metlab fertility experience really show?, in *Studies in Family Planning* 23:5 (1995), 292–310.

Chandrasekhar, Subrahmayan. The population problems of India and Pakistan, in *Eugenics Review* 41:2 (1949), 70–80.

Chowdhury, A. Mushtaque R., Abbas Bhuiya, Mahbub Elahi Chowdhury, Sabrina Rasheed, Zakir Hussain, and Lincoln C Chen. The Bangladesh paradox. Exceptional health achievement despite economic poverty, in *The Lancet* 382:9906 (2013), 1734–45.

Chowdhury, Mridul, and Radsheshyam Bairagi. Son preference and fertility in Bangladesh, in *Population and Development Review* 16:4 (1990), 749–57.

Chowdhury, Syeda, and Dipu Moni. A situation analysis of the menstrual regulation programme in Bangladesh, in *Reproductive Health Matters* 12:24 (2004), 95–104.

Cleland, John, Stan Bernstein, Alex Ezeh, Anibal Faundes, Anna Glasier, and Jolene Innis. Family planning. The unfinished agenda, in *The Lancet* 368:9549 (2006), 1810–27.

Connelly, Matthew. *Fatal misconception. The struggle to control world population*, Cambridge, Mass. 2008.

D'Costa, Bina. Victory's Silence, in *FORUM* 7:1, January 2013, <archive.thedailystar.net/forum/2013/January/victory.htm> 23 February, 2019.

D'Costa, Bina. War Crimes, Justice and the Politics of Memory in *Economic and Political Weekly*, 48:12,23 (2013).

Dixon-Mueller, R. Innovations in reproductive health care. Menstrual regulation policies and programs in Bangladesh, in *Studies in Family Planning* 19:3 (1988), 129–40.

Douthwaite, Megan, and Patrick Ward. Increasing contraceptive use in rural Pakistan. An evaluation of the Lady Health Worker Programme, in *Health Policy and Planning* 20:2 (2005), 117–23.

Drèze, Jean, and Amartya Sen. *An uncertain glory. India and its contradictions*, Princeton, NJ 2013.

Fikree, Fariyal, Amanullah Khan, Muhammad Kadir, Fatimah Sajan, and Mohammad Rahbar. What influences contraceptive use among young women in urban squatter settlements of Karachi Pakistan?, in *International Family Planning Perspectives* 27:3 (2001), 130–36.

Fikree, Fariyal, and Omrana Pasha. Role of gender in health disparity. The South Asian context, in *The BMJ* 328:7443 (2004), 823–26.

Finkle, Jason L. The political environment of population control in India and Pakistan, in *Political science in population studies*, ed. Richard L. Clinton, William S. Flash, and R. Kenneth Godwin, Lexington, Mass. 1972, 101–28.

Foucault, Michel. *The history of sexuality.* Vol. 1: An introduction, Paris 1976.

Fraser, Nancy. *Fortunes of feminism. From state-managed capitalism to neoliberal crisis*, London 2013.

Gordon, Linda. *Woman's body, woman's right. Birth control in America*, Charlottesville, Virg. 1990.

Guttmacher Institute. Menstrual regulation and unsafe abortion in Bangladesh fact sheet, March 2017, <www.guttmacher.org/fact-sheet/menstrual-regulation-unsafe-abortion-bangladesh>. 1 August 2019.

Hartmann, Betsy. *The poverty of population control. Family planning and health policy in Bangladesh*, London 1989.

Hartmann, Betsy. *Reproductive rights and wrongs. The global politics of population control*, Boston, Mass. 1995.

Hartmann, Betsy. Population control II. The population establishment today, in *International Journal of Health Services* 27:3 (1997), 523–40.

Hartmann, Betsy and Hilary Standing. *Food, saris and sterilization. Population control in Bangladesh*, London 1985.

Hossain, Naomi. *Aid-Lab. Understanding Bangladesh's unexpected success*, London 2017.

Hossain, Naomi. Post-conflict ruptures and the space for women's empowerment in Bangladesh, in *Women's Studies International Forum* 68 (2018), 104–12.

Huda, Fauzia, Yolande Robertson, Sabiha Chowdhuri, Bidhan Sarker, Laura Reichenbach, and Ratana Somrongthong. Contraceptive practices among married women of reproductive age in Bangladesh. A review of the evidence, in *BMC Reproductive Health* 14:69 (2017), 1–9.

Hussain, R., Fariyal Fikree, and H.W. Berendes. The role of son preference in reproductive behaviour in Pakistan, in *Bull World Health Organization* 78:3 (2000), 379–88.

Husain Sonia Husain, Samia Husain, and Rubina Izhar, Women's decision versus couples' decision on using postpartum intra-uterine contraceptives, in *Eastern Mediterranean Journal*, 25:5 (2019), 322–330.

Ibrahim, Nilima. As a war heroine, I speak, in *The Daily Star*, 27 March 2016, <www.thedailystar.net/supplements/independence-day-2016/war-heroine-i-speak-1199590>. 1 August 2019.

Joshi, Shareen, and T. Paul Schultz. Family planning as an investment in development. Evaluation of a program's consequences in Matlab, Bangladesh. Discussion Paper No. 951, prepared for the Economic Growth Center, Yale University, February 2007. <http://www.econ.yale.edu/~pschultz/SchultzJoshiEGCWorkingPaper951.pdf>.

Kabeer, Naila, Lopita Huq, and Simeen Mahmud. Diverging stories of "missing women" in South Asia. Is son preference weakening in Bangladesh?, in *Feminist Economics* 20:4 (2014), 138–63.

Kadir, Muhammad, Fariyal F. Fikree, Amanullah Khan, and Fatima Sajan. Do mothers-in-law matter? Family dynamics and fertility decision-making in urban squatter settlements of Karachi, Pakistan, in *Journal of Biosocial Science* 35:4 (2003), 545–58.

Kale, Rajendra. "It's a girl!"—could be a death sentence, in *Canadian Medical Association Journal* 184:4 (2012), 387–88.

Kandiyoti, Deniz. Bargaining with patriarchy, in *Gender and Society* 2:3 (1988), 274–90.

Karim, Lamia. *Microfinance and its discontents. Women in debt in Bangladesh,* Minneapolis, Minn. 2011.

Kamran, Iram, Mumraiz Khan, Zeba Tasneem. *Involving Men in Reproductive and Fertility Issues. Insights from Punjab*, Population Council: Islamabad (2013).

Khan, Ayesha. Policy-making in Pakistan's population program, in *Health Policy and Planning* 11:1 (1996), 30–51.

Khan, Shahnaz. Reconfiguring the native informant. Positionality in the global age, in *Signs: Journal of Women in Culture and Society* 30:4 (2005), 2017–37.

Khan, Shehla Aftab, and Nasreen Aslam Shah. Reproductive choices. Female bodies, male decisions. A case study of Pakistan, in *Pakistan Journal of Women's Studies* 23:2 (2016), 1–20.

Kumar, Santosh, and Suria Bano. Comparison and analysis of health care delivery systems. Pakistan versus Bangladesh, in *Journal of Hospital and Medical Management* 3:1 (2017) 1–7.

Mahmood, Naushin, and Karin Ringheim. Knowledge, approval and communication about family planning as correlates of desired fertility among spouses in Pakistan, in *International Perspectives on Sexual and Reproductive Health* 23:3 (1997), 122–29.

Mookherjee, Nayanika. Available motherhood. Legal technologies, "state of exception" and the dekinning of "war-babies" in Bangladesh, in *Childhood* 14:3 (2007), 339–54.

Mookherjee, Nayanika. History and the Birangona. The ethics of representing narratives of sexual violence of the 1971 Bangladesh war, in *Himāl: SouthAsian,* 9 November 2015, <http://himalmag.com/history-and-the-birangona-bangladesh/>.

Mumtaz, Zubia. Gender and reproductive health in Pakistan. A need for reconceptualisation, *PhD Thesis, London School of Hygience & Tropical Medicine, University of London* (2003).

Mumtaz, Zubia. Understanding gendered influences on women's reproductive health in Pakistan. Moving beyond the autonomy paradigm, in *Social Science & Medicine* 68:7 (2009), 1349–56.

Mumtaz, Zubia, and Sarah Salway. "I never go anywhere." Extricating the links between women's mobility and uptake of reproductive health services in Pakistan, in *Social Science & Medicine* 60:8 (2005), 1751–65.

Mumtaz, Zubia, Sarah Salway, Muneeba Waseem, and Nighat Umer. Gender-based barriers to primary health care provision in Pakistan. The experience of female providers, in *Health Policy and Planning* 18:3 (2003), 261–69.

Mumtaz, Zubia, Sarah Salway, Afshan Bhatti, Laura Shanner, Shakila Zaman, Lory Laing, and George T.H. Ellison. Improving maternal health in Pakistan. Toward a deeper understanding of the social determinants of poor women's access to maternal health services, in *American Public Health* 104:1 (2014), 17–24.

Mumtaz, Zubia, Umber Shahid, and Adrienne Levay. Understanding the impact of gendered roles on the experiences of infertility amongst men and women in Punjab, in *Reproductive Health* 10:3 (2013), 1–10.

Murphy, Michelle. *Seizing the means of reproduction. Entanglements of feminism, health, and techno science*, Durham, NC 2012.

Murphy, Michelle. *The economization of life*, Durham, NC 2017.

Nazneen, Sohala. Binary framings. Islam and struggle for women's empowerment in Bangladesh, in *Feminist Dissent* 3 (2018), 194–230.

Oldenburg, Philip. "A place insufficiently imagined." Language, belief and the Pakistan crisis of 1971, in *The Journal of Asian Studies* 44:4 (1985), 711–33.

Osborn, Richard. The Sialkot experience, in *Studies in Family Planning* 5:4 (1974), 123–29.

Pearson, Erin, Kathryn Andersen, Kamal Biswas, Rezwana Chowdhury, Susan Sherman, and Michele Decker. Intimate partner violence and constraints to reproductive autonomy and reproductive health among women seeking abortion services in Bangladesh, in *International Journal of Gynecology & Obstetrics* 136:3 (2016), 290–97.

Perry, Henry, Rose Zulliger, Kerry Scott, Dena Javadi, and Jessica Gergen, Katharine Shelley, Lauren Crigler, Iain Aitken, Said Habib Arwal, Novia Afdhila, Yekoyesew Worku, Jon Rohde, Zayna Chowdhury, and Rachel Strodel. Case studies of large scale community health workers programs. Examples from Afghanistan, Bangladesh, Brazil, Ethiopia, India, Iran, Nepal, and Pakistan, Rwanda, Zambia, and Zimbabwe, in *Maternal and Child Health Integrated Program*, January 2017, 1–114.

Raghavan, Srinath. *1971. A global history of the creation of Bangladesh*, Boston, Mass. 2013.

Rahman, Mizanur, and Julie DaVanzo. Gender preference and birth spacing in Matlab, Bangladesh, in *Demography* 30:3 (1993), 315–32.

Rahman, Mizanur, Siân Curtis, Nitai Chakraborty, and Kanta Jamil. Women's television watching and reproductive health behavior in Bangladesh, in *Population Health* 3 (2017), 525–33.

Riddell, Katrina. *Islam and the securitisation of population policies. Muslim states and sustainability*, London 2009.

Rizvi, Najma. Spectacular achievement, in *Development and Cooperation*, 19 March 2014, <dandc.eu/en/article/successful-family-planning-bangladesh-Holistic-approach-leads-lower-fertility-rates-rates>. March 2019.

Roberts, Dorothy. *Killing the black body. Race, reproduction and the meaning of liberty*, New York 1997.

Robinson, Warren. The "new beginning" in Pakistan's family planning programme, in *Pakistan Development Review* 26:1 (1987), 107–18.

Rozario, Santi. *Purity and Communal Boundaries. Women and Social Change in Bangladeshi Village*, London, UK (1992).

Saikia, Yasmin. *Women, War, and the Making of Bangladesh. Remembering 1971,* Durham, NC 2011.

Sathar, Zeba, Gul Rashida, Sabahat Hussain, and Anushe Hassan. Evidence of son preference and resulting demographic and health outcomes in Pakistan, Islamabad, *Population Council;* (2015) 1–39.

Schuler, Sidney, Syed Hashemi, and Ann Jenkins. Bangladesh's family planning success story. A gender perspective, in *International Family Planning Perspectives* 21 (1995), 132–37 and 166.

Sen, Amartya. What's happening in Bangladesh? in *The Lancet* 382:9909 (2013), 1966–68.

Shah, N.M. Past and current contraceptive use in Pakistan, in *Studies in Family Planning* 10:5 (1979), 164–73.

Solotaroff, Jennifer, and Rohini Prabha Pande. *Violence against women and girls. Lessons from South Asia,* Washington, DC 2014.

Star Online Report. Bangladesh ahead of India in social indicators. Amartya, in *The Daily Star,* 23 February 2015, <www.thedailystar.net/top-news/bangladesh-ahead -india-social-indicators-amartya-3540>. 21 February 2019.

Takeshita, Chikako. *The global biopolitics of the IUD. How science constructs contraceptive users and women's bodies,* Cambridge, Mass. 2012.

Tyler, Imogen. Introduction. Birth, in *Feminist Review* 93:1 (2009), 1–7.

UNICEF, 2017. Maternal and new born health disparities: Pakistan. https://data.unicef .org › country_profiles › Pakistan › country profile_PAK.

United Nations Development Program (UNDP). Improve maternal health where we are, n.d., <www.bd.undp.org/content/bangladesh/en/home/post-2015/millennium -development-goals/mdg5/>. 21 February 2019.

Wahed, Tasnuva, Anadil Alam, Salima Sultana, Nazmul Alam, and Ratana Somrongthong. Sexual and reproductive health behaviors of female sex workers in Dhaka, Bangladesh, in *PLoS ONE* 12:4 (2017), 1–17.

Weiss, Kenneth. How Bangladesh's female health workers boosted family planning, in *The Guardian,* 6 June 2014, <https://www.theguardian.com/global-development/2014/ jun/06/bangladesh-female-health-workers-family-planning>. March 2019.

World Bank. Contraceptive prevalence, any methods (% of women ages 15–49), <data .worldbank.org/indicator/SP.DYN.CONU.ZS?view=chart>. 3 February 2019.

World Health Organization (WHO). *Eliminating forced, coercive and otherwise involuntary sterilization. An interagency statement,* Geneva 2014).

Zhu, Nina, Elizabeth Allen, Annie Kearns, Jacquelyn Caglia, and Rifat Atun. Lady Health Workers in Pakistan. Improving access to health care for rural women and families. Working paper prepared as part of the Adding Content to Contact project, the Women and Health Initiative and the Maternal Health Task Force, Harvard School of Public Health, August 2014.

Reproduction: Health: India: Mid- to Late-Twentieth Century

Daksha Parmar and Sanjam Ahluwalia

Introduction

The second most populous nation in the world after China, India also has the third largest Muslim population in the world, after Indonesia and Pakistan, and has been center stage in the global discourse on overpopulation since the early twentieth century. Arguing on the basis of various census reports published since the nineteenth century, Western and Indian elites have expressed enormous concern over India's rapidly increasing population. Even when little reliable information was available on population growth, the "population problem" marked India. At the same time, there was also a growing concern for reducing maternal and infant mortality rates. Advocacy for increased distribution of birth control information has proved an effective means of reducing population growth and of improving the health of mothers and children, considered central to the constitution of a strong and healthy nation (Ramusack 1989). Advocacy for contraception has been based largely on Malthusian fears of population growth exceeding available resources. This has been interwoven with the eugenics movement, which called for restricting the multiplication of the unfit (Ahluwalia 2008). The publication of the 1931 census led to further intensification of birth control advocacy, in that it reported a marked increase in the Indian population within a decade. A number of middle-class Indian men and women advocated contraception as a solution to the rapidly increasing population. Indian birth control advocates formed alliances with Western advocates (e.g. Margaret Sanger, Marie Stopes, and Edith How-Martyn) to intensify propaganda for contraception. These Western advocates provided their Indian counterparts with different contraceptives and financial support for their advocacy. However, given the predominant influence of neo-Malthusian and eugenic ideas, the promotion of contraception mainly targeted the working class. In mapping the trajectory of birth control in India from 1877 to 1947, Ahluwalia (2008) argues that bourgeois nationalists, middle-class feminists, Western birth-control advocates, and colonial authorities identified the lower castes, the working class, women, Muslims, and the rural poor as the primary targets for contraceptive technology because they perceived these groups to have dangerously disruptive fertility practices.

© KONINKLIJKE BRILL NV, LEIDEN, 2018 | DOI:10.1163/1872-5309_EWIC_COM_002164

While policymakers expressed enormous concern about overpopulation, there was also a great deal of fear among colonialists and certain Indian elites, especially Hindus, over the increase in the population of particular religious groups, most commonly Muslims. Census data since 1871 provided information about the growth in the numbers of different communities (Cohn 1987). These details consolidated anxiety that Muslims were multiplying faster than Hindus. The practice of polygamy, widow remarriage, and low educational levels were among the factors identified as contributing to higher fertility among Muslims. Muslims, as such, were marked as sexually irresponsible subjects, whose procreative practices were not in the interest of the nation. There was a dominant understanding that higher fertility rates among Muslims would lead to a demographic imbalance, one that would threaten the interests of the majority Hindu community. As Ahluwalia and others have argued, the early twentieth century witnessed communalization of demographic issues in India (Ahluwalia 2008, Jeffery and Jeffery, 2005). In more contemporary times, right-wing Hindu political groups have effectively deployed the idea about "Muslim fertility," for political gains (Weigl-Jager, 2016).

Islam and Contraception in India

From the early twentieth century, there has been a dominant understanding among right-wing Hindus that Muslims have higher fertility rates, especially in comparison to Hindus, because, on religious grounds, they do not practice family planning (Moulasha and Rao 1999). This has led to a general assumption that Muslims blindly follow the religious doctrines that govern their lives. Even today it is widely thought (erroneously) that Islam forbids the use of contraception and that using contraception is considered a sin (*gunah*) in Islam (Weigl-Jäger 2016). According to Bhat and Zavier (2005), Muslims' adherence to the pronouncements of their religious leaders results in their higher fertility rates.

In fact, Islam allows for multiple views about contraception. Islamic texts are unclear on the use of and acceptance of different methods of birth control (Omran 1992, cited in Jeffery and Jeffery 2000). Some texts mention that Islam supports *azl*, or coitus interruptus, a practice that some believe is widely prevalent in India (Menon 1981). Most Muslims believe that sterilization is forbidden in Islam and that those who are sterilized are excluded from paradise (Jeffery and Jeffery 2000). Khan (1994, cited in Jeffery and Jeffery 2000) argues that even if there is religious opposition to sterilization (based on the belief that it brings about a permanent change in the body), this position has not found support among the different schools of Islamic jurisprudence. However, there is a dominant understanding that Islam accepts all forms of nonterminal family planning. Abortion until the end of the first trimester is acceptable, for until this point, the fetus is not a viable entity (Engineer 2004). The Quran does not unambiguously forbid contraception. In fact, it says that contraception is permissible where a couple want to avoid poverty and improve their standard of living, while also safeguarding women's health (Jeffery and Jeffery 2000). So Islam, rather than outright opposing and banning birth control, adopts a more nuanced view. Despite this, birth control continues to be a controversial issue for clerics and other religious leaders to advocate for in India (Jeffery, Jeffery, and Jeffrey 2008).

India's Family Planning Program and Muslims in India

India has the distinction of being the first country in the world to adopt an official family planning program aimed at reducing the birth rate within a short period. Since the 1950s, different contraceptive techniques have been experimented with, beginning with the rhythm method or safe period, to Intrauterine Contraceptive Devices (IUCDs), vasectomy, tubectomy, condoms, and injectable and hormonal contraceptives to control India's rapidly increasing population. The family planning program adopted a cafeteria approach based on clinical methods of trial and error. People chose from a variety of contraceptives that were most appropriate for their requirements. Camps were also set up to introduce people to contraceptives, giving them a chance to accept family planning. An important aspect of India's family planning program was the role of international foundations and agencies such the US-based Rockefeller Foundation, Ford Foundation, and Population Council. These international bodies provided financial support, technical expertise, and a supply of contraceptives to the Indian government, starting in the early 1950s (Rao 2004). In understanding the trajectory of India's family planning program, it is important to recognize that these foundations have played an active role in promoting and pushing for different types of contraceptives in order to limit the growth of India's population. For instance, after the 1961 census, which highlighted the massive increase in India's population, efforts were directed to intensify the family planning program with the introduction of new contraceptives popularly known as Intrauterine Contraceptive Devices (IUCDs), or Loops, funded by the Ford Foundation and the Population Council. The state vigorously promoted the dissemination and use of IUCDs, hailing them as a magic bullet.

Targets were set to insert the loop by organizing IUCD camps, and monetary incentives were offered to acceptors and doctors to achieve higher targets. However, the challenge of introducing IUCDs on a massive scale without effective health infrastructure or proper screening of women was not carefully considered. Many women came forward to accept IUCDs as they wanted to ensure control over their reproductive bodies. However, women were fitted with any size of IUCD, and their well-being was not the concern of health workers, who were under tremendous pressure to achieve listed targets (Ahluwalia and Parmar 2016). Many women thus experienced complications, particularly excessive bleeding, which led many of them to remove the IUCD. This led to a decline in the acceptance of IUCD insertion within two years of its experimentation. For Muslim women, the use of IUCDs led to a number of cultural conflicts. For instance, the urine drops that sometimes remain on the thread of the IUCD can pollute a woman's body, meaning she cannot offer prayer until she has taken a bath (Chattopadhyay-Dutt 1995, 134). The IUCD is a temporary method of birth control that enables women to space their pregnancies and regulate the size of their families. However, its zealous promotion without careful attention to the specific cultural location of Indian women led to an early disillusionment among women about the adoption of IUCDs. The failure of the IUCD led to a search for an alternative method of family planning, one that would facilitate the control of India's population within a short period. This is when the focus shifted to promoting vasectomy (i.e. the sterilization of men). Sterilization had been promoted since the 1950s, but it was only in the early 1970s that sterilization of men was largely intensified.

Starting in the early 1950s, the Population Council and the Ford Foundation had also provided enormous financial support to set up Demographic Research Centers across different states of India (Parmar 2016). One of the important areas of focus for most of these centers was research on fertility differentials between religious groups. Research also focused on understanding attitudes towards family planning and acceptance of different contraceptive methods. Throughout the 1950s and 1960s, the knowledge, attitude, and practice (KAP) surveys that these centers undertook highlighted that the adoption of family planning or knowledge of contraception among Muslims in India was unfavorable and lower than it was among Hindus. Among Indian Muslims, Islam's disapproval of contraception became the leading cause for lower rates of acceptance of family planning. The state thus directed its efforts to increasing acceptance of family planning by seeking to alter the attitudes of Muslims to contraception. For instance, as early as 1958, the Demographic Research Center at the Gokhale Institute of Politics and Economics in Poona conducted a study in Manchar, a small town in the north of Poona district, to understand the communication of family planning methods, with the financial assistance of the Population Council. It became clear from the study that Muslims constituted 10 percent of the total households surveyed in Manchar and that the average size of their family was the largest, with seven members in the household (Dandekar 1967). The Manchar study identified fifteen Muslim women with objections to family planning on religious grounds. Attempts to organize meetings with the men failed because they, too, responded by identifying religious objections to family planning. In response to Muslims' hesitation over family planning in the study area, Dr. M.C. Balfour of the Population Council sent a *fatwa* from Egypt to the Director of the Demographic Research Center, Professor Kumudini Dandekar, to translate and circulate in the study area. The *fatwa* was supportive of family planning and called for Muslims to adopt contraception. Despite this, few Muslims participated.

Data from this and other studies also made it clear that Muslims prefer spacing methods to sterilization, which is a permanent method of family planning (Mistry 1995). The acceptance of sterilization among men was particularly low. Even in the vasectomy camps, organized as a part of the intensification of family planning during the early 1970s, few Muslim men participated. For instance, Muslim men were underrepresented in Ernakulum vasectomy camps, which were widely regarded as pioneering and successful, and in which around 150,000 men underwent vasectomy operations (Krishnakumar 1972). During the National Emergency (1975–77), when people were coerced to accept sterilization, a number of Muslim men were forcibly sterilized, often resulting in outbreaks of violence. Riots occurred, for example, at Turkman Gate and Dujana House in Delhi, where forced sterilization of Muslim men was undertaken (Tarlo 2003). Police officers raided the Muslim-dominated village of Uttawar, in the state of Haryana, at 3 am one day in order to target men for sterilization at gunpoint. The villagers were awakened from their sleep with loudspeakers, and men above 15 years were ordered to assemble at the bus stop. After some sorting, men deemed eligible were taken to clinics to undergo vasectomy (Gatkins 1979). The forced sterilization of the villagers of Uttawar was a way to punish those who opposed the government's family planning program (Chadney 1988, 92). Since the state targeted Muslim men, those forcibly sterilized were largely poor Muslims living in slums and those belonging to lower castes (Tarlo 2003). Thus, during the Emergency, sterilization was a mechanism for disciplining Muslims, whose bodies were seen as hyper-fecund and who were identified as resistant to state-directed family planning programs and the state's objective of lower fertility rates.

The Hindu Right and Fertility Differentials in India

Over the years, the Hindu Right has generated a number of myths about the fertility of Muslims in India. They have claimed, for instance, that Muslims' higher fertility rates are part of a political agenda (Panandiker and Umashankar 1994). Members of the Right argue not only that the Muslim population is increasing rapidly but also that Muslims deliberately produce more children because they want to take over Hindu India (Jeffery and Jeffery 2006). Some political parties have in fact even called on Hindus to stop practicing family planning in order to improve the demographic balance. The Shiv Sena in Maharashtra, for instance, engages in hate speech with statements referring to Muslims as "wanton producers of too many children" (Lele 1995). The Sena has long opposed family planning because its leaders feared that it would work at the expense of Hindus and lead to the creation of another Pakistan (Morkhandi Kar 1967). The Sena espoused the creation of a Hindu nation underwritten with communal demographic overtones that represents Muslims as reproductively dangerous subjects, whose reproductive abilities need to be coercively controlled. This communalization of demography has become a common feature of Indian political discourse, leading to an unquestionable acceptance of differentials in religious fertility (Jeffery and Jeffery 2006). Religion has become a leading cause in the dominant explanation of Muslim opposition to family planning within Hindutva discourse.

In the early 1990s, with the demolition of Babri Masjid, communal discourse in India took center stage. In this context, the Hindu Right selectively appropriated the famous slogan of India's official family planning program, "Hum Do Hamare Do" (We Two and Our Two). This popular slogan was communalized with a pejorative representation of hyper-fertile Muslim women and polygamous Muslim men with the Hindu Right slogan "Woh Paanch Unke Pacchees" (They are five—one husband and four wives—and together they bear twenty-five children) (Gupta 2001). Viewed as resistant and noncompliant reproductive subjects, Muslims were portrayed as working against the interests of the national family planning program, whose main objective was to ensure smaller families and thereby stabilize India's population. By rejecting contraception, Muslims were acting against the interests of their nation. This communal propaganda with respect to family planning has widespread appeal in India; it directly feeds into an enormous fear about Muslims outnumbering the majority Hindu community. Strategic deployment of communalized demographic discourse fosters fear and generates hatred against Muslims (Rao 2010).

What needs to be highlighted within India's demographic trajectory since the late 1970s is the fertility transition, whereby the fertility differentials between Hindus and Muslims have diminished, with some acceleration in the 1980s (James and Nair 2005). Since the early 1990s, the decline in total fertility among Muslims has been sharper than among Hindus as Muslim women's use of contraception has increased more rapidly than it has among Hindu women (Krishnaji and James 2005). Despite this, the release of the provisional unadjusted figures from the 2000 census led to tremendous controversy over the increase in the numbers of Muslims in India (Moulasha and Rao 1999, Jeffery and Jeffery 2000, Krishnaji and James 2005). Conveniently ignored in this demographic controversy was the fact that the previous two censuses (1981 and 1991) had excluded the states of Assam and Jammu and Kashmir, the two states with a predominantly Muslim population, because of political turmoil (Engineer 2004). Instead, the selective highlighting of the 2001 census figures generated a fear that the Muslim population was increasing rapidly in India and that by 2050 Muslims would overtake Hindus in India.

Demographic scholars such as Rao argue that it is erroneous to generalize based on the Hindu-Muslim fertility differentials (Rao 2010). For instance, as per the National Family Health Survey-4 (2015–16), the total fertility rate for Hindus has declined from 2.6 children per woman in 2005–06 to 2.1 in 2015–16, while it has declined for Muslim households from 3.4 to 2.6 during the same period (IIPS 2017). There is also regional variation in the fertility levels of Muslims in India: Muslims in South India have lower fertility rates than Hindus in northern India (Jeffery and Jeffery 2000). Despite these demographic realities, the 2001 census figures selectively highlighted a community-based narrative to generate a fear of explosive Muslim growth. The resurgence of the Hindu Right in mainstream Indian politics has fueled this communalized demographic fear in more recent times.

Muslim Women and Reproduction in India

Within the dominant nationalist Hindu discourse, the Muslim practice of veiling (purdah) reflects the low status of Muslim women. Within this discourse, the poor health of Muslim women, particularly during childbirth, has also been framed as an effect of gender seclusion through the adoption of the purdah system. With marriage a universal life goal among both Hindus and Muslims in India, giving birth to the first child immediately after marriage enables a woman to secure her status within her marital family. Within this cultural context, it is difficult to promote the use of contraception within the initial years of marriage. Despite this shared cultural framework of heterosexual conjugality across religious communities, the issue of reproductive practices among Muslim women has become particularly contentious in contemporary India. Dominant communalized understanding frames Muslims as hyper-fertile with large families, and Muslim women as lacking reproductive agency in determining the number of children they desire, something that Muslim men are seen as largely determining (Jeffery, Jeffery, and Jeffrey 2008). Demographic history, however, seems to indicate that while Muslim women's use of contraception was lower in the first decades after independence, it has been increasing steadily over the years. Even where the use of modern contraception was low, women were able to ensure reproductive control over their bodies through natural methods of birth control such as *azl*, which is widely prevalent among Indian Muslims. Further, the cultural practice of sexual abstinence during menstruation has been another method widely popular among Muslim women. Muslim women usually abstain from sexual relations for six to seven days during and after menstruation in order to be free of pollution (Chattopadhay-Dutt 1995). Many Muslim women also practice sexual abstinence for forty days following childbirth. This has been found to be the case in studies of Tamil Muslims, who resume sexual activity only at the end of this restricted period (Van Hollen 2003). Abstinence is thus one of the methods of family planning culturally prevalent among Muslims. An indirect method of regulating one's fertility is by extending the duration of breastfeeding. These methods, of course, are risky and often result in unwanted pregnancies.

Studies on family planning in India have observed that Muslim women prefer spacing or temporary methods over terminal methods such as sterilization (Mistry 1995, Prasad and Nair 1998). This is because there are some religious restrictions on sterilization. The belief is that if a woman undergoes sterilization, her prayers will not be accepted, and she will be denied entry to paradise (Jeffery, Jeffery, and Jeffrey 2008). The IUCD, therefore, has been a more attractive method. In the early 1960s, when the IUCD was first introduced in India's family planning program, it was believed that women should have an IUCD fitted and forget about it. However, because women experienced complications with IUCDs, particularly in terms of heavy and irregular bleeding, most women rejected them (Ahluwalia and Parmar 2016). And since most Indian women are anemic, excessive bleeding further weakened and compromised their overall health. Though India's health care infrastructure has expanded over the years, it will be productive to identify the experiences of Muslim women who adopted IUCDs. A study by Prasad and Nair (1998) of Muslim women in the old city of Hyderabad, which has a high Muslim population, found that IUCDs were often accepted by rich and upper-class women, who can better deal with any side effects associated with their use. Poor women who have the desired number and composition of children in their family tend to accept sterilization because they lack the money or the time to seek medical treatment. In the Indian vernacular, "operation," or *nasbandi*, refers to sterilization (Weigl-Jäger 2016).

During the 1980s, studies on Muslim family planning in India noted that knowledge about contraception was very low. For instance, in their study in Bijnor in the early 1980s, Jeffery, Jeffery, and Jeffrey (2008) observed that there had been a slow increase in the use of modern contraception in the Muslim-dominated village of Jhakri. In the 1980s, it was 1 percent, increasing to 6 percent in the late 1990s. Sterilization was rare: in the 1990s, only two or three women were sterilized. Since then, however, there has been a significant increase in the use of contraception among Muslim women. Despite religious and theological beliefs against sterilization, many low-income Muslim women have accepted sterilization. This is mainly because most of the women want to ensure reproductive control over their bodies, for they find it challenging to provide proper care, food, and education to their children because of their poverty. It would be fair to argue that religious teachings alone do not shape Muslim women's reproductive decision-making. Rather, the socioeconomic context of their lives and their competing interpretations of the Quran have an important bearing on their reproductive choices. For instance, based on her ethnographic study in a Muslim-dominated slum in South Delhi, Weigl-Jäger (2016) argues that most Muslim women utilize their personal interpretation of the Quran to legitimize the use of contraception and justify their own reproductive decisions in order to achieve a small family. In their efforts to achieve their desired number of children, Muslim women in the slums have been found to visit gynecologists, get an IUCD inserted, accept sterilization, and undergo abortion—often despite opposition from family members. These women argue that the Quran stresses that if we are unable to provide proper food and education, then it is a sin to keep having more children. Women come forward to undergo sterilization for a number of reasons, including a desire to protect their health from the consequences of repeated pregnancies, the health risks associated with pregnancy, their fear of maternal death, and the expense of childbirth. As rational reproductive subjects, some Muslim women even undergo sterilization.

Thus, despite opposition to contraception based on their religious beliefs and teachings, a number of Muslim women accept different methods of modern contraception. The entire propaganda of seeing Muslim women as producing more children results in depicting Muslim women as blindly following the doctrines of their religious leaders (Jeffery, Jeffery, and Jeffrey 2008). This creates a notion that Muslim women are unwilling to limit their fertility and will adopt family planning only through coercion. This communalized understanding has resulted in increasing the vulnerability of Muslim women when they visit government health facilities. Out of fear that the doctors or the nurses at these health centers might scold or beat them, Muslim women who come there for childbirth often choose not to disclose the number of their living children. The health officials for their part look at Muslim women with suspicion and often view them as reproductively irresponsible women with multiple children (Van Hollen 2003). Most often, they force them to have a loop inserted immediately after their delivery, and if they learn that the woman already has three children, they sterilize them without their consent (Prasad and Nair 1998). Given such experiences with public health facilities, most Muslim women have withdrawn from using the services of government health facilities and tend, instead, to depend on private sector for family planning services.

Another common method of fertility regulation among Muslim women in India is abortion, locally referred to as *safai karna* (Unnithan-Kumar 1999). This is often resorted to when contraceptives or a natural method of family planning have failed. A study focused on the reproductive health practices of rural Muslim women in Jaipur found that Muslim women prefer to visit private doctors for abortion. Government health officials often believe that they are wasting their resources on repeatedly aborting the same women, who they believe rely on abortion as a form of contraception (Unnithan-Kumar 1999).

Conclusion

In India, depending on their socioeconomic context, Muslim women adopt different methods of family planning ranging from spacing methods to sterilization. However, the Indian government's family planning program has largely promoted sterilization as the main method of contraception because a sterilized woman becomes a quantifiable "target" that has been successfully met by health workers. The official program insufficiently emphasizes spacing methods, some of which are the preferred method of birth control of most Muslim women (Prasad and Nair 1998). Thus, there remains a high unmet need for proper and safe contraception among Muslim women in India. This contrasts starkly with the dominant portrayal of Muslims as hostile to state-sponsored family planning directives. A way forward to ensure reproductive health for all women, including Muslim women, would be to make the family planning program and maternal childcare services attentive and responsive to the varied needs and requirements of constituents across religious communities (Jeffery and Jeffery 2000).

Bibliography

Ahluwalia, Sanjam. *Reproductive restraints. Birth control in India, 1877–1947*, Urbana, Ill. 2008.

Ahluwalia, Sanjam, and Daksha Parmar. From Gandhi to Gandhi. Contraceptive technologies and sexual politics in postcolonial India, 1947–77, in *Reproductive states. Global perspectives on the invention and implementation of population policy*, ed. Rickie Solinger and Mie Nakachi, New York 2016, 124–55.

Bhat, Mari P., and Francis A. Zavier. Role of religion in fertility decline. The case of Indian Muslims, in *Economic and Political Weekly* 40:5 (2005), 385–402.

Chadney, James G. Family planning. India's Achilles' heel?, in *India. The years of Indira Gandhi*, ed. Yogendra Kumar Malik and Dhirendra Kumar Vajpayee, Leiden 1988, 84–98.

Chattopadhyay-Dutt, Purnima. *Loops and roots. The conflict between official and traditional family planning in India*, New Delhi 1995.

Cohn, Bernard S. The census, social structure and objectification in South Asia, in *An anthropologist among the historians and other essays*, New Delhi 1987, 224–54.

Dandekar, Kumudini. *Communication in family planning. Report on an experiment*, Gokhale Institute Studies No.49, Poona 1967.

Engineer, Asghar Ali. A handy tool for anti-minorityism, in *Economic and Political Weekly* 39:39 (2004), 4304–5.

Gatkins, Davidson. Political will and family planning. The implications of India's emergency experience, in *Population and Development Review* 5:1 (1979), 29–59.

Gupta, Charu. *Sexuality, obscenity, community. Women, Muslims, and the Hindu public in colonial India*, New York 2001.

IIPS (International Institute of Population Sciences). *National Family Health Survey 4 (2015–16)*, Mumbai 2017.

James, K.S., and Sajini Nair. Accelerated decline in fertility in India since the 1980s. Trends among Hindus and Muslims, in *Economic and Political Weekly* 40:5 (2005), 375–83.

Jeffery, Patricia, and Roger Jeffery. *Confronting saffron demography. Religion, fertility, and women's status in India*, New Delhi 2006.

Jeffery, Patricia, Roger Jeffery, and Craig Jeffrey. Disputing contraception. Muslim reform, secular change and fertility, in *Modern Asian Studies* 42:2/3 (2008), 519–48.

Jeffery, Roger, and Patricia Jeffery. Religion and fertility in India, in *Economic and Political Weekly* 35:35/36 (2000), 3253–9.

Khan, M.E. *Family Planning Among Muslims in India: A Study of the Reproductive Behavior of Muslims in an Urban Setting*. Delhi, 1979.

Krishnaji, N., and K.S. James. Religion and fertility. A comment, in *Economic and Political Weekly* 40:5 (2005), 455–58.

Krishnakumar, S. Kerala's pioneering experiment in massive vasectomy camps, in *Studies in Family Planning* 3:8 (1972), 177–85.

Lele, Jayant. Saffronisation of Shiv Sena. The political economy of city, state and nation, in *Economic and Political Weekly* 30:25 (1995), 1520–28.

Menon, Indu. *Status of Muslim women in India. A case study of Kerala*, Delhi 1981.

Mistry, Malika. Fertility and family planning among Muslims in India, in *Problems of Muslim women in India*, ed. Asghar-Ali Engineer, Bombay 1995, 160–74.

Morkhandi Kar, R.S. The Shiv-Sena. An eruption of sub-nationalism, in *Economic and Political Weekly* 2:42 (1967), 1906–9.

Moulasha, K., and Rama Rao. Religion-specific differentials in fertility and family planning, in *Economic and Political Weekly* 34:42 (1999), 3047–55.

Panandiker Pai, V.A., and P.K. Umashankar. Fertility control and politics in India, in *Population and Development Review* 20, Supplement: The New Politics of Population. Conflict and Consensus in Family Planning (1994), 89–104.

Parmar, Daksha. Controlling births and limiting population in Maharashtra, 1920–80. Ph.D. diss., Centre of Social Medicine and Community Health, School of Social Sciences, Jawaharlal Nehru University, New Delhi, 2016.

Prasad, Sheela and Sumanti Nair, Fertility Control and Muslim Women, in Political Environments # 2, 1995.

Ramusack, Barbara. Embattled advocates. The debate over birth control in India, 1920–1940, in *Journal* of *Women's History* 1:2 (1989), 34–64.

Rao, Mohan. *From population control to reproductive health. Malthusian arithmetic,* New Delhi 2004.

Rao, Mohan. On saffron demography, in *Economic and Political Weekly* 45:41 (2010), 27–29.

Tarlo, Emma. *Unsettling memories. Narratives of the emergency,* Berkeley, Calif. 2003.

Unnithan-Kumar, Maya. Households, kinship and access to reproductive health care among rural Muslim women in Jaipur, in *Economic and Political Weekly* 34:10/11 (1999), 621–30.

Van Hollen, Cecilia. *Birth on the threshold. Childbirth and modernity in south India,* Berkeley, Calif. 2003.

Weigl-Jäger, Constanze. Islam and contraception in urban north India. Muslim women's reproductive health behavior and decision-making, 2016, <http://crossasia-journals .ub.uni-heidelberg.de/index.php/izsa/article/viewFile/845/818>. 23 April 2018.

Primary Source

Dandekar, Dr Kumudini, Letter to Marshall Balfour 24th May 1960- India: GIPE, Dandekar Kumudini, 1958–66, 1968–76, Population Council-Accession:2, Foreign Correspondence, Box: 85, Folder: 809, Rockefeller Archive Centre Records, Tarrytown, New York.

Reproduction: Health: Indonesia

Linda Rae Bennett and Belinda Rina Marie Spagnoletti

Introduction

While not an Islamic state, Indonesia is home to the world's largest Muslim population. It is the world's fourth most populous nation, with a population of around 260 million. Approximately 90 percent of Indonesians identify as Muslim; Christians, Hindus, and Buddhists make up most of the remaining 10 percent. Indonesia is currently classified as a lower middle-income country and has a growing middle class. However, there are significant differences in economic development across its 34 provinces and between people living in urban centers and those in rural and remote areas. In 2017, it was estimated that more than 25.9 million Indonesians lived below the poverty line and that more than 20 percent of the population was vulnerable to falling into poverty (World Bank 2018).

Sunni Islam was introduced to the archipelago during the fourteenth and fifteenth centuries, spreading from the west across Sumatra and Java through to the northern and eastern islands. Islam in Indonesia is diverse and has often been described as syncretic. This religious dynamism is a product of a relatively young nation, characterized by extensive ethnic and linguistic diversity, and the flexibility of local people and cultures in developing unique Islamic worldviews. Academic observers have attempted to characterize Indonesian Muslims by describing them as either devout or practicing Muslims (*santri*) or as nominal or nonpracticing Muslims (syncretists) (Baswedan 2004). However, such characterizations are not necessarily relevant to the ways that Indonesian Muslims understand themselves. Many who might be characterized as syncretists by outsiders would describe Islam as central to their belief systems and daily lives.

Indonesian Islam has undergone rapid transformation over the past two decades, following a major political regime change and Islamic revivalism trends globally. Under Indonesia's first two presidencies, Sukarno (1945–67) and Suharto (1968–98), the political role of Islam was carefully contained. This shifted following Indonesia's dramatic economic and political crisis beginning in 1997. Following the downfall of the Suharto regime in 1998, strong calls for Islamic revivalism came from within Indonesian Islamic political parties, national Islamic organizations, and grassroots Muslim leaders. There was

© KONINKLIJKE BRILL NV, LEIDEN, 2019 | DOI:10.1163/1872-5309_EWIC_COM_002172

widespread consensus that a renewed commitment to Islam was necessary for national survival and renewal. This was articulated by Abdurrahman Wahid, a prominent Islamic cleric who became Indonesia's third president (1999–2001). Wahid encouraged Indonesian Muslims to express their religious devotion through purification by following the example of the prophet Muhammad by fasting every Monday and Thursday. Many Indonesians, particularly women, adopted this practice during Wahid's rule, and some still view additional fasting as an important part of their routine Islamic practice. Other visible trends associated with Islamic revivalism include a greater number of both Muslim men and women choosing to adopt more conservative modes of Islamic dress, higher attendance at Islamic study groups, a greater adherence to daily prayer and the other pillars of Islam, and increasing membership of formal Islamic organizations.

Women's status, roles, and freedoms are often at the forefront of Islamic debate in Indonesia (Robinson 2009). Some voices are highly progressive, while others represent positions that would ultimately curb the current freedoms and power that Indonesian Muslim women exercise (Davies and Bennett 2015). However, Indonesian Muslim women are important participants in these debates. Muslim women are active agents in a wide variety of informal and formal religious institutions, from neighborhood prayer groups to Islamic schools and national Islamic organizations. Although their contribution to the domestic sphere in terms of reproduction and parenting is typically viewed as their innate gender role, or *kodrat wanita* (the God-given roles of Muslim women), this has not resulted in the exclusion of women from public religious discourses or from working in the public domain. Indonesian women are highly active in Islamic welfare organizations, including grassroots women's Islamic groups, as well as the women's branches of Indonesia's two largest mass Islamic organizations, Nahdlatul Ulama (NU) and Muhammadiyah. The welfare work that Muslim women undertake within these organizations focuses on women's health and well-being, and includes running reproductive health clinics, family planning services, youth-oriented health services, and literacy and return-to-education programs, and assisting poor women with income generation.

Indonesian Muslim women engage with Islam in a multitude of ways that demonstrate their religious agency and are highly beneficial to their communities. Indonesia has a high proportion of female judges in sharia courts, which is important for women's status, considering the growing number of provinces that are implementing sharia bylaws (*perda*). Muslim women also play pivotal roles in the economic and political functions of Indonesia's Islamic organizations, and in developing the religious and political curricula within Islamic schools and universities.

Muslim women in Indonesia have historically enjoyed a high degree of economic, social, and spatial freedom (Sullivan 1994, Brenner 1998, Bennett 2005). It is often argued that the relative economic independence of women has supported their high physical mobility and more equal gender relations within families, compared with other Muslim cultures, where women have been more closely confined to the home (Manderson 1980, Blackburn 2004, Robinson 2009). Muslim women's reproductive roles, and their status as mothers, are highly valued throughout Indonesia's diverse cultures. Motherhood is the key indicator of adult status for women, and children are expected to both respect and adore their mothers. The popular hadith "Paradise lies under the feet of your mother" is often quoted to disobedient children.

The most reliable data sources that record reproductive health indicators in Indonesia are the Indonesian Demographic Health Surveys (IDHS), publications by the National Bureau of Statistics (BPS), and data collected by the Ministry of Health (Kemenkes) and provincial health departments. These data sources are reliable due to their representative sample sizes and rigor; yet, they rarely include analyses that are disaggregated by religion or ethnicity. However, we can assume that approximately 90 percent of the women included in nationally representative samples are Muslim. A range of important issues impacting on Muslim women's reproductive health—including polygamy, female genital mutilation, and the reproductive rights and health of lesbians and transgender women—are not addressed here, because they have been allocated a dedicated entry.

Comprehensive Reproductive/Sex Education

Provision of CRSHE in the Indonesian education system remains optional (UNESCO 2015). For secondary school students a version of CRSHE has been integrated into the national curriculum; yet, the content only partially reflects the international standard of CRSHE (UNESCO 2015). Inequities in terms of who has access to reproductive health education, and the comprehensiveness of education, have been confirmed by Utomo et al. (2014), who explored 1,762 primary school students' understandings of human reproduction across four provinces. This study found great variation in students' knowledge of how pregnancy occurs, with those at Islamic schools and those living in less developed provinces having poorer comprehension of the relationship between sex and pregnancy (Utomo et al. 2014). A major factor constraining improvements in the quality of CRSHE in Indonesia has been the lack of investment in teacher training (Bennett 2007). Although government investment in the provision of CRSHE remains weak and contested, this education gap for Indonesian youth is increasingly being addressed by civil society organizations and via social media, which provide educational materials and programs, as well as safe spaces for youth to discuss sexual and reproductive health and rights.

In the early 2000s, Indonesia was on the verge of implementing a more progressive adolescent reproductive health policy; however, progress has been delayed due to the growing influence of conservative Islam (Utomo and McDonald 2009). Although many parents, teachers, and religious leaders have sought for CRSHE to be actively discouraged, due to concerns that it may encourage premarital sex (Holzner and Oetomo 2004), such anxieties do not reflect the widely observed impact of CRSHE in other contexts, where young people who have received high quality CRSHE tend to have a later age of sexual debut when compared to their peers who have not received such education (Bennett 2007). Improving access to culturally and religiously appropriate CRSHE for Indonesian Muslim youth prior to marriage has the potential to promote equality in marital relationships, reduce the incidence of adolescent pregnancy, and support better reproductive health outcomes for women across the life course (Spagnoletti et al. 2018).

Maternal Health

Despite the cultural significance of motherhood for Indonesian Muslims, and the respect afforded to women when they become mothers, maternal mortality in Indonesia remains unacceptably high. Indonesia's Maternal Mortality Ratio (MMR) was estimated to be 126 maternal deaths per 100,000 live births in 2015 (MMEIAG 2018). Indonesia's MMR is among the highest in Southeast Asia, and in 2015 Indonesia failed to achieve its commitment to reduce MMR by 75 percent in response to the agenda of the Millennium Development Goals. The primary medical causes of maternal mortality in Indonesia are hemorrhage, hypertension, and infection (Soedarmono 2017). It is estimated that 78 percent of maternal deaths occur within 48 hours after delivery, and that at least 10 percent of those deaths could be avoided with adequate access to blood transfusions (Soedarmono 2017). Key socioeconomic drivers of poor maternal health and maternal mortality in Indonesia include poverty, undernutrition, and anemia among pregnant women, hard physical labor during pregnancy, lack of access to emergency obstetric care, and adolescent marriage and pregnancy.

There is significant variation in the MMR across Indonesia, with the most remote and least developed provinces having significantly higher MMR. Inequity in maternal health service quality and access is now well documented, with wealthier and urban women having greater access to and utilization of prenatal care, facility-based delivery, and C-section delivery compared with poor and rural women (Nababan et al. 2017). Despite these inequities, the number of Indonesian women giving birth with skilled birth attendants has increased from 36 percent of births in 1990 to 91 percent in 2015 (MMEIAG 2018). This has been partly due to the expansion of the national village midwife program, which has increased the availability of skilled birth attendants in rural and remote areas. The increase is also indicative of a strong trend among urban and middle-class women to give birth in hospitals, and their willingness to pay for private sector health services (Spagnoletti et al. 2018). Although women increasingly choose to deliver with skilled birth attendants, only 55 percent of births occur in health facilities (MMEIAG 2018). Despite the push to increase the number of births in facilities, the availability of emergency obstetric care in community health centers and hospitals remains very low across Indonesia. Without access to timely surgical intervention and blood transfusions, many women still die unnecessarily due to the low capacity of the health system, regardless of their choice to have a health facility delivery.

Improving the maternal health status of Muslim women in Indonesia requires sustained commitment to addressing both the biomedical and socioeconomic causes of poor maternal health and maternal mortality. This will necessarily involve increasing the number of health facilities that can provide emergency obstetric care and ensuring equitable geographical distribution of those facilities; poverty alleviation programs designed to reduce undernutrition and anemia; providing alternative income sources so that pregnant women do not need to undertake hard physical labor; improving family planning coverage to reduce unwanted pregnancy and unsafe abortion; and increasing access to antenatal and postnatal care.

Family Planning

Indonesia's formal family planning program commenced in the 1970s and has been led by the National Population and Family Planning Board (BKKBN), a government agency. It has been extremely successful in reducing Indonesia's total fertility rate (TFR) from 5.6 live births per woman in 1965 to 2.6 in 2002 (BPS et al. 2013, UN DESA 2013). According to the 2012 IDHS, the TFR has plateaued, remaining at 2.6 children per woman for the last decade. Indonesia's

REPRODUCTION: HEALTH: INDONESIA   357

two largest Islamic organizations, Muhammadiyah and NU, endorsed the national family planning program from its inception, contributing to the widespread acceptance of modern contraception by Muslim women and couples (Hull 2012). Although the use of modern contraception is normative for married Indonesian Muslims, it is rarely used prior to the arrival of a first child, which reflects the widespread belief that the primary purpose of marriage for Muslims is reproduction.

Since the 1990s, the family planning landscape in Indonesia has shifted toward the private sector; the 1991 IDHS reported that more than 75 percent of family planning services were accessed via the public sector, and today more than 70 percent of Indonesian women access family planning services via private providers (BPS et al. 2013). This has resulted from government decentralization; increased access to contraception via the private sector; and the transition from a population control approach to a reproductive rights approach, aligned with the 1994 International Conference on Population and Development Programme of Action (Hull 2012, Williams 2014). The 2012 IDHS reported on the contraceptive methods used by married women and sexually active unmarried women aged 15 to 45 years (BPS et al. 2013). It found that injectables were by far the most popular form of contraception (23.5 percent of surveyed women), followed by the pill (10 percent). Only 3 percent used an intrauterine device (IUD), 2.4 percent used implants, and 2.4 percent of women had been sterilized. Male-controlled methods were the least popular, with 1.3 percent using condoms and only 0.1 percent having had a vasectomy (BPS et al. 2013).

There have been calls for the national family planning program to address the recent plateauing of contraception uptake, the increasingly unmet need for family planning, and the persistently high rate of unintended pregnancy (Hull and Mosley 2009). Additionally, the trends of increased reliance on injectable contraceptives and the withdrawal method, while long-acting reversible contraceptive (LARC) use has been declining, have been noted as problematic in terms of the national fertility control goals (Hull and Mosley 2009, Weaver et al. 2013). The ongoing need for improvements in the quality of family planning services in the public and private spheres has also been noted in recent research with Indonesian Muslim women, with the lack of comprehensive family planning counselling highlighted as being of particular concern (Spagnoletti et al. 2018).

Emergency contraception (EC) is legally available in Indonesia; yet, the 2007 IDHS revealed that EC knowledge is extremely low (BPS and Macro International 2008). Moreover, EC is difficult to access as a prescription is required, and many Indonesian family planning providers have poor EC knowledge (Syahlul and Amir 2005). Increasing women's access to EC in Indonesia is imperative because it is the only contraceptive method that can be used after sex, and also because of the dwindling popularity of LARC. Another critical gap in access to family planning in Indonesia is the continued inability of unmarried Indonesians legally to access contraception. For Indonesian Muslims, pregnancy outside of wedlock is typically understood as socially and religiously unacceptable, despite the tendency toward later marriage and higher rates of premarital sex. Condemnation of premarital pregnancy has grave consequences for women and can lead to forced marriage or unsafe abortion, compounding the risks of unwanted pregnancy for single women (Bennett 2005).

Abortion

Abortion is criminalized in Indonesia under National Health Law 36 of 2009. There are three exceptions: if the pregnant woman's life is threatened; if the fetus has an untreatable genetic condition; or if the pregnancy resulted from rape. In instances where abortion is permissible, women must undergo professional counselling prior to the procedure and, in the case of rape, emergency medical treatment. Unless it is a medical emergency, abortion must be performed before six weeks' gestation by a recognized provider. If the pregnancy did not occur due to rape, spousal (or parental) permission is also required.

A 2005 fatwa issued by the Indonesian Islamic Council deemed abortion to be unlawful for Muslims, including termination of a pregnancy resulting from adultery (*zina*). The fatwa permits abortion in "emergency situations": if the pregnant woman suffers from a severe physical illness; if the pregnancy is life-threatening; if the fetus has an incurable genetic condition; or if the pregnancy is the result of rape as determined by the woman's family, a doctor, and an Islamic cleric. The fatwa rules that abortion due to fetal defects or rape must be performed before 40 days' gestation. As is the case globally, perspectives on abortion in Indonesia exist on a spectrum; there are conservative groups who claim that abortion is prohibited in Islam, while progressive Islamic women's groups (notably Fatayat NU) strongly advocate for women's right to access abortion up to 120 days' gestation through their interpretations of *fiqh* (van Doorn-Harder 2010).

Measuring abortion incidence in Indonesia is challenging, and the two most reliable studies—by Habsjah, and Hakim (2001) and Widyantoro and Lestari (2004)—were undertaken over a decade ago. More than one million Indonesian women are estimated to undergo induced abortion annually, and

REPRODUCTION: HEALTH: INDONESIA

the majority are married, educated women, aged over 20 (Widyantoro and Lestari 2004, Dalvie et al. 2009, Hull and Widyantoro 2010). Further complicating the measurement of abortion is the unknown extent of the provision of first trimester vacuum aspirated abortion—known as menstrual regulation, or *induksi haid*, which became popular in Indonesian cities in the 1970s (Hull and Hull 2001).

There are a range of well-known traditional practices to induce abortion, including vigorous abdominal massage, consumption of herbal tinctures purported to bring on menstrual bleeding (*jamu telat bulan*), and the consumption of foods traditionally avoided during pregnancy. Modern popular methods to induce abortion include the consumption of medications or other substances contraindicated during pregnancy, such as alcohol. Women living outside of urban areas have greatly reduced access to safe abortion and are more likely to attempt unsafe abortion methods. Unmarried Muslim women are also particularly at risk of experiencing unsafe abortion, as the imperative of hiding premarital pregnancy reduces their willingness to be seen accessing biomedical health care (Bennett 2001).

Gender-Based Violence and Reproductive Health

Several forms of gender-based violence are commonly directed toward Muslim women in Indonesia, substantially compromising their reproductive health and rights. These include the high incidence of unwanted sex in marriage, women's inability to negotiate condom use with their husbands, and men's extramarital sexual activity. These forms of gender-based violence have been documented among Muslim women of different ethnicities across Indonesia (Idrus and Bennett 2003, Andajani-Sutjahjo, and Idrus 2011, Nurmila and Bennett 2015, Platt 2017). In a study on women's maternal health and reproductive rights with 500 married Muslim women in Eastern Indonesia, 95 percent agreed that a husband having an affair constituted a form of domestic violence (Bennett, Andajani-Sutjahjo and Idrus 2011). This reflects both the commonality of extramarital sex for men in Indonesia, and women's characterization of this infidelity as a form of violence. The same study found that 60 percent of women had endured unwanted sex with their husband in the prior six months. This high prevalence of unwanted sex in marriage is related to a lack of awareness by both Muslim men and women that women are entitled to exercise sexual consent and refuse sex in marriage. Although many Indonesian women feel unable to refuse sex within marriage, an even higher proportion feel unable to request that their husband use condoms, for fear that it will either invoke suspicion from their spouse or be interpreted as accusing their spouse of infidelity (Jacubowski 2008).

Women's inability to refuse marital sex or insist on condom use, even when they know or fear that their husbands may be having extramarital sex, leaves them highly vulnerable to contracting a range of STIs. Moreover, the stigma associated with STIs and sexual health in Indonesia prevents many women from seeking treatment for STIs (Bennett 2015). Untreated chlamydia and gonorrhea (often asymptomatic for women) can lead to tubal blockage and female infertility. In the case of the human papilloma virus (HPV), women are rendered vulnerable to developing cervical cancer. Most women who contract HIV from their husbands report being unaware of the risk of HIV transmission within marriage. The situation for Indonesian Muslim women in relation to infertility, reproductive cancers, and HIV and AIDS is discussed below but should also be considered in the context of the gender-based violence that compounds women's vulnerability and inhibits their ability to protect themselves from STIs, including HIV.

HIV and AIDS

The total number of people living with HIV/AIDS in Indonesia in 2017 was estimated to be between 630,000 and 740,000; of these, 250,000 were women (UNAIDS 2018). Muslim women in Indonesia have become increasingly vulnerable to and affected by the national HIV and AIDS epidemic over the past decade. The sex ratio of the Indonesian epidemic has shifted, with the proportion of women living with HIV increasing from 31 percent in 2010 to 36 percent in 2016, while the proportion of men living with HIV declined from 68 percent to 63 percent in the same period (Kemenkes 2017, 201). The rate of new HIV infections among women has consistently increased since 2010; so, too, has the rate of infections among adolescents. This means younger women are particularly at risk of infection. The largest group of new infections reported since 2012 is heterosexual women self-described as housewives (Kemenkes 2018).

Indonesia's HIV-positive women are typically Muslim, poor, unemployed or employed in the informal sector, and financially dependent on others (Rahmalia et al. 2015). Additionally, HIV-positive women as a cohort are younger than HIV-positive men, and most are married (Rahmalia et al. 2015). More HIV-positive women report contracting HIV from their husbands, than men report contracting HIV from their wives (Rahmalia et al. 2015). HIV-positive women in Indonesia are also more often widows or divorcees than nonpositive women, which reflects the impact of HIV and AIDS on their lives. High levels of HIV-related stigma and discrimination directed toward women within the health system and community at large are now well documented in Indonesia (Nurachmah, and Rosakawati 2006, Waluyo et al. 2015) and have numerous and detrimental effects on women's health and livelihoods.

Women's vulnerability to HIV infection via their husbands is indicative of a shift in the key mode of HIV infection in Indonesia. Heterosexual sex is now the key mode of HIV infection; consequently, the continuing feminization of Indonesia's epidemic is a real threat based on new infection trends since 2012. The national HIV response in Indonesia has many gaps, as indicated by the 68 percent increase in AIDS-related deaths since 2012 (AIDS Data Hub 2018). Additionally, survival rates for Indonesian women who develop AIDS are lower than for men, indicative of women's poverty relative to that of men. In 2017, only 14 percent of Indonesians diagnosed with HIV were receiving antiretroviral therapy (ART), and only 13 percent of pregnant HIV-positive women had access to the WHO-recommended regime for prevention of mother-to-child transmission (Kemenkes 2017). A key reason for low access to ART includes low health system capacity (particularly at the primary health care level) for meeting the needs of HIV-positive individuals, including lack of adequately trained health personnel and low availability of essential medications. Outside of major metropolitan areas with tertiary referral hospitals, reliable and continuous access to ART is rarely available to those who most need to access health care in the public system. Numerous studies have also confirmed that early experiences of HIV- and AIDS-related stigma and discrimination within the Indonesian health system deters women from accessing HIV-related care, and that many women experience such stigma for the first time at the point of diagnosis (Mahendra et al. 2007, Sukmaningrum 2015, Waluyo et al. 2015).

Historically, the Indonesian response to HIV has been to target high-risk populations, namely, people who inject drugs, sex workers, men who have sex with men (MSM), and the transgender population. The social construction of HIV risk as only related to haram or "deviant" behaviors has led to a narrow and inaccurate understanding of HIV risk. This "othering" of risk has been widespread and has led many heterosexual women to assume they are not at risk. Yet, as noted above, many Muslim women in Indonesia experience a lack of sexual autonomy in marriage. Moreover, a large proportion of MSM in Indonesia are married to women. These conditions combine to heighten women's vulnerability to HIV transmission via their husbands. Thus, reducing Indonesian women's vulnerability to HIV and AIDS requires a dramatically improved health system response, the promotion of gender equity in marriage, and public acknowledgement of sexual behaviors that deviate from the ideals of Islamic sexual morality.

Infertility

Despite widespread acceptance of family planning and a strong trend toward smaller families, Indonesians overwhelmingly desire to have children, and the percentage of never-married women in Indonesia is the lowest in Asia (Jones 2010). The importance of motherhood for Indonesian women, combined with sexist assumptions about women's responsibility for reproduction, result in significant social suffering for infertile and childless women. Indonesian women in infertile marriages typically suffer higher degrees of depression and anxiety related to infertility than their male partners (Dwipayana 2011). Such women also tend to experience greater degrees of social exclusion due to being childless than do men (Bennett 2012). Indonesian statistics on divorce and polygyny also reveal that Muslim women in infertile unions are more vulnerable to both circumstances than women with proven fertility (Rutstein and Shah 2004, 44). Indonesian marriage law explicitly states infertility as a legal ground for divorce, for both men and women. However, the family court system does not typically request medical proof of who the infertile party is within a childless marriage. This lack of evidential requirement for determining the cause of infertility in a marriage frequently disadvantages women because they are often divorced by husbands who are unwilling to investigate or confirm male-factor infertility (Bennett 2012).

Approximately 15 percent of Indonesian couples will experience primary infertility during their reproductive years (Bennett et al. 2012). The WHO estimated the cumulative female infertility rate (combining primary and secondary infertility) in Indonesia to be as high as 22 percent of married women of reproductive age (Rutstein and Shah 2004). These rates are notably higher than those experienced in high-income countries with better access to affordable, comprehensive reproductive and sexual health care. Data on the causes of infertility in Indonesia, extrapolated from patient records, indicate that female factors account for 30 percent of infertility; male factors account for 30 percent of infertility; a combination of male and female factors are responsible for 10 percent of cases; and the causes of the remaining 30 percent of cases are unknown (Bennett et al. 2012).

The WHO recognizes STIs as "the main preventable cause of infertility worldwide, particularly in women" (WHO 2011); this is also the case for Indonesia, where the primary cause of female infertility is tubal blockage due to untreated

STIs (Perfitri 2013). In Indonesia, STI prevalence is high and increasing, while STI testing is very low and is not free of charge. Moreover, condom use is extremely low among the general population, heightening women's vulnerability to STIs. The detection and treatment of STIs is still a stigmatized area of reproductive and sexual health in Indonesia, one that must be addressed to prevent female infertility. Other preventable causes of infertility affecting Indonesian women include unsafe abortion and delivery-related complications.

Assisted reproductive technologies (ART), including in vitro fertilization (IVF) and intracytoplasmic sperm injection (ICSI), are available in Indonesia and are considered a halal option for married heterosexual couples who use their own gametes (sperm and ovum). In 2017, there were 30 government-registered infertility clinics across the country. ART is not government subsidized nor included under private medical insurance policies, so only around 10 percent of the population can afford such treatment. Research on barriers to accessing ART in Indonesia has identified a range of factors in addition to cost, including low confidence in ART success; the geographical location of clinics; lack of a well-established referral system; fear of receiving a diagnosis of sterility; low reproductive health literacy and inadequate patient education; and women's anxiety over vaginal examinations and invasive or painful treatments (Bennett et al. 2012, Bennett et al. 2015).

Islamic law has been highly influential in shaping the regulatory framework for ART in Indonesia. Religious debates surrounding the need for strict regulation of ART have centered on the protection of the rights of children born via ART, as well as respecting Islamic marriage laws, inheritance laws, and sexual morality. To ensure clarity of paternity, gamete donation of any kind is illegal in Indonesia, as is surrogacy. Posthumous access to gametes by a surviving partner is also illegal, as Islamic marriages are considered dissolved when one partner is deceased. Religion is also central to the coping strategies of Indonesian Muslim women living with infertility and childlessness (Bennett 2018).

Reproductive Cancers

Reproductive cancers are the leading cause of cancer-related deaths among Indonesian women, with breast cancer contributing to 21 percent of deaths each year, followed by cervical cancer and ovarian cancer (8 percent) (WHO 2014). The WHO estimates that there are approximately 50,000 new cases of breast cancer, 21,000 new cases of cervical cancer, and 10,000 new cases of ovarian cancer among Indonesian women annually (WHO 2014). However, ascertaining the true prevalence of reproductive cancers is hampered by the stalling of the national cancer registry, with the most recent population-level data captured in 2007 (WHO 2014). Survival rates for women affected by reproductive cancers in Indonesia are significantly lower than for women diagnosed and treated in high-income countries. For instance, the age-standardized death rate from cervical cancer in Indonesia is alarmingly high at 9.2 per 100,000 women, almost five times higher than Australia's rate of 1.99 per 100,000 women.

Low reproductive cancer survival rates for Indonesian women are directly linked to the limited availability of population-wide cancer screening and early treatment services. Despite having a cancer control policy firmly focused on expanding the coverage of breast and cervical cancer screening in Indonesia, these services are not widely available in the primary health care system, and are typically limited to large urban centers (WHO 2014). A number of community-based organizations teach women how to perform breast self-examination, as such checks are not routinely provided by midwives or GPs. Mammograms are available in both the public and private sectors, but again these services are concentrated in urban areas. Survival rates are significantly reduced by women's late diagnosis, and then compounded by the low cancer treatment capacity of the health system. The health system is unable to meet the increasing demand for treatment of reproductive cancers due to shortages in radiotherapy equipment, cryotherapy equipment, appropriate surgical expertise, and oncologists, and the availability and high cost of chemotherapy drugs. The consequence for women is prolonged waiting periods for treatment, during which their cancer is likely to progress further, diminishing their chances of survival. The cost of treatment for breast cancer and cervical cancer is partially covered by the national health insurance scheme. However, insurance coverage is limited to public hospitals with the longest waiting times, and thus those who cannot afford private cancer treatment are likely to wait the longest for treatment.

The HPV vaccine, which prevents transmission of the HPV types that cause cervical cancer, is licensed and available via the private sector in Indonesia. However, vaccination knowledge is low, and typically only women with high levels of formal education and high income can afford the cost of vaccination for their daughters and themselves. HPV vaccination pilot programs targeting young women in junior high school have been successfully undertaken in several large cities, including Manado, Medan, Jakarta, Surabaya, and Yogyakarta (Jaspers et al. 2011, GoI 2016). The Indonesian Coalition for Cervical Cancer Prevention (KICKS) is lobbying the GoI to include the HPV vaccine in the national immunization schedule (KICKS 2017).

Conclusion

Indonesian Muslim women typically exercise a high degree of mobility in the public sphere, routinely participate in paid work in both the formal and informal sectors, have increasingly higher educational attainment, and play important leadership roles in Islamic organizations locally and nationally. Yet, these positive indicators of gender equity for Indonesian Muslim women are not mirrored by their relatively poor reproductive health status and rights. The GoI continues to pay insufficient attention to the provision of CRSHE, safe abortion services, emergency obstetric services, STIs including HIV, female infertility, and reproductive cancers. The centrality of gender-based violence in compounding the reproductive morbidity of Muslim Indonesian women has also been largely ignored at official levels and requires explicit acknowledgement and attention in reproductive health policy and services. Significant inequalities also exist in terms of differential access to reproductive health care. Poorer women, women living in rural and remote areas, and unmarried women in Indonesia continue to have the most constrained access to care and subsequently the poorest reproductive and sexual health outcomes.

Bibliography

AIDS Data Hub (HIV and AIDS Data Hub for Asia Pacific). Indonesia country update, n.d., <www.aidsdatahub.org/Country-Profiles/Indonesia>. 14 October 2018.

Baswedan, Anies R. Political Islam in Indonesia. Present and future trajectory, in *Asian Survey* 44:5 (2004), 669–90.

Bennett, Linda Rae. Single women's experiences of premarital pregnancy and induced abortion in Lombok, Eastern Indonesia, in *Reproductive Health Matters* 9:17 (2001), 37–43.

Bennett, Linda Rae. *Women, Islam and modernity. Single women, sexuality and reproductive health in contemporary Indonesia*, London 2005.

Bennett, Linda Rae. Zina and the enigma of sex education for Indonesian Muslim youth, in *Sex Education* 7:4 (2007), 371–86.

Bennett, Linda Rae. Infertility, womanhood and motherhood in contemporary Indonesia. Understanding gender discrimination in the realm of biomedical fertility care, in *Intersections: Gender and Sexuality in Asia and the Pacific* 28 (2012), <http://intersections.anu.edu.au/issue28/bennett.htm>.

Bennett, Linda Rae. Sexual morality and the silencing of sexual health within Indonesian infertility care, in *Sex and sexualities in contemporary Indonesia. Sexual politics, health, diversity and representations*, ed. Linda Rae Bennett and Sharyn Graham Davies, London 2015, 148–66.

Bennett, Linda Rae. Infertility, adoption, and family formation in Indonesia, in *Medical Anthropology* 37:2 (2018), 101–16.

Bennett, Linda Rae, Sari Andajani-Sutjahjo, and Nurul I. Idrus. Domestic violence in Nusa Tenggara Barat, Indonesia. Married women's definitions and experiences of violence in the home, in *Asia Pacific Journal of Anthropology* 12:2 (2011), 146–63.

Bennett, Linda Rae, Budi Wiweko, Lauren Bell, Nadia Shafira, Mulyoto Pangestu, I.B. Putra Adayana, Aucky Hinting, and Gregory Armstrong. Reproductive knowledge and patient education needs among Indonesian women infertility patients attending three fertility clinics, in *Patient Education and Counseling* 98:3 (2015), 364–69.

Bennett, Linda Rae, Budi Wiweko, Aucky Hinting, I.B. Putra Adayana, and Mulyoto Pangestu. Indonesian infertility patients' health seeking behaviour and patterns of access to biomedical infertility care. An interviewer administered survey conducted in three clinics, in *Reproductive Health* 9:24 (2012), 1–8.

Blackburn, Susan. *Women and the state in modern Indonesia*, Cambridge 2004.

BPS (Statistics Indonesia) and Macro International. *Indonesia demographic and health survey 2007*, Calverton, Md. 2008.

BPS, BKKBN (National Population and Family Planning Board), Kemenkes (Ministry of Health), and ICF International. *Indonesia demographic and health survey 2012*, Jakarta 2013.

Brenner, Suzanne April. *The domestication of desire. Women, wealth, and modernity in Java*, Princeton, N.J. 1998.

Dalvie, S., A. Barua, N. Widyantoro, and I. Silviane. A study of knowledge, attitudes and understanding of legal professionals about safe abortion as a women's right in Indonesia. Study prepared for the Asia Safe Abortion Partnership, 2009, <http://asap-asia.org/pdf/Indonesia_Abortion_Booklet_Update.pdf>.

Davies, Sharyn Graham, and Linda Rae Bennett. Introduction. Mapping sex and sexualities in contemporary Indonesia, in *Sex and sexualities in contemporary Indonesia. Sexual politics, health, diversity and representations*, ed. Linda Rae Bennett and Sharyn Graham Davies, London 2015, 1–25.

Dwipayana, I. Different degrees of depression among husbands and wives in couples with infertility problems. Conference presentation at the 6th Asia Pacific Conference on Reproductive and Sexual Health Rights, Yogyakarta, October 2011.

GoI (Government of Indonesia). Application form for human papillomavirus vaccine (HPV) demonstration programme. Application for vaccine support to Gavi, the Vaccine Alliance, January 2016, <https://www.gavi.org/country/indonesia/documents/>.

Holzner, Brigitte M., and Dédé Oetomo. Youth, sexuality and sex education messages in Indonesia. Issues of desire and control, in *Reproductive Health Matters* 12:23 (2004), 40–49.

Hull, Terence H. Indonesia's demographic mosaic, in *Population dynamics in Muslim countries. Assembling the jigsaw*, ed. Hans Groth and Alfonso Sousa-Poza, Heidelberg 2012, 195–209.

Hull, Terence H., and Valerie J. Hull. Means, motives and menses. Uses of herbal emmenagogues in Indonesia, in *Regulating menstruation. Beliefs, practices, interpretations*, ed. Etienne Van de Walle and Elisha P. Renne, Chicago 2001, 202–19.

Hull, Terence H., and Henry Mosley. Revitalization of family planning in Indonesia. Government of Indonesia and United Nations Population Fund, 2009, <https://www.researchgate.net/publication/265396314_Revitalization_of_Family_Planning_in_Indonesia>.

Hull, Terence H., and Ninuk Widyantoro. Abortion and politics in Indonesia, in *Abortion in Asia. Local dilemmas, global politics*, ed. Andrea Whittaker, New York 2010, 175–98.

Idrus, Nurul I., and Linda Rae Bennett. Presumed consent. Marital violence in Bugis society, in *Violence against women in Asian societies*, ed. Lenore Manderson and Linda Rae Bennett, London 2003, 41–60.

Jacubowski, Nadja. Marriage is not a safe place. Heterosexual marriage and HIV-related vulnerability in Indonesia, in *Culture, Health and Sexuality* 10:1 (2008), 87–97.

Jaspers, L., S. Budiningsih, R. Wolterbeek, F.C. Henderson, and A.A.W. Peters. Parental acceptance of human papillomavirus (HPV) vaccination in Indonesia. A cross-sectional study, in *Vaccine* 29:44 (2011), 7785–93.

Jones, Gavin. Changing marriage patterns in Asia. Working Paper Series No. 131, Asia Research Institute, National University of Singapore 2010.

Kemenkes (Ministry of Health). *Indonesian health profile 2016*, Jakarta 2017.

Kemenkes. Laporan situasi perkembangan AIDS & PIMS di Indonesia (2017) [Report on the situation of the development of AIDS and sexually transmitted illness and infection in Indonesia (2017)]. Direktorat Jenderal Pencegahan dan Pengendalian Penyakit [Director General of Disease Prevention and Control], Jakarta 2018.

KICKS (Indonesian Coalition for Cervical Cancer Prevention). Lindungi putri kita dari kanker serviks dengan Program Imunisasi Nasional HPV segera! [Protect our daughters from cervical cancer with the HPV National Immunization Program right away!]. Change.org online petition by KICKS to President Joko Widodo, the Indonesian Minister of Health and Commission IX, 14 August 2017, <www.change.org/p/presiden-jokowi-lindungi-putri-kita-dari-kanker-serviks-dengan-program-imunisasi-nasional-hpv-segera>. 15 October 2018.

Mahendra, Vaishali S., Laelia Gilborn, Shalini Bharat, Rupa J. Mudoi, Indrani Gupta, Bitra George, Luke Samson, Celine C. Daly, and Julie Pulerwitz. Understanding and measuring AIDS-related stigma in health care settings. A developing country perspective, in *SAHARA-J:Journal of Social Aspects of HIV/AIDS* 4:616 (2007), 616–25.

Manderson, Lenore. Rights and responsibility, power and prestige, in *Kartini centenary. Indonesian women then and now*, ed. Ailsa T. Zainu'ddin, Clayton 1980, 69–92.

MMEIAG (Maternal Mortality Estimation Inter-Agency Group—WHO, UNICEF, UNFPA, World Bank Group, and United Nations Population Division). *Maternal mortality in Indonesia 1990–2015*. 2018.

Nababan, Herfina Y., Md Hasan, Tiara Marthias, Rolina Dhital, Aminur Rahman, and Iqbal Anwar. Trends and inequities in use of maternal health care services in Indonesia, 1986–2012, in *International Journal of Women's Health* 10 (2017), 11–24.

Nurmila, Nina, and Linda Rae Bennett. The sexual politics of polygamy in Indonesian marriages, in *Sex and sexualities in contemporary Indonesia. Sexual politics, health, diversity and representations*, ed. Linda Rae Bennett and Sharyn Graham Davies, London 2015, 69–88.

Perfitri. *Annual IVF Report*, Jakarta 2013.

Platt, Maria. *Marriage, gender and Islam in Indonesia. Women negotiating informal marriage, divorce and desire*, London 2017.

Rahmalia, Annisa, Rudi Wisaksana, Hinta Meijerink, Agnes R. Indrati, Bachti Alisjahbana, Nel Roeleveld, Andre J.A.M. van der Ven, Marie Laga, and Reinout van Crevel. Women with HIV in Indonesia. Are they bridging a concentrated epidemic to the wider community?, in *BMC Research Notes* 8:757 (2015), 1–8.

Robinson, Kathryn. *Gender, Islam and democracy in Indonesia*, London 2009.

Rutstein, Shea O., and Iqbal H. Shah. Infecundity, infertility and childlessness in developing countries. DHS Comparative Report No. 9, prepared for ORC Macro and WHO, Calverton, Md. 2004.

Soedarmono, Y.S.M. The Indonesian approach to reduce maternal mortality, in *ISBT Science Series* 12:1 (2017), 272–80.

Spagnoletti, Belinda, Linda Rae Bennett, Michelle Kermode, and Siswanto Wilopo. "I wanted to enjoy our marriage first... but I got pregnant right away." A qualitative study of family planning understandings and decisions of women in urban Yogyakarta, Indonesia, in *BMC Pregnancy and Childbirth* 18:353 (2018), 1–14.

Sukmaningrum, E. HIV disclosure experiences among women with HIV/AIDS in Jakarta, Indonesia. Unpublished Ph.D. diss., University of Illinois at Chicago, 2015.

Sullivan, Norma. *Masters and managers. A study of gender relations in urban Java*, St. Leonards 1994.

Syahlul, Dyna E., and Lisa H. Amir. Do Indonesian medical practitioners approve the availability of emergency contraception over-the-counter? A survey of general practitioners and obstetricians in Jakarta, in *BMC Women's Health* 5:3 (2005), 1–8.

UNAIDS (Joint United Nations Programme on HIV/AIDS). Indonesia country fact sheet, 2018, <www.unaids.org/en/regionscountries/countries/indonesia>. 6 April 2019.

UN DESA (United Nations Department of Economic and Social Affairs), *World population prospects. The 2012 revision*, New York 2013.

UNESCO (United Nations Educational, Scientific and Cultural Organization). *Emerging evidence, lessons and practice in comprehensive sexuality education. A global review 2015*, Paris 2015.

Utomo, Budi, A. Habsjah, and V. Hakim. Incidence and social-psychological aspects of abortion in Indonesia. A community-based survey in 10 major cities and 6 districts, year 2000. Study report, University of Indonesia, Jakarta 2001.

Utomo, Iwu D., and Peter McDonald. Adolescent reproductive health in Indonesia. Contested values and policy inaction, in *Studies in Family Planning* 40:2 (2009), 133–46.

Utomo, Iwu D., Peter McDonald, Anna Reimondos, Ariane Utomo, and Terry H. Hull. Do primary students understand how pregnancy can occur? A comparison of students in Jakarta, West Java, West Nusa Tenggara and South Sulawesi, Indonesia, in *Sex Education* 14:1 (2014), 95–109.

van Doorn-Harder, P. *Women shaping Islam. Reading the Qu'ran in Indonesia*, Urbana, Ill. 2010.

Waluyo, Agung, Gabriel J. Culbert, Judith Levy, and Kathleen F. Norr. Understanding HIV-related stigma among Indonesian nurses, in *Journal of the Association of Nurses in AIDS Care* 26:1 (2015), 69–80.

Waluyo, Agung, Elly Nurachmah, and Rosakawati. Persepsi pasien dengan HIV/AIDS dan keluarganya tentang HIV/AIDS dan stigma masyarakat terhadap pasien HIV/AIDS [Perceptions of HIV/AIDS patients and their families about HIV/AIDS and community stigma against HIV/AIDS patients], in *Jurnal Keperawatan Indonesia* [Indonesian Journal of Nursing] 10:2 (2006), 5–9.

Weaver, Emily H., Elizabeth Frankenberg, Bruce J. Fried, Duncan Thomas, Stephanie B. Wheeler, and John E. Paul. Effect of village midwife program on contraceptive prevalence and method choice in Indonesia, in *Studies of Family Planning* 44:4 (2013), 389–409.

WHO (World Health Organization). *Sexually transmitted infections*. Fact Sheet No. 110. 2011.

WHO. *Cancer country profiles*, Geneva 2014.

Widyantoro, Ninuk, and Herna Lestari. Laporan penelitian penghentian kehamilan tak diinginkan (KTD) yang aman berbasis konseling: penelitian di 9 kota besar [Research report on the safe, counselling-based termination of unintended pregnancy: findings from 9 major cities], Yayasan Kesehatan Perempuan [Women's Health Foundation], Jakarta 2004.

Williams, Lindy. W(h)ither state interest in intimacy? Singapore through a comparative lens, in *Sojourn: Journal of Social Issues in Southeast Asia* 29:1 (2014), 132–58.

World Bank, *Indonesia Overview*, 25 September 2018, <www.worldbank.org/en/country/indonesia/overview.> 14 October 2018.

Reproduction: Health: Indonesia

Linda Rae Bennett and Emma Barnard

Introduction

While Indonesia is not an Islamic state, it is home to the largest Muslim population in the world. Geographically, Indonesia spans over 5,000 kilometers from east to west and is constituted of over 17,000 islands, 6,000 of which are inhabited. The population has now reached 237 million and Indonesia is the world's fourth most populous nation. Today almost 90 percent of Indonesians identify Islam as their religion. The sex ratio of the Indonesian population is slightly higher for males at birth, but evens out by the age of 15, and women (73.6 years) have a higher life expectancy than men (68.5 years) of approximately five years (BPS 2007). Indonesia consists of 33 administrative provinces, and the central island of Java is the most densely populated being home to 60 percent of the nation's people.

Islam was introduced to the archipelago from the fourteenth and fifteenth centuries, and spread from the west across Sumatra and Java through to the northern and eastern islands. The island of Bali has resisted conversion and its indigenous people remain devout Hindus. The far eastern provinces are also characterized by lower levels of conversion and have higher proportions of Christians. However, both Hindus and Christians remain minority populations. Islam in Indonesia has always been dynamic and diverse and has often been described as syncretic. Studies of the relationships between *adat* (indigenous customs, laws and religion) and Islam have been popular since the 1960s (Geertz 1960). The diverse nature of Islam in Indonesia is a product of a relatively young nation, characterized by extensive ethnic and linguistic differences as well as the flexibility of local people, cultures and belief systems in developing unique Islamic world-views. Academic observers have attempted to characterize Indonesian Muslims by describing them as either devout or practicing Muslims (*santri*) and/or as nominal/non-practicing Muslims (syncretists) (Baswedan 2004). However, such characterizations are not always relevant to the ways that Indonesian Muslims understand themselves. Many who might be characterized as syncretists by outsiders would describe Islam as central to their belief system and daily spiritual practices.

Islam in Indonesia has been undergoing rapid transformations in recent decades. These changes have been enmeshed with the political and social upheaval of a major regime change, as well as the global trends of Islamic

© KONINKLIJKE BRILL NV, LEIDEN, 2012 | DOI:10.1163/1872-5309_EWIC_EWICCOM_001432

revivalism. During Indonesia's first two political regimes, under President Sukarno (1945–1967) and President Suharto (1968–1998, referred to as the New Order regime), the political role of Islam was kept carefully in check. These first two regimes were militaristic and authoritarian. Little democratic space was accorded for political and social debates, or the expression of public religious opinions on political, economic and social issues. This norm shifted radically as a consequence of Indonesia's dramatic economic and political crisis beginning in 1997, a crisis that was so severe it is referred to as *krisis total* (total crisis).

In 1997, President Suharto and his New Order regime came under severe criticism from the Indonesian population. This discontent erupted into extensive riots (known as the May riots) and eventually led to the ousting of Suharto in May 1998. The key criticisms of the New Order regime included extensive corruption, economic mismanagement of the nation, a perceived greed of the elite, and a lack of any true democratic participation of the masses. These failings were interpreted by many Indonesian Muslims as stemming from, and contributing to, a form of moral crisis in Indonesian society; a crisis that needed to be addressed by renewal of religious commitment and practice. Calls for Islamic revivalism came from within Indonesian Islamic political parties, national Islamic organizations, and Muslim leaders at the grassroots level.

Consensus that a renewed commitment to Islam was necessary for the survival and renewal of the nation was widespread, and was clearly articulated by the newly elected president Abdurrahman Wahid, a prominent Islamic cleric and leader of the nation from 1999 to 2001. Specifically, Wahid encouraged Indonesian Muslims to express their religious devotion through purification by following the example of the Prophet Muhammad of fasting every Monday and Thursday. Many Indonesians, particularly women, took up this practice during Wahid's rule and some still view additional fasting as an important part of their routine Islamic practice. Other visible trends associated with Islamic revivalism in the recent Reformasi era (1998 to the present) include a greater number of both Muslim men and women choosing to adopt more formalized versions of Islamic dress, higher attendance at Islamic study groups, a greater adherence to daily prayer and the other basic pillars of Islam, and increasing membership of formal Islamic organizations.

While the growing Islamization of Indonesia in recent times is clearly apparent, it has also been concurrent with a radical decentralization of state power, increasing democracy, and greater freedom in the media. This increasing devoutness of many ordinary Indonesian Muslims has not necessarily meant the encroachment of authoritarian or fundamentalist religious regimes on their lives. Rather, the opposite has been the case, with an expansion of political and religious pluralism and freedom of expression. Islam in Indonesia is constantly being interpreted by local, national and transnational voices in the Reformasi era, all of which represent claims to religious authority. Women's status, roles and freedoms are often at the forefront of contemporary Islamic debates. Some voices are highly progressive, while others represent positions that would ultimately curb the current freedoms and power Indonesian Muslim women exercise. However, the key issue to remember is that these debates are ongoing in any society, and that in Indonesia today Muslim women remain important participants in these debates.

Muslim women in Indonesia are active agents in a wide variety of informal and formal religious institutions from neighborhood prayer groups, to Islamic schools and national Islamic organizations. While their contributions to the domestic sphere in terms of reproduction and child rearing are typically seen as innate gender roles or *kodrat wanita* (the God-given roles of Indonesian Muslim women), this has not resulted in the exclusion of women from public religious discourses or from working in the public domain. Indonesian women are highly active in Islamic welfare organizations, including thousands of grassroots women's Islamic groups, as well as the various women's branches of Indonesia's two largest mass social Islamic organizations Nahdlatul Ulama (NU) and Muhammadiyah. The welfare work that Muslim women undertake within these organizations typically focuses on women's health and wellbeing, and includes the running of reproductive health clinics, family planning services, youth-oriented health services, literacy and return-to-education programs, as well as assisting poor women with income generation through skills building and credit schemes. In short, Indonesian Muslim women engage with Islam in a multitude of ways that demonstrate their religious agency and which are highly beneficial to their communities.

Indonesian *ulama* (male religious scholars and leaders) are understood to exercise primary authority in formal decision making regarding *sharia* (codified Islamic law), the pronouncement of *fatwas* (formal Islamic edicts) and in leading public religious sermons and debates. While Indonesian women do not share the same degree of formalized authority over public interpretations of Islam as Indonesian men, they are not excluded from positions of power within formal Islamic institutions. For instance, Indonesia has the highest proportion of female judges in *sharia* courts of any Islamic majority country. Indonesian *sharia* courts address issues of family law and welfare (state courts deal with criminal and corporate law), so the appointment of women as judges in the Islamic courts is a significant step in the negotiation and protection of Muslim women's rights in the family. Muslim women also play pivotal roles in the economic and political functions of large Islamic organizations, and in developing the religious and political curricula within Islamic universities.

In addition to the positions that Indonesian Muslim women occupy within formal religious institutions, they have also historically enjoyed a high degree of economic, social and spatial freedom within the diverse Muslim cultures of Indonesia. In central Javanese culture, women are typically understood to be the primary managers of household income and affairs, and men's role in domestic decision-making is often marginal (Sullivan 1994). In the Central Javanese city of Solo, Muslim women are also the leading entrepreneurs in family batik businesses, responsible for both production and the sale of their products (Brenner 1998). Even among very poor communities in outer islands such as Lombok, women are often responsible for generating and managing the main cash income of their families through their work as petty traders (Bennett 2005). It has often been argued that the relative economic independence of Indonesian women has supported their high physical mobility and more equal gender relations within Indonesian Muslim families, than has been the case in other Muslim cultures where women's roles have been more closely confined to the home (Manderson 1980).

Muslim women's reproductive roles, and their status as mothers, are highly valued throughout Indonesia's diverse cultures. Motherhood is a universal indicator of adult status in Indonesia and children are expected to both respect and adore their mothers. The popular *hadith* (recorded words of the Prophet), "paradise lies under the feet of your mother," is often quoted to disobedient children. Child bearing and child rearing are widely understood as the natural and positive roles of women.

Despite the importance of reproductive roles to women's identities and ideal notions of the family, the Indonesian state has not been as successful as it might have been in ensuring adequate reproductive health care and reproductive rights for its women citizens. The laudable achievements of the Indonesian government in terms of introducing family planning and combating high maternal mortality are discussed below. However, the larger picture is one that shows serious gaps in the provision of comprehensive reproductive health care, which is reflected in the relatively poor reproductive health status of Indonesian Muslim women. In brief, considerable improvements still need to be made in the following areas: the reduction of maternal mortality; ensuring that comprehensive maternal health services, including emergency obstetric care, are accessible to all women; ensuring greater access to family planning and improving the uptake of male methods; ensuring even access to safe abortion and emergency contraception; and substantially improving access to infertility care and treatment for reproductive cancers.

The poor reproductive health status of Muslim women in Indonesia cannot be adequately understood or addressed without consideration of the wider economic, political and geographical situation of the country. Indonesia is still very much a developing nation; 29 percent of its population live below the official poverty line (on incomes of US$28 per month or less) and 60 percent of the population can still be considered poor (BPS 2010). Health resources are scarce, the allocation of health financing in the national budget is inadequate, and health resources are unevenly distributed as a result of the vast geographical span of the country. In the current era of reform, the nation is in transition from a highly centralized authoritarian state, to a more decentralized and democratic system of governance. This process has made and will continue to make a huge demand on financial and human resources, and will require considerable time before the envisaged benefits of a decentralized health system become apparent. In addition to economic restraints and political change, the sheer size of the population also represents unique challenges for the provision of comprehensive reproductive health care.

The most reliable data sources that record reproductive health indicators in Indonesia are the Indonesian Demographic Health Surveys (IDHS), publications on specific health topics by the Bureau of Statistics (BPS), and data collected by the Ministry of Health (MOH) and Provincial Health Offices (PHO). While these data sources are reliable because of their representative sample sizes and attention to research design and rigor, they rarely include analysis of results that are segregated according to religion or ethnicity. Key indicators typically included in the analyses of government-generated data include socioeconomic status, education level, place of residence, age and marital status. Wherever possible, quantitative data that has been analyzed according to religion has been included in this discussion. However, the majority of national-level statistical information cited here refers more broadly to married Indonesian women of reproductive age, and does not distinguish results on the basis of religion. It can be assumed that approximately 90 percent of the women included in nationally representative samples are Muslim. It should be noted that the health status of Muslim women represented in such studies is very unlikely to be higher than that of non-Muslim women included in the same samples. The reason for this is that the majority of non-Muslim women living in urban areas, such as Balinese Hindus and ethnic Chinese Christians, tend to have considerably higher living standards, levels of education and better access to health services than their poorer Muslim counterparts.

Other important sources of data for this topic are qualitative studies of women's reproductive health, most prevalent in anthropological, sociological and gender studies literature. Qualitative research on women's reproductive health and roles in Indonesia has rarely revealed Islam as a key factor in impeding women's reproductive health. Rather, it has revealed the significance of poverty, faults in state policies and programs, low educational attainment and limited access to adequate services as key determinants of poor reproductive health for Indonesian Muslim women. This entry focuses on five interrelated areas of reproductive health affecting the lives of Muslim women in Indonesia. These are: maternal health, pregnancy and birthing; family planning; abortion and emergency contraception; female infertility; and reproductive cancers. While the issues of sexual health and gender-based violence are also intimately interconnected with reproductive health, they feature elsewhere in EWIC as entries in their own right, and thus are not included in the discussion here.

Maternal Health, Pregnancy and Birthing

Despite the enormous cultural significance of motherhood for Indonesian Muslims, and the respect accorded to women once they become mothers, maternal mortality in Indonesia remains unacceptably high. Indonesia's national Maternal Mortality Ratio (MMR) is currently estimated to be 228 maternal deaths per 100,000 live births. While the national MMR has slowly declined from 350 deaths in 2000 and 270 deaths in 2005, the current MMR among the poorest Indonesians (those in the lowest wealth quintile) is still estimated to be 700 deaths per 100,000 live births (BPS 2010). The MMR also varies significantly between provinces, with the most remote and least developed provinces still experiencing an alarmingly high mortality. Unacceptably high rates of maternal mortality are found in provinces with both Muslim majority populations (such as Nusa Tenggara Barat and West Java) and those with larger Christian populations (such as West Papua and Malaku). The most relevant factors in determining maternal health outcomes in Indonesia are access to maternal health services, geographical location and socioeconomic factors (BPS 2009).

Improvements in maternal health care over the past 15 years have included increases in the number of women receiving prenatal care, those being screened for high-risk pregnancies, and the proportion of women with skilled birth attendants at delivery. Yet only around 20 percent of community health centers (*puskesmas*) can provide basic emergency obstetric and neonatal care, despite the fact that these centers are the most popular location for birth outside of the home (MOH, PHO NTB and PHO NTT 2009). Poor access to emergency care is obviously a critical factor in high maternal mortality rates, as the primary cause of maternal death in Indonesia is still hemorrhage. Malnutrition and anemia among pregnant Indonesian women also remain serious problems that elevate the risks associated with childbirth and increase the likelihood of poor birth outcomes. Tetanus and malaria also contribute significantly to maternal and newborn mortality in Indonesia and tetanus immunization is not systematically provided to all pregnant women. Therefore, maternal health for Indonesian Muslim women needs to be understood in terms of its connection with the overall poor health status of the Indonesian population and the prevalence of health problems associated with poverty and low economic development.

Current government strategies for promoting maternal health are articulated in two major programs, the Safe Motherhood Program and the Making Pregnancy Safer Program. Key priorities in these programs include: reducing the numbers of home births and increasing skilled birth attendance at delivery; increasing the number of community health facilities that provide emergency obstetric and neonatal care; improving the coverage of family planning and reducing contraceptive failure to lessen the number of unwanted pregnancies; reducing the incidence of unsafe abortion; and increasing the coverage of tetanus immunization for pregnant women.

At the grassroots level, villages are also involved in communal preparation for birth which includes the planning and provision of transport to birthing facilities, as well as savings plans to assist with the costs associated with pregnancy and birth. These community-based interventions have seen significant improvements in birth outcomes in some areas, and are based on the concept of *desa siaga* (village cooperation and self-sufficiency in health matters), which is progressive in its insistence that all members of a community share the responsibility for maternal and child health. In provinces such as Nusa Tengara Barat, the notion of community responsibility for health has been directly supported by religious leaders and underpinned by the Islamic conception of responsibility to the *ummah* (the whole Muslim community).

Pregnancy-related rituals are widely practiced among the diverse ethnic groups of Indonesia (Tanner 1974, Niehof 1988). They are commonly conducted between the fifth and final months of gestation. Pregnancy rituals conducted in the second trimester typically indicate that a pregnancy is considered viable and usually involve purification rituals, where water is poured over a pregnant women's stomach. Later pregnancy rituals are understood as important preparation for birth and may also be related to connecting a child with ancestors. Pre-birth rituals are commonly directed at invoking protection for both mother and child from the physical dangers of childbirth, and from the malevolent spirits considered to be a threat when women are at their most vulnerable during childbirth. These rituals often combine Islamic prayer and local lay practices, to seek out protection from Allah, whilst warding off dangerous spirits via indigenous magic incantations. For Indonesian Muslims, the speaking of *shahadah* (declaration of Islamic faith) as soon as possible after a child's birth is obligatory, and is typically performed by the child's father or the closest male relative available. In cases where no suitable male relatives are present, a mother or close female elder may also welcome the child into the religion.

Over the past 30 years, the Indonesian government has aimed to reduce the popularity of home births and to promote delivery at government birthing centers and hospitals, with the support of skilled birth attendants. The logic for this has been that adequate emergency care cannot be provided for mothers and their children in the home environment or by traditional birth attendants. However, as only 20 percent of community-based health clinics can provide access to basic emergency obstetric and neonatal care, many women still do not receive adequate emergency coverage by choosing not to deliver at home. It is not surprising that around 50 percent of Indonesian births still occur at home. Such births are increasingly attended by village midwives (around 70 percent) and in many cases the roles of traditional birth attendants (TBAs) have shifted to assisting government midwives in home births (MOH, PHO NTB and PHO NTT 2009). In remote areas where the coverage of midwives is poor, TBAs still play a major role in attending births and delivering babies. Women who give birth at home are also typically supported by their female kin and birthing usually occurs in an all female space. For many women, a reluctance to deliver their baby in health facilities relates to the fact that few or no female kin may be permitted to support them in this setting, which is experienced as a significant loss. In the home birthing environment fathers are rarely present during delivery, but usually see both mother and child immediately after birth. Only in private, relatively expensive hospital birthing facilities are Indonesian fathers now invited to be present during delivery, although they are not expected to be.

Postpartum seclusion of 40 days (*nifas*) is strongly adhered to among Indonesian Muslims and is understood as both a religious requirement and also a period when mothers and their newborns are sheltered from the outside world while recovering from birth. Women are not typically expected to pray during *nifas*, but may do so after their postpartum bleeding has stopped. In many Indonesian ethnic groups Muslim women will return to their natal homes to give birth in the company of their mothers or close female kin, and so that they can also be supported through *nifas* by other women taking over the domestic burden of the household. Indonesian women who are unable to return to their natal families for childbirth, and who have no female kin present to support them during *nifas*, have been found to have higher rates of postnatal depression and greater difficulty coping with motherhood

(Andajani-Sutjahjo 2003). Thus, women's communal support surrounding childbirth and the postpartum period are extremely important in promoting maternal well being in Indonesia.

During the postpartum period poor Indonesian women, who must rely on the state maternal health system, are entitled to several postpartum visits in their home. However, at present only about 50 percent of the poor are receiving these visits and they tend to be focused on child survival rather than on supporting and educating mothers (MOH, PHO NTB and PHO NTT 2009). Home-based postpartum care is typically delivered by village midwives, traditional birth attendants, community health *kader* (volunteers) and female kin. Hence, the support received by women postpartum is typically offered exclusively by other women.

Over the past decade the average number of months of breastfeeding for Indonesian children between birth and two years has been declining at the national level (BPS 2010). The trend towards the use of formula, as opposed to exclusive breastfeeding, is greatest among women of higher socioeconomic status and for women in urban areas, because of their better access to formula milk and higher exposure to the commercial discourses that advertise formula milk. This trend is regrettable in light of persisting high infant mortality in Indonesia and the protection from infection provided by breast milk and exclusive breastfeeding. This is one area of maternal and child health in which the globalizing discourses of modernity are not assisting Indonesian women and their children to achieve better health outcomes.

Family Planning

Within Islamophobic discourses that draw upon, and create an irrational fear of, Islamic expansionism, Islamic nations are often assumed to have pronatalist population policies. Indonesia displaces this ill-informed assumption by providing an example of a predominantly Islamic nation where modern contraceptives have been promoted to achieve enormous success in the reduction of the total fertility rate (TFR) since the 1970s. Indonesia's TFR declined from 5.6 live births per woman in 1965–70 to 3.4 in 1985–90, and in recognition of this achievement President Suharto received the United Nations Population Award in 1989. Indonesian Islamic leaders and organizations have been involved in ongoing consultations with the National Family Planning Coordination Board (BKKBN) since its creation in 1965 (BKKBN and Department of Religious Affairs 1993). The result of this inclusive strategy has been widespread religious support for family planning, including support from the country's two largest Islamic organizations Nahdlatul Ulama (NU) and Muhammadiyah. At the community level, Indonesian Muslims have embraced the "two-child per family" ideal promoted by BKKBN, and the TFR is now estimated to be 2.6. Moreover, the state system has been heavily reliant on the participation of community leaders and volunteers for the distribution of contraceptives. Discussing family planning and contraceptive use is common among married Indonesian Muslim women and these matters are considered part of everyday life and are not stifled by taboo.

BKKBN focuses on female contraceptive methods and links family planning with safe motherhood and prosperity for small families. While a greater focus on male methods such as vasectomy and condoms is desirable, the emphasis on female methods is consistent with popular gender norms where reproduction and child rearing are considered to be central to women's identities and roles. Giving Indonesian women greater responsibility for family planning has had mixed results. It has undoubtedly increased women's control over their bodies and their reproductive autonomy. It has allowed women to safely space births, to limit family size, and to end their reproductive careers when they wish to. It has also been argued that many Indonesian women have benefited economically from being able to better manage income generation, child bearing and child rearing (Herartri 2005).

BKKBN has also attracted numerous critiques over the years. These critiques have included problems with the quality and continuity of care related to long-term methods such as IUDs and implants (Afandi et al. 1987). Questions have been raised over the target-driven nature of the system in its first three decades, when the focus was on increasing family planning acceptance and not on ensuring the recognition of women's reproductive rights (Smyth 1991). Concern over ensuring a true choice of contraceptive methods has also been voiced. Difficulties in guaranteeing a continuous supply of different methods meant at times that Indonesian women have had no real choice but to accept the single method being offered in a particular area.

More recently during the Reformasi era, BKKBN has reoriented its policies and programs to explicitly recognize the reproductive rights of women (BKKBN 2006). BKKBN currently aims to increase the overall quality of care, ensure a true choice of methods, and provide adequate counseling and information to all family planning clients. Both private and state providers meet the population's contraceptive needs with a strong continued commitment to the provision of free contraceptives to the poor. The private sector currently services a greater proportion of the population than the state system and is attractive to those who can afford it, because it offers a wider choice of methods and better access to short-term methods (Hayes 2010).

TABLE 1   Mix of contraceptive methods used by married women aged 15 to 45 years

Method	% of married women aged 15 to 45 using method
Pill	13.2
IUD	4.9
Injection	31.8
Condom	1.3
Implants	2.8
Female sterilization	3.0
Male sterilization	0.2
Periodic abstinence	1.5
Withdrawal	2.1
Other	0.4
Any method	61.4

SOURCE: IDHS 2007 (BPS 2008)

The contraceptive prevalence rate (CPR) in Indonesia for married women between the ages of 15 and 49 (including both modern and traditional methods) was reported as 61.4 percent in 2007 (BPS 2008). Modern contraceptive methods used in Indonesia include the pill, IUDs, hormone injections (Depo-Provera), condoms, hormone implants (Norplant), female sterilization and male sterilization. The CPR for modern methods is estimated to be 57.4 percent for married women of reproductive age. The popularity of different methods varies, with hormone injections being by far the most popular method among married women. Table 1 details the prevalence of different types of contraceptives used by married women recorded in the 2007 IDHS. The continued unpopularity of condoms as a contraceptive choice is a major concern for women in light of increasing HIV occurrence in the country and the fact that heterosexual contact is the main mode of HIV transmission in Indonesia.

Despite the strong commitment to making contraception available to Indonesians there is still an unmet demand for contraception among married women of childbearing age, which was estimated at the national level to be 9.1 percent in the 2007 IDHS. Indonesian women's access to modern contraceptives is also significantly influenced by economic and geographical factors. While the national CPR for modern methods among currently married women is 56.7 percent, it is only 43.4 percent for those women classified as extremely poor and 53.2 percent for those classified as moderately poor (Hayes 2010). Moreover, the CPR for married women living in more remote and less developed provinces can vary between 25 and 30 percent. The far eastern provinces of Indonesia, including Nusa Tengara Timur and Papua, have the poorest availability and uptake of modern contraceptives and also have Christian majority populations. Thus, access to adequate contraception for married Indonesian women is still limited by various factors including poverty, remote residence and also marital status.

The unmet need for contraception among unmarried people has not been measured, as single women do not have the legal right to access state sponsored family planning services. In this respect, the reproductive rights of unmarried Muslim women and men are directly affected by the perceived conflict between promoting the right to reproductive health for all citizens, and the moral dilemma of premarital sex which is understood as *haram* (prohibited for Muslims) and a form of *zina* (fornication or illicit sex). However, fears that access to contraception and reproductive/sex education for unmarried Indonesian Muslims will lead to greater sexual promiscuity are unsupported by the findings of extensive research into the effects of sex education and contraceptive availability for youth in developing country settings (Bennett 2007). On the contrary, there is now widespread evidence that reproductive sex education and access to comprehensive reproductive health care for Muslim youth can have numerous positive benefits including: later sexual initiation; greater use of condoms for protection against sexually transmissible infections (STIs) and HIV; and fewer unwanted pregnancies and unsafe abortions. While the introduction of compulsory comprehensive reproductive/sex education in Indonesian state schools is still to be achieved, reproductive biology is taught as part of the recommended science curriculum for junior high school students. In the Reformasi era, BKKBN has also increased its efforts towards raising the capacity of health educators to deliver quality reproductive sex education to youth in a range of contexts.

Despite continued attention to the provision of family planning in Indonesia, contraceptive failure remains a serious issue, which is reflected in high rates of unintended pregnancies and abortion. Estimates of contraceptive discontinuation and failure vary between 25 and 40 percent for different modern methods across Indonesia (BPS 2008). Contraceptive discontinuation and failure stem from a range of problems related both to the supply and use of contraceptives. Factors that directly impact on women's contraceptive cover include discontinuation as a result of side effects, changing between methods, and improper use of contraception due to poor knowledge. The current focus by BKKBN on better education and counseling should result in improvements in women's satisfaction with their family planning choices and reduce contraceptive failure.

Recent research indicates that the majority of Indonesian women (95 percent) typically decide on when to use contraception and what methods to use either individually or in consultation with their husbands (MOH PHO NTB and PHO NTT 2009). A small percentage of women (4 percent) have also indicated that midwives or general practitioners have been the key decision makers regarding what methods they use. However, there have been localized reports of Muslim women being denied their right to practice family planning when their husbands are absent. This has occurred in very poor and particularly devout communities, in which rural men often out-migrate to Malaysia to gain employment. This restraint of women's reproductive autonomy has involved local Islamic leaders instructing primary health care workers and volunteers not to offer free contraception to women whose husbands are abroad (Bennett 2005). The consequences are dire for women as they often experience yearly pregnancy when their husbands visit for brief annual holidays. When their husbands return to their migrant jobs women are left as the sole heads of growing families, with very little financial and social support.

In sum, Indonesia is characterized by widespread religious and social acceptance of modern family planning methods. Access to modern contraceptives has benefited Muslim women in Indonesia in a multitude of ways. However, significant discrepancies in access to the benefits of modern contraception still remain. Poverty, geographical location, and Islamic sexual morality (in relation to sex outside of marriage) still constrain the ability of different groups of Indonesian women to access adequate family planning services.

Abortion and Emergency Contraception

Technically, medicalized abortion in Indonesia is only legal in circumstances where the continuation of a pregnancy will put the woman's life at risk. Abortion on the grounds of psychological and social reasons is not yet legalized, despite the fact that safe medical abortion is routinely provided to married women who are understood to have unintended pregnancies as a result of contraceptive failure. Abortions provided in the first trimester are typically referred to as "menstrual regulation" and are tacitly accepted by the government as part of the state's responsibility to meet the family planning needs of its citizens and to limit population growth. Legally, induced abortion should only be provided by qualified obstetrician/gynecologists. In reality a wide range of providers perform abortions including reproductive specialists, general practitioners, government-trained midwives, and traditional birth attendants.

An accurate estimate of Indonesia's abortion rate is difficult to provide because of the limited availability of official statistics and the under-reporting of abortion. According to the 2007 IDHS, the abortion rate was reported to be only 12 percent of pregnancies for women between the ages of 15 and 45. However, the largest and most comprehensive study of abortion in Indonesia to date, which surveyed 1,446 women who had undergone abortions in nine Indonesian cities, reported the abortion rate to be 43 abortions per 100 pregnancies (Widyantoro and Lestari 2004, 5). Regardless of the difficulties in establishing an accurate abortion rate, it is evident that abortion is common in Indonesia and that it is also associated with significant reproductive morbidity. The World Health Organization estimates that there are 29 unsafe abortions per 100 live births in Indonesia (WHO 2007). Safe abortion providers are concentrated in urban areas, consequently regional, remote and very poor women all experience limited access to safe abortion (Widyantoro and Lestari 2004).

Unmarried women are particularly vulnerable to unsafe abortion. They are less likely to access safe medical abortion because of the shame associated with premarital pregnancy for Indonesian Muslims. Doctors who provide safe abortion are also more reluctant to do so for unmarried women whom they perceive as being pregnant as a result of immoral behavior (Bennett 2001). Unmarried women are also at greater risk of unsafe abortion since they have poorer access to the financial resources required for medicalized abortion. As unmarried Indonesians are not legally entitled to menstrual regulation offered by state family planning services, single women only have the options of accessing more costly services in the private sector, or attempting unsafe abortion. Between 12 and 15 percent of safe abortions recorded annually in Indonesia are conducted by unmarried women (Widyantoro and Lestari 2004). It is also estimated that up to 50 percent of all unsafe abortions attempted annually in Indonesian are undergone by unmarried women.

A range of traditional and popular practices for abortion persist in Indonesia. The most common traditional practices include: vigorous massage typically performed by TBAs; drinking herbal tinctures designed for monthly menstrual regulation (*jamu telat bulan*—herbs for late menstruation); the insertion of sharp objects per vagina; and the consumption of fruits and other acidic foods that are traditionally avoided during pregnancy. Popular abortion methods, that do not share the same cultural roots as traditional methods, include the consumption of medicines contraindicated during pregnancy and the consumption of alcohol and other substances thought to be harmful to a fetus.

The long history of abortion as a common practice among Indonesian women is reflected in the tolerance of, and support for, early safe abortion within some of Indonesia's most prominent religious organizations. For instance Fatayat NU, the young women's branch of Nahdlatul Ulama, has explicitly promoted the acceptance of abortion in the first 120 days of pregnancy. Fatayat NU bases this position on the following *hadith* (recorded words of the Prophet Muhammad):

> Truly the creation of human kind is assembled in a mother's womb for 40 days. After 40 days a clot of blood is formed, and after the third 40 days it is completed and turns into a clot of flesh then Allah assigns the angel to breathe the soul in and inscribes its livelihood, time of death, deeds, and good or bad destiny (educational poster by Fatayat NU and Ford Foundation 2002).

While progressive Islamic groups and women's NGOs are strong advocates for women's reproductive rights, including their right to safe abortion in Indonesia, there are also conservative "pro-life" groups who claim that abortion amounts to the homicide of Muslim children and is thus prohibited within the Qur'ān. Such groups make highly publicized attacks on "abortion doctors" for what they perceive to be the crime of murder. While anti-abortion elements do exist within Indonesian society, the prosecution of doctors who perform abortions is extremely rare, and campaigns to widen the circumstances under which abortion can be considered legal are ongoing and nationwide.

Medical (non-surgical) abortion, also commonly known as emergency contraception, offers a safe alternative to surgical abortion for women in the early weeks of pregnancy. Mifepristone (RU486) can be legally used in Indonesia when prescribed by a registered clinician. Despite its availability in Indonesia for several decades, it is not popular or well understood among Indonesian women. There is also very little support among Indonesian doctors for making emergency contraception more easily available by legalizing its supply as an over-the-counter drug (Syahlul and Amir 2005). The limited support for extending the availability of emergency contraception relates partly to confusion about how the drug actually works and whether it technically constitutes a form of abortion. It is not widely understood that emergency contraception is designed to interfere with ovulation and to prevent implantation, rather than to expel an established fetus. Improved education about, and awareness of, emergency contraception in Indonesia has the potential to increase access to this safe method of avoiding pregnancy and implantation, and subsequently could reduce the alarming incidence and impact of unsafe abortion.

Female Infertility

Estimates of infertility rates for Indonesia vary, with the most conservative rates being between 10 and 15 percent of the population of reproductive age (Wiweko 2009). These rates are extrapolated from the number of patients seeking biomedical fertility care and are likely to be underestimates, as many Indonesians, particularly the poor, do not seek biomedical treatment for infertility. The WHO has estimated the female infertility rate (combining primary and secondary infertility) to be 22.3 percent of married women between the ages of 15 and 45 (Rutstein and Shah 2004). The majority of data sources recording infertility in Indonesia tend to focus on women, and measure infertility within the wider context of maternal health indicators. However, the evidence to date suggests that female factors account for 30 percent of infertility, male factors account for 30 percent of infertility; a combination of male and female factors are responsible for 10 percent of cases; and the causes of the remaining 30 percent of cases are unknown (Hinting 2011). Despite the fact that the prevalence of female and male infertility is thought to be parallel, Indonesian women seek out both biomedical treatment and alternative therapies for infertility at much higher rates than men. This reflects the widespread assumption that reproduction is primarily a female responsibility in Indonesian society, and the popular misperception that female factors are typically the cause of a couple's infertility (Bennett 2012).

The cultural significance of infertility and childlessness for Muslim women in Indonesia cannot be overstated. Despite widespread acceptance of family planning and a strong trend towards smaller families, Indonesians overwhelmingly desire to have children. The numbers of never married women in Indonesia are lowest in the Asian region and this is understood partly as a function of women's aspirations to become mothers, as motherhood outside of wedlock is not religiously or socially sanctioned (Jones 2010). The importance of children and motherhood for Indonesian women, combined with sexist assumptions about women's responsibility for reproduction, result in significant social suffering for infertile and childless women. Recent research into women's experiences of infertility in Indonesia has revealed that women in infertile marriages typically suffer higher degrees of depression and anxiety related to infertility than their male partners (Dwipayana 2011). Infertile Muslim women in Indonesia also tend to experience much greater degrees of social exclusion and isolation as a result of being childless than do men (Bennett 2012). Moreover, statistics on divorce and polygyny rates in Indonesia reveal that women in infertile unions are more vulnerable to both occurrences than women with proven fertility. According to the 2000 IDHS, 3.0 percent of women aged between 15 and 45 who had living children reported being divorced at the time of the survey, while 11.2 percent of infertile women aged between 15 and 45 reported being divorced at the time of the survey (Rustein and Shah 2004, 44).

As yet, no systematic research into the causes of female infertility has been conducted at a population level in Indonesia. However, key causes of female infertility in less developed countries across the globe are becoming increasingly understood. The WHO now recognizes STIs (sexually transmitted infections) as: "the main preventable cause of infertility worldwide, particularly in women" (WHO 2011). In Indonesia, STI prevalence is high and increasing, and STI testing is very low and is not free of charge. Moreover, condom use is extremely low among the general population, heightening women's vulnerability to STIs. The detection and treatment of STIs is still a stigmatized area of reproductive health in Indonesia that requires much attention in order to reduce the preventable female infertility that results from untreated STIs. Other preventable causes of infertility affecting Indonesian women are the reproductive morbidity resulting from unsafe abortion and delivery-related complications. Each of these preventable causes of female infertility needs to be urgently addressed if the right of Indonesian women to reproductive health is to be adequately recognized.

Assisted reproductive technologies such as in vitro fertilization (IVF) and intracytoplasmic sperm injection (ICSI) were pioneered in Indonesia in the late 1980s and have become increasingly available over the past three decades. Indonesia currently has 16 infertility clinics that are all government regulated, and have state of the art technology. The clinics offer a wide range of diagnostic procedures, as well as IVF and ICSI to married Indonesian couples. The restriction of assisted reproductive technologies to married couples is based on Islamic jurisprudence that does not sanction sexual relations or the birth of children outside of marital unions. Islamic law has been a key source in developing the regulatory framework for the application of assisted reproductive technologies (ART) in Indonesia. Religious debates surrounding the need for strict regulation of ART have centered on the protection of the rights of children born via ART, as well as respecting Islamic marriage laws, inheritance laws and sexual morality. In order to ensure clarity of paternity, gamete donation of any kind is illegal in Indonesia, as is surrogacy. Post-posthumous access to gametes by a surviving partner is also illegal, as Islamic marriages are considered dissolved when one partner is deceased. Despite the role of Islam in the formation of clear and strict guidelines governing ART in Indonesia, there is widespread acceptance of adoption as a solution to infertility among Indonesian couples. This positive attitude towards adoption as a socially acceptable option for childless Indonesian Muslim couples, particularly when it is an intra-family adoption, is not as prevalent throughout the rest of the Muslim world. For instance, Inhorn (1994, 5) has documented how adoption is viewed as an unattractive option by infertile Egyptian couples because of the cultural and religious emphasis on the importance of biological paternity and inheritance rights.

Despite the availability of ART in Indonesia, utilization of these technologies remains very low relative to the size of the population. Singapore, for instance, with an estimated population of 5 million residents recorded 2,500 IVF cycles in 2010, while Indonesia with an estimated population of 237 million performed just 2,000 cycles in the same year (Wiweko and Bennett 2011). Recent research into the barriers that impede the access of Indonesian women to ART has identified numerous contributing factors. The financial structure of the existing infertility care system is a key barrier. It can be described as a high-cost, user-pays system, as infertility care is not government subsidized or included under medical insurance policies in Indonesia. Other significant barriers identified by infertile Muslim Indonesian women include: fear of receiving a sterile diagnosis; fear of vaginal examinations; fear of treatment failure as the success of ART is never guaranteed; fear of being made to feel ignorant or ashamed about infertility; concern over visiting a gynaecologist in light of negative reports from other patients; and strong religious faith that a child will come when Allah deems it to be the right time (Bennett 2010). Religion is also central to the coping strategies of Indonesian Muslim women facing infertility. Many believe that prayer and devout adherence to their religion will assist them in pleasing Allah and becoming worthy of being parents in Allah's eyes.

Reproductive Cancers

The 2005 IDHS found cancer of all types to be the fifth most common cause of mortality in adults for both sexes. It is also well established that the incidence of reproductive cancers is typically higher among women in developing countries than it is among women living in more wealthy settings, and Indonesia is no exception to this pattern (Jemal et al. 2011). The various types of cancers that manifest in women's reproductive system and organs include cervical cancer, ovarian cancer, uterine or endometrial cancer, vulvar cancer, vaginal cancer and also breast cancer. As yet there is no population-based cancer registry in Indonesia, which means that current data are derived from hospital records and therefore include only those people who have received cancer treatment. Despite the limitations of available data sources, patterns of prevalence for reproductive cancers are clear. The top four reproductive cancers affecting Indonesian women are: cervical cancer, accounting for 19.18 percent of all cancer cases recorded; breast cancer, 12.10 percent; ovarian cancer, 5.31 percent; and uterine cancer, 3.09 percent (Tjindarbumi and Mangunkusumo 2002). The significance of reproductive cancers as a major cause of both morbidity and mortality for women in Indonesia is reflected in the gendered proportions of cancer patients, where 65.5 percent of registered cancer patients are women and only 34.5 percent are men.

In response to the increasingly visible health burden and mortality resulting from cancer, and reproductive cancers in particular, the Indonesian government established the National Directorate for Cancer Control in 1995. Programs launched by this national body have specifically targeted women and reproductive cancers. In 2008, a voluntary national cervical and breast-screening program was launched. While there is now a growing consciousness among women that cancer screening is available, rates of uptake are lower than hoped. This may reflect a number of factors including: the fact that screening is not free; low awareness of the importance of early detection for successful treatment; the reluctance of women to undergo cervical screening because of the associated embarrassment; and the fact that older women often perceive themselves as being at low risk because their reproductive role has generally ended. Improvements in screening uptake for cervical cancer are critical for Indonesian women, as higher cancer-related morbidity in developing countries (compared to wealthier countries) is typically related to late diagnosis and treatment. In 1997, compulsory vaccination for the human papillomavirus (HPV) (a major cause of cervical cancer) was also integrated into existing child immunization programs, and the benefits of this initiative in terms of prevention will be reaped by younger generations of Indonesian women.

Two other government initiatives introduced to combat reproductive cancers include the ongoing expansion of technical capacity to respond to reproductive cancers in state-funded hospitals and a pilot project to establish a national cancer registry. While investment in the technical capacity of health services is critical, the population coverage of those services remains uneven and highly problematic. Those women who may suspect reproductive cancers are still required to travel to tertiary hospitals in large cities for diagnosis and treatment. Consequently, rural, remote and poor women, as well as the elderly, are at a higher risk of dying from undiagnosed and untreated reproductive cancers as a result of the additional expense and difficulties associated with substantial travel. Among those women who develop terminal cancer, many make the choice to die at home without access to home-based palliative care. In rural and remote areas there is even more limited access to drugs (such as

REPRODUCTION: HEALTH: INDONESIA 389

morphine) that are typically used in palliative care. For many women the desire to die in the care of their families and to prevent delaying their burial—as required for Muslims—results in much greater suffering than should be the case. Hence, the Indonesian response needs to focus not only on prevention and treatment of cancers, but also on providing humane palliative care for those women who lose their battle with reproductive cancers.

Conclusion

The poor reproductive health status of Muslim women in Indonesia reflects the country's status as a developing nation and the broader economic, political and geographical struggles it faces. Maternal health outcomes in Indonesia are shaped by access to maternal health services, geographical location and socioeconomic factors. Although maternal health is promoted by government policies and programs, and the MMR has declined in recent years, it remains unacceptably high. Recent improvements in prenatal care have been aimed at better detection of high risk pregnancies among Indonesian women. However, the major cause of MMR, postpartum hemorrhage, cannot be adequately tackled until the availability of emergency obstetric care is greatly expanded. Access to modern contraceptives has been pivotal to Indonesia's success in reducing the TFR since the 1970s. Although there is widespread religious and social acceptance of modern family planning methods, many women still struggle to access adequate family planning services. The gap in unmet need for modern contraceptives is greatest by far for unmarried women, and then for poor and remote women.

Early, safe abortion is available to married women for medicalized reasons and is tacitly supported as part of the state's commitment to family planning and population control. Unmarried women, women living in regional and remote areas and very poor women experience limited access to safe abortion, which contributes greatly to reproductive morbidity. Emergency contraception is available in Indonesia when prescribed by a registered clinician, but remains underutilized as an affordable safe alternative to unwanted pregnancy, primarily because of poor understanding of the method and its benefits. Infertility and childlessness for Muslim women in Indonesia is of enormous social, cultural and religious significance. Women are greater consumers of biomedical and alternative infertility treatment than men in Indonesia and although ART are available, the uptake of these technologies is still low. Reproductive cancers are a leading cause of morbidity and mortality for women, who constitute two-thirds of Indonesia's registered cancer patients. Despite the significant morbidity and mortality resulting from reproductive cancers, a nationwide population-based cancer registry is still to be established and treatment resources are limited. The last two decades have seen a larger investment in expanding government cancer treatment centers, but service coverage still remains uneven and inadequate for the size of the population.

While the most notable differences in access to reproductive health services and reproductive health outcomes for Indonesian Muslim women are determined by economic, political and geographical factors, the Islamic faith of Indonesian women plays important roles in determining how Muslim women negotiate and experience their reproductive health. For instance, explicit religious acceptance of safe abortion in the first three months of gestation underpins many Muslim women's ability to accept their decisions to terminate early pregnancies. Muslim cultural rituals during pregnancy are central to women's emotional and spiritual preparations for birth, and in the initiation of their newborns to the faith. Gendered Islamic understandings of female and male spaces also influence women's experiences when giving birth, and at times impact on women's decisions not to give birth in spaces where they cannot be supported by female kin. The Islamic custom of *nifas* is widely adhered to during the postpartum period by Indonesian Muslims, and is organized in a manner that provides much needed physical and emotional support for women who have recently given birth. Muslim women's choices in relation to accessing palliative cancer care is also shaped by strong attachments to their Muslim communities and their desire to leave the world in an Islamically prescribed manner. Islam is embedded in Indonesian Muslim women's reproductive lives and health in a myriad of ways simply because their faith is an inextricable part of their identities and the ways in which they live their everyday lives.

Bibliography

Affandi, B., S. S. I Santoso, Djajadilaga, W. Hadisaputra, F. A. Moeloek, J. Prihartono, F. Lubis and R. S. Samil. Five-year experience with Norplant, in *Contraception* 36:4 (1987), 417–28.

Andajani-Sutjahjo, S. Motherhood and women's emotional well being in Indonesia, Ph.D. thesis, University of Melbourne 2003.

Badan Pusat Statistik (BPS) [Statistics Indonesia]. *Indonesia demographic and health survey 2005*, Jakarta 2005.

Badan Pusat Statistik (BPS) [Statistics Indonesia]. Indonesia 2007. Results from the Demographic and Health Survey, in *Studies in Family Planning* 40:4 (2009), 335–40.

Badan Pusat Statistik (BPS) [Statistics Indonesia]. Health Indicators 1995–2010, 2010, <http://dds.bps.go.id/eng/tab_sub/view.php?tabel=1&daftar=1&id_subyek=30&no tab=33>, accessed 12 April 2012.

Badan Pusat Statistik (BPS) [Statistics Indonesia] and Macro International. *Indonesia demographic and health survey 2007*, Calverton, Md. 2008.

Baswedan, A. Political Islam in Indonesia. Present and future trajectory, in *Asian Survey* 44:5 (2004), 669–90.

Bennett, L. R. Single women's experiences of premarital pregnancy and induced abortion in Lombok, Eastern Indonesia, in *Reproductive Health Matters* 9:17 (2001), 37–43.

Bennett, L. R. *Women, Islam and modernity. Single women, sexuality and reproductive health in contemporary Indonesia*, Abingdon, U.K. 2005.

Bennett, L. R. *Zina* and the enigma of sex education for Indonesian Muslim youth, in *Sex Education* 4:17 (2007), 371–86.

Bennett, L. R. *Sudah menikah tetapi bukan keluarga.* Infertility and social suffering in Indonesia, paper presented at the 8th Annual Conference of the Indonesian Association of Obstetrics and Gynaecology (*PIT POGI 18*), Jakarta, 7–9 July 2010.

Bennett, L. R. Infertility, womanhood and motherhood in contemporary Indonesia. Understanding gender discrimination in the realm of biomedical fertility care, in *Intersections: Gender and Sexuality in Asia and the Pacific*, 28 (2012), <http://inter sections.anu.edu.au/issue28/bennett.htm>, accessed 12 April 2012.

BKKBN [National Population and Family Planning Board]. *Indonesian family planning reproductive health program. Shifting from demographic targets to reproductive rights*, Jakarta 2006.

BKKBN [National Population and Family Planning Board] and Department of Religious Affairs, *The Muslim ummah and family planning movement in Indonesia*, Jakarta 1993.

Brenner, S. A. *The domestication of desire. Women, wealth and modernity in Java*, Princeton, N.J. 1998.

Dwipayana, I. M. Different degrees of depression among husbands and wives in couples with infertility problems, paper presented at Claiming Sexual and Reproductive Rights in Asian and Pacific Societies—the 6th Asia Pacific Conference on Reproductive and Sexual Health Rights, Yogyakarta, 19–22 October 2011.

Fatayat NU and Ford Foundation. Educational poster on reproductive rights, Jakarta 2002.

Geertz, C. *The religion of Java*, Chicago 1960.

Hayes, A. The status of family planning and reproductive health in Indonesia, paper presented at UNFPA–ICOMP Regional Consultation. Family Planning in Asia and the Pacific. Addressing the Challenges, Bangkok, 8–10 December 2010.

Herartri, R. Family planning decision-making at grass-roots level. Case studies in West Java, Indonesia, Ph.D. thesis, Victoria University of Wellington 2005.

Hinting, A. and Bennett, L. R. Promoting male participation in Indonesian fertility treatment, paper presented at the 14th World Congress on Human Reproduction, Melbourne, 30 November–3 December 2011.

Inhorn, M. *Quest for conception. Gender, infertility and Egyptian medical traditions*, Philadelphia 1994.

Jemal, A., F. Bray, M. M. Center, J. Ferlay, E. Ward and D. Forman, Global cancer statistics, in *CA: A Cancer Journal for Clinicians* 61:2 (2011), 69–90.

Jones, G. Changing marriage patterns in Asia, ARI Working Paper No. 131, Asia Research Institute, National University of Singapore, Singapore 2010, <http://www.ari.nus.edu.sg/docs/wps/wps10_131.pdf>, accessed 12 April 2012.

Manderson, L. Rights and responsibility, power and prestige. Women's roles in contemporary Indonesia, in *Kartini centenary. Indonesian women then and now*, ed. A. T. Zainu'ddin, Melbourne 1980, 69–92.

Ministry of Health (MOH), Provincial Department of Health *Nusa Tengarra Barat* (PHO NTB) and Provincial Department of Health *Nusa Tengara Timur* (PHO NTT), *Measuring the fulfillment of human rights in maternal and neonatal health. Report on provincial and district laws, regulations, policies and standards of care*, Mataram 2009.

Niehof, A. Traditional medication at pregnancy and childbirth in Madura, Indonesia, in *The context of medicines in developing countries. Studies in pharmaceutical anthropology*, ed. S. Van Der Geest and S. Reynolds Whyte, Amsterdam 1988, repr. 1991, 235–52.

Rutstein, S. O. and I. H. Shah. *Infecundity, infertility and childlessness in developing countries*, DHS Comparative Report No. 9, ORC Macro and the World Health Organisation, Calverton, Md. 2004.

Smyth, I. The Indonesian family planning programme. A success story for women?, in *Development and Change* 22:38 (1991), 13–15.

Sullivan, N. *Masters and managers. A study of gender relations in urban Java*, Sydney 1994.

Syahlul, D. and L. Amir. Do Indonesian medical practitioners approve the availability of emergency contraception over-the-counter? A survey of general practitioners and obstetricians in Jakarta, in *BMC Women's Health* 5:3 (2005), 1–8.

Tanner, N. Matrifocality in Indonesia and Africa and among Black Americans, in *Woman, Culture and Society*, ed. Nancy Tanner, Michelle Zimbalist Rosaldo and Louise Lamphere, Stanford, Calif. 1974, 129–56.

Tjindarbumi, D. and R. Mangunkusumo. Cancer in Indonesia, present and future, in *Japanese Journal of Clinical Oncology* 32: 1 (2002), 17–21.

World Health Organisation (WHO). *Unsafe abortion. Global and regional estimates of incidence of unsafe abortion and associated mortality in 2003*, Geneva, 2007[5].

World Health Organisation (WHO). *Provincial reproductive health and MPS profile of Indonesia 2001–2006*, Jakarta 2008.

World Health Organisation (WHO). Sexually transmitted infections. Fact sheet N°110, August 2011, <http://www.who.int/mediacentre/factsheets/fs110/en/>, accessed 12 April 2012.

Widyantoro, N. and H. Lestari. *Laporan penelitian: penghentian kehamilan tak diinginkan yang aman berbasis konseling. Penelitian di 9 kota besar* [Research report. Understanding unwanted pregnancy and safe alternatives through counseling. Research in 9 large cities], Women's Health Foundation, Jakarta 2004.

Wiweko, B. Industry profile paper, resented at the Annual Meeting of the Indonesian Association for In Vitro Fertilization (PERFITRI), Jakarta, 6 July 2009.

Wiweko, B. and Bennett L. R. Fertility patients' patterns of treatment seeking. Understanding delays in presentation and barriers to access, paper presented at the 14th World Congress on Human Reproduction, Melbourne, 30 November– 3 December 2011.

Sexual Harassment

∵

Sexual Harassment: Bangladesh

Hana Shams Ahmed

Introduction

Despite the fact that sexual harassment is now legally recognized as a crime in Bangladesh, there is no legal redress in the vast majority of cases. A combination of familial, social, cultural and religious moral codes renders sexual harassment and most other forms of violence against women a source of shame for the victim instead of the perpetrator. These mores inform the attitudes and actions of law enforcement agencies, the courts and the state, which discourage women from registering complaints of sexual harassment out of fear of being stigmatized instead of being supported.

As in all societies, sexual harassment in Bangladesh is not limited to age, gender, class or social background. The form of sexual harassment considered in this entry, however, is the harassment of women and girls. Women and girls face sexual harassment within the home, often carried out by close relatives, as well as on the streets and in public places. The high rate of sexual harassment of women on the streets, in particular, gave rise to the popular term "Eve teasing" (more on this term later), the light-hearted tone of which makes instances of aggression or abuse against women seem like harmless two-way exchanges or mutual flirting. In recent years, cases of sexual harassment have been documented in schools, universities and other educational institutions. Over the last ten years, a number of charges of sexual harassment have been brought against teachers at universities in different parts of Bangladesh. But, in most of these cases, authorities proceeded to take action only after mass protests and other forms of organizing. And in some instances, cases were not prosecuted even when there was overwhelming evidence against a perpetrator. A combination of gendered legal practices, political pressure, and patriarchy together with a culture of shame and victim-blaming form a disagreeable environment for the application of legal redress and encourage a social climate in which sexual harassment continues to occur.

While there is growing awareness about sexual harassment in both the media and among the general public, sexual harassment continues to be a major problem in Bangladesh. The country is a rapidly industrializing one in which women are entering the workforce in larger numbers than ever before. Added to this is a post-1970s internationally supported emphasis on girls' education, which has played a significant role in bringing women out of their traditional roles at home. Given a lack of proper laws and training about issues

© KONINKLIJKE BRILL NV, LEIDEN, 2012 | DOI:10.1163/1872-5309_EWIC_EWICCOM_001437

of sexual harassment and violence against women both for the general public and for law enforcers, there has been an increase in cases of sexual harassment and general impunity for the perpetrators from any disciplinary legal measures. These incidents have affected the mobility and advancement of all women and girls. Women and girls report being harassed by close family members, by neighborhood boys when they go to school, at workplaces by their superiors, peers and subordinates, at markets and concerts, in other public places, on public transportation, over the internet, and on their mobile phones. For young girls, in particular, preventive measures taken by parents have proven to be mostly counterproductive, as these measures tend to focus on girls' and women's "modesty" and take fault away from the perpetrators.

Women's Rights in the Bangladesh Constitution and Related Laws

The Bangladesh constitution recognizes the right of women to participate equally with men in all spheres of life. For example, Article 10 of the constitution states, "Steps shall be taken to ensure participation of women in all spheres of national life." Article 19 states, "The State shall endeavor to ensure equality of opportunity to all citizens." Section 1 of Article 28 states, "The State shall not discriminate against any citizen on grounds only of religion, race, caste, sex or place of birth." Section 2 of Article 28 states, "Women shall have equal rights with men in all spheres of the State and of public life," while section 4 states, "Nothing in this article shall prevent the State from making special provision in favor of women or children or for the advancement of any backward section of citizens." There are several national laws that address issues concerning violence against women including the Domestic Violence (Protection and Prevention) Act, 2010, the Acid Crime Control Act, 2002, the Suppression of Violence against Women and Children Act, 2000 (amended 2003), the Dowry Prohibition Act, 1980, and the Penal Code, 1860. Each of these laws addresses specific aspects of violence against women. None of them, however, specifically addresses sexual harassment.

Bangladesh has a National Women's Development Policy that was updated in 2011. National laws such as the 2000 Women and Children Repression Prevention Act and international conventions such as the Convention on the Elimination of Discrimination against Women (CEDAW), which Bangladesh signed in 1984, promote legal action against individuals or groups perpetrating acts of violence against women. General Recommendation No. 19 of CEDAW notes: "Gender-based violence is a form of discrimination that seriously inhibits women's ability to enjoy rights and freedoms on a basis of equality with men ...

equality in employment can be seriously impaired when women are subjected to gender-specific violence, such as sexual harassment in the workplace."

Although Bangladesh has acceded to most of the CEDAW provisions, the government continues to maintain reservations on two articles of the convention, Articles 2 and 16.1.c. The former is particularly significant for confronting sexual harassment because it calls on state parties to take appropriate measures, including legislative ones, to abolish existing discrimination against women. Article 16.1.c urges state parties to take measures to eliminate discrimination against women in marriage and family arrangements and, specifically, to grant men and women equal rights in marriage and divorce. Despite intense lobbying by women's rights advocates, the Bangladesh government has refused to withdraw its reservations on these two articles.

The High Court Order

On 14 May 2009, responding to over ten years of street protests and media advocacy, the Bangladesh High Court issued a legal order outlining guidelines for the prevention of sexual harassment in public and private educational institutions, workplaces and public spaces. The judgment, known as the Sexual Harassment Guidelines, was issued by the joint bench of Justices Syed Mahmud Hossain and Qamrul Islam Siddiquee and was specifically aimed at addressing the sexual harassment of girls and women. The directive instructed all organizations and educational institutions to form a committee to implement and observe the Guidelines as law until the National Parliament passed a formal law. The Guidelines define sexual harassment as:

> (a) Unwelcome sexually determined behaviour (whether directly or by implication) as physical contact and advances; (b) attempts or efforts to establish physical relation having sexual implication by abuse of administrative, authoritative or professional powers; (c) sexually coloured verbal representation; (d) demand or request for sexual favours; (e) showing pornography; (f) sexually coloured remark or gesture; (g) indecent gesture, teasing through abusive language, stalking, jokes having sexual implication; (h) insult through letters, telephone calls, cell phone calls, SMS, pottering, notice, cartoon, writing on bench, chair, table, notice boards, walls of office, factory, classroom, washroom having sexual implication; (i) taking still or video photographs for the purpose of blackmailing and character assassination; (j) preventing participation in sports, cultural, organizational and academic activities on the ground of sex and/or for

the purpose of sexual harassment; (k) making love proposal and exerting pressure or posing threats in case of refusal to love proposal; (l) attempt to establish sexual relation by intimidation, deception or false assurance (BNWLA [Bangladesh National Women's Lawyer's Association] 2009).

The Bangladesh High Court's decision to pass these Guidelines was greatly influenced by similar guidelines issued by the Indian High Court in 1997 following the landmark case *Vishaka and others v. State of Rajasthan and others*, which dealt with the 1992 gang rape of Bhanwari Devi by a group of Thakurs.

More directly, the court order resulted from a Public Interest Litigation filed by BNWLA at the High Court on 7 August 2008, asking for guidelines for preventing sexual harassment and abuse at universities and workplaces (PIL No. 5916/2008). BNWLA filed the PIL following complaints of harassment from working women of different socioeconomic backgrounds and categories of work, including women working in the media, in the corporate sector, in the garment industries, and in universities.

A survey conducted by BNWLA of 200 female workers also discovered that 44.6 percent of women reported having been harassed in their place of work, sexually or otherwise; 27.8 percent of women said that they had not been harassed; and 27.6 percent refused to answer. Of the respondents who reported harassment, 30.06 percent were harassed by their employers, and 18.08 percent were harassed by their co-workers, many of whom were in subordinate positions. None of the women ever filed a complaint for fear of losing their jobs, risking their promotions, or being blamed for the harassment. According to BNWLA's report, many of these women had earlier experiences of being accused of not behaving or dressing in a proper way. In recognizing sexual harassment as a crime, the new court ruling empowers women to be able to work in an environment where everybody is aware of the punishment and refrains from engaging in such acts.

Studies on Sexual Harassment in Bangladesh

In Bangladesh, sexual harassment has only recently been recognized as an obstruction to women's right to education, work and freedom of movement. This is not to say that sexual harassment itself is a new phenomenon. However, in the developing economy context of Bangladesh, the large number of women entering the public sphere, which has always been considered a male space, is relatively new. Mandatory education for women is also a fairly recent phenomenon, which has gained more momentum since a democratic form of government was reinstituted in the early 1990s. Studies documenting cases of sexual harassment are few and provide few to no statistics on how many women are stalked and harassed and how this affects the quality of life of women and girls.

Although there have not been many quantitative studies documenting this, there is some evidence that sexual harassment and the fear of it keeps a substantive number of girls and women away from work and education, causes a high rate of school drop-outs, and leads to the practice of early marriages of girls. According to UNICEF (2011), about one-third of women aged 20–24 in Bangladesh were married by the age of 15; 66 percent were married by the time they were 18, and as many as 79 percent were married by the time they were 20. According to a report by the United Nations news agency Integrated Regional Information Networks (IRIN 2011), these figures are up by 2 percent since 2009. The report also quotes a social development adviser who states that the root causes of child marriage were "the prospect of reduced dowry payments and fears of sexual harassment" (IRIN 2011). Parents of lighter-skinned girls who are considered "prettier" face a particularly precarious situation, as they are constantly concerned that the girls will attract more harassment. Girls and women who refuse offers of marriage are also vulnerable. According to a media statistics report by the legal aid and human rights organization, Ain o Salish Kendra (ASK), in 2010 five women were mutilated by acid attacks following refusal of offers of marriage.

The number of reported sexual harassment cases, although high, probably represents only a small fraction of the actual number of incidents that take place. Such behavior is usually only reported to the police station, the media, or even to a parent or higher authority when it reaches an extreme or unbearable stage. Young girls are often afraid that their parents will punish them or blame their own behavior or clothing for the harassment. Often these fears are justified. Instead of taking action against the perpetrator, parents often react by stopping girls' education, forcing them to wear the *hijab* or *burka* when going out, or marrying them off at an early age. The consequences faced by the perpetrator are minimal, and he is left to pursue and pester women and girls. The emotional trauma faced by women as a result of being in a "blame-the-victim" environment is somewhat reflected in the alarming number of suicides by women.

In 2008, the BNWLA conducted a study involving 1,000 girls and women from all over the country. Their analysis of media reports revealed that between 2006 and 2008, at least twelve girls had committed suicide and sexual harassment was either a direct or indirect factor in each case; actual suicide figures are likely to be much higher. The study also found that 87 percent of respondents aged 10–18 and 82.5 percent of respondents aged 18–30 said that they had faced harassment (*Daily Star* 2008).

It is a well-known fact that crimes against women have typically not received much attention in the media in Bangladesh. In the last few years, however, the degree of media interest in women's rights violations has increased rapidly. Many more cases of sexual harassment, domestic violence, fatwa-related violence, and other forms of violence against women are being reported than ever before.

Media Reporting on Violence against Women

The reporting in the media of violence against women began in the 1980s. As Meghna Guhathakurta points out, much of it began as a subversive way of criticizing the dictatorship of General Hussain Mohammad Ershad, rather than out of a genuine concern for women's rights. Guhathakurta argues that the reason for the media's sudden interest in women's issues lay in the policies pursued by the autocratic regime of General Ershad, which had restricted political activity and enforced strict censorship of the news media to prevent political criticism or dissent. Thus, media attention was directed to gender-based violence as a way to criticize the government without being overtly political (Guhathakurta 1996).

Initially, media reports on violence related to women focused on dowry deaths, fatwa-based violence, acid attacks, and other forms of domestic violence. The national media did not turn its attention to sexual harassment as a form of violence against women until after the movement against sexual harassment at Jahangirnagar University, which began in the late 1990s. In the last few years especially, as a result of a rise in the number of women journalists as well as in cases of sexual harassment and related violence, there has been increasing media coverage of sexual harassment, stalking, and related suicides and murders. According to ASK's media statistics reports, during the period of January to October 2010, ten men and two women were murdered in connection with cases of sexual harassment. In November 2010, eight human rights organizations held a press conference to expose and protest against the rise in cases of sexual harassment and related violence. The organizations revealed 166 reports of sexual harassment, 26 cases of suicide among women, and one related suicide of a father whose daughter was being harassed throughout 2010. One case that garnered widespread media attention was the death of Chanpa Rani Bhowmik, who was run over and killed by a local man, Devashish Saha Rony, after she complained about his stalking of her two daughters (*Daily Star* 2010).

While national media has raised awareness of women's issues, it has also consistently promoted negative stereotypes of women. Women are commonly

SEXUAL HARASSMENT: BANGLADESH

portrayed as passive, emotional, and needy; a woman's youth is meant to be spent in search of a man to fulfill the role of guardian and breadwinner and once she is married a woman's role becomes that of procreator and home-maker. Films, television commercials and music videos present the game of pursuit as follows: the first step to winning a woman's heart is for the man to sweet-talk her, then to lure her with material gifts to prove that he has the eco-nomic means to take care of her, and when all else fails, to threaten her and her family with dire consequences. A common notion is that when a woman says no, she really means yes, and it is for the man to rise to the challenge. The lyr-ics from a music video by artist Tabiz Faruk show how sexual flirtation is often laced with violent threats:

> Hey girl who do you think you are?
> Think you are Queen Victoria?
> You don't like these Rajanigandha flower sticks
> When you get beating by hockey stick
> You'll learn
> How to take love by force
> Boss, should we give her a good lesson?
> No, wait.
> Ghee does not come up on straight finger
> Neither will a ring fit on a bent finger
>> translated, MOHAIEMEN 2011

Modesty, Victim-blaming, and the "Sunset Law"

On New Year's Eve 1999, Tumpa went to the Dhaka University campus with two male friends to celebrate the new millennium (although her real name was published in all the newspapers at the time, her name in this entry has been changed to respect her privacy). About a dozen men started hurling obscene remarks at her and soon attacked her, molesting her and ripping her clothes off her body, while a group of people, including police, looked on. She had to endure more than half an hour of assault before passers-by forced the police to rescue her.

The next day, photos of a joyful group of men pulling at a young woman's clothes were published in the national newspapers. The officer-in-charge of the local police station tried to defend the inaction of the police by laying the blame on the woman. He alleged that Tumpa was "improperly dressed and dancing," and this, in his opinion, justified the men's behavior. Even Joynal Hazari, a member of parliament from the ruling party, Awami League, went on record stating that Tumpa herself was to blame for the attack. A BBC report quoted him saying: "She should not have been out so late. What was she doing on the streets at that time of night?"(Chazan 2000).

Hazari's reference may have referred to perhaps the clearest form of institutionalized victim-blaming in Bangladesh—the archaic Shurjasto Ain (Sunset Law). This law was part of the 1920 Proctorial Rules enforced on women attending university and required women to return to their dormitories by sunset. The law, apart from being discriminatory against women, indirectly placed blame for any violence on the women themselves. There have been many demonstrations against the rule but it is still in place, although it is not enforced any more.

This tendency to blame the victim persists more than a decade later and at the highest levels of government. While handing out awards on Begum Rokeya Day at the Osmani Memorial Auditorium on 9 December 2010, Prime Minister Sheikh Hasina spoke about the alarming number of suicides that have resulted from sexual harassment: "One section of women wears too small clothes while another section covers their whole body, even their face and eyes ... both are unacceptable. We have to maintain our culture and tradition. Some so-called ultra-modern women don't bother to keep their modesty" (*Daily Star* 2010). The irony is that Begum Rokeya Day is meant to commemorate Begum Rokeya, a pioneering feminist and woman's rights advocate.

Critiquing the way women's ways of "being" in public spaces is misappropriated to excuse sexual harassment, Naeem Mohaiemen underlines how responsibility for criminal behavior is commonly taken away from the harasser or stalker. He argues that even the language of support comes with a "but"—that approval of women walking freely on the streets comes with the condition of "modest clothing"; anything less is seen as provoking, even deserving of negative attention. Mohaiemen points to a post on the Uttorshuri blog (a popular Bengali blog on political and social issues), where a very strong defense of women's rights still included the instruction: "Women need to be able to operate in this society [i.e., Bangladesh] openly without fear, harassment and intimidation. But at the same time—there needs to be a reciprocity of respecting the societal norms" (Mohaiemen 2009).

So what exactly is considered "inappropriate" or "immodest" in forms of clothing for women in Bangladesh? And who decides? Bengali-Muslim is the dominant cultural identity of the people of Bangladesh, and acceptable attire for women is largely defined by that identity. Saris and *salwar-kamiz* (traditionally, loose pants and long shirt, though this has been subject to fashion trends over the decades) and the *orna* (a long scarf) are the most common form of clothing for women. Although the *orna* has become part of most women's dress in Bangladesh along with the *salwar-kamiz*, the original need for it to be part of the "three-piece" was to cover a woman's breasts, so the contours of the breasts would be less visible. It is also often used to cover hair, as a loose form of *hijab*.

Many parents force their daughters to wear a *hijab* or the *burka* as a form of protection against the male gaze. This practice is particularly prevalent in rural areas where girls often go to school unaccompanied, which puts them at particular risk of being sexually harassed. In more urban areas a parent or guardian usually accompanies girls to their schools and coaching centers.

For a long time traditional fairs, markets, public transportation, indeed any crowded public place, were considered bastions of sexual harassment. No woman could claim to have been in any of these places without having been groped several times and in various parts of her body. Crowds provided a safe haven for perpetrators, allowing them to slip away undetected. The groping occurred so swiftly that by the time the woman turned around, the perpetrator would have disappeared into the crowd. Many women do not complain, for fear of not getting any support from those around or of creating an unnecessary commotion; and for those accompanied by parents, the fear of more restrictions being placed on them in the future. It was also generally accepted that it was a woman's responsibility to avoid being sexually harassed in public places by wearing modest clothes. Dina Siddiqi observes that with the stigma attached to open discussions of sexuality and the concern about honor, most women are reluctant to reveal experiences of a sexually exploitative nature. According to Siddiqi, dominant cultural practices militate against women's admitting to or seeking redress for incidences of harassment. Reluctance to press charges also comes from the awareness that it is difficult to verify allegations of sexual harassment (2003).

Taslima Nasrin was one of the first feminist writers in Bangladesh to write about sexual harassment in Bangladeshi society. She wrote about her personal experiences of being sexually harassed and molested and about raped women she had come across when she worked as a gynecologist. She received death threats from Islamic fundamentalists in Bangladesh for her views and for her criticism of Islam and religion in general. Nasrin currently lives in exile.

The Politics of Sexual Harassment

On 28 May 2011, Porimol Joydhor, a male teacher at one of Dhaka's leading girls' school, Viqarunnesa Noon School, molested a tenth grade student. The girl had gone to Joydhor's house for private lessons where he not only molested her, but took nude photos of her and threatened to expose her photos in public if she did not return. Fearful of the repercussions of having her photo circulated on the Internet, the girl returned to Joydhor's house on 17 June 2011, where he molested her once again. The girl finally spoke about the incidents with her friends, and news eventually traveled to her parents who immediately complained to the school authorities. The school's principal, instead of taking immediate action against the teacher, warned the parents not to pursue the complaint and instructed them to bury the incident. Some argue that this reaction may have been prompted by the fact that Joydhor was a former member of Bangladesh Chhatra League (BCL), the student front of the ruling party, Awami League. It took several rallies by students, parents and women's rights activists in front of the school and the Shahid Minar (Martyr's Monument) to bring the issue to the attention of the media. The school principal eventually dismissed Joydhor from the school and he was arrested. Two other teachers of the same school—Barun Chandra Barman of the Commerce department and Abdul Kalam Azad of the Religion department—were also suspended for what school authorities later termed "indecent behavior with students" (*Daily Star* 2011).

The movement against sexual harassment in educational institutions began at Jahangirnagar University, a public university, in 1998, when incidents of rape and sexual harassment were being carried out by a group of students belonging to the BCL. Here too, the university administration was initially too intimidated by the rapists' political affiliations to take any disciplinary action against them (Ahmed 2007). It took a nationwide movement including media reports and editorials and street protests by many students, teachers and activists for the authorities to finally acknowledge the problem. The anti-rape campaign went on for over 40 days and was said to be the longest such campaign in South Asia (Ahmed 2008). As part of this movement, teachers and activists drafted a policy against sexual harassment, which ultimately inspired the sexual harassment Guidelines issued by the High Court (*Daily Star* 2009).

Whether it is a case of sexual harassment, domestic violence, or fatwa-based or other kinds of violence against women, one notable fact that emerges in many instances is that the women or girls involved often remain silent until the violence reaches a breaking point. In the case of the incidents mentioned above, the political affiliations of the wrongdoers made seeking redress even more difficult. Writer Rahnuma Ahmed conducted research on abuses of power by BCL members. In particular, she documented how the ruling party's willingness to condone sexual crimes by BCL members had contributed to rising rates of sexual crimes across the country (Ahmed 2010).

(Ab)using Technology

In 2001, two young men, Shumon and Pintu, started what was at the time a new form of sexual violence in Bangladesh—homemade films created with hidden video cameras. Shumon, a Bangladeshi-American, came to Dhaka and filmed himself having sex with three different women. The duo then distributed their films among informal networks and also sold them in the markets in Dhaka (Hussain 2009).

Hidden cameras have also been discovered in bathrooms in public universities in Dhaka and recently, inside changing rooms of spas and beauty salons. The use of mobile phones cameras to harass women has in fact become an increasingly alarming problem in the urban as well as rural areas of Bangladesh.

Increasing Suicide Rates and Sexual Harassment

On 19 November 2010 a 13-year-old girl, studying in the fifth grade, committed suicide after her parents were assaulted by her stalker's family when they protested against the stalker's forceful entrance into their house. A 20-year-old man of the neighborhood used to stalk the girl on her way to school.

Throughout 2010, the media carried out a series of reports on suicides by young girls after they had been systematically stalked and harassed by men in their neighborhood. The Bangladesh Rural Advancement Committee (BRAC) conducted research that documented 3,000 incidents of human rights violations in 61 districts between 2006 and 2009. The research also found that 12 percent of the human rights violations resulted in suicide.

In January 2011, after a series of suicides, the High Court declared that stalking of girls and women would be deemed a punishable offence and directed the government to include stalking within the legal definition of sexual harassment (*Daily Star* 2011). The court also directed the government to enact laws to protect the victims and witnesses, to equip police stations to deal with stalking cases, to bring cyber cafés under registration because of the high rate of sexual harassment using mobile phone technology, and to address the mental trauma of victims.

From "Eve-teasing" to "Stalking" to "Sexual Harassment"—The Scuffle with Terminology

The origin and intended meaning of the term "Eve-teasing" are unclear. Although it likely originated in India, the term has over the years gained great popularity as a euphemism for sexual harassment in the Bangladeshi media. In the last few years especially, the term has become so popular in media usage that it has replaced the formal Bangla term for sexual harassment, *jouno nipiron*.

Women's rights advocates have duly noted that the usage of Eve-teasing is problematic. They argue that the playful tone of the term seems to detract from the seriousness of the crime and prevents people from appreciating the damaging physical and psychological effects of sexual harassment on women and girls. For example, Farah Mehreen Ahmad notes that Eve-teasing and related terms dilute the gravity of an act that infringes on basic human rights, which include the right to education, independence, mobility and life; and can lead to self-mutilation, suicide and murder. She also argues that the related term "street Romeo" imbues a deceptively playful, romantic accent to the harassers (Ahmad 2011).

Thus, along with the movement against sexual harassment, in late 2010, women's rights activists began a parallel movement to rid the media of the phrase Eve-teasing, holding several press conferences requesting media not to use it. Around the same time, the elite government crime-fighting force Rapid Action Battalion named their operation "Operation Romeo Hunt," to tackle sexual harassment on the streets. Historically, the police's record in tackling complaints of sexual harassment has been very poor. Incidents of police ignoring complaints, blaming the victims, asking for bribes, and generally not treating sexual harassment as a serious crime were not unusual. As a result of these efforts, the media shifted its usage to the term stalking, which encapsulates only one type of sexual harassment, and then finally turned to using the phrase sexual harassment. The use of Eve-teasing, however, has not completely disappeared.

Harassment and Sexual Assaults against Religious and Ethnic Minorities

Women's bodies have long been used as a form of war booty in conflict zones. So too, during Bangladesh's War of Independence from Pakistan in 1971, human rights violations and sexual violence against women were pandemic. As Bengalis were the political minority at the time, Bengali women were particularly vulnerable. In 2002, Dr. Bina D'Costa (academic and feminist researcher) interviewed Dr. Geoffrey Davis, an Australian doctor who performed abortions on rape victims in 1972 (D'Costa 2010). In the interview Dr. Davis revealed that at the time he was performing a hundred abortions a day in Dhaka, and he knew of many other cases of abortions being performed outside the capital or, for those who could afford it, in Calcutta. Dr. Davis also stated that he once heard a Pakistani military officer mention that there were instructions from military strategists to impregnate "as many Bengali women as they could" as they believed that "good Muslim" children would never fight against their fathers.

Following independence, Bengali Muslims, now a majority, also carried out systemic and brutal violence against the ethnic and religious minorities of Bangladesh. According to a recent judicial commission report, gangs affiliated with the Bangladesh Nationalist Party (BNP) and Jamaat-e-Islami coalition, which was in power at the time, raped over 200 women from mostly Hindu minority communities before the 2001 elections. Religious minorities are seen as a threat to BNP-Jamaat's vote bank. Bullying tactics, such as the looting of their houses, together with more grievous offenses, such as rape and sexual harassment, are used to intimidate minorities and prevent them from voting for the opposing party, the Awami League.

The Bangladeshi army also used tactics of sexual violence, among other ploys, to silence the rebellion taken up by the ethnic Jumma people to protest against the Bangladesh government's domination and marginalization of the people of the Chittagong Hill Tracts (CHT). Although the rebels and the government of Bangladesh signed a Peace Accord in 1997, the military still remains in the CHT, and the rape and sexual harassment of Jumma women and girls by Bengali settlers is condoned, even encouraged by the military as a tactic to sustain Bengali domination in a previously Jumma-inhabited area. Tania Haque has documented cases of the torture and murder of Jumma men by the Bangladeshi army on the pretext of suspecting them to be members of the rebel group Shanti Bahini (Peace Force). As a result, Jumma men and boys are reluctant to venture out, and outdoor chores are left to Jumma women instead. The result is even worse, as Jumma women have become the primary target on which to demonstrate the army's authority and domination over the region.

The Way Ahead

One of the demands of the 1998 mass movement against sexual harassment by the teachers and students of Jahangirnagar University was the formation of a policy against sexual harassment. This demand, along with heightened media awareness, brought sexual harassment within the purview of the law, was a milestone achievement for women's rights activists in Bangladesh. However it is clear that the law alone is not sufficient for confronting and criminalizing sexual harassment.

Confronting behaviors of sexual harassment ultimately begins at home. Many girls are raised not to be self-confident and do not have the support of their friends, family and co-workers to identify and report sexual harassment and intimidation without fear of reprimand or blame. Many women do not report sexual harassment fearing repercussions in the form of lower grades at academic institutions or loss of jobs. Many boys are not raised to respect girls and women as equal citizens and learn through the media to treat women as merely objects of sexual desire. Lawmakers and law enforcers, especially male police and judges, need to have mandatory gender sensitivity training.

The High Court's Sexual Harassment Guidelines have not been properly implemented so far. The Guidelines require all workplaces and educational institutions to have a committee by which to enforce complaints procedures. In reality, however, unless the Guidelines are made into laws, they will remain unenforceable and will have no effect on workplaces and educational institutions. Unless sexual harassment and other crimes against women are made punishable offences and law enforcers are trained, no words of protection promised by the Constitution are going to be powerful enough to make offenders realize the brutality of the crime that is sexual harassment.

Bibliography

Ahmad, Farah Mehreen. The economics of our loins, in *Forum Magazine* 5:7 (July 2011), <http://www.thedailystar.net/forum/2011/July/economics.htm>.

Ahmed, Hana Shams. Violating a sacred relationship, in *Star Weekend Magazine* 7:31 (1 August 2007).

Ahmed, Rahnuma. Of roses and sexual harassment, in *New Age*, 7 July 2008.

Ahmed, Rahnuma. Chhatra League's sexual offences. A widespread state of denial, in *New Age*, 19 April 2010.

BNWLA (Bangladesh National Women's Lawyer's Association). Judgment to prevent sexual harassment in educational institutions and workplaces, May 2009, <http://www.bnwlabd.org/highlighted-judgementsdirections/>, accessed 27 September 2012.

Chazan, David. Women students fight back, BBC News, 28 February 2000, <http://news.bbc.co.uk/1/hi/world/south_asia/660134.stm>.

D'Costa, Bina. 1971: Rape and its consequences, in *BDNews24.com*, 15 December 2010, <http://opinion.bdnews24.com/2010/12/15/1971-rape-and-its-consequences/>.

Guhathakurta, Meghna. Violence and victimization. Responses of the women's movement, presentation at conference, "Bangladesh 1971–1996: Past, present and future," School of Oriental and African Studies, University of London and ICS, 1996.

Haque, Tania. Militarization and the fate of women's body: A case study of the Chittagong Hill Tracts, in *Women and militancy. South Asian complexities*, ed. Amena Mohsin and Imtiaz Ahmed, Dhaka 2011, 41–59.

Hussain, Ahmede. Not child's play, in *Daily Star*, 13 November 2009.

IRIN (Integrated Regional Information Networks). Bangladesh. Parents still not heeding child marriage warnings, 5 April 2011, <http://www.unhcr.org/refworld/country,,IRIN,,BGD,,4d9ee2452,0.html>.

Mohaiemen, Naeem. Why should I be "modest"? in *Forum Magazine* 4:5 (May 2009).

Mohaiemen, Naeem. The poison of male violence, in *Daily Star*, 16 June 2011, <http://www.thedailystar.net/newDesign/news-details.php?nid=190093>.

Siddiqi, Dina M. The sexual harassment of industrial workers. Strategies for intervention in the workplace and beyond, Paper 26, Centre for Policy Dialogue, Dhaka, June 2003.

Daily Star. 81pc girls fall victim to eve teasing. Study, in *Daily Star*, 1 July 2008.

Daily Star. Sexual harassment: HC lays down guidelines, in *Daily Star*, 15 May 2009.

Daily Star. Chanpa Rani's killer Rony sent to jail, in *Daily Star*, 7 November 2010.

Daily Star. Stalking now sexual offence, in *Daily Star*, 27 January 2011.

Daily Star. Sexual assault charges rock leading school, in *Daily Star*, 6 July 2011.

UNICEF. *The state of the world's children 2011. Adolescence: An age of opportunity*, New York 2011.

Sexual Harassment: Egypt

Noha Roushdy

Introduction

Sexual harassment in public spaces in Egypt is currently one of the most endemic threats to the safety and mobility of women. According to recent studies, the majority of women in Egypt regularly experience some form of sexual harassment. Contrary to earlier speculations linking sexual harassment to a woman's attire or social status, these studies have unanimously confirmed that women from all walks of life, including conservatively dressed women, are habitually exposed to some form of sexual harassment in public spaces (Hassan and Shoukry 2008, Population Council 2011, UN Women 2013).

To date, sexual harassment is largely an urban phenomenon, most frequently taking place on the streets and on public transportation. The scope and nature of the harassment women report experiencing encompass a range of physical and verbal actions and behaviors that aim to incite or coerce women to engage in interactions of a sexual nature. Having one's body touched by strangers and receiving comments or verbal abuse of a sexual nature from them are the most frequently cited forms of sexual harassment women are exposed to in Egypt.

In 2014, a presidential decree rendered *al-taḥarrush al-jinsī* (sexual harassment) a crime punishable by no less than one year in prison. In its current legal definition (Article 306 (b) /2014), sexual harassment is distinct kinds of indecent public acts of sexual or pornographic nature that are "committed with the intension of the perpetrator receiving from the harassed benefit of a sexual nature." The criminalization of sexual harassment under Law 306 of the Egyptian penal code responded to the concerted efforts of civil society organizations, grassroots initiatives, and the media to document and report public sexual violence in the aftermath of the 2011 uprising (Langohr 2016).

Although criminalization has transformed the culture of impunity that used to surround sexual harassment in Egypt, it is only a partial victory for women's rights organizations that, for decades, have been calling for comprehensive legal and administrative reforms tackling sexual violence against women, of which street harassment is one form. For these organizations, a combination of structural and cultural factors has normalized and legitimized sexual harassment as an excusable masculine behavior in Egyptian society to an extent that exceeds the scope of the current legal framework (Ezzelarab 2014, FIDH et al. 2014).

© KONINKLIJKE BRILL NV, LEIDEN, 2016 | DOI:10.1163/1872-5309_EWIC_COM_002085

The arguments raised by pundits and scholars alike point to a patriarchal logic that assigns to women the full social and moral responsibility for both inciting sexual harassment and withstanding unwanted male attention (Ilahi 2008, Changing Masculinities 2011, Zaki and Abd Alhamid 2014). This logic patterns a dominant religious discourse that emphasizes *al-ḥayā' wal-ḥishma* (female sexual modesty) in dress and demeanor as moral and social armament against *fitna* (sexual temptation) and the resultant sexual misbehavior of men (Hoffman-Ladd 1987, El-Nadeem Center 2013, Hafez 2014a & b, Tadros 2015b). It is, moreover, consolidated by the ambiguous role of state institutions, which are expected to combat a crime they are frequently implicated in (Amar 2011, Carr 2014, Ezzelarab 2014, Hafez 2014a & b, Tadros 2015a & b).

Defining Sexual Harassment in Egypt: a Brief History

In Egypt, *al-taḥarrush al-jinsī* has emerged in public discourse as a recognizable form of violence against women fairly recently. It was foreshadowed by the methodical use of sexual violence to suppress political opposition in the late Mubarak era (Gad 2012, Kirollos 2013, Zaki and Abd Alhamid 2014, Abdelmonem 2015, Tadros 2015b). No form of sexual harassment, political or otherwise, is documented before the 2000s, when sexual harassment was considered one form, albeit a deplorable one, of *mu'akasa* (flirtation) (Kirollos 2013). However, observers suspect that sexual harassment had featured regularly during *mawālid* (saints' day celebrations), music concerts, and football game celebrations for much longer (Diab 2010, Gad 2012). One notorious case of mass assault on a woman in Cairo received significant media attention in 1992. A young woman getting on a bus with her mother and sisters in the popular Cairo district of *al-'Ataba al-Khaḍrā* was pulled away by four men who collectively assaulted her. The case became known as the case of *"fatāt al-'Ataba"* ("the Girl of 'Ataba") and made headlines in March 1992 (Sami 1992). The details of the attack strongly resemble the mass sexual assaults documented decades later.

In the early 2000s, civil society organizations, bloggers, and survivors began reporting and documenting incidents of sexual harassment, capturing the concurrent proliferation of *taḥarrush jama'i* (mass sexual harassment of women) on crowded streets during holidays and in protest areas (Rizzo, Price, and Meyer 2008, Abdelmonem 2015, Langohr 2015). The sexual assault of female protestors during an anti-Mubarak demonstration in 2005 is the earliest documented incident of sexual harassment. Experts and scholars commonly trace the emergence of sexual harassment as a subject of grassroots activism to this period (Amar 2011, Kirollos 2013, FIDH et al. 2014, Zaki and Abd Alhamid 2014). During this demonstration, organized by the Kifaya Movement to protest constitutional amendments supporting Mubarak's reelection, thugs collaborating with the security forces and under their direction sexually assaulted and harassed women protestors. Survivors of the attacks, dubbed "the attacks of Black Wednesday," reported being verbally abused before having their clothes torn and physically assaulted in full view of the police. This systematic targeting of female protestors in political conflict prompted the first organized response by Egyptian civil society organizations against sexual harassment. El-Nadeem Center for Rehabilitation of Victims of Violence, for example, filed lawsuits against police officers for committing acts of sexual assaults, and the Egyptian Initiative for Personal Rights filed a complaint before the African Commission on Human and People's Rights against the Egyptian government for failing to protect women protestors (Amar 2011, EIPR 2013).

The state's use of mobs of men to sexually assault female protestors on Black Wednesday reflected an emergent pattern of *taharrush jama'i* that was observed and documented in the following years during religious holidays in Cairo. These attacks involved mobs of men in a state of frenzy randomly attacking and sexually harassing women on crowded streets (Al-Sisi 2006). The attacks in Downtown Cairo on the 'Eid al-Fiṭr holiday in October 2006, for example, were purportedly triggered by the appearance of Dina, a well-known oriental dance performer, who was attending the première of a movie in which she was acting. The media initially accused Dina of having incited sexual harassment, claiming she had danced on the pavement of the movie theater. Three years later, when similar attacks were reported to have occurred during the 'Eid al-Aḍḥā holidays in Muhandisin, singling out Dina or any one woman for inciting mass sexual harassment became difficult to substantiate (Abdelhadi 2006, Ismail 2006, Ilahi 2008).

Responding to the escalating public sexual harassment, the Egyptian Center for Women's Rights (ECWR) initiated an extensive anti-sexual harassment campaign that produced groundbreaking evidence on the prevalence and intensity of sexual harassment, generating, for the first time in the Egyptian media, public debates over sexual harassment (Rizzo, Price, and Meyer 2008). In 2008, the organization published the findings of the first study on the proliferation of sexual harassment among Egyptian and foreign women living in Egypt (Hassan and Shoukry 2008). The finding showed that 83% of Egyptian women and 98% of foreign women living in the Greater Cairo area had been subjected to sexual harassment. The study presented vital evidence that a prevalent perception linking a woman's attire or demeanor to her exposure to sexual harassment contradicts women's actual experiences. In the following years, studies published by the Population Council (2011) and UN Women (2013) would corroborate the findings of ECWR's 2008 study.

In parallel to the rise of anti-sexual harassment activism, Egypt's judiciary sentenced a man, for the first time, to three years imprisonment and a fine for sexually harassing a woman on the street. The case of Nuha Rushdi al-Ustaz, a young filmmaker who physically handed her harasser to the police, became a landmark case for the battle against sexual harassment in Egypt. Al-Ustaz was not only the first who managed to report a case of sexual harassment, but she was also hailed for responding to the harassment by jumping on the minibus and physically dragging the driver who groped her out of the car and into the nearest police station (BBC News 2008). Notwithstanding some efforts to tarnish Nuha's credibility, her case and the by-then routine accounts of incidents of mass sexual harassments taking place in crowded spaces validated without a doubt that an escalation in the rate and severity of the forms of "flirtation" women were exposed to was taking place. It warned of an intensification of an everyday experience for women in Egypt that was still considered harmless masculine misbehavior.

In light of this historical context, the understanding of sexual harassment informing anti-sexual harassment activism in Egypt reflects a distinct local understanding of harassment that, on the one hand, differs from international definitions of sexual harassment and, on the other hand, encompasses a broader category of sexual violence than is entailed by the legal definition.

International definitions of sexual harassment target experiences of sexual violence linked to gender discrimination and sexual abuse in the workplace. They usually entail a reference to inappropriate advances promising favors in return for a sexual exchange of physical or verbal nature (US Equal Employment Opportunity Commission, n.d., BBC News 2006). The current Egyptian legal definition of sexual harassment resonates this international understanding of sexual harassment by emphasizing the promise of benefits in exchange for a sexual interaction. However, in line with the broader legal framework for sexual crimes, the full text of the law recognizes any "forward actions, insinuations or hints that are sexual or pornographic whether by signals, words or action and by any means including wired and wireless communication methods" to constitute a form of sexual harassment punishable by law, regardless of motivation ("Laws against Sexual Harassment in Egypt" 2016.

Conversely, the vernacular use of *al-taḥarrush al-jinsī* encompasses forms of sexual violence that are categorically different in the Egyptian penal code and go beyond the international understanding of sexual harassment. In addition to the above definition of sexual harassment, the vernacular use of *taḥarrush* may refer to acts of sexual assault and rape.

For example, in the case of Nuha Rushdi al-Ustaz, sexual harassment was not the crime for which the perpetrator was punished, although the case is commonly referred to as a case of sexual harassment. Instead, drawing on the existing sexual offenses recognized in the Egyptian penal code at the time, the perpetrator received the maximum prison sentence of three years for the crime of *hatk ʿirḍ* (indecent assault), one of the four main sexual offenses recognized in the Egyptian penal code to which sexual harassment was added. These include indecent public behavior (Article 278), the recently amended sexual harassment article on the use of lewd words, deeds, or gestures (Article 306 (a) and 306 (b)), as well as indecent assault (Article 268) and rape (Article 267). Because the Egyptian penal code only recognizes forced sexual intercourse that may lead to pregnancy as rape, the raping of women with objects, forced anal intercourse, and groping are indecent sexual assault. In the vernacular use of *taharrush* in the public sphere, almost any form of sexual violence short of the Egyptian legal definition of "rape" may be referred to as *al-taḥarrush al-jinsī* (Peoples 2008, Ebaid 2013, Fahmy et al. 2014, FIDH et al. 2014, Abdelmonem 2015). Attention to the ambiguity of the term as used in Egypt is critical to any understanding of the scope and range of sexual harassment in Egypt.

Sexual Harassment in the Everyday

In 2013, a poll by Thomson Reuters Foundation ranked Egypt as the "worst Arab country to be a woman." The poll, which surveyed gender experts in countries of the Arab League on their assessment of women's rights in different spheres, identified the prevalence of sexual harassment as one of the most critical issues undermining women's rights in Egypt. The poll's findings did not surprise an Egyptian public increasingly exposed to incidents of sexual harassment through the media. It actually validated the link between sexual harassment and the deteriorating quality of life for women in this country.

Studies of representative samples of the population established that the experience of sexual harassment is a universal experience for women in Egypt (Hassan and Shoukry 2008, Population Council 2011, UN Women 2013, Fahmy et al. 2014). According to these studies, street harassment is one of the most common forms of sexual harassment. It includes ogling, catcalling, sexual comments, and gestures, as well as following, touching, and indecent exposure. Exposure to these forms of sexual harassment is not limited to empty streets or late hours in the evening. Women experience sexual harassment at any hour of the day and most commonly on public transportation and crowded streets.

Even during Ramadan, sexual comments are cloaked in a religious rhetoric that curses women for tempting men to commit sins (Ilahi 2008).

Street harassment has become an intrinsic feature of walking in busy urban areas, particularly in Cairo and Alexandria. Although walking with a man is likely to limit a woman's exposure to sexual harassment, it does not prevent it. In fact, sexual harassment is a common cause for street fights when women are walking in the company of men. To preserve the reputation of the women, observers and passersby commonly urge men not to fight the harassers (Ilahi 2008).

Harassers are most commonly strangers. Although they are generally young men, older men, adolescents, and children also engage in sexual harassment (UN Women 2013). In most studies, women categorized their harassers as belonging to a profession that placed them on the streets: policemen and security forces, drivers, craftsmen, and school and university students (Hassan and Shoukry 2008, UN Women 2013). Subtle and indirect forms of harassment wherein the harasser is not a stranger to the victim are less commonly reported, which may be linked to the normalization of forms of sexual harassment that are implicit or not visibly aggressive. About 11% of respondents in the 2013 UN Women study reported having been harassed by a colleague, and 7% by a relative or friend. Women also reported having been asked to stay extra hours at work or pressured into accepting invitations for outings, meals, or rides (UN Women 2013).

Data on sexual harassment in the workplace suggests that street harassment is no more than the visible manifestation of a far more integrated environment of sexual harassment for women in public life in Egypt (Farag and Haridi 2004, New Woman Foundation 2016). Literature on women's experiences in the workforce suggests, moreover, that unwanted attention and inappropriate advances are not only widespread but also constitute an important social impediment to female employment (Hoodfar 1997, Barsoum 2002, Mostafa 2008).

Neither age, nor marital status, nor social class plays a significant role in protecting a woman from being sexual harassed. Nonetheless, because public transportation and the streets are two of the most commonly cited spaces for harassment, access to private cars and other private venues reduces the likelihood of harassment. In addition, how women dress or how they behave in public does not have a significant effect on whether they are subjected to harassment. Although studies have shown that women dressed in tight or revealing clothes are most likely to get harassed, there is no indication that a conservative attire intimidates harassers (Hassan and Shoukry 2008, Ilahi 2008, Population Council 2011, UN Women 2013).

In comparing the experiences of Egyptian and non-Egyptian women with sexual harassment, it becomes clear that the cultural identity and race of women play an important role in their sexual harassment experiences. Although the majority of Egyptian and non-Egyptian women in Egypt experience harassment, non-Egyptian women appear to be exposed to more explicit forms of sexual advances. While Euro-American women are more likely to report receiving direct sexual advances by men within their circle of acquaintances, sexual harassment against African and black Egyptian women is strikingly more aggressive and intense (Hassan and Shoukry 2008, Ilahi 2008).

Although sexual harassment on university campuses and in schools has not been adequately examined, evidence from existing studies, media coverage of sporadic incidents, and individual testimonies indicates that female students in pre- and post-college educational institutes and schoolteachers are regularly exposed to sexual harassment by male students (Sobhy 2012, Ezzelarab 2014, New Woman Foundation 2016). In 2014, a video showing an incident of sexual harassment on the main campus of Cairo University was widely circulated in the media and on online platforms. It showed a large group of male students pursuing a female student from the gates of Cairo University's main campus into a bathroom. Accounts by students who had witnessed the incident blamed the girl for inciting her harassment through her choice of clothing, a perception that was shared by the president of the University when asked to comment on the incident on TV. Although the president was later compelled to retract his comment, the incident revealed a punitive dimension to this incident of harassment as the girl was singled out because she was "known to dress provocatively" among students (Ezzelarab 2014, Langohr 2015).

Outside the walls of campuses, however, is where most female students experience sexual harassment on a daily basis (Sobhy 2012, UN Women 2013). Although preparatory and secondary schools in Egypt are commonly sex-segregated, schools for boys and girls are commonly close to one another. Consequently, female students are regularly exposed to unwanted attention and experience different forms of sexual harassment from boys attending adjacent schools (Sobhy 2012).

Other critical sites where sexual harassment takes place are seasonal spaces, such as *mawālid*, celebrations for football game victories, concerts, and markets. What these spaces have in common is their liminal nature: they are transitory gatherings of large numbers of people who are unknown to each other. As celebratory and festive spaces, such as the streets become when the Egyptian national football teams win a game or during a concert, they signal locations where nonnormative behavior is expected to take place, and hence become potentially risky for women. Women, who appear in these locations, especially if unaccompanied by men, are by virtue of their mere presence "fair game" because they have taken a risk by disregarding social norms on women's presence and comportment in public spaces (Ilahi 2008, Diab 2010, Gad 2012, Zaki and Abd Alhamid 2014).

Sexual Harassment in Protest Areas, 2011–14

The aftermath of the uprising that toppled the Mubarak regime in 2011 witnessed an intensification of sexual violence in protest areas, specifically in the vicinity of Tahrir Square in Cairo, which was the site of major political rallies. Between November 2012 and January 2014, more than two hundred and fifty incidents of mass sexual assaults were reported to have taken place during major political rallies organized in the interim period following the 2011 uprisings (Kingsley 2013, Begum 2014, FIDH et al. 2014). The escalation of these assaults coincided with the official withdrawal of the police from the area in January 2012 and continued throughout the period when the Supreme Council of the Armed Forces (SCAF) was in power (2011–12), under the short rule of the Muslim Brotherhood (2012–13), and during the presidency of General Abdel Fatah El-Sissi (2014 to the present).

Based on survivors' and other eyewitness accounts, these assaults differed significantly from everyday experiences of sexual harassments. Attackers in all accounts appeared to follow a clear and recurrent pattern wherein they formed a mob of men that would suddenly encircle a woman, isolate her completely from her surrounding, and take turns in assaulting her (El-Nadeem et al. 2013). The assaults involved attempting to tear the clothes off women's bodies, groping, and raping through the insertion of objects or fingers inside sexual organs.

In response to the unwillingness of state institutions to provide security for female protestors in Tahrir Square, young people formed several informal groups to secure the square and provide emergency rescue to women. The grassroots and volunteer basis of these initiatives suggested an unprecedented level of civic engagement with the battle against sexual harassment among Egyptian youth. Groups such as Operation Anti-Sexual Harassment (OpAnti-Sh) and Tahrir Bodyguards formed the nucleus of a more expansive anti-sexual harassment movement in Egypt that has played an important role in mobilizing public opinion against sexual harassment in following years, extending their work to cover Downtown Cairo during holidays, on the subway, and even in Alexandria (Zaki and Abd Alhamid 2014, Langohr 2014, 2015, Tadros 2015a).

The mob sexual assaults of Tahrir Square that started a year after the overthrow of Mubarak were not the only form of politically motivated sexual violence that women had been exposed to (Tadros 2015b). In fact, politically motivated sexual violence committed by state agents acting in their official capacities preceded the mob assaults/harassments.

Women protestors marching in Tahrir Square on International Women's Day in March 2011, only a month following the overthrow of Mubarak, were physically and verbally abused and subjected to forced "virginity tests" by military personnel. Samira Ibrahim, one of the survivors of the attacks, took the army physician who undertook the procedure to court. The doctor was charged with committing "acts in breach of public decency" but was later acquitted by a military court. His acquittal echoed official military statements, which defended the practice as precautionary lest the military be accused of violating protestors (Human Rights Watch 2011, Fleishman 2012, Ezzelarab 2014, FIDH et al. 2014, Hafez 2014b).

In November of the same year, soldiers brutally attacked and sexually assaulted female protestors during a raid on a sit-in near Tahrir Square. The widely circulated image of a soldier stripping the abaya off a female protestor, revealing her bra, and stepping on her chest—known in the media as the "blue bra girl"—became an iconic representation of the state's implication in sexual violence. Additionally, it exposed the degree to which the sexual harassment and assault of female protestors could be widely condoned and even supported on the pretext that the morality of women joining sit-ins is questionable. For example, in reaction to the wide circulation of the "blue bra incident" in local and international media outlets, some TV show presenters blamed the victim for not wearing full clothing underneath the abaya; others insisted that decent women should not have been at the location of the sit-in in the first place. "*Eih elli wadaha hinak*" (What business did she have there?), a phrase uttered by one TV presenter associated with the Freedom and Justice Party, was appropriated by activists as the catchphrase capturing the popular rhetoric justifying sexual harassment. In addition, members of the Shura Council (parliament's upper house) representing the political spectrum made public statements against survivors of sexual harassment, holding women responsible for having been in a risky environment, and blaming them for having mixed with men during demonstrations (Amaria 2011, Ghannam 2012, Hafez 2014a, FIDH et al. 2014, Zaki and Abd Alhamid 2014).

Attitudes toward Sexual Harassment

In October 2015, a young college student who was being followed by a man in a shopping mall was attacked and slapped on the face by her harasser when she refused to respond to his sexual advances. Sumaya, later known in the media as the "mall girl" (*fatāt al-mall*), appeared on a satellite channel show hosted by Riham Said, a young TV show hostess known to sensationalize stories of crime and sex. Sumaya told her story, and footage from security cameras was played showing her exchanging words with her harasser, in reaction to which he started violently slapping her before the security personnel pulled him away.

After Sumaya left the show, Riham Said displayed private pictures of Sumaya that had purportedly been sent to her by a stranger. In these pictures, Sumaya appeared holding a bottle of alcohol, in a man's arms, in a bathing suit on the beach, and posing sexually in bed. Before showing the pictures, Riham Said told her viewers that these pictures raised questions about Sumaya. She noted that ordinary women generally do not respond to sexual comments on the streets and that for someone to react as fiercely as Sumaya had, their moral standing needed to be impeccable. She said she was also grateful that the pictures had come her way before she magnified the case and attacked the police for having not protected Sumaya.

In response, Sumaya appeared on other TV shows, hysterical and speaking about being ostracized by her family, and how she had been afraid to walk the streets since the pictures had been made public. "I wish I let myself get beaten ... how many people who have this ... but everyone saw these pictures," she exclaimed. While online forums were quick to circulate the pictures of Sumaya, anti-harassment groups started a fierce online campaign against Riham Said. Within a week, the show's sponsors withdrew their money, leaving the channel's management no choice but to stop the show.

Sumaya's story is emblematic of the attitudes toward sexual harassment dominating Egyptian society. It also represents the remarkable transformation in social responses to sexual harassment. Sumaya's attempt at reporting her experience reflects the accumulation of years of concerted civil society efforts to raise awareness among women regarding the importance of reporting and speaking out. The reaction her act provoked reflects the extent to which sexual harassment is implicated in traditional social norms regarding women's sexual modesty and a political system where the police forces are beyond reproach. Riham Said did not only draw on a cultural logic that discredits a woman's essential right not to be sexually harassed regardless of her character; she also spoke to the right of the security forces not to protect women of questionable sexual modesty.

Notwithstanding her tarnished reputation as a "good girl," the support Sumaya received marks an unprecedented degree of civic commitment to combat sexual harassment and support women who report it. Yet it is unclear to what extent these transformations go beyond institutional and organized responses, and reflect changing attitudes toward sexual harassment on the community and individual level. In fact, Sumaya's incident showed that a woman's right not to be sexually harassed remains intimately linked to her sexual modesty and the extent to which she complies with dominant gender role expectations, and not merely what she was doing or wearing when she was subjected to the harassment.

The absence of a concrete and consistent anti-sexual harassment discourse unanimously supported by state institutions, religious authorities, and the media lies behind the contradictory and ambiguous attitudes toward victims of sexual harassment like Sumaya. Instead, since sexual harassment first emerged as a topic of public concern in the 2000s, social consensus over questions of accountability, prevention, and retribution has been stifled by conflicting arguments about the social factors behind the profusion of sexual harassment.

An initial position adopted and propagated by a number of prominent public intellectuals, journalists, and state officials at the beginning of the 2000s linked sexual harassment to the economic conditions stifling young men's access to marriage. This view grounded sexual harassment in poverty and the sexual frustration of the unemployed, identifying the unruly sexuality of disenfranchised and marginalized urban youth as the primary instigator of harassment (Ilahi 2008, Peoples 2008, Amar 2011, Zaki and Abd Alhamid 2014). This materialist understanding of sexual harassment was most popular before the aforementioned studies were published and before ample evidence showed that harassers come from all walks of life, including married men and educated professionals (Hassan and Shoukry 2008). This attitude, however, continues to guide a classist engagement with sexual harassment whereby social profiling of harassers as poor, uneducated, or unemployed overlooks the pervasiveness of sexual harassment and its entanglement in other forms of sexual violence that cut across social class.

A parallel and widespread argument grounds sexual harassment in social changes undermining traditional values and threatening public morality. The focus is on the values promoted in popular culture and on young people's access to sexually explicit content on television and the Internet as the driving social force behind harassment. This argument is most commonly reiterated in religious discourse and by conservative factions in society, which incorporate sexual harassment within a more general criticism of public and individual morality. For proponents of this argument, young men are agents within an immoral environment that not only makes sexually explicit content available and accessible, but also allows women to walk alone and dress inappropriately on the streets. This argument underlies a diverse range of attitudes toward sexual harassment that share, nonetheless, a fundamental appeal to normative gender role expectation as the solution to the problem. There again, attention shifts away from sexual harassment as an act of violence and a form of discrimination against women in public spaces toward reinstating an inequitable structure of patriarchy and protectionism (Schielke 2009, Ezzelarab 2014, New Woman Foundation 2016).

The third argument, advanced by activists and opposition groups, emphasizes the state's role in perpetuating sexual harassment. This argument includes positions that demand legal solutions and fiercer punitive measures to combat sexual harassment, as well as positions that stress the state's active role in perpetuating violence against women. While the former lend greater agency to state institutions and government representatives in combatting sexual harassment, the latter highlight the implications of state institutions in sexual violence. Proponents of the former approach include media personnel and civil society organizations that work in closer proximity with the state, including the state-funded National Council for Childhood and Motherhood. Feminist and some human rights organization have, on the other hand, pointed to the imbrication of sexual harassment in state politics. According to this latter approach, sexual harassment is one visible aspect of a structural condition wherein violence against women is not only condoned but also endorsed by state practices and regulations such as forced "virginity tests" and the use of sexual violence against protestors (Zaki and Abd Alhamid 2014).

Finally, street harassment of woman as a form of amusement is one of the most disconcerting attitudes underlying the prevalence of sexual harassment. Unlike other forms of sexual violence, street harassment is often associated with a socially accepted form of flirtation, wherein a woman's silence may be interpreted as concession to an advance. The harassment of women is, accordingly, regarded as a challenging form of flirtation, a way for men to test the extent to which a woman is open to the idea of an interaction, of sexual or romantic nature, with a man (Ilahi 2008, Ezzelarab 2014). In view of traditional norms and Islamic values on gender relations, judging a woman as willing to engage in any kind of relationship with a man she meets randomly in a public setting undermines her claim to sexual modesty. It is for this reason that girls have been traditionally taught not to respond in any way to men who subject them to *mu'akasat* (flirting) or *muḍāyaqāt* (harassment) on the streets. Any response by a woman may be interpreted as willingness to engage in an interaction. Even if a woman curses her harasser, for example, she will be judged as immodest for using a curse word, and hence susceptible to further harassment. Thus any response from a woman who is harassed draws attention to herself.

It will invite others to judge *her* comportment, what she did to incite her harassment. Then, factors ssuch as how she is walking, what she is wearing, with whom, where, and when will necessarily undermine her moral standing.

The 2011 Survey of Young People in Egypt showed, for example, that over 70% of young Egyptians aged 15–29 believe that women "deserve" to be harassed when they dress "provocatively." Notwithstanding evidence showing that women from all walks of life are harassed and that the majority of Egyptian women conform to one version or another of Islamic veiling, wearing tight and revealing clothes or makeup are two common items regarded as provocative (Population Council 2011, UN Women 2013).

Almost all men surveyed in the UN Women study attributed harassment to a woman's dress, beauty, or makeup. Thirty percent said that "the girl feels happy when harassed" and 15% claimed that girls had invited the harassment by showing interest in the harasser. Although the study showed that most men engage in forms of sexual harassment "to fulfill the sexual need," "out of habit," or as "the expression of manhood and confidence in one's self," there is no indication that men are reproached or claim some responsibility for the lack of safety women experience on the streets. The ensuing pattern of shaming women for failing to comply with the ideals of sexual modesty that men are excused from is one of the vital elements shaping public attitudes toward sexual harassment and defining women's responses to it.

Women's Responses to Sexual Harassment

The emergence and profusion of the hijab as an urban style adopted by college-educated and professional women in the late 1970s is considered one of the earliest ways through which women negotiated their growing participation in public life (ElGuindi 1981, Hoffmann-Ladd 1987). Until today, veiling and other conservative clothing styles represent one of the most essential ways through which women try to evade or limit their exposure to sexual harassment. Walking with a man or with a group of friends and using private cars, women-only transportation, or taxis are other ways through which women try to avoid sexual harassment. However, these practices not only reproduce the patriarchal underpinning justifying sexual harassment, but also offer impractical solutions to an everyday challenge for women from all walks of life.

Proponents of the social change argument also seek to address sexual harassment by appealing to male honor and chivalry. "Atardaha li Ukhtak?" ("Would you like this to happen to your sister?") is the slogan of a popular anti-harassment campaign from 2008 that ideally captured the emphasis on traditional values as a solution to sexual harassment. Men are asked to refrain from harassment not because it is a form of violence, an infringement on another person's civil rights, or a crime, but because these women are another man's sister. Instead of presenting sexual harassment as a behavior unacceptable by society, this rhetoric condones sexual harassment against women who the harassers would not liken to their sisters because of what they are wearing, what they are doing, or where they were walking when they were harassed. In fact, all studies have shown that men commonly agree that the streets are unsafe for their female kin, but that the majority of them nonetheless regard women at fault in incidents of harassment.

Women's responses to sexual harassment have shifted significantly since 2005, and sexual harassment is arguably among the most resonant and dynamic issue around which women in Egypt have mobilized in decades (Rizzo, Price, and Meyer 2008, Zaki and Abd Alhamid 2014, Tadros 2015a, Langohr 2016). Organized responses have varied over the course of the past ten years and have included litigation against institutions or individuals (Amar 2011, EIPR 2013), anti-sexual harassment awareness-raising activities (Rizzo, Price, and Meyer 2008), campaigns for legal reform or the institution of women-only public spaces (Changing Masculinities 2011, FIDH et al. 2013), training sessions and workshops for students and professionals (Langohr 2016), the documentation of incidents of sexual harassment, the publication of survivors' testimonies (El-Nadeem et al. 2013), and the formation of informal youth-led vigilante groups to protect women in protest areas (Tadros 2015a, Langohr 2016). These responses, largely initiated by organizations led by women, have broken the silence over sexual harassment in the public sphere, challenging widely held views that women should bear the shame of their harassment by remaining silent.

Although, still, relatively few women report sexual harassment to the police (UN Women 2013), outspoken survivors of public sexual violence have spoken in public about their experiences or published their testimonies, contesting the stigmatizing representation of victims of sexual harassment in the public sphere. The ECWR's 2008 study had revealed that the majority of women do nothing when subjected to sexual harassment (Shoukry and Hassan 2008). However, a UN Women study, conducted five years later, showed that 20% of victims did not remain silent, insulting their harassers. Although the majority of women, according to this study, claimed not to be affected to the extent that they would do anything about it, only about 15% mentioned their reputation as reason for their negative reaction (UN Women 2013).

Unfortunately, women's acts of resistance place them in more precarious zones of confrontation. Besides the fierce smearing campaigns that aim to tarnish the reputation of survivors who take their harassers to court and make a presence in the media, women are often brutally attacked if they fight their harassers (Ammar 2008, Kirollos 2013, Hafez 2014a, Abdelaziz 2015). In 2012, Eman Mustafa, twenty, was shot to death when she insulted the man who had groped her in a small village in Assiut; in 2013, Shoruk al-Turabi, was hit by her harasser's car in the city of Tanta (Ahmed and Malik 2012, Al-Mahdi 2013). To date, Eman and Shoruk are the only known victims who lost their lives fighting their harassers (Zaki and Abd Alhamid 2014).

Conclusions

Sexual harassment is one of the most endemic forms of sexual violence to which women are exposed in Egypt. Its emergence and profusion as an everyday experience for women living in urban areas is grounded in a combination of social, cultural, and political factors.

A culture of shaming victims of sexual violence, as well as the implication of security forces and state institutions in politically motivated sexual violence, has stifled large-scale societal responses against sexual harassment. Nonetheless, important strides have been made in shifting social attitudes toward sexual harassment from a form of flirtation to an act of violence against women at large. Throughout the 2000s, civil society organizations galvanized grassroots mobilization against sexual harassment. Increasing media coverage of incidents of mass sexual assaults during holidays and in protest areas compelled state institutions to respond to a growing public demand for a legal and official framework criminalizing sexual harassment.

Sexual harassment in Egypt is a complex social phenomenon rooted in the dynamic interplay between the political, social, and cultural structures underlying sexual violence in twenty-first century Egypt. Any effort to understand the mechanisms and structures behind its emergence and profusion needs to be grounded in a comprehensive understanding of the impact of patriarchal structures and violence in state governance and in the everyday regulation of social relations in Egypt.

Bibliography

Abdelaziz, Salma. Sexually harassed Egyptian woman wins via social media, in *CNN.com*, 20 October 2015, <http://www.cnn.com/2015/10/30/us/egypt-sexual -harassment-somaya-tarek-reham-saeed/>. 1 March 2016.

Abdelhadi, Magdi. Cairo street crowds target women, in *BBC News*, 1 November 2006, <http://news.bbc.co.uk/2/hi/middle_east/6106500.stm>. 1 March 2016.

Abdelhadi, Magdi. Egypt's sexual harassment "cancer," in *BBC News*, 18 July 2008, <http://news.bbc.co.uk/2/hi/middle_east/7514567.stm>. 1 March 2016.

Abdelmonem, Angie. Reconceptualizing sexual harassment in Egypt. A longitudinal assessment of El-Tahharush Al-Ginsy in Arabic online forums and anti-sexual harassment activism, in *Kohl: A Journal for Body and Gender Research* 1:1 (2015), 23–41.

Abdelmonem, Angie, Rahma Esther Bavelaar, Elisa Wynne-Hughes, and Susana Galan. The "Taharrush" connection. Xenophobia, islamophobia, and sexual violence in Germany and beyond, in *Jadaliyya*, 1 March 2016, <http://www.jadaliyya.com/pages/index/23967/the-taharrush-connection_xenophobia-islamophobia-a>. 1 March 2016.

Ahmed, Souad, and Mahmud Malik. إيمان ... دافعت عن شرفها وواجهت المتحرش بها فقتلها ببندقية آلية في أسيوط [Eman defended her honor and confronted her harasser who killed her with his automatic rifle in Assiut], in Al-Watan, 13 September 2012, <http://www.elwatannews.com/news/details/48479>. 1 March 2016.

Al-Mahdi, Basma. "اشفت تحرش تطالب الداخلية بنشر صور قاتل ضحية التحرش في الغربية" [I saw harassment" demands that the police release the picture of the murderer of harassment victim from Gharbiyya], in *Al-Masry Al-Youm*, 11 August 2013, <http://www.almasryalyoum.com/news/details/247575>. 1 March 2016.

Al-Sisi, Ayman. حينا تختلط الحقائق بالشائعات. التحرش الجنسي في وسط البلد [Sexual harassment in Downtown. Rumors and facts], in *Al-Ahram Newspaper*, 1 November 2006, <http://www.ahram.org.eg/Archive/2006/11/1/INVE1.HTM>. 1 March 2016.

Amar, Paul. Turning the gendered politics of the security state inside out? Charging the police with sexual harassment in Egypt, in *International Feminist Journal of Politics* 13:3 (2011), 299–328.

Amaria, Kainaz. The "girl in the the blue bra," in *NPR*, 21 December 2011, <http://www.npr.org/sections/pictureshow/2011/12/21/144098384/the-girl-in-the-blue-bra>. 1 March 2016.

Ammar, Manar. Noha Roushdy confirms Egyptian citizenship, in *Daily News Egypt*, 31 October 2008, <http://www.dailynewsegypt.com/2008/10/31/noha-roushdy-confirms-egyptian-citizenship>. 1 March 2016.

Barsoum, Ghada. The employment crisis of female graduates in Egypt. An ethnographic account, in *Cairo Papers in Social Science* 25:3 (2002).

BBC News. What is sexual harassment?, in *BBC News*, 16 August 2006, <http://news.bbc.co.uk/2/hi/africa/4791625.stm>. 1 March 2016.

BBC News. Egyptian sexual harasser jailed, in *BBC News*, 21 October 2008, <http://news.bbc.co.uk/2/hi/africa/7682951.stm>. 1 March 2016.

Begum, Rothna. How Egypt can turn the tide on sexual assault, in *Human Rights Watch*, 15 June 2014, <https://www.hrw.org/news/2014/06/15/how-egypt-can-turn-tide-sexual-assault>. 1 March 2016.

Carr, Sarah. Sexual assault and the state. A history of violence, in *Mada Masr*, 7 July 2014, <http://www.madamasr.com/sections/politics/sexual-assault-and-state-history-violence>. 1 March 2016.

Changing masculinities, changing communities, 2011. Cairo and Copenhagen: The Danish Egyptian Dialogue Institute and The Danish Center for Gender, Equality and Ethnicity, <http://nazra.org/sites/nazra/files/attachments/changing_masculinities_changing_communities.pdf>. 1 March 2016.

Diab, Mohamed. *678* (movie), Dollar Film, 2010.

Ebaid, Neama. Sexual harassment in Egypt. A neglected crime, MA thesis, American University in Cairo, Egypt 2013.

EIPR [Egyptian Initiative for Personal Rights]. Egypt held to account for failing to protect women demonstrators from sexual assault (press release), in *Egyptian Initiative for Personal Rights*, 14 March 2013, <http://eipr.org/en/pressrelease/2013/03/14/1657>. 1 March 2016.

ElGuindi, Fadwa. Veiling Infitah with Muslim ethic. Egypt's contemporary Islamic movement, in *Social Problems* 28:4 (1981), 465–85.

El-Messiri, Sawsan. *Ibn al-balad. A concept of Egyptian identity*, Leiden 1978.

El-Nadeem Center for Rehabilitation of Victims of Violence and Torture, Nazra for Feminist Studies, and New Woman Foundation. Sexual assault and rape in Tahrir Square and its vicinity. A compendium of sources, 2011–13 (joint report), Cairo 2013, <http://nazra.org/sites/nazra/files/attachments/compilation-_of_sexual-violence_-testimonies_between_20111_2013_en.pdf>. 1 March 2016.

Ezzelarab, Bahaa. The "legal woman." Sexual violence, the state and the law, in *Mada Masr*, 11 June 2014, <http://www.madamasr.com/opinion/"legal-woman"-sexual-violence-state-and-law>. 1 March 2016.

Fahmy, Amel, Angie Abdelmonem, Enas Hamdy, and Ahmed Badr. *Towards a safer city. Sexual harassment in Greater Cairo, effectiveness of crowdsourced data*, Cairo 2014.

Farag, Tarif Shawqi, and Adil Muhamad Haridi. 2004. "التحرش الجنسي بالمرأة العاملة: دراسة نفسية استكشافية علي عينة من العاملات المصريات" [The sexual harassment of working women: exploratory research on a sample of Egyptian women], Beni Souef, Egypt, <http://www.musanadah.com/images/taharesh.pdf>. 1 March 2016.

FIDH, Nazra for Feminist Studies, New Woman Foundation, and The Uprising of Women in the Arab World. Keeping women out. Sexual violence against women in the public sphere (joint report), Cairo, Egypt 2014, <https://www.fidh.org/IMG/pdf/egypt_women_final_english.pdf>. 1 March 2016.

Fleishman, Jeffrey. Egyptian army doctor acquitted of giving virginity tests to arrestees, in *Los Angeles Times*, 11 March 2012, <http://latimesblogs.latimes.com/world_now/2012/03/reporting-from-cairo-an-egyptian-military-tribunal-sunday-acquitted-an-army-doctor-of-giving-women-activists-virginity.html>. 1 March 2016.

Gad, Sawsan. We mold the collective memory of sexual assault, in *Egypt Independent*, 3 April 2012, <http://www.egyptindependent.com//opinion/we-mold-collective-memory-sexual-assault>. 1 March 2016.

Ghannam, Farha. Meanings and feelings: Local interpretations of the use of violence in the Egyptian revolution. In American Ethnologist 39: 1 (2012): 32–36.

Hafez, Sherine. a. Bodies that protest. The girl in the blue bra, sexuality and state violence in revolutionary Egypt, in *Signs* 40:1 (2014), 20–28.

Hafez, Sherine. b. The revolution shall not pass through women's bodies. Egypt, uprising and gender politics, in *Journal of North African Studies* 19:2 (2014), 172–85.

Harassmap. a. Laws against sexual harassment in Egypt, in *Harassmap.org*, n.d., <http://harassmap.org/en/resource-center/laws-against-sexual-harassment-in-egypt>. 1 March 2016.

Harassmap. b. What is sexual harassment?, in *Harassmap.org*, n.d., <http://harassmap.org/en/resource-center/what-is-sexual-harassment>. 1 March 2016.

Hassan, Rasha Mohammad, and Aliyaa Shoukry. *"Clouds in Egypt's sky." Sexual Harassment. From verbal harassment to rape. A sociological study*, Cairo 2008.

Hoffman-Ladd, Valerie J. 1987. Polemics on the modesty and segregation of women in contemporary Egypt, in *Journal of Middle East Studies* 19:1 (1987), 23–50.

Hoodfar, Homa. *Between marriage and the market. Intimate politics and survival in Cairo*, Berkeley, Calif. 1997.

Human Rights Watch. Egypt. Military "virginity test" investigation a sham, in *Human Rights Watch*, 9 November 2011, <https://www.hrw.org/news/2011/11/09/egypt-military-virginity-test-investigation-sham>. 1 March 2016.

Ilahi, Nadia. You gotta fight for your right(s). Street harassment and its relationship to gendered violence, civil society, and gendered negotiations, MA thesis, The American University in Cairo, Cairo 2008.

Ismail, Farag. الراقصة دينا تنفي مسؤليتها عن 'السعار الجنسي' بوسط القاهرة" [Dina denies responsibility over the sexual harassment in Downtown], in *Al-Arabiya*, 6 November 2006, <http://www.alarabiya.net/articles/2006/11/06/28863.html>. 1 March 2016.

Kandiyoti, Deniz. The fateful marriage. Political violence and violence against women, in *Opendemocracy.net*, 25 January 2016, <https://www.opendemocracy.net/5050/deniz-kandiyoti/fateful-marriage-political-violence-and-violence-against-women>. 1 March 2016.

Kingsley, Patrick. 80 sexual assaults in one day. The other story of Tahrir Square, in *The Guardian*, 5 July 2013, <http://www.theguardian.com/world/2013/jul/05/egypt-women-rape-sexual-assault-tahrir-square>. 1 March 2016.

Kirollos, Mariam. Sexual violence in Egypt. Myths and realities, in *Jadaliyya*, 16 July 2013, <http://www.jadaliyya.com/pages/index/13007/sexual-violence-in-egypt_myths-and-realities>. 1 March 2016.

Langohr, Vickie. New president, old patterns of sexual violence in Egypt, in *Middle East Research and Information Project*, 7 July 2014, <http://www.merip.org/mero/mero070714>. 1 March 2016.

Langohr, Vickie. Women's rights movements during political transitions. Activism against public sexual violence in Egypt, in *International Journal of Middle East Studies* 47 (2015), 131–35.

Langohr, Vickie. Why Egyptians have mobilized against public sexual violence, in *The Washington Post*, 6 April 2016, <https://www.washingtonpost.com/news/monkey-cage/wp/2016/04/06/why-egyptians-have-mobilized-against-public-sexual-violence>. 1 March 2016.

Leila, Reem. Unsafe Streets, in *Al-Ahram Weekly*, 9 October 2008, <http://weekly.ahram.org.eg/Archive/2008/917//eg6.htm>. 1 March 2016.

Mada Masr. Rights groups demand national strategy to fight sexual violence, in *Mada Masr*, 31 March 2014, <http://www.madamasr.com/news/rights-groups-demand-national-strategy-fight-sexual-violence>. 1 March 2016.

Mada Masr. Viewers outraged after TV anchor allegedly laughs at reports of sexual assault, in *Mada Masr*, 9 June 2014, <http://www.madamasr.com/news/viewers-outraged-after-tv-anchor-allegedly-laughs-reports-sexual-assault>. 1 March 2016.

Mada Masr. Trading blame over sexual assaults, in *Mada Masr*, 10 June 2014, <http://www.madamasr.com/news/trading-blame-over-sexual-assaults>. 1 March 2016.

Mostafa, Dalia A. *Roses in salty soil. Women and depression in Egypt today*, Cairo 2008.

Nazra for Feminist Studies. *"I'm coming back for you ... I want to kill you." One year of impunity. Violations against women human rights defenders in Egypt*, Cairo 2012.

Nazra for Feminist Studies. Testimonies on the recent sexual assaults on Tahrir Square vicinity, in *Nazra for Feminist Studies*, 13 June 2012, <http://nazra.org/en/2012/06/testimonies-recent-sexual-assaults-tahrir-square-vicinity>. 1 March 2016.

Nazra for Feminist Studies. Testimony from a survival of gang rape on Tahrir Square vicinity, in *Nazra for Feminist Studies*, 26 January 2013, <http://nazra.org/en/2013/01/testimony-survival-gang-rape-tahrir-square-vicinity>. 1 March 2016.

New Woman Foundation. مرصد الحقوق الاقتصادية والاجتماعية للنساء في العمل: التحرش الجنسي في أماكن العمل [Survey on women's economic and social rights. Sexual harassment in the workplace], 2016. <https://docs.google.com/document/d/1ldacwYqszhR6pDldAUW4gPf4AIM2vf7C1x00-6X7Ufk/edit>. 1 March 2016.

Peoples, Fatima Mareah. Street harassment in Cairo. A symptom of disintegrating social structures, in *The African Anthropologist* 15:1/2 (2008), 1–20.

Population Council. *Survey of young people in Egypt*, Cairo 2011.

Rizzo, Helen, Anne M. Price, and Katherine Meyer. *Targeting cultural change in repressive environments. The campaign against sexual harassment in Egypt*, Cairo 2008.

Roushdy, Noha. Three roads to patriarchy. Three roads to freedom, in *Mada Masr*, 11 August 2013, <http://www.madamasr.com/opinion/3-roads-patriarchy-—-3-roads-freedom>. 1 March 2016.

Sami, Ahmed. اعتداء على فتاة في وضح النهار في وسط القاهرة. جريمة العتبة الخضراء [Sexual harassment in broad daylight in Downtown Cairo. The crime of Al-'Ataba Al-Khaḍrā], in *Al Hayāt*, 13 April 1992, <http://daharchives.alhayat.com/issue_archive/Wasat%20magazine/1992/4/13/-اعتداء-على-فتاة-في-وضح-النهار-في-وسط-القاهرة-جريمة-العتبة-الخضراء-تهز-المجتمع-المصري.html>. 1 March 2016.

Schielke, Samuli. Ambivalent commitments. Troubles of morality, religiosity and aspiration among young Egyptians, in *Journal of Religion in Africa* 39:2 (2009), 158–85.

Sobhy, Hani. Education and the production of citizenship in the later Mubarak era. Privatization, discipline and the construction of the nation in Egyptian secondary schools, Ph.D. diss., University of London 2012.

Tadros, Mariz. Whose shame is it? The politics of sexual assault in Morsi's Egypt, 2013, Heinrich Boll Stiftung, <http://harassmap.org/en/wp-content/uploads/2015/07/Whose-Shame-Is-It.pdf>. 1 March 2016.

Tadros, Mariz. a. Contentious and prefigurative politics. Vigilante groups' struggle against sexual violence in Egypt (2011–13), in *Development and Change* 46:6 (2015), 1345–68.

Tadros, Mariz. b. Understanding politically motivated sexual assault in protest spaces. Evidence from Egypt (March 2011 to June 2013), in *Social and Legal Studies* 25:1 (2015), 1–18.

Thomson Reuters Foundation. POLL. Women's rights in the Arab world, in *Thomson Reuters Foundation*, 12 November 2013, <http://news.trust.org//spotlight/poll-womens-rights-in-the-arab-world>. 1 March 2016.

United Nations Secretariat. Prohibition of discrimination, harassment, including sexual harassment, and abuse of authority ST/SGB/2008/5, 2008, <http://www.un.org/womenwatch/osagi/fpsexualharassment.htm>. 1 March 2016.

UN Women. Study on ways and methods to eliminate sexual harassment in Egypt, UN Women.

US Equal Employment Opportunity Commission. Sexual harassment, n.d., <https://www.eeoc.gov/laws/types/sexual_harassment.cfm>. 1 March 2016.

Young, Chelsea. HarassMap. Using crowdsourced data to map sexual harassment in Egypt, in *Technology Innovation Management Review*, March 2014, 7–13.

Zaki, Hind Ahmed, and Dalia Abd Alhamid. a. استباحة النساء في المجال العام [Women as fair game in the public space. Part 1], in *Jadaliyya*, 8 January 2014, <http://www.jadaliyya.com/pages/index/15925/استباحة-النساء-في-المجال-العام-1>. 1 March 2016.

Zaki, Hind Ahmed, and Dalia Abd Alhamid. ٢ .b استباحة النساء في المجال العام [Women as fair game in the public space. Part 2], in *Jadaliyya*, 10 January 2014, <http://www.jadaliyya.com/pages/index/15944/2-العام-المجال-في-النساء-استباحة>. 11 March 2016.

الفيديوالكامل<القاهرة حقوق طالبة الجماعي بطالبة التحرش لحظة [*The Entire Video of Mass Sexual Harassment of the Law School Student*]. 2014, <https://www.youtube.com/watch?v=9OscMRLGbgc.>. 1 March 2016.

Sexualities

∵

Sexualities and Queer Studies

Samar Habib

Introduction

Muslim gender and sexual minorities have in the last decade displayed unprecedented visibility and political activism, through both self-representations and grassroots organizing in diasporic and local contexts. Consequently, a paradigmatic shift in the way queer genders and sexualities in Muslim contexts are studied is taking place in the academy.

In the last decade, we began to glimpse what is perhaps a uniquely new field of enquiry, that is, scholarship that emerges from the juncture of Islamic and queer/sexuality studies. The traditionally institutionalized field of Islamic Studies has not had an easy relationship with this emergent fusion and this new field is yet to be institutionalized in a process similar to the institutionalization of women's, gender and sexuality studies. Similarly, Queer Studies, in its current institutional configuration is also not unproblematically fusible with queer Islamic studies, or with queer Muslim scholarship, largely because sometimes, all that "queer" denotes in the latter is "gender and sexual minority persons," who for reasons of cultural specificity may not be suitably labeled "gay" or "lesbian." Often, in queer Islamic thought, there is not an outright rejection of the gender binary or even of normativity, nor is there an outright rejection of sexual identification or an essentialist view of sexuality and orientation, all of which tend to characterize queer discourse in Western contexts. This is necessitated by the fact that scholars who engage with Islam and gender and sexual diversity from a theological perspective cannot wholly circumvent the gender binary so evident in both scripture and living cultures of Islam. Additionally, the argument regarding the innateness of homosexuality and transgenderism is central to the theological rebuttals of prohibition (Bin Jahangir 2010, Kugle 2010), which traditionally relies on constructing homosexuality not as an orientation/identity but a chosen behavior (Abdul-Latif and Bin Jahangir 2012, Bin Jahangir 2010, Kelly 2010b, Zollner 2010). Nonetheless, Queer Islamic Studies has certainly earned its "queer" stripes, in that it builds on a collage of socio-cultural studies that highlight a gender and sexual continuum which is anything but privileging of gender and (hetero)sexual normativity, and one which spans 1,400 years of Muslim cultures across vast geographic and temporal expanses.

© KONINKLIJKE BRILL NV, LEIDEN, 2014 | DOI:10.1163/1872-5309_EWIC_COM_00019

Until recently, most scholars writing on the subject of Muslim sexualities were from Western and secular backgrounds. A perusal of Frédéric Lagrange's list of secondary references on this topic in this encyclopedia is a case in point (Lagrange 2003). Of course that is not to say that this scholarship holds any more or less value or analytical accuracy than writings carried out by (believing) Muslim gender and/or sexual minority scholars themselves. However, Islamic feminism of the late twentieth and early twenty-first century impacted the fields of gender and sexuality studies relevant to Islamic cultures, fostering queer Muslim scholarship. This is discussed in greater detail later. Another factor that has contributed to the rise of a queer Islamic studies framework can be seen in the rising visibility of queer Muslim counter cultures, both in diaspora and in homelands. There is an awakening across borders of a Muslim queer identity, and this has led to the activation of the "inclusive mosque" and the queer Muslim activist, vis-à-vis scholar. These two notable developments have led to a shift in research emphasis, methodologies, approaches and outcomes and will also be discussed in greater detail later.

The last decade's most remarkable outcome of the intersection of sexuality, queer and Islamic studies can be found in the emergent scholarly works engaging with Islamic theologies and the permissibility of gender and sexual diversity therein. While discussions of the permissibility of same-sex relations from a theological perspective in Abbasid and Andalusian texts were in circulation (Habib 2007), a revival and queering of such approaches was first revisited by Camilla Adang (2003) in her case-study on Ibn Hazm, and by Scott Kugle in his chapters in Omid Safi's collections *Progressive Muslims* (2003) and *Voices of Islam* (2007). Additional contributions in this area include several chapters in the two-volume edited collection *Islam and Homosexuality* (Habib 2010, Zollner 2010, Zanghellini 2010, Bin Jahangir 2010, Kelly 2010b, Musić 2010), and Scott Kugle's book-length theological treatise *Homosexuality in Islam* (2010). Muhsin Hendricks also contributed a seminal article on queer acceptance in Islam (2010), while Vanja Hamzić produced an article on Human Rights Law and "Islamic legal and social ethos" (2011). Mohamad Zahed published the book *Le Coran et la Chair* in 2012.

What is noteworthy is how authors from various disciplines, deploying a variety of methodologies and relying on differing textual evidences, often converged on the same result: this being that same-sex attractions and gender diversity can find a legitimate place in Islamic theological considerations. These conclusions, undertaken by secular scholars, as well as scholars of faith, commonly reject the unauthenticated (or severed) *ḥadīths* that are seen to prohibit homosexual relations. They also de-program the belief that the story of Lūt in the Qur'ān is a story about "homosexuals" or worse yet, a story about *all* homosexuals (Habib 2008). From this common ground, scholars who have written on this subject diverge in interests. Scholars of faith, who engage theology from a non-secular perspective proceed to highlight Qur'ānic verses describing and upholding diversity, and verses which refer to union between people in gender neutral terms (such as the word *zawj*, which means "pair"). Others emphasize the values of love and ethical conduct praised in the Qur'ān, or refer to the historical coexistence of the Prophet with gender non-normative "men"—*mukhannathūn*.

It should be noted, however, that two of the three *madhāhib* (schools of thought) which may be open to such suggestions are extinct in contemporary institutional Islam; these being, the Mu'tazila school of thought of the early Abbasid period and the Ẓahirī perspective (deployed by the Andalusian Ibn Ḥazm). Meanwhile, the Ḥanafī perspective, deployed by Scott Kugle, is popular in regions of Turkey and Southeast Asia as well as some parts of the Arabic-speaking world, but is not particularly influential elsewhere. Needless to say that Sufi Islam, which is often considered heretical and un-Islamic among mainstream Muslims, also has a propensity toward toleration of sensory pleasure and diverse manifestations of love, provided that these act as avenues toward communion with the divine, which is the ultimate Beloved.

Meanwhile, secular scholars who engage scripture from analytical perspectives rooted in historical contextualization and lexicography, further rely on historical studies of gender and sexually diverse communities across Muslim cultures and civilizations to demonstrate that there has been no homogeneously prohibitive dealing with gender and sexual variance. These studies often cite cultural scholarship on gender and sexuality in Muslim contexts, such as those undertaken by Murray and Roscoe (1997), El-Rouayheb (2005), Wright and Rowson (1997), to name but a few.

What has eased the development of this set of reformative ideas has been the emergence of what is now termed Islamic Feminist scholarship of the late twentieth and early twenty-first centuries. Although Islamic Feminist scholars can disagree considerably about the extent to which scriptures can be exonerated of patriarchy, the essence of the methodologies deployed in re-reading Islamic scripture paved the way for queering them in terms that are consistent with the internal logics of the faith. Essentially, in the works of Amina Wadud, Miriam Cooke, Leila Ahmad, Fatma Mernissi/Fatna Sabbah, Hiadeh Moghissi and Asma Barlas, the patriarchal and hegemonic tradition of interpretation is reconstructed in post-structural approaches to language, text and hermeneutics and in interrogating the historical constructions of prohibitory law and what makes a *real* Muslim. Amina Wadud (1999), for example, emphasizes that meaning is created at the juncture of text and reader and thus frees the Qur'ān from its millennium-old exegesis/*tafsīr*, placing it in dynamic relationship with a lived and living reading and interpreting experience. Wadud departs from the literalist methodology of traditional exegesis and considers themes and the "spirit" of the text as a whole. Meanwhile, Leila Ahmed (1993) interrogates the authority of *ḥadīth* and Qur'ānic exegesis long-used to justify restricting women to certain (domestic) functions in society, while also revisiting what she uncovers as the revolutionary character and actions of the Prophet, by situating these in their historical milieu.

Consequently, the tension between "queer" and "feminist" methodologies that can be glimpsed elsewhere in the academy seem to be largely absent here. This is perhaps because both queer and Islamic feminist approaches in the context of Islamic studies share a need to destabilize gender and sexual normativity without necessarily rejecting the gender binary altogether, at least so far. So much has remained unexplored with respect to the migration of conceptual tools from Islamic Feminist to Queer and Sexuality Studies. We do not yet know what a post-feminist, queer Islamic subjectivity looks like, or whether it is even possible, although Sufi philosophies of the dissolution of self and other reasonably carry such a fruitful possibility.

Why is There a Need for Queer Islamic Studies?

There is a need to reconceptualize the field of studying gender and sexual non-normativity in Muslim cultures given the proliferation of queer Muslim counter cultures and theologically-based enquiries in the last decade. There is also a need to broaden the scope of what is now known as Islamic Studies, necessitated by the emergence of a non-secular queer Muslim scholarship, though there is no immediately foreseeable way toward achieving this. On the one hand, traditional Islamic Studies suffers terribly from the burden of sometimes disguised, sometimes outright, homophobia. On the other, the cultural cringe in the West against Islam, and the endemic Islamophobic sweep should not be underestimated in the role they play in maintaining a dividing wall between what is called Islamic Studies and the liberal traditions of Women's, Gender, Sexuality, and/or Queer Studies (Habib 2013). However, this dividing wall is an imaginary line which has been repeatedly resisted, thwarted and subverted only because there is a growing momentum, on an international scale and in multiple local contexts, of subversive Muslim counter cultures and scholarships (for example, Farajajé 2012).

Queer Counter Cultures

These counter cultures can be observed through a number of outputs. Writings on Islam and gender and sexual minorities have increased considerably in the last decade, espousing not simply scholarly works, but activist paraphernalia, novels, television series and feature and documentary films. Nonetheless, there remains a disparity between the explosion of queer Muslim counter cultural outputs and scholarly documentation and analysis of these.

Gender and sexual non-normativity in Islamic cultures and theological apologetics is noted in classical works in ninth-century Abbasid Baghdad and eleventh-century Andalusia. But what is indeed a modern phenomenon, which is yet to be the subject of substantial scholarly treatment, is the emergence of designated worship spaces for queer Muslims. Several queer-inclusive mosques have been established throughout the world, the first of which appeared in Toronto, Canada, under the directorship of the Muslim LGBT organization, Salaam, founded by El-Farouk Khaki. This was followed by the Inner Circle, another queer-inclusive mosque and organization in South Africa, founded and headed by the openly gay Imam Muhsin Hendricks. In the United States, al-Fatiha, founded by Faisal Alam, organizes annual retreats for LGBT Muslims, while a queer-inclusive mosque was inaugurated in Washington, D.C. in 2011 and is headed by the openly gay Imam Daayiee Abdullah. In France, Homosexuels Musulmans oversees the publication of relevant literature on Islam and gender and sexual diversity, whilst also organizing an annual conference through a sister organization, CALEM, which gathers queer-friendly Muslim scholars and public figures annually. The founder of Homosexuels Musulmans, Ludovic Lotfi Mohamad Zahed, opened a queer-inclusive mosque in France in 2012. In England, the Muslim LGBT organizations, Iman and Yousef Foundation, provide a context of community formation and activism, while Sydney's famous Mardi Gras (Pride Parade) in Australia, witnessed its first of a kind "Muslims Against Homophobia" float (and group-formation) in 2011. To date, there has not been an intensive, book-length study of these various interlocked movements emerging in Muslims diasporic contexts.

Queering Muslim Marriage

The founder of Homosexuels Musulmans, Ludovic Lotfi Mohamad Zahed, has been the subject of vitriol and adulation alike, following his publicized same-sex *nikāh* (marriage) in 2012. It would be erroneous to presume that same-sex *nikāh* is a modern concept or phenomenon. Sufi *zawāyā* in Morocco and Tunisia have facilitated such marriages for at least two centuries. Police prosecution and persecution occurred for the first time in Morocco in 2008, when 46 pilgrims to the annual Darih Sidi Ali Bin Hamdoush festival, suspected of seeking same-sex marriage ceremonies, were ambushed and arrested (Bergeaud-Blackler and Eck 2011). Meanwhile, it has been suggested that same-sex *nikāḥ* also took place at the turn of the twentieth century at the Egyptian oasis of Siwa, although scholarship on the historicity of same-sex *nikāḥ* in Islam is, unfortunately, virtually non-existent. There is fertile ground for studies yet to be conducted on the existence of these sites of subversion of heteronormativity in Muslim societies, which require tools and methods of analysis that combine Islamic and sociological Queer studies. Naturally, such studies will invariably be locked into the sometimes irresolvable tension between essentialist and constructivist considerations of sexuality. On the one hand "queer" Muslims can be seen as part and parcel of a trend in globalization that has fixed in identity what have otherwise been fluid sexual acts in earlier centuries. On the other hand, it is perfectly viable to see contemporary queer Muslims as part of a historical continuum where it is not their prior existence which can be doubted, but rather the reliability of reports written *about* the subjects, rather than *by* them. Considerable theoretical tension surrounding the issue of whether same-sex *nikāḥ* or religious gender and sexual minority persons can be transgressive, or whether they simply reenact normativity in ways which cannot be really *queer*, is likely to emerge.

Measuring Counter Cultural Outputs

More scholarship that takes up this question is needed to investigate and analyze the literary and filmic outputs of the emergent queer Muslim counter cultures. In 2007, the first feature-length documentary on Islam and homosexuality was released to international audiences. Parvez Sharma's *A Jihad for Love* has now been seen by over 8 million people worldwide and in as many as 23 countries. While *A Jihad For Love* may have been seen by a large international audience, other, lesser known, documentaries relevant to Muslim gender and sexual minority persons include *Gay Muslims*, a UK Channel 4 2006 production; *Transsexual in Iran*, a BBC2 production released in 2008, and *Out in Iran* produced by CBC in 2007 (Beirne and Habib 2012).

The Lebanese film *Caramel* (2008), by Nadine Labaki, depicts a lesbian character and is a film moved by strong feminist themes. Religion does not feature centrally in this film, though its impact on social formations are clear to those familiar with Lebanese society. Rola Selbak's film from the United States, *Three*

SEXUALITIES AND QUEER STUDIES   441

Veils (2011), depicts a devout Muslim-American migrant struggling with her lesbian sexuality. The film's depiction of this character could very well have been a reflection on a number of Muslim lesbian narratives found in recent ethnographic studies (discussed later). The Egyptian television series *A Woman's Cry* (2007) sympathetically portrays, and is centered on, a male-to-female transgender heroine. This series was shown around the world on satellite television and it was entirely sympathetic to the character who undergoes a gender transition in a society still ill-equipped to deal with gender variance. Meanwhile the Lebanese drag queen, Bassem Feghali, reached international fame with a series of televised female impersonations, beginning on LBC Lebanese television, culminating in a television special for Ramadan and a series of theatrical appearances in Beirut's Monroe Hotel. None of these texts has received critical or scholarly attention despite the groundbreaking representations that they undertake. These motion pictures (and Feghali's theatrical presence) emerge after a significant hiatus in Arab cinema and show business in the treatment of the subject of same-sex relations and transgenderism (Habib 2007, Meniccuci 1998), providing further evidence of a paradigmatic shift that installs a queer Muslim subjectivity at the center of culture and scholarship.

In the literary world, recent novels and autobiographical writings have also emerged. Hanan al-Shaykh's novel *Misk al-Ghazāl* (1988) attracted considerable attention in the Western academy for its depiction of a transient lesbian relationship in an unnamed Gulf country. However, many of this novel's successors from the region have yet to garner similar attention and it has now become a rather outdated depiction of same-sex relations between women in Arabic literature. By contrast, Thānī al-Suwaydī's poetic novella, *Al-dīzil* (Diesel), was published in 1994 and is a first person narrative voice of a gender and sexually non-normative protagonist; it received virtually no critical attention (Habib 2007). Equally, Nawāl Sa'dāwī's *Jannāt wa-Iblīs* (Jannāt and the Devil, 2000), which also depicts a lesbian protagonist, has yet to receive due critical attention. *'Imārat Ya'qūbiyān* (2002) by 'Alā' Aswānī (made into an eponymous film, *The Yacoubian Building* in 2006) provides a representation of the demise of a homosexual man in Egypt as one of many character threads. *Al-Ākharūn* (2006), by Saudi writer Ṣabā al-Ḥirz, provides a lengthy engagement with a lesbian protagonist. *Rā'iḥa al-qirfa* (2007), by Samar Yizbak, from Syria, depicts a same-sex relationship between a domestic worker and her employer. *Banāt al-Riyāḍ* (2005), by Rajā' al-Sānī', depicts queer Saudi characters in passing but provides interesting insights into cultural and social homophobia of both the protagonist and the society in which she lives. Notably, each of the last four novels mentioned have appeared in English translation, producing a discursive impact well beyond the Arab world.

Abdella Taia's *Une Mélancolie Arabe* first appeared in French in 2008 and again in English translation in 2012. A novelized autobiography, Taia sets a stage for trauma and traumatization of a gender and sexual minority protagonist traversing the geographies of Morocco, France and Egypt. *Amīrāt Mansiyāt/ Forgotten Princesses* (2011) by Jamal Mutayyim and Samar Habib's *Rughum and Najda* (2012) are ficto-historical narratives set in the Umayyad and Abbasid dynasties respectively and clearly depict gender and sexual minority characters and themes. While mostly explicitly, sometimes implicitly, Islam plays a role in framing all of these narratives, often as a religion and a set of scriptures, but sometimes simply as a culture and community. Hanadi al-Samman's 2008 article, "Out of the Closet: Representation of Homosexuals and Lesbians in Modern Arabic Literature," fills a necessary gap in scholarship on contemporary Arabic novels dealing with gender and sexual transgression in Muslim contexts, but clearly so much more is needed.

Beyond the Gulf region, a new genre of autobiographical Arab queer writing has emerged, and this has largely been the work of grassroots NGOs, which did not exist in the last century. The latest of these is the autobiography of Hazim Saghia: *Memoirs of Randa the Trans* (2010). Three other autobiographical and literary book collections written by anonymous lesbian and/or transgender contributors of the Middle East and North Africa include *Ḥaqqī ʿan ʿAysh, ʿan Akhtar, an Akūn* (2007) and *Waqfa Banāt* (2010), both published anonymously in Haifa by the Palestinian Gay Women's organization, Aṣwāt. Meanwhile, the Lebanese organization, Meem, released *Barīd Mustʿajil* (2010). The strength of these autobiographical reflections on gender and sexuality is that they collect writings by Arab gender and sexual minorities from throughout the Arabic-speaking, Muslim-majority world. Other relevant literature in the vein of self-narrating Muslim and queer subjects include contributions in the edited collection *Islam and Homosexuality* by Badruddin Khan, Rusmir Musić and Omer Shah. Books published in a similar vein also include authors such as Badruddin Khan (1997), Rahal Eks (2008; 2012) and Afdhere Jama's collection of narratives, *Illegal Citizens* (2008). When, occasionally, Islam is not central in some of these autobiographical texts, it sometimes continues to feature in self-reflections and contemplations of queer "Muslims," be they believers or renunciates. When Islam does not prefigure as a religion, it manifests as a cultural identity and especially as a racial marker of otherness, when the subjects find themselves in (often Islamophobic) Western contexts. Activist organizations are also responsible for the proliferation of countless websites and blogs dedicated to queer issues in Islam and these, together with local grassroots organizations that are sprouting in clandestine ways in Muslim-majority countries, also require extensive scholarly documentation and analysis.

SEXUALITIES AND QUEER STUDIES

Further to the queer historical and literary studies of Islamic cultures of the past, the surge in contemporary counter cultural outputs, the establishment of visible queer Muslim communities, and the emergence of a queer Islamic exegesis in scholarship, there has been a rise in sociological and ethnographic enquiry into queer Muslim identities. The most quantitative of these may be Rudolf Pell Gaudio's *Allah Made Us* (2009), which provides an extensive ethnographic account of the lives of "sexual outlaws" in Northern Nigeria. The article by Tariq Bereket and Barry D. Adam (2008) asked 20 same-sex attracted Turkish men: "What joys and difficulties have you experienced regarding your sexual orientation in relation to Islam?" Meanwhile, the collection *Islam and Homosexuality* (Habib 2010) includes four chapters investigating questions of identity formation among transgender and/or same-sex attracted Muslims in diasporic contexts (Kelly, Khan, Al-Sayyad and Abraham). The same collection also includes three chapters looking at identity formation among same-sex attracted and/or transgender Muslims in Muslim-majority contexts (Luongo, Kramer, Maulod and Jamil). While all these studies cannot be justly or properly reviewed in this forum, what is noteworthy is the common recurrence of faith in Islam and/or retention of Muslim cultural heritage/identity among a disproportionate number of interviewees, a finding which can be at first surprising. Nevertheless, instances where "participation in the gay scene" results in a loss of religious convictions are also present in these studies (Bereket and Adam 2008, Kelly 2010a). Equally, the rejection of the gay scene, or the gay scene's rejection of religious individuals, tends to result in the problematization of gay or queer identification for non-heterosexual and/or gender nonconforming study participants (Abraham 2010). Overall, however, these studies reveal a broad spectrum of configurations of identities which are irreducible to binaries or generalization. Just as we come to expect multitudes in terms of gender and sexual expressions, so do we find multitudinous formulations of identity around Islam and queerness. For example, we also find study participants who live no contradiction between a deeply held faith and queer selves (Abu-Hatoum 2007, Musić 2010, Maulod and Jamil 2010, Lindström 2009).

Four social science dissertations on this subject are also worth noting. The first of these was completed by Nadine Naber in 2002 and has since been revised and published as a monograph in 2012. This work discusses numerous facets of "Arab San Francisco," including a significant investigation of the many slippages between "straight Arab" and "Americanized queer" that queer Arab community members of the San Francisco Bay Area unveil. Tellingly, these exhaustive and exhausting negotiations between familial obligation and personal self-assertion are also reflected throughout the more recent sociological/anthropological literature on this subject, in both diasporic and homeland contexts. Nayrouz Abu Hatoum's Masters thesis, completed in 2007, also looks at the liminality, what she calls "the borderzone," which queer Muslim self-narratives of this century seem to be communicating. Abu Hatoum's subjects were predominantly members of a close-knit queer Muslim community in Toronto, facilitated by the group Salaam. Meanwhile, Christina Lindström's "Narratives of Lesbian Existence in Egypt" (2009) concludes that same-sex attracted women in Egypt identify with a category of sexual orientation and simultaneously retain religious identification (four of her five participants were Muslim, one was of the Christian faith). Ghaida Moussa's Masters thesis, completed in 2011, looks at the intersection of race and sexuality among "queer Palestinian womyn." In Moussa's work, as well as the work of scholars engaging in diasporic and colonial contexts, Islam often (but not always) functions less as a religion than it does as a "racial" marker of otherness, as the study participants emphasize and interrogate Islamophobia in Western discourse and its impact on them.

Conclusion

Despite first impressions, gender and sexual minority counter cultures in Muslim majority contexts are by no means a result of postmodernity. The studies listed in Frederic Lagrange's secondary references all provided a range of treatments of gender and sexual diversity in pre-modern or early modern Islamic contexts. Specifically in relation to women and transgender persons, the scholarship of Afsaneh Najmabadi (2005), Saher Amer (2008), Fedwa Malti-Douglas (2001) and Habib (2009) have uncovered an extensive range of early or pre-modern texts written by scholars of Muslim civilizations across a range of historical localities and contexts. Therefore, the study of queer counter cultures is not new to the academy, nor are "queer Muslims" new to the world (contestations over the nomenclature notwithstanding).

However, the contemporary explosion and increased visibility of and interconnectivity between queer Muslim counter cultures globally necessitate a methodological shift in the academy to engender a new field of enquiry that is born of the union between Islamic and Queer/Gender/Women's/Sexuality studies. Islamic Feminist discourse, emerging in recent decades, has lent a credible theoretical framework of deconstructing patriarchy and traditional exegesis, which has facilitated the emergence of non-secular theological engagement with the permissibility and prohibition of gender and sexual diversity in Islam.

SEXUALITIES AND QUEER STUDIES

Queer Islamic Studies no doubt generates moral panics, whether from the homo/transphobia of traditional scholastic institutions of the study of Islam, or from the Islamophobia of managerial systems instituting otherwise liberal queer/gender/women's/sexuality research centers. Additionally, the term "queer" as it functions in Islamic Studies is not entirely commensurable with notions of the post-feminist, post-gender-queer we come to know in queer theoretical analysis of Western societies and subjects. Nevertheless, Queer Islamic Studies distinguishes itself from previous approaches to the study of gender and sexuality in Muslim contexts in that it is theologically engaged and coexistent with, perhaps even emergent from, living queer Muslim realities. These realities are now becoming evident throughout the scholarly field, which is attending to their examination in a variety of ways, whether through exegetical and theological enquiry, sociological and anthropological narratives of queer Muslim subjects, cultural studies of filmic and literary texts, or the ongoing probing of early or pre-modern Islamic world. Nonetheless, there is much work left to be done with respect to bringing scholarship up to date on counter cultural outputs, in what are truly invigorated and lively times for Islam, Muslims and the question of queer.

Bibliography

Abdul-Latif, Hussein and Junaid Bin Jahangir. Queering Muslim jurisprudence, Edmonton, Canada, unpublished.

Abraham, Ibrahim. "Everywhere you turn you have to jump into another closet." Hegemony, hybridity, and queer Australian Muslims, in *Islam and Homosexuality*, ed. Samar Habib, 2 vols., Oxford, Denver and Santa Barbara, Calif. 2010, 395–418.

Abu-Hatoum, Nayrouz. On the borderzone. Toronto's diasporic queer Muslims, M.A. thesis, York University 2007.

Adang, Camilla. Ibn Hazm on homosexuality. A case-study of Zahiri legal methodology, in *Al-Qantara* 24 (2003), 5–31.

Ahmad, Leila. *Women and gender in Islam. Historical roots of a modern debate*, New Haven, Conn. 1992.

Al-Sayyad, Ayisha A. "You're what?" Engaging narratives from diasporic Muslim women on identity and gay liberation, in *Islam and Homosexuality*, ed. Samar Habib, 2 vols., Oxford, Denver and Santa Barbara, Calif. 2010, 373–94.

Amer, Sahar. Cross-dressing and medieval same-sex marriage in medieval French and Arabic literatures, in *Islamicate sexualities. Translations across temporal geographies of desire*, ed. Kathryn Babayan and Afsaneh Najmabadi, Cambridge, Mass. 2008, 72–113.

Amer, Sahar. Medieval Arab lesbians and lesbian-like women, in *Journal of the History of Sexuality* 18:2 (2008), 213–36.

Amer, Sahar. *Crossing borders. Love between women in medieval French and Arabic literature*, Philadelphia 2008.

Anon. *Ḥaqqī ʿan ʿaysh, ʿan akhtar, an akūn* [My right to live, to choose, to be], Haifa 2007.

Anon. *Waqfa banāt* [Girls take a stand], Haifa 2010.

Anon. *Barīd mustʿajil. True stories* [Express post. True stories], Beirut 2010.

Aswānī, ʿAlāʾ. *ʿImārat Yaʿqūbiyān. Riwāya*, Cairo 2002; *The Yacoubian building. A novel*, trans. Humphrey Davies, Cairo and New York 2004.

Beirne, Rebecca and Samar Habib. Trauma and triumph. Documenting Middle Eastern gender and sexual minorities in film and television, in *LGBT transnational identities and the media*, ed. Chris Pullen, New York 2012, 41–58.

Bereket, Tarik and Barry D. Adam. Navigating Islam and same-sex liaisons among men in Turkey, in *Journal of Homosexuality* 55:2 (2008), 204–22.

Bergeaud-Blackler, Florence and Victor Eck. Les "faux" mariages homosexuels de Sidi Ali au Maroc. Enjeux d'un scandale médiatique, in *Revue des Mondes Musulmans et de la Méditerranée* 129 (2011), 203–21.

Bin Jahangir, Junaid. Implied cases for Muslim same-sex unions, in *Islam and Homosexuality*, ed. Samar Habib, 2 vols., Oxford, Denver and Santa Barbara, Calif. 2010, 297–326.

Eks, Rahal. *Khalil and Majnun*, West Hollywood, Calif. 2008.

Eks, Rahal. *Hussein and the nomad*, West Hollywood, Calif. 2012.

El-Rouayheb, Khaled. *Before homosexuality in the Arab-Islamic world, 1500–1800*, Chicago 2005.

Farajajé, Ibrahim Abdurrahman. In honour of the leadership of US-born African-American/African-Caribbean/African-Latin@ Muslim women in responding to HIV/AIDS, in *The Feminist Wire*, <http://thefeministwire.com/2012/08/in-honour-of-the-leadership-of-us-born-african-americanafrican-caribbeanafrican-latin-muslim-women-in-responding-to-hivaids/>, accessed 4 August 2012.

Gaudio, Rudolf Pell. *Allah made us. Sexual outlaws in an Islamic African city*, West Sussex, 2009.

Habib, Samar. *Female homosexuality in the Middle East. Histories and representations*, New York 2007.

Habib, Samar. Queer-friendly Islamic hermeneutics, in *Institute for the Study of Islam in the Modern World Review* 21 (2008), 32–33.

Habib, Samar. *Arabo-Islamic texts on female homosexuality*, Youngstown, N.Y. 2009.

Habib, Samar. Introduction. Islam and homosexuality, in *Islam and Homosexuality*, ed. Samar Habib, 2 vols., Oxford, Denver and Santa Barbara, Calif. 2010, xvii–lxii.

Habib, Samar. *Rughum and Najda*, West Hollywood, Calif. 2012.

Habib, Samar. Life, death and rebirth. The challenge of teaching female homosexuality and Islam in western Sydney and San Francisco, in *Kültür ve Siyasette Feminist Yaklaşımlar* [Feminist approaches to culture and politics] 19 (2013), n.p.

Hamzić, Vanja. The case of queer Muslims. Sexual orientation and gender identity in international human rights law and Muslim legal and social ethos, in *Human Rights Law Review* 11:2 (2011), 237–74.

Hendricks, Muhsin. Islamic texts. A source for acceptance of queer individuals into mainstream Muslim society, in *Equal Rights Review* 5 (2010), 31–51.

al-Ḥirz, Ṣabā. *al-Ākharūn* [The others], Beirut 2006; trans. Seba al-Herz, *The others*, New York 2009.

Jama, Afdhere. *Illegal citizens. Queer lives in the Muslim world*. West Hollywood, CA, 2008.

Jamal, Mutayyim. *Amīrāt mansiyāt. ʿĀʾisha bint Ṭalḥa wa-Sukayna bint al-Ḥusayn* [Forgotten princesses. Āʾisha bint Ṭalḥa wa-Sukayna bint al-Ḥusayn], Damascus 2011.

Kelly, Christopher Grant. The social construction of religious realities by queer Muslims, in *Islam and Homosexuality*, ed. Samar Habib, 2 vols., Oxford, Denver and Santa Barbara, Calif. 2010a, 223–46.

Kelly, Christopher Grant. Is there a "gay-friendly" Islam? Synthesizing tradition and modernity in the question of homosexuality in Islam, in *Islam and Homosexuality*, ed. Samar Habib, 2 vols., Oxford, Denver and Santa Barbara Calif. 2010b, 247–67.

Khan, Badruddin. *Sex, longing and not belonging. A gay Muslim's quest for love and meaning*, Oakland, Calif. 1997.

Khan, Badruddin. Longing, not belonging, and living in fear, in *Islam and Homosexuality*, ed. Samar Habib, 2 vols., Oxford, Denver and Santa Barbara, Calif. 2010, 23–36.

Khan, Mahruq Fatima. Queer, American, and Muslim. Cultivating identities and communities of affirmation, in *Islam and Homosexuality*, ed. Samar Habib, 2 vols., Oxford, Denver and Santa Barbara, Calif. 2010, 347–72.

Kramer, Max. Sexual orientation. The ideological underpinnings of the gay advance in Muslim-majority societies as witnessed in online chat rooms, in *Islam and Homosexuality*, ed. Samar Habib, 2 vols., Oxford, Denver and Santa Barbara, Calif. 2010, 133–62.

Kugle, Scott. Sexuality, diversity and ethics in the agenda of progressive Muslims, in *Progressive Muslims. On justice, gender and pluralism*, ed. Omid Safi, Oxford, 2003, 190–234.

Kugle, Scott. Sexual diversity in Islam, in *Voices of change*, vol. 5, *Voices of Islam*, ed. Vincent J. Cornell and Omid Safi, Westport, Conn. 2007, 131–68.

Kugle, Scott. *Homosexuality in Islam*, Oxford 2010.

Labaki, Nadine (dir.). *Sukar banat/Caramel*, DVD, Les films des tournelles et al. 2008.

Labīb, Rāʾid (dir). *Ṣarkha unthā/A woman's cry*, 26 episodes, Nāhid Farīd Shawqī 2007.

Lagrange, Frédéric. Sexualities and queer studies, in *Encyclopedia of women and Islamic cultures*, gen. ed. Suad Joseph, vol. 1, *Methodologies, paradigms and sources*, Leiden 2003, 419–22.

Lindström, Christina. Narratives of lesbian existence in Egypt. Coming to terms with identities, BA thesis, Stockholm University 2009.

Luongo, Michael. Gays under occupation. Interviews with gay Iraqis, in *Islam and Homosexuality*, ed. Samar Habib, 2 vols., Oxford, Denver and Santa Barbara, Calif. 2010, 99–110.

Malti Douglas, Fedwa. Tribadism/lesbianism and the sexualized body in medieval Arabo-Islamic narrative, in *Same sex love and desire among women in the Middle Ages*, ed. Francesca Canadé Sautman and Pamela Sheingorn, New York 2001, 123–41.

Malti Douglas, Fedwa. Homosociality, heterosexuality and Shaharazad, in *The Arabian nights encyclopaedia*, ed. Ulrich Marzolph and Richard Van Leeuwen, Santa Barbara, Calif. 2003, 38–41.

Maulod, Nur'Adlina and Nurhaizatul Jamila Jamil. "Because Allah says so." Faithful bodies, female masculinities, and the Malay Muslim community of Singapore, in *Islam and Homosexuality*, ed. Samar Habib, 2 vols., Oxford, Denver and Santa Barbara, Calif. 2010, 163–92.

Menicucci, Garay. Unlocking the Arab celluloid closet. Homosexuality in Egyptian film, in *Middle East Report* 206 (1998), 32–36, <http://www.merip.org/mer/mer206/egyfilm.htm>, accessed 30 March 2003.

Moussa, Ghaida. Narrative (sub)versions. How queer Palestinian womyn "queer" Palestinian identity, M.A. thesis, University of Ottawa 2011.

Murray, Stephen O. and Will Roscoe (eds.) *Islamic homosexualities. Culture, history and literature*, New York 1997.

Musić, Rusmir. Queer visions of Islam, in *Islam and Homosexuality*, ed. Samar Habib, 2 vols., Oxford, Denver and Santa Barbara 2010, 327–46.

Naber, Nadine. Arab San Francisco. On gender, cultural citizenship, and belonging, Ph.D. diss., University of California, Davis 2002.

Naber, Nadine. *Arab America. Gender, cultural politics, and activism*, New York and London 2012.

Najmabadi, Afsaneh. *Women with mustaches and men without beards*, Berkeley and Los Angeles 2005.

Saʿdāwī, Nawāl. *Jannāt wa-Iblīs* [Jannāt and the devil], Beirut 1992.

Ṣāghiyya, Ḥāzim. *Muthakirrāt Randā al-Trāns* [Memoirs of Randā the trans], Beirut 2010.

al-Samman, Hanadi. Out of the closet. Representation of homosexuals and lesbians in modern Arabic literature, in *Journal of Arabic Literature* 39:2 (2008), 270–310.

al-Sānīʿ, Rajāʾ ʿAbd Allāh. *Banāt al-Riyāḍ* [Girls of Riyadh], Beirut 2005; Girls of Riyadh, trans. Marilyn Booth, New York 2007.

Selbak, Rolla (dir.). *Three veils*, Three Veils Production Co. and Zahra Pictures 2011.

Shah, Omer. Reading and writing the queer Hajj, in *Islam and Homosexuality*, ed. Samar Habib, 2 vols., Oxford, Denver and Santa Barbara, Calif. 2010, 111–32.

Sharma, Parvez (dir.). *A jihad for love*, DVD, Halal Films 2007.

al-Shaykh, Hanān. *Misk al-ghazāl* [Musk of the gazelle] Beirut 1988; *Women of sand and myrrh*, trans. Catherine Cobham, London and New York 1989.

al-Suwaydī, Thānī. *Al-dīzil* [Diesel], Beirut 1994.

Taia, Abdellah. *Une mélancolie Arabe*, Paris 2008.

Wadud, Amina. *Qur'an and woman. Re-reading the sacred text from a woman's perspective*, New York 1999.

Wright, Jerry W. Jr. and Everett K. Rowson. *Homoeroticism in classical Arabic literature*, New York, 1997.

Yizbak, Samar. *Rā'iḥat al-qirfa* [The smell of cinnamon], Beirut 2008.

Zahed, Ludovic-Mohamad. *Le Coran et la chair* [The Qur'ān and the flesh], Paris 2012.

Zanghellini, Aleardo. Neither homophobic nor (hetero)sexually pure. Contextualizing Islam's objections to same-sex sexuality, in *Islam and Homosexuality*, ed. Samar Habib, 2 vols., Oxford, Denver and Santa Barbara, 2010, 269–96.

Zollner, Barbara. Mithliyyun or Lutiyyun? Neo-orthodoxy and the debate on the unlawfulness of same-sex relations in Islam, in *Islam and Homosexuality*, ed. Samar Habib, 2 vols., Oxford, Denver, Santa Barbara and Calif. 2010, 193–222.

Sexualities: Practices: Bangladesh

Shuchi Karim

Introduction

This entry provides an overview of women, gender, and sexualities in Bangladesh, with special focus on women's understanding, interpretations, and lived experiences of sexualities in their specific contexts. Sexuality is a fairly new area of research that recently emerged out of development and human rights discourses. To understand women and gender through the practices of sexualities in Bangladesh, it is necessary to pay attention to the region's colonial history, as well as its own combination of ethnicity and religion.

Women and Gender in Bangladesh: a General Overview

Bangladesh is a South Asian developing country, with a population of about 140 million. The majority (about 88 percent) of the people are Muslim, and over 98 percent speak Bangla (Bangladesh Bureau of Statistics 2007), making Bengalis the dominant ethnic group, thus forming, shaping and influencing the normative culture for gender and sexualities. Following independence in 1971, Bangladesh initially opted for a secular nationalist ideology in its constitution, but this was subsequently replaced by an increasing political commitment to Islam through a series of constitutional amendments between 1977 and 1988, and the secular status of the state has never been constitutionally restored (Mohsin 1997).

Like other South Asian countries, Bangladesh has a patriarchal society that dominates both private and public spheres of its members to different degrees. There is evidence of male bias and a double standard in areas ranging from the household to formal politics, in labor and employment, sexuality, marital choice, access to and ownership of income/assets. Common proverbs in Bangla reinforce cultural expectations regarding women's dependence on men—their father, husband, then son—throughout their lives (Baden et al. 1994). In reality, of course, to say Bangladesh has a fixed strict boxed frame of patriarchy would be far from the truth. The country's record on women's empowerment in education, the economy, and politics is impressive, as is the improvement in women's life expectancy. According to the United Nation Development program's Human Development Report 2011, Bangladesh ranked 112 out of 187 countries

---

© KONINKLIJKE BRILL NV, LEIDEN, 2012 | DOI:10.1163/1872-5309_EWIC_EWICCOM_001441

on the Gender Inequality Index. The traditional gendered separation of public and private in Bangladesh is being challenged with the increasing participation of women in education, the labor market, and politics (White 1992, Mahmud 2010). While women are not formally excluded from public spaces, women have to struggle against dominant cultural norms of femininity, sexuality, and class. If women transgress any of those norms for reasons other than economic, or question the character, morality, and dominance of men, they face hostile and sometimes violent consequences (Baden et al. 1994, Mohsin 2010, Azim 2010). The constitution guarantees equality to women in the public sphere, but governs private lives with personal laws that are religion-specific, and as Mohsin correctly points out, "it is the private sphere which regulates the lives of the majority of women" (2010, 15). Restrictions on marriage, sexuality, child custody and the like, through discriminatory personal laws, can and do restrict women's access to income, resources and empowerment opportunities. There has also been a rise in the "culture of violence," with a high increase in *fatwa*s (religious decrees) in rural areas which disproportionately target women with their extrajudicial calls for punishment for perceived moral transgressions (Human Rights Watch 2011).

Women, Gender and Sexual Normativity

Spatiality of Sexualities
Women's position, practices and negotiations within the (hetero)normative framework of life in Bangladesh largely influence aspects of sexualities. The spatiality of sexualities is mainly centered on the binary concepts of *ghor-bahir*, i.e. the binary concept of space as home and outside, or private and public. Home is the center of the family, and family is a socioreligious obligation, a responsibility that everyone must take on through marriage/s. Home is where purity, innocence, morality, and the core values of the family are practiced and preserved. It is a place of safety and protection, especially for women.

During the nineteenth-century Indian nationalist movement against British colonialism and especially in Bengal, "the new norm for organizing family life and determining the right conduct for women in the conditions of the modern world" was established by reconstructing the "classical" tradition and by putting women at the center of family life with the goal of upholding spirituality against materialism, by making women responsible for protecting and nurturing spirituality (Chatterjee 1989, 626–27). The "new woman" constructed by the nationalist movement remains the ideal informing today's dominant image of Bengali womanhood in Bangladesh. The explicitly gendered Bangla language and its proverbs position women within the private sphere of the household, responsible for the wellbeing of the family. Growing up, young girls are taught to be docile, caring, sacrificing, and have a restricted gender role that cannot be jeopardized at any cost. *Oshurjosporsha* (the woman untouched by the sun) is an archaic term but it retains significance as an ideal versus the *orokkhita* (the unprotected woman). This binary reveals a tension between the social sanction of space and sexuality, requiring strict disciplining, monitoring and chaperoning of sexual morality of women across Bengali society irrespective of religions. Restrictions of the spatial sexuality became a significant element in Bengali Muslim society.

Feminist scholars of Bengal (Amin 1996, Akhtar and Bhowmik 1998, Begum and Haq 2001) have shown that the transformation of Bengali Muslim women's roles and expectations over the last two centuries has been complex and far from linear or confined "within the binaries of the public and private sphere" (Azim 2010). This history is of particular relevance in understanding women and sexualities in contemporary Bangladesh. The *bhodromohila* (gentle woman; lady) is the precursor to today's ideal woman in Bangladesh, bound by the heteronormative prescriptions of gender and sexualities. Starting in the late nineteenth century, there were significant changes in the structure and formations of family, in marriage and gender relations. The fairly common polygyny of the nineteenth century was reorganized into monogamous matrimonial alliances, and in the twentieth century, this new arrangement established itself as the symbol of morality, equality and progressiveness (Ahmed and Chowdhury 2000). The sexual practices of men across classes in the nineteenth century were not only polygamous and polygenic, but within middle and affluent classes also included serial monogamy, marriage and sexual relations with maidservants, and regular visits to brothels. Women's sexual and marriage practices were far more limited compared to their male counterparts. Serial monogamy through marriages was practiced, but ideally a woman remained with one husband for her entire life. The sociopolitical history of the early twentieth century called for a respectable Muslim middle-class leadership, in opposition to the presumably immoral elite Muslim feudal leadership. This brought out the importance of education, the restructuring and reimagining of the household, and a new marriage system and sexual code of conduct. By 1950, sexual practices and sexual attitudes were attached to marriage, which was prescribed as the only space for sexuality. This new control of and attitude towards sexuality became the defining characteristics of the middle-class consciousness (Ahmed and Chowdhury 2000).

Today, sexuality is perceived and practiced within a tension of traditional perception of guilt and shame, and the urban-modernized-global Western cultural influences of desires. "Instilling attitudes of extreme modesty and feeling of shame (*lojja*) are part of girls' education in all classes of society ... shame is not only a desirable quality, it is an essential attribute of virtuous women which must be instilled in girls before puberty" (Blanchet 1996, 57). The code of conduct for female sexuality is based on shame and modesty. Threats of violence (inside and outside home) and a concern for family reputation and honor combine to impose certain restrictions on female sexuality while at the same time upholding an image of a liberal, modern, progressive Bengali identity. The ever increasing presence and interaction of both men and women in urban public spaces for work, education, and recreation are slowly giving way to relatively flexible social norms of gender, curiosity and opportunities regarding sex and expressions and new meanings of sexualities, which may challenge, if not always overtly, the Bengali notion of propriety.

Sexuality and Religion

According to Shuchi Karim (2011), religion does not play an important role in the life histories of middle-class, non-heterosexual men and women. Though people experience phases of religiosity over a lifecycle, they rarely face long-lasting major conflict between religion and sexuality. Individual women to whom religion is central find ways to negotiate the respective religious norms and rules that appear to be in conflict with their personal sexual desires, practices and identities. Religion is seen as a personal matter that needs to be approached and resolved in a personal spiritual way when it comes to sexualities. Religion is also used as a protection against outside scrutiny of one's sexual subjectivity. Women defying marriage normativity are seen using the image of piety (thus implying asexuality, modesty, purity and morality) to fight social pressures (Hasna Hena 2011, Karim 2011, 2010).

Heteronormativity: Homosociality and Marriage Normativity

Two crucial aspects of sexualities in Bangladesh are homosociality and marriage normativity. Each implies different meaning and practices for men and women, and for people of different sexualities. Homosociality and marriage normativity are part of growing up, of the gender training that takes place within the spaces of family households over different phases of an individual's lifecycle.

The dominant heteronormative framework of the Bengali culture, especially as set by the middle class, has its historical origin deeply embedded in its colonial history and its negotiation with modernity sets the ground of sociosexual morality for its members. At the heart of this lies the family-household with its norms of marriage, homosociability, gendered privileged visions of masculinity over femininity. It discourages sex outside marriage, but particularly suppresses female sexual expressions outside marriage. Marriage normativity and homosociability have different possibilities and consequences for men and women at different ages. Women who resist these roles, especially marriage normativity, are seen as social anomalies. Sex is an entitlement only within marriage, and women who do not marry are deprived of this entitlement and therefore must perform some degree of asexuality. Even though heterosexuality is compulsory and procreation is central to marital sexual relations, it still privileges males in sexual expressions outside heterosexuality, whereas women's non-heterosexual expressions are ignored to the point of denial (keeping the concept of penetrative sex as the only possible form of sex).

Homosociability can serve as a protective shield for both men and women's same-sex relations. Men's same-sex desires and relations are tolerated (if not fully accepted) as long as they conform to their heteronormative roles and responsibilities of marriage, children and family. Under heteronormativity, it is the "deviances" from heterosexuality that are most feared and monitored. Non-heterosexuality is tolerated because there is already an existent system of suppression and marginalization. This has special implication for single heterosexual women who can make use of neither homosocial nor marriage norms in order to assert their sexual agency in a socially negotiable manner (Alam 2001, Karim 2011). In contemporary Bangladeshi Bengali culture, unmarried/single men and women are expected to live with their parents and share common spaces, and it is culturally accepted and understood that the lives of unmarried children, especially daughters, need to be monitored by families. It does not matter how much one earns or how independent-thinking a person might be. For a single woman to live separately from the family within the same city is seen not only as unnatural and antisocial, but also as a potential threat to social morality. A women who does not take part in the institution of marriage, no matter her age or stage of economic independence, is denied adulthood within the family because she has not learnt responsibilities of *shongshar* (household/domesticity). This reduces her to a childlike entity for whom the family should still take major decisions and over whom they have control. Unmarried women's sexuality is seen as falling anywhere between hyper-sexualized to asexual. A woman is either considered a *ghorer lokkhi* (goddess of wealth, good omen, blessing at home) or a *ghorer khunti*, i.e., an additional bamboo pole in father's house (the proverb is in the traditional rural Bangladesh context where houses are made of bamboo poles and thatched roofs; to maintain such a frail structure, new supporting poles are needed every now and then). The proverb indicates not only the socioeconomic vulnerability of the father (who has failed to arrange a marriage for the daughter, which is understood as more of an economic failure than anything else), but it is also a shameful and hence undesirable situation for a daughter to stay at her father's house as an unmarried woman, turning into a "pole" which might be a support but which is completely contrary to her normative, expected social role of a dependent feminine entity. (Being a support to paternal family might be considered as a positive trait in modern societies, but in traditional Bengali culture, a father depending on a daughter is seen in a negative way). Marriage normativity is dominant and almost non-negotiable in oder ro avoid bringing down scorn, contempt and suspicion on the character of the woman in question.

Female sexual expressions are seen negatively and considered expressions of immorality, shamelessness and lewd. Yet experiences of premarital sex for women is evident and increasingly common, both in rural and urban areas (Aziz and Maloney 1985, Muna 1995), though it is always difficult to get admissions from young women. A study by Naripokkho (Azim 2001) inquiring about women's perception of their sex drive showed while 63 percent of women said "yes" to having sexual drives and desires, 2 percent said their sex drive was equal to but different from that of men, 9 percent said that women's sex drive was less than men's, 21 percent said that women did not have a sex drive, and 7 percent said that they did not know whether women had a sex drive. When asked whether women should express their sexual desire, only 8.6 percent said that they should, 30 percent said that a woman should only express her sexual desire to her husband, and 55 percent said that women should never express such desires. Research by Khan et al. (2002) on expression of female sexual desire in Bangladesh found that while many women confessed to having sexual desires, they considered it shameful to let their husbands know it. Some women stated that since their husbands demanded sex more frequently than than they themselves wanted it, they felt satisfied. However, if their husbands did not come to them for sex, they believed that it was best to wait and try to suppress or hide their own sexual desire.

Nocturnal Emissions, Masturbation and Talismanic Practices

In the Bangladeshi context, diametrically opposite norms of sexuality govern adolescent boys and girls. These social arrangements enable men to explore their sexuality at different ages while restricting female sexuality and its expressions (Muna 2005). Masturbation, though not encouraged, is acknowledged as a part of male sexual growth and emergence of male sexuality is often signaled through *shwopno-dosh* (nocturnal emissions) during puberty. A direct translation of the term would be faulty dream, or someone having the problem of wet dreams; ostensible cures for such "problems" or *dosh* can be found in abundance in newspapers, streets and leaflets everywhere. Wet dreams are considered a bodily malfunction and/or the evidence of satanic influence on young minds and bodies, also considered a cause of weakness in male body. Studies on adolescents and youth (Nahar et al. 1999, M. Ahmed et al. 2006) show that only a third of the respondents had prior information on menstruation or nocturnal emissions. Studies on male sexuality and vulnerability to HIV/AIDS show that young men regularly engage in homosexual activities such as exploratory play, mutual masturbation, penetrative anal sex, and the like (Gibney et al. 1999). Masturbation or *hasthomoythun* (hand massage, hand shake) is discussed as a common practice among boys and men. It is however rarely a mentionable topic of discussion for girls, and is often articulated as "unthinkable" or unheard of though there are acknowledgments of unspent female sexuality expressed as a negative term. While men easily described masturbation and body exploration as part of teenage sexual growth, not a single woman brought up this issue on their own during discussions. While girls/women rarely admit engaging in masturbation, they do admit their knowledge of such possibilities and hearsay stories of female masturbation practices (Reeuwijk and Idsert 2010, Alam 2001).

Alternative medicines, herbal treatments and talismanic practices to address sexuality-related problems and diseases are widely advertised and available. Starting from *shwopnodosh* (wet dreams), sexual weakness, erectile dysfunction, virility troubles, most of the offers of treatments are mainly targeted at male sexuality (Nahar et al. 1999, Alam 2001). Women's sexuality-related problems are usually seen within reproductive health-related problems such as infertility, miscarriages and white discharge (Rashid 2012). Religious sex manuals covering a wide range of topics such as conjugal life, normative sex, erotica, normative gender roles within sexual interactions, homosexuality, deviances, and so on are commonly available in Bangladesh. Books on talismanic treatments, magic, casting spells, and prescribing amulets are also available, targeting a population that otherwise does not have much access to sex education or reliable resources to help with sexual problems.

Women's Homoerotic Desires, Practices and Identities

In Bangladesh, male and female homosexuality tends to be ignored and not named. There is an uncomfortable cover-up, a denial. It should be noted that this was not always so. In the early twentieth century, there were in many parts of the country a much more casual approach to sexual encounters between men, and especially to relationships between adult men and young boys. These practices survive today in different pockets of society although they have become increasingly shameful and hidden (Blanchet 1996). The practice of adult males having relationships with other adult males, especially socially transgendered she/males, is common. Homosexuality in Bangladesh is a complex issue that involves the complicated play between class and gender much more than a simplistic reading of morality. The concept of a "moral society" within the middle class specifically explains why Law 377 (the anti-sodomy law) is not an issue. There is social understanding, simultaneous tolerance and denial of non-normative sexualities that are allowed to exist as long as they do not come to the surface (Hussain 2009). As long as an individual man lives by the norms of social morality in public, he remains a respectable member of his respective social class and/or group.

There is a silence regarding women's homoerotic desires and homosexual practices in Bangladesh. The socio-cultural-religious framework of Bangladeshi society is suppressive of agentic female sexual desires, expressions and practices in general; therefore, it is not surprising that female homoerotic practices are ignored. In recent years, because of emerging sexual rights discourses within the development sector, female homosexuality in Bangladesh has come to light, but not as much as male sexual diversity. A limited number of studies (Hasna Hena 2011, Rashid et al. 2011, Karim 2010) concerning women's homosexual practices show that women regard their journey of non-normative sexualities initially as an encounter of their own sexual subjectivity that stands in contradiction or opposition to a dominant model of heterosexual desires and related gender norms that are class-specific. Such contradictions create dilemmas and conflicts in women's minds as they try to make sense of non-heterosexual erotic desires and non-normative sexual identities. It is common to search for others like oneself, to look for a reference point of normalcy or community, and this quest is filled with dilemmas that derive from social construction and inculcation of what ought to be "normal" desire, i.e., heterosexual desire. Women become conflicted over whether sexual orientation is essentialist in nature or is a later-life construction stemming out of other experiences, especially from sexual violence or other negative experiences. It is not uncommon in women with same-sex desire to believe that sexual orientations can be compromised, reoriented, and negotiated; if given opportunities, they can be heterosexualized. Because of strict marriage-normativity, women, whatever their sexual desires and orientations might be, tend to agree to marriage and give heterosexuality a chance. Women thus go through a process of discovering sexual desires, facing dilemmas and internal conflicts regarding sexuality while going through heterosexualization processes from society.

Women create homes, support groups, or simple inner circles of friends to come together as a community. Sometimes these have intergenerational characteristics, some are based on professional commonalities or commonalities of education, marital status or simple family affiliations. In Bangladesh there exist two known support groups for women engaged in or interested in same-sex relations. The first one, Shawprava, is a Dhaka-based, non-registered group, mainly comprised of middle-class *shomopremee* (loving the same) women. The other one is Shomoy, a support group for female commercial sex workers who identify themselves as "lesbians" in their personal lives. There are also online communities for lesbian women in Bangladesh. The purpose of support groups like these is to create a social network and secure a safe private environment, breathing spaces that give women opportunities to find friendship, bonding and camaraderie. But they also provide all-important grounds for women to organize themselves, debate about the politics of sexual rights and identities, and extend support to fellow members of the community. The process of identity construction, and labeling oneself with a particular identity, is done at two levels: firstly, at the personal level and secondly, at a collective level that takes the personal to the level of the political. For example, the *shomopremee* women have debated the use of the label "lesbians," weighing the term's political correctness as well as its political usefulness in the broader sexuality rights movement/framework. They prefer to describe themselves as *shomo-premee*, with an emphasis on love and spirituality. The sex worker "lesbians" commonly use Bangla terms such a *nari-prem* (love for women) or *bon* (sister). But they have recently learned the term "lesbian" through various intervention programs such as those on HIV/AIDS, designed for sex workers. Their decision to be affiliated with sexual rights activities and to join a broader platform made them cautiously choose the English label of lesbian because it has greater universal currency (Karim 2012).

Women's sexualities in Bangladesh, as elsewhere, are lived in a fluidity that challenges the otherwise commonly understood "fixity" of sexual identities and practices. Non-heteronomative women find myriad ways in which they can strategize to live with their multiple diverse sexual desires, identities, and practices. Choices and agency are negotiated beyond the fixities of sexual identities and their materialistic manifestations in lives. Identities are expressed beyond "labels." Subtlety in defining oneself beyond the gender binary and/or sexual fixities is achieved through a day-to-day expressions of living arrangements, life styles, dress codes, associations and images that are more social in character than individual. Identities and their representations and meanings are still within the gender binaries of masculine-feminine, and are mostly kept in a simplified linear arrangements of gender and sexual performances, although within the non-heterosexual communities, expressions are much more explicit and labeled.

There exist multiple, ambiguous, paradoxical "sexual spaces" within the family-household. These are socio-symbolic inner worlds within which diverse sexual desires, identities and practices can be accommodated. However, the dynamics of gender, generational positioning, and class intersect to produce different possibilities for the existences and consequences of multiple sexualities. Family can become an ally, especially for middle-class non-heterosexual women (Hasna Hena 2011, Karim 2010).

Conclusion

The study of sexuality is still very new in Bangladesh and studies on women's sexualities are even fewer in number. There are major gaps in the knowledge base about sexuality and the socio-sexual conditions of people of different genders and sexualities in Bangladesh. There is almost no in-depth knowledge base concerning women's sexualities, its diversities and social practices. Spaces for alternative discourses that often stem out of different sites of resistances created by women through life's strategic lessons are absent in documented forms. The lived realities of sexualities can show us the processes of challenging norms, negotiating norms that are a process of not only strategic living but also of widening the possibilities of fighting stigma and discrimination. Women's sexualities, in particular, are not merely stories of victimhood, discrimination, and oppression; they are, in reality, also narratives of aspirations, strategies and empowerment. The porosity of the borders of normativity and deviances, between the public and private, are constantly challenged, negotiated and (re)created by women to accommodate non-normative desires, identities, and practices.

Bibliography

Ahmed, Masud Syed et al. Adolescents and youths in Bangladesh. Some selected issues, BRAC Research Monograph Series No. 31, Dhaka 2006.

Ahmed, Rehnuma and Manosh Lingo Chowdhury. Srenee ebong Onubader Khomota: Bangali Musolman Moddhobitto poribar o biye' [Class and the power of translation. Family and marriage in the Bengali Muslim middle class], in *Kortar shongshar. Naribadee rochona Songkolon'* [Master's house. Collection of feminist writings], ed. Sydia Gulrukh and Manosh Chowdhury, Dhaka 2000.

Akhtar, Shaheen and Moushumi Bhowmik (eds.). *Janana Mahfil. Women in concert. An anthology of Bengali Muslim women's writings, 1904–1938*), Calcutta 1998.

Alam, Mohammad Didarul. The secrets of young people. Exploring sexuality and health among adolescents in Bangladesh, MA thesis, Medical Anthropology Unit, Faculty of Social and Behavioural Sciences, University of Amsterdam 2001.

Amin, Sonia Nishat. *The world of Muslim women in colonial Bengal, 1876–1939*, Leiden 1996.

Amnesty International. Bangladesh. Landmark High Court ruling against fatwas, 5 January 2001, AI Index ASA 13/001/2001—News Service Nr. 3, <http://www .amnesty.org/en/library/asset/ASA13/001/2001/en/e7de6826-dc5b-11dd-bce7 -11be3666d687/asa130012001en.html>, accessed 31 October 2011.

Azim, Firdous. The new 21st century women, in *Mapping Women's Empowerment: Experiences from Bangladesh, India and Pakistan*, ed. Firdous Azim and Maheen Sultan, Dhaka 2010.

Azim, Safia. Naripokkho's pilot study on violence against women in Bangladesh, 2001, unpublished.

Aziz, Ashraful K. M. and Clarence Maloney. Life stages. Gender and fertility in Bangladesh, Dhaka 1985.

Baden, Sally, Cathy Green, Anne Marie Goetz, and Meghna Guhothakurata. BRIDGE background report on gender issues in Bangladesh, 1994, <http://www.bridge.ids .ac.uk/reports/re26c.pdf>, accessed 25 August 2011.

Bangladesh Bureau of Statistics. *Income and expenditure survey 2005*, Dhaka 2006.

Bangladesh Bureau of Statistics. *Statistical pocket book of Bangladesh*, Dhaka 2007.

Begum, Maleka and Azizul Haq. Ami naree. Tinshw bochhor-er Bangali nareer itihash (I am a woman. A three-hundred years history of Bengali women], Dhaka 2001.

Blanchet, Therese. *Lost innocence, stolen childhoods*, Dhaka 1996.

Chatterjee, Partha. Colonialism, nationalism and colonized women. The context in India, in *American Ethnologist* 16:4 (November 1989), 622–33.

Gibney, L. et al. Behavioural risk factors for HIV/AIDS in a low-HIV prevalence Muslim nation. Bangladesh, in *International Journal of STD & AIDS* 10 (1999), 186–94.

Hasna Hena. Women-loving-women. Issues and concerns in Bangladesh perspective, in *Women-loving-women in Africa and Asia. Trans/sign report of research findings*, ed. S. Wieringa, Amsterdam and The Hague 400–27.

Human Rights Watch. Bangladesh. Protect women against "fatwa" violence, July 2011, <http://www.hrw.org/news/2011/07/06/bangladesh-protect-women-against-fatwa -violence>, accessed 3 July 2012.

Hussain, Delwar. Gay, straight or MSM?, in *Guardian*, 6 August 2009. <http://www .guardian.co.uk/commentisfree/2009/aug/06/bangladesh-gay-sexuality>.

Karim, Shuchi. Living sexualities and not talking "straight." Understanding non-heterosexual women's sexuality in urban middle class Bangladesh, in *OIDA International Journal of Sustainable Development* 1:6 (2010), 67–78.

Karim, Shuchi. "Living sexualities." Non-hetero female sexuality in urban middle class Bangladesh, in *Sexuality in Muslim contexts*, ed. Anissa Hélie and Homa Hoodfar, Zed Books (forthcoming).

Khan, M. E., John W. Townsend and Shampa D'Costa. Behind closed doors. A qualitative study of sexual behaviour of married women in Bangladesh, in *Culture, Health & Sexuality. An International Journal for Research, Intervention and Care* 4:2 (2002), 237–56.

Mahmud, Simeen. Our bodies, our selves. The Bangladesh perspective, in *Mapping women's empowerment. Experiences from Bangladesh, India and Pakistan*, ed. Firdous Azim and Maheen Sultan, Dhaka 2010.

Mohsin, Amena. *The politics of nationalism. The case of the Chittagong Hill Tracts, Bangladesh*, Dhaka 1997.

Mohsin, Amena. Coming out of the private. Women forging voices in Bangladesh, in *Mapping women's empowerment. Experiences from Bangladesh, India and Pakistan*, ed. Firdous Azim and Maheen Sultan, Dhaka 2010.

Muna, Lazeena. *Romance and pleasure. Understanding the sexual conduct of young people in Dhaka in the era of HIV and AIDS*, Dhaka 2005.

Munthali, Alister and Bernie Zakeyo. Do they match? Young people's realities and needs relating to sexuality and youth friendly service provision in Bangladesh, April 2011, <http://www.rutgerswpf.org/sites/default/files/Do%20They%20Match %20Report%20Malawi%20-%20DEF_0.pdf>.

Nahar, Quamrun et al. Reproductive health needs of adolescents in Bangladesh. A study report, Operations Research Project Working Paper No. 161 ICDDR, B Working Paper No. 130, ISBN: 984-551-207-0, 1999.

Rashid, Sabina F., Hilary Standing, Mahrukh Mohiuddin and Farah M. Ahmed. Creating a public space and dialogue on sexuality and rights. A case study from Bangladesh, in *Health Research Policy and Systems* (2011), 9 (Suppl 1):S12 doi:10.1186/1478-4505-9-S1-S12.

Rashid, Sabina F., Hilary Standing, Mahrukh Mohiuddin and Farah M. Ahmed. Kal dristi. Stolen babies and "blocked uteruses." Poverty and infertility anxieties among married adolescent women living in a slum in Dhaka, Bangladesh, in *Anthropology & Medicine*, 14:2 (2007), 153–66.

UNDP, Country profile, Bangladesh, 2005, <http://www.un-bd.org/bgd/index.html>.

White, Sarah. *Arguing with the crocodile. Gender and class in Bangladesh*, London 1992.

Sexualities: Transsexualities: Middle East, West Africa, North Africa

Corinne Fortier

Introduction

Some societies recognize the existence of a third gender. The American anthropologist Gilbert Herdt (1994) introduced the term "third sex" or "third gender" in the 1990s, and in Quebec, the anthropologist Saladin d'Anglure (1985) applied the expression "third sex" after anthropologist Robert Ranulph Marett (Czaplicka 1914, 7, Saladin d'Anglure 2017, 50). This term is not used within societies as such but constitutes an anthropological category, as various emic terms are given to these individuals in different societies and during different historical periods.

Many terms have existed in the Muslim world for these third-gender persons, and they have varied through space and time. In addition to discussing these terms, this article will include a discussion of the social practices behind them, enriched by literary and cinematographic examples. Although these cultural realities appear different at first glance, they possess many similarities, especially regarding the figure of the "effeminate man," which is the most common.

Recent medical advances have made it possible for individuals to take hormones and undergo sex-change surgery (Fortier 2014a, 2014b). Differences of opinion between Sunni and Shiʻi Islam with regard to transsexualism will be analyzed. The situation of trans people—an umbrella term that includes individuals who identify as cross-dressers, transvestites, transgender, transsexual, or nonbinary, among other terms—living in Muslim countries will be presented.

Homosexuality, Third Gender, and *Khuntha* in Islam

It is impossible to speak about "third gender" and transsexuality in Islam without addressing the homosexuality and intersexuality with which they are associated (Fortier 2017a, 123). To clarify these concepts, which are confused in Islam, it is first necessary to return to Islamic texts (Qur'an, Sunna, fiqh) and to the etymology of the terms.

© KONINKLIJKE BRILL NV, LEIDEN, 2019 | DOI:10.1163/1872-5309_EWIC_COM_002185

SEXUALITIES: TRANSSEXUALITIES   463

The practice of naming masculine homosexuality in terms of anal inter-course is common in the Muslim world. The word for sodomy in Arabic, *liwāṭ* (Bosworth, Lewis, and Pellat 1986), as well as the term for one who engages in it, the sodomite or *lūṭī*, is related to the name of Lūṭ (Lot). This refers to the story found in both the Bible and the Qur'an according to which the people of Lot were destroyed by God, presumably for being devoted to this practice, which was considered an "abomination" (*fāḥisha*). The Qur'an (7:78–81) states: "And Lot, when he said to his people ...: 'See, you approach men lustfully in-stead of women; no, you are a people that do exceed (*musrif*)'" (Arberry 1980, 181). Although some gay Muslim scholars, such as the American historian of religion Scott Kugle (2010), affirm that this Qur'anic sura (verse) does not refer explicitly to homosexuality, this interpretation is still not popular among the general public and religious scholars in the Muslim world. Kugle and others have argued that punishment was incurred by God because the people of Lot engaged in rape and mistreated their women.

The Qur'an provides a clear affirmation of sex difference, as exemplified in the verse (92:1–4): "That which created the male and the female" (Arberry 1980, 595). Khalīl b. Isḥāq al-Jundī, an eighth/fourteenth-century Sunni jurist, speculates about the status of the *khuntha* (hermaphrodite) in the last lines of his *Mukhtaṣar* ("Compendium"), which is a reference for the Maliki school of jurisprudence (1995, 453). As it is obvious that there are no "true hermaphro-dites," or people born with a physical body fully combining both sexes, the term hermaphrodite is used here to translate the Islamic legal concept. To speak of "intersex" in such a context would be anachronistic because this term is new and related to the West. What seems to pose a problem for the Sunni jurist is not so much a person's sexual ambiguity as their gender ambiguity.

The need to identify an individual's gender identity derives from the fact that men and women do not enjoy the same legal rights, in particular regard-ing inheritance (Sanders 1991, 74–95). Thus Khalīl b. Isḥāq al-Jundī (1995, 453) tries to define the sexual characteristics of the person—the position of the urinary lacuna, the quantity and flow of urine, the thickness of the beard, the emission of sperm, and the appearance of menses and breasts—in order to determine whether the hermaphrodite is a man or a woman. But if it is im-possible to decide this at puberty, Khalīl b. Isḥāq al-Jundī asserts that the *khuntha* has the right in inheritance to half a man's share and half a woman's (ibid.). The *khuntha* is thus considered, in this context, as half man and half woman, belonging to both categories. In this case, there is indeed the recog-nition of a third gender. Islamic jurisprudence does not refer to an emascu-lation that would make the hermaphrodite body feminine; there is no need to mono-gender this hermaphrodite body (Fortier 2014a). But Khalīl b. Isḥāq al-Jundī recognizes it as a bi-gendered body with a special legal status different from that of men and women. Although it is not well known, this Islamic jurist creates a third legal status for hermaphroditism—that is, for what we would call intersex (Fortier 2017c).

Medinese Effeminates (*Mukhanaths*)

Already in Medina at the time of the Prophet, in the first/seventh century, the classical Arabic term *mukhannath*, meaning "the effeminate," was known through a hadith stating that Muhammad "cursed effeminate men (*al-mukhannathin mina al-rijal*) and mannish women (*al-mutarajjilat min an-nisa*)" (Nawawy 1991, 435). The etymology of this term refers to sweetness, curvature, and languidness, qualities that were considered specific to women (Bouhdiba 1979, 55). We find the same Arabic triliteral root *kh-n-th* in the word *khunthā* which designates the "hermaphrodite" in Muslim jurisprudence (*fiqh*).

This hadith provides evidence of the existence of men exhibiting effeminate behavior. The *mukhannath* did not necessarily cross-dress but demonstrated erotic movements and feminine ways of speaking (Lagrange 2008). As American historian Everett Rowson affirms: "There is considerable evidence for the existence of a form of publicly recognized and institutionalized effeminacy or transvestism among males in pre-Islamic and early Islamic Arabian society. Unlike other men, these effeminates or *mukhannathun* were permitted to associate freely with women, on the assumption that they had no sexual interest in them, and often acted as marriage brokers, or, less legitimately, as go-betweens" (1991, 671). They also practiced music, singing, and dancing (ibid., El-Feki 2013). In addition, these effeminate men could marry and have children (Mezziane 2008, 218), insofar as they were obliged, like everyone else, to perform their social and religious duties relating to marriage and reproduction (Fortier 2001, 2007, 2010b, 2011, 2013a, 2013b), even if they were not interested in women sexually.

The figure of the Medinese *mukhannath* existed in the Persian, Ottoman, Arabic, and African worlds. Although this figure was referred to by a vernacular term specific to each society and historical period—with the exception of Iran, where until the nineteenth century the word *mukhannath* itself was used (Najmabadi 2005, 5)—these terms often have an Arabic root, indicating the Arab-Persian influence of the *mukhannath* figure throughout time and space. Furthermore, these various local figures shared characteristics similar to the *mukhannath*, such as being beardless. Facial hair was considered as an immediately perceptible element that clearly demonstrated the physical difference between the sexes (Fortier 2010a, 95). The beard, and to a lesser extent the mustache (*shārib*) that is to some extent associated with it, were the visible marks of masculinity (Bourdieu 1972, 60 n4), and of the superiority that was attributed to men compared to women. Not to wear a beard could be considered a sign of effeminacy; a beardless man might be thought to fall short of the virile ideal. Another common feature of these different local figures was the practice of music, singing, and dancing, especially in ritual ceremonies, where they became objects of desire for men. The possibility of sharing both feminine and masculine spaces when such spaces were mostly gender segregated enabled them to act as matchmakers between men and women.

Afghan *Bacha Bereesh*

In Pakistan, Iran, Central Asia, and Afghanistan, there are *bacha bereesh* ("beardless boys," in Dari or Persian dialect). A beardless boy is seen as "asexual," feminine, and not totally masculine because facial hair is associated with masculinity, puberty, and sperm in many Muslim societies (Fortier 2010, 97–98). In Iran until the thirteenth/nineteenth century, beardless boys were also called by a specific name: *amrad*s (Najmabadi 2005, 15). They were objects of adult male desire, and their beauty was praised in homoerotic poems and painted in Persian miniatures (ibid.). In Afghanistan, according to Tiruvaloor Viavoori (2018, 5), they were outlawed under the Taliban regime as they were identified as homosexuals, but after the US invasion of Afghanistan in 2001, the traditional *bacha bereesh* witnessed a resurgence.

Afghan *bacha bereesh* wear make-up and cross-dress to dance in front of mature men during marriages or other private ceremonies. During their dancing performances, they wear belts around their waists to highlight their swaying hips, together with arm and ankle bracelets bearing little spherical bells that give rhythm to their movements. The men present during these private parties compete in poems and money to acquire the most handsome boy of the evening, who is considered the object of desire. This activity is called *bacha bāzī* (lit., boy game, from *bacha*, "child," and *bāzī*, "game"), and the men who play are called *bacha bāz* (De Lind van Wijngaarden and Rani 2011, 1064). In the Uzbek community of Afghanistan, this practice could also be called *bacabaozlik,* and the terms of address between an Uzbek dancing boy and his lover are *uka* ("younger brother") and *aka* ("older brother") (Baldauf 1990, 15).

In Afghanistan, pimps buy these boys from their parents when they are about eleven years old (Baldauf 1990, 15). Paradoxically, they sometimes offer to pay their dowry and wedding ceremony, because at puberty, *bacha bereesh* will stop their dancing performances to get married (ibid.). Pimps employ a master for one year to teach the *bacha bereesh* erotic songs and lascivious dances that they will perform in private circles in front of rich men who can pay for sex with them (ibid.). Although their consumption is forbidden by both Islam and the Afghan state, hashish and alcohol circulate at these parties and are given to the young boys to disinhibit them. Far from being a shameful activity, having one's own *bacha bereesh* is a sign of prestige, honor, and wealth for a man in Afghanistan (ibid.).

The documentary film *The dancing boys of Afghanistan* (by the Afghan journalist and filmmaker Najbullah Quraishi, 2010), shows this reality—as does the novel *The kite runner* (by the Afghan writer Khaled Hosseini, 2003), which inspired a movie of the same title. Baldauf (1990) and Quraishi demonstrate the existence of a poetic tradition in Afghanistan that celebrates the beauty of boys as they dance during these private traditions, a tradition that includes references to romance and sexual pleasure. Young boys' beauty, in particular their hair and the way they dance, is praised in poems and songs, as is shown in these verses from Quraishi's documentary:

> Now come and join the world of sin,
> Enjoy a life like sugar,
> Beautiful boys with no controversy.
> At this party shake your head,
> Beautiful boy, comb your hair and come to me. We love your dance and
>   hair,
> The clothes on your beautiful body.

As in Arabic and Persian courtship poetry, the language of love is commonly one of passion (Fortier 2004a, 76, 2004b, 241), where the lover "becomes crazy" and can "die from love": "I'll either reach my lover / Or drown in the river."

The following poem, also featured in Quraishi's documentary, refers explicitly to the underage status of the boy and to the idea of meeting his father as if he were a girl to marry:

> His body is so soft,
> His lips are so tender.
> He's touching the boy
> With his cotton clothes.
> Where do you live?
> So, I can get to know your dad.
> Oh boy! You've set your lover on fire.

SEXUALITIES: TRANSSEXUALITIES

A poetic joust to win the most beautiful *bacha bereesh* can arise between men on the occasion of these meetings, during which they express their feelings in a tender and sensual way by referring to the young man in terms of his physical characteristics—in the case of this excerpt from Quraishi's documentary, having a golden tooth:

> One man says:
> "The one with the golden tooth,
> Where are you?
> Why don't you come?
> I want to put my head
> On your tender breast."
> Another man says to challenge him:
> "Oh, my beloved, my beloved, my beloved.
> My beloved, let me hold you by myself,
> Let me put my arm around you and kiss you."

According to De Lind van Wijngaarden and Rani's research in Pakistan, the cultural difficulty for unmarried Pakistani men to have social or sexual relations with women seems to encourage such relationships and cultural practices as *bachabereesh*. Male relationships with women outside of marriage are strongly discouraged, while physical affection between males is socially tolerated. One of the boys they interviewed said clearly: "Sex with women gives children. Sex with men gives pleasure, so the difference is quite explicit" (2011, 1075).

De Lind van Wijngaarden and Rani remark that in Pakistan the boys are so dear to their "masters" that they are made part of their lives, and most of all they take them into their homes and lift the purdah (curtain) of their wives and daughters with them, and the boys eat their meals at the same table with them as if they were part of the family. The *bachabereesh* phenomenon in Pakistan is changing under the influence of globalization, with the exploitation aspects becoming more important and a decline in the cultural element of the phenomenon (2011, 1071).

Homosexual Unions in Siwa Oasis (Egypt)

Historically, gender segregation in the Siwi-speaking Berber society of the Siwa Oasis, Egypt, has been very strict—no man can see the face or hear the voice of a woman who is not his wife, sister, or daughter (Fortier 2012b, 78). Women remained in their high house of clay (*karshif*) and only ever went out to visit female relatives or for women's ceremonies, and then they are dressed in a cotton veil (*tarfutet*) that covers them completely from head to foot, leaving only one eye uncovered (ibid.). Control of women is still so strong in Siwa that no relation between the sexes is possible before marriage. Men aged between 12 and 24 constitute an age class called *zaggala*s (club bearers). Fortier argues that because of this extreme segregation between the sexes, *zaggala*s often engage in same-sex relations (Fortier n/p). Until the thirteenth/nineteenth century, the fortified village of Shālī in Siwa was forbidden to the members of this age class (Fakhry 1990). As they are supposed to be incapable of controlling their sexual desire, they would create disorder (*fitna*) if they entered this village, where only women, girls, children, and married men lived (Fortier 2012b, 78). Gardens that are located away from houses are their domain (Battesti 2006a, 159).

Every garden is the property of a married man, and it was a tradition that each man would take a young *zaggala* to help him in the farming of dates and olives but also as a sexual partner (Fortier n/p). The *zaggala* then became "his boy" (*akubi*) (ibid.). This kind of relation could lead to unions legitimized by the boy's father, to whom the owner of the garden paid a dowry superior to that given for a girl (ibid., Steindorff 1901, 12). Until 1928, it was not unusual for this agreement, which was sometimes called a marriage contract, to be written down, but after King Fu'ād I visited the oasis in that year, it became completely forbidden (Fakhry 1990 42). However, such agreements continued, but in great secrecy, and without being written down (ibid.). In Siwa society, not only women (Lévi-Strauss 1969) but also men can be exchanged by men, given that a father can decide to unite his son temporarily with a man in exchange for a dowry. Homosexual relations between *zaggala*s and owners are socially legitimate as long as they are framed by the payment of a dowry to the father (Fortier n/p). But if a boy is forced to have sexual intercourse without his consent, he could complain to his father, who would call upon the intermediation of the shaykh of the Arūsiyya brotherhood (*ṭariqa*), so that the offender would compensate the father and promise not to do it again (ibid.). Nowadays this kind of relation still exists, but the owner of the garden pays the *zaggala* directly for his work and sexual services (ibid.).

These practices entailed anal sex (*atchouki*) (Cline 1936, 43), a sexual act that married women were presumed not to practice because it was not related to procreation. Furthermore, men regarded women to be essentially for sexual reproduction and young boys for sexual pleasure (Fortier n/p). Sexual roles within these homosexual relations were clearly defined: the owner was active (*tiwyi*) and the *zaggala* passive (*guayashik*) (Ford and Beach 1951, 132). The *zaggala*, by being passive, was supposed, like a woman, to be penetrated and was not expected to have an orgasm. In sexual relations, either homosexual or heterosexual, pleasure was thus considered possible only for the one who was active (ibid.).

The most desirable young men were those who had curves, particularly around the bottom—the male body part considered the most erotic by other men—and also those with chubby cheeks and round, hazel eyes (Ford and Beach 1951, 132). Although there is no particularly important poetic tradition in Siwa, a Siwi poet named Youssef Ahmed described in the 1980s the beauty of a young man, in particular his eyes, but also the shape of his flanks when they were revealed by his *jalabiyya* (long garb like a dress worn by men) (Fortier n/p). Although this poem is in the Berber language, similar to classical Arabic poetry, the first name of the beloved is pronounced Bid'allah (or "God's slave" in Arabic):

> Bid'allah, whose eyes are like a calf (Bid'allah tawan naghi),
> His jalabiyya lifted up when he rode his bike towards Lamraghi (ishumar yuna Lamraghi).

In a longer version of this poem, collected by Fathi Malim (2001, 101), it is written, as in the Arabic poetry (Fortier 2018, 56): "O beautiful boy, you are the remedy of our sufferings."

Masculine sociability in the garden was accompanied by the consumption of hashish and date alcohol ('*aragui*) (Battesti 2006b, 168). Boys sang and forced their voices at some moments as if they were shouting like women (Fortier n/p). Some lined their eyes with kohl (ibid.). Some wrapped a scarf around their hips to emphasize their feminine swaying and began to dance by making graceful gestures with their arms in the style of women, and others joined and danced together, smiling and touching each other (ibid., Ford and Beach 1951, 132). At one moment during the dance, they made certain movements peculiar to men, throwing themselves on the ground and moving their bottoms in rhythm as if they were mimicking a sexual act (Tsai 2013). Until the 1980s, the *zaggalas* cross-dressed in the streets during marriage ceremonies until they reached the age of 18 and were ready for their own marriage (Fortier n/p). Siwa was relatively isolated and very remote. When a road was constructed in the 1990s, it began to open up to tourism. From then on, because of its homosexual tradition, gay tourists started to come and even settle in Siwa, with certain consequences on the life of their inhabitants in many aspects related to sexual commodification of young men's and boy's bodies (Fortier n/p).

Turkish *Köçek*s and Egyptian *Khawal*s

The Turkish word *köçek* is derived from the Persian word *kuchak*, meaning "little," "small," or "young." The *köçek* of the eleventh/seventeenth century was a handsome young boy who cross-dressed in feminine attire and was employed as an entertainer for dancing (Popescu-Judetz 1982, 48, Van Dobben 2008, 43). Before that, male dancers were called by the Arabic/Persian term *raqqāṣ* (dancer), suggesting an Arabic or Persian influence of this third-gender figure. The culture of the *köçek*s, which flourished from the eleventh/seventeenth to the thirteenth/nineteenth centuries, had its origin in the customs of the Ottoman palaces, and in particular in the harems (Van Dobben 2008, 43). *Köçek*s were allowed into the harems because they were not yet considered men (ibid., 48). Their performances took place on the occasion of wedding or circumcision celebrations, feasts, and festivals, as well as for the pleasure of the sultans and aristocracy.

The *köçek*s were recruited from among the ranks of the non-Muslim subject nations of the Ottoman Empire, such as the Jews, Romani, Greeks, Albanians, Armenians, and others (Van Dobben 2008, 45). A *köçek* began training around the age of seven or eight and was considered accomplished after about six years of study and practice. A dancer's career would last as long as he was beardless—a characteristic already noted in other cultural contexts—and retained his youthful appearance (Shay 2005, 56, 2014, 25). The *köçek*'s style of music and dance imitated that of female entertainers and the outward appearance and behavior of women (Shay 2014, 30). In the first part of their performances, the dancers would move to slow music using a veil or a shawl (Van Dobben 2008, 48). The second part would be livelier, and the dancers would shimmy their shoulders and hips (ibid.). Ottoman miniature paintings from the tenth/sixteenth to twelfth/eighteenth centuries show young boys around the age of ten or twelve with long hair, dancing in small groups and playing wooden clappers with their hands (ibid.).

European observers who saw the *köçek*s described them as suggestive, sensual, and attractive, affecting the movements and looks of women, and their dancing as "sexually provocative" (Boone 2014, 102). The *köçek*s were available sexually, often to the highest bidder, in the passive role (Ze'evi 2006, 86). In certain levels of Ottoman society, homoerotic sexual attraction was not a taboo subject (Van Dobben 2008, 32). With the suppression of harem culture at the end of the thirteenth/nineteenth century, *köçek* dance and music lost the support of its imperial patrons and gradually disappeared (Schmitt 1992, 84–85).

In accounts comparable to those of the Ottoman *köcek*s, there were *khawal*s in Egypt until the early thirteenth/nineteenth century (Boone 2014, 188).

*Khawal*s were effeminate young male dancers who performed with castanets. Their hands were painted with henna, their long hair dressed in braids, their facial hair plucked, and their faces decorated with make-up, especially kohl. According to Hanna (1988, 42), they cross-dressed and had the mannerisms of women dancers (*ghawazee*). In the streets, when not engaged in dancing, they often even veiled their faces, not from shame, but merely to look like women. They performed at functions such as weddings, births, circumcisions, and festivals. They were perceived as sexually available; their male audiences found their ambiguity seductive (Hanna 1988, 57–58). *Khawal* refers in dialectal Egyptian Arabic to their passive sexual role in anal sex.

Indian and Pakistani *Hijra*s

Hijra (Punjabi, *khusra*), used in India and Pakistan, is an Urdu term of Arabic origin (Jaffrey 1996, 25) meaning someone who has emigrated or left his tribe or social group, which suggests the Arabic/Persian influence of such a third-gender figure. In Pakistan they are also known as eunuchs or *khwāja sara* in *urdu*, as they had been part of the Mughal court and harem (Frembgen 2011). *Hijra*s can be of any religion: Muslim, Hindu, Sikh, or Catholic, but a lot of *hijra*s are Muslims, especially in Pakistan but also in India, for example in Hyderabad, where the anthropologist Gayatri Reddy (2005) did her fieldwork.

*Hijra*s perceive themselves as a distinct community with a special identity: "neither man nor woman" (Nanda 1990, 49–53). They are born as male and stand out through their female dress (sari) and effeminate behavior (Reddy 2005, 51). Some boys are taken or recruited from poor families by *hijra*s at the age of six to be castrated at the age of fifteen or sixteen (Jaffrey 1996, 25, 37), and some *hijra*s voluntarily choose this identity and castration (Reddy 2005, 75, 95, Revathi 2010, 22, 85).

When a young *hijra* leaves his family, he severs links with his caste, enters a new household, receives a new name, and is sometimes ritually initiated, through the removal of his genitals (Reddy 2005, 56–57, Frembgen 2011). Nowadays, some *hijra*s are not castrated and may decide at some moment in their life to undergo this ritual to be reborn as a "real *hijra*" (Reddy 2005, 92–93). The ritual of emasculation involves the complete removal of the penis and the testicles (ibid., 94). Traditionally, this emasculation was performed by *hijra*s known as midwives (*daiammas*), but most *hijra*s nowadays go to biomedical doctors (ibid.).

*Hijra*s belong to a guru, who often exploits and controls them and sometimes abuses them physically (Reddy 2005, 159). A new entrant into the *hijra* community in India goes through a ritual (ibid., 157–60). In Pakistan, in the presence of a larger group of *hijras*, the left nostril of the female-dressed disciple is pricked with a needle by her guru and a black thread is passed through (Frembgen 2011). The new disciple is then presented with shawls and money to buy bangles by all those present (ibid.). Within the caste hierarchy of the *hijras*, those gurus with the largest number of disciples (*chelas*), and the most beautiful, female-looking among them are ranked in the highest positions (ibid.). It is considered essential for a guru to perform the pilgrimage to Mecca, after which he only wears white, or at least no loud colors (ibid.). In India, *hijras* wear green saris, the color of Islam for special occasions, and even burqas over their saris (Reddy 2005, 104).

Hijras in India and in Pakistan want to look as much like women as possible (Reddy 2005, 124). For this purpose, they adopt feminine names, wear saris, adornments, jewelry, and heavy make-up, and put henna on their hands. They speak in loud and high-pitched voices like women. They walk in a sensual way, adopting an exaggerated feminine hip-swaying walk (ibid., 131). They sometimes make obscene gestures, which women cannot perform because of modesty. The physical feminization of their bodies is often limited to plucking their beards, shaving their bodies, and growing their hair long (ibid., 126–28). Today, however, most of them take female hormones to develop breasts (Lal 1999, 128, Reddy 2005, 127).

Their activities consist in begging on the streets and singing and dancing during festivities such as the birth of a son, the ritual circumcision of a boy, and especially weddings and engagements, even if not officially invited to do so, to ensure fertility and good luck (Reddy and Nanda 2009). Singing and handclapping is accompanied by the playing of a small drum. The language of these fertility songs is often rude and full of sexual innuendo. When a new house is built or a new shop is opened, they will also appear and perform, playing an auspicious role by blessing and bestowing fertility. People will give them money when they ask for it, because they fear their power to curse and thus to confer inauspiciousness. If somebody dares to turn them away without giving any money, they will clap their hands loudly in strong rhythms and shout abusive curses to frighten him (Reddy 2005, 55). *Hijras* are believed by Muslims, Hindus, Sikhs, Catholics, and others in South Asia to have sacred powers.

In addition to these rites of passage, *hijras* are also invited to private, male-only parties where they sell sex. Some eke out a living in circuses, dancing in the "well of death" surrounded by motorbikes roaring round the vertical walls of the drum. According to their customary rules, *hijras* in Pakistan have to hand over one-third of their income and gifts such as jewelry and sweets to their guru (Frembgen 2011). Some have lovers or "husbands" that they meet

SEXUALITIES: TRANSSEXUALITIES 473

sometimes (Reddy 2005, 64). Like wives, they generally perform women's work for their "husband": cooking, sewing, cleaning, and passive sex (ibid., 74).

In Pakistan, the right to include "T" for trans on their identification document was acquired by the *hijras* in 2010—after the Indian state of Tamil Nadu, which approved it in 2008, but before Nepal, which approved it in 2011. In 2018, the Pakistani parliament passed the Transgender Persons (Protection of Rights) Act, which established broad protections for trans people. They may choose to self-identify as male, female, both, or neither. They may express their gender according to their own preferences, and they can have their gender identity of choice indicated on their identity documents. The act defines a "transgender person" as someone with a "mixture of male and female genital features or congenital ambiguities," or a male who "undergoes genital excision or castration," or, more broadly, "any person whose gender identity and/or gender expression differs from the social norms and cultural expectations based on the sex they were assigned at the time of their birth," which allows people to self-identify as such. Discrimination based on gender identity in employment and public housing is forbidden under the new law. Nevertheless, this legal recognition does not change the reality of wide social stigma.

Omani *Khanith*

The Norwegian anthropologist Unni Wikan (1977, 1982) has described the *khanith* in Oman. The Omani Arabic term comes from the classical Arabic triliteral root *kh-n-th*, a root that also provides the words *khunthā* and *mukhannath*, as we saw above. Like the *mukhannath* of Medina, *khanith* are not cross-dressers, because wearing women's clothes, including the mask (*batula*) and the veil that women commonly wear, could get them into trouble (Wikan 1982, 43).

Omani *khanith* behavior falls between that of men and women (Wikan, 1982, 27). According to Wikan, although the facial expressions, voice, laughter, movements, and swaying walk of the *khanith* imitate those of women, *khanith* wear clothing that is a mixture of men's and women's styles. They wear the ankle-length tunic of men but are belted tightly at the waist as women would do. Men generally wear white clothing, women wear brightly colored, patterned clothes; *khanith* wear unpatterned colored clothes. Men wear their hair cut short and women wear it long; *khanith* wear their hair mid-length. Men comb their hair back from their faces, whereas women comb it diagonally from a center parting; *khanith* comb theirs forward from a side parting and oil it in the manner of women (ibid.). It is important to note that these descriptions of the behavior and styles of men, women, and *khanith* as described by Wikan refer to the overall dominant trends of the period he wrote in and have probably shifted tremendously over the years.

Thus, the *khanith* demonstrate their intermediate gender role in many aspects of their public self-presentation. They are regarded by Omanis as neither men nor women, but with characteristics of both. *Khanith* are born as boys; they have male genitals and do not, like the *hijras*, practice castration. *Khanith* have masculine names and are referred to in the masculine grammatical gender form. Under Islamic jurisprudence they have all the rights of a man. They also worship in the mosque with men.

In other ways, however, *khanith* are like women. Their appearance is judged by standards of female beauty: white skin, shiny black hair, large eyes, and full cheeks. In Omani society, where women are in seclusion (purdah) and men and women are strictly segregated in social interaction, *khanith* are classed with women for many social purposes. They visit with women where other men would not be allowed to do so, and they may walk down the street arm in arm with a woman. They do women's work in their households and are complimented and feel flattered by attention to their cooking and housekeeping abilities. And in this society, where eating is considered an extremely intimate act, they eat with women. Furthermore, on festive occasions they join the women in singing and dancing, and they can also play a matchmaker role between men and women. And significantly, only they, and never other men, are allowed to view the face of a bride on her marriage night.

As they are not subject to the feminine codes of modesty, they do not cover their hair (Fortier 2017b, 241) like women. And because their mobility is not controlled like that of women, they can freely move around outside their houses, though only during the day. As they are not considered men, they do not sit down with them in public and do not play musical instruments reserved for men. But they can sing, dance, and prostitute themselves for men. According to Wikan's research into their activity as prostitutes, they take the passive sexual role associated with being a woman. Indeed, in Oman one of the important distinctions between a man and a woman is that men take an active, penetrative role in sexual intercourse, whereas *khanith*, like women, are viewed as passive receivers. Because it is the active role in sexual intercourse that is the essential characteristic of a man, *khanith* are not men.

The most important reason *khanith* are considered "not men" has to do with the fact that in Oman, the definition of a man centers on sexual potency, demonstrated through marriage. On the morning after a wedding there must be public verification of the consummation of a marriage, by showing a bloody

SEXUALITIES: TRANSSEXUALITIES   475

handkerchief which proves that the bride is a virgin. It is only by this public demonstration of his ability to perform sexual intercourse in the male role, as penetrator, that a person is validated as a man (Fortier 2012a, 61).

This definition of masculinity, however, makes it possible for a *khanith* to become a man. If he chooses to marry, and if he can demonstrate publicly in the approved way that he is indeed potent in the masculine sexual role, a *khanith* moves into the category of man. He is recognized as a man only if, once married, he manages to deflower his wife. That means that masculinity in this society is defined mainly by sexuality, and in this particular case by penetrative sexuality.

This gender identity is not definitive or fixed. When he asked about the gender role of a particular individual, Wikan (1977) was occasionally told "X was once a *khanith*, but now he is a man." And a *khanith* who becomes a man can become a *khanith* again, if his spouse dies, for example. This contrasts with the Western social and legal idea of fixed and irreversible gender identity, because a person can have been a boy and subsequently become a *khanith*, and then become a man, and even, although this is rarer, become a *khanith* again.

Mauritanian *Gūrdigan*

The figure of an effeminate man exists in the Moorish society of Mauritania under the Wolof term *gūrdigan*, which means "man-woman." It is composed of the term *gūr*, meaning "man," and *digan*, meaning "woman." One of the physical signs indicating femininity in this society, as in other societies discussed above, is the absence of a beard. The term for beard (*laḥya*) in Moorish society, whose members speak an Arabic dialect called *ḥassāniyya*, is used to designate a man by metonymy. And the local expression for a man without a beard is related to the fact of being effeminate, *mistandhi*—from the Arabic *nisā'*, "woman." Furthermore, not only do *gūrdigan* shave their beards, but as women, they epilate their forearms (Fortier 1998, 212).

In addition, they possess certain characteristics of women like corpulence, in a society that practiced force-feeding until the 1970s (Fortier 1998, 209). They make effeminate gestures like hand movements and hip-swaying. They play an important part in marriage ceremonies, where they play tom-toms (*ṭbal*) and dance. They frequent feminine salons and play the role of entertainers and matchmakers between men and women. Although they do engage in same-sex acts, in a country like Mauritania where homosexuality is a taboo subject, some are married.

Gūrdigan also exist in Senegal (Broqua 2017). More generally, there are similar figures in other African countries (Murray and Roscoe 1997): *tché-té mousso-té* ("neither man nor woman") in the Dyula of the Ivory Coast, *kodjo-besia* (the term *besia* evoking "the feminine inside the masculine") in Ghana (Geoffrion 2013), *mke-si mume* (lit. the woman is not the man) in the Kiswahili of the African east coast (Gueboguo 2006), and the *dan daudu* ("the sons of Daudu") in Hausa, referring to men who act as women and have sexual intercourse with other men in Nigeria (Gaudio 2009).

Afghan *Bacha Posh*

If men who tend to be perceived as women exist in these societies, the opposite is much rarer. *Bacha posh* (lit. dressed up as a boy, in Dari or dialectal Persian) are Afghan girls who, from the age of about eleven, are obliged by their parents to dress like boys, have their hair cut short, and go without the scarf that other girls wear (Nordberg 2014, 9). They can behave like boys, play sports outside the house, and do not need to perform domestic chores like other girls (ibid.). For parents who only have girls, having one of their daughters pretend to be a boy, allowing her to go out more freely in the masculine public place (Fortier 2012b, 73–74), is important as it provides the family with help in work or shopping. They can also escort their mothers to places they she could not go without their husbands or sons. Thus *bacha posh* are widely accepted in society as they are seen as a solution to the problem of not having a boy in the family (Nordberg 2014, 7).

The *bacha posh* conform to parents' expectations, but as soon as the girls begin to have feminine physical attributes, their masculine way of life is supposed to end, and they return to the feminine domestic place to marry and procreate (Nordberg 2014, 7). Women raised as a *bacha posh* often have difficulty making the transition from life as a boy and adapting to the traditional constraints placed on women in Afghan society. Many girls do not want to go back once they have experienced freedom as a boy. Some of them decide to confront family pressure and keep their menswear, like Ukmina Manoori (2014). Manoori had an extraordinary male destiny: she waged war against the Soviets, assisted the mujahidin, and ultimately became one of the elected council members of her province (ibid.).

This practice has been the subject of numerous films, including *Osama* (an Afghan movie by Siddiq Barmak, 2003); the documentary film *Bacha Posh, you will be a boy my daughter* (by the French journalist Stéphanie Lebrun, 2012);

SEXUALITIES: TRANSSEXUALITIES

and *Breadwinner* (an animated drama film by Nora Twomey, 2017, based on the best-selling eponymous novel by the Canadian writer Deborah Ellis, 2015).

The *Mustarjils* of the Marsh Arabs

In *The Marsh Arabs*, Wilfred Thesiger writes about women called *mustarjils*, an Arabic term meaning "becoming man," among the ethnic group of Maʿdān (2007, 165) in the south of Iraq, in the Tigris and Euphrates delta. The Maʿdān said they became men because they were "women with men's hearts" (ibid.). This expression, which means that women have the character and behavior of men, also exists in the Piegan society of Canada (Lewis 1941, 174), but the anthropological context is very different, because in the Piegan case it concerns menopausal widows with the status of a man who can marry a woman (Héritier-Augé 1985, 16), whereas Maʿdān women with "men's hearts" were young and unmarried. A member of this community told Wilfred Thesiger (2007, 165):

> A *mustarjil* is born a woman, Amara explained. "She cannot help that; but she has the heart of a man, so she lives like a man."
> "Do men accept her?"
> "Certainly, we eat with her and she may sit in the *mudhif* [men's meeting house]. When she dies, we fire off our rifles to honour her. We never do that for a woman. In Majid's village there is one who fought bravely in the war against Haji Sulaiman."
> "Do they always wear their hair plaited?"
> "Usually they shave it off like men."
> "Do *mustarjils* ever marry?"
> "No, they sleep with women as we do."

Once, however, we were in a village for a marriage, when the bride, to everyone's amazement, was in fact a *mustarjil*. In this case she had agreed to wear women's clothes and to sleep with her husband on the condition that he never asked her to do women's work. The *mustarjils* were much respected.

It seems that it was the choice of these women to become men. Thesiger also cites the case of a man in Maʿdān society who dressed as a woman, practiced women's activities, and wanted to be castrated. The work of a couple of German anthropologists, Sigrid Westphal-Hellbush and Heinz Westphal (1962), is consistent with Thesiger's observations about *mustarjils*. They affirm that many *mustarjil*s declare their decision to lead a manly life after puberty, and this decision is generally accepted without opposition from the community. The young girl, if she has not already begun to live like a boy, henceforth dresses as a man and procures weapons for herself to take part in hunting and war campaigns. But the acknowledgment of a *mustarjil* as a man refers exclusively to her lifestyle, as her status is still that of a woman, for rules of inheritance, for example. As Thesiger wrote, she cannot marry as a man but only as a woman to assume her maternal and procreative role, and she cannot return to her former manly life after that.

Sex Change or Reassignment Surgery across the Region

In the West, terms to designate transsexuality have been developed only recently, more precisely in the nineteenth century. They are a recent development also in the Muslim world. According to Massad (2007), local activists, under the influence of international LGBTQI associations, have translated the Western term "transsexual" into Arabic as *mutaḥwwīl*, derived from the verb *taḥwwīl*, meaning "to transform or shift shape."

In Egypt, after the case of a student of al-Azhar University who had undergone surgery in the 1980s, in 1988 the Grand mufti (the highest government-appointed religious authority) of Egypt, Muḥammad Sayyid Ṭanṭāwī (d. 2010), issued a fatwa. Although the fatwa concerned a transgender person, in fact it authorized surgery not for transsexual people but for intersex individuals, because it concerned an operation aiming to "reveal the male or feminine organs hidden for purposes of treatment":

> The rulings derived from these and other noble hadiths on treatment grant permission to perform an operation changing a man into a woman, or vice versa, as long as a reliable doctor concludes that there are innate causes in the body itself, indicating a buried (*matmura*) female nature, or a covered (*maghmura*) male nature, because the operation will disclose these buried or covered organs, thereby curing a corporal disease which cannot be treated, except by this operation.
>
> SKOVGAARD-PETERSEN 1997, 318, see also ALIPOUR 2017a, 95, and TOLINO 2017, 235

Consequently, surgery understood as uncovering an already existing nature (some would label it "intersex") was legalized, whereas surgery arising from one's personal desire to change sex was considered illegal. Intersex surgery is practiced in certain countries, like Egypt (Skovgaard-Petersen 1997, 320) or

SEXUALITIES: TRANSSEXUALITIES

Tunisia (Redissi and Ben Abid 2013, 239), shortly after the birth of the child, as is the case in numerous Western countries, where it is, however, condemned by intersex associations on the basis that it violates the right to bodily integrity and individual autonomy (Fortier 2017c, 95).

The context behind the Egyptian fatwa helps to explain Ṭanṭāwī's position. The case concerned a medical student at al-Azhar University originally named Sayyid who became Sally. Egyptian doctors decided to operate on her after having detected his "psychological hermaphroditism" (*al-khunūtha al-nafsiyya*) (Dupret 2001, 54, 2013, 266). This concept seems to be connected to the Muslim notion of physical hermaphroditism discussed above. Here, however, it was applied not to the anatomical plan but to the psyche. The equivalent in the West would be the psychiatric category of gender dysphoria developed by the psychiatrist Norman Fisk in 1970 (Fortier 2014b, 275, Fortier and Brunet 2012, 82), a condition that has since been removed from the categories of psychological disorders.

After Sally's surgery, al-Azhar sued the doctors, on the grounds that they had practiced harmful mutilation (Skovgaard-Petersen 1997, 322). The mufti argued that the suffering of a transsexual person could be cured by psychological treatment rather than by surgery, which attacked the body's integrity. Additionally, al-Azhar accused the doctors of having performed this surgery on her so that she could maintain legitimate homosexual relations as a transsexual. The doctors responded to this accusation by declaring that they had submitted her to an anal examination proving that she did not practice anal intercourse. This anal examination is also practiced by Egyptian police on presumed homosexuals to prove their "crime of sodomy," even though there is no law specifically banning homosexuality in Egypt.

However, the Egyptian court agreed with the doctors, and Sally obtained her legal gender identity change, as identity cards in Egypt cannot be modified until successful completion of the sex change surgery. Despite this, the al-Azhar faculty of medicine, which is gender segregated, refused either to readmit Sally to the masculine section or to transfer her to the feminine section (Skovgaard-Petersen 1997, 323–25), so she lodged a complaint against al-Azhar for discrimination with the International Court of Justice of The Hague. It was only after a ruling of the Administrative Court that al-Azhar's decision was revoked and Sally was allowed to take her final exams at any university (ibid., 331).

More generally, in 2013, the Egyptian Medical Syndicate issued a new code of ethics that permitted trans people who could prove they have "gender identity disorder" to have "sex reassignment surgery." Applicants are required to have carried out the relevant medical and hormonal checks and must have had a minimum of two years of psychiatric consulting, at the end of which they obtain a report from the psychiatrist to confirm they have "gender identity disorder." The committee that approves sex change surgery consists of five members, two psychiatrists, a urologist, a specialist in heredity and chromosomes, and a member of the al-Azhar board. "Sex reassignment surgery" is possible in Egyptian government hospitals, such as the Cairo University Hospital, free of charge. However, this is probably because al-Azhar often refuses to perform transsexual surgery. And some trans people do not come forward because they "fear the stigma of homosexuality" (Islam 2015).

Although Sunni Islam forbids the castration of eunuchs, Ottoman harems, which existed from 1300 to 1922, avoided the prohibition by performing this practice on slaves sold in Turkey by non-Muslims, in particular Christian or Jewish traders. The fact that they were castrated allowed them to guard the women in the harems without the risk of reproduction. Even there, eunuchs were characterized by their lack of facial hair and their feminine corpulence, and they also played the role of matchmakers between men and women (Cheikh Moussa 1982, 415).

In Turkey, where Islam is not the state religion, transsexual surgery performed within the framework of a medical protocol, which can end in a change of legal gender identity, has been practiced since 1988 (Zengin 2014, 57). It was not the case before this date, as is shown by the example of the transsexual singer Bülent Ersoy (b. 1952), who was affectionately nicknamed the "diva" or "oldest sister" by the Turkish public. Since 1988 as a result of this legislative change for transsexuals, she took advantage to return to her country to perform; she had been forbidden from doing so until that point after undergoing sex change surgery in London in 1981. Zeki Müren, a cross-dressing singer and actor (d. 1996), was very popular in Turkey; a museum is dedicated to him in Bodrum (Stokes 2010).

In North Africa, as in Turkey, cross-dressing singers such as the Algerian rai singer Cheb Abdou are very popular—Algeria is a country where it is common to see cross-dressing dancers in marriage ceremonies with the *shikhat*, women musicians (Virolle Souibes 1995, 90). In Morocco, in public places such as Jāmaaʿ al-Fnāʾ square in Marrakesh, it is common to see cross-dressers dancing with tambourines while wearing black veils (niqab) on their faces so as not to be recognized (Bailleul 2015).

In Morocco, sex-change surgery already existed from the 1950s to the 1970s, initiated by a doctor who had settled in Casablanca, Georges Burou (d. 1987). He operated on Coccinelle (Ladybird) (d. 2006), a famous French music hall star in the cabaret "Le Carrousel" of Pigalle in Paris, at a time when in France no surgeon would agree to practice sex-change surgery because it was illegal (Foerster 2006, 98, Pruvot 2007, 187).

SEXUALITIES: TRANSSEXUALITIES   481

Although transsexual surgery is forbidden in Sunni Islam, it is licit in Shi'i Islam. In 1976, Iran's medical council limited surgery to intersex cases (Najmabadi 2014, 49), but this situation changed after the revolution in 1979 (Saeidzadeh 2016, 251). Transsexual surgery was allowed in 1982 by a fatwa issued by the Supreme Guide of Iran, Ayatollah Khomeini (d. 1989), at the instigation of a trans woman. This woman, Maryam Khatoun Molkhara (Tait 2005), wrote repeatedly to the ayatollah to explain her situation, that of "a woman imprisoned in a man's body" (Fortier 2014b). She asked him to authorize sex-change operations, which he did by a letter that became a fatwa: "There is no Islamic obstacle to sex change surgery, if it is approved by a reliable doctor" (Saeidzadeh 2016, 252). Maryam Khatoun was immediately given an Iranian veil or chador to wear (Najmabadi 2014, 165), even though she had not yet undergone sex-change surgery.

In fact, Khomeini had issued another fatwa on this subject long before, in 1964, in his *Tahrir al-wasila*, translated and quoted by Mehrdad Alipour (2017a, 96, 2017b 170):

> It seems that male-to-female sex-reassignment surgery is not forbidden (*ḥarām*) [in Islam] and neither is the reverse operation, nor is it forbidden for a *khunthā* (hermaphrodite/intersex) undergoing [this surgery] to be attached to one of the sexes [female or male]; and [if one asks] is a woman/man obliged to undergo the sex-reassignment surgery if the woman finds in herself [sensual] desires similar to men's desires or some evidence of masculinity in herself—or if a man finds in himself [sensual] desires similar to the opposite sex or some evidence of femininity in himself? It seems that [in such a case] if a person really [physically] belongs to a [determined] sex, sex-reassignment surgery is not an obligation (*wājib*), but the person is still entitled to change his/her sex into the opposite gender.

At the beginning of 1984, judicial and medical institutions started to regulate the process of gender transition under the supervision of Iran's judicial power (Saeidzadeh 2016, 251). Many people interpreted this gesture as a recognition of transsexuals, but others saw this practice as an avenue to normalize and reify heterosexuality instead (Jafari 2014, 33). In a country where homosexuality is illegal, the legality of transsexuality pushes certain effeminate gays and lesbians to become trans (Bahreini 2008). Obeying a rigorous medico-psychiatric protocol that ends in a legal change of gender identity ensures that the transsexual surgery is taken care of by the government (Saeidzadeh 2016, 254). But, after having obtained a medical certificate, it is possible to live as a transgender person without necessarily going for surgery, as Afsaneh Najmabadi writes: "Legal and religious authorities know fully well that many certified trans people do very little, beyond living transgender lives, once they obtain their certification: at most they may take hormones" (2014, 175).

In Iran, FtM (female-to-male) transsexuals are more readily accepted than MtF (male-to-female) transsexuals, because becoming a man is considered upward social mobility, given the superiority of men in society. On the other hand, even after transsexual surgery, MtF transsexuals are perceived as homosexuals and called by the pejorative Persian *kunis*, which references sodomy. The suspicion of homosexuality behind transsexuality remains a constant.

Conclusion

The clear segregation between the sexes that exists in some Arab-Islamic societies facilitates the existence of in-between gender figures (*mukhannath, khanith*, eunuchs, *gūrdigan*, etc.). These individuals are characterized physically by their lack of facial hair and their round forms and feminine body movements. They can enter feminine spaces because of their capacity to sing, play, and dance, particularly at marriage ceremonies, and also because their supposed lack of virility does not risk spoiling the virtue of women or creating illegitimate children (*zinā*). The fact that they can share masculine spaces as much as feminine ones has made them favored matchmakers between men and women.

Furthermore, in certain societies, the social duty of virginity before marriage and the idea that men have irrepressible sexual desires favor premarital homosexuality, which is accepted because it helps to reduce the sexual desire for women that might threaten society, on condition that this homosexuality is practiced discreetly and not claimed as an identity (Murray 1997, Whitaker 2006). It is also tolerated insofar as it is only temporary, as men must perform their social duty by entering into marriage.

However, in certain societies, as in Siwa or Afghanistan, this homosexuality may continue after marriage, as women's main sexual role is restricted to procreation and producing sons. Some boys (*köçeks, khawals, bacha bereesh*) are dedicated through their cross-dressing to entertain men and to satisfy their pleasure in a relationship based on domination, not only through age difference (adult/beardless) but also through gender (virile man/effeminate boy), social position (rich/poor), sexuality (active/passive), and perspective (male gaze / being looked at).

This category of boys (*bacha bereesh*) or effeminate men (*hijra*s or *kusra*s) is the product of certain masculine erotic desires, which, far from being socially repressed, are legitimate and are even considered a sign of virile potency associated with social power. Furthermore, allowing sexual relations with these boys rather than with women is a way to avoid the dangers of adultery and illegitimate descent inherent to any relation with a woman. And because these effeminate men are not subject to feminine codes of modesty, they can show themselves more active than women in seducing men and engaging in certain sexual practices that women refuse.

Bibliography

Alipour, Mehrdad. Islamic shariʿa law, neotraditionalist Muslim scholars and transgender sex-reassignment surgery. A case study of Ayatollah Khomeini's and Sheikh al-Tantawi's fatwas, in *International Journal of Transgenderism* 18:1 (2017a), 91–103.

Alipour, Mehrdad. Transgender identity, the sex-reassignment surgery fatwās and Islamic theology of a third gender, in *Religion and Gender* 7:2 (2017b), 164–79.

Arberry, Arthur John (trans.). *The Koran interpreted*, London 1980.

Bahreini, Raha. From perversion to pathology. Discourses and practices of gender policing in the Islamic Republic of Iran, in *Muslim World Journal of Human Rights* 5:1 (2008), <https://doi.org/10.2202/1554-4419.1152>.

Bailleul, Adeline. Saïd, homme "danseuse" de la place Jemaa el-Fna, HuffPost Maroc video, 4:01, posted 19 June 2015, <https://www.youtube.com/watch?v=zp6tg_H6ghM>.

Baldauf, Ingeborg. Bacabozlik. Boy love, folksong and literature in Central Asia, in *Paidika* 2:2 (1990), 12–31.

Battesti, Vincent. "Pourquoi j'irai voir d'en haut ce que je connais déjà d'en bas?" Centralités et circulations. Comprendre l'usage des espaces dans l'oasis de Siwa, in *Égypte Monde Arabe* 3 (2006a), 139–81.

Battesti, Vincent. De l'habitation aux pieds d'argile. Les vicissitudes des matériaux et techniques de construction à Siwa (Égypte), in *Journal des Africanistes* 76:1 (2006b), 165–85.

Boone, Joseph A. *The homoerotics of Orientalism. Mappings of male desire in narratives of the Near and Middle East*, Columbia, NY 2014.

Bosworth, Clifford Edmund, Bernard Lewis, and Charles Pellat (eds.), Liwāṭ, in *Encyclopédie de l'Islam* 5 (1986), 782–85.

Bouhdiba, Abdelwahab. *La sexualité en Islam*, Paris 1979.

Bourdieu, Pierre. *Esquisse d'une théorie de la pratique, précédée de trois études d'ethnologie kabyle*, Geneva 1972.

Broqua, Christophe. Goor-jigéen. La resignification négative d'une catégorie entre genre et sexualité (Sénégal), in *Socio* 9 (2017), 163–83.

Butler, Judith. *Gender trouble. Feminism and the subversion of identity*, New York 2007.

Cheikh Moussa, Abdallah. Gahiz et les eunuques ou la confusion du même et de l'autre, in *Arabica* 29 (1982), 184–214.

Cline, Walter. Notes on the people of Siwa, Menasha, Wis. 1936.

Czaplicka, Maria. *Aboriginal Siberia. A study in social anthropology*, Oxford 1914.

De Lind van Wijngaarden, Jan Willem, and Bushra Rani. Male adolescent concubinage in Peshawar, northwestern Pakistan, in *Culture, Health and Sexuality* 13:9 (2011), 1061–72.

Dumont, Louis. *Homo Hierarchicus. The caste system and its implications*, Chicago, Ill. 1980.

Dupret, Baudouin. Sexual morality at the Egyptian bar. Female circumcision, sex change operations, and motives for suing, in *Islamic Law and Society* 9:1 (2001), 42–69.

Dupret, Baudouin. Disposer de son corps. Excision, virginité, transsexualisme et transplantation en droit égyptien, in *Islam et révolutions médicales. Le labyrinthe du corps*, ed. Anne-Marie Moulin, Marseille 2013, 253–75.

Ellis, Deborah. *The breadwinner*, Toronto 2015.

El-Feki, Shereen. *Sex and the citadel. Intimate life in a changing Arab world*, New York 2013.

Fakhry, Ahmed. *Siwa Oasis*, Cairo 1990.

Foerster, Maxime. *Histoire des transsexuels en France*, Paris 2006.

Ford, Clellan S., and Frank A. Beach, *Patterns of sexual behavior,* New York 1951.

Fortier, Corinne. Le corps comme mémoire. Du giron maternel à la férule du maître coranique, in *Journal des Africanistes* 68:1–2 (1998), 199–223, <https://www.persee.fr/doc/jafr_0399-0346_1998_num_68_1_1169>. 8 August 2018.

Fortier, Corinne. "Le lait, le sperme, le dos. Et le sang?" Représentations physiologiques de la filiation et de la parenté de lait en islam malékite et dans la société maure de Mauritanie, in *Les Cahiers d'Études Africaines* 55(1):161 (2001), 97–138, <http://etudesafricaines.revues.org/68>. 8 August 2018.

Fortier, Corinne. "O langoureuses douleurs de l'amour." Poétique du désir en Mauritanie, in *Sentiments doux-amers dans les musiques du monde*, ed. Michel Demeuldre, Paris 2004a, 15–25.

Fortier, Corinne. Séduction, jalousie et défi entre hommes. Chorégraphie des affects et des corps dans la société maure, in *Corps et affects*, ed. Françoise Héritier and Xanthakou Margarita, Paris 2004b, 237–54.

Fortier, Corinne. Blood, sperm and the embryo in Sunni Islam and in Mauritania. Milk kinship, descent and medically assisted procreation, in *Body and Society* 13:3 (2007), 15–36.

Fortier, Corinne. La barbe et la tresse. Marqueurs de la différence sexuée (société maure de Mauritanie), in *Les Cahiers du Laboratoire d'Anthropologie Sociale* 6 (2010a), 94–104.

Fortier, Corinne. Le droit musulman en pratique. Genre, filiation et bioéthique, in *Droit et Cultures* 59 (2010b), 11–38, <http://droitcultures.revues.org/1923>. 8 August 2018.

Fortier, Corinne. Filiation versus inceste en islam. Parenté de lait, adoption, PMA, reconnaissance de paternité. De la nécessaire conjonction du social et du biologique, in *L'argument de la filiation aux fondements des sociétés méditerranéennes et européennes*, ed. Pierre Bonte, Enric Porqueres, and Wilgaux Jérome, Paris 2011, 225–48.

Fortier, Corinne. Sculpter la différence des sexes. Excision, circoncision et angoisse de castration (Mauritanie), in *Penser le corps au Maghreb*, ed. Monia Lachheb, Paris 2012a, 35–66.

Fortier, Corinne. Vulnérabilité, mobilité, voile et ségrégation des femmes dans l'espace public masculin. Point de vue comparé (France-Mauritanie-Égypte), in *Gouvernance locale dans le monde arabe et en Méditerranée; quels rôles pour les femmes?* ed. Sylvette Denèfle and Monqid Safaa, Cairo 2012b, 71–102.

Fortier, Corinne. Genre, sexualité et techniques reproductives en islam, in *Normes religieuses et genre. Mutations, résistances et reconfiguration XIXᵉ-XXIᵉ siècle*, ed. Florence Rochefort and Sanna Maria Eleonora, Paris 2013a, 173–87.

Fortier, Corinne. Les ruses de la paternité en islam malékite et dans la société maure de Mauritanie, in *Islam et révolutions médicales. Le labyrinthe du corps*, ed. Anne-Marie Moulin, Marseille 2013b, 157–81.

Fortier, Corinne. Inscribing trans and intersex people in the dominant binary categories of gender, *Etropic* 13/2 (2014a), 1–13, <http://dx.doi.org/10.25120/etropic>. 8 August 2018.

Fortier, Corinne. La question du "transsexualisme" en France. Le corps sexué comme patrimoine, in *Les Cahiers de droit de la santé* 18 (2014b), 269–82.

Fortier, Corinne. Intersexuation, transsexualité et homosexualité en pays d'islam, in *Homosexualité et traditions monothéistes. Vers la fin d'un antagonisme?* ed. Martine Gross and Bethmont Rémy, Geneva 2017a, 123–37.

Fortier, Corinne. Derrière le "voile islamique," de multiples visages. Voile, harem, chevelure. Identité, genre et colonialisme, in *Écrire et penser le genre en contextes postcoloniaux*, ed. Anne Castaing and Gaden Élodie, Berne 2017b, 233–58.

Fortier, Corinne. Intersexués, le troisième genre en question en France et au-delà, in *Socio* 9 (2017c), 91–106.

Fortier, Corinne. Seduction, the expenses of love. Seduction, poetry and jealousy in Mauritania, in *Reinventing love? Gender, intimacy and romance in the Arab world*, ed. Corinne Fortier, Aymon Kreil, and Maffi Irene, Berne 2018, 47–69.

Fortier, Corinne, and Laurence Brunet. Changement d'état civil des personnes trans en France: Du transsexualisme à la transidentité, in *Droit des familles, genre et sexualité*, ed. Nicole Gallus and Van Gysel Alain-Charles, Limal 2012, 63–113.

Fortier, Corinne, and Safaa Monqid. Le corps féminin en contexte arabo-musulman: Entre autonomisation et domination, in *Corps des femmes et espaces genrés arabo-musulmans*, ed. Corinne Fortier and Monqid Safaa, Paris 2017, 9–19.

Frembgen, Jürgen Wasim. The third gender in Pakistan. Dancers, singers and performers, in Fikrun wa Fann (Goethe Institute), January 2011, <http://www.goethe.de/ges/phi/prj/ffs/the/ger/en7089001.htm>. 8 August 2018.

Gaudio, Rudolf Pell. *Allah made us. Sexual outlaws in an Islamic African city*, Chichester, UK 2009.

Geoffrion, Karine. "I wish our gender could be dual": Male femininities in Ghanaian university students, in *Cahiers d'études africaines* 209–10 (2013), 417–43.

Gueboguo, Charles. L'homosexualité en Afrique. Sens et varitions d'hier à nos jours, in *Socio-logos* 2006, <http://journals.openedition.org/socio-logos/37 8.8.2018>.

Hanna, Judith Lynne. *Dance, sex, and gender. Signs of identity, dominance, defiance, and desire*, Chicago, Ill. 1988.

Herdt, Gilbert. Introduction. Third sexes and third genders, in *Third sex, third gender. Beyond sexual dimorphism in culture and history*, ed. Gilbert Herdt, New York 1994, 21–81.

Héritier-Augé, Françoise. Le sang du guerrier et le sang des femmes. Notes anthropologiques sur le rapport des sexes, in *Les Cahiers du Grif* 29 (1985), 7–21.

Hosseini, Khaled. *The kite runner*, London 2003.

Islam, Salma. The untold story of Egypt's transgender community, in *Egyptian Streets*, 12 July 2015, <https://egyptianstreets.com/2015/07/12/the-untold-stories-of-egypt-transgender-community/>. 8 August 2018.

Jafari, Farrah. Transsexuality under surveillance in Iran. Clerical control of Khomeini's fatwas, in *Journal of Middle East Women's Studies* 10:2 (2014), 31–51.

Jaffrey, Zia. *The invisibles. A tale of the eunuchs of India*, New York 1996.

Khalīl b. Isḥāq al-Jundī. *Le précis de Khalīl*, Beirut 1995.

Kugle, Scott. *Homosexuality in Islam. Critical reflection on gay, lesbian and transgender Muslims*, London 2010.

Lagrange, Frederic. *Islam d'interdits, islam de jouissances*, Paris 2008.

Lal, Vinay. Not this, not that. The hijras of India and the cultural politics of sexuality, in *Social Text* 61 (1999), 119–40.

Lévi-Strauss, Claude. *Elementary structures of kinship*, Boston, Mass. 1969.

Lewis, Oscar. Manly-hearted women among the North-Piegan, in *American Anthropologist* 43 (1941), 173–87.

Malim, Fathi. *Oasis Siwa from the inside. Traditions, customs and magic*, Cairo 2001.

Manoori, Ukmina. *I am a bacha posh. My life as a woman living as a man in Afghanistan*, New York 2014.

Massad, Joseph. *Desiring Arabs*, Chicago, Ill. 2007.

Mezziane, Mohammed. Sodomie et masculinité chez les juristes musulmans du IX^è au XI^è siècle, in *Arabica* 55 (2008), 276–306.

Murray, Stephen O. They will not to know. Islamic accommodations of male homosexuality, in *Islamic homosexualities. Culture, history and literature*, ed. Stephen O. Murray and Will Roscoe, New York 1997, 14–54.

Murray, Stephen O., and Will Roscoe. *Boy-wives and female husbands. Studies of African homosexualities*, New York 1998.

Najmabadi, Afsaneh. *Women with mustaches and men without beards. Gender and sexual anxieties of Iranian modernity*, Berkeley, Calif. 2005.

Najmabadi, Afsaneh. *Professing selves. Transsexuality and same-sex desire in contemporary Iran*, Durham, NC 2014.

Nanda, Serena. *Neither man nor woman. The hijras of India*, Belmont, Calif. 1990.

Nawawy, Mohammed. *Les jardins de la piété. Les sources de la tradition islamique*, Paris 1991.

Nordberg, Jenny. *The underground girls of Kaboul. In search of a hidden resistance in Afghanistan*, New York 2014.

Popescu-Judetz, Eugenia. Kocek and cengi in Turkish culture, in *Dance Studies* 6 (1982), 46–69.

Pruvot, Marie-Pierre. *Marie parce que c'est joli*, Paris 2007.

Quraishi, Najbullah. The dancing boys of Afghanistan, Bruxelles Laique video, 02:52, posted 11 August 2011, <https://vimeo.com/27586143>. 8 August 2018.

Redissi, Hammadi, and Ben Abid Slah Eddine. L'affaire Samia ou le drame d'etre "autre." Commentaire d'une décision de justice, in *Islam et révolutions médicales. Le labyrinthe du corps*, ed. Anne-Marie Moulin, Marseille 2013, 237–51.

Reddy, Gayatri. *With respect to sex. Negotiating hijra identity in South India*, Chicago, Ill. 2005.

Reddy, Gayatri, and Serena Nanda. Hijras. An "alternative" sex/gender in India, in *Gender in cross-cultural perspective*, ed. Caroline B. Brettell and Carolyn F. Sargent, Upper Saddle River, NJ 2009, 275–82.

Revathi, A. *The truth about me. A hijra life story*, London 2010.

Rowson, Everett K. The effeminate of early Medina, in *Journal of the American Oriental Society* 111:4 (1991), 671–93.

Saeidzadeh, Zara. Transsexuality in contemporary Iran. Legal and social misrecognition, in *Feminist Legal Studies* 24:3 (2016), 249–72.

Saladin d'Anglure, Bernard. Du projet paradi au sexe des anges. Notes et débats autour d'un "troisième sexe," in *Anthropologie et Sociétés* 9:3 (1985), 139–76.

Saladin d'Anglure, Bernard. Un pionnier du troisième sexe social. Entretien avec Bernard Saladin d'Anglure, by Laëtitia Atlani-Duault, in *Socio* 9 (2017), 37–74.

Sanders, Paula. Gendering the ungendered body. Hermaphrodites in medieval Islamic law, in *Women in Middle Eastern history*, ed. Nikki Keddie and Baron Beth, New Haven, Conn. 1991, 74–95.

Schmitt, Arno. *Sexuality and eroticism among males in Moslem societies*, New York 1992.

Shay, Anthony. The male dancer in the Middle East and Central Asia, in *Belly dance. Orientalism, transnationalism and harem fantasy*, ed. Anthony Shay and Barbara Sellers-Young, Costa Mesa, Calif. 2005, 51–84.

Shay, Anthony. *The dangerous lives of public performers. Dancing, sex, and entertainment in the Islamic world*, London 2014.

Skovgaard-Petersen, Jakob. *Defining Islam for the Egyptian state. Muftis and fatwas of the Dār al-Iftā'*, Leiden 1997.

Steindorff, George. Durch die Libysche Wuste Zur Amonoase, Leipzig 1904.

Stokes, Martin, *The republic of love. Cultural intimacy in Turkish popular music*, Chicago, Ill. 2010.

Tait Robert, A fatwa for freedom, *The Guardian*, 27 July 2005, <http://www.the guardian.com/world/2005/jul/27/gayrights.iran>. 8 August 2018.

Thesiger, Wilfred. *The Marsh Arabs*, London 2007.

Tiruvaloor Viavoori, Jayantika Rao. Resurgence of bacha bazi in Afghanistan. Socio-cultural and political factors, Ph.D. diss., Faculty of Humanities, International Studies, Middle East, Leiden University 2018.

Tolino, Serena. Transgenderism, transsexuality and sex-reassignment surgery in contemporary Sunni fatwas, in *Journal of Arabic and Islamic Studies* 17 (2017), 223–46.

Trash, Jimmy. Bülent Ersoy. The remarkable untold story of a Turkish icon, transgender diva and unintentional revolutionary, in *Huffington Post Gay Voices*, 19 December 2012, <http://www.huffingtonpost.com/network-awesome/bulent -ersoy-remarkable-story_b_2330277.html>. 8 August 2018.

Tsai, Venus. Belly dance by man in Siwa/Egypt, video 2013. <https://www.youtube .com/watch?v=59NB6CPdaMk>. 18 September 2019.

Van Dobben, Danielle J. Dancing modernity. Gender, sexuality and the state in the late Ottoman Empire and early Turkish Republic, M.A. thesis, University of Arizona 2008.

Virolle Souibes, Marie. *La chanson raï. De l'Algérie profonde à la scène internationale*, Paris 1995.

Westphal-Hellbush, Sigrid, and Heinz Westphal. *Die Ma'dan. Kultur und Geschichte der Marschenbewohner im Süd-Iraq*, Berlin 1962.

Wikan, Unni. Man becomes woman. Transsexualism in Oman as a key to gender roles, in *Man* 12 (1977), 304–19.

Wikan, Unni. *Behind the veil in Arabia. Women in Oman*, Baltimore, Md. 1982.

Whitaker, Brian. *Unspeakable love. Gay and lesbian in the Middle-East*, London 2006.

Ze'evi, Dror. *Producing desire. Changing sexual discourse in the Ottoman Middle East, 1500–1900*, Berkeley, Calif. 2006.

Zengin, Asli. Sex for law, sex for psychiatry. Pre-sex reassignment surgery psychotherapy in Turkey, in *Anthropologica* 56:1 (2014), 55–68.

Space: Female Space

∴

Space: Female Space: Arabian Peninsula

Jocelyn Sage Mitchell, Sean Foley, Jessie Moritz, and Vânia Carvalho Pinto

Introduction

The place of women in the Arabian Peninsula has been "'imagined' rather than real.... In this 'imagining', Gulf women were placed under the full custody of male relatives, their movements constrained, and their presence in the public sphere conceptualized as non-existent" (Sonbol 2012, 7). Taking this insight as a starting point, this entry highlights emerging research that challenges the imagined place of women in the Arabian Peninsula. Building on extensive recent fieldwork, this research crosses disciplines and source materials to understand the ways that gender intertwines with and contests the production of dominant powers and public-private boundaries in the region.

This entry first surveys the public powers of private women's spaces in the region, both physical and virtual, assessing the ways in which patriarchal norms can advantage or disadvantage the women who participate in these networks. Examples here include the dominance of women on certain platforms of Saudi Arabia's online community and the potential of women's private *majālis* (gatherings) in Qatar to function as sites of civic engagement. Second, this entry explores the relationships between state-sponsored feminism and the state's gendered response to women who challenge state authority in the public space. Recent research in the United Arab Emirates explores how the state, in line with national visions of human development, has symbolically appropriated the achievements of female intellectuals in both national and international spaces. Research in Bahrain and Oman during the Arab Spring reveals the limits of this enhanced public role by examining the role of women and the response of the state in a contested public space: opposition street demonstrations. Throughout this entry, the abstract concepts of gender and space are grounded in empirical evidence to advance the current understanding of gendered spaces in the Arabian Peninsula.

Physical Spaces of Private Seclusion and Public Influence

Private women's spaces in the Arabian Peninsula were once seen as symbolic of the forced exclusion of women from civic life. Today many scholars see these spaces as part of vast networks with surprising powers to advantage women in

© KONINKLIJKE BRILL NV, LEIDEN, 2016 | DOI:10.1163/1872-5309_EWIC_COM_002073

the public sphere. Whether physical or virtual, the irony of these spaces is that while patriarchal norms of society may necessitate their creation, participation within them may result in female empowerment and engagement in the wider public sphere.

The role of these private spaces in the societies of the Arabian Peninsula can be understood by analyzing the patriarchal mechanisms that helped to create them. Many explanations have been offered for these mechanisms. The structural effects of oil wealth, in particular the distribution of welfare benefits, reduce both the supply and demand of women's economic participation (Ross 2012). Governments have employed their oil wealth to buttress religious and cultural traditions by funding parallel institutions to enforce sex segregation and by hiring foreign workers over local women (al-Rasheed 2013). The importance of the legal system in propagating patriarchy is emphasized in works on kinship networks (Charrad 2009), in discussions of Islam, gender, and policy (al-Malki et al. 2015), and in the "Shadow Report" (Independent Group of Concerned Citizens 2013) submitted to the UN Convention on the Elimination of All Forms of Discrimination against Women (CEDAW). Research has shown the power of societal norms—shared by men and women alike—that favor men over women in the political and economic spheres (al Fardan 2015, Monir 2016, al-Tamimi 2016). Although women in the Arabian Peninsula outperform their male counterparts in education, they remain underrepresented in the workforce and the political arena (Foley 2010, Ridge 2014). Original, nationally representative survey data has demonstrated that three out of every four Qatari women agree that there is social pressure on them to focus on family instead of work (Mitchell et al. 2015). These societal norms can discourage women from entering the public sphere either through onerous structural barriers to gender-mixed environments (al Fassi 2016) or "symbolic annihilation" through the absence of female presence in the media (Mir and Paschyn 2016).

While these patriarchal mechanisms result in segregated private spaces for women in the region, participation in these spaces may give women the ability and the opportunity to influence the public sphere. A landmark study of Ottoman history argues against the "erroneous assumption that the seclusion of women precluded their exercise of any influence beyond the physical boundaries of the harem itself" (Peirce 1993, 6). Rather, the evidence that women in protected spaces were able to shape imperial politics profoundly encourages a reevaluation of the Western notion of public/private space. Likewise, the activism of female Islamists in Yemen, "conducted in ways that are spatially private but substantively public in intent and effect," is part of a gradual transformation of the public sphere by the private (Yadav 2010, 1). The Yemen case study suggests a reconsideration of "the designations of public and private more generally" in order to understand how spatially separated women can nevertheless transcend physical boundaries to influence the public arena (Yadav 2010, 2, see also Khouri 2015).

In this vein, recent work has focused on the potential public power of segregated spaces within the home. Typically, domestic spaces are not seen as part of traditional civil society (e.g., Krause 2008, 8–9). Groundbreaking work on "protected spaces" in Kuwait has made the important argument that *dīwānīyyāt* (gathering spaces within the home; known as *majālis* throughout the rest of the Arabian Peninsula) are "a plausible substitute for civil society in the public space" as they "institutionally, legally, and normatively are off-limits to state intervention" (Tétreault 1993, 277–79). Formal civil society organizations are often repressed in the authoritarian regimes of the Middle East (Norton 1994, 1995), especially in the oil-rich regimes of the region. Given the importance of extended family and tribal networks in the Arabian Peninsula for driving public engagement in economy and polity (Saad al-Deen 1988, Herb 1999, al Shawi 2002), the observation on the protected space of the in-home *dīwānīyya* represents a crucial link in the larger study of the interconnectedness of the public and private in civil society in the region (Tétreault 1993). Several recent works have highlighted the connection between the *dīwānīyya* and political participation (Alhajeri 2010, Segal 2012, al-Nakib 2014). Likewise, evidence from Qatar demonstrates that male participation in *majālis* can result in beneficial exchanges and networking, akin to participation in civil society organizations (al-Dosari 2012, Small 2015).

Most research on these in-home gatherings has focused on male participation and has neglected female engagement in these spaces. When female participation in *majālis* is studied, it is often through the lens of exceptional and elite women and their gatherings (e.g., Ahmed 1992, Mernissi 1993, Peirce 1993, Lienhardt 2001, 62, 171–72, Fay 2012, Stowasser 2012). The emphasis on elite use of these spaces overlooks the fact that the *majlis*, one of "the most unique and important forms of social organization and political dialogue [to] endure in the Gulf region" (Kane 2011, 56), is a natural setting of social life for ordinary women as well as men in the region.

This gap in the literature has spurred multi-method research to study the prevalence, activities, and effects of Qatari female participation in *majālis*, including ethnographic participant-observation and two nationally representative, randomly sampled surveys of Qatari citizens in 2014 and 2015 (Mitchell et al. 2015). The survey evidence demonstrates that *majlis* participation is a significant part of most Qatari women's lives, with more than eight out of ten women participating in at least one gathering. Within these gatherings, women participate in activities that develop their skills in interacting with the public sphere, such as sharing opinions, making decisions, gathering and sharing important information, and giving presentations. Further exploration of the link between *majlis* participation and increased feelings of freedom of speech and political efficacy, through a combination of survey data and individual interviews, suggests that the *majlis* can function as a site of civic engagement for Qatari women and men alike (al Thani 2016). Different *majālis* have different impacts on political and social engagement. In particular, the family *majlis*, due to its hierarchical and traditional nature, appears to replicate rather than challenge the status quo, while participation in social and neighborhood *majālis* may build more confidence and individualism among their members (Mitchell 2015, see also al Sulaiti 2015). In sum, participation in these segregated spaces may provide opportunities for skill building and engagement with the public sphere, but these opportunities are nuanced and contextual, and this research could benefit from further investigation into the processes that link these opportunities to broader societal involvement.

Virtual Private Spaces and Female Entrepreneurism

The Internet has emerged in Saudi Arabia as a powerful social force during the first decades of the twenty-first century, with the rise of Arabic social media platforms, faster Internet speeds, and the proliferation of smartphones. By late 2014, Saudis were among the top users per capita globally of Twitter, YouTube, and other social media platforms (Ayish and Mellor 2015, 42–43).

When explaining this phenomenon, Western scholars have focused on young male entrepreneurs, portraying the new online world as a male space. With the exception of recent work on Saudi Arabia's online community (Foley 2015) and on online entrepreneurs in Qatar and other states of the Arabian Peninsula (al-Malki 2015), no other scholarly work has investigated the success of online businesswomen and performers in Saudi Arabia. Indeed, it is widely assumed that women lack public roles separate from that of their spouses or male family members (al-Malki 2015, 16–17).

Saudi women have had tremendous success in online retail, where they draw on what Saudi fashion designer Marriam Mossalli terms the "innate creativity" of the Kingdom's society and a knack for thinking "outside the box" (Dhillon 2015). One can see this creativity in the way Saudi women use Instagram, the online photo-sharing site, to buy and sell cosmetics and other products, shop for weddings, and advertise lifelike clay sculptures of food and cakes (Vingiano 2013). Saudi female online businesses boast thousands (and sometimes millions) of followers on Instagram—often exceeding their male counterparts (Almashabi and Nereim 2015, Foley 2015). Saudi women are also heavy users of Snapchat, the video messaging application. They like the fact that Snapchat allows them to both control who views their online posts and limit how long posts are available to be seen (Foley 2015).

For Saudi female entrepreneurs, e-commerce offers several advantages over a traditional brick-and-mortar business. The Kingdom has a strong on-line infrastructure, and millions of Saudi consumers spend considerable time online. The legal infrastructure is equally strong, for Saudi copyright laws are consistent with global norms, respected, and rigorously enforced (Foley 2015). Women can post pictures on Instagram and other social media applications without fear that their work will be stolen by a competitor. Nor are women ex-pected to register their online businesses with the government (Amos 2015). By contrast, women who open public shops or offices must secure a male guard-ian to represent them before government agencies and to sign official docu-ments on their behalf (Almashabi and Nereim 2015).

Women's online retail operates in an unregulated commercial and social space. These businesses can be managed from anywhere, freeing women from the hassle of commuting in communities that are spread out and congested, and where travel for them can be time-consuming and expensive, especially given that Saudi women cannot drive and consequently must depend on hired drivers, male family members, or taxis (Amos 2015). Online commerce permits Saudi women to earn a regular income while respecting their religious lead-ers' frequent injunctions against the interaction of unrelated men and women (Foley 2015). While it is often difficult to maintain strict gender segregation in a brick-and-mortar store or in a public office, women can limit online both whom they interact with directly and who has access to any of their personal information, including their gender. Abdulaziz al-Shalan, who heads the mar-keting department for one of Saudi Arabia's top YouTube production compa-nies, Telfaz11, estimated in 2014 that at least 30 percent of the company's online male subscribers were actually women (Foley 2015).

Ironically, these conservative social norms, which some Saudi women and many Western analysts maintain are an impediment to the advancement of women, have further enhanced the market position of women on Instagram. In Saudi Arabia, foreigners and Saudis alike are rarely alone, for they are al-ways with others. They spend most of their social lives with their families or a close circle of lifelong friends of the same sex, or *šalla*. This time is spent in homes, hotels, restaurants, desert camps, or the farms outside of the large cities (Foley 2015).

The architecture of Saudi cities, where 80 percent of Saudis live (Elliot-House 2012, 69), reinforces the sense of shared social space. Housing develop-ments for Saudis are usually tightly packed together in low-rise neighborhoods that often link extended families, tribes, or the people of a given region. Most businesses, family compounds, government offices, universities, and family homes have a *majlis*. Many Saudi homes have an eating area and *majlis* exclusively for men and one for women (al-Naim 2006, 139).

Saudis have recreated this core social institution in their social media, especially in Instagram, which permits account holders to limit who can see individual accounts and even specific posts. Saudi women include the same people who are in their *šalla* or who would attend a *majlis* at their homes (Foley 2015). Because Saudi social and familial networks are large, the online networks built on them are also large, compelling some women to turn to Instagram as a way of communicating to a large audience simultaneously (Johnson and Alluri 2015). The men who manage Telfaz11 and other online companies do not see these networks, because they are men in a patriarchal society. As Amy Roko, a leading female Saudi online performer, has observed, "there is no way that a man could ever access a female *šalla*" (Foley 2015). The same conservative religious and social principles that justify the ban on women driving in Saudi cities also allow for Saudi women to defeat men commercially on Instagram.

Saudi businesswomen have a dominant presence on the online platform, and they are unlikely to lose it anytime soon. Although the Saudi government will likely seek to regulate women's online commerce as it regulates YouTube channels, Riyadh is unlikely to push female entrepreneurs too hard, because their businesses help to address decisive social challenges, including women's driving and high levels of female unemployment.

Female Intellectuals as Symbolic Public Figures in National and International Spaces

There has been widespread interest in recent years in the public symbolism of high-achieving women in the Arabian Peninsula. Usually referred to as "women leaders," "women achievers," or even "trailblazers" (e.g., Augsburg, Claus, and Randeree 2009 on the UAE, Thompson 2015 on Saudi Arabia), this group includes women who may be highly educated, who may have achieved senior positions, and who may have entered into predominately male professional fields, such as the military or the "hard sciences." These women have been attaining rising domestic and international prominence as their governments began publicly recognizing their accomplishments, through both awards ceremonies as well as encouraging statements reproduced in the local media. In acting in such a way, the governments of the Arabian Peninsula are indicating that these life choices are culturally appropriate, as they purportedly show that women can succeed professionally while adhering to their country's traditions, religion, and culture.

The study of this "achievers" group is still characterized by a certain homogenizing tendency, as many women, from all walks of life and professions, are being "bundled up" together under this label. Such an amalgamation teaches us very little about the effective scope of opportunities and constraints different groups of women face within public spaces. There is an important subgroup within the latter that is seldom the focus of analytical examination in its own right: the intellectuals. Works on intellectual women in other areas of the world also tend to be scarce (Bünnig et al. 2015, 7).

Female intellectuals, in addition to their professional careers, also perform a wide range of activities, including lecturing, public speaking, social advocacy, writing opinion articles on several topics, and volunteering. Similarly to their male intellectual colleagues—and this is particularly so in postcolonial societies—female intellectuals are called upon to reconcile modernity with tradition and religion. Indeed, reflecting on society, being concerned about its advancement, and offering solutions to the above issues are hallmarks of intellectual endeavour. These hallmarks are discussed in diverse case studies, including on Malaysia (Alatas 1977), Turkey and Iran (Parsi 2000), Southeast Asia (To 2006, 42), Islamic intellectuals in general (Dudoignon, Hisao, and Yasushi 2006, viii), and female intellectuals (cooke 2001, 152).

Women as individuals who operate in the public eye, however, are also ascribed the responsibility of representing their culture and showing that coordinating public duties with tradition is possible. Such expectations are quite prevalent, given that these women operate within a discursive environment where an emancipatory rhetoric coexists with discriminatory laws and traditional interpretations (International Federation for Women's Rights 2010). Women are often seen as symbols of both modernity and culture, as well as of religion and resistance against Western values (e.g., Kandiyoti 1991, Yuval-Davis 1997, Derichs and Thompson 2013).

Female intellectuals' gendered insertion and participation into public life is mirrored by similar experiences within the international sphere. For domestic audiences, the lives and achievements of female intellectuals are meant to signal the successes of the government's gender regime: the state's proposed configuration of gender relations. For international audiences, their attainments are geared towards enhancing their country's international status. For the small, dependent countries of the Arabian Peninsula, the amalgamation of soft power as a means to achieve status, to enhance it, or both, is an important goal (Neumman and de Carvalho 2015, 1–21). This has been particularly so since the attacks of September 11, as international audiences began scrutinizing more closely the domestic arrangements within the Arabian Peninsula.

The UAE is the country that has followed a more significant policy in this regard, closely followed by Saudi Arabia, especially regarding women's political participation (al-Rasheed 2013). Research indicates that in the UAE, female intellectuals are located within a complex interplay of state sponsorship of women's rights, contradictory cultural and governmental messages, and a society that views women as symbols of authenticity (Carvalho Pinto 2015). In addition, their professional achievements—depicted both as positive statistics as well as markers of progress—have been discursively and symbolically appropriated by the state. This articulation is then deployed in the international arena as a means to inform the construction of a positive international image for the UAE. Status becomes a key dimension with which to analyze the gendered characteristics of the international spaces where female intellectuals operate. The gendered dimensions of their countries' foreign policies can be fruitfully analyzed as determining or even deriving from this engagement. Other interesting focus areas include the study of how women intellectuals navigate these politics of representation, and whether they perceive them as imposed or as part of their national duty. Preliminary research indicates both (Carvalho Pinto 2015).

It is well known that an important hallmark of feminist international relations research is focused on "finding" women and revealing their often-invisible contributions to global politics (e.g., True 2005, Enloe 2014). The Arabian Peninsula governments offer a slightly different empirical angle to the study of women and international politics: women achievers as embodying (physically and symbolically) the successes of their countries' gender regimes. It can be argued that this is merely a continuation of the research focused on women as symbols of modernity (e.g., Jayawardena 1994), but that research could well benefit from fresh insights derived from the Arabian Peninsula.

The Contested Public Space of Street Demonstrations

The status, behavior, and even appearance of women in the Arabian Peninsula are intimately linked to ideas of modernization and progress, which prompt states to place women "front and center" in development strategies. As discussed in the preceding section, this is partly to reinforce domestic legitimacy, but it also reinforces a global brand presenting them as liberal and open in order to attract foreign investment (Krause 2009, Hamade 2013). This process of state-sponsored empowerment denotes a context in which women are seen as "instruments to be empowered," and where the state's aim is "to showcase women as empowered by their enlightened leadership" (Schedneck 2014, 135).

At the same time, state-sponsored feminism is a form of managed empowerment unlikely to fundamentally challenge patriarchal dominance. Examining state responses to women who joined a contested public space— reformist street demonstrations during the Arab Spring—reveals the limits of state-sponsored empowerment, particularly where the state has taken repressive, gendered responses to their political activism. This section outlines this process with reference to two states in the Arabian Peninsula: Bahrain and Oman.

While descriptions of street demonstrations in the Arabian Peninsula tend to highlight male participation, the opposition activism of women from this region is not a new phenomenon. Bahraini women helped organize anti-British strikes in the 1960s (Alfoory 2014), and participated in strikes, formal petitions, and demonstrations during the 1994–99 Uprising (Fakhro 1997). Bahraini women were present in large numbers from the inception of demonstrations at Pearl Roundabout in 2011, have continued to turn out en masse at demonstrations organized by the formal opposition societies (al-Wefaq, Waad, and a number of smaller societies that formed an opposition bloc in 2011), such as an all-women protest in September 2011, and have been regular attendants at weekly demonstrations since then (Bassiouni et al. 2011, Moritz 2015). Fewer women have participated in demonstrations organized by informal political groups such as Haq, al-Wafaa, and the 14 February Youth Coalition, but even here women play an important role in shaping street mobilizations. The 14 February Youth Coalition, for example, rationalizes its violent tactics by citing a January 2012 speech made by Shia cleric Isa Qasem in response to reports that Bahraini women protesters had been attacked, in which he said it was permissible to use violence to "defend" the community (Matthiesen 2013, 63).

Individual Bahraini women have also become prominent opposition voices. Farida Ghulam, wife of Ibrahim Sharif, the General Secretary of the secular nationalist political society Waad, led public campaigns in 2011 to free her husband from jail. Ghulam's activism is critical to understanding women's participation in the public space of street demonstrations, for two reasons. First, it is emblematic of an advantage women have in opposition: as noted in research on Tunisia, women are particularly effective at continuing demonstrations in the face of violence against male protesters, often using the incarceration of their male kin as a mobilizing tool (Chomiak 2014, 51). Second, her activism as a wealthy, Sunni woman occupying a senior position in Bahrain's largest secular political society challenges the narrative prevalent in state and loyalist media that depicts the protests as orchestrated by poor, male, and violent Bahraini Shia (Moritz 2015).

This individual activism often came at a cost: state harassment and repression. As an example: Bahraini teacher's union leader Jalila al-Salman and several colleagues who had organized strikes and street protests were arrested during night raids in March 2011. Al-Salman claims she was not given time to cover herself properly, and then once incarcerated she was threatened with rape unless she confessed to having deliberately undermined the security of the state (Bassiouni et al. 2011). Her case exemplifies the type of gendered response women activists experienced, in which modesty and purity were attacked or threatened. A series of over 130 interviews conducted in 2013 and 2014 with protesters, loyalists, and state officials from Bahrain, Oman, and Qatar suggests these tactics were common across the Arabian Peninsula (Moritz 2015). While this research found that in most cases the state was more likely to react violently towards male demonstrators (potentially because the state-sponsored empowerment strategy complicates mass-scale overt violence towards women), the gendered nature of the attacks against female activists nevertheless highlights both the limits of state tolerance for female dissent and the use of misogynistic forms of repression.

Omani society, in comparison to Bahrain's, is much less politically active, particularly because political organizations have been banned since the end of the Dhofar War in 1976. As a more conservative and traditional society, Omani women also face greater societal constraints in joining public demonstrations, particularly overnight sit-ins. The nature and scale of "opposition" demonstrations in Oman also differ from those in Bahrain: recent works have found that Omani protesters consistently emphasize their loyalty to the Sultan even while advocating for moderate reform (al-Farsi 2011, Valeri 2015).

There is almost no work on Omani women's participation in Arab Spring protests. An exception is recent research that has found that their presence in street demonstrations varied markedly by region (Moritz 2015). In general, protests in Muscat attracted greater numbers of Omani women than did demonstrations in other regions of Oman, even as male protesters greatly outnumbered female protesters overall. This can be explained by several factors. Muscat's more cosmopolitan culture and more diverse population may have weakened societal barriers to attendance in a traditionally male-dominated space. This was reflected in the reform demands of the Muscat demonstrations, which included calls for Omani women married to foreigners to be able to pass citizenship to their children. By comparison, there was greater evidence of a conservative trend within Salalah demonstrations, such as a call to end co-education of the sexes in Omani schools (al-Hashimi 2013). While most Dhofari women refrained from joining the major demonstrations in Salalah, some mobilized around more specific causes, such as a protest by the Omani Women's Association in Salalah decrying the alleged corruption of their director. Specific concerns related to the context of regional demonstrations also reduced women's presence in these protests, including the rapid escalation into violence in Sohar, and the concern in Dhofar that protesters would be associated with Marxist elements (Moritz 2015).

Although women formed only a small minority in most Omani street demonstrations in 2011, the Omani state nevertheless demonstrated a tendency to repress women's political activism when it threatened state authority. As in the rest of the Arabian Peninsula, this repression often took a gendered response. In April 2011, for example, Basma al-Rajhi, a journalist who participated in street demonstrations in Muscat, was detained by security forces alongside another prominent reformer. She alleges she was beaten and tortured, after which she was taken to a police hospital and given a virginity test, "because they want to create a picture of me, that I am not a fighter but something else" (Salisbury 2012).

Though the level and nature of their participation have varied, Bahraini and Omani women have engaged with the contested space of street demonstrations. While there remains a dearth of literature on female engagement with street protests in the Arabian Peninsula since 2011, the gendered state response to women's mobilization in opposition generates important implications for understanding state-sponsored empowerment and access to public space. Most critically, it highlights the underlying purpose of state-sponsored empowerment, in that the state only "sponsors" female empowerment in the public space where this empowerment enhances, rather than threatens, state authority.

Conclusion

Connecting in-depth, contextual knowledge from across the Arabian Peninsula with broader theoretical questions about gender and space in the world today, this entry highlights some of the opportunities and challenges facing women as they seek to access and influence the public sphere. On the one hand, unexpected sources of public influence can be found in the physical rooms of private women-only *majālis* or the virtual spaces of online e-commerce platforms, lending an ironic twist to the patriarchal norms that helped create these separate spaces. On the other hand, when women are welcomed onto the public stage through inclusive government rhetoric and actions, they can find their achievements appropriated as symbols of both national progress and international status. Further, as women use their physical presence in the public sphere to challenge state authority through reformist protests, the state attempts to repress their participation by targeting their modesty, purity, and honor. In all of these dynamic interactions, a focus on gendered spaces, understood broadly, sheds new light on the complex world of today's women of the Arabian Peninsula.

Bibliography

Ahmed, Leila. *Women and gender in Islam. Historical roots of a modern debate*, New Haven, Conn. 1992.

Alatas, Syed Hussein. *Intellectuals in developing societies*, London 1977.

Alfoory, Samyah. The 2011 Bahraini uprising. Women's agency, dissent, and violence, Georgetown Institute for Women, Peace, and Security Research Paper No. 5, Sept. 2014.

Alhajeri, Abdullah Mohammad. The development of political interaction in Kuwait through the 'diwaniyas' from their beginnings until the year 1999, in *Journal of Islamic Law and Culture* 12:1 (2010), 24–44.

Almashabi, Deema, and Vivian Nereim. Saudi businesswomen tap Instagram to bypass men, attract clients, in *Bloomberg Business*, 17 August 2015, <http://www.bloomberg.com/news/articles/2015-08-17/saudi-businesswomen-tap-instagram-to-skirt-men-attract-clients>. 18 August 2015.

Amos, Deborah. Saudi women can't drive to work, so they are flocking to Instagram, in *NPR*, 11 May 2015, <http://www.npr.org/sections/parallels/2015/05/11/405885958/saudi-women-cant-drive-to-work-so-theyre-flocking-to-the-internet>. 7 April 2016.

Augsburg, Kristin, Isabell A. Claus, and Kasim Randeree. Leadership and the Emirati woman. Breaking the glass ceiling in the Arabian Gulf, in *International Economics Series*, Vol. 4, Muenster 2009.

Ayish, Mohammad, and Noha Mellor. *Reporting in the MENA region. Cyber engagement and social media*, London 2015.

al-Azri, Khalid. *Social and gender inequality in Oman. The power of religious and political tradition*, New York 2013.

Bassiouni, Mahmoud Cherif, Nigel Rodley, Badria al-Awadhi, Philippe Kirsch, and Mahnoush H. Arsanjani. Report of the Bahraini independent commission of inquiry, 23 November 2011, <http://www.bici.org.bh/BICIreportEN.pdf>. 14 April 2016.

Bünnig, Jenny, Barbara Holland-Cunz, Sigrid Metz-Göckel, and Amrei Sander. Vorwort. Intellektuelle frauen [Introduction. Intellectual women], in *Gender. Zeitschrift für Geschlecht, Kultur und Gesellschaft* [Gender. Journal for Gender, Culture and Society] 3 (2015), 7–11.

Carvalho Pinto, Vânia. Emirati female intellectuals. On challenges, spaces for advancement, and production of gendered discourse, Paper presented at the Annual Meeting of the Middle East Studies Association, Denver, Colo., Nov. 2015.

Charrad, Mounira M. Kinship, Islam, or oil. Culprits of gender inequality?, in *Politics & Gender* 5:4 (2009), 546–53.

Chomiak, Laryssa. Architecture of resistance in Tunisia, in *Taking to the streets. The transformation of Arab activism*, eds. Lina Khatif and Ellen Lust, Baltimore, Md. 2014, 22–51.

cooke, miriam. *Women claim Islam. Creating Islamic feminism through literature*, New York 2001.

Derichs, Claudia, and Mark R. Thompson (eds.). *Dynasties and female political leaders in Asia. Gender, power, and pedigree,* London 2013.

Dhillon, Kam. Meet Marriam Mossalli. The conversation, in *Not Just a Label*, 4 April 2015, <https://www.notjustalabel.com/editorial/meet-marriam-mossalli>. 7 April 2016.

al-Dosari, Rawda. Civic engagement culture among young Qatari men. Al-majlis as a case study, M.A. thesis, Qatar Faculty of Islamic Studies, Hamad bin Khalifa University 2012.

Dudoignon, Stéphane A., Komatsu Hisao, and Kosugi Yasushi. Preface, in *Intellectuals in the modern Islamic world. Transmission, transformation, communication*, eds. Stéphane A. Dudoignon, Komatsu Hisao, and Kosugi Yasushi, New York 2006, vii–xiii.

Elliot-House, Karen. *On Saudi Arabia. Its people, past religion, and fault lines—and future*, New York 2012.

Enloe, Cynthia. *Bananas, beaches, and bases. Making feminist sense of international politics,* Berkeley, Calif. 2000, 2014[2].

Fakhro, Munira A. The uprising in Bahrain. An assessment, in *The Persian Gulf at the Millenium*, eds. Gary Sick and Lawrence Potter, New York 1997, 167–88.

al Fardan, Sara Fahad. Qatari women and leadership. The effect of culture, law and education on a changing political and economic context, M.Sc. thesis, King's College London 2015.

al-Farsi, Sulaiman. *Democracy and youth in the Middle East. Islam, tribalism, and the rentier state in Oman*, London 2011.

al Fassi, Hatoon. Municipal elections. New challenges facing Saudi women, Presentation at Women's Studies Circle in Qatar, Georgetown University School of Foreign Service in Qatar, Education City, Doha, Qatar, 17 Feb. 2016.

Fay, Mary Ann. *Unveiling the harem. Elite women and the paradox of seclusion in eighteenth-century Cairo*, Syracuse, NY 2012.

Foley, Sean. *The Arab Gulf states. Beyond oil and Islam*, Boulder, Colo. 2010.

Foley, Sean. Women are killing us on Instagram. Gender, social space, and Saudi Arabia's online community, Paper presented at the Annual Meeting of the Middle East Studies Association, Denver, Colo., Nov. 2015.

Hamade, Mona. Gender and late rentierism in the UAE, Conference presentation at Gulf Research Meeting, Cambridge, Jul. 2013.

al-Hashimi, Said Sultan (ed.). *al-rabi' al-'Umani. Qira'a fi al-sayyaqat wa-l-dalalat* [*The Omani Spring. A reading of the contexts and meanings*], Beirut 2013.

Herb, Michael. *All in the family. Absolutism, revolution, and democracy in the Middle Eastern monarchies*, Albany, NY 1999.

Independent Group of Concerned Citizens. Qatar shadow report, Submitted to United Nations Convention on the Elimination of Discrimination on Women (CEDAW), 2013, <http://tbinternet.ohchr.org/Treaties/CEDAW/Shared%20Documents/QAT/INT_CEDAW_NGO_QAT_16177_E.pdf>. 10 April 2016.

International Federation for Women's Rights. Women's rights in the United Arab Emirates (UAE), Submitted to the 45th Session of the Committee on the Elimination of Discrimination Against Women (CEDAW) on the occasion of its first examination of the UAE, January 2010, <https://www.fidh.org/IMG/pdf/UAE_summaryreport_for_CEDAW.pdf/>. 2 March 2015.

Jayawardena, Kumari. *Feminism and nationalism in the Third World*, London 1986, 1994[2].

Johnson, Ben and Aparna Alluri. Using technology to empower women in Saudi Arabia, in *Marketplace Tech*, 25 March 2015, <http://www.marketplace.org/topics/tech/using-technology-empower-women-saudi-arabia>. 1 April 2016.

Kandiyoti, Deniz. Identity and its discontents. Women and the nation, in *Millennium: Journal of International Studies* 20:3 (1991), 429–43.

Kane, Tanya. Transplanting education. A case study of the production of 'American-style' doctors in a non-American setting, Ph.D. diss., University of Edinburgh 2011.

Khouri, Rami G. Pioneering Qatari women transcend private, public spheres, *Agence Global*, 16 September 2015, <http://s4ir.mj.am/nl/s4ir/157zt.html>. 10 April 2016.

Krause, Wanda. *Women in civil society. The state, Islamism, and networks in the UAE*, New York 2008.

Krause, Wanda. Gender and participation in the Gulf, LSE Kuwait Programme on Development, Governance, and Globalisation in the Gulf States, No. 4, Sep. 2009, 1–38.

Lienhardt, Peter. *Shaikhdoms of Eastern Arabia*, ed. Ahmed Al-Shahi, New York 2001.

al-Malki, Amal Mohammed, Amira el Azhary Sonbol, Hatoon Alfassi, Batool M. Khalifa, and Nada Adeeb Omar Eltaiba. Islam, gender, and policy, Panel discussion at Qatar Faculty of Islamic Studies, Hamad bin Khalifa University, Education City, Doha, Qatar, 20 Oct. 2015.

al-Malki, Fatema. Unveiling the Arab woman. How women cultural entrepreneurs use social media in the Gulf states, M.A. diss., King's College London 2015.

Matthiesen, Toby. *Sectarian Gulf. Bahrain, Saudi Arabia, and the Arab Spring that wasn't*, Stanford, Calif. 2013.

Mernissi, Fatima. *The forgotten queens of Islam*, trans. Mary Jo Lakeland, Minneapolis, Minn. 1993.

Mir, Sadia, and Christina Paschyn. Women's symbolic annihilation and documentary media practice. A Qatari case study, Paper for presentation at the Arts and Humanities Conference, International Institute of Social and Economic Sciences, Venice, Italy, 27–30 Apr. 2016.

Mitchell, Jocelyn Sage. *Majaalis al-hareem*. Civic sites of social and political engagement?, Paper for presentation at the annual meeting of the Middle East Studies Association, Denver, Colo. 21–24 Nov. 2015.

Mitchell, Jocelyn Sage, Christina Paschyn, Sadia Mir, Kirsten Pike, and Tanya Kane. In *majaalis al-hareem*. The complex professional and personal choices of Qatari women, in *DIFI Family Research and Proceedings* 4 (2015), <http://www.qscience.com/doi/pdf/10.5339/difi.2015.4>. 14 April 2016.

Monir, Malak. Where are the educated Qatari women in the workforce?, Paper for presentation at the Middle Eastern Studies Student Association annual conference, Georgetown University School of Foreign Service in Qatar, Education City, Doha, Qatar, 17 Mar. 2016.

Moritz, Jessie. Women in protest. Bahraini and Omani women in the Arab Spring, Conference presentation at Middle East Studies Association, Denver, Colo. Nov. 2015.

al-Naim, Mashary A. The home environment in Saudi Arabia and Gulf states. The dilemma of cultural resistance, Identity in transition. Working Paper No. 11, 2006, Centro Di Richerche Sul Sistema Sud E IL Mediterraneo Allargato (CRiSSMA), Research Centre on the Southern System and Wider Mediterranean, Facoltà Di Scienze Politiche, Università Cattolica, Milan, Italy.

al-Nakib, Farah. Public space and public protest in Kuwait, 1938–2012, in *City: Analysis of Urban Trends, Culture, Theory, Policy, Action* 18:6 (2014), 723–34.

Neumann, Iver B., and Benjamin de Carvalho. Introduction. Small states and status, in *Small state status seeking. Norway's quest for international standing,* eds. Benjamin de Carvalho and Iver B. Neumann, New York 2015, 1–21.

Norton, Augustus Richard (ed.). *Civil society in the Middle East*, vol. 1, Leiden 1994.

Norton, Augustus Richard (ed.). *Civil society in the Middle East*, vol. 2, Leiden 1995.

Parsi, Rouzbeh. Reforming society. Intellectuals and nation-building in Iran and Turkey, in *Between Europe and Islam. Shaping modernity in a transcultural space,* eds. Almut Hoefert and Armando Salvatore, Multiple Europes Series No. 14, Berlin 2000, 109–42.

Peirce, Leslie P. *The imperial harem. Women and sovereignty in the Ottoman Empire*, New York 1993.

al-Rasheed, Madawi. *A most masculine state. Gender, politics, and religion in Saudi Arabia*, New York 2013.

Ridge, Natasha. *Education and the reverse gender divide in the Gulf states. Embracing the global, ignoring the local*, New York 2014.

Ross, Michael. *The oil curse. How petroleum wealth shapes the development of nations.* Princeton, NJ 2012.

Saad el-Din, Ibrahim (ed.). *Al-mujtama' wa'd-daula fi'l-watan al-'arabi* [*Society and state in the Arab world*], Beirut 1988.

Salisbury, Peter. Insulting the Sultan in Oman, in *Foreign Policy*, 19 October 2012, <http://foreignpolicy.com/2012/10/19/insulting-the-sultan-in-oman/>. 14 April 2016.

Schedneck, Jillian. 'Empowering' or 'empowered' Emirati women? State-sponsored feminism and self-perceptions of women's achievements in the public sphere, in *The contemporary Middle East: Revolution or reform*, eds. Adel Abdel Ghafar, Brenton Clark, and Jessie Moritz, Melbourne 2014, 132–155.

Segal, Eran. Political participation in Kuwait. *Diwanniya, majlis* and parliament, in *Journal of Arabian Studies: Arabia, the Gulf, and the Red Sea* 2:2 (2012), 127–41.

al-Sharif, Manal. Saudi activist Manal al-Sharif on why she removed the veil, in *The Daily Beast*, 30 October 2014, <http://www.thedailybeast.com/articles/2014/10/30/saudi-activist-manal-al-sharif-on-why-she-removed-the-veil.html>. 7 April 2016.

al Shawi, Ali A. Hadi. Political influences of tribes in the state of Qatar. Impact of tribal loyalty on political participation, Ph.D. diss., Mississippi State University 2002.

Small, Nancy. Qatar's globalized citizenry and the *majlis* culture. Insights from Habermas's theory of the development of a public sphere, in *Deconstructing global citizenship. Political, cultural, and ethnic perspectives*, eds. Hassan Bashir and Phillip W. Gray, Lanham, Md. 2015, 285–302.

Sonbol, Amira el-Azhary (ed.). *Gulf women*, London 2012.

Stowasser, Barbara Freyer. Women and politics in late Jahili and early Islamic Arabia. Reading behind patriarchal history, in *Gulf women*, ed. Amira el-Azhary Sonbol, London 2012, 69–103.

al Sulaiti, Tamador. *Majlis al hareem.* Part of civil society?, in *Northwestern Undergraduate Research Journal Online* 2015–2016, 2 December 2015, <http://www.thenurj.com/majlis-al-hareem-part-of-civil-society>. 13 April 2016.

al-Tamimi, Noor. Where are the Qatari women in politics?, Poster presentation at the Qatar Foundation Annual Research Conference, Doha, Qatar, 21–22 Mar. 2016.

Tétreault, Mary Ann. Civil society in Kuwait. Protected spaces and women's rights, in *Middle East Journal* 47:2 (1993), 275–91.

al Thani, Nayla. 2016. *Majlis* participation and influence, Poster presentation at the Qatar Foundation Annual Research Conference, Doha, Qatar, 21–22 Mar. 2016.

Thompson, Mark. Saudi women leaders. Challenges and opportunities, in *Journal of Arabian Studies* 5:1 (2015), 15–36.

To, Lee Tai. The role of Asian intellectuals in a globalized economy. A commentary, in *The power of ideas. Intellectual input and political change in East and Southeast Asia*, eds. Claudia Derichs and Thomas Heberer, Copenhagen 2006, 36–45.

True, Jacqui. Feminism, in *International society and its critics,* ed. Alex J. Bellamy, Oxford 2005, 151–62.

Valeri, Marc. The Ṣuḥār paradox. Social and political mobilisations in the Sultanate of Oman since 2011, in *Arabian Humanities* 4 (2015), <http://cy.revues.org/2828>. 13 April 2016.

Vingiano, Ali. This Saudi woman has an amazing Instagram, in *BuzzFeed*, 9 December 2013, <http://www.buzzfeed.com/alisonvingiano/this-saudi-woman-has-an-amazing-instagram#.xnl8kk1JL>. 30 March 2016.

Yadav, Stacey Philbrick. Segmented publics and Islamist women in Yemen. Rethinking space and activism, in *Journal of Middle East Women's Studies* 6:2 (2010), 1–30.

Yuval-Davis, Nira. *Gender and nation*, London 1997.

Space: Female Space: Pakistan

Sarwat Viqar

Introduction

Much of the scholarship on female space in Pakistan has conceptualized and historicized the subject through the lens of nation and religion. More broadly, the trajectory of women's spatial practices in the public realm in Pakistan is rooted in regional South Asian traditions and histories, most significantly in the colonial transformations of space and society. A key element of this transformation, with respect to gender, as posited by Partha Chatterjee, was the reworking of the private and public sphere and its associated meanings, in which women's place in society was framed within the struggle between a dominant colonial modern and a resistant native traditional (Chatterjee 1989). The resultant social space, with its corresponding spatial elements, was delineated into an inside (*andar*) and an outside (*bahir*). Chatterjee also points out that while the distinction between a male public sphere and a female domestic sphere is of course not exclusive to South Asia, what is significant is the way in which women's place in the home became a central site of struggle over meanings of sovereignty and nationhood. Thus, carried over from colonial times, the *andar/bahir* distinction has dominated discourses and practices associated with female space in Pakistan. For Indian Muslim communities who migrated in large numbers to Pakistan, and whose cultural narratives significantly shaped female space in Pakistan, the segregation and seclusion of women was a key element of their distinct identity as Muslims. Muslim respectability was contingent upon the way women appeared (or did not appear) in public and the extent to which they were seen as occupying the "protected" space of the home (Rouse 1996). Consequently, as Ayesha Jalal points out, the stability of the family unit became a core element of maintaining the Islamic social order (Jalal 1991). The social control of women's lives was thus normalized through this public/private dichotomy. In Pakistan today, women's participation and presence in public life unfolds within intense debates over women's rights and their access to the public sphere. These contestations show an imbrication of gender with religious norms, and the question of women's greater freedom often becomes a conflict between statehood, religion, and secularism.

The military government of General Zia-ul-Haq that came to power in 1977, and the subsequent Islamicization initiatives, marked a major turning point

© KONINKLIJKE BRILL NV, LEIDEN, 2019 | DOI:10.1163/1872-5309_EWIC_COM_002196

for women and public space in Pakistan. Far-reaching and draconian legislation like the Hudood and Zina ordinances initiated a series of measures that restricted women's access to public space and regulated the forms of their appearance outside the home. The Hudood Ordinances replaced parts of the secular British-era Pakistan Penal Code and added crimes of adultery (*zina*) and fornication, punishable by whipping, amputation, and stoning to death. The *zina* provisions of the laws became very controversial as victims of rape were accused of adultery and punished under the ordinance. While the hijab was not made mandatory, women in public services, including in the media, were required to cover their heads and dress modestly overall. Consequently, the discourse of *chadar and chardiwari* (veil and home) that was popularized during the regime, circulates through the social space and has been used to curtail women's mobility, as well as their access to the courts and legal protection from harassment, rape, and violence. The strong inscriptions of religion in legal structures have meant that women's mobility has been heavily influenced by the Zina and Hudood laws. Further, as Farida Shaheed (2010) has posited, even though the majority of women in Pakistan are not affected by the legal purview of the state, official inscriptions of religion in state structures have permeated the social and cultural sphere and given license to non-state social actors to act as moral enforcers in public.

This article discusses different aspects of how female space has been conceptualized and studied by scholars, paying particular attention to issues of female space and mobility in urban and rural areas; lifecycle observances and sociality; sex work and public performance; empowerment discourses and strategies emphasizing women-only spaces; and feminist activism for women's different access to different forms of public space.

Urban Space

The gendered nature of public space in Pakistan has been problematized as placing limitations on women's mobilities. Much work on female space in Pakistan is focused on women's access to economic, social, and physical infrastructure. This work is concerned with restrictions to women's mobility in public space that hinder their access to jobs, health services, and public transportation. Zubia Mumtaz and Sarah Salway (2005), in their study of women's mobility and its links to reproductive health services, argue that women's mobility is dictated not so much by physical geography as by social geography. This social geography consists of norms of movement that are ruled by kin- and clan-based affiliations that translate into the notion of *biradiri*, an iteration of community and kinship relations that is particular to many regions of South Asia.

Kamran Asdar Ali (2012) shows how low-income women in Karachi who move into the public realm to seek employment find themselves subjected to a new bodily and emotional discipline that they must maintain if they are to safely negotiate their way through the city. In addition to this gendered discipline, women in public spaces also encounter the violent and unpredictable political economy of a complex urban environment from which they had previously been shielded.

In their study addressing intersections of gender, mobility, and violence in urban Pakistan, Nausheen Anwar, Sarwat Viqar, and Daanish Mustapha find that mobility is inherently gendered in Pakistan and that women negotiate the public space of the city relying on various coping strategies (2018). These coping strategies are shaped not only by the threat of violence but also by deeply entrenched cultural narratives governing gender roles. The authors also point out that the inner lanes and streets of neighborhoods are potential spaces of safety for women, where they are surrounded by the familiar world of family and kin, as well as spaces of control, where transgressions are surveilled. Since women's proper place is deemed to be the private space of the home, women's unaccompanied presence in public is seen as a transgression. However, in an urban context like Karachi, with the largest working women population in the country, as well as the highest literacy rate, women are very much part of the public presence in the city. Through adopting various strategies—from donning the veil or hijab, to modifying the trajectories of their commutes—women manage to move through the public space of the city. Negotiating public transport is fraught with challenges for women because it is a highly masculinized space in Pakistan. Women generally report experiencing the space of public buses as hostile and intimidating (Hasan and Raza 2015). As Anwar, Viqar, and Mustapha point out, "At play, is a geographic fear associated with the outside for women" (2018, 24). Conversely, the inside is represented as an ideal space of safety for women, belying the truth of the pervasive violence faced by women in domestic spaces. As the invocation of the outside as a dangerous space for women is imbricated with the threat of sexual violence, it became clear in the study that women are increasingly adopting various veiling practices—the hijab, niqab, and burqa—to create a "shield" against harassment and violence.

More recent work questions the current conceptual framework that privileges a Westernized notion of "freedom of movement," as well as challenging assumptions about what mobility means in public and private—the public/private dichotomy (Mumtaz and Salway 2005, Viqar 2018). This work examines women's possibilities for a quotidian engagement in public life despite the constraints that have been so well-documented in other studies. In doing so, it also interrogates not only the notion of public and private but also the taken-for-granted association between freedom, agency, and unaccompanied mobility. In ethnographic accounts of women's public lives in the neighborhood of Karachi's old city, Sarwat Viqar identifies some of the ways in which women's membership in various collective arrangements operating in the neighborhood structures forms of engagement in public life. Women from largely lower-middle-class and working-class backgrounds participate in political, religious, and cultural activities that emanate from the various sovereign arrangements that manage and regulate life in the neighborhood. Their public participation in these activities crisscrosses the various domains of politics, religion, and culture, bringing into question the delineations that are generally used to separate these categories (Viqar 2018).

Rural Space

The idea that domestic space is the ideal realm for women is even more entrenched in rural areas. In reality, however, the association of women with the secluded space of the home is not absolute. Women generally venture out from the home due to extenuating circumstances related to poverty and the need to earn a livelihood, and when they do, they are not seen as "respectable" women (Chaudhry 2010). Thus socioeconomic factors mitigate women's mobilities as women from large land-owning families conform more to the gendered public/private dichotomy than low-income rural women who have to step out of the home to earn a living. Also, as Mumtaz and Salway (2005) point out, women's mobility outside the home does not automatically conform to the notion of "freedom of movement," the discourse of which, the authors suggest, is an expression of a Westernized notion of autonomy. They find that many women walk unaccompanied in a variety of spaces—a lack of mobility as such is not the main problem. Women who walk alone, it turns out, do not automatically report a higher use of reproductive services. Rather, Mumtaz and Salway emphasize the need to understand the larger social context within which women's mobility is restricted. As they put it, "The identity of the people who share a space at a particular moment in time determines whether the space is classified as 'bahar' (outside) or 'ander' (inside) space" (Mumtaz and Salway 2005, 1758). In the case of rural Punjab and Sindh, where their study was undertaken, the social context is one of large income disparities between the landowning and the laboring agricultural class, and of the association of public space with sexual threats and violence toward women, as well as with cultural codes of honor. Class hierarchies, they find, play a significant role in shaping women's experiences—and their ability to access contraception and antenatal care. Richer women, they find, are able to move around more freely and with less fear of being targeted for gendered violence, than can poorer women.

Sarah Halvorson (2005) shows that the socialization process that young girls in a rural region in Gilgit in Northern Pakistan undergo is a key factor in preparing them for their private and public roles in village life. In Gilgit, young girls are socialized not only in tasks typically associated with women's traditional role in the home, but also through the work they do outside the home, on the farm and in the fields, work that takes them through the public spatial geography. While their presence on the streets and in the fields around the village is highly circumscribed, women's sphere of movement from home to the outside has undergone significant changes due to transformations in the local and regional political economy.

Spaces of Sociality

Pashtun women play a significant role in constructing a space of sociality in *gham-khadi* observances, as Amineh Ahmed (2005) shows in her detailed ethnographic study. *Gham-khadi* refers to wedding, birth, or funerary gatherings among Pashtuns and is "a place where a number of normative and definitional conceptions of gender, personhood, propriety and tradition are knotted—and are beginning to unravel" (Ahmed 2005, 942). Ahmed argues that the world of *gham-khadi* observances, which involves both celebration and mourning, is also one that intersects with the public and political lives of family members. It involves the negotiation of social status through collective cooperation, the consumption of the feast-meal, and ritual and performance in which gifting plays a significant role. While both men and women participate in *gham-khadi*, Ahmed points out that it is women who exercise control over the proper forms and behaviors to be maintained during the observances and, in doing so, they enact individual agency. These forms and behaviors have implications for the political careers of their husbands and other male family members, which, by extension, influence the fortunes and public image of the family and the tribe.

Space, Sexuality, and Entertainment

Some aspects of the oppressive nature of women's appearance in public are echoed in *The dancing girls of Lahore* (2005), in which Louise Brown explores the complexities of the lives of sex workers in Heera Mandi, Lahore's red-light district. Not neatly adhering to the norms associated with either the domestic or public realms, these women occupy spaces that are networks of relationships and associations that cannot be easily categorized. While the space of sex work is universally stigmatized, Brown's account reveals the everyday dilemmas women face and the choices they make in order to survive while aspiring to better futures. Brown also points out the long tradition of courtesanship in South Asia that underpins modern sex work in its close association with dance as an art form. However, the practices that were tolerated and even patronized by courtly culture in the precolonial days, were later criminalized under British law. This criminalization was based on colonial indifference to the dance arts drawn upon by courtesans, as well as driven by the Victorian purity movement that spread from England to the colonies. This attitude prevailed despite "the decorum and modesty of their performances" (Brown 2005, 36).

Fouzia Saeed (2010) traces the lives of another group of women whose profession keeps them in the public eye. These women are in the performing arts, working as singers, dancers, and actresses in the local theatre companies that travel around the province. They perform for mostly all-male crowds, with women rarely in the audience of these spectacles. Saeed concludes that "women in the Lok theatre were economic assets; for the owners they were the crowd-pullers; for their men (husbands, fathers, lovers and brothers), they were lucrative investments to be tapped at whim" (Saeed 2010, 44).

The Politics of Women-Only Spaces

Women-only spaces have been among the strategies for women's empowerment in gender equality initiatives that are being implemented with transnational support. These initiatives are also seen as responding to local cultural needs. However, in their study of women workers in a garment factory in Karachi, Kanchana Ruwanpura and Alex Hughes (2016) show how women's empowerment discourses and practices circumscribe women within their stereotypical gender roles as wives, mothers, and potential brides rather than as women workers. The authors argue that, in actual practice, women-only work spaces serve to further entrench women's gendered roles in society as their work roles need to be justified as necessary for the maintenance of nationhood and the economy. There is also a strong discourse of empowered spaces as safe spaces, which in the context of industrial work discipline, the authors argue, can be used to regulate and mold a docile female workforce. The study thus raises important questions about how transnational gender empowerment discourses can be translated into local contexts in a way that creates new modes of gendered subjectivities.

Feminist Activism and Reclaiming Public Spaces

Recent years have seen an emerging activism around women's right to public spaces, led by young, middle-class feminists seeking to occupy and reclaim spaces that have traditionally been the reserve of men. Girls at Dhabas, a group with a strong social media presence, take their cues from similar moves in India, where initiatives for women to reclaim the public spaces of cities are meant to highlight the ways in which women's movement in public spaces has been controlled and regulated. The idea of occupying public space, city streets, and parks purely as a mark of leisure is at the forefront of these attempts to reclaim public spaces. Feminist scholars writing in the context of Indian cities have argued that even though women's labor in public space is an essential part of the urban economy, yet their presence is often made invisible through practices of surveillance and exclusion (Phadke, Khan, and Ranade 2011). The authors further posit that an important element of women reclaiming public spaces is to assert their right to "loiter" in public space. The Pakistani feminist group Girls at Dhabas has garnered social media attention as young women exercise their right to enjoy leisure time in *dhabas* (roadside teastalls), post pictures of their exploits, and argue for women's unimpeded right to the city (Iqbal 2015, Ansari 2018).

Nida Kirmani and Ayesha Khan (2018) argue that feminist activism in Pakistan has been victim to a false binary that casts women's engagement in public life as falling into either of two categories: women's involvement in conservative religious movements or as liberal, secular feminists in the Western mold. They point out that, in fact, gender-based resistance has continued throughout the country in multiple forms that do not conform to this binary. Peasant-based rural women in Punjab actively participate in the larger peasant movement, the Anjuman-e-Mazarain, which resists land dispossession and demands ownership rights. Protests and sit-ins are organized by the Lady Health Workers (LHW) to demand adequate wages and regularization as federal employees. As the authors highlight, "LHWs' mobilization is possibly the most sustained, widespread, and successful example of women-led collective action in Pakistan's recent history, yet somehow their endeavor has operated quite independently from the women's rights movement and the NGO sector" (Kirmani and Khan 2018, 170). The third example they use is the Tribal Women's Association, formed in 2012, which brings together women of diverse backgrounds from the FATA (Federally Administered Tribal Areas) region of Pakistan to demand political representation at different levels of government, including reforms to the traditional *jirgah* system because of its patriarchal structure. Finally, the authors point to emerging transgender activism as another example of feminist activism, specifically because it challenges the binary biological categorization of sex and the conflation of sex with gender.

Conclusion

Female space in Pakistan remains understudied as the spatial geography of women's lives has not garnered a great deal of attention from scholars. The important work that does exist has foregrounded both the constraints and the potentialities that exist in women's trajectories across different territorial scales, rural and urban. Women's mobility remains a major focus of concern as numerous studies indicate that women face a complex array of challenges in negotiating public space, whether for access to essential services, work, or leisure. The social geography of family and community relations establishes the norms and conditions for women's movement in space that is always contingent upon adherence to these norms. In rural areas, the social geography of clan and tribe is much more determinant in regulating women's movement. These social geographies, however, are not static but subject to the changing regional and national political and economic landscape.

In more nuanced studies, the public aspect of women's lives is represented as more complex, as private and public domains often intersect and women create agentive possibilities in these interstices. There has generally been more focus on the ways in which women's movement, presence, and activities in public space are restricted and less engagement with the forms of public life that tend to exist under the radar or do not seem to fit the conceived notions of private and public, individual and community. In urban areas, while women face daunting challenges related to mobility and access to basic services and employment, their mobility and participation in public life is made possible through complex negotiations with urban social and physical geographies.

The leisurely or even transgressive aspects of women's use of space—for example, related to sexuality—are areas of study much deserving of attention, but they remain understudied in the context of Pakistan. On the other hand, there is an emerging focus on the spaces of feminist activism, which have also become the flashpoint for debates on religion and secularism and the meaning of women's rights in Pakistan.

Bibliography

Ahmed, Amineh. Death and celebration among Muslim women. A case study from Pakistan, in *Modern Asian Studies* 39:4 (2005), 929–80.

Ansari, Natasha. Girls at Dhabas. Challenging issues of safety, or "respectability" in urban Pakistan? in *Open Democracy*, 27 April 2018, <https://www.opendemocracy.net/5050/natasha-ansari/girls-at-dhabas-safety-respectability-urban-pakistan>. 31 May 2019.

Anwar, Nausheen, Sarwat Viqar, and Daanish Mustapha. Intersections of gender, mobility and violence in urban Pakistan, in *Social theories of urban violence in the Global South*, ed. Jennifer E. Salahub, Markus Gottsbacher, and John de Boer, London 2018, 15–31.

Asdar Ali, Kamran. Women, work and public spaces. Conflict and co-existence in Karachi's poor neighbourhoods, in *International Journal of Urban and Regional Research* 36:3 (2012), 585–605.

Brown, Louise. *The dancing girls of Lahore. Selling love and saving dreams in Pakistan's Pleasure District*, New York 2005.

Chatterjee, Partha. Nationalism, and colonized women. The contest in India, in *American Ethnologist* 16:4 (1989), 622–33.

Chaudhry, Lubna N. Women and poverty. Salient findings from a gendered analysis of a quasi-anthropological study in rural Punjab and Sindh, in *Pakistani women. Multiple locations and competing narratives,* ed. Sadaf Ahmed, Karachi 2010, 47–119.

Halvorson, Sarah J. Growing up in Gilgit. Exploring the nature of girlhood in Northern Pakistan, in *Geographies of Muslim women. Gender, religion and space,* ed. Ghazi Walid-Falah and Caroline Nagel, New York 2005.

Hasan, Arif, and Mansoor Raza. *Karachi. The transport crisis*, Karachi 2015.

Iqbal, Ameerah. Girls at Dhabas. A much-needed campaign, in *TNS: The News on Sunday*, 13 September 2015, <http://tns.thenews.com.pk/girls-at-dhabas-much-needed-campaign/#.XPGm2NNKgWp>. 31 May 2019.

Jalal, Ayesha. The convenience of subservience. Women and the state of Pakistan, in *Women, Islam and the state*, ed. Deniz Kandiyoti, London 1991, 77–114.

Kirmani, Nida, and Ayesha Khan. Moving beyond the binary. Gender-based activism in Pakistan, in *Feminist Dissent* 3 (2018), 151–91.

Masood, Ayesha. Negotiating mobility in gendered spaces. Case of Pakistani women doctors, in *Gender, Place and Culture* 25:2 (2018), 188–206.

Mumtaz, Zubia. Gender and social geography. Impact on lady health workers' mobility in Pakistan, in *BMC Health Services Research* (2012), 12:360.

Mumtaz, Zubia, and Sarah Salway. "I never go anywhere." Extricating the links between women's mobility and uptake of reproductive health services in Pakistan, in *Social Science and Medicine* 60 (2005), 1751–65.

Phadke, Shilpa, Samira Khan, and Shilpa Ranade. *Why loiter? Women and risk on Mumbai streets*, India 2011.

Rouse, Shahnaz. Gender, nationalism(s) and cultural identity. Discursive strategies and exclusivities, in *Embodied violence. Communalising women's sexuality in South Asia*, ed. K. Jayawardena and M. Alwis, New Delhi 1996, 42–70.

Ruwanpura, Kanchana N., and Alex Hughes. Empowered spaces. Management articulations of gendered spaces in apparel factories in Karachi, Pakistan, in *Gender, Place and Culture* 23:9 (2016), 1270–85.

Saeed, Fouzia. Women in *Lok* (folk) theatre, in *Pakistani women. Multiple locations and competing narratives*, ed. Sadaf Ahmed, Karachi 2010, 25–46.

Shaheed, Farida. Contested identities. Gendered politics, gendered religion in Pakistan, in *Third World Quarterly* 31:6 (2010), 851–67.

Viqar, Sarwat. Women's public lives and sovereign arrangements in Karachi's inner city, in *Gender, Place and Culture* 25:3 (2018), 416–33.

Sports

∵

Public Spaces and Gender: Sport and Activism: United States

Stanley Thangaraj

Introduction

Most common (mis)conceptions of Muslims, especially in United States society, frame them outside the normative boundaries of citizenship. With rising Islamophobia, the connections between citizenship and the representation of the Muslim American (terrorist) become that much more disparate. In particular, the tension between the two and the constant maintenance of a dichotomous relationship is further nurtured, perpetuated, and made legible through sporting practices. Sport, with its long ties to patriotism and production of the normative (read as white, male, middle-class, heterosexual, and Christian, Lorde 1995) citizen, is a key but often overlooked site to examine how Muslim American communities manage identity and belonging. Sport offers us a site to think critically through "cultural citizenship" (Maira 2009, Thangaraj 2015, 2014) that allows for different and expansive renditions of US citizenship which accommodates Muslim-ness, sport, and claims to American-ness simultaneously. The affinity to basketball and other American sports were a key aspect of claiming US belonging for Muslim American men.

This entry looks at the diverse sporting practices in Muslim America. It centers on the (dis)engagement of Muslim Americans with sporting cultures and the ways by which Muslim communities construct different and differential gendered relations to racialized sport. In the process, it becomes evident how public spaces in US society are differently and differentially experienced and claimed across the gendered divide in Muslim America. This entry is not representative of all of Muslim America but rather draws on focused explorations of Muslim American sporting practices in Nashville, Tennessee and Atlanta, Georgia. In the process of looking at Muslim America, we can decipher how the public sphere is already one that is political, racialized, gendered, and differentially experienced. Sports, as activities celebrating and underscoring public performances, stand in for nation. Furthermore, the language of meritocracy fosters notions of sport as neutral, almost apolitical (Burdsey 2011, Carrington 2010, Ratna 2011). Yet, the lives of Muslim American men and women shed light on how public sport is religiously demarcated, gendered, and racially contained to exclude a variety of subjects. The entry into and marginalization in

© KONINKLIJKE BRILL NV, LEIDEN, 2015 | DOI:10.1163/1872-5309_EWIC_COM_002027

sport provide important insights into how Muslim American men and women experience sport cultures differently.

While sport offers an understanding of consumptive practices of mainstream American sports and practices of cultural citizenship, Muslim American women have different relations to it and the public sphere (Farooq Samie 2013, 2011). Diasporic South Asian Muslim and Kurdish Muslim American communities open up spaces for various performances of gendered sporting Muslim identity, but sometimes within a problematic concoction of masculinity and the male body (Brooks 2009). Whereas sport might not be the way for female Muslim communities to engage with public space in explicit and physical ways, one must not fall into the stereotypical renditions of Muslim women. Muslim women are not powerless dupes who are always only victims of patriarchy and Islam. They are part of sporting cultures, but their presence is not always easily decipherable through normative readings (Thangaraj 2015). Furthermore, some Kurdish American and South Asian American Muslim women found pleasure in claiming public spaces other than sport, for asserting citizenship and performing their politics. By visualizing a wider gamut of public and political performances, they express their radicalness that can also work alongside piety (Mahmood 2005). Muslim women find public spaces other than sport for claiming their American identity while simultaneously challenging the dominant racializations of them. Their male counterparts, on the other hand, find private spaces of sport to claim their American identity.

Sport and Gendered Citizenship

The interpellation of sport as masculine has become a hegemonic discourse by which men are given privileges through the domination of and exclusion of women from sporting cultures (Thangaraj 2015, Ratna 2011). Within the United States, sports such as basketball, ice hockey, football, and softball are often construed as naturally masculine venues. Women who participate in these sports are labeled as "butch" or "lesbian," which acts as a regulating force that disciplines athletes into heterosexual femininity, delegitimizes the achievements of female athletes, closes the possibilities for femininity, and limits female participation in those sports (Rand 2012). Furthermore, diasporic communities sometimes have more conservative notions of gender and sport than their ancestral communities in places of origin. As a result of the taken-for-granted nature of sport as for men, Muslim American women do not attend to basketball as they might other sports that are seen in US society as feminine, such as tennis and volleyball (Thangaraj 2015).

Within the larger Muslim South Asian American basketball communities in Atlanta, there was no mention or evidence of well-known female athletes. They did not participate heavily in mainstream sports, but instead played a variety of games—which were already discursively connoted as not intense, not competitive, and not as aggressive as sport. When South Asian American women played basketball, it was often in highly gender-segregated spaces where women played against other women (Karim 2009, Thangaraj 2010b). The mainstream mosques held inter-mosque and intra-mosque basketball tournaments where young girls and young women would play their co-gender peers. Jamilah Karim (2009) explains that African American mosques, as a result of their involvement in the civil rights movement and association with the Nation of Islam, did not practice the strict gender-segregation of the mainstream international mosques that had a large community of immigrants from Africa, the Middle East, and South Asia. Some African American Muslim girls and young women have gone on to play high school and collegiate basketball. In contrast, the Muslim basketball tournaments held in Atlanta by South Asian American Muslims were gender-segregated and the separate sexes did not share the same basketball court. Similarly, there was not the same investment for girls compared to boys in performing cultural citizenship through mainstream sport. As a result, the media recognition of Muslim American men and Muslim men far exceeds the coverage of Muslim American women athletes.

Even within the South Asian American community, there is a disproportionate amount of attention given to men both within and outside South Asian communities (Farooq Samie 2013, Thangaraj 2010b). For example, there is disproportional attention given to Sikh Canadian players Sim and Tanveer Bhullar, both 7 footers. Sim played collegiate basketball for New Mexico State and is now in the developmental league of the National Basketball Association. While at New Mexico State, Sim did not set any records or receive greater international recognition. On the contrary, Madeleine Venkatesh, a Christian South Asian American women played in the highly coveted Division I collegiate conferences and set local collegiate records. Yet she is invisible in discourses of South Asian American athletic spectacularity.

While the discourse of "butch" regulates and constricts the possibilities for femininity in basketball (Thangaraj 2010b), this does not happen to all South Asian diasporas equivalently. In the United Kingdom, basketball does not carry the same weight and significance as it does in the United States. As a result, there are different gendered affective connections to basketball in the United Kingdom, while soccer and cricket might be policed much more rigorously instead. In her sophisticated ethnography of sport among South Asian communities in the United Kingdom, Samaya Farooq Samie (2013) highlights the relationship Pakistani British women have to basketball that differs from Pakistani American communities. Whereas soccer and cricket present sites of regulation where national masculinity is managed, the Muslim South Asian Britains who play basketball do not feel constrained by the discourse of "butch." In contrast to the US case, British South Asian women who play soccer and cricket are interpellated as "butch" and "lesbian" (Puar and Rai 2004). For the female Muslim players, the homosociality of basketball allowed safe spaces to offer their own renditions of femininity, bodily integrity, and (hetero)sexiness (Farooq Samie 2013). However not all diasporic Muslim communities celebrated muscular and toned female bodies as representations of diaspora/nation. The representations in the diasporas have tended to be conservative thereby allocating them to a particular domesticity, passivity, and delineating them as holders of (unchanging) tradition/culture (Gopinath 2005, Naber 2012).

The lack of female Muslim sporting figures in the diaspora does not equivalently translate across to home/ancestral nations. There are many countries with openly head-covering female athletes and bearded Muslim men (Farooq Samie and Sehlikoglu 2014, Farooq Samie 2013), as well as Muslim tennis players such as Sania Mirza (Shankar 2013). For many of the recent Olympics, there have been head-covering women's teams: Turkey's volleyball team and Iran's soccer team, for example. FIFA (International Federation of Association Football) found the presence of head-covering women on Iran's national team unacceptable and took back their opportunities to play. They banned head-covering as the Iranian team readied themselves to play Jordan in the 2011 qualifying rounds (see <http://religionclause.blogspot.com/2011/06/soccer-official-bans-islamic-head.html>). Institutional regulation of gender and sexuality at the level of international sport shows how Muslim women are policed by Western nations, who promise liberation from patriarchy (Nguyen 2011). Cases such as this illustrate how the Western anxiety over Islam already makes impossible the possibility of Muslim women's agency in their own nation and in their own sporting cultures. A certain kind of conservatism is already mapped onto the bodies of Muslim women, be it in home nations or diasporas. The Muslim public, as a result, is already racialized and seen as out of bounds for women's agency and active participation. While Muslim American women may not always occupy sporting publics, they do find important ways to claim other types of public spaces. Their iteration of self is one that collapses American-ness, Muslim-ness, and political activism.

Islam, Femininity, and Public Space

Research on South Asian American sporting cultures demonstrates that women occupy a wide assortment of spaces (Thangaraj 2015, 2014, 2010b).

Similarly, Kurdish American women in Nashville were very active in public spaces and politically progressive venues. As Muslim South Asian Americans practice gender-segregation much more strictly than their Muslim African American peers (Karim 2009), they were not present in the sporting spaces as athletic participants (Thangaraj 2015, 2010b). Women who came to the tournaments often came as sisters, girlfriends, and spouses to cheer the men playing on the court or field. At the various South Asian American tournaments, a few older Muslim South Asian American women would come to support their sons. For the most part, diasporic female Muslim bodies were not celebrated or showcased within the sporting realms of basketball. However, as post-9/11 hysteria continued to exclude and ostracize Muslim men in various public forums—such as sporting venues—Muslim South Asian American women took to mainstream public spaces at the very moment their brothers, fathers, husbands, partners, and friends were increasingly being detained, deported, and incarcerated. Whereas the mainstream media depicts Muslim women as always victims to Islamic patriarchy who have no agency for themselves, South Asian American and Kurdish American women were principled civil rights activists who claim American publics while staking out their own renditions of American identity in a country governed by the Judeo-Christian ethos (Rana 2011). Instead of expressing a version of Muslim identity and assimilation into US society that demanded secularity, they chose to don the hijab against the wishes of men (brothers, fathers, spouses) in their community. Part of their claim to public space is the performance of Muslim piety in Atlanta and Nashville.

Since 2001, the increasingly expansive global "war on terror" has been accompanied with depictions that demonize Muslim men while representing Muslim women has helpless, powerless victims of theocratic rule (Rana 2011, Alsultanly 2012, Naber 2012). Accordingly, such discourses take Muslim women's oppression as convention, one that can be undone with Western (often military) influence. The young Muslim American women, both South Asians and Kurds, do not see Islam, feminism, and liberation as antithetical, dichotomous, and impossible alternates. Peek (2010) demonstrates how Muslim American women took to head covering, the hijab, the veil, and burkas after the increasingly racial profiling of their communities post-9/11. By donning hijabs, Muslim American women were politicized in public arenas as a way to simultaneously offer critique of the rise of Islamophobia while demonstrating their solidarity with Muslim men who felt the increasing burden of the US state into their communities. Alongside head-covering, Muslim women also increased their political presence in the public sphere with increased participation in non-profit and activist organizations.

Muslim women in Atlanta and Nashville express their politics with performances of Islamic feminism that challenge the simplistic binaries of second wave feminisms (Karim 2009). Instead of seeing Islam as the source of disempowerment, Muslim South Asian American women locate the radical and progressive elements within the Qur'an. The Muslim South Asian American women did not separate Islam from modernity and radicalness but rather saw it as part of that algorithm. They did not pose religion against the state—it was not diametrically opposed to democracy, but rather a key element of it. Their embrace of Islam as part of a public performance of citizenship was contrary to how public spaces were seen as conventionally masculine. By entering the white public space, their presence and politics expanded the contours of American-ness beyond its racial (white), religious (Christian), class (middle-class), and gender (male) parameters.

Muslim South Asian American and Kurdish American women, both those who wore headscarves and those who did not, were at various major public events in Atlanta and Nashville. In 2007, the US Social Forum (meeting of progressive activists and scholars) was held in Atlanta. Thousands of activists, community organizers, and scholars (students, teachers, and faculty) arrived in the city to discuss the growing poverty globally, the Western imperialisms at play, and the localized politics of racism and xenophobia. In the process, there were many creative, expansive, and pleasurable opportunities for coalition building. Many South Asian American activists arrived, most of them were women. South Asian American activists from New York (of which several were Muslim) affiliated with Desis Rising Up and Moving (DRUM) worked alongside Atlanta's South Asian American radical leftists to discuss matters of the "missing" (Maira 2009) and detention of their community members. At the 2007 Social Forum, Ehsanul Sadequee's mother and sister chaired a panel on Islamophobia, the increasing detention of Muslim South Asian Americans, and the unjust incarceration of American-born and Atlanta native Ehsanul. After going to Pakistan for wedding service, he was unlawfully detained and incarcerated. He had written widely about the growing problematic known as the "war on terror," translated a few Arabic texts, and, like his sister, advocated for civil rights for Muslims in the United States. On the flight back, he was detained and put in a secret detention center and then in the Atlanta federal penitentiary before his trial. After being found guilty of having terroristic ambitions without full due process, Ehansul was sentenced to 17 years at a secret prison, affiliated with the Corrections Corporation of America (CCA), in Terra Haute, Indiana. At the Social Forum, Ehsanul's mother wore a head scarf and pleaded, with tears on her face and bitterness in her voice, for better politics that were attuned to the intersections of race, religion, and gender. Ehsanul's sister demonstrated the connections between the "global war on terror" and the localized experiences of detention, detainment, and racial profiling. She

PUBLIC SPACES AND GENDER: SPORT AND ACTIVISM: UNITED STATES   529

was a tireless advocate for immigrant rights and worked with non-profit organizations to provide resources for women of color.

The pleas of both the mother and the sister work, complicate, and challenge the semantics of "terror" and "terrorist." Often, especially in mainstream Western media, the figure of the Muslim man is singularly projected as "terrorist" whose acts terrorize white women and corrupt public space (Alsultany 2012). Contrary to these simplistic depictions, many Muslim American women refuse to shy away from public spaces; rather they find meaning, solidarity, and strength from advocacy in those realms. In addition, some Muslim women, such as Ehsanul's mother, enter the public arena with a headscarf and thus accentuate their difference from the commonsensical public feminine heroine who is white, middle-class, heterosexual, and Christian.

In addition to Ehsanul's sister and mother, other Muslim South Asian American women take on activist roles. For example, young Muslim women played active roles in the local masjids and the Islamic Speakers Bureau, participated in non-profit work, and were key organizers in the Movement to End Israeli Apartheid-Georgia (MEIA-GA). Al-Farooq Masjid, the largest mainstream Muslim mosque, instituted the Islamic Speakers Bureau as a result of the advocacy of a Muslim woman. The Islamic Speakers Bureau goes to organizations, schools, and institutions across Georgia enlightening locals about the complex lives of Muslims, the different readings of the Qur'an, and dismantling Islamophobic stereotypes. Fatima Ahmed and her daughter, Abda Ahmed, attended a MEIA-GA organizing event and took notes and raised several questions about how fighting for Muslim rights was related to US imperialism and Israeli apartheid. Fatima discussed the reasons for her attendance: "It is my obligation as an American and as a Muslim." As she looked around, she added, "I am sad that more Muslim men are not here. They do not feel safe to come out to this [MEIA-GA event]. I am going to have a talk with the Imam [at Abdulla Masjid in Gwinnett County]." Other Muslim activist women shared a frustration with the lack of men's presence at these important meetings. Yet, clearly, like Fatima, they identified the hostile nature of public space that gave them, as Muslim women, more freedoms to enter it than men. Their presence in public spaces challenges the mainstream American imagination.

In Nashville, Kurdish American women activists were key figures in the Kurdish community, and in the larger Tennessee community. As Kurds in Nashville come from South Kurdistan (the area known as Iraq), they are refugees and enter through refugee clauses rather than immigration clauses (Nguyen 2012, Vang 2010). While weaving their refugee experiences into the narrative of Muslim identity, Kurdish American head-covering activists expressed women of color politics that included wide coalition-building (Lorde 1995).

Working with various immigrant and refugee rights organizations and serving on the board of various non-profit organizations, Kurdish American women advocated for civil rights for communities of color, for Muslims, for immigrants, and for refugees. The post-9/11 racial hysteria had an impact on Kurdish communities, who do not identify as Arab. There have been several instances of hate directed toward Kurdish communities, such as burning down mosques, attempting to pass anti-Shar'ia bills in the Tennessee Legislature, and the opposition to expanding an old mosque in Murfreesboro, Tennessee (20 miles southeast of Nashville). In response, head-covering Muslim Kurdish American activists have become the key political figures and public figures in Nashville. Their presence at immigrants' rights rallies and their organization of protests following the acquittal of George Zimmerman (a gun zealot accused of killing black teenager, Trayvon Martin) illustrates a strong political commitment to civil rights. Commitment of this sort to social justice is part of the Islamic feminism they practice. The South Asian and Kurdish women in Atlanta and Nashville emphasize one of the five pillars of Islam, *zakāt* (charity and service), as a critical part of their everyday performance of self.

Playing through Citizenship with US Popular Culture

With the Islamic commitment to charity (*zakāt*), young Muslim Americans of various Islamic branches grew up with social service. However, once Muslim American youth finished high school, the young Muslim women continued their social justice organizing and went from the private realms of the mosque into the public realm of social service while the men entered the private realms of their professions. The stereotyping of South Asian Americans as "terror" and "terrorists" (as a noun and a classification) has a profound effect on these communities, especially the men, by fixing their bodies outside the racial, gendered, classed, and sexual realm of American-ness. Even in the intimate realm of sport where bodies collide and there is pleasure in such physical proximity, South Asian American men are imagined to be playing South Asian sports. Accordingly, often these young men heard whites asking, "Don't you guys play cricket?" The assumption that South Asian Americans consume cricket, and other South Asian cultural forms such as Bollywood, fixes their tastes and identity in symbolic and physical territories of South Asian-ness (Thangaraj 2015, 2010a). On the contrary, members of Atlanta's South Asian American community, especially the young men playing in basketball leagues, partake in various forms of popular culture that collapsed American-ness and South Asian-ness into South Asian American-ness (see Thangaraj 2010a, 2010b). However, there are communities of young Muslim South Asian American men in Atlanta and across the United States who gravitate to the sport of cricket and Bollywood cinema as their expressions of "cultural citizenship" (Maira 2009). In contrast, some choose to participate in basketball as positions of counter-identification from cricket players.

The young Muslim Pakistani American men on the two teams Atlanta Outkasts and Atlanta Rat Pack did not play cricket (Thangaraj 2015, 2010a), other than as a rare occurrence at their mosque. Even during the encounters with cricket at the mosque, Mustafa, one of the key players in Atlanta's South Asian community, mentioned, "I almost got into a fight. I can't do that any-more." He then alluded to how basketball was his "true love." Many Muslim American men gravitated to and chose basketball as the site for performing their version of American identity. The basketball players frequently brought up the subject of cricket, but always as counter-identification. Whereas they understand the basketball gym and basketball court as a quintessential site of American-ness, they also configured South Asian men playing cricket on soccer and football fields as not American enough. For example, when driving to an Asian American basketball tournament, one of the key players on team Atlanta Rat Pack, Imran, pointed to a group of young South Asian American men playing cricket on one of the Georgia Institute of Technology's recreation-al fields: "They play every Sunday. FOBs play cricket. They play every week-end at Georgia Tech [Georgia Institute of Technology]." Imran translated the pejorative term "Fresh Off the Boat" (FOB) that was used to label the "boat people" from Vietnam to mark a generational divide between himself and other South Asian immigrants. In this instance, he underscores which group of Muslim men could properly claim public spaces and cultural citizenship. Second generation South Asians in the United States solidify "foreignness" and un-American masculinity onto the bodies of recent male immigrants, mostly international students who play cricket. Their depiction of them as "freshy off the boat," was also a classed judgment of masculinity. Cricket players were rep-resented as immigrants without the class resources or the cultural constitu-tion to buy into either American-ness or "basketball cool" (Thangaraj 2015). Again, it is not to say that South Asian American men cannot play cricket and identify as American, but rather that basketball players engage in "intra-ethnic Othering" (Abelmann 2009) of men within South Asian America by position-ing cricket players as less capable, less manly US subjects. By conceptualizing cricket on different territorial and national terms, South Asian American bas-ketball players racialized cricket players as a different class of immigrants in the United States.

With the popularity of basketball, the ease with which basketball games are organized, and the ways in which basketball communicated ideas about race and masculinity (Brooks 2009), many young men actively partook of basketball play and corresponding social interactions. Given the gamut of basketball circuits in Atlanta, these young South Asian American men participated in a variety of ethnically and religiously exclusive leagues such as Indo-Pak Basketball (South Asian American league), Asian American leagues, and Muslim tournaments. Within these ethno-religious spaces, the South Asian American players could express their versions of American-ness and masculinity. Practices of cultural citizenship, such as playing basketball, extended the limits of American citizenship onto South Asian American bodies and South Asian American places. However, such cultural citizenship in Atlanta's South Asian American basketball cultures were possible only in private, co-ethnic only leagues that limited various racial, gendered, and sexual "Others." There had to be a creation of an ethnic Muslim public that was private in order to perform their renditions of American identity.

Masjids as Sites of American-ness

The masjids (mosques) were key sites of Muslim-only basketball tournaments that included participants from a wide-ranging religious, ethnic, and national spectrum. South Asian American men played against their Muslim peers in religiously bounded tournaments and leagues at the local mosques. Contrary to popular belief, Muslim South Asian American centers of worship were not sites of latent "terror cells" and nor were they areas in need of extra-governmental surveillance (Rana 2011). For South Asian Americans, sport participation was a "racial project" (Carrington 2010, Omi and Winant 1994) that contested mainstream racializations of Muslim South Asian Americans as socially inept or dangerous masculinities while trying to gain entry into American-ness in a much more complete manner. As part of citizenship in the United States is predicated on legibility within the black–white racial dichotomy, the practice of basketball by these racial subjects reconfigures the boundaries of belonging by inverting the relationship between race and ability (Saskietewa Gilbert 2010). From the early construction and to the early years of Al-Farooq Masjid (the first mainstream, international mosque in Atlanta), sports were central to the spiritual training of Muslim men within the arena of American-ness. While many of the newly arriving immigrants played cricket, Muslim South Asian American men, who were born or grew up in the United States, socialized into American masculinity through their social interactions on the masjid basketball court. Young Muslim American women played games and were not in the same sporting spaces as the young men (Thangaraj 2015).

PUBLIC SPACES AND GENDER: SPORT AND ACTIVISM: UNITED STATES 533

The Muslim community hosted several co-religious basketball tournaments in Atlanta. On 15 August 2009, India's Independence Day, Angul, an organization for Muslim youth, structured a 3-on-3 basketball tournament in a Gwinnett County public gym (Thangaraj 2010b). On the days of Pakistani and Indian Independence days (14 and 15 August respectively), instead of going to the independence day parades and festivities across Atlanta, the young South Asian American men chose instead to play basketball. They committed their entire days to playing in various tournaments that weekend—this was their source of pleasure. Some members of Atlanta's Muslim South Asian American community enjoyed partaking of basketball in less-structured co-ethnic only spaces other than these tournaments.

In addition to the tournaments, various Muslim Americans took part in much more pedestrian experiences of basketball. From early summer to late fall, Imran (21 years old), Amir (also 21 and teammate of Imran's from Atlanta Rat Pack), and their collegiate peers and Muslim friends would gather on Friday evenings. The young men arrived, after the completion of *jumma* (sacred Friday prayers for Muslims), at Imran's parents' immaculate 10,000 square foot home. At the back of the hoouse, there was a beautiful outdoor half-court basketball court. Arriving with their professional clothes and other attire, the mostly affluent collegiate students of Pakistani American and Middle Eastern American descent, played a few hours of National Basketball Association (NBA)'s EA videogame as the precursor for the real thing. Each of them would take on the racialized character of mostly the African American professional players in the videogame and challenge each other. After a few hours, the players would slip off their athletic slides (a kind of sporting flip-flop) and don their basketball shoes. In the blistering and muggy Atlanta heat, the young men competed intensely against each other while drenched in sweat.

Partaking of basketball was routine and part of the fabric of South Asian American masculinity. Participation in basketball was part and parcel of an American-ness that Muslim American players never questioned. Instead, it was the larger US public that doubted the American-ness of Muslim men. One of the key elders in Atlanta, Dr. Abdul, emphasized, "This [post 9/11 racial hysteria] has awakened Muslims to the need to interact with the community at large and explain the teachings of Islam instead of having radicals explain Islam. We are extra vigilant with our own behavior and stay away from all forms of extremism and violence and actions to strengthen the fabric of this society ... we as Muslims [must be] perceived as an asset to society." The US public spaces are such that they are coded with whiteness and saturated in a Judeo-Christian ethos that continues to depict South Asian American bodies as antithetical to American-ness. Public realms, such as multi-racial leagues and collegiate tournaments, are not sites of post-racial times. Rather, participants in public, multi-racial sporting cultures use racialized language of the "nerd" and "terrorist" to marginalize South Asian American men.

For Kurdish Americans in Nashville, their status as "Middle Eastern" locates them within a racial discourse of "white" and "Caucasian" (Jamal and Naber 2008, Gualtieri 2009). Their refugee status and struggles do not allow them the same mobility promised via normative whiteness. At the Salahadeen Center, the first international mosque in Nashville, Kurdish American men socialized and formed various sport teams. Most Kurdish American men were not public figures like their Kurdish sisters. However, they had a much more intimate engagement with sports, both US and global. At the Nashville International Center for Empowerment (refugee resettlement organization) fund-raiser soccer tournament, the Kurdish team and Muslim Somali teams beat out the Vanderbilt University club team, Bhutanese teams, Myanmar teams, and local teams to play for the championship. The captain of the Kurdish team explained that they play soccer and basketball primarily. Participation in these two sports was a way for Kurdish American men to balance, manage, and negotiate their American identity and their global histories.

The soccer tournaments in Nashville, Indo-Pak Basketball tournaments, recreational basketball at the masjids, and basketball at Imran's house provided safe spaces to perform renditions of being masculine, Muslim, and American that countered the racial formation of "Muslim looking" (Rana 2011, Naber 2012, Thangaraj 2014). In the safety of this exclusive space, these young men partook of physical, aggressive, and tough play. In these Muslim spaces, the young men could safely perform the multiplicity of American-ness, weaved through different ethnic and national registers, and sporting masculinity. Only by closing basketball and soccer off to the general public could they articulate the masculine and racial contours of American-ness. The heightened state surveillance and racial hysteria concerning Muslims made social exclusivity one of the few methods to open up venues to articulate a complicated American-ness inclusive of Muslim-ness. To be sure, there are a few male elders at the forefront of civic engagement with American society on many fronts. For example, the major forums and inter-faith dialogues in Atlanta were organized, structured, and facilitated by the male elders at Al-Farooq Masjid. Yet not all South Asian American and Kurdish American men had the disposition to enter public spaces and challenge the restrictive contours of American-ness. As their retreat to private sporting spaces challenges their racialization, Muslim South Asian American women resist their own racializations by entering the very public spaces that ostracize their brothers.

Conclusion

The discursive production of the "war on terror" and its relevant subject, the "terrorist," has deep implications for how race, gender, and religion operate in US society. For Muslim men, their inward movement to certain insularity constituted an important recourse by which to perform cultural citizenship. However, such an insular projection expands the contours of American-ness, but in quite limited ways. In this case, sporting venues allow for a reconfiguration of American and Muslim masculinity as convergent subjectivities but do so through the production of basketball as masculine. In this space, Muslim American men play with the boundaries of masculinity where their toughness, athleticism, and aggression are still part of the US national fabric. However, the very exclusivity of these spaces then erases the possible visibility of these performances of American-ness for the greater American public. In a different vein, Muslim South Asian American women have occupied public spaces as the means to stake out their American-ness. They interject Islamic feminism into white Christian spaces. Their visibility and presence inverts the relationship between femininity and Islam. These Muslim women express a politics of empowerment centered on their Islamic faith and identity. As a result, they, as the supposed victims of the Islamic terror, call into question the very Islamophobic equation that equals oppression with religion. In contradiction, they emphasize that the apparatus of oppression and disempowerment is the imperial state, and not the terror within or outside of US borders.

Bibliography

Abelmann, Nancy. *The intimate university*, Durham, N.C. 2009.

Alsultany, Evelyn. *Arabs and Muslims in the media. Race and representation after 9/11*, New York 2012.

Brooks, Scott. *Black men can't shoot*, Chicago 2009.

Burdsey, Daniel (ed.). *Race, ethnicity, and football*, Abingdon, U.K. 2011.

Carrington, Ben. *Race, sport and politics. The sporting black diaspora*, London 2010.

Davis, Angela. *Women, culture, politics*, New York 1985.

Farooq Samie, Samaya. "Tough talk," muscular Islam, and football. Young British Pakistani Muslim masculinities, in *Race, ethnicity, and football*, ed. Daniel Burdsey, Abingdon, U.K. 2011, 145–60.

Farooq Samie, Samaya. Hetero-sexy self/body work and basketball. The invisible sporting women of British Pakistani Muslim herita, in *South Asian Popular Culture* 11:3 (2013), 257–70.

Farooq Samie, Samaya and Sertac Sehlikoglu. Strange, incompetent and out-of-place. Media, Muslim sportswomen and London 2012, in *Feminist Media Studies* (2014), 1–19.

Gopinath, Gayatri. *Impossible desires*, Durham, N.C. 2005.

Gualtieri, Sarah M.A. *Between Arab and white. Race and ethnicity in the early Syrian American diaspora*, Berkeley, Calif. 2009.

Jamal, Amaney and Nadine Naber. *Race and Arab Americans before and after 9/11*, Syracuse, N.Y. 2008.

Karim, Jamillah. *The American Ummah*, New York 2009.

Lorde, Audre. *Sister outsider. Essays and speeches*, Berkeley, Calif. 1995.

Mahmood, Saba. *Politics of piety. The Islamic revival and the feminist subject*, Princeton, N.J. 2005.

Maira, Sunaina. *Missing*, Durham, N.C. 2009.

Naber, Nadine. *Arab America. Gender, cultural politics, and activism*, New York 2012.

Nguyen, Mimi. The biopower of beauty. Humanitarian imperialisms and the global feminisms in an age of terror, in *Signs* 36:2 (2011), 359–83.

Nguyen, Mimi. *The gift of freedom. War, debt, and the other refugee passages*, Durham, N.C. 2012.

Omi, Michael and Howard Winnant. *Racial formation in the United States*, New York 1994.

Peek, Lori. *Behind the backlash. Muslim Americans after 9/11*, Philadelphia 2010.

Puar, Jasbir and Amit Rai. The remaking of a model minority, in *Social Text* 22:3 (2004), 75–104.

Rana, Junaid. *Terrifying Muslims*, Durham, N.C. 2011.

Rand, Erica. *Red nails, black skates*, Durham, N.C. 2012.

Ratna, Aarti. Flying the flag for England? National identities and British Asian Female footballers, in *Race, ethnicity, and football*, ed. Daniel Burdsey, Abingdon, U.K. 2011, 117–30.

Saskiestewa Gilbert, Matthew. Hopi footraces and American marathons, 1912–1930, in *American Quarterly* 62:1 (2010), 77–101.

Shankar, Shalini. "Affect and Sport in South Asian American Marketing." *South Asian Popular Culture* 11.3 (2013): 231–42.

Thangaraj, Stanley. "Ballin' Indo-Pak Style: Pleasures, Desires, and Expressive Practices of "South Asian American" Masculinity." *International Review for the Sociology of Sport* 45:3 (2010a).

Thangaraj, Stanley. Lifting it up. Popular culture, Indo-Pak basketball, and South Asian American institutions, in *Cosmopolitan Civil Societies. An Interdisciplinary Journal* 2:2 (2010b), 71–91.

Thangaraj, Stanley. We're 80% more patriotic. Atlanta's Muslim Community and the performances of cultural citizenship, in *Routledge international handbook on race, class, and gender*, ed. Shirley Jackson, Abingdon, U.K. 2014, 220–30.

Thangaraj, Stanley. *Desi hoop dreams. Pickup basketball and the making of Asian American masculinity*, New York 2015.

Vang, Chia Youvee. *Hmong America. Reconstructing community in diaspora*, Urbana, Ill. 2010.

Sports: Turkey: 19th to Early 20th Centuries

Ilknur Hacısoftaoğlu

Introduction

This entry analyzes policies related to women in sport in early twentieth-century Turkey. It charts the progress made and the problems faced by women in Turkey during that time. It also outlines sport policies in order better to explain the position of women in the sporting milieu. It further explores the dynamics of the period for women in sport through analyzing magazines and newspapers popular at the time, as well as statements of significant politicians.

Beginning in the late Ottoman period (1789–1918), Turkey underwent radical social changes, that were institutionalized in the republican period (1923–45) and that affected every component of society, including the position of women. During the late Ottoman period upper class Ottoman women, using opportunities made available to them, were able to transform their position in society—spaces opened up for them to express their thoughts, allowing them to prove their intellectual abilities and to object to tradition and push the established boundaries (Toska 1998). The last 20 years of the Ottoman state witnessed a rise in the feminist movement among Muslim women. In that period *Şukufezar* [*The garden of flowers*], a magazine with an entirely female editorial board, and *Hanımlara Mahsus Gazete* [*Newspaper for women*] were published as the first examples of their kind. They focused on women's education, mostly in terms of how it could empower the family, later shifting to how it could empower women as women (Osmanağaoğlu 2015). For example, *Kadınlar dünyası* [*The world of women*] used the word "feminism" to define its political approach and tried to act as a vehicle for developing politics in relation to the rights of women (Çakır 2011).

In the late Ottoman period women struggled to become citizens and sought the abolition of religious regulations in the law. Changes during this period were inspired by the modernization processes evident in many Western countries. The sociopolitical transformation in this period, and the struggle of Ottoman women, led to the enactment of what became known as the Hukuk-u Aile Kararnamesi [Family Law Decree]; the first codification legalized decree in Ottoman-Muslim family law (Yazıcı 2015). Although abolished in 1919, the law regulated the legal age for marriage (18 for women and 17 for men), making obligatory the presence of a public officer at the marriage ceremony and giving couples the right to divorce. It was the first legal regulation related to women's rights (Osmanağaoğlu 2015).

During the republican period, regulations referring to shari'a were omitted. This development directly affected women's position in society and was another symbol of the "modernization" of the new system. It replaced the "old" notion of women or the "old" women, who had access to the public space through strict rules, with the "new" women, who had gained equality with men before the law. The Civil Law (1926) severed all links with shari'a, giving women the right to divorce, forbidding polygamy, and providing women with equal custody and inheritance rights. However, this law maintained certain aspects of patriarchy: it made the husband the head of the household and made the wife's working life dependent on her husband's permission. Nonetheless, patriarchy was no longer religiously referenced. Additionally, in 1924, the unity of education law [Tevhid-i Tedrisat Kanunu] was came into force and by the law the legal regulation guaranteeing equal opportunities to girls and boys in education were passed. These and others initiated significant changes in women's lives. At first, few women were able to use these benefits, but more were included within the process. Women were given the right to vote in local elections in 1930 and in national elections in 1934, before women's suffrage in many Western countries. In all of these regulation changes, the struggle of women in the late Ottoman period was readily apparent, and the republican elite were keen to continue to improve the rights of women. According to Osmanağaoğlu (2015), this enthusiasm among the founders of the republic was less about women's rights as such and more about correcting the dominant image in the Western world of the Oriental woman and promoting women's reproductive role as mothers in the building of a new nation. On the other hand, for the Women's Movement in Turkey, these developments were insufficient, in that women were excluded by the state from preparing women's policies, even though the movement had played a key role in securing rights for women. The critical voice of the women's movement was all but muted, and the central state shaped almost all women's policies.

The social transformations experienced by women in the late Ottoman period and during the early republic can be well understood from many different fields, including education and occupation, as well as sports and bodily practices. Sport, the focus of this entry, can offer insights into most of the social developments related to women at the time. To understand how the situation for women was affected through their participation in sport, it is necessary to study the politics of sport in the country at the time, as well as the general status of women in society. Accordingly, sport in the late Ottoman and early republican periods are described in the following section.

Sport in the Late Ottoman (1789–1918) and Early Republican (1923–45) Periods

Modern sport has evolved in Europe since 18th century and came to be embedded in the major elements of modernization itself—industrialization, urbanization, and nationalism as well as bureaucratization and rationalization of the system. Developments in modern sport began to take root in the Ottoman Empire considerably later than they did in Europe, mostly following the Tanzimat reforms which promulgated between 1839–1876 and seen as the first step for the modernization/westernization process of the empire by the historians. Sport was embodied in the case of modernizing of many institutions including the elements mentioned above in that era. Before this time, sport in the Ottoman Empire had existed for a considerable time but with no organizational structure, and comprised only the traditional sports, like wrestling and archery, which were practised in Islamic monasteries.

When the Union and Progress Party (UPP, İttihad ve Terakki Partisi) was elected as the government of the constitutional monarchy in 1908, modernization efforts in sport were accelerated. The first Western sport to be accepted was gymnastics; coaches coming from Europe to teach in the empire's most famous schools contributed considerably to the development of the sport in the country. Selim Sırrı Tarcan, who was tutored by some of these coaches, strove to develop gymnastics, establishing the empire's first sport school (Darülirfan, or the house of culture) and organizing the Turkish Olympic Committee. To increase his knowledge of gymnastics, he went Higher Institute of Physical Education in Sweden in 1909, where he studied for a year in a physical education teaching department. Thanks to his close relationship with the UPP government, he was able to establish physical education courses in some military schools and Mekteb-i Sultani [Galata Palace Royal School] which was/is one of the oldest schools in Ottoman Empire and Turkeyand managed to have the course included on the syllabus (Okay 2003).

The UPP's politics enabled modern sport and physical education to be introduced into the country, but sport politics was largely driven by the party's nationalist agenda rather than by a desire to Westernize. The UPP was the first supporter of Turkist politics, and it ensured the new generation's education had a basis in nationalism. Trade, education, music, games, children's books, and literature were all used in raising a nationalist generation. Gymnastics and sport came to serve the same agenda (Okay 2003), institutionalized and disseminated through youth unions. The drive to develop sport, which had started after the Tanzimat reforms, was interrupted with the outbreak of the War

SPORTS: TURKEY: 19TH TO EARLY 20TH CENTURIES

of Independence (1919–1923), and the issue remained off the agenda until the early years of the republic. In the aftermath of the war, the government viewed sport as important in forging a strong Turkish nation and used it to prepare Turkish citizens' bodies for possible future war. Daver, a famous author and sport person of the time, defines one of the fundamental duty of Turkish athletes was to defend their homeland (Daver 1937, 15).

Sport came to be seen as important not only in preparing for war but also for building the body of a new nation (Akın 2004). The words of Mustafa Kemal Atatürk, the founder of the republic, reflected these thoughts, while also targeting the creation of the new man: "To raise a strong and virtuous generation that is faithful to positive sciences, like fine arts, increasing his/her skills in physical education as well as in the education of the mind, is the clear goal of our main policies" (Atatürk 1935, in Güneş 2003, 21) (*All translations are by the author unless otherwise indicated*).

The drive to develop Turkish sport was taken up in earnest by the state, which established the Turkish Training Associations Union (TİCİ) on 31 July 1922. It was the first significant Turkish sporting organization. However, although it was influenced from its inception by the politics of the government, particularly after its status was changed to a "union for public welfare" in 1924, in April 1936, during TİCİ's eighth congress, the government abolished the union, accelerating the process of putting sport completely under governmental control.

During this congress, accusations were made by government representatives that interclub conflicts were harming the development of sports and it was believed that TİCİ's uncentralized structure impeded the development and spread of sport (Fişek 1985). In a speech in 1937, the Prime Minister, İnönü, said the following about the organization, despite being its one-time honorary president: "An organization had appeared known as the Training Associations Union, and that organization dissolved, keeping the country away from sport in weakness, unaccountability and anarchy" (Turan 2003, 321).

In TİCİ's place, the government established Türk Spor Kurumu [the Turkish Sports Administration] (TSK) in 1936, and the government's control of sport came to have a structure. The government tightened its control by appointing the provincial presidents of the Republican People's Party which was the ruling and only party in the country, as regional presidents of the TSK. It appointed General Ali Hikmet Ayerdem president of the organization.

To disseminate its policies, TSK published *Türk Spor Kurumu Dergisi* (*Turkish Sport Administration Magazine*). The words of Nasuhi Baydar, the manager of the magazine and one of the important sport personalities of the time, summarized the motive behind sport policies: "Turkish athlete must be in a position as a guide for all citizens in the country" (Baydar 1937, 1). However, in spite of the efforts to organize sport through central politics, the party's governors were dissatisfied with the development of sport during the TSK period. TSK was seen only as a transitional organization, one step toward building a more controlled and structured sport field. In 1939, the government established the Beden Terbiyesi Genel Direktörlüğü [Physical Education General Directorate] (BTGD), and the process of the state taking control of sport was complete. According to Osman Şevki Uludağ, this was a necessary step in the organization of sport, which had become removed from its national mission and was in a state of anarchy (Taner 1939, 37). The stated purpose behind the establishment of the BTGD was:

> to guide and manage the games, gymnastics and sporting activities that provide for the development of the physical and moral capabilities of citizens according to national and revolutionist needs ... Many Western countries have accepted the hygiene of their race and the raising of citizens of high quality in physical terms as the most important element of their home country's defense and economic development, and thus have given primary importance to sports and physical education.
>
> TANER 1939, 2

In the common discourse around politics in sport during the early republican era in Turkey by both the TSK and BTGD, sport was viewed as a public duty. In the official magazines published by the organizations, engaging in sport was considered an obligation. Tarcan, for example, in one of these magazines, underlined the duties to be realized by every citizen for his/her nationhood, and defined the state's will to provide the moral and physical education of youth as a part of its role in the regulation of public duties. For him, sport provided the moral discipline required for the building of a common future (Tarcan quoted in BTGM 1942, 36). These magazines, in this regard, put forward an ideal of a militant citizen, framed in an understanding that every citizen is owned by and obligated to the state and bounded to the state's existence, as defined by Üstel (2002). Sport was viewed as a vehicle for the creation of such citizens, and so any desires for personal success or to gain popularity as an athlete were not tolerated. Magazines mainly emphasized sports like gymnastics, skiing, and camping—which were seen as mandatory for building up the Turkish physique—rather than soccer, which it was believed turned people into a passive audience. In short, the era's sport policy emphasized mass sports and recreational sports rather than the more popular sports.

The government attempted to formulate systematic policies for organizing sport, including enacting Beden Terbiyesi Kanunu [the Physical Education Law], which made physical education and sport obligatory for Turkish citizens. Males between the ages of 12 and 45, and females between the ages of 12 and 30, were obliged to participate regularly in physical education and sport. Although plans were made to build sport facilities and to train teachers and staff to provide opportunities and guidance to the public, due to the social and economic conditions not all of the targets were met (Tarakçığlu 2014).

So, the ultimate aim of the political sport agenda was to discipline the body of the nation in order to make it healthy, robust, and ready for war. As in other historical examinations, it is important to focus on the policies related specifically to women as a separate research subject, since historical explorations of an era tend to focus on the history of men. Looking at history through a gender lens can reveal a different story, and in doing so for the issue of policies related to sport, the differences for women are readily apparent.

Sport Policies for Women in the Early Republican Period

The republican regime attempted to clearly define the new woman of the republic. Legislation was enacted to address not only women's social status but also their daily lives, including detailed programs about bodily practices (for example, apparel selection, sports and exercise, and so forth). The discourse around regulating the female body focused on women's duties and responsibilities, since the new citizens were considered largely to be responsible to the state for the benefit of the Turkish nation. Every Turkish woman, as a new citizen, was obliged to fall in line with a set of "idealized" and "civilized" symbols, images, and rituals (Çolak 2005), and sport, being about the regulation of the body, was considered the arena in which they were to be demonstrated.

Along with that tendency, gender equality was also pursued in sport regulations. The Physical Education Law (1938) was one of the strongest signs of state policies treating sport as a duty, and it made sport obligatory for girls and boys alike. The main actors in the drawing up of sport-related policies were men, as could clearly be seen in the publications and state discourses of the era, although sport was hailed as an activity for both women and men, as in education; and women were expected to be seen in sport as men's partners, friends, and assistants. The inclusion of women in physical education schools was also an example of that. In 1926 in Kız Öğretmen Okulu [Girls School of Teacher Training] in Capa, a physical education course was opened and continued for four seasons. 45 female and 102 male physical education teachers were trained and appointed to the schools (Cumhuriyet Halk Partisi 1938). Additionally, the Department of Physical Education was opened in 1932–33, and the school started to accept female students in 1936–37 (Ergin 1977).

Taking a closer look, however, discourse on the level of participation of the two genders contained both differences and commonalities. First, women's participation in sport always came with certain circumstances and restrictions and which sports were deemed proper for women were defined and rationalized in detail. In most of the articles published in the magazines, the specific conditions for the participation of women in sports were described. According to Tarcan, writing in 1943, women—whose most important duty was to give birth and raise children—should develop their stomach, hips, and pelvis, and should avoid activities that develop their chest and legs, as this would masculinize them. So, women should not engage in contact sports such as boxing, wrestling, soccer, or rugby, as women who partake in these sports are masculine and therefore ugly. Thus the limits of women's participation in sports were clearly drawn by Tarcan. Another writer, writing in 1940, considered swimming, aquatics, tennis, walking, light body movements, and light track and field events to be appropriate sports for women; heavy exercise and competition were unhealthy. Sports that beautified women and made their body more proportioned were to be recommended (Baba 1940, 11).

The idea of sport as an activity for the beautification of women also often appeared in sport discourse in early 20th century with gymnastics suggested as one of the key activities in the creation of the ideal body for women. Magazines of that period often included guides for women, showing them how to do gymnastic exercises and explaining the potential benefits. Urban women did gymnastic exercises at home, sometimes even together with other women. Particularly in the country's larger cities, such as Istanbul and Ankara, women were increasingly influenced by Western body ideals and aesthetics which started to value slender, slim and graceful body in 20th century (Seid 1994), and would try to change their bodies accordingly (Pfister and Hacısoftaoğlu 2017).

A 1937 article claimed that gymnastics would not destroy a woman's figure by making it bigger and provided information on how sport actually regulates the body, giving it a female appearance, by making the muscles more elastic (TSK Magazine 1937, 11). Another article, "For ladies. To make the ankles thinner and to lose the leg fat," suggested the right gymnastic movements for women: "Making one's ankles thinner, decreasing body fat and gaining beautiful legs is a powerful wish in the heart of every woman. Anyway, what woman wants to be ugly in any part of her body? It is very difficult to define an ugly leg, but the first thing that comes to mind that it should definitely not be fat and thick" (Anonymous 1938, 6).

This described female body image was influenced by Western ideas. But women in early republican Turkey also involved themselves in politics as a symbol of difference from the West—since the differences from the West were defined around the concepts of honor and *namus* which was seen as belong to the feminine space (Üşür 2004). On the other hand, women represented the Western face of Turkish modernization; women's policy was an apparatus to fight against the West's Oriental image of Turkey. This conflict was related to the Westernization conception of the period, which was shaped around the idea of being Westernized in spite of the West. In that contested terrain, attempts were made to form the female Turkish body according to the Western ideal. Beauty pageants and competitions, for example, promoted the image of a modern and civilized Turkey abroad, but at the same time redefined the concept of honor and expanded the public limits within which women could move (Shissler 2004). In sport, too, an arena for the creation of a Westernized body, women were defined with their function, but politics provided a way for the entry of sport into the realm of women.

Women were also encouraged to participate in sport to improve their reproductive capacity. The benefits of sport for women were depicted in the previously mentioned article "Women Gymnastics" (1937); first in terms of emphasizing body regularity and proportion. Second, increasing of body endurances was added to benefits of sport. The article makes a last but highly important point: creating a strong body for maternity was another important benefit of gymnastics. The article dwelled on women's maternal role, and discussed sport's potential benefit to the organs, detailing the exercises needed to protect the organs, and stating that because every woman had to be a mother, women should look after themselves: "In brief, those with the determination and willpower in physical education will not be content with classical beauty, and will gain qualifications by being a robust and healthy mother" (TSK Magazine 1937, 11).

Fertility control and the discipline of citizens' bodies were key points in the central politics of the early years of the republic, as in other modernization projects. According to Yuval-Davis (1997), capitalism considers men to be patriots and soldiers defending the country, and laborers increasing production, while women reproduce the nation, and are imagined as fertile mothers and loyal wives. It is apparent that the population policies of the nineteenth century were formulated based on women's sexuality and the female body (Balsoy 2013), and since that period, political efforts to regulate the reproductive capacity of women have come to feature heavily in discourses related to changing society. In the early republican period, in concordance with modernization and the nationalist agenda, pronatalist policies were adopted, and a new regulation was put in place in 1930 prohibiting abortion and the use of contraceptives (Ünal and Cindoğlu 2013). This new "reproduction" discourse posited women as mothers of the nation and saw sport as strengthening women's bodies for that function. Atatürk hailed strong Turkish women and spoke of their duty to raise powerful generations: "Turkish women should be the most enlightened, most virtuous, most dignified women in the world. The duty of Turkish women is to raise powerful generations who are capable of protecting and defending the country with their minds, muscles and ambition" (Ataturk Research Centre 2006, 362). Sport was considered important to building new, strong, and robust women who could give birth to a healthy generation.

In 1943 İnönü described the government's approach to women's sport as follows: "What we want from our girls is to make families stronger, to create them as indestructible castles ... We want young women to be like their mothers who carried munitions with their strong bodies while wearing a flower on their heads" (İnönü 1929, 936). Although the discourse related to women in sport was built around these themes, some female athletes engaged in regular sport as a discipline in their lives.

Female Athletes as Symbols of Modernity

Women's participationin sport had an additional meaning: it symbolized the public presence of modern Westernized Turkish women (Yarar Cantek, and Özgüven 2009). The appearance of female athletes in the highly masculine area of sport served to prove that women were the equal of men. Furthermore, by representing Turkey internationally, female athletes were excellent representatives of the modern face of the new Turkey. In the 1920s, Turkish women began to compete in such upper-class sports as tennis, swimming, fencing, rowing, and volleyball, all of which were considered appropriate for women. Women at the time—particularly those from elite families—enjoyed participating in sport in the same events as men, although in small numbers (Pfister and Hacısoftaoğlu 2017). Magazines at the time tried to encourage women to participate in sport by presenting female athletes as role models, with the "sporting woman" being portrayed as the "new woman," and used as an "advertisement" for the reformers' modernization project (Pfister and Hacısoftaoğlu 2017).

It is no surprise that Turkish women began participating in international competitions following these developments in the 1930s, with one particular platform, the Olympic Games, serving as an ideal opportunity to present the nation to the world. Male Turkish athletes had been participating at the Olympic Games since 1908, with numbers increasing from one in 1908 to 31

FIGURE 1   Girls running at the İnönü Races. Issue 40 of *Physical Education and Sport Magazine*

in 1932, and to 48 in 1936 (Türkiye Milli Olimpiyat Komitesi 2016). In 1936, 36 years after the introduction of women's competitions to the Games, two female fencers joined the Turkish Olympic team—Suat Fetgeri Aseni and Halet Çambel—symbolizing the republic's support for women in the modernization project. The two fencers lost their matches and failed to win any medals (Sports Reference 2017), but as the first female Turkish athletes to have participated in the Olympics, they inspired future generations in Turkey. They received little attention in the media at the time, but their participation has been appreciated in later years by the media and researchers (Pfister and Hacısoftaoğlu 2017).

Discourse related to gender equality in public life concentrated mostly on women's expertness and occupational identities. The strong emphasis on women's working under the same conditions as men permeated the sporting field. The benefits that the new republic offered women were often noted in articles about women in sports. Jale Taylan, who wrote regularly in the magazine of the Physical Education and Sport Directory, stated that it was necessary to recognize the participation of both girls and boys in sport:

This determination, this strength is naturally born in us, as the girls of today, because we are not those "poor little women" anymore. When it's our turn, we like to quarrel as well and to evaluate our young strengths in nature ... They ski like the wind with their very small skis down hills with steep slopes, without fear. Even though most of them find themselves falling in snow down the hill, their eyes glitter with happiness and glee. You do not differentiate between boys and girls there. In fact, not long ago it was a screaming girl's voice that was saying, "Let's see who can be first down the hill!" Never ever should someone older join them and tell them, "Stand away, these kinds of things are too dangerous for girls," as this would discourage the child. The girl, as she gets older, will understand naturally what she is capable of ... There is neither a "dame" nor "cavalier" in skiing. A real skier girl becomes always a friend of a boy. (Taylan 1940, 18–19)

For Çığıgil (1942, 36), skiing was a sport that brought women closer to the male character, and proved that women could always be friends to men. The zeitgeist of that era led to a burgeoning of many ideas (in spite of their differences between them) about the equality of women and men even in sport, a traditionally masculine area, in both Turkey and around the world. Despite the tendency to have different aims for women and men in sport, discourse on direct gender equality was able to find a place for itself. Even women who engaged in sports considered "inappropriate for women" were covered in the newspapers of the time. A 1936 interview with the first Turkish female boxers is a good example of this, with both boxers stating that women are active in all areas of the society, and asking "Why should sport be an exception?" (Es 1936). Even though it would be unthinkable today, at that time a woman could play in a male volleyball team: Sabiha Rıfat played in Fenerbahçe's male volleyball team during her education in an engineering faculty. In a magazine of the period that event was presented as a reason for congratulating the team for forming a mixed sex team: "The captain of the Fenerbahçe female team, Suphiye Rıfat [Sabiha Rıfat] was included in the team. We congratulate Fenerbahçe since it brought a change to the country's sport by competing with a mixed sex team" (Spor Alemi 1929, 5, in Dağlaroğlu 1987).

Conclusion

Policies related to women in sport, like those focusing on women's issues in general, have always changed with historical developments. In modern times, they have been seen mostly as an apparatus for disciplining the female body. In Turkey, particularly in the 19th and early 20th centuries covered in this article, sport was one of the most significant vehicles for the formation of a new,

SPORTS: TURKEY: 19TH TO EARLY 20TH CENTURIES

preferred female body. The beauty of the female body, as well as its capacity for reproduction, was at the forefront of these policies, with the aim being to raise healthy generations by making women stronger and more vigorous: "appropriate" sports for women were discussed in these policies in terms of the reproductive capacity of the female body, as well as the fear of the masculinization of the female form through sport. Sport was seen as a duty of the citizens of the new republic. But it is also important to focus on women as active subjects. The hegemonic discourse regarding women in sport was built through central state policies; however, discussions and practices of gender equality in the sporting space encouraged women to participate in sport as the equal of men. Female athletes emerged as epitomes of modern Turkey and participated in international tournaments for the first time. Women's participation in sport from childhood was deemed vital in the modernization efforts of the new society.

Above all, girls, it seems, enjoyed participating in sport, as is demonstrated by the image that accompanies this article. For this reason, if nothing else, it is important to understand women's perspectives on this issue.

Bibliography

Akın, Yiğit. *Gürbüz ve yavuz evlatlar. Erken cumhuriyet'te beden eğitimi ve spor [Robust and vigorous children. Physical education and sports in early republican Turkey]*, Istanbul 2004.

Anonymous. Bayanlar için [For ladies], in *Türk Spor Kurumu Dergisi [Turkish Sports Administration Magazine]* 91 (1938), 6.

Atatürk Araştırma Merkezi, Atatürk Kültür, Dil ve Tarih Yüksek Kurumu [Atatürk Research Centre, Atatürk Culture, Language and History Supreme Institution]. *Atatürk'ün söylev ve demeçleri [Atatürk's speeches and statements]*, 3 vols, Ankara 2006.

Baba, Nüzhet. Kadınlar hangi sporları yapmalı. Sporda yaş meselesinin oynadığı rol [Which sports should women do? The role of age in sport], in *Beden Terbiyesi ve Spor Dergisi [Physical Education and Sport Magazine]*, 13 (January 1940), 11–12.

Balsoy, Gülhan. *The politics of reproduction in Ottoman society, 1838–1900. The body, gender, and culture*, London 2013.

Baydar, Nasuhi. Sporda yenmek ve yenilmek [Winning and losing in sport], in *Türk Spor Kurumu Dergisi [Turkish Sports Administration Magazine]* 61 (1937).

Cumhuriyet Halk Partisi [Republican People's Party]. *Onbeşinci Yıl Kitabı [The book of fifteenth year]*, İstanbul 1938.

Çakır, Serpil. *Osmanlı kadın hareketi [Ottoman women's movement]*, Istanbul 2011.

Çığıgil, L. O. Genç kızlarımız ve bir spor olarak kayak [Our girls and skiing as a sport], in *Beden Terbiyesi ve Spor Dergisi* [*Physical Education and Sport Magazine*] 43 (July 1942), 36.

Çolak, Yılmaz. Citizenship between secularism and Islamism in Turkey, in *Citizenship in a global world. European questions and Turkish experiences*, eds. Fuat Keyman and Ahmet İçduygu, London 2005, 242–66.

Dağlaroğlu, Rüştü. *1907–1987 Fenerbahçe spor kulübü tarihi* [*1907–1987 The history of Fenerbahçe Sport Club*], Istanbul 1987.

Daver, Abidin. Türk sporunda kutlu bir inkılap başlıyor [A blessed revolution is starting in Turkish sport], in *Turkish Sport Administration Magazine* 1937, 57, 15.

Ergin, Osman. *Türkiye maarif tarihi* [*The education history of Turkey*], Istanbul 1977.

Es, H. F. Genç kızlarımız arasında müthiş bir boks merakı başladı [An interest for boxing has started among our girls], in *Akşam* 1 August 1936, 7.

Fişek, Kurthan. *100 soruda Türkiye spor tarihi* [*History of Turkey in 100 questions*], Istanbul 1985.

Güneş, İhsan. *Türk parlemento tarihi. TBMM 5. Dönem (1935–1939)* [*The history of the Turkish Parliament. Fifth period (1935–1939)*], Ankara 2003.

İnönü, İsmet. *Türkiye Büyük Millet Meclisi Kararları* [*The Grand National Assembly of Turkey Parlimantary Acts*. 14 December 1929, Number 531, 936.

Kadın cimnastikleri [Women gymnastics], in *Türk Spor Kurumu Dergisi* [*Turkish Sport Administration Magazine*] 72 (1937), 15.

Okay, Cüneyd. Sport and nation building. Gymnastics and sport in the Ottoman state and the Committee of Union and Progress, 1908–1918, in *The International Journal of History of Sport* 20:1 (2003), 152–56.

Osmanağaoğlu, Hülya (ed.). *Feminizm kitabı* [*The book of feminism*], İstanbul 2015.

Pfister, Gertrud and Hacısoftaoğlu, İlknur. Women's sport as a symbol of modernity. A case study from Turkey, in *International Journal of the History of Sport* 33:13 (2017), 1470–82 (published online 6 April 2017).

Seid, Roberta P. Too "Close to the bone": The historical context for women's obsession with slenderness, in *Feminist Perspectives on Eating Disorders,* ed. Patricia Fallon, Melanie A. Katzman and Susan C. Wooley, New York 1994, 3–16.

Shissler, A. Holly. Beauty Is Nothing to Be Ashamed of. Beauty contests as tools of women's liberation in early republican Turkey, in *Comparative Studies of South Asia, Africa and the Middle East* 24:1 (2004), 107–22.

Sports Reference. Halet Çambel, in *Sports Reference*, n.d., <http://www.sports-reference.com/olympics/athletes/ca/halet-cambel-1.html>. 9 February 2017.

Taner, Cemil. Beden terbiyesi teşkilatının çalışma esasları [*Working essentials of the Physical Education Administration*], in *Beden Terbiyesi ve Spor Dergisi* [*Physical Education and Sport Magazine*] 1 (January 1939), 2.

Tarakçığlu, Sait. A failed project in Turkey's sports history. The law on physical education of 1938, in *International Journal of the History of Sport* 31:14 (2014), 1807–19.

Taylan, Jale. Kadın sporu olarak kayak [Skiing as a woman's sport], in *Beden Terbiyesi ve Spor Dergisi* [*Physical Educaton and Sport Magazine*] 16 (April 1940), 18–19.

Toska, Zehra. Cumhuriyet'in kadın ideali. Eşiği aşanlar ve aşamayanlar [The ones who could exceed the threshold and the ones who couldn't], in *75 yılda Kadınlar ve Erkekler* [*Women and men in 75 years*], ed. Ayşe Berktay Hacımirzaoğlu, Istanbul 1998, 71–88.

Turan, İlhan. *İsmet İnönü. Konuşma, demeç, makale, mesaj ve söyleşiler* [*İsmet İnönü. Speech, statement, article, message and interviews*], Ankara 2003.

Türkiye Milli Olimpiyat Komitesi. Olimpiyat Oyunları, in *Türkiye Milli Olimpiyat Komitesi*, n.d., <http://www.olimpiyatkomitesi.org.tr/Olimpiyat-Oyunlari/1/5>. 30 October 2016.

Ünal, Didem, and Dilek Cindoğlu. Reproductive citizenship in Turkey. Abortion chronicles, in *Women's Studies International Forum* 38 (2013), 21–31.

Üstel, Füsun. Türkiye cumhuriyeti'nde resmi yurttaş profilinin evrimi [The evolution of the legal citizen profile in the Turkish republic], in *Modern Türkiye'de Siyasi Düşünce-Milliyetçilik* [*Political thought in modern Turkey*], iv, *Milliyetçilik* [*Nationalism*], ed. Tanıl Bora, Istanbul 2002, 275–83.

Üşür, Serpil. Otoriter Türk modernleşmesinin cinsiyet rejimi [The gender regime of authoritarian Turkish modernization], in *Doğu-Batı* [East-West] 7:29 (2004), 203–04.

Yarar, Betül, Funda Şenol Cantek, and Petra Holzer Özgüven. Türkiye'de modernleşme süreci içinde ve spor alanında toplumsal cinsiyete dayalı yeni beden ekonomisi ve kadının toplumsal kimliğinin kuruluşu ve dönüşümü [New gendered body economy and construction and transformation of social identity of women in modernization period of Turkey and in sports field], in *The Scientific and Technological Research Council of Turkey* (*TUBİTAK*) *Research Project Report*, project number: 106K026, 2009.

Yazıcı, Abdurrahman. Osmanlı Hukuk-ı Aile Kararnamesi (1917) ve Sadredding Efendi'nin eleştirileri, in *Ekev Akademi Dergisi* [*Ekev Academy Journal*] 19 (2015), 567–84.

Yuval-Davis, Nira. *Gender and nation*, Thousand Oaks, Calif. 1997.

Sports: Turkey

Sertaç Sehlikoglu

Introduction

This entry reviews Turkish women's involvement in professional and non-professional sports through a historical lens. It demonstrates how sports have been perceived as more than a matter of developing physical fitness, health, and team spirit and have become part of certain political agendas of various public actors in the region. By doing so, it also reveals the operations that have objectified women's bodies through sports, "thereby negating and distorting women's own experience of their corporeality and subjectivity" (Mahmood 2005, 158). Once the meanings that nation-building projects attribute to women and their bodies are clearly identified, it is then easier to analyze the ways in which women negotiate the meanings, ideologies, and discourses in question. In order to identify these meanings, this entry will begin with an overview of the history of sports and women's involvement in them, starting from the end of the nineteenth century in the Middle East, and particularly in Turkey.

Sports in Transition: From Colonialism to Nationalism

It is curious how several branches of the modern sports, such as archery, wrestling, horseback riding, racing, and swimming, were for centuries part of the official military training of men in the Middle East and are still considered "traditional" sports in the region (Fişek 1985, Di-Capua 2006). They were mainly available to men, and were associated with "honor, bravery, and male group spirit" as virtues of masculinity (Di-Capua 2006, 440).

In the mid-1800s, several Western sports clubs were established for men in the major cities of the Middle East, such as Cairo, Alexandria, Istanbul, and Beirut. These sports clubs were established under the roof of European colonial organizations such as embassies and schools (Fişek 1985, Yurdadön 2004, Di-Capua 2006,). The clubs provided opportunities for their —predominantly male—members to play Western sports, including cricket, hockey, soccer, tennis, and basketball. In Iran, Western sports were first played by the teams established by the South Persia Rifles during the British occupation in 1916 (Guttmann 2004). With this particular colonial encounter, the idea of such

© KONINKLIJKE BRILL NV, LEIDEN, 2016 | DOI:10.1163/1872-5309_EWIC_COM_002076

physical activities as "sports," an involvement for pleasure and health purposes, was introduced to the Middle East.

An important characteristic of Western sports clubs was their civilizing mission (Fişek 1985, Yurdadön 2004, Di-Capua 2006, Atalay 2007), which included promoting gender equality and increasing women's visibility in the Middle East (Sfeir 1985, Yarar 2005, Di-Capua 2006, Talimciler 2006). Women, whose close male relatives (i.e., fathers) were members of these sports clubs, also had access to the facilities, which made them the first women to start playing Western sports, at the end of 1800s (Yıldız 2002, Di-Capua 2004, Atalay 2007).

By the late nineteenth century, an anticolonial rhetoric started emerging in the Middle East against Western sports clubs. Western sports practiced under the auspices of Western powers became a matter of contestation in the period of anticolonial movements. Many started arguing that the British and American sports clubs were acting as venues to "damage" young minds, by allowing Western culture to infiltrate into local social life. With such nationalist sentiments, Ottoman governors prohibited the public from participating in these clubs and sports of the "imperial powers" (Fişek 1985). This anticolonial sentiment, however, did not ban the various branches of sports introduced to the Middle East. Rather, the activities, clubs, and various branches of sports were nationalized. Shortly after, starting in the early 1900s, Western sports clubs were gradually replaced by Arab (Palestinian, Lebanese, Egyptian, and North African), Turkish, and Iranian clubs promoting nationalism as part of the anticolonial movements in the region.

Both national and colonial sports initiatives perceived sports as a tool to shape and transform the nation, only with different ideological agendas. While colonialism aimed to civilize the colonized, the new nationalist projects aimed to modernize, improve, and advance the young bodies by creating a healthy nation through sports. According to Di-Capua, the *ahālī* spirit "promoted the European idea that a physically and mentally healthy individual is a precondition for the well-being of a robust nation, for the nation itself was the sum of these healthy individuals" (Di-Capua 2006, 440).

The first three decades of the Turkish Republic were characterized by the republican project, which would come to be referred to as Kemalism after Kemal Atatürk's death, and it involved building a secular and proud European/ Western nation state through a set of reforms. As a reflection of this nationalist movement against cultural colonialism, the first purely national sportsclub of Turkey, Guard Force (*Muhafiz Gücü*), was founded in 1920. Guard Force was established by and for military people, training men in marathon, sprint, equestrian and, in later years, in non-military-related branches such as basketball, football, and volleyball. Another notable investment in sports by the state of

Turkey was the formation of *Türkiye İdman Cemiyetleri İttifâkı* (The Alliance of Exercise Association of Turkey) in 1922, which became responsible for managing sports activities in Turkey. As will be discussed below, the republican project has invested in sports not only at the institutional level, but also at the discursive level.

Turkish Modernity and Nation Building through Women's Sports

In Kemalist discourse, many modernist values, such as physical fitness (i.e., involvement in sports), gender equality, and progressive thinking, are suggested to be characteristics of "the Turks"—referring to pre-Islamic Turkic ethnicities—that were forgotten during Ottoman rule (see Atalay 2007, 26). According to this discourse, the republican ideology restores the original national characteristics of Turks back to the Turkish nation (see Navaro-Yashin 2002, 15). Among those national characteristics of Turks, sport is also defined as an important duty of all devout subjects of the nation, a perspective that persists in both popular and academic work from the 1990s on sports in the early republican period. The following quote from a graduate dissertation submitted to Marmara University is a good example of this perspective: "The word 'Turk' is associated with bravery, heroism, soldier and conquest in the entire world. The core part of these qualities are, assuredly, the discipline of body and sportsmanship" (Hergüner 1993, 35).

The nationalist overtone is a result not only of the anticolonialist nationalist rhetoric of the early 1900s, but also of the fact that the first managers of sports clubs were ex-military men who had fought during World War I and the Turkish War of Independence. Thus the strong patriotic reinterpretation of sports was partly inevitable because the founders of such clubs had formerly pursued similar physical activities as part of their military training.

The founder and first President of the Turkish Republic, Kemal Atatürk, is said to have been influenced by the eugenics discourse of his contemporaries in the early twentieth century, as well as by the mind/body dichotomy of Enlightenment philosophy (Alemdaroğlu 2005, 64). In his speech at the opening ceremony of the Alliance of Exercise Association of Turkey in 1938, Atatürk claimed that sports are crucial in the world because they "concern[s] the improvement and development of the race" and are "also a matter of civilization," two good reasons why he considered it essential for the country he meant to build (Tuzcuoğulları, 2001, 55, 57–58). According to Atatürk, the bodies of Turkish people "remained in the East while their thoughts inclined towards the West" (Cantek 2003, 33). Hence the body had to be molded into better shape, in accordance with European standards, in order to complete the project of creating a modern nation. His claims also reflected the prevalent ideologies of the time in the region concerning sports and creating fit bodies through regular physical exercise.

Another important characteristic of this period was the gradual acceptance of the idea of women's participation in sport—not only in Turkey, but also in several parts of the Middle East (and Europe). Countries such as Iran and Turkey, where the physical changes in women's public visibility and bodies were considered indicators of the achievements of modernist nationalist projects, invested in women's sports as a pillar of the project after the 1920s. In Iran, Reza Shah Pahlavi promoted sports for women both at amateur and professional levels, and this enabled Iranian sportswomen's participation in games for the first time in 1939. In 1926, Turkey opened its first national course to educate professional sportswomen in Istanbul (Çapa Teacher's School for Girls). The course lasted nine months and successful students were sent to Europe for further education.

The First Turkish Sportswomen: Elite and Engineered

Sport was a crucial tool in Atatürk's nation-building project, and women's involvement was essential. As future mothers of the next generation, women were expected to have healthy and strong bodies. Moreover, women's fit bodies were no longer hidden behind curtains and veils, and international competitions were the perfect venue to display the physical transformation of the Turkish nation into a Western, modern, and secular society, all pillars of the new republican ideology.

In the 1920s and 1930s, sport was predominantly seen as a masculine activity, not only in the Middle East, but also in the Western world. In Turkey, the normative culture of sexuality compelled women to control their physical activities in public, including running, jumping, swimming, and so forth (Sehlikoglu 2016). However, as discussed above, women's participation in sports was significant in the republican project. This dilemma was resolved with the particular patriotic approach to sports in the early republican period, whereby the first sportswomen were perceived as heroic figures devoted to their nation. Their devotion was about stepping into a masculine zone to fulfill their duties of establishing a nation, and about overcoming their gendered barriers.

FIGURE 1
Suat Fetgeri Aşeni (second left, circled) and Halet Çambel (right, circled) with other sportswomen participating in the 1936 Summer Olympics in Berlin
ARIPINAR ET AL. 2000, 44

After the 1920s, a very limited number of women from elite families became involved in Western sports, both as professionals and as amateurs. The first sportswomen were the relatives of members and managers of those clubs and they became involved in sports with the personal encouragement of Kemal Atatürk himself. There are anecdotes about managers who sought to find female members through their male members to satisfy Atatürk's request (Atalay 2007).

Women who were professionally involved in sports came from wealthy, educated, and prestigious families, and most of them had other professions as well. Suat Aşeni and Halet Çambel, for instance (Figure 1), who represented the Turkish Republic in Berlin in 1936, were the first Turkish women to participate in the Olympic Games in fencing. Suat Aşeni was the daughter of a wrestler and military man Ahmet Fetgeri Aşeni, who was also the founder of one of the largest national sports clubs of Turkey, Beşiktaş Gymnastics Club (BJK). Halet Çambel was born in Berlin, and her family was able to afford private courses in fencing for her. Later, she became the first and one of the most well-known professors in archeology in Turkey (Tuzcuoğulları, 2001, 10). Another leading sportswoman, Sabiha Rıfat, who became the first female volleyball player in 1929, was one of the very few female members of a national (and men's) sports club, Fenerbahçe. Rıfat was an educated woman from an elite family and was part of the construction team for Anıtkabir, Atatürk's mausoleum, as the first female engineer of Turkey.

A special issue of the popular Turkish daily newspaper *Hürriyet*, published on the occasion of the seventy-fifth anniversary of the Republic in 1998, focused on sports and women in the early republican period in an article entitled "*Kafesten Pistlere*" (From the wooden cage to the track). The *mashrabiyya* or in the Turkish case, *kafes,* which can be translated as "wooden cage," was previously used when gender segregation was being practiced. It ensured that women would not be seen by men while women could watch the men in such places as mosques, palaces, and certain houses. The transformation of women's rural-looking, veiled, "unhealthy," and therefore uncivilized bodies into civilized, disciplined, and liberated bodies was perceived not only as an indicator of the westernization and modernization of the country, but also as a way to create and define the new ideal Turkish woman (Kandiyoti 1989, Göle 1996, Alemdaroğlu 2005) (Figures 2a–c). A major resource on Turkish women's involvement in the Olympic Games makes the following point, which has been cited by several researchers: "The Turkish Republic, which proceeded on the pathway of modernization with giant steps, had to show the world that the Turkish woman now was no longer under the *çarşaf* (black veil) or behind the *kafes* (wooden curtain)" (Arıpınar, Atabeyoğlu, and Cebecioğlu 2000, 7). Thus women's participation in sports was perceived as a way to represent and demonstrate to the global (especially Western) gaze that the Turkish nation was succeeding in modernizing itself (Yarar 2005, Talimciler 2006, Atalay 2007).

The fruits of the Turkish modernization project were presented to the widest international interest at the 1936 Summer Olympics in Berlin. Nationalism was at its peak during this pre-World War II period, and the 1936 Summer Olympics were crucial in the history of Turkish sportswomen. As previously mentioned, Alemdaroğlu suggests that Atatürk was highly influenced by Hitler's ideology about eugenized bodies (2005, 64). The 1936 Summer Olympic Games are particularly interesting for Turkish sports because they were where the first fruits of "eugenics a-la-Turca" were presented to an international gaze. This happened on eugenics' home turf, Germany, where Hitler transformed eugenic theory into a nationalist project, according to Alemdaroğlu. It is important, however, to distinguish between this "eugenics a-la-Turca"—a secular republican "body-building" project focused on the outer shape and appearance of bodies—and conventional eugenics, which seeks to meddle in a population's genetic composition, as suggested by the term itself.

When it comes to male bodies, it is possible to claim that transformation through sports was largely concerned with creating strong bodies fit for different kinds of "service" to the country. However, in the case of women, their healthy, fit, urban-looking bodies were discursively portrayed as the physical representation and manifestation of the new country, which had cut its ties from the Ottomans and "turned its face to the West." The sportswomen of the early republican period were also the mothers of a fit and "pure" next

FIGURE 2A
1926 in city of Izmir, Turkey: Teachers' School for Girls, Second Grades during Physical Education (Terbiye-i Bedeniyye) Class
PERSONAL ARCHIVE, SERTAÇ SEHLIKOGLU

FIGURE 2B
1926 in city of Izmir, Turkey: Teachers' School for Girls, Third Grades during Physical Education (Terbiye-i Bedeniyye) Class
PERSONAL ARCHIVE, SERTAÇ SEHLIKOGLU

FIGURE 2C
1926 in city of Aydın, Turkey: Halide Hatun Teachers' School for Girls, Fourth and Fifth Grades during Physical Education (Terbiye-i Bedeniyye) Class
PERSONAL ARCHIVE, SERTAÇ SEHLIKOGLU. (THE NOTE AT THE BOTTOM STATES THIRD GRADES AS WELL)

generation of the nation, with their bolstered reproductive capability and mothering skills. Reproducing a pure nation, according to eugenics discourse, which, as already suggested, had some influence on Kemal Atatürk's thinking, is "an honor and privilege, if not a duty" (Kevles 1995, 184) for any woman who has the capacity to give birth. In short, the Republican state turned women's bodies into both the arena and the subject of Turkish identity formation.

Women's Sports as Sexual Acts: Resistance and Counter-Resistance

Although the state elite emphasized the importance of women participating in sports, the number of Turkish women involved in sports remained fairly low until the mid 1990s (Fişek 1985, Harani 2001, Baydar 2002, Amman 2005). However, due to the lack of statistics about the number of women involved in professional or amateur sports, it is hard to provide an exact number or percentage. Still, it is possible to draw some conclusions from the news published in sports magazines during that time. In 1930 in Turkey, for instance, only two of the thirty-five athletes who participated in the series of athletic contests organized by Galatasaray Club were women (Yarar 2005). These contests were for amateurs who participated in sports as a hobby, yet female participation was still very low.

Public opinion shaped by gendered cultural norms was undoubtedly at play regarding the resistance towards women's involvement in sports in Turkey until only two decades ago. From the 1930s to the late 1970s, the majority of parents did not allow their daughters to join sports teams or compulsory physical education classes in public schools (Pfister and Fasting 1999, Amman 2005). This was partly linked to the popular belief that young women who were involved in sports would lose their womanhood (Hergüner 1993, 10) and become masculinized. Di-Capua (2006) also documents the public rumors that physical exercise could damage the hymen and result in the loss of virginity (2006, 440). Also, with reference to the cultural context, the bodily movements of women are coded as sexual; therefore, these codes limit women's public behavior and movements. Because scholars insist that it is the families (mainly fathers) who prevent their daughters participating in sports, it is difficult to find out whether girls wanted to participate in any form of sports themselves, but we do know that there was a public resistance in general in the Middle East (Hergüner 1993, Pfister and Fasting 1999, Amman 2005). The compulsory physical education classes were often opted out. Hoşer tells how, as recent as "[i]n 1970, in one of the most prestigious schools of Istanbul, a total of 3 out of 25 girls are doing sports in the gymnastics class; two German and a Turkish girl, the rest have fake medical reports that allow them not to attend. The boys of the same class are fully attending" (Hoşer 2000, 3, translated by Sehlikoglu). Teenage girls attending compulsory physical education classes in high school still faced sexual harassment from their male classmates as late as 1980 (Hoşer 2000, 42). The social pressures were influencing professional sportswomen as well, taking forms of sexual harassment. Many women's volleyball teams were violently harassed by male spectators (Hoşer 2000, 43–45).

Contested Exercise: Selected Recent Debates and fatwas on Muslim Women and Physical Exercise

Although fewer myths and misconceptions about women's involvement in sports circulate today, it still is perceived as a sexually charged act and is subjected to clerical scrutiny in Islamic contexts. Heteronormative sexual norms continue to exercise power over women's physical activity in public and in private spheres. Since the 1990s, this general social resistance to women's involvement in sports has been reinforced by an emerging neo-Islamist ideology.

By the 1930s, the religious social circles in Turkey assumed the role of preserving tradition and started to build the cornerstones of Islamist ideology early during the republican era. According to this ideology, the transformation of Turkish women during the early republican era represented a process of degeneration and distancing from their traditional roles. The word *fitne* or *fitnah* (secession/chaos) thus came to embody the process of women's emancipation from domestic life. It also became synonymous with unveiling and gaining access to public realms. Women's participation in sports was not acceptable, because sports took women outside of these normative boundaries. As republican ideology tried to transform Turkish women by imposing unveiling and new dress codes upon them in order to make them "modern," Islamic ideology emphasized the "protection" of women through their veiling and the preservation of their traditional roles in the household. This ideological struggle turned women's bodies into an arena where opposing lifestyles and values were contested: the one represented by republican, secular, modernist ideals, the other embedded within Islamic, traditionalist discourses. However, as social resistance has faded in recent years, new spaces (gender-segregated or mixed-gender) and possibilities have opened up to accommodate and welcome women into the world of physical education, exercise, fitness, and sports (Sehlikoglu 2016a).

An Interesting Case: Exercise Fest as the Reflection of the Changing Ideologies in Turkey

In discussions about the nationalist project of Turkey and sports, Idman Bayramı (Exercise Fest) is an interesting example that embodies the changing ideologies and approaches concerning sports dating back to the late Ottoman period. The Fest had begun to be celebrated as Idman Bayramı (Exercise Fest) in the last years of the Ottoman Empire, in 1916 and 1917, on 12 May. In these first two Fests, only men were allowed to participate. The purpose was to celebrate and welcome spring with the spirit of youth (Armağan 1998, 2012).

FIGURE 3
The first celebration of Gymnastics Fest, name of which is now "Atatürk's Dat" after the date was pushed to 19th of May, 1938
PERSONAL ARCHIVE, SERTAÇ SEHLIKOGLU

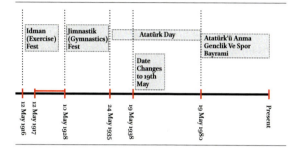

FIGURE 4
Table showing the changes in the name and dates of the fest that is known today as "Remembrance of Atatürk, Youth and Sports Fest" (Atatürk'ü Anma, Gençlik ve Spor Bayramı) since 1980. (Sehlikoglu)

After a break of ten years, the young republican country decided to continue the Fest in 1928, on 10 May, with a more Western name, Jimnastik Bayramı (Gymnastics Fest) (Figure 3). Changing the name from an Arabic to a French (*gymnastique*) word was also meant to symbolically reflect Turkey's westernization. In 1938, Atatürk decided that the Fest should be celebrated on 19 May, which marks the beginning of the Turkish War of Independence. Therefore, the Fest transformed from a celebration of the coming of spring into a remembrance of the War of Independence. As it turned out, 19 May 1938 marked Atatürk's last public appearance. The celebrations continued throughout the next decades of the Republic. After the third military coup in 1980, the name of the Fest was switched to "Remembrance of Atatürk, Youth and Sports Fest." Once again, the event and its name were convenient tools to create and manage a collective memory (Figure 4).

In the gymnastics fests of the early republican period, the appearance of girls used to have symbolic meaning as a representation of liberated female bodies. Today, the length of girls' shorts and skirts becomes a disputed subject every 19 May. Longer skirts are criticized as a symbol of "Islamization" in Turkey. Comparisons of the length of the skirts of today with the length of those of the 1950s are made in the mass media after every 19 May Fest. Another question the media poses every year is whether the governing neo-Islamist party (AKP) members are watching the Fest or closing their eyes when the girls are performing their shows.

Over the last decade, Turkish women have become increasingly interested and involved in exercise, as observed in middle-aged women walking fast on the streets and public parks with their robes and sneakers; images of older women on daytime TV programs exercising with the hosts of women's shows; a proliferation of healthy lifestyle, fitness, exercise, and weight-loss products on the market; and exercise and beauty tips on the national news channels. The number of women-only gyms, pools, sports centers, and exercise sessions increased twenty-fold between 2005 and 2012 in Istanbul. The demands of women of ages from fifteen to late fifties and from different socioeconomic classes in Turkey to exercise in segregated spaces have opened up a whole new market. "What is at stake is not women's desire to lose weight or become fit. The core aspect of women's desire is to feel (italic) healthier, slimmer, and even stronger which is, in their mind, is already associated with a better, a more advanced self" (Sehlikoglu 2014, 2016b).

Conclusion: Sports Education and Women's Bodies: Encounters with Patriarchies

In Turkey, both secular modern and Islamist ideologies lay claim to women's bodies through sports. In this counting, women's bodies have long been the target of multiple patriarchy—including both Islamic traditionalism and secular nationalism. On the one hand, Islamic ideology enforces ethical standards of modest dress, confinement to domestic spaces, and gender segregation. On the other hand, Turkish secular nationalism enforces modern Western outfits and mingling with the opposite sex. Although veiled women have been caught between these patriarchies, they have been able to act as agents of a neo-Islamist movement that seeks to integrate religious and modern identities as a hallmark of Turkish Islam. Since the establishment of the Republic in 1923, the construction, formation, and representation of women's bodies have been politicized by both the secularists and the traditional Islamists, and have revealed a wide range of cultural meanings, mores, and power dynamics at play.

Women's sports have been considered as more than an individual act not only in the context of Turkey, but also elsewhere in the Muslim world. The debates surrounding women's sports and physical activity are very much related to broader discussions including, but not limited to, modernity, nationalism, and nativeness, because physical exercise is based on defining, shaping, and reshaping women's appearances and bodies and on using the body as the stage for representations of the nation at large. Focusing on the discursive and cultural productions of the nation-state, Sirman argues that "women were made part of the nation through the control of their bodies and, through cultural elaborations of femininity, the definition and control of the cultural boundaries of the nation" (Sirman 2005, 149).

The state seeks to build the bodies of its citizens through its myriad institutional and discursive apparatuses. As Das and Poole have pointed out, "sovereign power exercised by the state is not only about territories, it is also about bodies" (2004, 10). Putting women's bodies at the center of nationalist debates, in effect makes them embodied representational subjects of certain national identities. This investigation will be helped by calling to mind Giorgio Agamben's use of a Foucauldian framework in looking at "the individual as a simple living body become what is at stake in society's political strategies" (1998, 3), because it allows us to think about the role of the sovereign as formulator of subjects. In a parallel vein, Anthias and Yuval-Davis (1989) problematize the role of the nation-state in a way that is fruitful for this discussion, because it exposes the ways in which it treats women as second-class citizens while simultaneously locating them at the center of nationalist projects.

Acknowledgments

I would like to thank Ceren Ilikan for her translation to modern Turkish from Ottoman resources of Late-Ottoman and Early-republican period.

Bibliography

Abdelrahman, Nail Abdel. *Women and sport in Islamic society*, Alexandria, Alexandria University 1992.

Agamben, Giorgio. *Homo sacer. Sovereign power and bare life*, Palo Alto, Calif. 1998.

Aitchison, Cara. Feminist and gender research in sport and leisure management. Understanding the social-cultural nexus of gender-power relations, in *Journal of Sport Management* 19 (2005), 422–41.

Alemdaroğlu, Ayça. Politics of the body and eugenic discourse in early Republican Turkey, in *Body & Society* 11 (2005), 61–76.

Alexandris, Konstantinos, and Monika Stodolska. The influence of perceived constraints on the attitudes toward recreational sport participation, in *Loisir et société* 27:1 (2004), 197–217.

Amman, Tayfun. *Kadın ve Spor* [*Woman and sport*], Istanbul 2005.

Anthias, Floya, and Nira Yuval-Davis. *Woman-Nation-State*, London 1989.

Arıpınar, Erdoğan, Cem Atabeyoğlu, and Tuncer Cebecioğlu. *Olimpiyat Oyunlarında Türk Kızları* [*Turkish girls in Olympic Games*] 4, ed. Türkiye Milli Olimpiyat Komitesi, Istanbul 2000.

Armağan, Mustafa Hakkı. *19 Mayıs 'ın bilinmeyen tarihi* [Unknown History of 19th May], Zaman Daily, May 19, 1998.

Armağan, Mustafa Hakkı. Republished: *19 Mayıs'ın bilinmeyen tarihi* [Unknown History of 19th May], in *Küller Altında Yakın Tarih: Vahdettin'den Mustafa Kemal'e Unutulan Gerçekler (Near History Under the ashes, forgotten truths from Vahdettin to Mustafa Kemal)*, Timaş Publishing, İstanbul 2012, 91–96.

Atalay, Ayşe. Osmanlı Ve Genç Türkiye Cumhuriyeti Döneminde Sporda Batılılaşma Hareketleri [Westernization movements in sports during the Ottoman empire and early-Republican Turkey], in *Spor Yönetimi ve Bilgi Teknolojileri Dergisi* 2:2 (2007), 30–35.

Atalay, Ayşe. Türkiye'de Osmanlı Döneminde Ve Uluslaşma Sürecinde Kadın Ve Spor [Women and sports during the Ottoman era and during the process of nationalization in Turkey], in *Spor Yönetimi ve Bilgi Teknolojileri Dergisi* 2:2 (2007), 24–29.

Baydar, Gülsüm. Tenuous boundaries. Women, domesticity, and nationhood in 1930s Turkey, in *Journal of Architecture* 7 (2002), 229–44.

Benn, Tansin, Gertud Pfister, and Haifaa Jawad (eds.). *Muslim women and sport*, London 2010.

Cantek, Funda Şenol. *Yaban'lar ve Yerliler* [The Strangers and the Natives]. İletişim Yayınları, İstanbul, 2003.

Dareini, Ali Akbar. Iran President, clerics battle over women's sports. *Associated Press*, 2010 <http://archive.boston.com/news/world/middleeast/articles/2010/12/06/iran_president_clerics_battle_over_womens_sports/>. 20 September 2016.

Das, Veena, and Deborah Poole. *Anthropology in the margins*. Santa Fe, N.Mex. 2004.

Di-Capua, Yoav. Sports, society, and revolution. Egypt in the early 1950s, in *Rethinking Nasserism,* eds. Elie Podeh and Onn Vinclair, Gainesville, Fla. 2004, 144–62.

Di-Capua, Yoav. "Sports. Arab states", in *Encyclopedia of Women & Islamic Cultures*, ed. Suad Joseph. (2006) <http://dx.doi.org/10.1163/1872-5309_ewic_EWICCOM_0207a>. 21 September 2016.

Dworkin, Shari L., and Michael A. Messner. Just do... what? Sport, bodies, gender, in *Gender and sport. A reader*, eds. Sheila Scraton and Anne Flintoff, New York, NY 2002, 17–29.

Fişek, Kurthan. *Devlet Politikası ve Toplumsal Yapıyla İlişkileri Açısından Spor Yönetimi. Dünyada - Türkiye'de* [*Sports management in Turkey and in the world vis-à-vis state politics and relationships with social structure*], Ankara 1980.

Fişek, Kurthan. *100 Soruda Türkiye Spor Tarihi* [Turkey's History of Sports in 100 Questions], Gerçek Publications, Ankara, 1985.

Göle, Nilüfer. *The forbidden modern. Civilization and veiling*, Ann Arbor, Mich. 1996.

Guttmann, Allen. *Sports. The first five millennia*, Boston, Mass. 2004.

Harani, Yavuz. Türk Kadının Sporla İmtihanı [Turkish women's challenge in sports], in *Hürriyet*, 13 January 2001.

Hargreaves, Jennifer. *Sport, culture, and ideology*, London 1982.

Henderson, Karla, and Deborah Bialeschki. The meanings of physical recreation for women, in *Women in Sport and Physical Activity Journal* 3:2 (1994), 22–38.

Hergüner, Gülten. Spor Yapmalarını Etkileyen Sosyo-Kültürel Faktörler. Samsun Ili Uygulaması [Socio-cultural factors that affect women's involvement in sports. The case of the city of Samsun], Ph.D. diss., Marmara University 1993.

Hoodfar, Homa. *The role of sport in resisting, accommodating, and in the remaking of Muslim women. A symposium report*, Montreal 2008.

Hoodfar, Homa (ed.). *Women's sport as politics in Muslim contexts*, London 2015.

Hoşer, Firdevs. 2000. Sport ve Kadın Özel 2000 Ajandası. İstanbul: Kadın Eserleri Kütüphanesi.

Kay, Tess. Daughters of Islam, sisters in sport, in *Geographies of Muslim identities. Diaspora, gender, and belonging*, eds. Cara Aitchison, Peter E. Hopkins, and Mei-po Kwan, Hampshire 2007, 125–41.

Kandiyoti, Deniz. "Women and the Turkish State: Political Actors or Symbolic Pawns?". In *Woman-Nation-State* edited by Floya Anthias and Nira Yuval-Davis. London: Macmillan, 1989, 126–149.

Kevles, D.J. *In the name of eugenics. Genetics and the uses of human heredity*, Cambridge, Mass. 1995.

Koca, Canan, and Ilknur Hacısoftaoğlu. Religion and the state. The story of a Turkish elite athlete, in *Muslim women and sport*, eds. Tansin Benn and Gertud Pfister, London 2009, 198–210.

Koca, Canan, and Ilknur Hacısoftaoğlu. Struggling for empowerment. Sport participation of women and girls in Turkey, in *Muslim women and sport*, eds. Tansin Benn and Gertud Pfister, London 2009, 154–66.

Mahfoud, Amara. An introduction to the study of sport in the Muslim world, in *Sport and society. A student introduction*, ed. Barrie Houlihan, London 2008, 532–53.

Mahmood, Saba. *Politics of piety. The Islamic revival and the feminist subject*, Princeton, NJ 2005.

Messner, Michael. A., and Donald F. Sabo. *Sport, men, and the gender order. Critical feminist perspectives*, Champaign, Ill. 1990.

Navaro-Yashin, Yael. *Faces of the state. Secularism and public life in Turkey*, Princeton, NJ 2002.

O'Reilly, Jean, and Susan K. Cahn. *Women and sports in the United States. A documentary reader*, Boston, Mass. 2007.

Pfister, Gertrud. Equality and social missions. Muslim women and their opportunities to participate in sport and physical activities, in *Spor Bilimleri Dergisi* 19:4 (2008), 250–60.

Pfister, Gertrud, and Kari Fasting. *Opportunities and barriers for sport for women in Turkey. A pilot study*, Las Vegas, Nev. 1999.

Raval, Sadha. Gender, leisure, and sport. A case study of young people of South Asian descent—a response, in *Leisure Studies* 8:3 (1989), 237–40.

Saavedra, Martha. Women and sports in Senegal, Sudan, and Nigeria, in *The role of sport in resisting, accommodating, and in remaking Muslim women*, ed. Homa Hoodfar, Montreal 2008.

Sehlikoğlu, Sertaç. Highlights/Muslim women in sports, in wlUML *Newsletter*, ed. Nandita Dutta, 12, London 2011.

Sehlikoğlu, Sertaç. Imagining the Self as Sporting Body. Cultural Anthropology Fieldsights-Field Notes March 2, 2014 <https://culanth.org/fieldsights/495-sports -deviation> 12 October, 2016.

Sehlikoğlu, Sertaç. Exercising in comfort. Islamicate culture of Mahremiyet in everyday Istanbul, in *Journal of Middle East Women's Studies* 12:2 (2016a), 143–165.

Sehlikoğlu, Sertaç. Desiring Muslim Women: Agency and Feminist Theory, in *Senior Research Seminar* at the Division of Social Anthropology, University of Cambridge (2016b).

Sfeir, Leila. "The status of Muslim women in sport: conflict between cultural tradition and modernization." *International Review for the sociology of sport* 20, no. 4 (1985), 283–306.

Sirman, Nükhet. The making of familial citizenship in Turkey, in *Citizenship in a global world. European questions and Turkish experiences*, eds. E. Fuat Keyman and Ahmet İçduygu, London 2005, 147–172.

Snape, Robert, and Phil Bink. Re-thinking sport. Physical activity and healthy living in British South Asian Muslim communities, in *Managing Leisure* 13 (2008), 23–35.

Talimciler, Ahmet. İdeolojik Bir Meşrulaştırma Aracı Olarak Spor Ve Spor Bilimleri [Sports and sport sciences as a tool to gain legitimacy], in *Spor Yönetimi ve Bilgi Teknolojileri Dergisi* 1:2 (2006), 674–723.

Tuzcuoğulları, Cemal. *Atatürk ve Spor [Ataturk and sports]*, Ankara 2001.

Walseth, Kristin. Young Muslim women and sport. The impact of identity work, in *Leisure Studies* 25:1 (2006), 75–94.

Walseth, Kristin, and Kari Fasting. Islam's view on physical activity and sport. Egyptian women interpreting Islam, in *International Review for the Sociology of Sport* 38:1 (2003), 45–60.

Walseth, Kristin, and Kari Fasting. Sport as a means of integrating minority women, in *Sport in Society* 7:1 (2004), 109–29.

Wiley, Caroline G.E., Susan M. Shaw, and Mark E. Havitz. Men's and women's involvement in sports. An examination of the gendered aspects of leisure involvement, in *Leisure Studies* 22:1 (2000), 19–31.

Yarar, Betül. Civilized women and light sports. Modernization, women, and sport in the early Republican period of Turkey, in *Kadın-Woman* 2000 12:1 (2005), 1–36.

Yıldız, Doğan. *Çağlarboyu Türkler'de Spor [Sports amongst Turks through the ages]*, Istanbul 2002.

Yurdadön, Ergun. Sport in Turkey. The post-Islamic Republican period, in *The Sport Journal* 7:1 (2004).

Index of Names

14 February Youth Coalition (Bahrain)   501
Abbottabad   328
'Abd al-Majīd (Ottoman Sultan)   212
Abdou, Cheb   480
Abdul, Dr.   533
Abdullah, Daayiee   439
Abi Zaʿbal (Egypt)   213
ABIM (Angkatan Belia Islam Malaysia,
    Muslim Youth Movement of
    Malaysia)   121–122
Abu Hatoum, Nayrouz   444
Abu-Lughod, Lila   77, 89, 92
Ackerman, Susan   3–4
Adam, Barry D.   443
Adang, Camilla   436
Adibah v. Abdul Rani case (Malaysia)   117
Adil, Adnan   327–328
Afghanistan
    girls raised as boys in   476–477
    homosexual relations with boys
        in   465–467
Agamben, Giorgio   563
Ahluwalia, Sanjam   340, 341
Ahmad, Farah Mehreen   408
Ahmadu, Fumbai   48, 52
Ahmed, Amineh   252, 514
Ahmed, Fatima and Abda   529
Ahmed, Leila   438
Ahmed, Rahnuma   406
Ahmed, Youssef   469
Ain-O-Shalish Kendra (Law and Mediation
    Center, Bangladesh)   71, 401, 402
Al-Ākharūn (al-Ḥirz)   441
Akhter, Farida   304–305, 319, 324–325, 326
Akhter, Shameem   308, 309
Alam, Faisal   439
Alam, Shamsul   68
Albasman, Faleh Ghazi   89
Aldosari, Hala   77, 78, 80, 86
Alemdaroğlu, Ayça   557
Algeria, cross-dressing in   480
'Alī, 'Abdullah Yūsuf   173
Ali, Kamran Asdar   512
'Alī, Mustafa   214
Ali, Parveen Shaukat   248

Ali, Salma   73
'Alī Pāsha, Mohammad (Viceroy of Egypt)
    213
Alipour, Mehrdad   481
Alkhateeb, Sharifa   169, 170
Allah Made Us (Gaudio)   443
Alliance of New Men (LLB, Indonesia)   110
Ameen, Nusrat   67, 68
Amer, Saher   444
Amin, Rahman Mohd   8
Amirat Mansiyat (Forgotten Princesses,
    Mutayyim)   442
Amnesty International   64, 90
Amry, Shareem   122–123
Andajani-Sutjahjo, Sari   102
Andalusia, gender diversity and
    homosexuality in   439
Angul (Muslim youth organization, United
    States)   533
Anjuman-e-Mazarain (Pakistan)   516
Anthias, Floya   563
Anwar, Nausheen   512
APGWA (Association for Promoting Girls' and
    Women's Advancement in the
    Gambia)   192
APWA (All Pakistan Women's Association)
    318
Arab Families Working group   286, 291
*Arab Human Development Report: The
    Empowerment of Arab Women*
    (2005)   285, 289
Arab states
    abortion in   286
    activism on gender equality in
        290–291
    contraceptive use by women in   285
    fertility rates in   285–286, 292
    declines in   283–284
    health care in, women's access to   286,
        290
    Islamism in   290
    marriage in, increases in age of
        284–285
    maternal mortality in   280
    patriarchy in   282–283

INDEX OF NAMES

Arab states (cont.)
  population and health sciences studies
    of 278–279, 292
  families 283–285, 286, 288
  reproductive health of
    women 279–282
  youth 287–288
Arabian Peninsula *see* Gulf states
al-Arabiya.net 91
Arendt, Hannah 315
Arıpınar, Erdoğan 557
Aşeni, Ahmet Fetgeri 556
Aşeni, Suat Fetgeri 547, 556
Ash, Luiza 233
Assiut (Egypt) 426
Aswānī, ʿAlāʾ 441
Aşwāt (Palestine) 442
Atabeyoğlu, Cem 557
Atatürk, Mustafa Kemal 541, 546, 553,
    554–555, 556, 557, 561
Atlanta 525, 527–528, 531, 532–533, 534
Aurat Foundation (Pakistan) 133
Australia
  deaths from female reproductive cancers
    in 364
  Islam and homosexuality in 439
Awami League (Bangladesh) 406, 409
Awang, Halimah 9
Aydın (Turkey) 558
Ayerdem, Ali Hikmet 541
Azad, Abdul Kalam 406
al-Azhar University (Cairo) 479
Aziz, Azalina 125

Baby Friendly Hospital Initiative 6
Badawi, Abdullah 125
Bagdad 439
Bahrain
  Arab Spring uprisings in, role of women
    in 493, 501–502
  guardianship of women in 78
  violence against women in
    awareness campaigns on 88, 91
    against domestic migrant
      workers 90
    domestic violence 81, 87
    state violence against activists 84–85
Bakhtiar, Laleh 173

Baldauf, Ingeborg 466
Balfour, M.C. 344
Balochistan Province (Pakistan) 141
Banāt al-Riyāḍ (al-Sānīʿ) 441
Bangladesh
  adoption from 323
  divorce in, women's rights to 69
  family planning in 301–304, 311, 316,
    324–326, 328–330, 332–333
    abortion 323, 331–332, 408–409
    contraceptive use 301, 303, 304–306,
      311, 317–318, 325–326, 333
  female sexualities in 450, 451–459
  fertility rates in 317, 325
  gender equity in 65, 450–451
  legal reforms in 70–71, 73–74
  marriage in 67, 401, 452, 453–454
  minorities in, violence against 409
  motherhood in 308, 311
  patriarchy in 450
  reproductive health in 301, 303, 316
  son preference in 330–332
  violence against women in 308
    domestic violence in 63–65, 66–74
    sexual harassment 397–410
    wartime rape 322–324, 408–409
  womanhood ideals in 451–452
  women's rights in 304–306, 306–311, 398
Barīd Mustʿajil (anon.) 442
Barlas, Asma 66
Barman, Barun Chandra 406
Baydar, Nasuhi 541–542
BCHR (Bahrain Center for Human Rights)
    84, 85
BCL (Bangladesh Chhatra League) 406
Beaugrand, Claire 83
Beersheba 216
Beijing
  Platform for Action 289
  World Conference on Women in
    (1995) 137, 187
Bellman, Beryl 49
Benevolent Society (Turkestan) 231
Bennett, Linda 106–107, 108
Bereket, Tariq 443
Berlin Olympics (1936) 556, 557
Bernard, Carl Ambrose 212
Beşiktaş Gymnastics Club (Turkey) 556

INDEX OF NAMES

Beverly, Elizabeth A.   39
Bhowmik, Chanpa Rani   402
Bhullar, Sim and Tanveer   525
Bhutto, Benazir   250, 322, 327
Bhutto, Zulfikar Ali   135, 319, 320–321
Bijnor (India)   348
Bin Laden, Osama   328
Black Wednesday (Egypt)   414
Blackburn, Susan   110, 111
Bledsoe, Caroline H.   34
Blumfeldt (midwife)   232–233
BNP (Bangladesh Nationalist Party)   409
BNWLA (Bangladesh National Women's
   Lawyer's Association)   400, 401
Boddy, Janice   50
Bodrum   480
Boone, Sylvia Ardyn   49
BRAC (Bangladesh Rural Advancement
   Committee/Building Resources Across
   Communities)   328, 407
Brown, Louise   514–515
Bukhara   147
Bulatova, Fotima   233
Burkina Faso, breastfeeding in   31, 34
Burou, Georges   480
Bux, Fehmida and Allah   136

Cairo   414, 419
   al-Azhar University   479
   Tahrir Square protests   419–420
   University   418
Çambel, Halet   547, 556
Cameroon, breastfeeding in   30, 33
Caramel (film)   440
Casamance region (Senegal), female genital
   mutilation in   193, 194–195
Casey, Conerly   86
Cebecioğlu, Tuncer   557
CEDAW (Convention on the Elimination of
   All forms of Discrimination against
   Women)
   reservations
      by Bangladesh   65, 399
      by Gulf states   87
   signatories of
      Bangladesh   65, 398–399
      Pakistan   138
      Tajikistan   149
   on violence against women   398–399

Chan Ah Moi case (Malaysia)   115
Charara, R.   258
Chatterjee, Partha   510
China, breastfeeding in   6
Chittagong Hill Tracts (Bangladesh)   409
Chowdhury, Mushtaque   328
Çiğigil, L.O.   548
Cleland, John   324, 329
Clinton, Hillary   193
Clot, Anthoine Barthelemy   213
Coccinelle (Ladybird)   480
Çocuk Beslemek (Child-feeding, Münir)
   23–25
Çocuk Büyütmek (Child-rearing, Rahmi)
   20–23
Contestations (electronic newsletter)   290
Corea, Gena   310
Côte d'Ivoire, breastfeeding in   30
Cuba, breastfeeding in   6

The Dancing Boys of Afghanistan (film,
   Quraishi)   466–467
The Dancing Girls of Lahore (Brown)
   514–515
Dandekar, Kumudini   344
D'Anglure, Saladin   462
Das, Veena   563
DaVanzo, Julie   8, 11
Daver, Abidin   541
Davis, Geoffrey   408–409
D'Costa, Bina   408
De Lind van Wijngaarden, Jan Willem   467
Delhi   348
Depo-Provera (injectable contraceptive)
   325
Dettwyler, Katerine A.   32, 38
Dhabas (Pakistani women's group)   516
Dhofar (Oman)   503
Di-Capua, Yoav   553, 559
Dina (oriental dance performer, Egypt)   414
Dixon, Paul   84
Al-dizil (Diesel, al-Suwaydī)   441
Douglas, Mary   47, 211
Drop the Knife (anti female genital
   mutilation event, Gambia)   192
DRUM (Desis Rising Up and Moving, United
   States)   528
Dushanbe   152
Dziegielewski, S.F.   169

ECWR (Egyptian Center for Women's Rights)
  414–415, 425
Egypt
  adoption in 387
  Arab Spring in 286
  health care in 213
  homosexuality in 479
    with effeminate boys 467–469,
      470–471
  intersex/transsexuality surgery
    in 478–480
  Islamist movement in 286
  reproductive technologies in 310
  sexual harassment in 291, 412–426
El Saadawi, Nawal 247, 441
El-Nadeem Center for Rehabilitation of
  Victims of Violence (Egypt) 414
El-Sissi, Fatah 419
Emzirmek (Breastfeeding, Ömer) 19
Ershad, Hussain Muhammad 324, 402
Ersoy, Bülent 480

Fahmy, Khaled 213
Faqir, Fadia 218
Fargues, Philippe 283, 286
Faridah (bte Dato Talib) 119
*Faridah bte Dato Talib v. Mohamed Habibullah
  bin Mahmood* case (Malaysia) 118
Al-Farooq Masjid (mosque, United States)
  529, 532, 534
Faruk, Tabiz 403
Al Fassi, Hatoon 83–84
fatāt al-ʿAtaba case (Egypt) 413
Fatayat NU (Indonesia) 384
al-Fatiha Mosque (United States) 439
FDAP (Family Planning Association of
  Pakistan) 318, 319
Feghali, Bassem 441
The Female Circumcision Controversy
  (Gruenbaum) 53
Fenerbahçe sport club 548, 556
Ferme, Mariane 56
FIFA (International Federation of
  Association Football) 526
Fisk, Norma 479
Fitrat, Abdurauf 240
Ford Foundation 342, 343, 384

*Forensic Medicine and its Function in applying
  Criminal Law in Palestine* (al-Hadidi and
  Hamdi) 219
Fortier, Corinne 468
Foucault, Michel 306
France, Islam and homosexuality in 439
Franklin, Sarah 307
Fraser, Nancy 330
Fuʾād I (King of Egypt) 468
Full Stop (advertising agency) 91

Gadit, Amin 258
Galatasaray sport club (Turkey) 559
Galtung, Johan 76
Gambia
  breastfeeding in 34
  female genital mutilation in 56, 190–192,
    196
GAMCOTRAP (Gambia Committee on
  Traditional Practices) 192
Gardner, Andrew M. 89–90
Gaudio, Rudolf Pell 443
Gay Muslims (documentary) 440
Gender Inequality Index, Bangladesh's
  ranking in 450–451
Genesis (Bible book), on breastfeeding 15
Georgia (United States) 529
Ghana, female genital mutilation in 185
al-Ghanim, Khaltham Ali 91–92
al-Ghermeizi, Ayat 85
al-Ghomgham, Israa 84
Ghulam, Farida 501
Giacaman, Rita 285
Gilgit (Pakistan) 514
*Global Burden of Diseases, Injuries, and Risk
  Factors Study* (Charara et al) 258
Gokhale Institute of Politics and Economics
  (India) 343–344
Gonashyastha Kendra (People's Health
  Center, Bangladesh) 325
Gorenstein, M. I. 239
Gosselin, Claudie 54
Grant, James 326
Great Britain
  Islam and homosexuality in 439
  mandate rule of Palestine by 217–218,
    220

INDEX OF NAMES

Muslim female sport activities in 525–526

Gruenbaum, Ellen   49, 53–54, 56

Guard Force sport club (*Muhafiz Gücü*, Turkey)   553

Guhathakurta, Meghna   402

Guinea, female genital mutilation in   185

Guinea-Bissau
  breastfeeding in   30, 36, 38
  coming of age rituals in   50, 53
  female genital mutilation in   50, 56
  Islamic education in   54–55

Gulf Affairs (magazine)   87–88

Gulf states
  Arab Spring uprisings in   85
    role of women in   493, 500–503
  guardianship of women in   77–78, 79–80, 493
  private female spaces in   493–496, 503–504
  state-sponsored feminism in   493, 498–501
  violence against women in   76–77, 80–81, 82–85, 87–89, 91–92
    domestic violence   78–80, 81–82, 86–87
    against female domestic migrant workers   89–91

Habib, Samar   442, 444

Habibie, Bacharuddin Jusuf   101

Habibullah, Mohamed   118

Habsburg Empire, health care in   212

Habsjah, A.   358–359

al-Hadidi, Moa'men   219

Hairun v. Omar case (Malaysia)   116, 117, 118

al-Hajeri, Falah   79

Hakim, V.   358–359

Hakimi, M.   102

Hall, Stuart   306

Halvorson, Sarah   514

Hamdi, Nazeeh   219

Hamzić, Vanja   436

Ḥanafī school of law   437

Hanımlara Mahsus Gazete (Newspaper for women, Ottoman Empire)   538

Hanna, Judith Lynne   471

Ḥaqqī ʿan ʿAysh, ʿan Akhtar, ʿan Akūn (anon.)   442

Haque, Tania   409

Hartmann, Betsy   324, 325

Harvest Infertility Care Ltd. Clinic (Bangladesh)   310

Hashim, Rahmah   121

Hasina, Sheikh   404

Hasnah v. Saad case (Malaysia)   116

Hasnah v. Zaaba case (Malaysia)   117–118

Hassan, Aasiya   168, 179

Hassan, Ibrahim Pasha   213

Hazari, Joynal   403–404

Hendricks, Muhsin   436, 439

Heng Seai Kie   125

Herdt, Gilbert   462

Hergüner, Gülten   554

Hernlund, Ylva   56

al-Ḥirz, Ṣabā   441

Hitler, Adolf   557

Holzhausen, Walter   326

Homosexuels Musulmans (France)   439

Hoşer, Firdevs   559

Hossain, Syed Mahmud   399

Hosseini, Khaled   466

HRCP (Human Rights Commission of Pakistan)   133

Hudood Ordinances (Pakistan)   135, 138, 246, 321, 511

Hughes, Alex   515

"Hum Do Hamare Do" sloban (We Two and Our Two, India)   345

Human Development Index, Bangladeshi scores on   316

Human Laboratory (BBC documentary)   326

Human Rights Watch   78, 81–82, 88

Hürriyet (newspaper, Turkey)   556

Hussein, N.   261

Hyderabad   347, 471

Ibn ʿAbbās   16

Ibn Ḥazm   436, 437

Ibn Isḥāq al-Jundī, Khalīl   463–464

Ibn Mālik   202, 205

Ibn Sīnā   17

Ibrahim, Anwar   123

Ibrahim, Samira   420

ICPD (International Conference in Population and Development) 289–290, 303, 322, 357
Idrus, Nurul I. 106, 108
ILO (International Labor Organization) 6–7
Iman and Yousef Foundation (Great Britain) 439
'Imārat Ya'qubiyān (The Jacoubian Building, Aswānī) 441
Inayatulla, Attiya 321
India
  demographic research in 343
  family planning in 340, 342–344, 349
    abortion 349
    contraceptives use 340, 342–343, 347–348
    Hindu opposition to 345
    by Muslims 343–344, 347–349
  female feticide in 331
  fertility rates in, of Muslim population 341, 345–346
  Hindu nationalism/Hindu Right in 345–347
  homosexual relations with effeminate boys in 471–473
  population growth in 340
    of Muslim population 341
  women's access to public spaces in 516
Indonesia
  divorce in 107, 111, 362, 385–386
  family planning in 356–358, 378–382, 389
    abortion 358–359, 382–384, 389, 390
    contraceptive use 357–358, 379–382
  fertility rates in 356, 378–379
  gender equity in 354, 365, 372–373
  health care in 364, 374, 376, 388–389
  health of women in
    HIV/AIDS infections 360–362, 380
    maternal health 355–356, 375–378, 389
    reproductive cancers 363–364, 387–389, 390
    reproductive health 354–365, 373, 374–375, 389–390
  infertility in 362–363, 385–387, 389
  Islam in 352

  Islamic revivalism/Islamism in 352–353, 370–372
    women's activism in 353–354
  Islamization in 370
  marriage in 102–105
  motherhood in 354, 373
  poverty in 352, 374
  sex education in 354–355
  sexually transmitted illnesses in 360–362, 363, 386
  violence against women in
    domestic violence 100–102, 105–111
    sexual violence 359–360
  women's organizations in 100, 101, 110
    Islamic 353–354, 372, 384
Inhorn, Marcia 310, 387
Inner Circle Mosque (South Africa) 439
İnönü, İsmet 541, 546
Instagram 498
Iran
  contraceptive use in 285
  effeminates in 465
  fertility rates in 283
  health care in 280
  higher education in, female participation in 285
  sport in 552
    by women 555
  transsexual surgery in 481–482
IRIN (Integrated Regional Information Networks) 401
Islam and Homosexuality (Badruddin Khan et al eds) 442, 443
Islamic Speakers Bureau (United States) 529
Ismail (Khedive of Egypt) 213
Ismail, Zaleha 122
Istanbul 555
  medical school in 212
Izmir 558

Jadaliyya (website) 290
JAG-VAW (Joint Action Group against Violence Against Women, Malaysia) 121
Jahan, Roushan 73
Jahangirnagar University (Bangladesh) 402, 406
al-Jāhiz 16

INDEX OF NAMES

Jaipur 349
Jalal, Ayesha 510
Jamaat-e-Islami (Bangladesh) 409
Jammeh, Yaya 190–191
Jannāt wa-Iblīs (Jannāt and the Devil, El
Saadawi) 441
Janson, Yu E. 231
Jayakumari case (Malaysia) 115
Jeffery, Patricia, Roger and Craig 348
Jenkins, Rachel 257
Jerusalem 214, 216
Jhakri (India) 348
A Jihad for Love (film, Sharma) 440
Johnson, Lyndon B. 302
Johnson, Michelle C. 50, 54–55
Jong, Ferdinand de 55
Jorio, Rosa de 57
Josiah, Ivy 124
Joydhor, Porimol 405–406
JUI-F (Jamiat Ulema-e-Islam-Fazl, Pakistan)
140
Julekha Begum 68

Kabeer, Naila 330
Kadınlar dünyası (The world of women,
women's magazine, Ottoman
Empire) 25–26, 538
Kadınlık ve Analık (Womanhood and
motherhood, Tevfik) 26
Kakute, Peter Nwenfu 39
Kamarulzarman, Ibrahim 10
Kane, Tanya 495
Karachi 268, 512, 513, 515
Karim, Jamilah 525
Karim, Lamia 329–330
Karim, Shuchi 453
Khaki, El-Farouk 439
Khan, Ayesha 516
Khan, Ayub 319, 320, 327
Khan, Badruddin 442
Khan, Imran 316
Khan, M.E. 341–342, 455
Khan, Murad 268
Khan, Shehla Aftab 322
Khan, Yahya 320
Khatib-Chahidi, Jane 36
al-Khawaja, Abdulhadi 84
al-Khawaja, Maryam 84–85

al-Khawaja, Zainab 85
Khomeini, Ayatollah Ruhollah 481
Kifaya Movement (Egypt) 414
Kirmani, Nida 516
The Kite Runner (Hosseini) 466
Kiz Öğretmen Okulu (Girls School of Teacher
Training, Turkey) 543–544
Kokand 235
Kolosov, T. A. 238
Komnas Perempuan (National Commission
on Women, Indonesia) 101, 102, 109, 110
Kovaleva (midwife) 239
Kristeva, Julia 211
Kugle, Scott 436, 437, 463
Kurmysheva, Fotima 233
Kuwait
domestic migrant workers in 91
guardianship of women in 78
trauma after Iraqi invasion in 85–86
violence against women in
domestic violence 80, 86–87
honor killings 88–89

Labaki, Nadine 440
Lagrange, Frédéric 436, 444
Lahore 515
Lamentations (Bible book), on
breastfeeding 15
The Lancet (journal) 290
LBH-APIK (Legal aid institute—association
of Indonesian women for justice) 100
Lee, Raymond 3–4
Lestari, Herna 358–359
LeVine, Robert A. 33
Libya, Arab Spring in 286
Lim Kit Siang 123
Lindström, Christina 444
Loh Cheng Kooi 125
Lūṭ/Lot, Qur'anic/Biblical story of 463

Ma'dān ethnic group (Marsh
Arabs) 477–478
Mahdiyah, Wan Norsiah 10
Mai, Mukhtār 133
Malaysia
breastfeeding in 3, 4–11
divorce in 116–119
domestic violence in 114–128

Islam in 3–4
marriage in 120
Mali
breastfeeding in 31, 32, 38
female genital mutilation in 51, 54, 56, 185
Malicounda (Senegal), female genital mutilation abandoned in 193
Malim, Fathi 469
Malti-Douglas, Fedwa 444
Manchar (India) 344
Manderson, Lenore 9
Manoori, Ukmina 476
Marett, Robert Ranulph 462
Marks, Miriam 287–288
Marmot, Michael 279
The Marsh Arabs (Thesiger) 477
Mary (mother of Jesus), breastfeeding by 15
Masood, Ayesha 252
Massad, Joseph 478
Matlab (Bangladesh) 325, 329
Mauritania, effeminate men/boys in 475–476
Medina 464–465
Meem (Lebanon) 442
MEIA-GA (Movement to End Israeli Apartheid-Georgia) 529
Mekteb-i Sultani (Galata Palace Royal School, Turkey) 540
Une Mélancolie Arabe (Taia) 442
Melching, Molly 195
Memoirs of Randa the Trans (Saghia) 442
Mevlan, Nuriye Ulviye 25
Middle East, sport in 552–553
Mifepristone (medicine) 384
Millennium Development Goals
in Bangladesh 316
gender equity in 288–289
in Indonesia 355
Mirza, Ilyas 257
Mirza, Sania 526
Misk al-Ghazal (al-Shaykh) 441
Mitra Perempuan (Women's friend) Crisis Centre (Indonesia) 100
Modanlou, H.D. 17
Mogannam, Mogannam 218
Mohaiemen, Naeem 404
Mohamad, Mahathir 125

Mohamed Habibullah bin Mahmood v. Faridah bte Dato Talib case (Malaysia) 118–119
Mohsin, Amena 451
Molkhara, Maryam Khatoun 481
Mommersteeg, Geert 54
Morocco
cross-dressing in 480
same-sex marriage in 440
transsexual surgery in 480
Mossalli, Marriam 496
Mostofi, Mani 90
Moussa, Ghaida 444
Muftah (website) 290
Mugford, Gerry 258
Muḥammad (Prophet)
fasting by 353, 371
on female genital mutilation 189
funerary prayers for 205–206
funerary rites by 205, 210
Muhammadiyah (Indonesia) 353, 357, 372, 379
Muhandisin (Egypt) 414
Mukhtaṣar (Compendium, Ibn Isḥāq) 463
Mumtaz, Khawar 250
Mumtaz, Zubia 511, 513
Münir, Refik 23–25
Müren, Zeki 480
Musawah (website) 290
Muscat 502, 503
Musharraf, Pervez 133
Muslim Alliance of North America 179
Mustafa, Eman 426
Mustapha, Daanish 512
Mutayyim, Jamal 442

Naber, Nadine 443
Naciri, Mohammad 87
Nadir, A. 169
Nair, Sumanti 347–348
Najashi (Christian king) 205
Najmabadi, Afsaneh 444, 482
Nalivkin, Vladimir Petrovich and Maria Vladimirovna 232
Naqvi, Haider 268
Naripokkho (women's groups, Bangladesh) 63, 455
Nashville 527–528, 529–530, 534

INDEX OF NAMES

Nasrin, Taslima 405
National Women Lawyers' Association (Bangladesh) 64
Navot, Orit 217
Nazra for Feminist Studies (Egypt) 291
Nestlé (company) 38
New Arab Demography project 283
New Mexico 525
New Straits Times (Malaysia) 120–121
New Women Research Centre (Egypt) 291
New York 528
Ng Yen Yen 122
Ngieng Shiat Yen v. Ten Jit Hing case (Malaysia) 123
Nigeria, homosexuality in 476
Nor, Rahim 122
Norplant, use in Bangladesh of 304–305, 326
North Africa, cross-dressing in 480
NU (Nahdlatul Ulama, Indonesia) 353, 357, 372, 379
Nurmila, Nina 107
Nusa Tengara Barat province (Indonesia) 376
Nusa Tengara Timur province (Indonesia) 381

Obaid-Chinoy, Shireen 134
Odhikar (NGO, Bangladesh) 63
Oman
    Arab Spring uprisings in, role of women in 493, 502–503
    domestic violence in 81–82, 87
    effeminate boys in 473–475
    female genital mutilation in 82
    guardianship of women in 78
    violence against domestic migrant workers in 90–91
Omar, Napsiah 120
Ömer, Besim 19
One Roof (awareness campaign) 91
OpAnti-Sh (Operation Anti-Sexual Harassment, Egypt) 419
Open Asia (research center) 146, 152
Osmanağaoğlu, Hülya 539
al-Otaibi, Maryam 79
Ottoman Empire
    breastfeeding in 14, 18–27

    feminist movement in 538–539
    forensic medicine in 212–214
    funerary rites in 210–211
    homosexuality with boys in 470–471
    motherhood in 14, 18–21, 25–26, 27
    Shariʿa courts in 18
    sport in 540
Ottoman medicine. Healing and medical institutions (Shefer-Mossenson) 214
"Out of the Closet: Representation of Homosexuals and Lesbians in Modern Arabic Literature" (article, al-Samman) 442
Out in Iran (documentary) 440

Pahl, Jan 72
Pakistan 257, 315
    arranged marriages in 204, 252
    divorce in 134
    education of girls in 251, 252–253
    family law in 134
    family planning in 316, 318–322, 327–328, 333
        abortion 331, 332
        contraceptive use 317–318, 320, 322, 333
    female spaces in 510–517
    fertility rates in 317
    funerary rites in 205–207
    gender equity in 137–138, 258–259
    homosexuality with boys in 467, 471–473
    honor of women in 246–247, 248, 251
    Islamization in 135, 246
        impact on women 321, 510–511
    maternal mortality in 316
    mental health in 257–258
        care system 257, 265–268
        of women 258, 259–265, 268, 269
    nationalism in, women as embodiment of 245–246
    partition of 315, 320
        wartime rape committed in 322–324, 408–409
    poverty in 261
    purdah/gender segregation in 247–249, 251, 252, 510
    son preference in 330–332

INDEX OF NAMES

Pakistan
  violence against women in   131–134,
    135–137, 138–143
      domestic violence   263–264
      honor killings/crimes   133, 135–136,
        138, 201, 202–205, 207–208
  women's dress in   249–250, 511
Palestine
  funerary rites in   209, 215, 221
  health care in   215–216, 218, 278
  legal system in   217–218
  postmortem practices in   209, 214–217,
    218–222
Paliyenko, Dorofey Stepanovich   231, 232,
  239
Papua (province of Indonesia)   381
Paris   480
Pasamanickam, Sarasa   122
Pathways of Women's Empowerment
  290–291
Peek, Lori   527
Peirce, Leslie P.   494
People Opposed to Violence Against Women
  (Indonesia)   101
Pew Research Center   168n1, 179
Piegan society (Canada)   477
PML-N (Muslim League Nawaz, Pakistan)
  140
Poole, Deborah   563
Poona district (India)   344
Population Council   342, 343
Poslavskaya, A. V.   235
Prasad, Sheela   347–348
Predtechenskaya, A. N.   239
The Progress of Arab Women (Unifem)   289
Public Health in the Arab World (Jabbour
  et al)   282
Punjab province   268, 513
Purabi, Dr.   306

Qasem, Isa   501
Qatar
  guardianship of women in   78
  labor force participation by women
    in   494
  violence against women in   80–81
    against domestic migrant
      workers   90

      domestic violence   81, 87
  women's *majālis* (gatherings) in   493,
    495–496
Qatif rape case   84
Quetta   328
Quraishi, Najbullah   466–467

Rahma (Mercy, awareness campaign)   91
Rahmah, Hashim   122
Rahman, Mujipur   322–323
Rahmi, Mustafa   20–23
Rāiʿha al-qirfa (Yizbak)   441
al-Rajhi, Basma   503
Rani, Abdul   117
Rani, Bushra   467
Rao, Mohan   346
Rasmussen, Susan   48
Raykova (midwife)   232–233
Raymond, Janice   307
Razack, Sherene H.   89
al-Rāzī, Fakhr-al-Dīn   16
Reddy, Gayatri   471
Reproductive Health Matters (journal)
  290
Reproductive Health Working Group   291
Republican People's Party (Turkey)
  541–542
RESURJ (Realizing Sexual and Reproductive
  Justice)   291
Reza Pahlavi (Shah of Iran)   555
Riḍa, Moḥammad Rashīd   213–214
Riddell, Katrina   318, 321
Riesman, Paul   35
Rıfat, Sabiha   548, 556
Rifka Annisa (Women's friend, Indonesia)
  100, 110
Les rites de passage (Van Gennip)   211
Robinson, Warren   316
Rockefeller Foundation   342
Roko, Amy   498
Rony, Devashish Saha   402
Rowe, William S.   108
Rowland, Robyn   307
Rowson, Everett   464
Rozario, Santi   329
Rughum and Najda (Habib)   442
Rushdie, Salman   315
Ruwanpura, Kanchana   515

INDEX OF NAMES

Saʿdāwī, Nawāl *see* El Saadawi, Nawal
Sadequee, Ehsanul 528–529
Sadik, Nafis 321, 326
Sadoi Farghona (newspaper, Turkestan) 233
Saeed, Fouzia 515
Saeed, Nazeeha 85
Safi, Omid 436
Saghia, Hazim 442
Said, Riham 421
Saikia, Yasmin 323
Salaam (LGBT organization, Canada) 439, 444
Salahadeen Center (mosque, United States) 534
Salalah (Oman) 502–503
Salleh, Abdul Latif 9
al-Salman, Jalila 502
Salway, Sarah 511, 513
Samarkand 147, 235, 236, 237
Samie, Samaya Farooq 525–526
al-Samman, Hanadi 442
San Francisco 443
al-Sānī', Rajā' 441
Saudi Arabia
    citizenship laws in 83
    female activists in, arrests of 83–84
    guardianship of women in 78, 79–80
        protests against 88
    online platforms of, and empowerment of women 493, 496–498
    violence against women in 79–80, 83–84
        against domestic migrant workers 91
        domestic violence 86
Saving Face (film, Obaid-Chinoy) 134
Sawar, Samia 133
Schwarz, Aleksandr Lvovich 235, 236
Selbak, Rola 440–441
Sen, Amartya 316
Senegal
    breastfeeding in 30, 35
    coming of age rituals in 49, 50–51, 55–56
    female genital mutilation in 193–196
        ban on 191, 193, 195
Shah, Nasreen Aslam 322
Shaheed, Farida 249, 250, 511
Shaheed Benazir Bhutto Centres for Women (Pakistan) 141

al-Shalan, Abdulaziz 497
Shālī (Egypt) 468
Shame (Rushdie) 315
Shanti Bahini (Peace Force, Bangladesh) 409
Sharif, Ibrahim 501
Sharif, Nawaz 135
Sharma, Parvez 440
Shasthya Shebika program (Bangladesh) 328–329
Shawprava (support group for lesbians, Bangladesh) 458
al-Shaykh, Hanan 441
Shefer-Mossenson, Miri 214
Shemyakina, Olga 154–155
Shiv Sena (political party, India) 345
Shomoy (support group for sex workers, Bangladesh) 458
Shorokhova, Antonina Alekseevna 230, 233
Shurjasto Ain (Sunset Law, Bangladesh) 404
Siddiqi, Dina 405
Siddiquee, Qamrul Islam 399
Sierra Leone, coming of age rituals for Muslim girls in 47, 52
Sindh province 513
    honor killings in 202–205
    mental health care in 268
Singerman, Diane 287
Sirman, Nükhet 562–563
Sister Fa 188
Siwar Oasis (Egypt), homosexuality in 467–469
Snapchat, female use of, in Saudi Arabia 497
Sohar (Oman) 503
Solo (Indonesia) 373
Sonbol, Amira El-Azhary 76, 493
South Africa, queer-inclusive mosques in 439
South Asia, transgenders in 473
Soviet Union, rule of Tajikistan by 145, 147–148, 157
Stalin, Joseph 147
sub-Saharan Africa
    coming of age rituals for Muslim girls in 45–57
    female genital mutilation in 45, 46, 49–51, 52, 56–57

578   INDEX OF NAMES

Sudan, female genital mutilation in   50, 52,
    53–54, 56
Suhandjati, Sri   107, 108
Suharto, Muhammad   100–101, 352, 371, 378
Sukarno, Ahmed   352, 371
Sukkur (Pakistan)   203
Şukufezar (The garden of flowers, women's
    magazine, Ottoman Empire)   538
Sultana, Mirza   310
Sultana, Nasrin   73
al-Suqair, Moodhi   87–88
Suvarov, Ivan Petrovich   230
al-Suwaydī, Thānī   441
SuWep (Sudanese Women Empowerment for
    Peace)   291

Tahrir al-wasila (Khomeini)   481
Tahrir Bodyguards   419
Tahrir Square (Cairo), women sexually
    assaulted on   419–420
Taia, Abdella   442
Tajikistan
    civil war in   148–149
    divorce   162
    domestic violence in   145–146, 152–163
    economic development in   149–150
    Islamization in   151–152, 159, 163
    Soviet rule of   147–148, 157
    women's rights in   150–151
Tan, Kok Leong   7–8
Taner, Cemil   542
Tanta (Egypt)   426
Ṭanṭāwī, Muḥammad Sayyid   478, 479
Tarcan, Selim Sırrı   540, 542, 544
Tashkent   230, 231–233, 235, 236, 238–239
Taylan, Jale   547–548
Telfazıı (company, Saudi Arabia)   497, 498
Tennessee   530
Téreault, Mary Ann   89
Tevfik, Kenan   26
Thesiger, Wilfred   477, 478
Thomson Reuters Foundation   416
Three Veils (film)   440–441
TİCİ (Turkish Training Associations Union)
    541
Togo, female genital mutilation in   185
Toronto   439, 444

Tostan (human rights NGO, Senegal)   191,
    193, 194, 195–196
Transsexual in Iran (documentary)   440
Tribal Women's Association (Pakistan)
    516–517
TSK (Türk Spor Kurumu)   541–542
Tunisia
    Arab Spring uprisings in   286
    transsexual surgery in   478–479
al-Turabi, Shoruk   426
Türk Spor Kurumu Dergisi (Turkish Sport
    Administration Magazine)   541–542
Turkestan
    diseases in   234–235, 236–237
    health care in   237–240
       childbirth assistance   231–233
       traditional   229
       Western   230–234, 235–236, 238–239,
       240
Turkestanskiye vedomosti (newspaper)   230
Turkey
    gender equity in   539, 547–548
    Islamization in   560, 561
    motherhood in   545–546
    sport in   540–543, 553–555
       by women   538, 543–546, 552,
       555–562
    transsexual surgery in   480
Türkiye İdman Cemiyetleri İttifâkı (The
    Alliance of Exercise Association of
    Turkey)   554
Turner, Victor   45, 47

Uludağ, Osman Şevki   542
UMNO (United Malays National
    Organisation)   125
UNFPA (United Nations Fund for Population
    Activities)   302, 303, 305, 321, 325
UNIFEM (United Nations Development Fund
    for Women)   150, 289
United Arab Emirates
    citizenship laws in   83
    domestic violence in   79
    guardianship of women in   78
    state-sponsored feminism in   493, 500
United Kingdom *see* Great Britain

INDEX OF NAMES

United States
> family planning programs funded
> > by 302
> mosques in 525, 529, 532–533, 534
> > queer-inclusive 439
> Muslims in 168–169, 179, 523
> > domestic violence among 167–168,
> > > 169–179
> > men
> > > sport activities by 530–533, 534,
> > > > 535
> > > stereotyping of 530–531
> > women
> > > agency of 527–530, 535
> > > sport activities by 523–525,
> > > > 526–527
Upjohn (company) 325
UPP (Union and Progress Party, Turkey)
> 540
US Social Forum 528–529
al-Ustaz, Nuha Rushdi 415, 416
Utomo, Budi 354
Uttawar (India) 344
Uttorshuri blog 404

Van Gennep, Arnold 45, 46, 52, 211
Venkatesh, Madeleine 525
Viavoori, Tiruvaloor 465
"Violence against Women in Tajikistan"
> (WHO et al) 146, 152–155
Viqar, Sarwat 512–513
Vishaka case (India) 400
"VisualizingPalestine" campaign 278

Wadud, Amina 65–66, 438
WAF (Women's Action Forum, Pakistan)
> 136
Waheed, Begum Saeeda (Saida) 318
Wahid, Abdurrahman 353, 371
Wanita MCA (Malaysian Chinese
> Association) 122
Wanita MIC (Malaysian Indian Congress)
> 122
Waqfa Banāt (anon.) 442
Warwick, Ellen 250
Washington 439
WCC (Women's Crisis Centre, Malaysia)
> 124–125

Weigl-Jäger, Constanze 348
Weiss, Anita M. 251
Weiss, Kenneth 329
West
> autonomy notions in 513
> influence of
> > on body ideals for women 544–545
> > on health care 212, 230, 238–239, 240
> > on sport 552–553
> Islamophobia in 438, 523
> media representations of Muslim men
> > in 529
> Muslim women viewed by 527
> transsexuality in 478
West Africa
> abortion in 34
> breastfeeding in 29–40
> effeminate boys/men in 476
> female genital mutilation/cutting
> > in 185–187, 189–197
> initiation rituals in 48–49, 54–55
> motherhood in 32
Westphal, Heinz 477–478
Westphal-Hellbush, Sigrid 477–478
WGNRR (Women's Global Network for
> Reproductive Rights) 291
Whittemore, Robert D. 39
WHO (World Health Organization)
> on abortion 383
> on Baby Friendly Hospital Initiative 6
> on breastfeeding 5
> on domestic violence 152–155
> on female genital mutilation 185, 186
> on infertility 362, 385
> on reproductive cancers of women 363
> on social determinants of health 280
> on suicide 258
Wick, Livia 278
Widyantoro, Ninuk 358–359
Wieringa, S. 111
Wikan, Unni 473, 475
Wilkinson, Richard G. 279
A Woman's Cry (television series) 441
"Women Gymnastics" (article) 544, 545
Women and Memory Forum (Egypt) 291
World Conference on Women, in Beijing
> (1995) 137, 187

Yadav, Stacey Philbrick 494
Yazbak, Mahmoud 217
Yemen, contraceptive use in 285
Yizbak, Samar 441
Yunus, Mohammad 329
Yuval-Davis, Nira 545, 563

Zahed, Mohamad 436, 439
Zahrat al-Khaleej (The flower of the Gulf, magazine) 88

Zainah, Anwar 122
Zakaria, Rafia 251
Ze'evi, Dror 214–215
Zhu, Nina 327, 328
Zia ul-Haq, Muhammad 135, 246, 321, 510–511
Ziguinchor (Senegal) 195
Zimmerman, George 530
Zurayk, Huda 279

Index of Subjects

abortion
  acceptability within Islam of 331, 342
  in Arab states 286
  in Bangladesh 323, 331–332, 408–409
  in India 349
  in Indonesia 358–359, 382–384, 389, 390
  in Pakistan 331, 332
  in West Africa 34
acid crimes
  in Bangladesh 63–64, 401
  in Pakistan 134, 138
activism
  against domestic violence/violence against women
    in Bangladesh 408
    in Egypt 412
    in Gulf states 88, 91
    in Indonesia 101, 110
    in Malaysia 119–120, 122–123, 124–125
    in Pakistan 136–137, 138, 142–143
  against female genital cutting 188, 189
  on gender equality 290–291
  against honor killings 207–208
  against sexual harassment, in Egypt 419, 425–426
  women's
    in Arab Spring uprisings 493, 500–503
    on human rights, in Gulf states 83, 84–85
    Islamic/Islamist
      in Indonesia 353–354, 372, 384
      in Yemen 494–495
    in Ottoman Empire 538–539
    in United States 528–530
    on women's rights
      in Egypt 412
      in Pakistan 133, 516–517
      in Palestine 220–221
      in Saudi Arabia 83–84
administrative violence against women, in Gulf states 83
adoption
  in Egypt 387

  in Indonesia 386–387
  international, from Bangladesh 323
adultery *see* extramarital sex
adulthood, initiation rituals for reaching 52, 55, 57
advertising of infant formula products 7, 38
advice literature, on breastfeeding 19–26, 27
African American Muslims 168, 174, 525
agency of Muslim women, in United States 527–530, 535
agricultural labor by women, in Tajikistan 150
anatomy, teaching of 213
anemia, among women in Turkestan 237
animals, milk used for baby/infant feeding from 19–20, 31
anxiety disorders 258
Arab Americans 170
Arab Spring uprisings 286, 292
  in Egypt 286
    sexual assaults against women protesters in 413–414, 419–420
  in Gulf states 85
    role of women in 493, 500–503
  modesty demands on women protesters in 419–420, 502
  and youth bulge theory 287, 288
Arabic language
  literature on homosexuality in 441–442
  online information sharing platforms in 290
  scientific journals in 290
armed conflicts
  in Arab states 280–281
  Tajik civil war 148–149
arranged marriages
  in Pakistan 204, 252
  in Tajikistan 156
ART (antiretroviral therapy) for HIV patients, availability of 361
arts
  used for campaigns against female genital cutting 188
  see also performing arts

582 INDEX OF SUBJECTS

ARTS (assisted reproductive technologies)
301
   in Bangladesh 306–311
   in Indonesia 363, 386–387, 389
asexuality expectations of single
     women 454
   see also chastity of women
authoritarian regimes
   in Arab states 287–288
   in Indonesia 371
   in Tajikistan 157
autobiographical writings, queer 442
autonomy
   of victims of domestic violence 127
   of women
     reproductive 382
     Western notions of 513
autopsies
   in Ottoman Empire 211–212, 213–214
   in Palestine 214–215, 216, 218–222
avlods (kinship networks, Tajikistan) 146–
     147, 151
   and domestic violence 160–162
   men as head of 159

babies
   bonding with mothers of, and
     breastfeeding 36–37
   food suitable for 30–31
   health of, and breastfeeding 33, 39
baby friendly hospitals 6
bacha bereesh (beardless boys) *see* effeminate
   men/boys
Bambara people 31
basketball players in United States
   Muslim men 531–533, 534
   Muslim women 525–526
beards, as sign of masculinity 465
beautification of women, sport as 544
beauty pageants and competitions, in
   Turkey 545
Begum Rokeya Day celebrations
   (Bangladesh) 404
benefits
   of breastfeeding 5, 33, 39–40
   of sex education 381
Bengal language 452
benzodiazepines, use of 266–267

Bible, on breastfeeding 15
biopolitics
   in Bangladesh 326
   of reproductive health 326, 333
births *see* childbirths
blood money 218
bodies, female
   control over
     and contraceptive use 301, 304–306
     and honor killings/crimes 202–205
     in Indonesia 379
     and nationalism 323
     and reproductive
       technologies 306–311
     in Tajikistan 157
   postmortem examination of 212, 216,
     217
     opposition to 213–214, 215, 218, 221
   reproductive processes of, and mental
     health 260
   transformation through sport of 544–
     545, 557
   as war booty 408
bonding
   between initiates 47
   between mother and child 36–37
boxing, by women 548
boys
   effeminate/homosexual relations
     with 465–476, 482–483
   raising of, in Bangladesh 410
   see also sons
breast cancer, in Indonesia 363, 364, 388
breastfeeding
   benefits of 5, 33, 39–40
   in Indonesia 378
   in Malaysia 3, 4–11
   in Ottoman Empire 14, 18–27
   in Turkestan 233–234
   in West Africa 29–40
burial customs *see* funerary rites

campaigns
   anti-female genital cutting 188, 189
   anti-sexual harassment
     in Bangladesh 406
     in Egypt 414, 424–425
   anti-violence against women

INDEX OF SUBJECTS

in Gulf states 88, 91
in Indonesia 101
in Malaysia 119–120
on neonatal mortality 278
for safe abortions 384
cancers, female reproductive 363–364, 387–389, 390
caring burden of women 262
castration
of effeminate boys 471
of slaves 480
cervical cancer, in Indonesia 364, 388
charity, Islamic 530
chastity of women
emphasis on, in Pakistan 246
see also modesty demands on women
childbirths
medical assistance/health care for women at
in Indonesia 356, 375–378, 390
in Turkestan 231–233
mental illness caused by 260
in Palestine 278
sex ratio at 330
sexual abstention period after 347
spacing of, and breastfeeding 33
children
abuse of, in Tajikistan 154, 156–157
adoption of
from Bangladesh 323
in Indonesia 386–387
from adulterous relations 202
breastfeeding of 5, 16, 33, 233–234
and infant mortality 39–40
and personal development 37
custody of, in Gulf states 83
gendered preferences for 330–332
health care for, in Turkestan 233–235
malnourishment of, in Pakistan 260
number of
and breastfeeding 10
and mental illness 264
unregistered, in Tajikistan 155
see also boys; girls; youth
Christianity
of Arab Americans 170
breastfeeding promoted in 15
in Indonesia 381

circumcision
female *see* female genital cutting
male 54
citizenship
cultural, of Muslim Americans 531–533, 535
in Gulf states 82–83
civil law, in Bangladesh 72–73
civil society organizations, in Gulf states 495
civilizing mission, of sport clubs 553
classes, social
and domestic violence 108, 131–132
and family planning 340
and female genital cutting 53–54
and sexual harassment 422
and women's mobility and access to public spaces 250, 513–514
coitus interruptus, acceptability within Islam of 341
colonialism 76n1
sport promoted by 552–553
views of women's inferior status in Islam of 245
colostrum 30
communities
membership of, initiation rituals for 53
role in pregnancy and childbirth care of 376
condoms, use of, in Indonesia 380
confinement, illegal, of women 204
contraception
Islamic teachings on 303, 341–342
use of 316, 317
in Arab states, by women 285
in Bangladesh 301, 303, 304–306, 311, 317–318, 325–326, 333
in India 340, 342–343, 347–348
in Indonesia 357–358, 379–382
in Pakistan 317–318, 320, 322, 333
copyright laws, in Saudi Arabia 497
coroners, in Palestine 219–220
corpses
forensic examinations of 214–215, 216–217
in Ottoman Empire 211–212, 213–214
in Palestine 209, 214–217, 218–222
washing of 210

cottage industries, female, in Pakistan 251

counter cultures, Muslim queer 439, 440–443, 444

cricket sport 530, 531

criminal law
in Bangladesh 71–72
in Egypt 415–416
in Gulf states 80, 81, 82, 92
in Pakistan 138
in Palestine 218

criminalization
of domestic violence 115, 121, 125–126, 127, 128
of sexual harassment 410, 412, 415

cultures
and female genital cutting 189
and Islamic teachings 172
Muslim American 169, 172, 175
male 531–533, 535
West African, breastfeeding views of 29–30

custody of children, in Gulf states 83

customary law
on female sexuality 202
in Indonesia 104–105
in Pakistan 139, 141

dancing
by boys for men's pleasure 465–466, 469, 470
prostitution associations of 515

daughters, neglect of, in Pakistan/Bangladesh 330–332

death
unnatural
postmortem examinations of 206–207, 211, 214–217, 221–222
of women 220–222
see also mortality

democratization
in Indonesia 101
in Tajikistan 151

demography
of Arab states 283–288, 292
in India 343

depression 258
among Pakistani women 260

detention, of Muslim Americans 528–529

diasporas, South Asian 525–526

discrimination of women
in Bangladesh 69
in Gulf states 82–83
in Kuwait 80
in Pakistan 135, 142

diseases
female reproductive cancers 363–364, 387–389, 390
mental 257–258, 259–260
sexually transmitted 360–362, 363, 386
in Turkestan 234–235, 236–237

divorce
customs/practices
in Indonesia 385–386
in Ottoman Empire 18
husband initiated
in Pakistan 134
in Tajikistan 162
legislation, in Indonesia 362
women's rights to/wife initiated
in Bangladesh 69
in Indonesia 107, 111
in Malaysia 116–119

divorcees, female, stigmatization of 111, 159, 175, 263

dīwānīyyāt (gathering spaces within the home) 495

domestic violence 146
in Bangladesh 63–65, 66–74
in Gulf states 78–80, 81–82, 86–87
in Indonesia 100–102, 105–111
in Malaysia 114–128
in Pakistan 131–134, 136–137, 139–140, 263–264
in Tajikistan 145–146, 152–163
in United States 167–168, 169–179

domestic workers, violence against 89–91

dower/mahr
in Bangladesh 68
in Tajikistan 161

doya (traditional birth attendant) 232, 240

dress
cross-dressing 480
of effeminate boys 471, 473
of Muslim women
in Malaysia 4
in Pakistan 249–250, 511

INDEX OF SUBJECTS

and sexual harassment   403–405,
   417, 425
in Turkey   561
in United States   527
dry nursing   35
dry season   48
duppatta (thin gossamer veil), in Pakistan
   249, 250
Dyula peoples, female genital cutting
   practices of   56

economic contribution of women, in
   Indonesia   373
economic development, in
   Tajikistan   149–150
economic policies, impact on health of
   women of   281–282
economic rights of women   187
education
   Islamic, for girls   47–48
   low levels of, and mental
      illness   261–262
   of medical doctors   212, 213
   of midwives   232
   physical education   540, 543
      for girls   543–544, 558, 559
   sex education   354–355
   for women/girls
      in Arab states   285
      in Bangladesh   400
      in Pakistan   251, 252–253
      in Tajikistan   149–150, 159
effeminate men/boys   462, 464–476,
   482–483
elderly
   in Arab states   288
   depression among   262–263
elites
   Ottoman   25
   Turkish   556–558
embryos, freezing of   309
emergency contraception (EC)
   in Bangladesh   331–332
   in Indonesia   357–358, 359, 384, 389
empowerment of women
   in Bangladesh   450–451
   development projects' focus on   303,
      329–330

in Gulf states
   and online platforms   493, 496–498
   through private spaces   494–496,
      503–504
   and state-sponsored
      feminism   500–501
in Ottoman Empire   538
in virtual private spaces   496–498
in women-only workplaces   515–516
entrepreneurs, female
   in Indonesia   373
   in Saudi Arabia   496–497, 498
equality, of genders *see* gender equity
erotic poetry, on beauty of boys   466–467,
   469
ethnicities
   belonging to/membership of, and
      initiation rituals   53–54
   in Malaysia   3, 8
eugenics theory   557, 558
eunuchs   480
"Eve teasing" (sexual harassment
   euphemism)   397, 407–408
extended families
   abuse of women by members of   132,
      175–176
   American Muslim   175–176
   in Malaysia   10
   in Pakistan   262–263
   in Tajikistan   146–147
extramarital sex
   children born from   202
   condemnation of   358
   by men, as domestic violence   359
   unlawfulness of   201–202, 246, 321
   by women
      and contraceptives use   381
      and honor killings/crimes   202–205
      stigmatization of   156, 161, 454, 455
   see also zina

faith healers
   in Pakistan   266
   in Turkestan   229, 236
families
   in Arab states, changes in   283–285, 286,
      288
   decreasing size of, in Malaysia   10

faith healers (cont.)
  extended
    abuse of women by members of   132,
      175–176
    American Muslim   175–176
    in Pakistan   262–263
    in Tajikistan   146–147, 162
    husbands as heads of, in Indonesia   103,
      104
family ideals
  in Indonesia   103
  in Malaysia   120
family law
  in Bangladesh   69
  in Gulf states   78
  in Malaysia   117, 118
  in Ottoman Empire   538–539
  in Pakistan   134
family planning
  in Bangladesh   301–304, 311, 316,
    324–326, 328–330, 332–333
  in India   340, 342–344, 349
  Hindu opposition to   345
  in Indonesia   356–358, 378–382, 389
  in Pakistan   316, 318–322, 327–328, 333
faskh divorce (annulment of marriage)
  116–117, 118
fasting, of Muḥammad   353, 371
fatwas
  on abortion   358
  on autopsies/postmortem
    examinations   213–214
  in Bangladesh, violence against women
    related to   63
  on family planning   344
  on transsexual surgery   478, 479, 481
female genital cutting   186, 196
  in Gulf states   82
  as human rights violation   187–188
  illegality of   186–187, 191
  and Islam   50–51, 56, 57, 189–190,
    191–192, 193, 194
  in sub-Saharan Africa   45, 46, 49–51, 52,
    53–54, 56–57
  in West Africa   185–187, 189–197
feminism
  Islamic
    in Arab states   286

    impact of   436, 444
    scholarship of   437–438
    in United States   530, 535
    in Ottoman Empire   538–539
    in Pakistan   516
    state-sponsored
      in Gulf states   493, 498–501
      in Turkey   543
    see also women's groups and
      organizations
fencing, by women   547
fertility rates
  in Arab states   285–286, 292
    declines in   283–284
  in Bangladesh   317, 325
  in Egypt, of Islamists   286
  in India, of Muslims   341, 345–346
  in Indonesia   356, 378–379
  in Pakistan   317
  in Palestine   218, 285
  in Turkestan   231, 235
  see also population growth
fertility songs, by effeminate boys   472
feticide, female, in Pakistan   331
filming of women, as form of sexual abuse
  407
films
  on girls behaving like boys   476–477
  on queer Muslim counter
    cultures   440–441
fitne/fitnah (secession/chaos), female sport
  activities seen as   560
flirtation, sexual harassment likened to
  403, 415, 423
folk medicine *see* healing practices,
  traditional
food
  for babies   30–31
  and breastmilk   31, 32
  insecurity, in Tajikistan   150, 151
football *see* soccer
forced marriages, in Tajikistan   155
forced sterilization, in India   344
forensic medicine   211
  in Egypt   213
  in Ottoman Empire   212–214
  in Palestine   214–215, 216–217, 219, 222

INDEX OF SUBJECTS

Fulani people, breastfeeding/baby feeding
practices of 30, 31, 33, 34, 36, 37
funerary rites 209–210
exclusion of women from 206–207, 210,
252
in Ottoman Empire 210–211
in Pakistan 205–207
in Palestine 209, 215, 221

gang rapes 133
gastrointestinal diseases 236–237
gay scene, and religiosity 443
gender ambiguity
in Islam/Muslim world 462, 463–465,
482
of men/boys
in Afghanistan 465–467
in Egypt 467–469, 470–471, 478–479
in India 471–473
in Oman 473–475
in Ottoman Empire 470
in West Africa 475–476
of women/girls
in Afghanistan 476–477
in Arab world 477–478
gender diversity, permissibility in Islam of
436–437
gender dysphoria 479
gender equity
in Bangladesh 65, 450–451
in Gulf states 87–88
and health of women 280
in Indonesia 354, 365, 372–373
in Islam/Muslim world 65–66, 290–291
in Millennium Development
Goals 288–289
in Pakistan 137–138, 258–259
in Tajikistan 149–150, 162, 163
in Turkey 539, 547–548
gender identities 463
fluidity of 475
formation of 458
and initiation rituals 54
gender roles, in Bangladesh 307, 450, 452
gender segregation
in Egypt 467–468
in Gulf states 494
among Muslim Americans 524–525

in Pakistan 246, 249, 252
on Saudi Arabian social media 497–498
in Senegal 49
in Tajikistan 160, 163
in Turkey 556–557
see also purdah
gendering
of ARTs promotional material 306–308
of sport activities 525–526
gham-khadi gatherings (Pashtun life event
gatherings) 514
girls
circumcision of see female genital cutting
education of
in Pakistan 251, 252–253
in Tajikistan 159
health of, in Turkestan 234–235
initiation/coming of age rituals for 45–
57, 189, 192
marriage of
in Bangladesh 401
in Pakistan 204
in Tajikistan 155–156
in Turkestan 239–240
physical education of, in Turkey 543–
544, 558, 559
raising of
in Bangladesh 410
as boys, in Afghanistan 476–477
in Tajikistan 161
victims of sexual harassment, in
Bangladesh 401
virginity of, importance for family honor
of 247
see also daughters
goiter disease 235, 238
grandmothers, in West Africa 35
guardianship
of children, by mothers 83
of women, in Gulf states 77–78, 79–80,
88, 493
gymnastics, in Turkey 540
by women 544, 561
gynecology, in Turkestan 230, 239

ḥadīths
on adultery 202
on female genital cutting 50, 189

ḥadīths (cont.)
    feminist interpretations of   438
    on gender ambiguity   464
    on homosexuality   436–437
harems, access to   470
head-covering by women
    in sport   526
    see also veiling by women
healing practices
    Islamic/spiritual   229, 238
    mystical   229, 236
    traditional
        in Bangladesh   456
        in Pakistan   266
        in Turkestan   229, 237–238, 240
health   257
    of children, in Pakistan   260
    socio-economic determinants of   279–280, 281–282
    of women
        in Arab states   279–282
        in Bangladesh   301, 303
        breastfeeding   22–23, 24, 26, 33
        in Pakistan   258, 259–265, 268, 269
        in Saudi Arabia   79–80
    see also mental health; reproductive
        health
health care
    in Arab states, access for women to   86, 290
    in Egypt   213
    in Indonesia   364, 374, 376, 388–389
    in Ottoman Empire, reform of   212
    in Pakistan   257, 257–258, 265–268, 327
    in Palestine   215–216, 218, 278
    in Turkestan   229, 230–240
    see also medicine
health sciences *see* population and health
    sciences
health workers, female
    for contraception/reproductive
        health   317–318, 322, 327–330
    in Pakistan   516
hermaphroditism   479
    see also gender ambiguity
heteronormativity, in Bangladesh   454
higher education, female participation in
    285

hijabs *see* veiling by women
Hindu nationalism/Hind Right in India
    341, 345–347
Hindus, in Bangladesh, violence against
    409
historical studies, of gender and sexuality in
    Islam   437
HIV/AIDS, among women in Indonesia
    360–362, 380
homes
    births at, in Indonesia   377
    as female space   451, 495
        in Pakistan   510–511, 513
    matrimonial, exclusion of abusive
        husbands from   115
    in Saudi Arabia   497–498
homicide on women
    in India   331
    in Palestine   215, 216, 220–221
    see also honor, killings/crimes
homophobia, Islamic/Muslim   438
homosexuality
    in Afghanistan   465–467
    in Bangladesh   454, 456–457
    in Egypt   467–469, 470–471, 479
    female *see* lesbianism
    in Islam/Muslim world   435, 436–437, 463, 482
        with boys   465–476
        cultural expressions of   440–442
    in Nigeria   476
    in Ottoman Empire   470–471
    in Pakistan   467, 471–473
homosociality   453–454
    of basketball   526
honor
    killings/crimes
        in Gulf states   88–89
        in Pakistan   133, 135–136, 138, 201, 202–205, 207–208
        in Tajikistan   161
    women as embodiment of   105, 111, 156, 161, 171–172, 175, 218
    in Pakistan   246–247, 248, 251
hormone implant contraceptives   304–305, 326
hormone injection contraceptives   325, 380

INDEX OF SUBJECTS

hospitals
    baby friendly   6
    for cancer treatment, in Indonesia   388
    in Turkestan   230, 231–232, 239
households
    female headed
        in Indonesia   382
        in Tajikistan   150–151, 162
    incomes of, women as managers of   373
    male headed, in Indonesia   103, 104
    in Pakistan   247–249
HPV (human papilloma virus)   360
    vaccine   364, 388
human rights activism
    against female genital cutting   188, 189
    in Gulf states   83, 84–85
    in Pakistan   136
human rights organizations, in Bangladesh
    70
human rights violations, female genital
    cutting as   187–188, 196
husbands
    abusive, exclusion from matrimonial
        home of   115
    divorce initiated by
        in Pakistan   134
        in Tajikistan   162
    as heads of families, in Indonesia   103,
        104
hymens, as proof of virginity   247

iddah (waiting period), for widows   252
identities
    American, of Muslim American
        men   531–535
    gender   54, 458, 463, 475
    sexual, formation of   443, 458
Idman Bayramı (Exercise Fest, Turkey)
    560–561
imams, gay   439
infant formula products, use of   7, 38
infectious diseases, in Turkestan   236
infertility   307
    in Indonesia   362–363, 385–387, 389
    in Turkestan   231, 238
    in West Africa   35
    of women, stigmatization of   308, 309,
        362, 385

    see also ARTs (assisted reproductive
        technologies)
infidelity *see* adultery
inheritance rights in Islam, and gender
    ambiguity   463
initiation rituals *see* rituals, coming of age/
    initiation
internet
    information sharing platforms on,
        Arabic   290
    Saudi platforms on, empowerment of
        women on   493, 496–498
intersex individuals, surgery for   478–479
Islam
    in Bangladesh, and violence against
        women   65–66
    breastfeeding promoted by   8, 15–16
    and coming of age rituals   55–56
    and culture   172
    and female genital cutting   50–51, 56, 57,
        189–190, 191–192, 193, 194
    gender diversity/ambiguity in   462,
        463–465
    gender equity in   65–66
    in Indonesia   352
    in Malaysia   3–4
    patriarchy in   77
        colonial views of   245
    personal accountability to God in   172
    and sexuality   324, 453
    in sub-Saharan Africa   47–48
    teachings of
        on adultery   201
        on contraception/birth control   303,
            341–342
        and domestic violence
            justifications   176–177
        on funerary rites   205–206
        on homosexuality   435, 436–437, 463
        on marriage   172
        on reproductive technologies   310,
            386
    in United States   169, 174–175
    of women   527–528
Islamic education
    in sub-Saharan Africa, for girls   47–48
    in West Africa   54–55

Islamic feminism
  in Arab states   286
  impact of   436, 444
  in United States   530, 535
Islamic law
  on adultery   201–202
  on domestic violence   116
  protection of breastfeeding mothers in
    17–18
  on reproductive technologies   363
  on witnesses   117
  see also Shariʿa
Islamic medicine
  in Pakistan   257
  in Turkestan   229
Islamic Studies
  feminist   437–438
  queer/sexuality studies in   435–436
Islamism
  in Arab states   290
  in Egypt, high fertility rates in   286
  in Indonesia   352–353, 370–372
  in Pakistan   139
  in Turkey   560, 562
  in Yemen, female activism in   494–495
Islamization
  in Indonesia   370
  in Pakistan   135, 246
    impact on women   321, 510–511
  in Tajikistan   151–152, 159, 163
  in Turkey   560, 561
Islamophobia   438
  in United States   523
IUDs (intra-uterine devices), use of
  in Bangladesh   325
  in India   342–343, 347–348
  in Pakistan   319
IVF (In-Vitro Fertilization), risks of   309,
    310

Jimnastik Bayramı (Turkey)   561
jirgas (tribal council, Pakistan)   204
Jola people
  coming of age rituals of   47, 49, 50–51,
    55–56
  female genital cutting practices of   193,
    194–195
judges, female, at Shariʿa courts   372

Jumma people (Bangladesh), sexual violence
  against   409
jurisprudence
  on domestic violence
    in Bangladesh   68–69, 73
    in Malaysia   115–119, 123
  on rape, in Gulf states   84
  on sexual harassment, in
    Bangladesh   399–400
justice
  social, activism on   528–530
  tribal, in Pakistan   204

karo kari custom   202–205
Kemalism   553
Kenana people   53–54
kinship, through breast milk   17, 35–36,
    39–40
knowledge
  production of   306
  secret   47, 49
kola nuts, consumption of   30
Kurdish Americans
  American identities of   534
  women
    activism by   529–530
    sport activities by   527

labor force participation of women
  in Bangladesh   67
  in Gulf states   494
  in Malaysia   9
  and marriage   284–285
  in Pakistan   251
labor migration
  to Gulf states   89–91
  from Tajikistan   150, 162
land ownership, by women, in
  Tajikistan   150–151
leadership, religious
  in Bangladesh   333
  in Pakistan   206, 333
  in United States   178–179
legal aid, by human rights organizations, in
  Bangladesh   70
legal systems
  in Kuwait   88
  in Pakistan   140–141
  in Palestine   217–218

INDEX OF SUBJECTS 591

lesbianism
    in Bangladesh 457–459
    Muslim 440–441
liberalization of the economy, in
    Tajikistan 149
liminality 444
literacy rates, in Pakistan 257
literature
    advice on breastfeeding 19–26, 27
    on Muslim homosexuality 441–442
loitering in public spaces, women's rights to
    516

magazines
    sport 451–452
    women's
        on breastfeeding 18–19, 25–26
        in Ottoman Empire 538
majālis (gatherings), of women, in
    Qatar 493, 495–496
malnourishment
    in Pakistan 260
    in Tajikistan 150
Mande people/culture 29
    breastfeeding practices of 35–36
    female genital cutting by 54
Mandinga/Mandinka people *see* Mande
    people/culture
    breastfeeding practices of 30, 31, 34, 35,
        36
    coming of age rituals of 50, 53, 55
    female genital cutting practices by 50,
        56, 190, 191–192
marital rape
    criminalization of, in Gulf states 81, 82
    in Indonesia 106–107, 108, 359
    in Malaysia 126–127
    in Tajikistan 156
marriage
    age of
        in Arab states 284–285
        early age
            in Bangladesh 401
            impact on women of 284
            in Pakistan 204
            in Tajikistan 155–156
            in Turkestan 239–240
        increases in 284–285

minimum age, in Pakistan 134
arranged
    in Pakistan 204, 252
    in Tajikistan 156
conflict solving in 177
customs and practices
    in Bangladesh 67, 452
    in Indonesia 102–105
forced, in Tajikistan 155
initiation rituals in preparation of 52
Islamic teachings on importance of
    172
legislation on
    in Malaysia 120
    in Pakistan 134
normativity of, in Bangladesh 453–455,
    457
restrictions, milk kinship 17, 36, 39–40
same-sex, in Muslim world 439–440,
    468–469
masculinity
    beards as sign of 465
    in Indonesia 104
    of Muslim Americans 532, 533, 535
    in Oman 474–475
    of sport 524, 532, 552
mass sexual assaults on women, in Egypt
    413–414, 419–420
masturbation 455, 456
maternal mortality 280
    in Indonesia 355–356, 375–378, 389
    in Pakistan 316
    in Tajikistan 150
maternity leave, in Malaysia 6–7
media coverage
    of sport activities
        by Muslim Americans 525
        by Turkish women 556–557
    of violence against women
        in Bangladesh 402–403, 406, 407
        in Egypt 413, 420, 420–421, 426
        in Malaysia 120–121, 122–123
media representations
    of Muslim American women 527
    of Muslim men 529
mediation of conflicts, in Bangladesh 69
medical advice, on breastfeeding
    19–25, 26

medical doctors
  childbirth assistance by   231
  female
    in Pakistan   252–253
    in Turkestan   230
  training of, in Ottoman Empire   212, 213
medicine
  forensic   211
    in Egypt   213
    in Ottoman Empire   212–214
    in Palestine   214–215, 216–217, 219, 222
  patriarchy in   307
  Western, in Turkestan   230–234, 238–239, 240
  see also healing practices; health care
medicines
  for breastfeeding mothers   31
  for emergency contraception   384
  for psychiatric disorders   266–267
men
  activism by   110, 207–208
  groups of, sexually assaulting women   413–414
  identities of, women taking on   477–478
  see also masculinity
Mende peoples, initiation rituals of   47, 49, 52
menstruation, sexual abstinence after   347
menstruation regulation (MR) *see* emergency contraception (EC)
mental health in Pakistan   257–258
  care system   257, 265–268
  of women   258, 259–265, 268, 269
midwives
  in Indonesia   377
  in Turkestan   231, 232–233
migrant workers
  female, violence against   89–91
  from Tajikistan   150, 162
military training, and sport   554
milk
  from animals, for baby/infant feeding   19–20, 31
  breastmilk
    alternatives for   37–38, 40
    food influences on   31, 32
    Islamic views of   16–17

    kinship relations through   17, 35–36, 39–40
    West African views of   29
  infant formula   7, 38
milk kinship   17, 35–36, 39–40
minorities
  Hindu, in Bangladesh   409
  Muslim
    in India
      family planning by   343–344, 347–349
      population growth among   341
    in United States   168–169, 523
      agency of women   527–530, 535
      domestic violence among   167–168, 169–179
      female sport activities   523–525, 526–527
      men, American identities of   530–535
mobility of women, restrictions on, in Pakistan   246, 247, 250, 253, 321, 511–513, 517
modernity, women athletes as symbols of   546–548
modernization
  in Malaysia   3, 11
  in Ottoman Empire   540
  in Turkey   545, 557
modesty demands on women
  and female protesters in Arab Spring uprisings   419–420, 502
  and female sexuality/sexual harassment   403–405, 421–422, 423–424, 453
  questioning of   286–287
morality discourses, and sexual harassment   422
mortality rates
  of female reproductive cancers   363, 364, 388
  of infants/neonatals
    and breastfeeding   39–40
    in Palestine   278
    in Tajikistan   150
  maternal   280
    in Indonesia   37–85, 355–356, 389
    in Pakistan   316

INDEX OF SUBJECTS

in Tajikistan 150
in Palestine 218
in Tajik civil war 148, 149
mosques
queer-inclusive 439
in Tajikistan 151–152
in United States 525, 529, 532–533, 534
motherhood
in Bangladesh 308, 311
in Indonesia 354, 373
in Ottoman Empire 14, 18–21, 25–26, 27
in Turkey 545–546
in West Africa 32
womanhood synonymous with 308
mothers
bonding with babies through
breastfeeding 36–37
custody/guardianship rights of 83
depression of, in Pakistan 260, 261, 264
mortality rates of 280
in Indonesia 355–356, 375, 389
in Pakistan 316
in Tajikistan 150
mourning by women, in Pakistan 206
murder *see* homicide
music, used for campaigns against female
genital cutting 188
Muslims
in India
family planning by 343–344,
347–349
fertility rates of 341, 345–346
in Indonesia 352
in United States 167–169, 179, 523
domestic violence among 167–168,
169–179
men
American identities of 531–535
stereotyping of 530–531
women
agency of 527–530, 535
sport activities by 523–525,
526–527
mustarjils (women behaving as men)
477–478
Muʿtazila school of law 437

natality 315
nation-states
female citizens of 563
Indonesian 103
nationalism
and control over women's bodies 323
in Gambia 191
and motherhood 545–546
and sport 553–555
in Turkey 540, 541, 553–555, 562
by women 562–563
women as embodiment of 245–246
neolocal marriages 105
nuclear families, in Malaysia 10

obedience of women, Islamic duty of 66,
79, 173–174
obstetrics
in Indonesia 377, 389
in Turkestan 232–233, 239, 240
oil wealth of Gulf states 494
Olympic Games, Turkish female
participation in 546–547, 556, 557
online platforms *see* internet
oral catarrhal diseases 237
ovarian cancer, in Indonesia 363, 388

palliative care, in Indonesia 388–389, 390
Pashtun people 514
paternity leave, in Malaysia 7
patriarchy
in Arab states 282–283
in Bangladesh 450
in Egypt 426
in Gulf states 493–494
in Islam 77
Qurʾān interpretation 173
in medical science 307
in Pakistan 132
in Tajikistan 151, 160–161
in Turkey 539, 562
performing arts
female participation in, in Pakistan 515
use for campaigns against female genital
cutting of 188
perpetrators, of sexual harassment 401
personal status law *see* family law

personal/personhood development
  and breastfeeding   37
  and initiation rituals   53
physical education, in Turkey   540, 543
  for girls   543–544, 558, 559
piety, female Muslim   453
  in United States   527–528
poetry, erotic, on beauty of boys   466–467,
    469
police
  handling of complaints on violence
    against women by
      in Bangladesh   69, 72
      honor killings/crimes   204–205
      in Malaysia   122–123, 124
      in Pakistan   138–139, 140
      sexual harassment   403, 408, 425
  in Palestine   220
political parties
  in Bangladesh   409
  in India, Hindu   345
  in Pakistan, Islamic   140
politics
  biopolitics
    in Bangladesh   326
    of reproductive health   326, 333
  female participation in, and private
    spaces of women   494–496
  Palestinian, and health care   278
  of revolt   287–288, 292
  sexual violence/harassment in
    in Bangladesh   405–406
    in Egypt   413, 414, 419–420, 422
  and sport, in Turkey   540, 541–543,
    545–546
polygyny
  in Bangladesh   452
  in Indonesia   107–108
  in Pakistan   132
  in Tajikistan   154–155
  in United States   177
population control programs see family
  planning
population growth
  in Bangladesh, declines   326
  in India   340
    of Muslim population   341

problematization of   278, 292, 302, 316,
    340
  see also fertility rates
population and health sciences   277, 278
  on Arab states   278–279, 292
    families   283–285, 286, 288
    reproductive health of
      women   279–282
    youth   287–288
population policies
  in Ottoman Empire   14, 19, 20
  in Turkey   544–545, 545–546
postmortem practices
  in Ottoman Empire   211–212, 213–214
  in Palestine   209, 214–217, 218–222
  see also funerary rites
poverty
  in Arab states   280
  and family planning   302
  in Indonesia   352, 374
  in Pakistan   261
  and sexual harassment   422
  in Tajikistan   150, 158
power
  abuse of, and sexual harassment   406
  of women see empowerment of women
prayer
  funerary   205–206
  by women, and female genital
    cutting   50–51, 191
pre-Islamic society
  breastfeeding in   4–5
  health care in   229
pregnancy
  and breastfeeding   34, 39
  rituals related to, in Indonesia   376–377
  out of wedlock, condemnation of   358
prenatal care, in Indonesia   377, 389
prenatal depression   260
prevention, of sexual harassment   399
private spaces
  distinction from public spaces
    in Bangladesh   451
    in Pakistan   246, 247, 510
  female empowerment in, in Gulf
    states   493–496, 503–504
  virtual, empowerment of women
    on   496–498

INDEX OF SUBJECTS

pronatalist policies *see* population policies

property
- rights of women to, in
  - Tajikistan 150–151
- women seen as 132

prosecution of violence against women
- domestic violence
  - in Bangladesh 68–70, 71, 72, 73
  - in Malaysia 115–119, 123, 124, 127
- honor killings/crimes 205
- sexual crimes
  - in Bangladesh 397
  - in Egypt 415, 416
  - in Gulf states 84
  - in Pakistan 133, 135, 136

prostitution
- by boys 466, 472
- dancing associated with 515
- in Tajikistan 156
- *see also* sex workers

protests *see* Arab Spring uprisings

psychiatry, in Pakistan 268

psychological violence against women, in
Tajikistan 153

puberty rituals for Muslim girls, in sub-
Saharan Africa 45–57

public health
- in Arab world 279–282
- in Pakistan 267
- in Palestine 218

public opinion, on sport activities by
women 559–560

public spaces
- breastfeeding in 10, 33
- distinction from private spaces
  - in Bangladesh 451
  - in Pakistan 246, 247, 510
- sexual harassment of women in 412,
  415, 416–419, 423
- women's access to
  - in Bangladesh 400, 452
  - in Gulf states 493, 500–503, 504
  - in Indonesia 353–354, 365, 372–373
  - of Muslim American women 524,
    527–528, 529, 535
  - in Pakistan 247, 250–251, 321,
    510–514, 516–517

public sphere, in United States 523

public transport, women's use of 512

punishments, extrajudicial, against women
63

purdah (seclusion of women)
- in India 346
- in Pakistan 247–249, 251, 252, 510

Queer Islamic Studies 435–445

Qurʾān
- interpretation
  - and patriarchy 173
  - by women/gender-sensitive 65–66,
    437–438
- translations of 173
- verses
  - on adultery 201
  - on breastfeeding 4, 8, 16
  - on contraception 342
  - on funerary rites 205
  - on gender differences 463
  - on homosexuality 436–437, 463
  - on male dominance over women/
    patriarchy 77, 104, 172–173
  - on marriage restrictions 17
  - on obedience of women 66, 79,
    173–174

Qurʾānic education/schools
- in sub-Saharan Africa, for girls 47–48
- in West Africa, initiation into 54–55

racism, in United States 530

rape
- in Bangladesh 322–324, 408–409
- in Egypt 416
- in Gulf states 81, 82, 84
- in Indonesia 101, 106–107, 108, 110, 359
- in Malaysia 126–127
- in Pakistan 133, 136, 138
- in Tajikistan 156

refugees
- in Arab states 281
- Rohingya, sexual violence
  against 331–332
- in United States 529–530

registration, of children/births, in
Tajikistan 155

religion
- in Malaysia 3
- in United States 169

religiosity, and sexuality   453
religious abuse   176–177
reproductive health   315, 316–317
  in Arab states   279–282
  in Bangladesh   301, 303, 316
  and biopolitics   326, 333
  female health workers for   327–330
  in Indonesia   354–365, 373, 374–375,
    389–390
  and mental health   260
  and sport activities by women   545,
    557–558
  and women's rights   304–306, 316, 379
reproductive rights of women   304–306,
  316, 379
reproductive technologies *see* ARTs (assisted
  reproductive technologies)
revolts/revolutions
  in Bangladesh   409
  in Indonesia   371
  see also Arab Spring uprisings
rights of women
  to access public spaces   516–517
  in Bangladesh   304–306, 306–311, 398
  to divorce   69
  economic   187
  in Ottoman Empire   538–539
  in Pakistan   134, 135, 139, 142
  to property, in Tajikistan   150–151
  reproductive   304–306, 316, 379
  in Saudi Arabia   83–84
  in Tajikistan   150–151
  in Turkey   539
risks
  of contracting HIV/AIDS   361
  factors
    for domestic violence   171
    for mental illness of
      women   260–264
  of female genital cutting   186, 193
  of reproductive technologies   309–310
  of sexually transmitted
    diseases   362–363
rituals
  coming of age/initiation, for girls   45–
    57, 189, 192
  funerary, in Pakistan   205–207

pregnancy related, in
  Indonesia   376–377
  rites of passage   46, 189, 211
  women's roles at   252
Rohingya refugees, sexual violence against
  331–332
rural areas, in Pakistan
  mental health care in   267
  women's access to public spaces in
    513–514

ṣabr (patience)   177
sacred forests, coming of age rituals in   55
safety, of abortions   359, 383, 389, 390
Sande people, initiation rituals for girls by
  47, 56
sardars (feudal landlords, Pakistan)   204
screening for cancer, in Indonesia   364, 388
seclusion of women
  postpartum, in Indonesia   377–378, 390
  see also purdah
secrecy, related to initiation rituals   48–49
secret knowledge   47
sex education   381
  in Indonesia   354–355
sex workers
  in Bangladesh   458
  in Pakistan   515
  in Tajikistan   156
  see also prostitution
sexual harassment
  in Bangladesh   397–410
  in Egypt   291, 412–426
  in Gulf states   80–81
  in Indonesia   110
  in Turkey, of sportswomen   559
sexual identities, formation of   443, 458
sexual intercourse
  abstention from
    during breastfeeding   15–16, 33–34,
      39, 347
    after childbirth   347
    after menstruation   347
  coitus interruptus   341
  consent to, by women in marriage   106
  same-sex, man-boy   468–469, 482–483
  see also extramarital sex

INDEX OF SUBJECTS

sexual violence
   in Bangladesh   322–323, 409
   in Indonesia   359–360
   against Rohingya refugees   331–332
   in Tajikistan   155
   see also rape
Sexuality Studies, Islamic   435–445
sexuality/sexualities
   female
      in Bangladesh   450, 451–459
      control of   51, 202–205
   of female sport activities   559–560
   and Islam   324
   male, in Bangladesh   455–456
sexually transmitted illnesses (STIs), in
   Indonesia   360–362, 363, 386
shame, as female women   453
Shari‘a
   abolition of, in Turkey   539
   application of
      to adultery   201–202
      in Malaysia   119
Shari‘a courts
   female judges at   372
   in Malaysia   116, 118–119, 121
   in Ottoman Empire   18
   in Palestine, records of   214
   protection of breastfeeding mothers by
      17–18
shelters for victims of domestic violence
   110–111, 124, 141
Shi‘i Islam
   suppression of, in Bahrain and Saudi
      Arabia   84–85
   on transsexual surgery   481
single women
   access to contraceptives by   381
   in Arab states, increases in   283–284
   asexuality expectations of   454
   in Bangladesh   454–455
   stigmatization of   111
   vulnerability to mental illness of   263
skiing, by women   548
skin diseases, in Turkestan   236
soccer
   head-covering by women players in   526
   by Muslim Americans   534
social events, women's roles at   252

social justice activism, of Muslim American
   women   528–530
social media use, in Saudi Arabia   496–497,
   498
social sciences, on Muslim homosexuality
   and gender diversity   443–444
socio-economic factors
   and health   279–280, 281–282
   and sexual harassment   422
son preferences, in Pakistan/
   Bangladesh   330–332
South Asian Americans   170
   detention of   528–529
   female agency of   527–529
   female sport activities by   524–525,
      526–527
   men
      cultural citizenship of   531–533
      stereotyping of   530–531
South Asian Britains   526
spaces
   female, in Pakistan   510–517
   gendering of, and gender
      ambiguity   465
   see also private spaces; public spaces
spatiality
   in Pakistan   514
   of sexualities   451–453
sperm, breastmilk likened to   16–17
sport
   masculinity of   524, 532, 552
   in Middle East   552–553
   and nationalism   553–555, 562–563
   in Ottoman Empire   540
   in Turkey   540–543, 553–555
      by women   538, 543–546, 552,
      555–562
   in United States
      by Muslim American men   530–533,
      534, 535
      by Muslim American women   523–
      525, 526–527
stalking   407
state-building, in Indonesia   103
statelessness, in Gulf states   83
states, culpability for sexual violence of
   422

statistics
    on childbirths, in Turkestan   231
    on domestic violence/violence against
        women
            in Indonesia   102
            in Malaysia   125
            in Pakistan   133, 142
            in Tajikistan   152–155, 156
            in United States   170, 173–174
    on female sport activities, in Turkey   559
    on illnesses, in Turkestan   234–235
    on reproductive health, in
        Indonesia   374
    on sexual harassment
        in Bangladesh   400, 402
        in Egypt   414–415, 417
    on suicide by women, in
        Bangladesh   407
status of women
    in Bangladesh   66–68, 454–455
    in Gulf states   493
    in Islam, colonial views of   245
    in Ottoman Empire   538–539
    in Palestine   220
    in Tajikistan   150–151, 157–158
    in Turkey   543
stereotyping
    of Muslim women
        in Bangladesh   402–403
        in India   348–349
    of South Asian American men   530–531
sterilization
    female
        in Bangladesh   304, 326
        in India   347–349
    Islam on   341–342
    male
        in India   343, 344
        in Pakistan   318, 319
stigmatization
    of sexually transmitted diseases and HIV/
        AIDS   360, 361, 386
    of women
        divorcees   111, 159, 175, 263
        and extramarital sexual
            relations   156, 161, 454, 455
        infertile   308, 309, 362, 385
        mentally ill   264–265

victims of domestic violence   105
victims of sexual harassment   425
structural adjustment programs, health
    impact of   281
students, female, sexual harassment of   418
Sufism, tolerance towards homosexuality and
    gender diversity in   437, 439–440
suicide
    rates of, in Pakistan   258
    by women
        in Bangladesh   401, 407
        in Pakistan   132–133
superovulation, risks of   309, 310
surgery, transsexual   478–482
symbolic significance of female genital
    cutting   189
syphilis, in Turkestan   237

taboos, on breastfeeding and breastmilk
    32–33
taklik divorce (wife initiated)   116
talaq (repudiation, unilateral divorce by
    husband)
        in Pakistan   134
        in Tajikistan   162
Tanzimat Reforms (Ottoman Empire)   19
TBAS (traditional birth attendants)
        in Indonesia   377
        in Turkestan   232, 240
teacher training, in Turkey   543–544
television series, on transgenderism   441
terrorists, stereotyping of Muslim American
    men as   530
third-gender persons   462
    in Islam   463–464
    see also effeminate men/boys; gender
        ambiguity; hermaphroditism
thyroid disease, in Turkestan   234–235
torture of women activists, in Bahrain   85
traditional birth attendants see TBAs
traditional medicine see healing practices,
    traditional
transgenderism/transsexuality
    in Iran   481–482
    Muslim/in Islam   435, 462
    films on   440, 441
    in South Asia   473
    surgery   478–482

INDEX OF SUBJECTS

599

in Turkey 480
in West 478
transitional states, dangers of 47
translations, of Qur'ān 173
trauma
in Kuwaiti society 85–86
of Muslim Americans 171
in Tajik society 163
tribal justice, in Pakistan 204
Tuareg peoples
female genital cutting rejected by 51
initiation rituals for girls of 48

ulema
on autopsies/postmortem
examinations 213–214
on breastfeeding 16–17
in Indonesia 372
in Palestine, silence on murder of women
by 218
see also fatwas
universities, sexual harassment at 418
unsafe abortions 359, 383
urban areas
breastfeeding in 9, 38, 40
sexual harassment in 417
women's access to public spaces
in 511–513
uterine cancer, in Indonesia 388
uxorilocal marriages 105

vaccination, for HPV 364, 388
vasectomy see sterilization, male
veiling by women
in Bangladesh 405
in Egypt 425
in Pakistan 249–250, 511, 512
in Turkey 560
in United States 527
victims of violence against women
domestic violence
assistance for 110–111, 124, 141, 177–179
protection of 126, 127
stigmatization of 105
honor killings 204–205, 207
sexual harassment
blaming of 401, 403–405, 413, 420,
421, 426
violence against 425–426

wartime rape, rehabilitation of 323
violence
against children, in Tajikistan 154,
156–157
against minorities, in Bangladesh 409
against women 398–399
in Bangladesh 308
domestic violence 63–65, 66–74
sexual harassment 397–410
sexual violence 322–323,
331–332, 409
wartime rape 322–324, 408–409
in Egypt 412–426
in Gulf states 76–77, 80–81, 82–85,
87–89, 91–92
Arab Spring uprisings 502, 503
against domestic migrant
workers 89–91
domestic violence 78–80, 81–82,
86–87
in Indonesia 359
domestic violence 100–102,
105–111
sexual violence 359–360
in Malaysia, domestic
violence 114–128
in Pakistan 131–134, 135–137, 138–143
domestic violence 263–264
honor killings/crimes 133,
135–136, 138, 201, 202–205,
207–208
in Tajikistan, domestic
violence 145–146, 152–163
in United States, domestic
violence 167–168, 169–179
see also homicide on women; honor,
killings/crimes; rape
virginity
importance for family honor of 247
proof of 52, 474–475
tests performed on female protesters
of 420, 503
virilocal marriages 52, 104–105
volleyball, by women 548

war
bodies of women as booty in 408
and maternal mortality 280
see also armed conflicts

"war on terror"   528–529
wartime rape, in Bangladesh   322–324, 408–409
washing, of corpses   210
water, breastmilk links of   30–31
weaning from breastmilk
    in Turkestan   234
    in West Africa   34–35
websites *see* internet
weddings, in Pakistan   251
welfare work by women, in Indonesia   353, 372
Westernization, in Turkey   545, 546, 561
wet nursing   39–40
    Islam on   16–17
    in West Africa   29, 30, 36
widows, *iddah* (waiting period) of   252
wilāya (male guardianship), in Gulf states   77–78, 79–80, 493
witnesses, female, admissibility of   117, 135
wives
    divorce initiated by, in Malaysia   111, 116–119
    obedience obligations of   66, 79, 173–174
Wolof peoples, female genital cutting
    rejected by   51, 190, 193
womanhood
    in Bangladesh   451–452

in Ottoman Empire   14
in Turkey   556–557
women's groups and organizations
    in Arab states   291
    in Bangladesh   458
    in Indonesia   100, 101, 110
        Islamic   353–354, 372, 384
    in Malaysia   121–122, 124–125
    in Pakistan   136–137, 142–143, 516–517
    in Palestine   220
    in Turkey   539
    see also feminism
workplaces
    sexual harassment at   417
    women-only   515–516

youth
    in Arab states   287–288
    bulge theory   287, 288
    see also children

Zabarma people   53–54
Ẓahirī school of law   437
zakat (Islamic charity), in United States   530
zina (unlawful sexual intercourse)   107–108, 381
    Pakistani laws on   135, 246, 321, 511

Printed in the United States
By Bookmasters